THE
GREENWOOD GUIDE
TO AMERICAN
POPULAR CULTURE

THE
GREENWOOD GUIDE
TO AMERICAN
POPULAR CULTURE

Volume III

Edited by M. Thomas Inge and
Dennis Hall

GREENWOOD PRESS
Westport, Connecticut • London

Library of Congress Cataloging-in-Publication Data

The Greenwood Guide to American popular culture / edited by M. Thomas Inge and Dennis Hall.
   p.   cm.
    Includes bibliographical references and index.
     ISBN 0–313–30878–0 (set : alk. paper)—ISBN 0–313–32367–4 (v. 1 : alk. paper)—
  ISBN 0–313–32368–2 (v. 2 : alk. paper)—ISBN 0–313–32369–0 (v. 3 : alk. paper)—
  ISBN 0–313–32370–4 (v. 4 : alk. paper)
    1. Popular culture—United States. 2. Popular culture—United States—History—Sources.
  3. Popular culture—United States—Bibliography. I. Inge, M. Thomas. II. Hall, Dennis.
E169.1.H2643 2002
306.4'0973—dc21   2002071291

British Library Cataloguing in Publication Data is available.

Library of Congress Catalog Card Number: 2002071291
ISBN: 0–313–30878–0 (set)
       0–313–32367–4 (v. 1)
       0–313–32368–2 (v. 2)
       0–313–32369–0 (v. 3)
       0–313–32370–4 (v. 4)

First published in 2002

Greenwood Press, 88 Post Road West, Westport, CT 06881
An imprint of Greenwood Publishing Group, Inc.
www.greenwood.com

Printed in the United States of America

The paper used in this book complies with the
Permanent Paper Standard issued by the National
Information Standards Organization (Z39.48–1984).

10 9 8 7 6 5 4 3 2 1

For
Donária Carvalho Inge
and
Susan Hall

They stood by their men.

CONTENTS

Contents

Contents

JAZZ

William Kenney and Jeffery Wasick

Jazz first attracted public attention in the United States in 1917, when the Victor Talking Machine Company issued a recording of a group of white musicians from New Orleans who called themselves the Original Dixieland Jazz Band. Recorded in a bright, brassy, and often playfully vulgar style, this double-sided 78 rpm disc set the country to talking about "jazz." In subsequent years, commercialized jazz liberally mixed with popular dance music became the dominant form of American popular music in the Roaring Twenties and the Big Band era. After World War II, however, jazz, in the new guise of bebop, began to evolve into a form of art music to which most people listened rather than danced. Bebop's emphasis on musical innovation set in motion a fragmentation of jazz into myriad experimental style categories like traditional jazz, hard bop, cool, free jazz, and fusion, each with its devoted adherents. At the present time, Wynton and Branford Marsalis have done much to bring back a neo-bebop style, making it jazz's dominant influence.

As this chapter explains, jazz most often has reached the public in mediated form via phonograph recordings, radio broadcasts, movies, television, music videos, and newspaper and magazine articles. If the record companies did not invent the word "jazz," they certainly introduced the term into popular discourse. Scholars have come substantially to agree that the musical styles that have been called "jazz" have been commercialized forms of vernacular music in which Americanized elements of West African traditions have mixed with Africanized elements of American music to form an original musical syncretism.

HISTORICAL OUTLINE

The prehistory of this synthesis reveals the mingling of myriad strains of musical activity and sensibility, among which African American ones played a particularly important role. These gradually came together with diverse European American influences to produce jazz. Within African American cultures, a number of characteristics exerted a formative influence on music-making in the British colonies and in the United States. Among these was the call-and-response or antiphonal form in which the traditional European American distinction between performer and audience largely disappeared. Furthermore, African Americans, despite the variety of their origins, tended to retain elements of West African traditions that integrated the amazing power of music into the fabric of their daily lives. Barred from the worlds of concert music in North America, African Americans developed vernacular music traditions, associating music strongly either with religion or with social dancing. They also evolved original, independent, and highly creative approaches to musical instruments through which they tended to produce sounds related to those made by the human voice. Finally, West African traditions of polyrhythmic elaboration, the simultaneous multilayered sounding of different rhythmic patterns, brought a complex and transforming foundation to the sounds of the Americas.

Various European American ethnic groups also brought with them to the New World musical traditions that contributed to the creation of jazz. Most important in many ways were the musical instruments themselves and the tradition of playing composed music from written scores. For most of its history, moreover, jazz was made largely, if by no means solely, on traditional European musical instruments. The banjo, many kinds of drums, and the xylophone originated in West Africa. Moreover, for all the analysis of improvisation in jazz, that key aural tradition actually developed in conjunction with, and in tension with, musical literacy. For example, the traditions of the European American marching and concert bands influenced New Orleans jazz, while Tin Pan Alley sheet music and orchestrations dominated the white dance band tradition that contributed so much to the swing era.

Whatever the origins of its elements, early jazz is neither purely West African nor entirely European but an original musical and cultural synthesis achieved in the United States that has flourished as both a form of entertainment and a form of musical art. This is what makes jazz such an important and distinctive element of the broader popular cultures of the United States and the world. The musicians and groups that have embraced the jazz label have been those who prized instrumental, rhythmic, harmonic, and melodic growth and experimentation. This, in turn, also explains why current popular culture and popular music studies should not take jazz for granted as just one among many stylistic genres in a wide spectrum of popular music styles. While they have been deeply suspicious of pretentious claims to art, jazz musicians have consistently sought to make music artfully. Moreover, their status as musicians of great popularity may be questioned; the vast majority stopped playing for masses of adoring fans back in the 1940s, when the Big Bands collapsed. For over fifty years now jazz usually has been played for small listening audiences, far removed from the latest popular fads in popular music. At this time, about 3 percent of all compact disc sales involve jazz recordings. Jazz has established itself as a major force in concert hall music at the Lincoln Center for the Performing Arts and in major concert halls around the world. Many, if not all, would agree with Grover Sales that jazz is "America's classical music," at least in the sense that it has been an indigenous music requiring constant practice and creative focus to play with any enduring skill and originality.

The prehistory of jazz usually begins with ragtime, from which early New Orleans jazz took several influences. Ragtime is a heavily structured form of written music designed primarily for the piano, although a variety of wind ensembles played ragtime orchestrations from the "Red Back Book." Ragtime arose in the 1890s and had declined by 1910. The first published ragtime composition was William H. Krell's "Mississippi Rag" (1897), but the genre's greatest composer was Scott Joplin, famous for having written "Maple Leaf Rag" (1899) and many others. Ragtime was quickly commercialized by Tin Pan Alley, most notably in Irving Berlin's "Alexander's Ragtime Band" (1912). As a result, one must distinguish between ragtime-influenced popular songs like Berlin's and a more instrumentally challenging form of piano music usually referred to as classic ragtime. The core works of this genre include the compositions of Joplin, James Scott, and Joseph Lamb, many of whose compositions were originally published by Missourian John Stark.

The classic study of ragtime is Rudi Blesh and Harriet Janis, *They All Played Ragtime*, but more recent scholarship has enriched our knowledge of the musical core and historical context of the ragtime movement. John Hasse, editor of *Ragtime: Its History, Composers, and Music*, provides an invaluable compendium of research and interpretation on the genre as a whole. Edward A. Berlin, who has devoted his life to ragtime performance and research, has written the definitive biography of ragtime's greatest composer, *King of Ragtime: Scott Joplin & His Era*. At the same time, Susan Curtis, *Dancing to a Black Man's Tune*, offers greater depth on the relationship of ragtime to turn-of-the-century historical trends. Scott DeVeaux and William Howland Kenney, editors of *The Music of James Scott*, analyze both the music and the life of ragtime's second most important composer, whose prolific output shows Joplin's influence. Kenney's history of Scott's ragtime in southwestern Missouri argues that the music in many ways reflected both the terrifying race relations of that time and the region's simultaneous pursuit of cultural refinement.

The role of the blues in the prehistory of jazz has raised some of the most contentious issues in jazz studies. On the one hand, many influential works, such as Albert Murray, *Stompin' the Blues*, Amiri Baraka, *Blues People*, and Gunther Schuller, *Early Jazz*, insist that early jazz was so heavily dependent upon the blues that jazz could not be said to have existed without it. These same writers have interpreted the blues as the indispensable precursor of jazz, a deeply ingrained historical musical practice that provided the foundation for many different styles of vernacular music. Since the origins and development of the blues have been traced exclusively to African Americans, many have concluded that the only "authentic" jazz has been, still is, and should always be that played by blacks. According to this influential line of thought, as summarized by James Lincoln Collier, whites can be involved in playing jazz only on "sufferance."

That white American males should have to take second place to anyone may appear, particularly to the white American males, as an outrageous affront, but however much the cultural contrivance of a racially troubled country, the idea of black artistic superiority in jazz has endured from the start and offered a window of creative opportunity to African American musicians. White jazz musicians and fans who complain about the lack of respect that they find in jazz would do well to study musical and entertainment history, particularly the history of minstrelsy and the history of race in the media. There one finds ample evidence of a society

Bessie Smith. Courtesy of the Library of Congress

that enjoyed the idea that blacks made authentic music while denying to those authentic music makers the fruits of their labors in the music business. American racial attitudes created this reverse racism in music, and musically inclined African Americans are seizing the opportunities that society has presented.

African Americans have a very strong claim to artistic dominance in jazz. The blues surely did provide one particularly rich musical resource for improvisation and, depending upon one's point of view, arguably contributed the single most influential one. An uncounted number of blues-oriented guitarists and pianists performed very largely improvised, aural, vernacular music, providing the rhythmic beat for social dancing at lumber camps, rent parties, juke joints, and picnics throughout the United States at the turn of the century. Moreover, soon after World War I, William Christopher Handy commercialized and reified "the blues" from aural traditions in such famous sheet music and recording hits as the "St. Louis Blues," "Memphis Blues," and "Beale Street Blues." White Tin Pan Alley songwriters quickly followed Handy's example and incorporated elements of the blues into the songs (or at least the song titles) that they published in sheet music. Finally, jazz and blues intriguingly intertwined in the first recorded blues. African American female vocalists such as Mamie Smith, Bessie Smith, and Gertrude "Ma" Rainey made the first blues recordings beginning in 1920, and a number of influential early jazz musicians accompanied them.

But the blues-created-jazz hypothesis must remain a hypothesis, at least as it applies to the nineteenth-century roots of twentieth-century musical practice. Although the term "blues" can be traced back to seventeenth-century England, there is little evidence of its use by African Americans before 1920. Although a small number of African Americans recorded in the 1890s, when commercial recording began, none of them recorded anything that they or the record companies, much less music writers, then or thereafter called "blues" until 1920. Recordings are essential when documenting musical practice in the past. Without them, one has recourse only to written commentaries about past musical practice. The recorded evidence indicates that the blues first appeared in 1920, well after ragtime, which first appeared in 1894, and jazz, which first appeared in 1917, had been well established.

Moreover, the connections between blues and jazz reveal a central conundrum characteristic of both jazz practice and jazz studies. Many jazz greats—William "Count" Basie, Charlie Parker, Thelonius Monk, and John Coltrane among them—made the blues a core ingredient of their performance careers. Other essential jazz leaders, such as Coleman Hawkins and Dizzy Gillespie, did not. To insist upon blues as a uniform ethnic group musical characteristic skirts too closely to overly sweeping generalizations about race since no one would deny that Hawkins and Gillespie were master jazz artists.

The traditions of nineteenth-century minstrelsy in the greater white society had long encouraged the popular idea that "blacks" played "authentic" vernacular music, which whites might imitate and appropriate to their purposes. White people controlled the media and entertainment businesses and therefore drew upon the traditions of minstrelsy to create marketing categories that funneled African Americans into the blues and jazz. Many of these musicians welcomed the chance to further develop their blues in jazz performances and recordings. Nevertheless, others—Danny Barker, Alberta Hunter, Blue Lu Barker, Billy Eckstine—preferred to work on different kinds of musical problems and therefore sometimes felt constrained by what they saw as racial stereotyping in the recording industry, which prevented them from giving expression to the full range of their musical sensibilities. In the name of the blues, for example, record producers of the 1920s routinely denied to African Americans the right to "cross over" the boundaries of marketing labels to record more mainstream popular numbers. Whether or not all African American musicians would have preferred to devote their careers to blues and jazz, they were offered precious few alternatives and therefore deserve credit for their exceptional, unmatched historical contributions to those genres.

Another look at the idea of "authenticity" in jazz history reveals that those granted the status of being the most authentic in jazz often remained an éminence grise artfully placed just behind the more commercial white performers and recording artists. This or that popular star musician was often said to have studied with a legendary black artist, on the strength of which he claimed a measure of "authenticity" that his skin color would otherwise deny to him. When "authentic" jazz musicians had the misfortune to die, their recordings continued to make money for recording companies. Being an "authentic" jazz musician has often merited more press copy than high-paying gigs.

The powerful political role of race in jazz has had beneficial effects on some whites. The process by which these whites slowly come to grips with the role of race in jazz defines much of the nonmusical element of the jazz experience for them. Those who, in the habitual round of daily experience, would otherwise have had few contacts with blacks involve themselves in the heavily racialized world of jazz. Some may seek out black musicians from whom to learn and with whom to play and even move on from musical associations to a deeper and more comprehensive understanding of race in the wider world around jazz. Such jazz experiences can alter their understanding of themselves, of American history, and of their African American countrymen and countrywomen.

Jazz Journalism

From the first appearance of jazz as a music style, journalists began to comment on it in the music trades press. For many years thereafter, newspaper and magazine writers dominated jazz commentary. After World War II, however, musicologists and sociologists began to infiltrate the journalists' territory. Finally, during the 1990s academic scholars from a wide variety of disciplines that included history, musicology, literature, sociology, black studies, and American studies began to fashion a variety of new interdisciplinary approaches to jazz. Their efforts redirected attention away from individual musicians and recordings by particular bands onto the broader cultural terrain in which jazz appeared: the media, music business, race relations, and cultural life of urban America. This growing body of writing, a combination of history and/or literature with methods borrowed from ethnomusicology, has brought jazz studies into the mainstream of North American culture studies. As this chapter is being written, the focus of jazz studies appears to be shifting even further toward explicit investigations of the role of race, gender, and social class in the cultural processes that have shaped the music's performance, publicity, audiences, and critical stature. This less musical and more social and historical approach has allowed scholars to reintegrate jazz into the fabric of time and place.

The journalistic interest in interviews, concert reviews, and music reporting did much to create an evidential and conceptual foundation for "jazz writing." Jazz criticism began during the second decade of the twentieth century with the founding of such American music trade magazines such as *The Phonograph Monthly Review*, *Metronome*, and *Downbeat* and the leading entertainment weeklies, *Variety* and *Billboard*. R. D. Darrell contributed the first articles of musical analysis of jazz records to a variety of phonograph trade publications and thereby became the founder of the American tradition of jazz journalism.

The idea of writing books about jazz first arose in France and Belgium, where Andre Coeuroy, Robert Goffin, and Hugues Panassie interpreted jazz records as a North American reflection of West African musical traditions, modified by what they condemned as a repressive racism in the United States. Panassie, the most prolific of the group (*Hot Jazz*, *The Real Jazz*), interpreted jazz as a mysterious racial essence "untarnished by the slightest design . . . the spontaneous urge of a whole people." The primitivism and racial separatism of his stance, a good-natured adoption of the views of his friend the American expatriate reed man Mezz Mezzrow, served to undermine the idea of jazz as a conscious musical art form and totally divorced it from any influence from the white-dominated entertainment complex of the United States. Panassie's emphasis on jazz as black music would be echoed by many American writers (Baraka, Williams, Levine) and would stimulate substantial controversy and further scholarly analysis.

Writers in the United States before World War II tended to divide into those who wrote about jazz as music and those who interpreted its cultural and historical dimensions. Winthrop Sargeant led the former school and was among the first to systematically introduce musical notation to his pages. Wilder Hobson later pursued some of the same methods as Sargeant and added the linguistic metaphor that jazz was like a language: what it communicated depended upon what the listener knew about its form. Those with listening habits formed by European concert hall music needed to learn more about jazz forms in order to avoid value judgments.

During the depression, a new group of journalistic writers arose. They included John Hammond, Bill Simon, Otis Ferguson, George Hoefer, Frederick Ramsey, and Charles Edward Smith. This group tended to reflect the influence of Popular Front politics of the time. They associated jazz with the plight of America's oppressed groups, saw swing as an antifascist force both at home and abroad, and found evidence of racial and ethnic pluralism and integration in jazz's collective improvisation and spontaneous individuality. They also differed over their estimates of the relative degree of authenticity and commercialism in jazz recordings, broadcasts, and concerts.

Jazz's French connection resurfaced in the 1950s, when the composer/violinist Andre Hodeir began publishing about jazz. Playing a role easily as influential as his predecessor Panassie, Hodeir's *Jazz: Its Evolution and Essence* cut through knotty critical problems by clarifying the harmonic and rhythmic principles of bebop. Hodeir also offered a lucid explication of what had been the great holy mystery of jazz writing—swing—and freed jazz writing of Panassie's mysticism.

The journalistic tradition flourished well into the 1950s and 1960s. Whitney Balliett's stylistically elegant biographical articles in the *New Yorker* documented the lives of important jazz stylists, usually of the years before the appearance of bebop. The spare, finely tuned articles of Martin T. Williams rivaled the stylistic elegance of Balliett and surpassed the latter in communicating a sense of the major lines of musical influence and confluence connecting what he convincingly demonstrated to be the greatest instrumental stylists. Williams crowned the efforts of earlier jazz journalists by creating in his collected articles and his Smithsonian Institution record sets a canon of musicians whose recordings documented the evolution of a musical art form called jazz.

CRITICAL AND CULTURAL STUDIES

Two books by Martin Williams served as jazz's first textbooks: *Where's the Melody? A Listener's Introduction to Jazz* (1966) and *The Jazz Tradition* (1983). These widely read books championed an artfully developed canon of autonomous jazz stylists. In subsequent years, most other texts have not stayed long in print, perhaps due to the mounting scholarly wars over what came to be seen as artificial, ahistorical critical concepts. As this chapter goes to press, the leading texts currently available on the market are Ted Gioia, *The History of Jazz* (1997), Mark Gridley, *Jazz Styles: History and Analysis* (1997), Lewis Porter et al., *Jazz: From Its*

Origins to the Present (1992) and the long-awaited *Visions of Jazz: The First Century* (1998) by Gary Giddins, perhaps the leading jazz journalist at this time.

The proudly independent tradition of jazz journalism owes much to the work of poet Amiri Baraka, whose collected columns in *Blues People* (1967) and *Black Music* (1967) explored the relationship between blues, jazz, and the black experience of American life. His latter book was the first full-length study of jazz by a black writer. Stanley Crouch, currently a major force in jazz programming at New York's Lincoln Center for the Performing Arts, wrote about jazz for the *Village Voice* during the 1970s and 1980s, collecting many of his best pieces in *Notes of a Hanging Judge*. So, too, Gary Giddins, a protégé of Martin Williams, collected his articles from *Village Voice* and *New York Magazine* in such books as *Riding on a Blue Note* and *Rhythm-a-ning* and *Visions of Jazz: The First Century*. Canadian Gene Lees, *Down Beat* editor from 1959 to 1961, founded in 1981 the *Gene Lees Jazz-letter*, which offers perceptive essays on jazz.

The gravitation of jazz writing toward the major concerns of academic discourse in the humanities, a development not always applauded by the journalists, got under way in 1952, when Marshall Stearns, then a professor of English at Hunter College, founded the Institute of Jazz Studies (IJS), based on his own extensive collection of records and other documents. Stearns, while teaching medieval literature, had pursued graduate-level courses on music and on African and African American history and culture. He contributed articles to a wide variety of music journals and subsequently published in 1956 a major history, *The Story of Jazz*, a formative contribution to the formal study of jazz influenced by the methods of ethnomusicology.

The collections of the Institute of Jazz Studies matured rapidly and in 1966 found an academic home at Rutgers University in Newark, New Jersey. By the 1970s, IJS had become the premier jazz archive in the world. Much of its preeminence was earned under the leadership of Dan Morgenstern, who before his tenure as director (1976–   ) had been editor of both *Metronome* and *Down Beat* and a lecturer on jazz at Brooklyn College and the Peabody Institute. Morgenstern launched in 1973 the scholarly *Journal of Jazz Studies*, which became in 1982 the *Annual Review of Jazz Studies*, and a monograph series at the Scarecrow Press, leading jazz further into a working alliance with higher education. In great part because of the influence of IJS, an important monograph series on jazz was founded under the direction of Sheldon Meyer at Oxford University Press. The Oxford connection influenced a number of other university presses, most notably those at the University of California and the University of Chicago. At the same time, such major foundations as the National Endowment for the Humanities, the American Council of Learned Societies, and the Guggenheim Foundation began supporting selected jazz research projects.

Jazz is a musician's music, demanding and usually offering only musical and aesthetic rewards to most of its practitioners. As such, jazz continues to be interpreted as this country's most original art form, particularly by artists in other media. Jazz literature is both collected and interpreted in a number of excellent collections, including Richard N. Albert, *From Blues to Bop: A Collection of Jazz Fiction* (1990), Marcella Breton, *Hot and Cool: Jazz Short Stories* (1991), Sascha Feinstein and Yusef Komunyakaa, *The Jazz Poetry Anthology*, 2 vols. (1991, 1996), Art Lange and Nathaniel Mackey, *Moment's Notice: Jazz in Poetry and Prose* (1993),

Dizzy Gillespie. Courtesy of the Library of Congress

and Robert Gottlieb, *Reading Jazz: A Gathering of Autobiography, Reportage, and Criticism from 1919 to Now* (1996).

Composer, conductor, and writer Gunther Schuller, president of the New England Conservatory, cofounder, with pianist/composer John Lewis, of the Lenox School of Jazz in Massachusetts, and champion of Third Stream music, also pioneered the musicological analysis of jazz. Schuller demonstrates the music's African-based foundations to a skeptical discipline too exclusively anchored in European art music. Schuller's *Early Jazz: Its Roots and Musical Development* (1986) and *The Swing Era: The Development of Jazz, 1930–1945* (1989) set the standard for a formal musical evaluation of jazz based on sound recordings.

Gunther Schuller's work inspired an entire generation of students and jazz fans who read and reread his books while replaying the records to which they referred. No one did more than Schuller to convince the reading public that jazz was a musical art form. His scholarly influence can be found in Mark Tucker's monograph *Ellington: The Early Years*, in Lewis Porter's musical analyses of tenor saxophonists Lester Young and John Coltrane, and in Scott DeVeaux's work on bebop, described in more detail later.

But the scholarly investigation of jazz also shifted away from the concerns of jazz musicologists, following instead the emerging lines of the culture studies movement within the humanities. The pioneers of this new approach followed the leads in Amiri Baraka's *Blues People*, situating jazz within the evolution in race relations, racial attitudes, and ethnicity in the United States. Baraka's work was extended and enriched by Lawrence Levine's widely influential *Black Culture and Black Consciousness: Afro-American Folk Thought from Slavery to Freedom* (1977), which linked blues and jazz to the secularization of black expressiveness brought on by the continuing twentieth-century migrations to northern industrial cities. Levine's *Highbrow/Lowbrow: The Emergence of Cultural Hierarchy in America* (1990) provided a compelling model for understanding the rise to dominance of European concert hall music and the corresponding denigration of jazz and blues.

Neil Leonard's *Jazz and the White Americans* (1962), while documenting the cultural pressures that influenced the interpretation of jazz as art form, traced the tensions between creative jazz musicians and the country's musical establishment. He portrayed such struggles as parts of a Hegelian dialectic that produced forms of homogenized, commercialized jazz when that of the black innovators was rejected as too shocking. According to Leonard's model, jazz innovators were likely to be vilified, copied, and exploited.

Having published the first scholarly cultural analysis of the production of jazz, Leonard then turned in *Jazz, Myth, and Religion* to the music's reception among primarily white jazz fans. Here he traced a fascinating pattern of secular religion in which devotees transformed African American musical entertainment into a true faith that served as a replacement for mainstream organized churches. This important study of audience thought and behavior remained an isolated beacon to which scholars turned only ten years later.

The cultural studies approach to jazz has tended to divide into those who emphasize jazz as a socially and culturally rebellious force and those who argue that it reflected and energized major developments in American life. Historian Kathy Ogren's *The Jazz Revolution* (1989), for example, portrays jazz as a revolutionary force that seriously disrupted American society and culture. Lewis A. Erenberg, *Swingin' the Dream* (1998), similarly portrays jazz as a powerful populist force taking its origins and energy from a democratic youth movement. James Lincoln Collier's *The Reception of Jazz in America* (1988), on the other hand, argues that leftist jazz writers had created the false notion that the American middle class had rejected jazz. In doing so, he argued, they had identified it too exclusively with the discontents of oppressed groups in the United States. In *Red and Hot: The Fate of Jazz in the Soviet Union, 1917–1980*, S. Frederick Starr also documented how susceptible jazz had been to the shifting dogmas of Soviet Russian governmental hegemony.

Three recent books have done much to integrate jazz into some of the most important themes in the twentieth-century history of the United States: the social construction of race, race relations, migration, cultures of consumption, and urban politics. As summarized by John Gennari, "Recovering the 'Noisy Lostness': History in the Age of Jazz," *Journal of Urban History* 24: 2 (January 1998), 226–34, historians have begun to revise the idea of jazz as a socially rebellious counterculture. Instead, they have emphasized its integration into the major patterns of migration and urbanization in the United States. Burton Peretti's *The Creation of Jazz* (1994) has described the role that jazz played in the major patterns of African American migration, out of the South and into major urban areas across the country. So, too, William Howland Kenney's *Chicago Jazz: A Cultural History, 1904–*

1930 (1993) portrayed jazz activities as integral parts of the growth of Chicago's leisure time entertainment institutions in the era of the Great Migration. Ann Douglas, *Terrible Honesty: Mongrel Manhattan in the 1920s* (1996), provides a rich cultural context for what was the single most important center of jazz activity in that era. In *Swing Changes* (1994), David Stowe argued that Big Band swing reflected and itself generated a national cultural consensus based largely on the New Deal coalition of working-class white ethnics, African Americans, Jews, and progressive intellectuals. Michael Denning's *The Cultural Front* (1996) included an insightful chapter on "Cabaret Blues," which integrated 1930s jazz into the period's politics of resistance to corporate cultural hegemony.

Analyzing representations of jazz in literature, cinema, and cultural discourse, Jon Panish, in *The Color of Jazz: Race and Representation in Postwar American Culture* (1997), follows a growing movement toward whiteness studies, arguing that the cultural mythology found in the representation of jazz serves to secure the hegemonic power of whiteness in the United States. This kind of cultural interpretation of jazz representations draws upon pioneering works by David Roediger, *The Wages of Whiteness* (1999), Homi Bhabha, *The Location of Culture* (1994), and Eric Lott, *Love and Theft* (1993).

Krin Gabbard brought jazz writing together with elements of cinema studies discourse in *Jammin' at the Margins* (1996). His book interpreted the ways in which film makers and screenwriters had marginalized the roles of famous jazz performers while using black jazz men and women as pawns in the dramatization of white gender identity rituals. Those simply seeking information on jazz scenes and performances in the movies also should consult David Meeker, *Jazz in the Movies* (1977). Gabbard's two edited volumes, *Jazz among the Discourses* and *Representing Jazz* (1995), collected examples of scholarly efforts to reexamine the journalists' jazz canon of great artist-auteurs while highlighting the impact of the media on popular perceptions of jazz.

More than any other author, Scott DeVeaux most successfully crossed the frontier between musicological and cultural analysis of jazz. Using both recorded solo transcriptions and historical data, DeVeaux's *The Birth of Bebop* (1997) deftly demonstrates how the social and economic inequalities faced by exceptionally gifted and accomplished black musicians deeply influenced the evolution of bebop.

The cultural studies approach to understanding jazz has yet to accord sufficient interpretive importance to the role of gender. The first books to insist on women's contributions to jazz were Sandra Lieb, *Mother of the Blues: A Study of Ma Rainey* (1981), Linda Dahl, *Stormy Weather: The Music and Lives of a Century of Jazzwomen* (1992), and Daphne Duval Harrison, *Black Pearls: Blues Queens of the 1920s* (1988). Angela Y. Davis, *Blues Legacies and Black Feminism* (1998), following leads suggested by Lieb and Hazel Carby, extends the subject's boundaries from female contributions to jazz's role in replacing rigid gender definitions with a greater flexibility. Leslie Gourse, *Madame Jazz*, describes contemporary realities for female jazz musicians. We await several more biographies of female performers and also anticipate studies of the ways in which jazz has encouraged certain heightened images of masculinity. A recent article by David Ake, "Re-Masculating Jazz: Ornette Coleman, 'Lonely Woman,' and the New York Jazz Scene in the Late 1950s," *American Music* 16: 1 (1998), 25–44, ably demonstrates the possibilities in a culture studies approach to gender in jazz.

Methodologically complex cultural approaches to jazz studies cast many of the genre's most basic assumptions into question. Many books on jazz have explored a particular style category, as in David Such's study of the avant-garde and Stowe's and Erenberg's on Big Band swing. Analysis of exactly how such style labels came into being in the first place and how they came to occupy such prominent positions in a critical jazz canon risks dismantling the architecture of jazz history. Some journalists fear that the scholars will eventually dismiss the term "jazz," thereby casting the musicians and their recordings into a critical and historical vacuum in which their marvelous creativity may the more easily be forgotten. The scholarly urge to deflate the promotional edge in journalistic jazz writing, to dismantle the critics' carefully crafted stories of a jazz continuum through time, and to expose the unacknowledged racial biases among white jazz writers risks destroying jazz's written reputation without replacing it with any other more coherent model.

The cultural studies approach to jazz has established one major new interpretation: jazz was and is a mediated music, part of a vast music business network that heavily influences our perceptions of the music. In order to put jazz into its most immediate cultural context, scholars will want to continue to investigate the media. Among those that have been particularly influential are the recording companies, radio and television broadcasters, the major band booking agencies, dance hall and nightclub entrepreneurs, the show business and music trades press, and jazz writers, who are the gatekeepers of the popularity polls.

Music Business

Several scholars have pointed the way toward this essential dimension of jazz studies. The third volume of Russell J. Sanjek's *American Popular Music and Its Business* (1988) and his *Pennies from Heaven: The American Popular Music Business in the Twentieth Century* (1996), written with David Sanjek, offer crucial information. Evan Eisenberg, *The Recording Angel* (1988), and William Howland Kenney, *Recorded Music in American Life: The Phonograph and Popular Memory* (1999), sketch patterns in the influence of record producers on the music and in the ways that listeners receive records. The autobiographies of jazz record producers Milt Gabler, John Hammond, and Teddy Reig must not be overlooked, and jazz scholars also ought to read those of producers in other popular genres, since the same industry-wide imperatives shaped most of the popular genres.

While awaiting a book on jazz and radio, those interested in the business, cultural, and communications contexts that radio imposed upon musical performance should read Michele M. Hilmes, *Radio Voices: American Broadcasting, 1922–1952* (1997), Daniel J. Czitrom, *Media and the American Mind* (1982), J. Fred MacDonald, *Don't Touch That Dial! Radio Programming in American Life, 1920–1960* (1979, 1982), and Susan Smulyan, *Selling Radio: The Commercialization of American Broadcasting, 1920–1934* (1994).

Discographies

Since the last edition of this chapter, giant strides have been taken in publishing jazz reference works. Without recordings, no aural evidence of jazz would exist, so discographies, which are listings of recordings with their personnel, instrumentation, tunes, company names, and identification numbers, inevitably play a crucial role in jazz research. The genre was invented by Charles Delaunay, and its template was created by discographer Brian Rust, whose *Jazz Records, 1897–1942* (1970), *The American Dance Band Discography, 1917–1942* (1976), and, with Allen Debus, *The Complete Entertainment Discography, from the Mid-1890s to 1942* (1973) defined the field. Rust's work also included *The American Record Label Book* (1983), in which one can learn about the histories of the various recording companies and their many different labels. Rust's legacy was carried forward chronologically by Jorgen Grunnett Jepsen, *Jazz Records, 1942–1965* (1966), Walter Bruyninckx, *Sixty Years of Recorded Jazz, 1917–1977*, Erik Raben, *Jazz Records, 1942–1980* (1987), and Tom Lord, *The Jazz Discography* (1992).

In addition to these sweeping, comprehensive discographies, several of a more specialized nature should not be overlooked. These books include Richard S. Sears, *V-Discs: A History and Discography* (1980), which catalogs the records issued by the U.S. government during World War II, Jan Leder, *Women in Jazz: A Discography of Instrumentalists, 1913–1968* (1985), Michel Ruppli, ed., *Atlantic Records: A Discography* (1979), and Richard Spottswood, ed., *Ethnic Music on Records* (1990), which covers recordings produced in the United States, 1893–1942. Discographies of blues recordings include R.M.W. Dixon and J. Goodrich, *Blues and Gospel Records, 1902–1942*, and Mike Leadbitter and Neil Slaven, *Blues Records, 1943–1966*. Finally is David Meeker, *Jazz in the Movies: A Guide to Jazz Musicians, 1917–1977*. As documentary films and videos have proliferated, Meeker's listing will be updated.

REFERENCE WORKS

Further research will begin with the major jazz reference works. The most useful, at least in beginning any project, is *The New Grove Dictionary of Jazz* (1994), edited by Barry Kernfeld. This single volume holds 4,500 articles, 1,800 discographies, 1,000 cross-references, 220 photographs, and 100 musical examples. Roger D. Kinkle's edited *The Complete Encyclopedia of Popular Music and Jazz, 1900–1950* offers four volumes that include alphabetical entries for performers and songwriters as well as a year-by-year chronology of popular tunes and Broadway musicals. Colin Larkin's edited *The Guiness Encyclopedia of Popular Music* (1995) places jazz entries within the broader context of popular music, as does Donald Clarke's edited *The Penguin Encyclopedia of Popular Music* (1990). Critic and pianist Leonard Feather collected biographical materials for his essential, multivolume *The Encyclopedia of Jazz*. John Chilton offers detailed biographical entries that are particularly strong on early jazz musicians in *Who's Who of Jazz: Storyville to Swing Street*. Valuable information on jazz musicians is collected in Eileen Southern, ed., *Biographical Dictionary of Afro-American and African Musicians* (1982).

A limited number of bibliographical guides organize references to the literature of jazz. The most useful is Donald Kennington, *The Literature of Jazz: A Critical Guide*, a comprehensive survey of published works up to 1980. That resource may be compared to Carl Gregor Herzog, ed., *International Jazz Bibliography: Jazz Books from 1919 to 1968*, and Alan P. Merriam and Robert J. Benford, *A Bibliography of Jazz*. Eddie S. Meadows, *Jazz Reference and Research Materials*, and Bernhard Hefele, *Jazz Bibliographie*, may also prove useful in some cases.

At the present juncture, anthologies of jazz recordings have become a major casualty of the culture wars. Culture studies scholars have particularly attacked as an artificial construction the canon of great jazz artists whose work has been made into the jazz tradition. With the racial, ethnic, gender, and social class dimensions of jazz history under such intense scrutiny, many scholars have wondered whether the white males who dominated jazz journalism had sufficient omniscience to impose such artistic pronouncements. This scrutiny has had the beneficial effect of creating intense discussion of how selections and omissions came to be made in past anthologies of jazz records. It has had the unfortunate effect of lowering demand for anthologies like the *Smithsonian Collection of Classic Jazz*, a set of five compact discs with accompanying 120-page booklet. This set was made readily available by its publisher and sold well with the imprimatur of the Smithsonian Institution. Although no longer in print, it will very likely continue to be widely used in academe in the absence of any other available anthology.

Photographs, whether artfully posed or simply publicity snapshots, communicate a visual impression of jazz musicians and their cultures. William Claxton, William Gottlieb, Herman Leonard, and Francis Wolff specialized in LP jazz art photos, often used on album covers, and each man achieved considerable levels of sophistication. Two major photo collections provide a visual survey of the sweep of jazz history: Orrin Keepnews and Bill Grauer Jr.'s edited *A Pictorial History of Jazz* (1966), long out of print, and Frank Driggs and Harris Lewine's edited *Black Beauty, White Heat: A Pictorial History of Classic Jazz*.

A great deal of jazz history was documented in the trade journals *Metronome*, *Down Beat*, and *Jazz Review* and the show business papers *Billboard* and *Variety*. A variety of interpretive approaches to jazz continues to appear in scholarly journals. As previously mentioned, the Institute of Jazz Studies' journal, *Annual Review of Jazz Studies* (1982–   ), has been the leading voice in jazz scholarship, but valuable articles on the subject are no longer limited to such specialized journals. Important work has appeared regularly in the *Black Music Research Journal*, edited by Samuel Floyd at Columbia College in Chicago. Floyd's *Black Music Research Newsletter* should not be overlooked. The Sonneck Society for the Study of American Music publishes *American Music*, in whose pages one can trace the methodological shift from musicology to culture studies. The *Journal of Popular Music Studies* of the International Association for the Study of Popular Music, a British organization, is an essential source, as is *Popular Music and Society*, published by the Popular Culture Center at Bowling Green State University. For several years now, the good news has been in seeing articles on jazz in the major humanities and social science journals; the bad news has been that the *American Quarterly* has not been among them.

Many listeners around the world became convinced of the enduring worth of jazz and created important collections of records and other documents. These numerous collections, listed in *The New Grove Dictionary of Jazz*, edited by Barry Kernfeld, house important primary and secondary sources on particular facets of jazz history. The single most important, comprehensive jazz research archive, however, is the Institute of Jazz Studies, housed in the Dana Library of Rutgers University at Newark, New Jersey. IJS offers an outstanding collection of sound recordings, historical documents, and photographs. The typescripts of interviews with jazz musicians made for the Jazz Oral History Project form an archival core

Ruth Brown and Taylor Collins. © Painet

as vital for historians as is the monumental IJS collection of sound recordings for musicologists. The Schomberg Center for Research in Black Culture, just across the river from Newark in the New York Public Library, houses crucial resources on jazz activity in Harlem. Information on other important jazz archives across the country and in Europe will be found in the *New Grove Dictionary of Jazz*.

The William Ransom Hogan Jazz Archive (www.tulane.edu/~lmiller/ JazzHome.html), headed by Bruce Raeburn at Tulane University in New Orleans, holds a rich trove of oral interviews with the founding generation of musicians from that city and its environs. As New Orleans has long been interpreted as the birthplace of jazz, the Hogan archive, also a fully stocked jazz reference center, remains of primary importance to historical jazz writing.

Several archives place their jazz resources within larger collections that represent the social and cultural contexts in which jazz musicians worked. Few would deny the influence of the recording industry on jazz, and the definitive collections of the Division of Recorded Sound, directed by Samuel A. Brylawski at the Library of Congress (LC), command the attention of jazz researchers. This collection, housed close by LC's stunning Music Division and a short distance from the Copyright Division in the Madison building, offers overwhelming evidence of the communications, business, and legal framework that produced jazz.

With the resources outlined in this chapter, it will be easier than ever before for those who wish to learn more about jazz to ground their efforts in solid primary and secondary sources. Jazz writing offers an unprecedented occasion to explore the interplay of music, race, and art in a historical context. Let us hope that jazz journalism and jazz scholarship both will serve to broaden and deepen the audience for the music and manage to avoid killing jazz with bitter racial wrangling. Learning to listen carefully and to play the music well can be a major lifelong challenge but one that is also a great elemental pleasure. All jazz writing should be at least partially devoted to reminding everyone of the unsurpassed rewards to be discovered in the music.

BIBLIOGRAPHY

Anthologies of Jazz Records

Giants of Jazz. Time-Life Records, STL.JOI-STL.J28. Alexandria, Va.: Time-Life Records, n.d.

Jazz Piano: A Smithsonian Collection. Washington, D.C.: Smithsonian Collection of Recordings, 1989.

The Jazz Singers: A Smithsonian Collection of Jazz Vocals from 1919–1994. Washington, D.C.: Smithsonian Collection of Recordings/Sony Music Special Products, 1998.

Louis Armstrong: Portrait of the Artist as a Young Man. Washington, D.C.: Smithsonian; New York: Columbia Legacy, 1994.

Morgenstern, Dan, comp. *The Greatest Jazz Records of All Time*. Philadelphia: Franklin Mint, n.d.

The New World Anthology of American Music. New York: New World Records, 1975–1978.

Schuller, Gunther, and Martin T. Williams, comps. *Big Band Jazz: From the Beginnings to the Fifties*. Washington, D.C.: Smithsonian Institution, 1983.

Williams, Martin T., comp. *The Smithsonian Collection of Classic Jazz*. Washington, D.C.: Smithsonian Institution, 1987.

Books and Articles

Ake, David. "Re-Masculating Jazz: Ornette Coleman, 'Lonely Woman,' and the New York Jazz Scene in the Late 1950s." *American Music* 16: 1 (1998), 25–44.

Albert, Richard N., ed. *From Blues to Bop: A Collection of Jazz Fiction*. Baton Rouge: Louisiana State University Press, 1990.

Albertson, Chris. *Bessie*. New York: Stein and Day, 1972.

Allen, Daniel. *Bibliography of Discographies*. Vol. 2: *Jazz*. New York: R. R. Bowker, 1981.

Allen, Walter C. *Hendersonia: The Music of Fletcher Henderson*. Highland Park, N.J.: Privately published, 1973.

Armstrong, Louis. *Louis Armstrong: A Self-Portrait: The Interview by Richard Meryman*. New York: Eakins Press, 1971.

———. *Satchmo: My Life in New Orleans*. New York: Da Capo Press, 1986.

Armstrong, Louis, with Horace Gerlach. *Swing That Music*. London: Longmans, Green, 1936.

Baker, Dorothy. *Young Man with a Horn*. Garden City, N.Y.: Sun Dial Press, 1938.

Balliett, Whitney. *Dinosaurs in the Morning: 41 Pieces on Jazz*. Philadelphia: J. B. Lippincott, 1962.

————. *Ecstacy at the Onion: Thirty-one Pieces on Jazz.* Indianapolis: Bobbs-Merrill, 1971.

————. *The Sound of Surprise: 46 Pieces on Jazz.* New York: E. P. Dutton, 1959.

Baraka, Imamu Amiri. *Blues People.* New York: William Morrow, 1967.

————. *Black Music.* Cambridge, Mass.: De Capo Press, 1998.

Basie, William "Count," and Albert Murray. *Good Morning Blues: The Autobiography of Count Basie.* New York: Random House, 1985.

Bechet, Sidney. *Treat It Gentle: An Autobiography.* New York: Da Capo Press, 1978.

Berendt, Joachim. *The Jazz Book: From New Orleans to Rock and Free Jazz.* New York: Granada, 1983.

Berger, Monroe, Edward Berger, and James Patrick. *Benny Carter: A Life in American Music.* Metuchen, N.J.: Scarecrow Press and Institute of Jazz Studies, 1982.

Berlin, Edward A. *King of Ragtime: Scott Joplin & His Era.* New York: Oxford University Press, 1994.

————. *Ragtime: A Musical and Cultural History.* Berkeley: University of California Press, 1984.

Bhabha, Homi K. *The Location of Culture.* London and New York: Routledge, 1994.

Blancq, Charles. *Sonny Rollins.* Boston: Twayne, 1983.

Blesh, Rudi. *Shining Trumpets: A History of Jazz.* 2nd ed. New York: Alfred A. Knopf, 1958.

Blesh, Rudi, and Harriet Janis. *They All Played Ragtime.* 4th ed. New York: Oak, 1971.

Breton, Marcela, ed. *Hot and Cool: Jazz Short Stories.* London: Bloomsbury, 1991.

Bruyninckx, Walter. *Jazz: Modern Jazz, Bebop, Hard Bop.* Mechelen, Belgium: 60 Years of Recorded Jazz Team, 1985.

————. *Jazz: Modern Jazz, Modern Big Band.* Mechelen, Belgium: Copy Express, 1985.

————. *Jazz: Progressive Jazz, Free-Third Stream Fusion.* Mechelen, Belgium: Copy Express, 1984.

————. *Jazz: Swing, 1920–1985; Swing, Dance Bands and Combos.* Mechelen, Belgium: Copy Express, 1985.

————. *Jazz: Traditional Jazz, 1897–1985.* Mechelen, Belgium: Copy Express, 1985.

————. *Sixty Years of Recorded Jazz, 1917–1977.* Mechelen, Belgium: Copy Express, 1977.

Charters, Samuel B. *The Bluesmen.* New York: Oak, 1967.

————. *The Country Blues.* New York: Holt, Rinehart, and Winston, 1959. Reprint. New York: Da Capo Press, 1975.

————. *Jazz: New Orleans, 1885–1963.* Rev. ed. New York: Oak, 1963.

————. *The Poetry of the Blues.* New York: Oak, 1963.

————. *Sweet as the Showers of Rain.* New York: Oak, 1977.

Charters, Samuel B., and Leonard Kunstadt. *Jazz: A History of the New York Scene.* Garden City, N.Y.: Doubleday, 1962.

Chilton, John. *Who's Who of Jazz: Storyville to Swing Street.* London: Bloomsbury Book Shop, 1970.

Clarke, Donald, ed. *The Penguin Encyclopedia of Popular Music*. London, England, and New York: Penguin Books, 1990.

Collier, James Lincoln. *Duke Ellington*. New York: Oxford University Press, 1987.

———. *Louis Armstrong: An American Genius*. New York: Oxford University Press, 1983.

———. *The Making of Jazz: A Comprehensive History*. Boston: Houghton Mifflin, 1978.

———. *The Reception of Jazz in America: A New View*. Brooklyn: Institute for Studies in American Music, Conservatory of Music, Brooklyn College of the City University of New York, 1988.

Condon, Eddie, and Thomas Sugrue. *We Called It Music: A Generation of Jazz*. New York: Da Capo Press, 1986.

Cooper, David E. *International Bibliography of Discographies*. Littleton, Colo.: Libraries Unlimited, 1975.

Crouch, Stanley. *Notes of a Hanging Judge: Essays and Reviews, 1979–1989*. New York: Oxford University Press, 1990.

Curtis, Susan. *Dancing to a Black Man's Tune: A Life of Scott Joplin*. Columbia: University of Missouri Press, 1994.

Czitrom, Daniel J. *Media and the American Mind: From Morse to McLuhan*. Chapel Hill: University of North Carolina Press, 1982.

Dahl, Linda. *Stormy Weather: The Music and Lives of a Century of Jazzwomen*. 2nd ed. New York: Limelight Editions, 1992.

Dance, Stanley, ed. *The World of Count Basie*. New York: Scribner's, 1980.

———. *The World of Duke Ellington*. New York: Scribner's, 1970.

———. *The World of Earl Hines*. New York: Scribner's, 1977.

———. *The World of Swing*. New York: Scribner's, 1974.

Davis, Angela Y. *Blues Legacies and Black Feminism: Gertrude "Ma" Rainey, Bessie Smith, and Billie Holiday*. New York: Pantheon Books, 1998.

Davis, Elizabeth A., ed. *Index to the New World Recorded Anthology of American Music*. New York: W. W. Norton, 1981.

Delaunay, Charles. *New Hot Discography*. New York: Criterion, 1948.

de Lerma, Dominique-Rene. *Bibliography of Black Music*. 4 vols. Westport, Conn.: Greenwood Press, 1981–1984.

Denning, Michael. *The Cultural Front: The Laboring of American Culture in the Twentieth Century*. London and New York: Verso, 1996.

DeVeaux, Scott. *The Birth of Bebop: A Social and Musical History*. Berkeley: University of California Press, 1997.

DeVeaux, Scott, and William Howland Kenney, eds. *The Music of James Scott*. Washington, D.C.: Smithsonian, 1992.

Dixon, R.M.W., and J. Goodrich. *Blues and Gospel Records, 1902–1942*. 3rd ed. Chigwell, England: Storyville, 1982.

Dodds, Warren, and Larry Gara. *The Baby Dodds Story*. Los Angeles: Contemporary, 1959.

Douglas, Ann. *Terrible Honesty: Mongrel Manhattan in the 1920s*. New York: Noonday Press and Farrar, Straus, and Giroux, 1996.

Driggs, Frank, and Harris Lewine, eds. *Black Beauty, White Heat: A Pictorial History of Classic Jazz*. New York: William Morrow, 1982.

Eisenberg, Evan. *The Recording Angel: The Experience of Music from Aristotle to Zappa*. New York: Penguin Books, 1988.

Ellington, Duke. *Music Is My Mistress*. Garden City, N.Y.: Doubleday, 1973.

Ellington, Mercer, with Stanley Dance. *Duke Ellington in Person: An Intimate Memoir*. Boston: Houghton Mifflin, 1978.

Erenberg, Lewis. *Steppin' Out: New York Nightlife and the Transformation of American Culture*. Chicago: University of Chicago Press, 1984.

———. *Swingin' the Dream: Big Band Jazz and the Rebirth of American Culture*. Chicago: University of Chicago Press, 1998.

Evans, David. *Big Road Blues: Tradition and Creativity in the Folk Blues*. Berkeley: University of California Press, 1982.

Fahey, John. *Charley Patton*. London: Studio Vista, 1970.

Feather, Leonard. *The Book of Jazz: A Guide to the Entire Field*. New York: Horizon Press, 1965.

———. *The Encyclopedia of Jazz in the Sixties*. New York: Horizon Press, 1967.

———. *The New Edition of the Encyclopedia of Jazz*. New York: Horizon Press, 1960.

Feather, Leonard, and Ira Gitler. *The Encyclopedia of Jazz in the Seventies*. New York: Horizon Press, 1977.

Feinstein, Sascha, and Yusef Komunyakaa, eds. *The Jazz Poetry Anthology*. Vol. 1. Bloomington: Indiana University Press, 1991.

———. *The Second Set: The Jazz Poetry Anthology*. Vol. 2 Bloomington: Indiana University Press, 1996.

Ferris, William. *Blues from the Delta: An Illustrated Documentary of the Music and Musicians of the Mississippi Delta*. New York: Da Capo Press, 1983.

Floyd, Samuel A., and Marsha J. Reisser, eds. *Black Music in the United States: An Annotated Bibliography of Selected Reference and Research Materials*. Millwood, N.Y.: Kraus International, 1983.

Gabbard, Krin. *Jammin' at the Margins: Jazz and the American Cinema*. Chicago: University of Chicago Press, 1996.

———. *Jazz among the Discourses*. Durham, N.C.: Duke University Press, 1995.

———. *Representing Jazz*. Durham, N.C.: Duke University Press, 1995.

Gennari, John. "Recovering the 'Noisy Lostness': History in the Age of Jazz." *Journal of Urban History* 24: 2 (January 1998), 226–34.

Giddins, Gary. *Rhythm-a-ning: Jazz Tradition and Innovation in the '80s*. New York: Oxford University Press, 1986.

———. *Riding on a Blue Note: Jazz and American Pop*. New York: Oxford University Press, 1981.

———. *Visions of Jazz: The First Century*. New York: Oxford University Press, 1998.

Gillespie, John Birks "Dizzy," with Al Fraser. *To Be or Not to Bop: Memoirs*. Garden City, N.Y.: Doubleday, 1979.

Gioia, Ted. *The History of Jazz*. New York: Oxford University Press, 1997.

Gitler, Ira. *Swing to Bop: An Oral History of the Transition in Jazz in the 1940s*. New York: Oxford University Press, 1985.

Gottlieb, Robert, ed. *Reading Jazz: A Gathering of Autobiography, Reportage, and Criticism from 1919 to Now*. New York: Pantheon Books, 1996.

Gourse, Leslie. *Madame Jazz: Contemporary Women Instrumentalists*. New York: Oxford University Press, 1995.

Gridley, Mark C. *Jazz Styles: History and Analysis*. 6th ed. Upper Saddle River, N.J.: Prentice-Hall, 1997.

Hadlock, Richard. *Jazz Masters of the Twenties*. New York: Macmillan, 1965.

Hammond, John, with Irving Townsend. *John Hammond on Record: An Autobiography*. New York: Ridge Press, 1977.

Harris, Sheldon. *Blues Who's Who: A Biographical Dictionary of Blues Singers*. New Rochelle, N.Y.: Arlington House, 1979.

Harrison, Daphne Duval. *Black Pearls: Blues Queens of the 1920s*. New Brunswick, N.J.: Rutgers University Press, 1988.

Harrison, Max. *Charlie Parker*. London: Cassell, 1960.

Hasse, John Edward, ed. *Ragtime: Its History, Composers, and Music*. New York: Schirmer Books, 1985.

Hefele, Bernhard, ed. *Jazz Bibliographie*. Munich: Saur, 1981.

Herzog, Carl Gregor, ed. *International Jazz Bibliography: Jazz Books from 1919 to 1968*. Strasbourg, France: P. H. Heitz, 1969.

Hilmes, Michele. *Radio Voices: American Broadcasting, 1922–1952*. Minneapolis: University of Minnesota Press, 1997.

Hobson, Wilder. *American Jazz Music*. New York: Da Capo Press, 1976.

Hodeir, Andre. *Jazz: Its Evolution and Essence*. New York: Grove Press, 1956.

Hodes, Art, and Chadwick Hansen, eds. *Selections from the Gutter: Jazz Portraits from "The Jazz Record."* Berkeley: University of California Press, 1977.

Holiday, Billie, and William Dufty. *Lady Sings the Blues*. Garden City, N.Y.: Doubleday, 1956.

Jepsen, Jorgen Grunnett. *Jazz Records, 1942–1965: A Discography*. Holte, Denmark: Knudsen, 1966.

Jones, LeRoi. *Black Music*. New York: Morrow, 1967.

Jones, Max, and John Chilton. *Louis: The Louis Armstrong Story, 1900–1971*. Boston: Little, Brown, 1971.

Jost, Ekkehard. *Free Jazz*. Graz: Universal Edition, 1974.

Keepnews, Orrin, and Bill Grauer Jr., eds. *A Pictorial History of Jazz*. 2nd rev. ed. New York: Crown, 1966.

Keil, Charles. *Urban Blues*. Chicago: University of Chicago Press, 1966.

Kenney, William Howland. *Chicago Jazz: A Cultural History, 1904–1930*. New York: Oxford University Press, 1993.

———. *Recorded Music in American Life: The Phonograph and Popular Memory*. New York: Oxford University Press, 1999.

Kennington, Donald. *The Literature of Jazz: A Critical Guide*. Chicago: American Library Association, 1971.

Kernfeld, Barry, ed. *The New Grove Dictionary of Jazz*. New York: St. Martin's Press, 1994.

Kinkle, Roger D., ed. *The Complete Encyclopedia of Popular Music and Jazz, 1900–1950*. 4 vols. New Rochelle, N.Y.: Arlington House, 1974.

Kirkeby, Ed. *Ain't Misbehavin': The Story of Fats Waller*. New York: Dodd, Mead, 1966.

Kofsky, Frank. *Black Nationalism and the Revolution in Music*. New York: Pathfinder, 1970.

Lange, Art, and Nathaniel Mackey, eds. *Moment's Notice: Jazz in Poetry and Prose*. Minneapolis: Coffee House Press, 1993.

Larkin, Colin, ed. *The Guinness Encyclopedia of Popular Music*. 2nd ed. Enfield, Middlesex, England: Guinness; New York: Stockton Press, 1995.

Leadbitter, Mike, and Neil Slaven. *Blues Records, 1943–1966*. New York: Oak, 1968.

Leder, Jan, comp. *Women in Jazz: A Discography of Instrumentalists, 1913–1968*. Westport, Conn.: Greenwood Press, 1985.

Leonard, Neil. *Jazz and the White Americans: The Acceptance of a New Art Form*. Chicago: University of Chicago Press, 1962.

———. *Jazz, Myth, and Religion*. New York: Oxford University Press, 1987.

Levine, Lawrence W. *Black Culture and Black Consciousness: Afro-American Folk Thought from Slavery to Freedom*. New York: Oxford University Press, 1977.

———. *Highbrow/Lowbrow: The Emergence of Cultural Hierarchy in America*. Cambridge: Harvard University Press, 1990.

Lieb, Sandra R. *Mother of the Blues: A Study of Ma Rainey*. Amherst: University of Massachusetts Press, 1981.

Litweiler, John. *The Freedom Principle: Jazz after 1958*. New York: William Morrow, 1984.

Lomax, Alan. *Mr. Jelly Roll: The Fortunes of Jelly Roll Morton, New Orleans Creole and "Inventor of Jazz."* New York: Grove Press, 1950.

Longstreet, Stephen. *Sportin' House: A History of the New Orleans Sinners and the Birth of Jazz*. Los Angeles: Sherbourne Press, 1965.

Lord, Tom. *Clarence Williams*. Essex, England: Storyville, 1976.

———. *The Jazz Discography*. West Vancouver, B.C.: Lord Music Reference, 1992.

Lott, Eric. *Love and Theft: Blackface Minstrelsy and the American Working Class*. New York: Oxford University Press, 1993.

MacDonald, J. Fred. *Don't Touch That Dial!: Radio Programming in American Life, 1920–1960*. Chicago: Nelson-Hall, 1979, 1982.

Machlin, Paul S. *Stride: The Music of Fats Waller*. Boston: Twayne, 1985.

Marquis, Donald M. *In Search of Buddy Bolden, First Man of Jazz*. Baton Rouge: Louisiana State University Press, 1978.

Massagli, Luciano, Liborio Pusateri, and Giovanni M. Volonte. *Duke Ellington's Story on Records, 1923– *. Milan: Musica Jazz, 1967.

Meadows, Eddie S., ed. *Jazz Reference and Research Materials: A Bibliography*. New York: Garland, 1981.

Meeker, David. *Jazz in the Movies: A Guide to Jazz Musicians, 1917–1977*. New Rochelle, N.Y.: Arlington House, 1977.

Mellers, Wilfrid. *Music in a New Found Land*. New York: Alfred A. Knopf, 1967.

Merriam, Alan P., and Robert J. Benford. *A Bibliography of Jazz*. 1954. Reprint. New York: Da Capo Press, 1970.

Mezzrow, Milton, and Bernard Wolfe. *Really the Blues*. Garden City, N.Y.: Doubleday, 1972.

Murray, Albert. *Stompin' the Blues*. New York: Vintage Books, 1982.

Nanry, Charles, with Edward Berger. *The Jazz Text*. New York: Van Nostrand Reinhold, 1979.

Ogren, Kathy J. *The Jazz Revolution: Twenties America & the Meaning of Jazz*. New York: Oxford University Press, 1989.

Oliver, Paul. *Blues Fell This Morning.* London: Cassell, 1960. Reprinted as *The Meaning of the Blues.* New York: Collier Books, 1963.

———. *Savannah Syncopators: African Retentions in the Blues.* New York: Stein and Day, 1970.

———. *The Story of the Blues.* Radnor, Pa.: Chilton Books, 1982.

Ostransky, Leroy. *Jazz City: The Impact of Our Cities on the Development of Jazz.* Englewood Cliffs, N.J.: Prentice-Hall, 1978.

Panassie, Hugues. *Hot Jazz: The Guide to Swing Music.* Trans. Lyle Dowling and Eleanor Dowling. New York: Witmark, 1936.

———. *The Real Jazz.* New York: Smith and Durrell, 1942.

Panish, Jon. *The Color of Jazz: Race and Representation in Postwar American Culture.* Jackson: University Press of Mississippi, 1997.

Pepper, Art. *Straight Life: The Story of Art Pepper.* New York: Schirmer Books, 1979.

Peretti, Burton W. *The Creation of Jazz: Music, Race, and Culture in Urban America.* Urbana: University of Illinois Press, 1994.

Porter, Lewis. *John Coltrane: His Life and Music.* Ann Arbor: University of Michigan Press, 1998.

———. *Lester Young.* Boston: Twayne, 1985.

Porter, Lewis, and Michael Ullman, with Ed Hazell. *Jazz: From Its Origins to the Present.* Englewood Cliffs, N.J.: Prentice-Hall, 1992.

Raben, Erik, ed. *Jazz Records, 1942–1980: A Discography.* [S.l.]: Stainless/Wintermoon; Copenhagen, Denmark: Jazz Media Aps, 1987.

Ramsey, Frederic, and Charles Edward Smith, eds. *Jazzmen.* New York: Harcourt, Brace, 1939.

Reig, Teddy, with Edward Berger. *Reminiscing in Tempo: The Life and Times of a Jazz Hustler.* Metuchen, N.J.: Scarecrow Press: Institute of Jazz Studies, Rutgers University, 1990.

Roediger, David R. *The Wages of Whiteness: Race and the Making of the American Working Class.* London and New York: Verso, 1999.

Rose, Al, and Edmond Souchon. *New Orleans Jazz: A Family Album.* Baton Rouge: Louisiana State University Press, 1967.

Rowe, Mike. *Chicago Blues: The City and the Music.* New York: Da Capo Press, 1981.

Ruppli, Michel, ed. *Atlantic Records: A Discography.* Westport, Conn.: Greenwood Press, 1979.

Russell, Ross. *Bird Lives! The High Life and Hard Times of Charlie (Yardbird) Parker.* New York: Charterhouse, 1973.

———. *Jazz Style in Kansas City and the Southwest.* Berkeley: University of California, 1971.

Russell, Tony. *Blacks, Mutes, and Blues.* New York: Stein and Day, 1970.

Rust, Brian. *The American Dance Band Discography, 1917–1942.* New Rochelle, N.Y.: Arlington House, 1976.

———. *The American Record Label Book.* New York: Da Capo Press, 1983.

———. *Jazz Records, 1897–1942.* London: Storyville, 1970.

Rust, Brian, and Allen Debus. *The Complete Entertainment Discography, from the Mid-1890s to 1942.* New Rochelle, N.Y.: Arlington House, 1973.

Sanjek, Russell. *American Popular Music and Its Business*. New York: Oxford University Press, 1988.

Sanjek, Russell; updated by David Sanjek. *Pennies from Heaven: The American Popular Music Business in the Twentieth Century*. New York: Da Capo Press, 1996.

Sargeant, Winthrop. *Jazz: Hot and Hybrid*. New York: Da Capo Press, 1975.

Schuller, Gunther. *Early Jazz: Its Roots and Musical Development*. New York: Oxford University Press, 1986.

———. *The Swing Era: The Development of Jazz, 1930–1945*. New York: Oxford University Press, 1989.

Sears, Richard S. *V-Discs: A History and Discography*. Prepared under the auspices of the Association for Recorded Sound Collections. Westport, Conn.: Greenwood Press, 1980.

Shapiro, Nat, and Nat Hentoff, eds. *The Jazz Makers*. New York: Rinehart, 1957.

Skowronski, JoAnn, ed. *Black Music in America*. Metuchen, N.J.: Scarecrow Press, 1981.

Smulyan, Susan. *Selling Radio: The Commercialization of American Broadcasting, 1920–1934*. Washington, D.C.: Smithsonian Institution Press, 1994.

Southern, Eileen, ed. *Biographical Dictionary of Afro-American and African Musicians*. Westport, Conn.: Greenwood Press, 1982.

———. *The Music of Black Americans: A History*. 2nd ed. New York: Norton, 1983.

Spottswood, Richard K., ed. Foreword James H. Billington. *Ethnic Music on Records: A Discography of Ethnic Recordings Produced in the United States, 1893 to 1942*. Urbana: University of Illinois Press, 1990.

Starr, S. Frederick. *Red and Hot: The Fate of Jazz in the Soviet Union, 1917–1980*. York: Oxford University Press, 1983.

Stearns, Marshall W. *The Story of Jazz*. New York: Oxford University Press, 1976.

Stewart-Baxter, Derrick. *Ma Rainey and the Classic Blues Singers*. London: Studio Vista, 1970.

Stowe, David W. *Swing Changes: Big-Band Jazz in New Deal America*. Cambridge: Harvard University Press, 1994.

Such, David G. *Avant-Garde Jazz Musicians: Performing "Out There."* Iowa City: University of Iowa Press, 1993.

Sudhalter, Richard M., and Philip R. Evans. *Bix: Man and Legend*. New Rochelle, N.Y.: Arlington House, 1974.

———. *Lost Chords: White Musicians and their Contribution to Jazz, 1915–1945*. New York: Oxford University Press, 1999.

Tirro, Frank. *Jazz: A History*. 2nd ed. New York: Norton, 1993.

Titon, Jeff Todd. *Early Downhome Blues: A Musical and Cultural Analysis*. Urbana: University of Illinois Press, 1977.

Travis, Dempsey J. *An Autobiography of Black Jazz*. Chicago: Urban Research Institute, 1983.

Tucker, Mark. *Ellington: The Early Years*. Urbana: University of Illinois Press, 1991.

Ulanov, Barry. *Duke Ellington*. New York: Creative Age Press, 1946.

Vance, Joel. *Fats Waller: His Life and Times*. Chicago: Contemporary Books, 1977.

Waller, Maurice, and Anthony Calabrese. *Fats Waller*. New York: Schirmer Books, 1977.

Wells, Dicky, and Stanley Dance. *The Night People: Reminiscences of a Jazzman*. Boston: Crescendo, 1971.

Williams, Martin. *Jazz Masters in Transition, 1957–1969*. New York: Da Capo Press, 1982.

———. *The Jazz Tradition*. 2nd rev. ed. New York: Oxford University Press, 1983.

———. *Where's the Melody? A Listener's Introduction to Jazz*. Rev. ed. New York: Pantheon, 1966.

Periodicals

American Music. Champaign-Urbana, Ill., 1983– .

Annual Review of Jazz Studies. Newark, N.J., 1982– .

Audio. Philadelphia, 1947.

Billboard. Los Angeles, 1894– .

Black Music Research Journal. Chicago, 1980– .

Black Music Research Newsletter. Chicago, 1977– .

The Black Perspective in Music. Cambria Heights, N.Y., 1973– .

Coda. Toronto, 1962– .

Downbeat. Chicago, 1934– .

Esquire. New York, 1933– .

Gene Lees Jazzletter. 1981– .

Guitar Player. Cupertino, Calif., 1967– .

High Fidelity/Musical America. Great Barrington, Mass., 1951– .

Jazzforschung/Jazz Research. Grasz, Austria, 1969– .

Jazz Magazine. Northport, N.Y., 1976– .

Jazz Review. New York, 1958–1960.

Journal of Jazz Studies. Newark, N.J., 1973–1981.

Journal of Popular Music Studies. London, 1989– .

Metronome. New York, 1885–1961.

Modem Drummer. Clifton, N.J., 1977– .

Musician, Player & Listener. Boston, 1977– .

New Yorker. New York, 1925– .

Popular Music and Society. Bowling Green, Ohio, 1976– .

Popular Music Journal. Cambridge, England, 1982– .

Rolling Stone. New York, 1967– .

Saturday Review. New York, 1924– .

Stereo Review. New York, 1958– .

Variety. New York, 1905– .

Web Sites

Institute of Jazz Studies: www.libraries.rutgers.edu/rul/libs/jazz/jazz.shtml

Schomberg Center for Research in Black Culture, New York Public Library: http://www.nypl.org/research/sc/sc.html

William Ransom Hogan Jazz Archive: http://www.tulane.edu/~lmiller/JazzHome.html

LEISURE VEHICLES, PLEASURE BOATS, AND AIRCRAFT

Bernard Mergen

The subject of recreational travel is large and complex; it is also a matter of considerable economic and social importance. Despite periods of high rates of inflation and gasoline shortages, the manufacture and sales of pickup trucks, motor homes, vans, sport utility vehicles, snowmobiles, trail bikes, motorcycles, motorboats, and airplanes have increased enormously. Bicycles, sailboats, canoes, gliders, and balloons have also proliferated. Statistics showing the number of participants in cycling, boating, flying, vanning, and "truckin'," while impressive, tell only part of the story. For the student of American popular culture, the study of recreational travel, pleasure boating, and flying offers ways of combining some of the major issues of our time in research that has public policy as well as academic usefulness.

The issue of leisure—what it is and what it means in our society—is the most obvious area of investigation. How do people conceive of and use their nonwork time? What are the relationships between such variables as class, race, age, sex, and region and the use of recreational vehicles, pleasure boats, and aircraft? What are the appeals of speed, fantasy, and competition in the kind of play associated with the use of these artifacts of modern technology? A second issue, commercialism, raises the question: To what extent is our leisure time manipulated by businesspeople interested in selling machines without regard to safety or environmental damage? The leisure vehicle industry—manufacturing, marketing, and servicing—is inextricably linked to both national and international economics. What role should the government play in the regulation of these industries? What control is necessary of individual owners of planes, boats, and vehicles? The third major issue, the conservation of natural resources, raises the question of the future. How will those subcultures that support each of the recreational vehicle, boat, and aircraft types respond to shortages of fuel and restrictions on land and water use? In 1974, a group of recreation and natural resource experts developed a set of future leisure environments for the U.S. Forest Service that included restriction of off-road vehicles in public recreation areas and the banning of private aircraft from metropolitan airports by 1980. At the same time, they predicted that airstrips and helicopter ports at most popular recreation areas and small private submarines would be as common as snowmobiles today by the year 2000. By 2050, their report concluded, only foot travel would be allowed in major public parks, but hovercraft would be widely used, as would jet-powered backpacks and single-seat, low-speed helicopters.[1]

Recreational vehicles are a product of our economy, technology, and value system. They must be studied in the context of many related activities, especially when we see that persons' choice of a leisure activity is often closely related to their work, social class, educational level, age, and family status. The use of a camper, van, boat, or plane is obviously related to such ancillary activities as hunting, fishing, scuba diving, photography, amateur radio operating, and camping. As the history of boating, flying, cycling, and recreational driving reveals, each activity has unique origins. Unlike less mechanized and less expensive pastimes, their present is a product of past decisions made deliberately and consciously by individuals who had much to gain and often much to lose.

HISTORICAL OUTLINE

Of the forms of transportation considered in this chapter, boating was clearly the earliest. The pleasure yacht was introduced into England in the seventeenth century by the Dutch, and by 1713 American shipbuilders had developed the schooner, a small, fast ship that could be used for fishing and coastal freight. Impromptu races between fishermen inspired wealthier colonists to invest in "well-fitted pleasure boats" through the eighteenth century. In Ireland and England the aristocracy organized yachting clubs to regulate the growth of pleasure boating and to supervise races among members. Many historians point to George Crowninshield's brigantine, *Cleopatra's Barge*, built in 1816, as the first American yacht, but Thomas Doubleday was sailing his twenty-foot sloop in Cape Cod Bay in the same year. The two basic types of pleasure boating, the day sailor and the ocean cruiser, seem to have appeared simultaneously.

By the 1830s, the first-generation American yachtsmen were testing their ships in competition and making technical improvements based on their experience. Robert L. Stevens, Edwin A. Stevens, and John C. Stevens, sons of the great inventor, turned their talents to sailing, and their boat, *Gimcrack*, designed by George Steers, became the first ship of the fleet of the New York Yacht Club when it was organized in 1844. Seven years later, Steers' yacht, *America*, astounded the British by winning the Queen's Cup at Cowes.

The end of the Civil War signaled the beginning of ostentatious yachting by American millionaires. The transatlantic race among *Vesta*, owned by Pierre Lorillard Jr., *Fleetwing*, owned by George and Franklin Osgood, and *Henrietta*, which belonged to James Gordon Bennett Jr., drew national attention in 1866. The 1870s witnessed the diffusion of yachting across the nation and the founding of clubs on both coasts, the Gulf of Mexico, and the Great Lakes. One of the first journals devoted to water sports, *Aquatic Monthly and Nautical Review*, appeared in 1876, with news of rowing contests and yacht club regattas. By 1884, yachting was firmly in the hands of professional marine architects such as Edward Burgess and Nathaniel Greene Herreshoff and devoted amateur sailors such as George I.

Land Rover. Courtesy of FreeFoto.com

Tyson and Malcolm Forbes. Burgess' *Puritan*, which successfully defended the America's Cup in 1885, broke with the tradition of broad-beam, shallow-draft sloops by adding a lead keel and reducing the waterline length. Five years later, Herreshoff continued this trend toward narrow, deeper-hulled craft in his *Gloriana*. Like most changes in yacht design, these were made solely to increase speed and to circumvent the rules regarding size, weight, and sail area.

The 1880s was also a decade of steam yachts and naphtha-powered motor launches, heralding the age of motorboating in the twentieth century. In the 1890s, journals such as *American Yachtsman* and *Rudder* helped to popularize small boat racing as well as cruising. Joshua Slocum's solo voyage around the world in 1895–1898, the poetry of John Masefield, and the popular spy novel *The Riddle of the Sands* (1903) by Erskine Childers all helped to create a romantic image of the sea and encouraged thousands of young men and women to take up sailing. Professional marine photographers such as N. L. Stebbins and Henry Greenwood Peabody published their work in books and magazines for thousands more who would never walk a deck or hoist a sail but who participated vicariously in every America's Cup challenge and Bermuda Race. Although the automobile caused a brief decline in yachting, the work of L. Herreshoff, William Gardner, who developed the "Star" class sailboat in 1911, and John Alden, whose designs led to the construction of more than 5,000 boats, contributed to the democratization of yachting. Sailing dinghies led the revival of yachting in the 1920s and 1930s. Collegiate racing, junior racing, and ladies racing all became an accepted part of yacht club activities. The artist Rockwell Kent made several voyages, one of which, to Greenland in a thirty-three-foot cutter, is described and illustrated in *N by E*. The gasoline engine brought new kinds of boating activity, as exemplified by Gar Wood's *Miss America* speedboats, which were approaching 100 miles per hour by 1928. Flying and yachting were pursued by many, both in the United States and abroad, as the journals *Flugzeug und Yacht* and *Aviation and Yachting* suggest.

Although the depression and World War II disrupted yachting, the postwar years were a bonanza for the boating industry. New technology produced safer, less expensive boats of all types. In the late 1970s almost 50 million Americans participated in some kind of boating. *Boating* claimed a circulation of over 200,000, and *Sail* about 170,000. *Canoe*, the publication of the American Canoe Association, which celebrated its centennial in 1980, had 30,000 subscribers. Although the variety of boating activities makes it difficult to generalize about the people who own and operate the "Snipes," "Sunfish," "Lightnings," Tempests," and various motorboats, it is clear that the traditional, masculine world of yachting is being replaced by a familial one. The past twenty years have seen the publication of innumerable books with titles like *Family under Sail: A Handbook for First Mates*, by Jane Kirstein, *The Woman's Guide to Boating and Cooking*, by Lael Morgan, and *How to Be a First-Rate Mate: A Sailing Guide for Women*, by Gloria Sloane. This trend affects the other forms of recreational travel as well.

Cycling also began as a male activity but eventually became a vehicle (literally) of women's liberation. Today bicycling is generally considered a family activity, and even motorcycling is promoted as a way to meet "the nicest people." Cycling, like ballooning, was French in origin, and the two remained linked until late in the nineteenth century. Neither developed very rapidly. In 1817, Baron Karl von Drais de Sauerbrun developed a bicycle with a fork over the front wheel to allow steering by handlebars; still later, in 1839, Kirkpatrick Macmillan, a Scottish blacksmith, added cranks attached to a system of rods and levers.

Almost a generation later, in the 1860s, Pierre Lallement and Pierre Michoux placed the cranks and pedals on the front wheel to create the highly successful velocipede. The next cycle, the ordinary or penny-farthing, with its large front wheel, required skill and practice to operate. Acrobats were quick to incorporate it into their acts, and French cycling instructors helped to give bicycling a continental, high-status image. Bicycles were promoted at the Philadelphia Centennial Exhibition, and in 1877 Colonel Albert A. Pope began his campaign for the bicycle and better roads. Two years later, *Bicycling World* began publishing news and technical information, becoming the official journal of the League of American Wheelmen (LAW) in 1880.

Improvements in bicycle design in 1884 led to the cycling boom of the 1890s. The LAW had over 100,000 members by the end of the century, many of them women whom reformers encouraged to discard their corsets and confining garments and take up cycling as healthful exercise. Almost as suddenly as it had begun, the cycling mania ceased, as bicyclists left their wheels to younger brothers and sisters and took up motoring. Not until 1972 did bicycles again outsell automobiles. Since the 1980s, off-road bicycling, or mountain biking, has increased in popularity and added significantly to the number of bicycle owners and riders.

Although inventors had tried to attach steam engines to bicycles and tricycles since the late 1860s, it was not until 1885 that Gottlieb Daimler successfully attached a gasoline engine to a frame similar to a velocipede. Further improvements made cheap, reliable motorcycles widely available by 1906, when *Motorcycle Illustrated* began publication. From the beginning, motorcycles were associated with a violent, libidinous, antisocial male subculture. As Sam Brooks points out in his excellent study of the motorcycle in American culture, the association of the motorcyclist with the lone horseman of western mythology was strong, despite the fact that motorcyclists tended from the beginning to form clubs and ride in groups. By 1912, Andrew Carey Lincoln and Lieutenant Howard Payson had created a fictional world of "motorcycle chums" for boys to read about and emulate. Perhaps, as Brooks suggests, the appeal of the motorcycle was even deeper than the image of the cowboy. "To the practiced and regular rider," wrote Brooks, quoting the authors of an 1898 book on cycling, "the motorcycle becomes so far like the lower part of the centaur that steering is almost unconscious and the balancing a matter of instinctive bodily sway."[2]

Curiously, motorcycling made a comeback in the 1960s under the stimulus of economic prosperity and an aggressive advertising campaign by Japanese manufacturers. Today the image of the motorcyclist is paradoxically split between the outlaw "Hell's Angels" and "Easy Rider" type and the weekend touring cyclist. The problems posed by the current popularity of cycling are neatly summarized in a recent publication of the Bureau of Outdoor Recreation (now the Heritage Conservation and Recreation Service). Noting that different users consume trails "psychologically" in different ways, the report argues that bicyclists, like hunters, are goal-oriented, needing point-to-point trails in which the trail is more important than the scenery. Motorcyclists and snowmobilers are more concerned with the stimulus from their machines, so their trails should emphasize difficulty of terrain.[3]

Snowmobiles are second only to motorbikes in popularity among off-road or all-terrain recreational vehicles. In the early 1970s the A. C. Nielsen Company found that snowmobiling was the third fastest growing sport in the United States, just behind tennis and skiing, with more than 7 million participants driving almost 1 million machines. Yet snowmobiles are only a small part of the leisure vehicle industry. Since the perfection of the Model A, the automobile industry has encouraged the development of pleasure driving. In 1914, the *Ford Times* claimed that "campers received motor-morphic medicine because of the laws of motion. Babies were put in cradles, children rode rocking horses, savages swayed to sinuous dances, and grandmother rocked ceaselessly in a rocking chair."[4] As auto camping caught on, car owners began to modify and customize their machines. Trailers were custom-made by cutting an old car in half and hitching the rear seat and wheels to another automobile. Home-built vans were made to look like Pullman cars, clapboard cottages, and prairie schooners. By 1930, the Covered Wagon Company of Mt. Clemens, Michigan, was mass-producing trailers, and a new industry was born.

Although trailer owners had organized as early as 1919, as the Tin Can Tourists, the 1930s was the decade of rapid expansion and public awareness. *Trailer Travel Magazine* began publication in 1936, and popular periodicals such as *Fortune*, *Harper's*, *The Nation*, and *Time* discovered "The Trailer Epidemic." Wally Byam's Airstream trailer made its appearance in 1935, a product of new technology and styles. Until the 1950s, recreational vehicles were limited to trailers and converted automobiles and trucks. Developments of the past forty years have redefined the term. Today the recreational vehicle (RV) may be defined as "a permanent compartment carried by a motorist to cook and/or sleep in."[5] This includes pickup campers, motor homes, camping trailers, travel trailers, and fifth-wheel trailers. It excludes the off-road and all-terrain vehicles such as jeeps, dune buggies, snowmobiles, and trail bikes. Vans, too, should be considered another category. The reasons for these distinctions are partly technical and partly sociological. RV owners tend to be older, married with children, and in the middle-income group. The image that the RV industry seeks to project is solidly "middle American." "In their own small way," wrote a spokesman in 1979, "RVs have strongly contributed to the rejuvenation of family life. Children find out how much fun parents can really be and that regular TV is not a necessity. At the same time RVs are an aid in bringing families together in a wholesome outdoor setting. Children are also learning the fundamentals of conservation and ecology."[6]

Off-road vehicle owners, on the other hand, tend to be younger, less affluent, and a good deal noisier. They seek action, adventure, and speed. Although the jeep appeared in 1940, the greatest diffusion of four-wheel-drive vehicles has taken place since 1980. *Off-Road* magazine, which began publishing in 1969, claimed a circulation of 125,000 a decade later and was closely followed by *4 Wheel Drive & Sport Utility*, published by *Road and Track*, and *Pickup, Van and 4-Wheel Drive*. The impact of off-road vehicles tends to be localized and seasonal, but in some parts of the country the organizations and subcultures associated with them are highly visible and politically powerful. Perhaps most visible on city streets are the vanners in their customized, elaborately painted and decorated vehicles. According to one observer, vanners are often former hot-rodders who have turned to vanning after getting married and having children and who find the results of their customizing more satisfying. The pleasure of customizing a van is "glancing over your shoulder and seeing you're surrounded by an environment of your own making. . . . Whether for families or for single people, the van is a playground for personality, a space to shape fantasy."[7]

Since 1990, a whole new category of vehicles has been created by the automobile industry, the SUV, or sport utility vehicle. Automobile manufacturers in Asia, Europe, and North America are competing aggressively in design and advertising for a share of a seemingly insatiable market. Dozens of models bearing names such as "Tahoe," "Explorer," "Tundra," "Trail Blazer," "Expedition," "Pathfinder" are clearly meant to appeal to the fantasies of harried commuters caught in suburban traffic jams. SUVs are controversial because they are larger than other passenger vehicles and thus create a safety hazard for smaller cars, they are not fuel-efficient, and they were not, until the year 2000, subject to the same emission controls. Yet, owners are generally enthusiastic, citing their own safety, passenger comfort, and image.

Of all the fantasies in which humans have indulged, perhaps the greatest is flight. Flying for pleasure may date from Icarus and Daedalus or the twelfth-century Chinese, but for Americans the connection is again French. Following Jacques and Joseph Montgolfier's balloon ascent in 1783, French balloonists gave frequent demonstrations in the United States. The first American balloonist is said to have been thirteen-year-old Edward Warren, who volunteered to ride in a balloon constructed by Peter Carnes. His ascent, made at Bladensburg, Maryland, on June 24, 1784, preceded Josiah Meggs' in New Haven, Connecticut, by a year. For the next forty-seven years only Frenchmen attempted flights in the United States. In 1835, however, John Wise began to generate interest in ballooning by selling rides in his hot air balloon, *The Meteor*. Within a few years Wise had a rival in the person of Thaddeus Sabieski Constantine Lowe, known as Professor Carlincourt, whose balloon, *Enterprise*, became the model for several that Lowe built for the Union army. After the Civil War, Wise continued his career as showman and scientific experimenter until his disappearance in a balloon over Lake Michigan in 1879.

Experiments in gliding were also being conducted by Americans and Europeans in the late nineteenth century. In the 1890s Octave Chanute made over 7,000 glider flights in Dune Park, Indiana, and in 1894, Charles Proteus Steinmetz of General Electric organized the first club, the Mohawk Aerial Navigation and Exploration Company. Although Germans and Russians were far ahead of Americans in developing the technology of gliders, the fact that the Wright Brothers succeeded in attaching a motor to one of their gliders overshadows the other achievements. Most of the energy of American inventors and engineers went into perfecting the airplane, yet gliders continued to play a role in the general development of aviation. In 1928, Charles Lindbergh lent his enormous prestige to Hawley Bowlus, who designed sailplanes that were competitive with European models. Anne Morrow Lindbergh was the first American woman to obtain a glider pilot license, while Richard Du Pont used his family connections to bring the best German ideas on soaring to the attention of Americans. When World War II broke out, however, there were only 165 glider pilots in the United States, compared to 186,000 in Germany. In the past thirty years, soaring as a pastime and for competition has become increasingly popular, and American pilots have set altitude and distance records. *Soaring and Motorgliding* magazine claims a circulation of 16,000. Moreover, the development of flexible-wing, kitelike gliders by Francis M. Rogallo and others in the late 1940s has led to the boom in hang gliding, a less expensive and more accessible recreation than monoplane gliding.

Flying private airplanes for pleasure, however, remains the most popular of all forms of airborne recreational travel. From 1911, when John and Alfred Moisant opened the first flying school in the United States, to the present, millions of Americans have received pilot's licenses. As of 1999 the Aircraft Owners and Pilots Association listed 616,342 pilots in the United States, of whom 247,605 held private pilot licenses and may be considered recreational flyers. Although owning a plane is expensive—a new, two-seat Diamond Katana cost around $90,000 in 1998, and a four-seat Cessna 172 sold for $170,000—a number of manufacturers have provided small planes suitable for pleasure flying since 1907, when Alberto Santo Dumont, the Brazilian flier and aeronautical engineer, introduced his *Demoiselle*. In 1937, Piper Aircraft Corporation began to manufacture the small planes that have become synonymous with private flying. Cessna, Beechcraft, Grumman, and, in the 1950s, Lear Jet joined Piper in providing a wide range of models for business and pleasure flying. Most recently, Cirrus Design revived the dream of highways in the sky by introducing a small plane equipped with a parachute that should lower the plane to a survivable landing if other options fail.

Yacht. Courtesy of FreeFoto.com

REFERENCE WORKS

Good bibliographies on the history of leisure vehicles, pleasure boats, and aircraft are hard to come by. There are many reference works, guides, and abstracts for these subjects, but they usually cover only the most technical matters. The cultural and social dimensions of recreational travel, topics of interest to students of American popular culture, have generally been ignored. Standard references such as *Readers' Guide*, the *Social Science Index*, and the *Humanities Index* yield some useful materials, as do some of the computer-based bibliographic search services. Since leisure vehicles, boats, and planes are used outdoors, bibliographies on the environmental impact of outdoor recreation often cover the subject.

Alison Wellner's *Americans at Play: Demographics of Outdoor Recreation and Travel* contains an array of statistics that help place recreational travel—off-road driving, boating, snowmobiling—in the context of other recreation. For example, boating, with 60.1 million participants in 1995, is the third most popular outdoor activity after walking and sightseeing, but recreational travel in general has shown steady increases in the past twenty years. *Rural Recreation and Tourism Abstracts*, an English publication, covers a wide range of activities and is especially useful for comparative studies. Geoffrey Wall's "Impacts of Outdoor Recreation on the Environment," Council of Planning Librarians Exchange Bibliography no. 1363, is a good, brief survey of books and articles published in the 1970s. Gerald Morris and Llewellyn Howland's *Yachting in America: A Bibliography* fills a long-standing gap. Similarly useful are Gale Research Company's *Bicycling: A Guide to Information Sources*, edited by Mark and Barbara Schultz, and *Recreation and Outdoor Life Directory*, edited by Paul and Steven R. Wasserman. Richard D. Christensen's *Motorcycles in Magazines, 1895–1983* provides 2,500 titles from trade journals and popular science magazines.

Flying is better provided with research tools. William B. Gamble's *History of Aeronautics: A Selected List of References to Material in the New York Public Library* and N. H. Randers-Pehrson and A. G. Renstrom's *Aeronautic Americana: A Bibliography of Books and Pamphlets on Aeronautics Published in America before 1900* provide exhaustive guides to the early days of flight. These works have been updated in Dominick Pisano and Cathleen Lewis, *Air and Space History: An Annotated Bibliography*.

The Pocket Encyclopedia of World Aircraft in Color: Private Aircraft, Business and General Purpose since 1946, by Kenneth Munson, provides brief historical sketches of each of the several hundred airplanes described. It is a literate, well-illustrated guide. Less encyclopedic and more personal is Jules Bergman's *Anyone Can Fly*, which explains why airplanes fly and how to fly a small plane and describes several types of aircraft. *Fly: The Complete Book of Sky Sailing* by Rick Carrier and *The Encyclopedia of Hot Air Balloons* by Paul Gamson are also how-to books with chapters on the history of their respective types of flying. Carrier also lists the names of several manufacturers, organizations, and publications concerned with soaring and hang gliding.

Associations can provide the student of leisure vehicles, pleasure boats, and aircraft with much valuable information. The Boat Owners Association of the United States, 880 Pickett Street, Alexandria, Va. 22304, and the American Canoe Association, Denver, Springfield, Va. (http://www.aca-paddler.org) are among the most important in their fields. The League of American Wheelmen, founded in 1880, is now operating out of offices at 1612 K Street, NW, Washington, D.C. 10006 (http://www.bikeleague.org), and the Motorcycle Industry Council is now located at 2 Jenner Street, Suite 150, Irvine, Calif. 92618 (http://www.yearbooknews.com). The American Motorcyclist Association, 13515 Yarmouth Drive, Pickerington, Ohio 43147 (http://www.ama-cycle.org) and the International Snowmobile Hall of Fame, 192 County Road 59, Bovey, Minn. (http://www.amsnow.com) are also useful. The Aircraft Owners and Pilots Association, 421 Aviation Way, Frederick, Md. 21701 (http://www.aopa.org) and the Balloon Federation of America, P.O. Box 400, Indianola, Iowa 50125 (http://www.bfa.net) are the leading organizations in their fields. This list is merely suggestive; there are many other national, regional, and local groups representing manufacturers, retailers, and consumers.

Four encyclopedic collections of outdoor pastimes from the second half of the nineteenth century contain material on leisure travel. The earliest, John Henry Walsh's *Encyclopedia of Rural Sports*, has sections on yachting, riding, driving, and pedestrianism. *The Book of American Pastimes*, published by Charles A. Peverelly in 1866, describes the uniforms of various yacht clubs and gives details of several early races. *The Tribune Book of Open Air Sports*, edited by Henry Hall in 1887, begins with a chapter entitled "Why We Want to Be Strong" by William Blaikie and contains sections on canoeing, cycling, and ice yachting. The chapter on yachting was written by Hall, who is identified as a special agent for the U.S. Census on Shipbuilding. The prolific John D. Champlin teamed with Arthur E. Bostwick to produce *The Young Folks' Cyclopaedia of Games and Sports* in 1890. Cycling and sailing are well covered.

RESEARCH COLLECTIONS

There are major research collections in several museums and libraries. Within the Smithsonian Institution, the Museum of American History has research materials on cycling and sailing. Especially important are the drawings made during the late 1930s by members of the Historic American Merchant Marine Survey, a project designed to record all types of American sailing craft. The National Air and Space Museum has extensive collections of primary material, including a large number of photographs of early aircraft. John Allen's *Aviation and Space Museums of America* provides details on several other collections of aeronautical materials. The Mariners Museum in Newport News, Virginia, has some good material on pleasure boats, and the Maritime Museum Association of San Diego has the luxury motor yacht *Medea* on display. The Henry Ford Museum has an extensive collection of vehicles relating to recreational travel. Contact the curators at 20900 Oakwood Blvd., Dearborn, Mich. 48121. Further information may be found in Allan Lee, *American Transportation: Its History and Museums*, and Robert B. Jackson, *Waves, Wheels, and Wings: Museums of Transportation*.

HISTORY AND CRITICISM

The handful of general histories of recreational travel includes Cindy Aron, *Working at Play: A History of Vacations in the United States*, which provides an overview, and John Jakle's *The Tourist: Travel in Twentieth-Century North America*, which is especially good on the importance of the automobile. For detailed examinations of highway and roadside, see Warren Belasco, *Americans on the Road*, Christopher Finch, *Highways to Heaven*, and Phil Patton, *Open Road*. Roger White's essay on early campers and recreational vehicles in *American Heritage* suggests that the auto camping experience needs to be investigated still further. In a class by itself, Hal Rothman's *Devil's Bargains: Tourism in the Twentieth-Century American West* is a meticulously researched and clearly written critique of the impact of recreational travel.

Finally, one general periodical, *Popular Mechanics*, stands out as indispensable for the study of leisure vehicles and boating. Since 1902 *Popular Mechanics* has been providing craftsmen with ideas and plans and small boys and girls with hours of pleasant dreaming. Its present circulation of 1,736,000 is too large to ignore, and its influence on American popular culture has yet to be explored.

There is no comprehensive history of American pleasure boating, but Douglas Phillips-Birt's *The History of Yachting* is a good beginning. Although written from a British point of view, it gives adequate attention to American yachting. The best studies are Arthur Hamilton Clark's *The History of Yachting, 1600–1815* and Howard I. Chapelle's *American Sailing Craft*. The former is as literary as the latter is technological; both are classics. From Clark we learn that *yacht* comes from the

Dutch *jaght*, which in turn comes from *jagen* and refers to the swift horses used in hunting. Pepys' diary for 1660 contains the word. Chapelle describes all the types of fishing and commercial ships—New Haven sharpies, skipjacks, friendship sloops, Cape Cod cat boats, and Gloucester schooners—many of which became prototypes for pleasure boats. Additional technical details on yachts of the nineteenth century are provided by William Stephens in his essential *American Yachting*.

More limited aspects of yachting are treated in Reginald Crabtree's *The Luxury Yacht from Steam to Diesel* and Alfred F. Loomis' *Ocean Racing: The Great Blue-Water Yacht Races, 1866–1935*. More important are studies of the men who designed and promoted yachting. The best of these is Bill Robinson's *The Great American Yacht Designers*, which describes the work of Nathaniel Herreshoff, Clinton Crane, John Alden, Philip Rhodes, Bill Tripp, Ray Hunt, Bill Lapworth, and Olin Stephens. Each of the men deserves a full-length biography, as do Edward Burgess, William Gardner, Sherman Hoyt, and many others. Samuel Carter's *The Boatbuilders of Bristol: The Story of the Amazing Herreshoff Family of Rhode Island* is a bit uncritical, but his subjects were indeed amazing. Karl Friederich Herreschoff [*sic*], adopted by Frederick the Great, immigrated to Rhode Island in 1786 and married the daughter of the wealthy merchant John Brown. For over fifty years, his sons and grandsons dominated yachting as no family has ever dominated a sport. *An L. Francis Herreshoff Reader* and other books by L. Francis Herreshoff help complete the portrait of this arrogant and talented family. A biography of John Rushton and a history of canoeing in the nineteenth century are provided by Atwood Manley in *Rushton and His Times in American Canoeing*. The work of another energetic small boat traveler, Lewis Ransome Freeman, should also be mentioned, and the incomparable Ruben Gold Thwaites.

Histories of yacht clubs begin with Benjamin Adams' *Amateur Yachting*, an account of the Quaker City Yacht Club in 1886, which encourages Americans to take up yachting as preparation for war. *Sherman Hoyt's Memoirs* is an excellent autobiography of a man who began sailing with the Seawanhaka Yacht Club in 1894 and went on to compete in several America's Cup races in the 1920s and 1930s.

Maritime photography is a subject worthy of study by itself. Edward Burgess' *American and English Yachts* is beautifully illustrated with the work of N. L. Stebbins, "Maritime and Landscape Photographer." *Representative American Yachts*, by Henry Greenwood Peabody of Boston, is a collection of 100 magnificent photographs. Frances Benjamin Johnston was invited to photograph the Kaiser's Cup race of 1905, and her excellent photos are in the Prints and Photographs Division of the Library of Congress, as is the collection of Charles E. Bolles of Brooklyn and additional work by Peabody and Stebbins.

Recent research on the economic and social significance of boating includes Elwell B. Thomas' *This Business of Boating*, which provides details on getting into the boat and marina business. Donald Field and Joseph O'Leary provide some interesting information on the social context of boating in their essay in the *Journal of Leisure Research*. Field and O'Leary found that family groups were more important in visiting the beach and swimming, whereas friendship groups were disproportionately represented in fishing. In power boating, family-friendship groups were overrepresented.

Among the many journals published for yachting and power boating, *American Yachtsman*, *Rudder*, and *Yachting* stand out in the early years. All contain club news, technical information, and occasional essays and verse. In 1888, young Hamlin Garland published "My Cabin" in *American Yachtsman*, one stanza of which reads:

> My cabin cowers in the onward sweep
>   Of the terrible northern blast;
> Above its roof wild clouds leap
>   And shriek as they hurry past:
> The snow-waves hiss along the plain;
>   Like hungry wolves they stretch and strain;
> They race and ramp with rushing beat;
>   Like stealthy tread of myriad feet.

In the 1970s, Bernard Goldhirsh challenged the established publishers with *Sail* and *Motorboat*. With a circulation of 174,000 in 1999, *Sail* is one of the most widely read sailing magazines in the world. *Yachting* survives, but *Rudder* merged with *Sea*. *Motorboat* is second to the Ziff-Davis Company's *Boating*. All these magazines offer well-illustrated feature stories on cruising and racing, how-to articles, and equipment evaluations. Comparisons with England, France, and Germany may be made by perusing *Yachting World*, *La Revue Nautique*, and *Die Yacht*. The *American Neptune* is a scholarly quarterly devoted chiefly to commercial maritime history.

Boating continues to inspire some of the best travel writing. In the last decade of the twentieth century, Peter Jenkins sailed the Gulf Coast from the Florida Keys to Brownsville, Texas, and described his journey in *Along the Edge of America*; Alvah Simon steered his thirty-six-foot, steel-hulled cutter into the waters off Baffin Island, where he spent a winter frozen in the ice; while Robert Sullivan paddled his kayak along the New Jersey shore opposite Manhattan and recorded his experiences in *The Meadowlands: Wilderness Adventures at the Edge of a City*. Two well-known land travelers also became watermen. William Least Heat-Moon, author of the best-selling automobile journey *Blue Highways*, crossed the United States in a twenty-two-foot dory, *Nikawa*, an Osage word meaning river horse. His book, *River-Horse*, is an account of the country and its people as he traveled four months and 5,000 miles from Astoria, New York, to Astoria, Oregon. Jonathan Raban's shorter voyage up the Inside Passage from Puget Sound, Washington, to Alaska in the thirty-five-foot ketch *Penelope* produced a more introspective book, *Passage to Juneau: A Sea and Its Meanings*. Both should be compared to earlier accounts of inland sailing by Bill and Kathy Dimond, Charles and Alice Mary Hadfield, Stephen Jones, Michael Poole, and Joe Upton.

The history of the bicycle is told in Robert A. Smith's *A Social History of the Bicycle: Its Early Life and Times in America*, Frederick Alderson's *Bicycling: A History*, Seamus McGonagle's *The Bicycle in Life, Love, War and Literature*, and more recently in James McGurn's *On Your Bicycle: An Illustrated History of Bicycling*. Industry journals such as *American Bicyclist and Motorcyclist* and participants' magazines such as *Outing* (which incorporated *Wheelman* in 1884) and *Bicycling* provide a good overview of technological and social changes. A recent account of

RV in Arizona. © Painet

bicycling around the world by David Duncan gives some indication of new developments in this mode of travel.

The motorcycle has received less judicious treatment, although Sam Brooks' dissertation, "The Motorcycle in American Culture: From Conception to 1935," is a good beginning. Brooks' thesis, that motorcycle riders were from the beginning likely to defy accepted social conventions, needs further testing, but the image of the motorcycle rider as a rebel has been sustained by writers such as Tom Wolfe and Hunter S. Thompson. Thierry Sagnier tries to counter that image in *Bike! Motorcycles and the People Who Ride Them*, but even he admits that the motorcycle is part of the youth cult in the 1970s. Magazines such as *Easyriders* and *Rider* present contrasting images of the motorcycle rider as outlaw and family member. The British have always taken a more serious view of motorcycling, as Richard Hough and L. J. Setright illustrate. An enjoyable account of a cross-country motor scooter trip is Peter S. Beagle's *I See by My Outfit*, while Malcolm Forbes' *Around the World on Hot Air and Two Wheels* recounts the famous publisher's ballooning and motorcycling adventures.

Recent motorcycle diaries of note include Ed Culberson's *Obsessions Die Hard: Motorcycling the Pan American Highway's Jungle Gap*, an account that focuses on the difficulty of riding his BMW R80 G/S through the Darien Gap, and Patrick Symmes' *Chasing Che*, which records the vicissitudes of following the Argentine revolutionary Ernesto Guevara's 1952 motorcycle journey through Chile, Bolivia, and Peru. Two authors who try to explain their fascination with motorcycles provide contrasting perspectives. Melissa Holbrook Pierson's *The Perfect Vehicle: What It Is about Motorcycles* covers the history of motorcycling and its current status as well as her own riding experiences. Brock Yates focuses on the most famous brand and its grip on the American imagination in *Outlaw Machine: Harley-Davidson and the Search for the American Soul.*

Homes on Wheels is a sympathetic study of the contemporary RV subculture by Michael Aaron Rockland, of the American Studies Department of Rutgers University. Rockland interviewed some of the 10 million Americans who travel and live in recreational vehicles, as well as some of the 800 entrepreneurs who build them. The book is illustrated with photographs by Amy Stromsten. The recreational vehicle industry has also been surveyed by Carlton Edwards, a professor at Michigan State University, and Al Griffin, a popular writer. Edwards' *Homes for Travel and Living* is a compendium of history, commercial and technological information, and legal matters. His bibliography is very useful, and he raises many important points, such as the potential for mobile homes to provide low-cost housing. The shift from vacationing to year-round living, satirized by Lucille Ball and Desi Arnaz in the film *The Long, Long Trailer* in 1954, continues, and its consequences need to be studied. Ted J. Born's "Elderly RV Campers along the Lower Colorado River: A Preliminary Typology" suggests that public campgrounds have become a kind of ghetto for the retired poor, and Sheila Johnson's *Idle Haven: Community Building among the Working Class Retired* also emphasizes the economic problems of mobile home dwellers. The lessening importance of trailers has been noted by David Thornburg in *Galloping Bungalows: The Rise and Demise of the American House Trailer*, while Allan Wallis argues a similar fate for mobile homes in *Wheel Estate.*

In contrast, Arnold Wolfe's breezy *Vans and Vanners* is a participant observer's sanguine report on the seminomadic life of customized van owners. The nation's estimated 300,000 vanners are sociable, belonging to more than 400 clubs, which sponsor "fox hunts," a kind of hide-and-seek played by the van drivers with the aid of CB radios; "radio rallies," which include various kinds of competition; "truck-ins," bacchanals that sometimes tarnish the family image of vanning; and "caravans," migrations of vanners across hundreds of miles of highway for the sheer joy of driving and camping together. Caravanning is like having your neighborhood on wheels, according to Wolfe, who described the typical vanner:

> Only 5 percent of the more than 2,500 vanners at the Third National Truck-in at Bowling Green listed their occupation as "professional." Only 7.5 percent of these vanners have college degrees, though nearly eight out of ten are under thirty years old. More than three out of ten indicated their work was connected with automobiles or automobile products, while more than 56 percent said they were "craftsmen, foremen or kindred workers; operatives or production workers; laborers" and "service workers."[8]

The elaborate painting of vans, or "trickin'," is the most public feature of vanning. Wolfe's book is well illustrated with color photographs that indicate a preference for western landscapes and tropical beaches in the murals that adorn the sides of many vans. The iconography of the van needs to be studied, but it may be that there is less than meets the eye. Customized vans have been around for more than sixty years, and, if the photographs in T. H. Watkins' essay in *American West* are any indication, they have always looked like picture postcards on wheels.

The desire to live their adventure fantasies motivates the owners of four-wheel drive and off-road vehicles. Studies of snowmobile and four-wheel drive vehicles repeatedly emphasize the desire to escape the ordinary, to live the American Dream of exploring the unknown, and to identify with a rugged, military image. These were the conclusions of Gregory Hill in an article in *Journal of Leisure Research* and of the Task Force on Off-Road Recreational Vehicles, sponsored by the secretary of the interior. Hill discovered that snowmobilers in central New York state drove as much at night as in the day. Other studies have shown that snowmobilers spend more time in their activity than other recreational vehicle owners and more money on their equipment than bicyclists, campers, or tennis players. Not surprisingly, Timothy B. Knopp and John D. Tyger found significant differences in attitudes toward the environment between snowomobilers and cross-country skiers, but a startling statistic was that although over 50 percent of the ski tourers had graduated from college, only 10.2 percent of the snowmobilers had completed sixteen years of school. Further research needs to be done on what appear to be enormous social class differences among recreation subcultures.

When Joseph-Armand Bombardier of Valcourt, Quebec, first put a Model T engine and a propeller on a sleigh in 1922, he began the snowmobile industry. Although, as Clarke Wallace points out in his *The Complete Snowmobiler*, the basic design was not perfected until 1958, the impact since then has been swift and widespread. Leonard Reich, "Ski-Dogs, Pol-Cats, and the Mechanization of Winter: The Development of Recreational Snowmobiling in North America," is an authoritative history of snowmobiles. *Snowsports* magazine claims to reach 1 million readers, and an article on names for snowmobiles suggests that homemade versions probably preceded the mass-produced models of the past three decades. What is called the "snowsled" in New England is the "auto-neige" in French Canada, while "snowbug" and "snowbuggy" are popular in Michigan. "Power toboggan" is used in Manitoba, "iron dog" in Alaska, and "snow machine" in the Midwest. In Minnesota "snowcats" and "ski-dogs" fight it out, but some old-timers prefer "power sled."[9] Other topics of interest to folklorists, anthropologists, and students of popular culture are raised in Pertti J. Pelto's *The Snowmobile Revolution: Technology and Social Change in the Arctic*, a study of the effect of the snowmobile on Finnish Lapps in the 1960s. Pelto found that the machines had produced great changes in the economy and social structure, leading to greater class stratification. John McPhee mentions similar changes in the lives of Alaskans in *Coming into the Country*.

The use of the ordinary family car for recreational travel and self-discovery has produced a rich genre of literature, from Edith Wharton's *A Motor Flight through France* in 1908, to William Fox's *Driving by Memory* in 1999. For Wharton, unexpected encounters on backroads restored the romance of travel, while driving on the often-empty highways of the western states inspires Fox to comment on the influence of the desert on highway design and roadside architecture. Novelists Theodore Dreiser and John Steinbeck have also written books of their automobile travels. Lesley Hazleton's *Driving to Detroit: An American Automobile Odyssey*, which chronicles her six-month journey in a Ford Expedition from Seattle to the motor city by way of the Bonneville Salt Flats and a Houston junk yard, and James Morgan's *The Distance to the Moon: A Road Trip into the American Dream*, which describes his forty-seven-day jaunt from Florida to California in a Porsche Boxter, are good examples of what Christopher Finch has called auto biography. Less ambitious accounts of car trips include Estella Copeland's *Overland by Auto in 1913*, Kathryn Hulme's *How's the Road?*, and books by Francis Line and Richard McAdoo.

Ancillary to books on driving are those that celebrate the highway itself. Beginning with George R. Stewart's paean to U.S. 40 in 1953, several highways have received book-length treatments. Michael Wallis and Qunita Scott, with Susan Croce Kelly, have praised Route 66, Drake Hokanson rediscovered the Lincoln Highway, Jim Lilliefors and Wulf Berg cruised Highway 50, Thomas and Geraldine Vale surveyed U.S. 89 from Canada to Mexico, while Andrew Malcolm did the same for U.S. 1 from Maine to Florida, and Angus Gillespie and Michael Rockland looked for America on the New Jersey Turnpike. Jerry Bledsoe confined his wanderings to U.S. 64, North Carolina's longest highway. In the mid-1980s Thomas Vale and Thomas Schlereth both rediscovered U.S. 40.

A definitive history of ballooning, *The Eagle Aloft* by Tom Crouch, and two books on aviation, Roger Bilstein's *Flight in America 1900–1983* and Joseph Corn's *The Winged Gospel: America's Romance with Aviation, 1900–1950*, provide a solid foundation for future studies. Jeremiah Milbank's *First Century of Flight in America* is on early ballooning, and Will Hayes' *The Complete Ballooning Book* brings the story down to the present. For important personal accounts, see John Wise, *Through the Air: A Narrative of Forty Years Experience as an Aeronaut*, and Charles McCarry, *Double Eagle*. Some of the adventures of the pioneering Wise have been mentioned earlier. His book is well illustrated with engravings. *Double Eagle* is the story of the first successful transatlantic balloon flight by Ben Ambruzzo, Maxie Anderson, and Larry Newman. Magazines such as *Ballooning* and *Buoyant Flight* contain information on significant flights, races, clubs, and equipment. A model for scholars interested in the social significance of activities such as ballooning is Claudia Kidwell's "Apparel for Ballooning with Speculations on More Commonplace Garb," in *Costume: The Journal of the Costume Society*.

Soaring and hang gliding are described in six books. Derek Piggott's *Gliding: A Handbook on Soaring Flight* appeared first in 1958 and remains a useful introduction. *On Silent Wings* by Don Dwiggins is the best general history, and D. S. Halacy, *With Wings as Eagles: The Story of Soaring*, and James E. Mrazek, *Hang Gliding and Soaring: A Complete Introduction to the Newest Way to Fly*, are useful supplements. Mrazek, a World War II glider infantry battalion commander, brings considerable experience to his subject. The most recent accounts are *Hang Gliding*, by Martin Hunt and David Hunn, and *A Hole in the Wind: Hang Gliding and the Quest for Flight*, by Hank Harrison.

Personal accounts of private piloting from 1937 to 1999 provide some sense of the history of pleasure flying. These include George Hutchinson's *Flying the States*, Alma Heflin McCormick's *Adventures with the Compass*, Douglas Bond's *The Love and Fear of Flying*, Mary Bernheim's *A Sky of My Own*, Diane Ackerman's *On Extended Wings*, and Burton Bernstein's *Plane Crazy*. Recent accounts of the joys of private flying include Laurence Gonzales, *One Zero Charlie: Adventures in Grass*

Roots Aviation, focused on Galt Airport in Illinois; Mariana Gosnell, *Zero Three Bravo: Solo across America in a Small Plane*; and Rinker Buck, *Flight of Passage: A Memoir*, which recounts the cross-country flight that he made in 1966 with his brother Kernahan when they were both teenagers. More literary accounts that explore some of the deeper psychological aspects of flying may be found in William Langewiesche's *Inside the Sky: A Meditation on Flight* and Henry Kisor's *Flight of the Gin Fizz: Midlife at 4,500 Feet*. Kisor flew a thirty-year-old Cessna 150 in a replication of Cal Rodgers' epic 1911 flight.

Dominick Pisano's *To Fill the Sky with Pilots* provides a history of the Civilian Pilot Training Program of the 1930s. There is great need for biographies and histories of manufacturers and pilots. Devon E. Francis' *Mr. Piper and His Cubs* is only a modest beginning. *American Aviation Historical Society Journal* contains some good essays on private flying, but most of the history of recreational air travel is still locked in the memories and personal papers of the pioneers. *Flying*, with a circulation of 380,000, is the most important trade journal, with *Air Progress*, *AOPA Pilot*, and *Sport Aviation* providing equally valuable information.

ANTHOLOGIES AND REPRINTS

Sports in North America: A Documentary History brings together primary material from many sources. Volume 4, edited by George B. Kirsch, covers the years 1860–1880, when yachting and bicycling were becoming popular. David Seybold, *Boats: An Anthology* is a collection of twenty-five stories, poems, and essays by Peter Matthiessen, Annie Dillard, Tim Cahill, and others.

NOTES

I would like to thank the following individuals for their help in preparing the original version of this chapter: Julia Herron, administrator, Member Communications and Publications, Recreational Vehicle Industry Association; Judy Hinds, editor, Recreational Vehicle Dealers Association; John Haifley, *Tempest* sailor; Robert Humphrey, Department of Anthropology, George Washington University; Dom Pisano, National Air and Space Museum; Tom Narbeth, assistant reference librarian, George Washington University; Donald Berkebile, curator, National Museum of American History; and Andrew Mergen, Department of Justice. This revision has replaced about one-third of the original references with new and updated material.

1. Elwood L. Shafer, George H. Moeller, and Russell E. Getty. "Future Leisure Environments." U.S. Department of Agriculture, Forest Service Research Paper, NE-301. Upper Darby, Pa., 1974, 7.

2. Sammy Kent Brooks, "The Motorcycle in American Culture: From Conception to 1935" (Ph.D. diss., George Washington University, 1975), 38.

3. Bureau of Outdoor Recreation, "America's Trails," *Outdoor Recreation Action* 42 (Winter 1976), 39.

4. Reynold M. Wik, *Henry Ford and Grass Roots America* (Ann Arbor: University of Michigan Press, 1972), 27.

5. Al Griffin, *Recreational Vehicles* (Chicago: Regnery, 1973), 7.

6. James B. Summers, "The RV Industry and Its Future," *RVDA News* 12 (June 1979), 4.

7. Arnold Wolfe, *Vans and Vanners* (Matteson, Ill.: Greatlakes Living Press, 1976), 2.

8. Ibid., 47.

9. *Snowsports* (October 1972), 19.

BIBLIOGRAPHY

Books and Articles

Ackerman, Diane. *On Extended Wings*. New York: Atheneum, 1985.

Adams, Benjamin. *Amateur Yachting*. Philadelphia: B. F. Adams, 1886.

Alderson, Frederick. *Bicycling: A History*. New York: Praeger, 1972.

Allen, John. *Aviation and Space Museums of America*. New York: Arco, 1975.

Aron, Cindy S. *Working at Play: A History of Vacations in the United States*. New York: Oxford University Press, 1999.

Badaracco, R. J. "ORV's: Often Rough on Visitors." *Parks and Recreation* 11 (September 1976), 32–35, 68–75.

Baldwin, Malcolm F. *The Off-Road Vehicle and Environmental Quality: A Report on the Social and Environmental Effects of Off-Road Vehicles, Particularly Snowmobiles*. Washington, D.C.: Conservation Foundation, 1970.

Beagle, Peter S. *I See by My Outfit*. New York: Viking, 1965.

Belasco, Warren J. *Americans on the Road: From Autocamp to Motel, 1910–1945*. Cambridge: Massachusetts Institute of Technology Press, 1979.

Berg, Wulf. *US 50, Coast to Coast*. Suffolk, Va.: W. Berg Press, 1996.

Bergman, Jules. *Anyone Can Fly*. Garden City, N.Y.: Doubleday, 1976.

Bernheim, Mary Lilias Christian. *A Sky of My Own*. New York: Macmillan, 1974.

Bernstein, Burton. *Plane Crazy: A Celebration of Flying*. New York: Ticknor and Fields, 1986.

Bilstein, Roger. *Flight in America 1900–1983: From the Wrights to the Astronauts*. Baltimore: Johns Hopkins University Press, 1984.

Bledsoe, Jerry. *From Whalebone to Hot House: A Journey along North Carolina's Longest Highway, U.S. 64*. Charlotte, N.C.: East Woods Press, 1986.

Bond, Douglas. *The Love and Fear of Flying*. New York: International Universities Press, 1952.

Born, Ted J. "Elderly RV Campers along the Lower Colorado River: A Preliminary Typology." *Journal of Leisure Research* 8 (Fall 1976), 256–62.

Brooks, Sammy Kent. "The Motorcycle in American Culture: From Conception to 1935." Ph.D. diss., George Washington University, 1975.

Buck, Rinker. *Flight of Passage: A Memoir*. New York: Hyperion, 1997.

Burgess, Edward. *American and English Yachts*. New York: Scribner's, 1887.

Butler, R. W. "The Impact of Off-Road Vehicles on Travel." *Journal of Travel Research* 13 (Spring 1975), 13–16.

Byam, Wally. *Trailer Travel Here and Abroad: The New Way to Adventurous Living*. New York: McKay, 1960.

Carrier, Rick. *Fly: The Complete Book of Sky Sailing*. New York: McGraw-Hill, 1974.

Carter, Samuel. *The Boatbuilders of Bristol: The Story of the Amazing Herreshoff Family of Rhode Island*. Garden City, N.Y.: Doubleday, 1970.

Chadwick, Henry. *Beadle's Dime Hand-Book of Yachting and Rowing*. New York: Beadle, 1867.

Champlin, John D., and Arthur E. Bostwick. *The Young Folks' Cyclopaedia of Games and Sports*. New York: Holt, 1890.

Chapelle, Howard I. *American Sailing Craft*. New York: Kennedy, 1936. Reprint. Camden, Maine: International Marine, 1975.

Christensen, Richard D. *Motorcycles in Magazines, 1895–1983*. Metuchen, N.J.: Scarecrow Press, 1985.

Clark, Arthur Hamilton. *The History of Yachting, 1600–1815*. New York: Putnam's, 1904.

Copeland, Estella M. *Overland by Auto in 1913*. Indianapolis: Indiana Historical Society, 1981.

Corn, Joseph. *The Winged Gospel: America's Romance with Aviation, 1900–1950*. New York: Oxford University Press, 1983.

Crabtree, Reginald. *The Luxury Yacht from Steam to Diesel*. New York: Drake, 1974.

Crouch, Tom. *The Eagle Aloft: Two Centuries of the Balloon in America*. Washington, D.C.: Smithsonian Institution Press, 1983.

Culberson, Ed. *Obsessions Die Hard: Motorcycling the Pan American Highway's Jungle Gap*. Kissimmee, Fla.: Teak Wood Press, 1991. Reprint. North Conway, N.H.: Whitehorse, 1996.

Dimond, Bill and Kathy. *Across the U.S.A.—by Boat*. New York: John Day, 1970.

Dreiser, Theodore. *A Hoosier Holiday*. New York: John Lane, 1916. Reprint. Bloomington: University of Indiana Press, 1997.

Duncan, David. *Pedaling to the Ends of the Earth*. New York: Simon and Schuster, 1986.

Dwiggins, Don. *On Silent Wings*. New York: Grosset and Dunlap, 1970.

Editors of Flying Magazine. *Best of Flying*. New York: Van Nostrand Reinhold, 1977.

Edwards, Carlton. *Homes for Travel and Living*. East Lansing, Mich.: Carl Edwards, 1977.

Fallows, James. "Turn Left at Cloud 109." *The New York Times Magazine* (November 21, 1999), 84–87.

Field, Donald, and Joseph O'Leary. "Social Groups as a Basis for Assessing Participation in Selected Water Activities." *Journal of Leisure Research* 5 (Spring 1973), 16–25.

Finch, Christopher. *Highways to Heaven: The Auto Biography of America*. New York: HarperCollins, 1992.

Forbes, Malcolm. *Around the World on Hot Air and Two Wheels*. New York: Simon and Schuster, 1985.

Fox, William L. *Driving by Memory*. Albuquerque: University of New Mexico Press, 1999.

Francis, Devon E. *Mr. Piper and His Cubs*. Ames: Iowa State University Press, 1973.

Freeman, Lewis Ransome. *By Waterways to Gotham: The Account of a Two Thousand Mile Voyage by Skiff and Outboard Motor from Milwaukee to New York*. New York: Dodd, Mead, 1926.

———. *Waterways of Western Wandering: Small Boat Voyages down the Ohio, Missouri, and Mississippi Rivers*. New York: Dodd, Mead, 1927.

Gamble, William B., ed. *History of Aeronautics: A Selected List of References to Material in the New York Public Library*. New York: Arno Reprint, 1971.

Gamson, Paul. *The Encyclopedia of Hot Air Balloons*. New York: Drake, 1978.

Gillespie, Angus, and Michael Rockland. *Looking for America on the New Jersey Turnpike*. New Brunswick, N.J.: Rutgers University Press, 1989.

Gonzales, Laurence. *One Zero Charlie: Adventures in Grass Roots Aviation*. New York: Simon and Schuster, 1992.

Gosnell, Mariana. *Zero Three Bravo: Solo across America in a Small Plane*. New York: Knopf, 1993.

Griffin, Al. *Recreational Vehicles*. Chicago: Regnery, 1973.

Hadfield, Charles, and Alice Mary. *Afloat in America: Two Enthusiasts Explore the United States and Canada by Waterway and Rail*. North Pomfret, Vt.: David and Charles, 1979.

Halacy, D. S. *With Wings as Eagles: The Story of Soaring*. Indianapolis: Bobbs-Merrill, 1975.

Hall, Henry, ed. *The Tribune Book of Open Air Sports*. New York: Tribune, 1887.

Harrison, Hank. *A Hole in the Wind: Hang Gliding and the Quest for Flight*. Indianapolis: Bobbs-Merrill, 1979.

Hayes, Will. *The Complete Ballooning Book*. Mountain View, Calif.: World, 1977.

Hazleton, Lesley. *Driving to Detroit: An American Automobile Odyssey*. New York: Free Press, 1998.

Heat-Moon, William Least. *Blue Highways*. Boston: Little, Brown, 1982.

———. *River-Horse*. Boston: Houghton Mifflin, 1999.

Herreshoff, L. Francis. *An L. Francis Herreshoff Reader*. Camden, Maine: International Marine, 1978.

Hill, Gregory. "Central New York Snowmobilers and Patterns of Vehicle Use." *Journal of Leisure Research* 6 (Fall 1974), 280–92.

Hokanson, Drake. *The Lincoln Highway: Main Street across America*. Iowa City: University of Iowa Press, 1988.

Hough, Richard, and L. J. Setright. *History of the World's Motorcycles*. New York: Harper and Row, 1973.

Hoyt, Charles Sherman. *Sherman Hoyt's Memoirs*. New York: Van Nostrand, 1950.

Hulme, Kathryn. *How's the Road?* San Francisco: Privately printed, 1928.

Hunt, Martin, and David Hunn. *Hang Gliding*. New York: Acro, 1977.

Hutchinson, George R. *Flying the States*. Chicago: A. Whitman, 1937.

Jackson, Robert B. *Waves, Wheels, and Wings: Museums of Transportation*. New York: H. Z. Walck, 1974.

Jakle, John. *The Tourist: Travel in Twentieth-Century North America*. Lincoln: University of Nebraska Press, 1985.

Jenkins, Peter. *Along the Edge of America*. Nashville: Rutledge Hill Press, 1995. Reprint. Boston: Houghton Mifflin, 1997.

Johnson, Sheila. *Idle Haven: Community Building among the Working Class Retired*. Berkeley: University of California Press, 1971.

Jones, Stephen. *Drifting; Being the Author's Account of His Voyages in Dooryards, Alleys, Bayous, Millraces, Swamps, Sumps, Rivers, Creeks, Canals, Lakes, Bays & Open Sewers about the Historic Lands of New Orleans, Valley of the Swans, Cape May, Yorktown, Jamestown, Mystic, Noank, and Westerly, Rhode Island*. New York: Macmillan, 1971.

Keith, J. E. "Snowmobiling—A Look at Participants." *Journal of Travel Research* 17 (Fall 1978), 30.

Kent, Rockwell. *N by E.* New York: Brewer and Warren, 1930. Reprint. Middletown, Conn.: Wesleyan University Press, 1978.

Kidwell, Claudia. "Apparel for Ballooning with Speculations on More Commonplace Garb." *Costume: The Journal of the Costume Society* 11 (1977), 73–87.

Kirsch, George B. *Sports in North America: A Documentary History.* Vol. 4: *Sports in War, Revival and Expansion 1860–1880.* Gulf Breeze, Fla.: Academic International Press, 1995.

Kirstein, Jane. *Family under Sail: A Handbook for First Mates.* New York: Macmillan, 1970.

Kisor, Henry. *Flight of the Gin Fizz: Midlife at 4,500 Feet.* New York: Basic Books, 1997.

Knopp, Timothy B., and John D. Tyger. "A Study of Conflict in Recreational Land Use: Snowmobiling vs. Ski-Touring." *Journal of Leisure Research* 5 (Summer 1973), 6–17.

Langewiesche, William. *Inside the Sky: A Meditation on Flight.* New York: Pantheon, 1998.

Lee, Allan E. *American Transportation: Its History and Museums.* Charlottesville, Va.: Hildesigns Press, 1993.

Lewis, David, and Laurence Goldstein, eds. *The Automobile and American Culture.* Ann Arbor: University of Michigan Press, 1983.

Lilliefors, Jim. *Highway 50: Ain't That America.* Golden, Colo.: Fulcrum, 1993.

Lincoln, Andrew Carey. *The Motorcycle Chums in the Land of the Sky.* Chicago: M. A. Donohue, 1912.

Line, Francis R. *Scrapbook on America.* Irvine, Calif.: Wide Horizons Press, 1990.

Loomis, Alfred F. *Ocean Racing: The Great Blue-Water Yacht Races, 1866–1935.* New York: William Morrow, 1936. Reprint. New York: Arno, 1967.

Malcolm, Andrew. *U.S. 1.* New York: St. Martin's, 1991.

Manley, Atwood. *Rushton and His Times in American Canoeing.* Syracuse, N.Y.: Syracuse University Press, 1968.

McAdoo, Richard B. *Eccentric Circles: Around America in a House on Wheels.* Boston: Houghton Mifflin, 1991.

McCarry, Charles, with Ben Ambruzzo, Maxie Anderson, and Larry Newman. *Double Eagle.* Boston: Little, Brown, 1979.

McCormick, Alma Heflin. *Adventures with the Compass.* Boston: Little, Brown, 1942.

McGonagle, Seamus. *The Bicycle in Life, Love, War and Literature.* New York: Barnes, 1968.

McGurn, James. *On Your Bicycle: An Illustrated History of Bicycling.* London: Murray, 1988.

McPhee, John. *Coming into the Country.* New York: Farrar, Straus, and Giroux, 1977.

Milbank, Jeremiah. *First Century of Flight in America.* Princeton, N.J.: Princeton University Press, 1943.

Morgan, James. *The Distance to the Moon: A Road Trip into the American Dream.* East Rutherford, N.J.: Riverhead Books, 1999.

Morgan, Lael. *The Woman's Guide to Boating and Cooking*. Freeport, Maine: B. Wheelwright, 1968. Rev. ed. Garden City, N.Y.: Doubleday, 1974.

Morris, Gerald E., and Llewellyn Howland III. *Yachting in America: A Bibliography Embracing the History, Practice, and Equipment of American Yachting and Pleasure Boating from Earliest Beginnings to circa 1988*. Mystic, Conn.: Mystic Seaport Museum, 1991.

Mrazek, James E. *Hang Gliding and Soaring: A Complete Introduction to the Newest Way to Fly*. New York: St. Martin's Press, 1976.

Munson, Kenneth. *The Pocket Encyclopedia of World Aircraft in Color: Private Aircraft, Business and General Purpose since 1946*. New York: Macmillan, 1969.

National Transportation Safety Board, Bureau of Surface Transportation Safety. *Safety Aspects of Recreational Vehicles*. Washington, D.C.: Government Printing Office, 1972.

Oliver, Smith Hempstone, and Donald H. Berkebile. *The Smithsonian Collection of Automobiles and Motorcycles*. Washington, D.C.: Smithsonian Institution, 1968.

———. *Wheels and Wheeling: The Smithsonian Cycle Collection*. Washington, D.C.: Smithsonian Institution, 1974.

Olyslager Organization. *The Jeep*. London: F. Warne, 1971.

Partridge, Michael. *Motorcycle Pioneers: The Men, the Machines, the Events, 1860–1930*. New York: Acro, 1977.

Patton, Phil. *Open Road: A Celebration of the American Highway*. New York: Simon and Schuster, 1986.

Payson, Howard. *The Motorcycle Chums around the World*. New York: Hurst, 1912.

Peabody, Henry Greenwood. *Representative American Yachts*. Boston: Henry G. Peabody, 1893.

Pelto, Pertti J. *The Snowmobile Revolution: Technology and Social Change in the Arctic*. Menlo Park, Calif.: Cummings, 1973.

Peverelly, Charles A. *The Book of American Pastimes*. New York: Privately printed, 1866.

Phillips-Birt, Douglas H. C. *The History of Yachting*. London: Elm Tree Books, 1974.

Pierson, Melissa Holbrook. *The Perfect Vehicle: What It Is about Motorcycles*. New York: Norton, 1999.

Piggott, Derek. *Gliding: A Handbook on Soaring Flight*. New York: Macmillan, 1958.

Pirsig, Robert. *Zen and the Art of Motorcycle Maintenance*. New York: William Morrow, 1974.

Pisano, Dominick A. *To Fill the Sky with Pilots: The Civilian Pilot Training Program, 1939–46*. Urbana: University of Illinois Press, 1993.

Pisano, Dominick A., and Cathleen S. Lewis. *Air and Space History: An Annotated Bibliography*. New York: Garland, 1988.

Poole, Michael. *Ragged Islands: A Journey by Canoe through the Inside Passage*. Vancouver: Douglas and McIntyre, 1991.

Porter, Luther Henry. *Wheels and Wheeling*. Boston: Wheelman, 1892.

Raban, Jonathan. *Passage to Juneau: A Sea and Its Meanings*. New York: Pantheon, 1999.

Randers-Pehrson, N. H., and A. G. Renstrom. *Aeronautic Americana: A Bibliogra-

phy of Books and Pamphlets on Aeronautics Published in America before 1900. New York: Aeronautic America, 1943.

Reich, Leonard S. "Ski-Dogs, Pol-Cats, and the Mechanization of Winter: The Development of Recreational Snowmobiling in North America." *Technology & Culture* 40:3 (July 1999), 484–516.

Robinson, Bill. *The Great American Yacht Designers.* New York: Alfred A. Knopf, 1974.

Rockland, Michael Aaron. *Homes on Wheels.* New Brunswick, N.J.: Rutgers University Press, 1980.

Rothman, Hal K. *Devil's Bargains: Tourism in the Twentieth-Century American West.* Lawrence: University Press of Kansas, 1998.

Sagnier, Thierry. *Bike! Motorcycles and the People Who Ride Them.* New York: Harper and Row, 1974.

Schlereth, Thomas J. *U.S. 40: A Roadscape of the American Experience.* Indianapolis: Indiana Historical Society, 1985. Reprint. Knoxville: University of Tennessee Press, 1997.

Schultz, Mark, and Barbara Schultz, eds. *Bicycling: A Guide to Information Sources.* Detroit: Gale Research, 1979.

Scott, Qunita, and Susan Croce Kelly. *Route 66: The Highway and Its People.* Oklahoma City: University of Oklahoma Press, 1988.

Seybold, David, ed. *Boats: An Anthology.* Boston: Atlantic Monthly, 1997.

Shafer, Elwood L., George H. Moeller, and Russell E. Getty. "Future Leisure Environments." U.S. Department of Agriculture, Forest Service Research Paper, NE-301. Upper Darby, Pa., 1974.

Simon, Alvah. *North to the Night: A Year in the Arctic Ice.* New York: McGraw-Hill, 1998.

Sloane, Gloria. *How to Be a First-Rate Mate: A Sailing Guide for Women.* New York: Quadrangle, 1974.

Slocum, Joshua. *Sailing Alone around the World.* New York: Century, 1900. Reprint. New York: Dover, 1956.

Smith, Robert A. *A Social History of the Bicycle: Its Early Life and Times in America.* New York: American Heritage Press, 1972.

Snowmobile and Off-the-Road Vehicle Research Symposium. Sponsored by the Department of Park and Recreation Resources and the Agricultural Experiment Station, Michigan State University, and the Bureau of Outdoor Recreation, Department of the Interior. East Lansing, Mich., 1971.

Steinbeck, John. *Travels with Charlie in Search of America.* New York: Viking, 1962.

Stephens, William. *American Yachting.* New York: Macmillan, 1904.

Stewart, George R. *U.S. 40: Cross Section of the United States of America.* Boston: Houghton Mifflin, 1953. Reprint. Westport, Conn.: Greenwood, 1973.

Stubelius, Svante. *Airship, Aeroplane, Aircraft: Studies in the History of Terms for Aircraft in English.* Göteborg, Sweden: Elanders Boktryckeri Aktiebolag, 1960.

Sullivan, Robert. *The Meadowlands: Wilderness Adventures at the Edge of a City.* New York: Scribner's, 1998.

Symmes, Patrick. *Chasing Che.* New York: Penguin, 2000.

Task Force on Off-Road Recreation Vehicles. Washington, D.C.: Government Printing Office, 1971.

Thomas, Elwell B. *This Business of Boating*. Cambridge, Md.: Cornell Maritime Press, 1949.

Thompson, Hunter S. *Hell's Angels*. New York: Random House, 1967.

Thornburg, David. *Galloping Bungalows: The Rise and Demise of the American House Trailer*. Shoe String/Archon, 1990.

Thrasher, W. E. *Ballooning: A Pictorial Guide and World Directory*. Homestead, Fla.: Thrasher Balloons, 1978.

Thwaites, Reuben Gold. *Historic Waterways: Six Hundred Miles of Canoeing down the Rock, Fox, and Wisconsin Rivers*. Chicago: McClung, 1888.

Upton, Joe. *Journeys through the Inside Passage: Seafaring Adventures along the Coast of British Columbia and Alaska*. Portland, Oreg.: Alaska Northwest Books, 1998.

Vale, Thomas R. *U.S. 40 Today: Thirty Years of Landscape Change in America*. Madison: University of Wisconsin Press, 1983.

Vale, Thomas, and Geraldine R. Vale. *Western Images, Western Landscape: Travels along U.S. 89*. Tucson: University of Arizona Press, 1989.

Vaughan, Rodger. *Ted Turner: The Man behind the Mouth*. Marion, Ohio: Sail Books, 1979.

Wagenvoord, James. *Bikes and Riders*. New York: Avon, 1972.

Wall, Geoffrey. "Impacts of Outdoor Recreation on the Environment." Council of Planning Librarians Exchange Bibliography No. 1363. Monticello, Ill.: N.p., October 1977.

Wallace, Clarke. *The Complete Snowmobiler*. New York: Scribner's, 1971.

Wallis, Allan D. *Wheel Estate: The Rise and Decline of Mobile Homes*. New York: Oxford University Press, 1990.

Wallis, Michael. *Route 66: The Mother Road*. New York: St. Martin's, 1990.

Walsh, John Henry. *Encyclopedia of Rural Sports*. Philadelphia: Potter and Coates, ca. 1867.

Wasserman, Paul, and Steven R. Wasserman, eds. *Recreation and Outdoor Life Directory*. 2nd ed. Detroit: Gale Research, 1983.

Watkins, T. H. "Home on the Road." *American West* 13 (September–October 1976), 36–49.

Wellner, Alison S. *Americans at Play: Demographics of Outdoor Recreation and Travel*. Ithaca, N.Y.: New Strategist, 1997.

Wharton, Edith. *A Motor Flight through France*. New York: Scribners, 1908.

White, Roger. "At Home on the Highway." *American Heritage* (December 1985), 98–105.

Wise, John. *Through the Air: A Narrative of Forty Years Experience as an Aeronaut*. Philadelphia: To-day, 1873.

Wolfe, Arnold. *Vans and Vanners*. Matteson, Ill.: Greatlakes Living Press, 1976.

Wolfe, Tom. "Sissy Bars Will Be Lower This Year." *Esquire* (February 1971), 60–63.

Yates, Brock W. *Outlaw Machine: Harley-Davidson and the Search for the American Soul*. Boston: Little, Brown, 1999.

Zonker, Patricia. *Murdercycles*. Chicago: Nelson-Hall, 1978.

Periodicals

Air Progress. Canoga Park, Calif., 1941–1998.

American Aviation Historical Society Journal. Santa Ana, Calif., 1956– .

American Bicyclist and Motorcyclist. Northbrook, Ill., 1879– . (Began as *Motorcycle Illustrated*; title and place vary).

American Neptune. Salem, Mass., 1941– .

American Yachtsman. New York, 1887–1908.

AOPA Pilot. Frederick, Md., 1958– .

Aquatic Monthly and Nautical Review. New York, 1872–1876.

Aviation and Yachting. Detroit, 1933–1948 (title varies).

Aviation History. Leesburg, Va., 1990– .

Ballooning. Ashville, N.Y., 1968– .

Balloon Life. Seattle, 1986– .

BicycleUSA. Washington, D.C., 1989– .

Bicycling. Emmaus, Pa., 1962– .

Bicycling World. Philadelphia, 1879– .

Boating. New York, 1956– .

Buoyant Flight. Akron, Ohio, 1952– .

Canoe. Denver, 1973– .

Canoe & Kayak. Stamford, Conn., 1978– .

Cruising World. Newport, R.I., 1974– .

Cycle World. Newport Beach, Calif., 1961– (title varies).

Easyriders. Agoura Hills, Calif., 1971– (title and place vary).

Flugzeug und Yacht. Vienna, Austria, 1923–1926.

Flying. New York, 1927– .

Ford Times. Detroit, 1908–1917.

4 Wheel Drive & Sport Utility. Anaheim, Calif., 1971– .

Motorboat. Boston, 1973– .

Motorboating and Sailing. New York, 1907– .

Motorcycle Illustrated. See *American Bicyclist and Motorcyclist*.

Mountain Biking. Canoga, Calif., 1986– .

Off-Road. Anaheim, Calif., 1969– .

Outing. New York, 1882–1923.

Parachutist. Alexandria, Va., 1956– .

Pickup, Van and 4-Wheel Drive. Newport Beach, Calif., 1972–?

Popular Mechanics. New York, 1902– .

La Revue Nautique. Paris, 1926–1939, 1944– .

Rider. Maple Grove, Minn., 1974– .

Rudder. See *Sea*.

Rural Recreation and Tourism Abstracts. Farnham Royal, England, 1976– .

Sail. Boston, 1970– .

Sailing. Port Washington, Wis., 1966– .

Sea (Combined with *Rudder*). Irvine, Calif., 1890– .

Skylines. Ashville, N.Y., 1989– .

Snow Goer (*Snowsports, Snowmobile*; title varies). Maple Grove, Minn., 1965– .

Soaring. Hobbs, N.Mex., 1937– .

Soaring and Motorgliding. Santa Monica, Calif., 1973– .

Sport Aviation. Hales Corner, Wis., 1951– .
Today's SUV. Anaheim, Calif., 1991– .
Trailer Life. Ventura, Calif., 1941– .
Trailer Travel Magazine. Chicago, 1936– (continued as *Woodall's Trailer Travel*, Highland Park, Ill., 1976–?).
Truckin'. Anaheim, Calif., 1975– .
Van World Magazine. Encino, Calif., 1975– .
Die Yacht. Berlin, 1904– .
Yachting. Greenwich, Conn., 1907– .
Yachting World. London, 1894– .

Association Web Sites

Aircraft Owners and Pilots Association, http://www.aopa.org
American Canoe Association, http://www.aca-paddler.org
American Motorcyclist Association, http://www.ama-cycle.org
Balloon Federation of America, http://www.bfa.net
Boat Owners Association of the United States, http://www.boatus.com
International Snowmobile Hall of Fame, http://www.amsnow.com
League of American Wheelmen, http://www.bikeleague.org
Motorcycle Industry Council, http://www.yearbooknews.com

LIVING HISTORY
AND BATTLEFIELD
REENACTMENTS

Randal Allred

Living history is loosely defined, at best. It describes a class of cultural or scholarly activities that re-create or reenact historical events or environments in order to make them seem alive for the spectator. Often, these events are staged for the tourist trade or for educational purposes, yet such reenactments do not necessarily require spectators, in spite of their quasi-theatrical nature, as in the case of battle reenacting, an activity that is arguably pursued for the benefit of the reenactor, primarily. Some kinds of living history, however, such as the outdoor museum, are designed especially for instruction and require an audience. Such living-history events or presentations create a virtual historical world that focuses on experience (whether for the participant or for the spectator) that provides a kind of virtual time travel. Like theater, living history's very artificiality attempts to create the illusion of verisimilitude and induce a willing suspension of disbelief in order to include this vicarious experience. Such environments are also used for research to test theories of material history, as in experimental archaeology.

Battle reenactments, historical pageants, and living-history communities (Outdoor Museums) such as the Farmers Museum, Colonial Williamsburg, Conner Prairie, Mystic Seaport, Plimoth Plantation, the Fortress of Louisbourg in Nova Scotia, and Old Sturbridge, Massachusetts, are all examples of living history. The difficulty in defining the discipline lies in the fact that it has not been a discrete, unified discipline up until recently and in the fact that so many endeavors at representing culture in a historical context such as museums, festivals, fairs, and even national historical parks blur considerably the boundary lines if we were to consider drawing them. Living history has strong links to the heritage industries, historical preservationism, tourism, and modern mythmaking in the best patriotic tradition. The study of it occurs in anthropology, archaeology, history, museum studies, folklore, gender studies, ethnology, literature, theater, psychology, political science, and cultural studies in general. Living history facilities and events do not flourish only in the United States by any means, but Americans have given historical reenactment a special fervor and flavor in our national obsession with acquiring a tangible sense of our past, in our quest for identity.

We are best served by remembering that living history is simply one kind of manifestation of the cultural representations that characterize human endeavors to explore or even reify the past. It is essentially imitative and creative at the same time. Its very effort to create the illusions of authenticity, in fact, draws attention to its very artificiality. It is not precisely art—although it depends, like theater, on a willing suspension of disbelief and visual aesthetics—nor is it always historical scholarship. It is necessarily a hybrid of the imaginative and the scholarly. The living-historian's insistence on authenticity creates a dissonant tension in relation to the performer's insistence on aesthetic harmony and unity. In its pageant form, it has goals and effects far different from those of a more conventional theatrical production; it is intended for instruction and reinforcing cultural and political values, rather than mere entertainment. Living history is manifested in the battlefield guide in a Confederate uniform at Gettysburg, the tanner in Williamsburg, the tattoo drill on Signal Hill in St. John's, Newfoundland, the joust at a Renaissance fair, and the staged gunfights in the streets of the re-created frontier town of Dodge City, Kansas, or Old Tucson, Arizona.

Living history is linked to, but does not include, conventional museums, historical preservation, or any representations of history in literature, film, or other art media. The Web site for the Association for Living History, Farm and Agricultural Museums offers this insight by way of definition:

> Some people equate "Living History" with costumed role-players portraying life in a different time. Some think that it is only the group of folks who put on uniforms of past wars and have a good time reenacting battles. While the past cannot change, history which is an interpretation of the past is always changing. What we call "Living History" is a relatively recent development in the interpretation of history. ("So What Is Living History?")

Some living-history museums are created to reflect a particular culture and lifestyle, and others, such as Colonial Williamsburg and Plimoth Plantation, document a specific time and place (Reid).

It is important to recognize that living history is interpretation and reenactment, not necessarily commemoration, although both activities often go hand in hand. Commemoration is remembering and even celebrating without necessarily reenacting. Living history, however, is the staging or simulation of the event or culture itself, with or without a celebratory context.

Unlike museum artifacts, the events of living history tend to produce their own curators and defenders. In the case of battle reenactments, the actors themselves are the primary researchers and scholars and, in many cases, the spectators as well. Jay Anderson offers this definition, which also differentiates among the several uses of living history:

> Living History can be defined as an attempt by people to simulate life in another time. Generally, the other time is in the past, and a specific reason is given for making the attempt to live as other people once did. The reasons vary, but the three most common ones are: to interpret material culture more

effectively, usually at a living history museum; to test an archaeological thesis or generate dates for historical ethnographies; and to participate in an enjoyable recreational activity that is also a learning experience. (3)

Anderson goes on to indicate how folklorists would see living history as an interesting form of expressive culture that finds use as a research tool for understanding the past as well as a medium for acting out in a socially acceptable way behavior not commonly encountered in the contemporary world, such as dressing up as a knight or soldier or mountain man.

HISTORICAL OUTLINE

Living history is as old as civilization itself and found ancient manifestation, for example, in the mock naval battles that the Romans staged in the flooded Coliseum. In traditional societies, especially those that preserved traditions orally, often the dramatic re-creation of a historical or even mythical event—a famous victory of a past hero over the society's traditional enemies, for instance—formed the basis of a religious ritual. Such dramatic reenactments were also often part of the storytelling that served both as social bonding and as instruction to youth. The rise of passion plays and related festivals in medieval Europe fulfilled much the same cultural purpose.

In the nineteenth century, Buffalo Bill Cody's Wild West Show featured mock battles that were highly stylized portrayals of thrilling frontier fights to titillate the audience. Historical pageants gained increased importance in American communities as the frontier disappeared and the pioneer generation began to wane; the pageants served to institutionalize and mythologize the community past. Around the turn of the century, agricultural and mechanical expositions began to offer hands-on exhibits of traditional methods of farming, weaving, and other folk arts. After World War I, a particular and focused interest in the demonstration of history began to give rise to open-air museums such as Colonial Williamsburg in Virginia (a pet project of John D. Rockefeller) and the Farmers Museum. Soon, other living-historical communities such as Old Sturbridge Village in Massachusetts and Greenfield Village in Michigan (Henry Ford's pet project) began operation, catering to the tourist trade.

Civil War reenactments began just a few years after the Civil War, as veterans of both sides began to hold reunions and encampments to commemorate famous battles. Often, veterans' groups such as the Grand Army of the Republic sponsored such events, and the reenactments began to be more meticulous at representing the authentic details of camp life in wartime (Cullen 182). They became increasingly popular during the 1880s, and Jim Cullen remarks that they took on the sanitized and highly sentimentalized view of the war that often accrues to such public events. Increasingly, the draw of such events was the camaraderie that soldiers felt for their comrades and erstwhile enemies. "Although encampments may have been stylized, to say the least, they did affirm a sense of community all too lacking in more conventional social arrangements" (Cullen 182). These staged battles, more ritual than historical, often accompanied community festivals and historical pageants and the staging of historical tableaux. As the twentieth century began, the interest in pageants increased, and in 1913 the American Pageant Association was formed in order to provide standards and guidance for what was becoming a professional enterprise. Pageants increased but increasingly became the tool of business and local chambers of commerce. So the American Pageant Association dissolved itself in 1930 (Fried 3). Pageants as an enterprise—in fact, all living-history enterprises—began to hit their stride in the years following World War II, when public concern intensified over maintaining the high pitch of patriotism that the nation had felt during the war years. Although there has been a slight decline in recent years, every summer still offers to the tourist numerous historical pageant events, usually outdoor, for their entertainment, from the Church of Jesus Christ of Latter-Day Saints' Hill Cumorah pageant in upstate New York portraying the story of the *Book of Mormon*, to *Ramona*, a tale of race and forbidden love in early California.

The earliest "open air" museum may have been Skansen in Sweden, opened in 1891, which was designed to "preserve the material culture, especially the buildings" of an era ("So What Is Living History?"). Artur Hazelius, the founder, offered a motto for this kind of cultural simulation: "Know yourself by knowing the past." Many other outdoor museums and "folk parks" developed all over Europe, dedicated to the research and preservation of fading traditional arts such as roof thatching, construction, weaving, traditional farming methods, home textiles, animal husbandry, and related lifestyles. First-person interpreters were on hand to demonstrate, even to "live" the lifestyle, in order to put it into the context of a specific economy and society.[1] Soon, such folk parks began to appear in North America. After a tour of Hazelius' tableaux, George Francis Dow began a living-history house in Salem, Massachusetts, which grew to a village during the first decades of the twentieth century (Anderson, *Time Machines* 25–27). This kind of activity took on a grander scale after World War I, beginning, according to Kathryn Boardman, with Henry Ford, who promoted hands-on learning in folk arts and founded Greenfield Village in Michigan, a fictional village of authentic buildings and interpretations of the past. He also restored Wayside Inn (of Longfellow fame) in Massachusetts, in addition to other projects. In 1933, the Witter Agricultural Museum was established at the New York State Fair, which "set weavers and spinners to work demonstrating historic processes in a gallery museum" (Boardman). J. D. Rockefeller's purchase of property toward the restoration of Colonial Williamsburg, beginning in 1926, led to the completion of the full Williamsburg experience during the 1940s and 1950s (although Williamsburg continues to grow and revise) (Fried 100). From the 1930s to the 1960s, commemorative events such as the 350th anniversary of the founding of Jamestown (Fried 103), commemorations of Champlain's and Hudson's voyages, and anniversaries of Hamilton's birth, the founding of Philadelphia, and the Declaration of Independence all gave stimulus to the reenacting trend. The American Heritage Foundation, founded in 1947 and dedicated to a "civic reawakening" in American culture, fostered and promoted many such events (Fried 21, 31–32). National and state parks began to employ living-history-style interpretation at many sites, which has become since then a staple of presenting the nation's history at historical sites. In 1970, the Association for Living History, Farm and Agricultural Museums (ALHFAM) began, with help from the Smithsonian. ALHFAM became an "umbrella organization" for such farms and outdoor museums in 1981 (Anderson, *Time Machines* 38–39). As of this writing, the Web site of ALHFAM lists ninety-five

Dressed as medieval knights. © Painet

such outdoor museums in the United States that have Web sites on the Internet. There are sixteen in Canada and many more in Europe.

Battle reenactment began to find a new generation of enthusiasts, the actual veteran generation of Civil War soldiers being mostly gone by 1935, when the National Park Service sponsored a reenactment of the Battle of Chancellorsville, using personnel from the U.S. Marines and Army and the Virginia Military Institute (Cullen 183).

In the 1930s, the rise of the National Muzzle Loading Rifle Association spawned groups that went beyond shooting to include the costumes and tactics of Civil War soldiers, Revolutionary War soldiers, mountain men (who prefer to be called "buckskinners"), Indian wars combatants, and shooters of other eras. But the approach of the 1960s Centennial of the American Civil War created a demand for authentically staged battles. According to Anderson, the North–South Skirmish Association (an outgrowth of the National Muzzle Loading Rifle Association), a group dedicated to live-fire competitions among authentically dressed Civil War units, became the core of the units that participated in these "sham battles." The First Battle of Bull Run was reenacted on the very grounds of the battlefield park on July 22, 1961, sponsored and partly planned by Karl Betts, the executive director of the Civil War Centennial Commission (CWCC). This event was sanctioned by General Ulysses S. Grant III (Ret.), who was chair of the CWCC. But the professional scholars and other members on the CWCC disliked the spectacle of a cheap-thrills storybook war, and so the commission headed in other directions and opposed battle reenactments as part of the war's commemoration (Fried 131–32). This, on top of the bizarre and bitter events of the CWCC National Assembly in Charleston,[2] led the commission to oust Betts and replace him with James I. Robertson. Grant resigned in the wake of bitter feelings, and historian Allan Nevins replaced him (Fried 132–33). When Nevins and Robertson encountered recurrent zeal for reenactments (especially from President Kennedy, who liked them), the CWCC adjusted yet again and adopted a stance of neutrality concerning them. Many reenactments were staged by various public and private entities during the years 1961–1965, with mixed results. The reenactment of Pickett's Charge at Gettysburg in 1963 ended not in victory or defeat but in the two sides gathering for a flag salute and singing patriotic songs (Bodnar, *Remaking* 220). As Cullen has pointed out, the tensions and divisions between professional and amateur historian on the authenticity and appropriateness, not to say the value, of battle reenactments during these years survive in "different forms" to the present (183). The scholarly historian objects to the glorification and veneration of the violence by staging an imitation of it; the amateur historian (co-opting the title living-historian), using the rationale of experimental archaeology, argues that simulating and participating in the actual experience, with as many of the sensual cues as possible, are the only way to understand the original event.

After the centennial, battle-reenacting enthusiasm was largely restricted to hardcore devotees who wanted to avoid the gaudy pageantry and commercialized spectacles of the centennial and thus began researching their avocation in earnest. Gray work clothes, cheap souvenir kepis, and anachronistic weapons were abandoned in favor of more authentically researched reproduction clothing and weapons. This curious mix of hobbyism and amateur historical research has come to characterize the movement up to our day, to the point that when filmmakers want to obtain accurate images for their movies, they go to the reenactors, whose knowledge of the uniforms, weapons, accoutrements, and manifold minutiae of the daily life of the soldier is usually greater than that of any academic historian or filmmaker.[3]

Since the political and cultural atmosphere of the 1960s and 1970s and the experience of Vietnam did not encourage open displays of America's historical patriotic violence, reenacting faded into the private intensity of personal hobbyism and small units and clubs. Quietly, a thriving cottage industry dedicated to supplying the reenactor emerged. Manufacturing concerns such as Dixie Gun Works and Navy Arms, as well as Parker-Hale of England and Euroarms of Italy, began to make reproduction rifles and parts of Civil War-vintage weapons with careful accuracy. Small firms such as C&D Jarnagin of Corinth, Mississippi, made uniforms, leathers, shoes, tinware, and other personal items, meticulously researched from existing original uniforms and historical records.

With the approach of the 1970s, however, came rising enthusiasm for the bicentennial of the American Revolution, according to Anderson in his book *Time Machines*. Reenactors paid closer attention to this war than before, and a new group, the Brigade of the American Revolution (BAR), organized itself in the early 1960s and applied stringent standards of a professional quality on the reenactment units and their weapons, uniforms, cantonments, drill, and tactics (145–47). This group staged a number of events during the bicentennial years, but the crowning event was the reenactment of the siege and battle of Yorktown, the last major engagement of the Revolution, in 1981. Prominent among the spectators were Presidents Reagan and Mitterand of the United States and France, respectively, while the BAR organized and choreographed a battle using thousands of reenactors from hundreds of units to represent with authentic showmanship the American, French, and British troops who fought in the original battle (Anderson, *Time Machines* 146–47). In what many connoisseurs of living history believe was the movement's "finest moment in time," Anderson explains, the whole event featured a well-staged battle (including the British surrendering in a poignant ceremony), in addition to several days of encampment, reenacted surgery demonstrations, parades, period games, and other events as part of the eighteenth-century milieu orchestrated for the event (147).

Meanwhile, new Civil War groups had formed, dedicated to the same stringent standards for authenticity as the BAR. The North-South Skirmish Association remained focused on live-fire shooting competitions, but most other groups such as the National Regiment departed from this focus by staging reenacted battles. Most of these, by participating in what became annual reenactment events, established a network of surprising unity and cohesion.

In the 1980s, the American Civil War Commemoration Committee, a coalition of the National Regiment, and a number of other reenacting groups organized a series of planned events for the 125th anniversary of the war, from 1986 to 1990. Napoleonic Tactics, a firm founded by reenactor Pat Massengill, brought Civil War reenactment choreography into a new age of professionalism. The ACWCC hired Napoleonic to organize and stage the event. Massengill's company did not enjoy a happy career and eventually folded after the dissatisfaction over too many errors in organizing such complex events took its toll. The first Bull Run event (125th anniversary) was the largest battle reenactment up until that time. In heat that reached 105 degrees Fahrenheit in fields only a few miles from the original battlefield, over 10,000 reenactors performed the historic battle before a crowd of spectators that exceeded, by some counts, 40,000. Enthusiasm only grew, however, and the next year's Antietam event in Maryland and the reenactment of Shiloh (which included an authentic march over the same roads by a small band of exhausted Confederates in a light snowfall) also attracted large numbers of hobbyists. The 125th anniversary reenactment of Gettysburg attracted nearly 13,000 reenactors and set once again a record for the largest reenactment staged in North America. Attracting over 100,000 spectators during the three days of staged portions of the three days of the historic battle, Gettysburg seemed to be the crowning event of the 125th, and was accompanied by articles in major national magazines. The events included footage shot by a variety of film companies. Some of this footage appears in the film *Glory*.

The 130th anniversary followed (1991 to 1995), and the even bigger 135th anniversary (1996–2000) followed that. These events may have exceeded even the 125th anniversary numbers. Some regional festivals in the eastern United States are built around an annual reenactment of the local battle. The attendant industry surrounding this phenomenon has earned new respectability and, in some cases, prosperity, on a limited scale. When Fields and Zwick made their monumental film *Glory*, they hired Ray Herbeck, a reenactor who worked on other Civil War films as a technical adviser, to get the details right. He guided them to C&D Jarnagin, a reenactors' outfitter, for the film's uniforms.

Civil War battle reenactors are found in every state of the union and in a number of foreign countries. They differ from outdoor museum interpreters in that they are almost exclusively lay practitioners. Reenacting is more than a hobby, as it assumes the identity of a culture itself with its own unique traditions, language, and rituals. Its practitioners collect or make their own authentic reproductions of Civil War uniforms and equipment in order that they may portray any of a number of characters found in a camp or battle scene: soldier, sutler, surgeon, musician, vivandiere, chaplain, camp follower, photographer, undertaker, or soldier's wife. Reenactors include women as well as men. Women increasingly participate as soldiers, and authentically so; research has shown that a small handful of women fought in both armies, mostly incognita. Reenactors also often give demonstrations, lectures, and shows; stage encampments; and speak at schools and clubs, educating the public. In this way, they serve the same function as living-history interpreters at outdoor museums or living-historical farms.

As with other living-historians, the passion for authenticity is strong with reenactors, who even have their own jargon as part of having formed a distinct discourse community. A "farb" is a reenactor who is not authentic; that is, there is something about his or her "impression" that is too modern or otherwise anachronistic and that would identify him or her as a twenty-first-century person, such as a jacket of the wrong color or fabric or a model of rifle that was not in military use during the Civil War. Reenactors are typically not scholars but read copiously on the subject, often having large personal libraries. They research the elements of their individual impressions with meticulous zeal and are, as Dennis Hall has expressed it, "down-right learned in their own way" (8).

Reenacting has its own economy, with publications such as the *Camp Chase Gazette* and a number of cottage industries (such as C&D Jarnagin or Dixie Gun Works) that manufacture authentic-pattern shirts, uniforms, accoutrements, weapons, tents, horse tack, and wagons, to name a few. Several Web rings dedicated to reenacting testify to the considerable Internet traffic for this avocation, much of it by vendors but also an enormous amount by private individuals plying their own specialized knowledge. A few consulting firms, such as now-defunct Napoleonic Tactics, Inc., have sporadically appeared to provide expert battle reenactment choreography.

One of the fundamental issues in reenacting that scholars address is the question of what the attraction is. "It is often the realism of the hobby that attracts," according to Randal Allred, the discomfort of long underwear and wool clothing, "bad food, floorless tents, cold comfortless nights, insects, diarrhea, and drilling in humid Pennsylvania heat" (6). One reenactor expresses the attraction of the hobby: "One can read of past events, or view photos & paintings as part of a learning experience, but to participate or view in a small way the ways things [actually] looked can bring a knowledge as few other things can" (Cornell). Rory Turner, in a groundbreaking 1990 article, offers insights into the attraction of it and how it allows participants to occasionally "be in the same position as those who fought long ago" (126).[4] This time warp, according to Turner, is only part of the draw, however. Also involved is the attraction of having a play identity (126). There is also opportunity for performance, political camaraderie, escape from modern life and its tensions, group identity, and, in Turner's observation, "a remarkable arena for self-expression and creativity":

> They have created a bloodless war, a war within which they can have a good time and learn something about themselves. The pain, violence, and misery of war have been extracted, leaving camaraderie, exhilaration, and a certain beauty. This playful war becomes a place where reenactors can move away from their everyday life identities by becoming someone else for a brief period. This is a process of self-exploration and confirmation. What the Civil War was about and the issues it raised . . . form the themes of this self-examination. (134)

While viewing Civil War reenacting as perhaps the most salient example, we must not ignore the fact that battle reenactment covers a much broader base. Units in many nations reenact the American Civil War, the American Revolution, the French and Indian War, both world wars, the Indian Wars of the United States, and the English civil war. In Britain alone, organizations such as the Sealed Knot and the English Civil War Society stage battles and other historical events from the earliest of the Viking invasions up through the Wars of the Roses, the English civil war, the American Revolution, Napoleonic Wars, the Zulu War, the Boer War, and the world wars, all with the passion for detailed authenticity that marks American organizations. In fact, the English Civil War Society, according to one story, seceded from the Sealed Knot over a dispute on historical accuracy (Milne 12). At the time of this writing, a brief cruise through the Web sites and related news items shows events as varied as mountain man rendezvous, Viking raids, pioneer wagon treks, Renaissance fairs, Shackleton's voyage on the *Endurance* to Antarctica, the 1874 westward trek by the Royal Canadian Mounted Police, Thomas Jefferson's speeches and memoirs on stage, and Civil War battles, all being reenacted. There are organizations that specialize in reenacting periods and events as diverse as the Spanish-American War, the Boxer Rebellion, Confederate blockade runners, and Spanish colonial forces in the pre-1840s Southwest.

Even a cursory glance at the World Wide Web uncovers innumerable groups dedicated to reenacting the past in some fashion, whether in depicting a lifestyle, an event, or an era or even a forgotten craft or skill. For example, besides the long-lived and wittily named Society for a Creative Anachronism (medieval through the Jacobite Rebellion), there are Angelcynn (Anglo-Saxon era of British history), the Sealed Knot (English civil war), the Bitter Creek Outlaws (Old West gunfighting group), Guild of Santa Maria (portraying an ambassador and entourage from the Medici court, mid–1500s), Oregon Trail Travelers (self-explanatory), Ship's Company (to crew the restored USS *Constellation*), and even St. Sebastian's Guild, which is dedicated to "the craft and skill of longbow archery of the sixteenth century."

The critical issues among those who study living history, both as a form of historical research and as a cultural phenomenon of postmodern nostalgia, focus on the matter of representation, authenticity, and the revision of history. Scholarly attention to these phenomena deals in what Barbara Kirschenblatt-Gimblett calls "the distinctions between doing and showing, demonstrating and performing, presenting and representing" (4). In exploring such distinctions, the future of living-history study will likely focus on a number of concerns in cultural studies theory, recent scholarship on the representation of history and culture, postcolonial theory, and the ongoing debate among historians concerning the validity of reenacting, outdoor museums, and experimental archaeology.

It became apparent in the late nineteenth century that perhaps the actual recreation of certain social structures or economic enterprises would best help the archaeologist or anthropologist venture into the past to discover the realities of past cultures. Jay Anderson tells of one effort in recent times to reconstruct a Dutch barn in New York state that had been burned by an arsonist. The builder, Richard Babcock, decided to do it using traditional tools and methods. But without a record of the process, he had to rediscover or surmise technique and found it a thornier problem than he had imagined. "The problem was to get inside the head of a colonial carpenter and see things his way. Given the specific jobs that had to be done and the tools and men at hand, what techniques would have been devised?" (*Time Machines* 77).

This notion of experimental archaeology makes living-history sites and events valuable resources for research, argue its proponents. We can realize little about the realities of the interdependence or even hierarchies of the various trades in a nineteenth-century town until we try to run a buggy-making shop and have to depend on carpenters, blacksmiths, wheelwrights, sawyers, and tanners for our parts and supplies. The realities of command structure and communication on the battlefield in the Civil War cannot fully be grasped or put into context until we try the experiment of maneuvering a brigade-sized unit on the field, in coordination with other brigades, amid the smoke, noise, confusion, and distance of a nineteenth-century battlefield. How can we rediscover the diet or culinary ingredients of rural people unless we try out the foodstuffs that they had on hand? Can we understand the suicide rate among merchant seamen in the age of sailing ships without the experiment of voyaging across the Atlantic in such a craft? This is the rationale offered by living historians for living history as a viable, even indispensable method of history. John Coles of Cambridge University offers these examples:

> By building copies of houses, palisades, and fortresses, we can appreciate better the scale of ancient enterprise, and the organizations of labor required. By constructing and using replicas of boats and wagons we can understand the problems of communication and colonization in early times. And by trying to actually live as our ancestors did . . . we may become aware of our prehistory, or past problems concerned with wood supplies and shelter, and the inventive nature of man. . . . By reproducing his actions, archaeologists can better understand not only his technical abilities but also his reasons for choosing one course of action rather than another. (1–2)

This same sort of hypothetically historical reenactment as experiment was exemplified by Magnus Anderson, a Norwegian sailor and editor who, in 1893, built a replica of the recently excavated Gokstad ship in the Viking style and sailed the tiny, twenty-four-meter-long craft across the Atlantic to Newfoundland (where, half a century later, at L'Anse aux Meadows, the discovery of a Viking settlement would lend credibility to Anderson's venture) and then on through the Great

Battlefield reenactment. © Painet

Lakes to Chicago, where World's Fair crowds greeted his ship with enthusiasm (Anderson, *Time Machines* 107–8). Similar voyages have since become fairly common in our century, with Thor Hyerdahl's famed *Kon Tiki* (1947) and *Ra II* (1970) expeditions and Tim Severin's sailing of an Irish curragh across the Atlantic to North America in 1976. Further maritime reenacting, based on more copious historical documentation than these, found form in the voyage of Plimoth Plantation's authentically reconstructed *Mayflower II* across the Atlantic, captained by Alan Villiers, in 1957, Elizondo and Marx in the *Niña II* in 1962, and the more recent voyage completely around the world of the Australian-built replica of the *HM Bark Endeavor* (of Captain James Cook fame) in 1996–2000.

REFERENCE WORKS

Because of living history's amorphous nature, its interdisciplinarity, and its recent advent, few useful print guides address this topic comprehensively. The heading "Living History" is used only twice, for example, in the *Social Sciences Index* during the last eight years. Other periodical articles are often listed under "Historical Reenactment." Ormond Loomis' *Sources on Folk Museums and Living Historical Farms* (1977) focuses on the folk park/museum side of living history, as does Rath and O'Connell's *Interpretation: A Bibliography on Historical Organization Practices*. A fine bibliography, "Selected Readings on Living History Interpretation," is to be found on-line at the ALHFAM Web site, compiled by Stacy Flora

Roth (http://www.voicenet.com/~frstprsn/alhfam/lhbiblio.htm). It is fairly extensive and useful, although it, too, restricts itself largely to sources dealing with living-historical interpretation at outdoor museum sites. Material on battle reenactments as a cultural phenomenon has not been assembled largely because there has been too little written about it yet. On reenacting, researchers will find the notes in Jim Cullen's *The Civil War in Popular Culture* to be useful, as well as those of Richard M. Fried in *The Russians Are Coming! The Russians Are Coming! Pageantry and Patriotism in Cold-War America* (1998).

Jay Anderson's collection of essays, *A Living History Reader*, volume 1, is the only significant anthology of shorter pieces on living history. Among the articles collected therein are pieces by the major figures in the field, such as Anderson himself, James Deetz, and David Lowenthal. Anderson's lead-off article ("Living History") offers a succinct, yet comprehensive, definition of the discipline, and sections follow on the beginnings (the rise of the cultural museum), forts, farms, villages, experimental programs (such as experimental archaeology projects), and concerns, which features articles about the issues and controversies in the study of living history, such as cultural responses, authenticity, representations of the past, changing museum paradigms, and the cultural commodification of nostalgia.

Perhaps the most significant reference tool extant is Anderson's *The Living History Sourcebook*, published in 1985. Written to be useful to the lay as well as the scholarly researcher, this work begins with Anderson's Preface and moves into Part One ("Into the Time Warp"), which lists living-history museums and annual events, with discussion on each. Part Two ("Pointing the Way") is a series of pithy and succinct reviews of all of the significant books and articles on the subject up until 1985, as well as an evaluation of periodicals (such as *Living History* and *Civil War Times Illustrated*) that have appeal or other connections to living-historical topics. Part Three ("Suiting Up") reviews reenactment and living-history organizations, both lay and professional. Anderson also evaluates suppliers and vendors of historical reproduction artifacts, clothing, and other goods for the living-historical practitioner. He adds a section on books and collections of historical costume sketches and patterns. Part Four ("Fun and Games") discusses historical films that have content of interest to the living-historian as well as historical simulation war games and history games, such as the complex board games published by the late great Avalon Hill Company. The Afterword ("Serious Play") reprises Anderson's article of that title, published also in *A Living History Reader*, as well as an extensive and useful Glossary.

Another recent encyclopedic item is an excellent general introduction by Marcella Bush Treviño ("Civil War Reenactors") in volume 1 of the *St. James Encyclopedia of Popular Culture*, edited by Tom and Sara Pendergast. Treviño recognizes and stresses the value for reenactors of the popular accessibility of their avocation: "Civil War reenactors understand that popular history is a valuable form of communication . . . viewing their participation as a learning experience both for them and for their audience" (522).

HISTORY AND CRITICISM

This discussion of published scholarship on living history must necessarily be divided into four sections: Museums (outdoor museums, folk parks, and experimental archaeology), Pageants, Cultural Studies and Theory, and Battle Reenacting, which focuses on Civil War reenacting as the salient manifestation of that avocation. Most of the serious work in this field has appeared within the last two decades, since the rise of scholarly interest in this area has paralleled the rise in cultural studies.

Museums

The article that first coined the term "living history" appeared as the transcript of a 1931 presidential address that Carl Becker gave to the American Historical Society, entitled "Every Man His Own Historian," published in his book of the same title in 1935. Becker held that each generation must posit a "living history," an essentially imaginative representation of the past that reflects the present's influence and needs. Living history is "that pattern of remembered events, whether true or false, that enlarges and enriches [society's] collective specious present" (252). History must appeal to the senses, emotions, and imagination of the people in order to be relevant. As museums, both in North America and abroad, began to experiment with cultural representation after World War II, more research on the ramifications appeared. Robert Asher published a significant article in *American Anthropologist* entitled "Experimental Archaeology" (1961), the first scholarly work on this subject, wherein he defines the concept of "imitative experiment," that is, the valid use of simulation for historical and anthropological research. He offered several examples of experimental projects, influencing the work of John Coles, the most prominent scholar on this topic, in his *Archaeology by Experiment* (1973) and *Experimental Archaeology* (1979). Freeman Tilden's important *Interpreting Our Heritage* (1967) advocates the emphasis on first-person interpretation, that live interpretation brings the artifacts of the past alive. The first reference works on living history appeared about this time: Ormond Loomis' *Sources on Folk Museums and Living Historical Farms* came out in 1977, and Rath and O'Connell's *Interpretation: A Bibliography on Historical Organization Practices* in 1978. The first significant "how-to" work on developing interpretation methods at historical sites and outdoor museums was *Interpretation of Historical Sites*, by William T. Alderson and Shirley Paine Low in a revised edition in 1976.

In the 1980s, a surge in research on living history produced works that began to more energetically explore the museum as a tool for cultural definition and historical rhetoric and to confront the question of whether we thereby represent or sanitize history. Michael Wallace published an article ("Visiting the Past: History Museums in the United States") addressing this question. A revisionist, Wallace argued that the conventional museum was built and supported by the ruling classes and would portray history that privileged its sponsors and benefactors. He criticized most museums like Williamsburg for not having changed enough to represent a pluralistic conception of U.S. history, for example, ignoring the implications of slave life in Virginia and its impact on current attitudes toward race.

By far the most important and seminal article of this period was a piece by Jay Anderson, the most influential scholar of this period, in *American Quarterly* and later reprinted as the keynote article in his *Living History Reader*, Volume 1 (1991). In "Living History: Simulating Everyday Life in Living Museums," Anderson classes all attempts to simulate the past as part of the same discipline. He offers a brief history of the movement and then discusses the three functions of living-history activity: "research, interpretation, and play" (3). The interpretation potential is what has driven most of the growth in outdoor museums, in the desire to educate and inspire the public. Research potential is clear, too, in the reproduction of the material culture of a time or any of a number of experimental archaeology projects. Nor does Anderson dismiss the "play" potential of living history. "The use of living history as an enjoyable recreational activity that is also a learning experience will continue whether or not the National Park Service, museum curators, or academic historians approve of it" (10). For reasons as diverse as camaraderie, travel, outdoor fun, and profit, playacting in another time and place will remain popular because of what it offers: "part revival, revitalization movement, ethnohistorical secular ritual, and nostalgic response to future shock" (10).

Soon after this, Anderson produced his book *Time Machines: The World of Living History*, in 1984, to date the best overview of the development and range of living history. It covers everything from battle reenacting to living-history farms. "Although it's usually a great adventure for the participants, time traveling can also be a significant historical exercise" (*Time Machines* 10). On this premise, Anderson expands on the threefold function of living history outlined in his 1982 article. Part One discusses Living History Museums; Part Two, Living History as Research; and Part Three, Living History as Play, in other words, reenacting. This book is the first substantial effort to bring all manifestations of living history together. He begins with the outdoor museum villages of northern Europe as the foundation of living history, moving into the American manifestations in Williamsburg and Plimoth Plantation, as well as the historical farms. Anderson downplays the scorn that European anthropologists have for *folklorismos*, or "fakelore"— "pseudo traditions being passed off as the real thing" (22). Such experiences provide the investigator with the aesthetic appeal of the simulation and therefore the imaginative leap of faith needed. Anderson, perhaps echoing Carl Becker's bias in favor of history that "lives," does not reject any simulated event that will plausibly evoke an authentic encounter with a bygone cultural time and place. He discusses the problems with curating outdoor museums, such as enforcing authenticity among interpreters and the fine line between teaching and merely entertaining visitors.

Anderson moves into Part Two, which discusses the research potential of such living-history sites in the experimental possibilities of "trying it out." An experiment in rediscovering the recipe for authentic beer from the Elizabethan period finally succeeded when tried in the setting of the Plimoth Plantation community, with the expertise of the living-historians there (85–87). Other experiences, including living in a Stone Age house, helping to build and sailing in a Viking longship, rebuilding the *Mayflower*, and planting ancient strains of grain with the same techniques and challenges endured by ancient farmers, illustrate the value of the first-person experience: experimental archaeology.

Part Three offers a detailed look at historical reenactment, especially in North America, and the concurrent rise of interest in black powder firearms hobbies and the phenomenon of "weekend warriors," the reenacting hobbyists. From Civil War to medieval reenactors, to living-history farms in Iowa, the attraction of personal participation continues to grow. Anderson concludes with a section listing

"Sources and Resources," which includes a selected annotated list of living-history sites and suppliers of reproduction historical gear.

The ongoing controversy between living-historians and traditionalists begins to broaden into the more recent trends in historical and textual theory. In 1989, David G. Vanderstel, senior historian at Conner Prairie, published "Humanizing the Past: The Revitalization of the History Museum," in which he discusses the uses of the history museum in light of the shift in historical research from political history to behavioral history, to the importance of the individual experience. He warns of the dangers of assuming that the mere collection and cataloging of data and artifacts constitute an accurate picture of the past: "While artifacts are surviving elements of past cultures and provide some immediate answers to any inquiry (such as size, shape, material and use), a more pressing problem for the historian is defining *exactly* what any individual or group knew or felt" (19). More important than looking at the quilting frame as the device that held the quilt is the problem of finding out what happened around the frame during a quilting bee, for example (21). To get away from Frederick Jackson Turner's "romanticized" history of the westward conquest, the living-historian must use his or her resources to emphasize rural history and the impact of daily material culture on how people actually lived, behaved, and felt. Vanderstel acknowledges the limitations of living history in that it often replicates only the "artifactual settings and mechanical settings" of a period (23). There must be a symbiosis: living history should depend on behavioral and social history, "for innovative, interdisciplinary research and theories, *and* behavioral history should look to its associate [living history] as a laboratory in which to test hypotheses and to experiment with past processes," since both deal with the grassroots historical emphasis on ordinary people (23). In this same issue, Kate F. Stover published an article entitled "Is It Real History Yet?: An Update on Living History Museums," in which she discusses the status of living-history museums in the eyes of critics, citing (as an example) the onetime lack of blacks in the portrayal of colonial life in Williamsburg and the danger of nostalgia governing the selective interpretations of some sites. Stover observes that many living-history museums have responded to this criticism by incorporating elements of social and racial conflict inherent in the times represented (14).

At the same time, museum scholarship entered a new phase with the publication of Leon and Rosenzweig's important *History Museums in the United States: A Critical Assessment* (1989), wherein Warren Leon and Margaret Piatt contribute a piece on "Living History Museums." In this, they discuss the various criticisms of living-history museums, noting that they range from complaints that they focus too much "on the gritty, mundane reality of the past," to the challenge that they "prettify and sanitize history" (64). Leon and Piatt acknowledge that both ends of the spectrum have valid points. One of the problems, for instance, is that such museums do not portray nineteenth-century urban life or the connected immigrant experience, for the most part. Leon and Piatt further explore the problems of incomplete interpretations, the nostalgic expectations of audiences, staffing problems, romanticizing the past, and whether such sites should represent the typical as opposed to the actual, among others. The authors acknowledge the value of living-history museums in allowing audiences to engage the past meaningfully, however.

In 1993, Stephen Eddy Snow (*Performing the Pilgrims*) investigated the use of role-playing in the living-history museum, using Plimoth Plantation as his case study. Snow's approach looks at role-playing as theater and how such performance dramatizes our collective myths and reinforces popular histories. When Plimoth switched over from third-person to first-person interpretation, it led to more emphasis on capturing an authentic portrayal of the times. Snow compares the living-history performer to a method actor who has to experience the character's lifestyle in order to see the role more clearly. Snow's significant study is enhanced by the fact that he himself worked for some time at Plimoth as a living-historian and portrayed characters such as William Bradford in various reenacted events.

Thomas A. Woods wrote a 1995 article ("Museums and the Public Good: Doing History Together") that looks at two revisionist exhibitions at the Smithsonian in order to examine the role of the public in revising history. "History has always been pragmatic in the sense that historians revise and rewrite constantly to meet their own needs and the needs of a new generation," observes Woods. He cites Becker's 1932 address and reminds us that popular history engages its audience, which in turn influences the shaping of it. This engaging of the audience is the strength of popular history.

More recently, Richard Handler and Eric Gable produced *The New History in an Old Museum: Creating the Past at Colonial Williamsburg* (1997). Handler and Gable have collected a number of previously published journal articles and reshaped them into a more comprehensive critique of Williamsburg and its underlying rationale for the version of history presented there. Relying on interviews of resident staff and scholars at Williamsburg, the authors engage in critical evaluations of revisionist efforts to more rigorously portray colonial life authentically at Williamsburg, arguing that the changes toward a more socially accurate impression have been only cosmetic and that Williamsburg's vision of the past is still rooted firmly in the idealistic atmosphere and patriotic propaganda of the 1950s. Essentially, the elitism of the park's narrative of history persists. An excellent review of this book by John Michael Vlach (1998), however, argues that Handler and Gable are ignoring positive changes in the "thick, multistranded tale" presented at Williamsburg and that the authors offer little in the way of constructive proposals that could revise the park's text in a more meaningful way. This is but one example of the ongoing scholarly debate on the texts presented by living-history museums and historical revision and the cultural imperatives informing them.

There has been much scholarly activity on the issue of performance and technique itself. Among these are *The Good Guide: A Source Book for Interpreters, Docents, and Tour Guides*, by Alison L. Grinder and E. Sue McCoy (1985); *On Interpretation: Sociology for Interpreters of Natural and Cultural History*, by Gary E. Machlis and Donald R. Field (1992); and particularly Stacy Flora Roth's 1998 work, *Past into Present: Effective Techniques for First-Person Historical Interpretation*. Roth points out that historical reenactment has long been part of human history but that the difference now is that it has become far more "technical" and that "our needs and purposes for simulation have evolved," in that we use living history now as a scholarly tool to probe the personal and deeper meanings of the past (1–2). She discusses motivation for living-historians, interplay between interpreters and audience, audience appeal, and authenticity, among many other pertinent issues.

Pageants

The scholarship on historical pageants is found in a region whose borders blur with those of cultural studies in general, New Historicism, theory, literary theory, and theater. But several works deserve particular mention, as they deal with America's conscious construction of the historical past in the service of glorifying and bolstering history in its popular and broadly accepted versions. Beginning with the question, Where do Americans get their ideas about history?, David Glassberg examines the culturally sponsored and preserved versions of history and the processes whereby such readings of history are made and adopted. In *American Historical Pageantry: The Uses of Tradition in the Early Twentieth Century* (1990), Glassberg offers a comprehensive historical look at the pageant phenomenon in American culture during its heyday from the turn of the century to World War II, examining "American historical pageants in terms of their creators' explicit purposes and symbols; their implicit depiction of the nature of history, of society, and of social change; and the patterns of social relationships entailed in producing collective-historical imagery in public" (3). Glassberg points out that historical pageants in this period, unlike public celebrations in other periods, had a unique use for history: "the belief that history could be made into a dramatic public ritual through which the residents of a town, by acting out the right version of their past, could bring about some kind of future social and political transformation" (4). In other words, it did not merely portray history but was meant to shape the future as well by reinforcing certain community values, in a progressive, Whig-like faith in the machinations of events. Glassberg indicates that the historical rhetoric behind these pageants assumed that there was some fundamental tradition to "discover" that would lead us to meaningful reform in the future (4).

Glassberg examines a number of pageants from this era as community products, especially "The Masque of Saint Louis," as well as the imagery engendered by them and the civic forces behind such enormous productions. In his conclusion, he ponders the idea that the pageant as an overarching expression of the community's perceived values would unite and offer a sense of cohesion in the midst of rapid change and confusing diversity. The pageant attempted to reinforce traditional values (or, perhaps, invent them) yet show how these values inevitably would lead to progress and change for a better society (283). Glassberg also makes the connection with other forms of living history, in the restoration of historical towns and even Disneyland's Main Street, as being kindred with historical pageants in the effort to use an idealized past as an escape from the present.

In 1992, John Bodnar published *Remaking America: Public Memory, Commemoration, and Patriotism in the Twentieth Century*. Bodnar covers much of the same species of public commemorations that Richard Fried would address six years later. In his Preface, Bodnar discusses the role of ideology in shaping popular perceptions about history and the emerging role of social history. "I had always assumed that social history—the study of small worlds and individual lives—had contributed much that was new to the field of American history" (xi). But he was surprised to find social history coming under attack during the 1980s from a conservative ideological emphasis (during the Reagan era) on traditional patriotism and the need to believe in a monolithic view of patriotic history. Bodnar's purpose is to "understand the link between everyday life and political issues" (xii). He examines the phenomena of pageantry, monuments, and other manifestations of popular history in twentieth-century America. Of particular interest is Chapter 8, which looks at the celebrations of the Civil War Centennial and the American Revolution Bicentennial as pageants used to reflect—and reinforce—popular values in the representation of national history. He emphasizes how, during the 1960s and 1970s, even though Vietnam and the racial tensions of the rising civil rights movement were not explicitly mentioned, these two commemorative events "were never far from the disunity that was manifested in the era" (206). President Lyndon B. Johnson, when he created the American Revolution Bicentennial Commission (ARBC) in 1966, offered the analogy that the Vietnam War was a similar struggle and that Americans were obligated by the principles of our heritage to help them in their fight for freedom as well (229).

In regard to the Civil War Centennial, Bodnar notes the conflicts and political changes that continually impinged upon that celebration. An example of contemporary influences was the battle reenactments at first Manassas and Gettysburg, where historical accuracy was altered in favor of reconciliation: in the former event, instead of the Union forces breaking and retreating, both armies came together to sing "God Bless America." National unity, heroism, and reconciliation were emphasized in order to diminish sectional acrimony. Bodnar identifies an essential tension between the need to orchestrate a national past to celebrate and the concurrent need of subcultures and local interests to refashion the commemoration to meet its own needs. He follows up on many of these issues in his 1996 book, *Bonds of Affection: Americans Define Their Patriotism*.

Fried authored *The Russians Are Coming! The Russians Are Coming!* in 1998, in which he examines the broad spectrum of patriotic activity in the United States since World War II, particularly in the context, as the title suggests, of America's concept of itself as the bastion of democracy against the communist threat. Pageants, in Fried's work, take on a much broader definition than merely dramatic stage productions of historical events. His purpose is to "plumb the way citizenship activists struggled to define what it was we had to defend and then to convey the message to others. Their varied efforts to do so consumed huge amounts of energy and, whether profoundly or lightly, touched many American lives" (xi). Fried's Introduction discusses Americans' love of pomp and ceremony and our attempts to construct a historical tradition in spite of having so little of it. He discusses the rise of historical pageants that Glassberg so ably explicates, in addition to anniversaries, commemorative days, and especially patriotic holidays, which proliferated early in this century.

Flag Day, I Am an American Day, and other observances found fertile ground during the 1930s and 1940s, when threats to freedom and personal liberties abroad made Americans value their liberties more keenly. But after the war, new fears about communism surfaced, and new civic organizations, such as the Freedoms Foundation of Valley Forge and the American Heritage Foundation (founded in 1947), arose to foster patriotic activity and publication. Along with the Jaycees, American Legion, the Veterans of Foreign Wars, and other groups, patriotic festivals and projects dedicated to beating communism sprang up across the country, including Loyalty Day, Law Day, and others. Fried spends an entire chapter on a town-sized pageant—or reenactment of sorts—when the town of Mosinee, Wisconsin, staged a takeover by communists for forty-eight hours on May Day 1950. Sponsored by the American Legion, this event "briefly inspired anti-communists to believe they had hit upon a new and striking form of anti-communist theatre" (67). The media poured in, and the Mosinee event transfixed the nation in debate for a short time, calling into question the Red Menace and whether or not it could happen in any American town. In the 1950s, celebrations ran the spectrum from reenactments of Jamestown's founding (including a pageant), to staging pageants on the life of George Washington and reenactments of the Battle of New Orleans. Fried also outlines the Civil War Centennial and the controversies over who has control over the kind of Civil War that the country would celebrate—including the most bitter debates over whether or not we would stage pageants and battle reenactments.

After that era, Cold War pageantry began to decline. A blurring of unity and purpose in the post–world war years, as Fried indicates, combined with political factionalism and strife in the 1960s and the Vietnam era, did not provide fertile ground for public celebrations of America's glories and unity. In spite of Kennedy's call for participatory democracy, public fervor on national holidays began to decline, and some holidays disappeared altogether. As the troubles of the 1960s increased, groups like the American Heritage Foundation (AHF) became increasingly irrelevant, and after the strife-filled year of 1968, the AHF ceased to be. This basic change in American attitudes has remained with us in the forms of our patriotic displays.

Cultural Studies and the Heritage Industry

In recent years, what we used to call "revisionist" history is now the vehicle by which we critically reexamine and call into the question the machinery and cultural paradigms that we use to represent history in the context of our own times. Warren Susman's *Culture as History* (1984) looks at the problem of history's being shaped by current cultural values and the need for myth. Using Lincoln's dictum that "we cannot escape history" as a theme, Susman speculates that most Americans do not really care to escape history (3). "From the founding of the colonies, Americans have sought almost as a kind of secular conversion justification and sanctification from history," and that control of the historical narrative is tantamount to control of the broader range of social enterprises (3). In exploring the "problem of history and culture," Susman presents several essays on traditional historical technique, the frontier myth, the Puritans, and other pertinent issues.

Historians call into question the competing histories of events, such as the disgrace of postbellum America, when the forces of emancipation (the federal army and white America) were used to reverse a good measure of freedom for newly freed slaves and to drive Native Americans from their inherited lands (Appleby, Hunt, and Jacob 130). The "revisionist" scrutiny would lift the veil on assumed historical interpretations and challenge them. Joyce Appleby, Lynn Hunt, and Margaret Jacob, in *Telling the Truth about History* (1994), examine closely the foundations of history making, suggesting that since "it is the historians who do research on the past, write the histories, and teach the nation's youth," then we

Reenactment of the Battle of Little Bighorn, ca. 1905. Courtesy of the Denver Public Library

should more closely question whether or not historians are unwittingly "agents of the state" (155). This calls to mind criticisms of many outdoor museums, particularly the popular Colonial Williamsburg, for being too "white" and for being too zealous in reinforcing the cultural values of mainstream America and the heritage industry than in portraying an early Virginia fraught with the contradictions and ironies of racial and class separation, for example. Appleby, Hunt, and Jacob offer this observation: "These clashes make the writing of the history of one's own country different from other historical work, for with it, a relatively open-ended scholarly inquiry collides with the vigilant censor of national self-interest and the group pressure of celebratory self-fashioning" (156).

It is with this "celebratory self-fashioning" that the relevance of living history as performance enters this discussion. Directors and curators of living-history sites have in recent years begun to reconsider the assumptions and motives for their practices, from the pristine, park-like Williamsburg, to the more stark and bucolic realism of Plimoth Plantation and Fortress Louisbourg in Nova Scotia. Race relations and portrayal have been issues at the former, and recent changes at Williamsburg have prompted more than one observer to notice the changes. The aforementioned 1997 study by Handler and Gable (*The New History in an Old Museum: Creating the Past at Colonial Williamsburg*) is one prominent example of this kind of scrutiny. Peter Feverherd, in 1999, pointed out that "Williamsburg has developed a reputation perhaps undeserved for a kind of Disneyfied history, a place where the good guys and bad guys are easy to identify, providing weary travelers with a respite from today's more ambiguous headlines" (31). But he goes on to point out the park's efforts, belatedly, to include more realism, especially in regard to the portrayal of black slavery in early Virginia. Indeed, he relates a *Washington Post* story (July 7, 1999) of a recent reenactment at Williamsburg where the militia were trying to break up a slave gathering. This sort of reenactment becomes personal and compelling to the spectators, who, in this instance, tried to step in and disarm the militia who themselves had to step out of character to diffuse the tensions (Feverherd 31).

Peter Burke, in his *History and Social Theory* (1993), discusses collective identity as "a concept which has become increasingly prominent in a number of disciplines" and how the use of urban or village rituals, such as the Bastille Day celebrations in France every year, can "no longer be dismissed as mere antiquarianism" (57). They serve a very relevant social function in the present time. "The power of memory, of imagination and of symbols notably language in the construction of communities is increasingly recognized." This is especially true in the formation and maintenance of national identities and nationalistic imperatives (57). This is a theme echoed by Fried, Cullen, and others.

This discussion has part of its roots in David Lowenthal's *The Past Is a Foreign Country* (1985), which looks at the past not as fixed but rather as a malleable text ("largely an artifact of the present"), the product of our own cultural need for the comforting trappings of a meaningful past. Lowenthal points to the heritage craze in the public and commercial architecture of the 1970s and 1980s; memorabilia, relics, and antiques; and the zeal for genealogy in recent years as signs of an increasing need for the "trappings of history" to give our present society more substance (xv–xvi). He identifies the invention of the past as something of recent origin, marked by the notion that things of antiquity have more charm and beauty than the cultural markers of the present—hence, the preservation movement in its many varieties. Among many other matters, he discusses the power of nostalgia and its risks, American nostalgia for Old World antiquity, the textuality of history and history-making, and the revisionism inherent in relic preserving.

Lowenthal later addressed many of the same issues in his *Possessed by the Past: The Heritage Crusade and the Spoils of History*, in 1996. He cautions against the heritage trend, that in spite of the benefits to us of links to tradition and roots, it can also be "oppressive, defeatist, decadent. . . . Miring us in the obsolete, the cult of heritage allegedly immures life within museums and monuments . . . undermining historical truth with twisted myth" (ix–x). That is how the partisan argument goes. Lowenthal looks at why heritage is a "growth industry" of late, and how the politics and economics of preservation postulate an exclusionary text for what gets saved and what does not (x). As examples, he offers the sanitized version of the past that would have been offered by Disney's planned American Historyland in northern Virginia or the failure of a Civil War encampment to reflect "underlying social and political issues" (103).

Perhaps the most significant discussion of these theoretical issues in recent years is Greg Dening's *Performances*, published in 1996. Dening, an ethno-historian, offers a look at the semiotics and poetics of history-making. In presenting the past, "bringing past and present together," the past is not replicated but changed into a representation. Dening observes that "history or the past transcribed into words and signs is the way we experience the present. We make sense of the present in our consciousness of the past" (xiv–xv). Our ability to read the signs "with political astuteness" is essential to our social survival. Since history is not the past but the telling of the past and the shaping of it into "story," then all presentation of history is therefore storytelling (34–35) or the interpretation and narrative-making of our present need. Dening organizes his remarks around "Making a Present of the Past (History's Anthropology)," "Presenting the Past (History's Theatre)," and "Returning to the Past Its Own Present (History's Empowering Force)" (xv). The implications of these ideas for living-history enterprises are large and at the heart of what its practitioners do and why they do it.

Also significant is Barbara Kirschenblatt-Gimblett's *Destination Culture: Tourism, Museums, and Heritage*, published in 1998. She presents several essays that take an ethnographic look at the "logic of exhibition" in museums, fairs, historical simulations, and heritage-oriented tourism, all "in the context of lively debates about the death of museums, ascendancy of tourism, production of heritage, limits of multiculturalism, social efficacy of the arts, and circulation of value in the life world" (1). For instance, she posits that exhibitions, by nature, "are fundamentally theatrical, for they are how museums perform the knowledge they create" (3). Plimoth Plantation is a case for scrutiny, "where the year 1627 'lives' forever." Plimoth, according to Kirschenblatt-Gimblett, is "an unscripted ensemble performance," but one in which the performers are obliged to forget anything that has happened after 1627, even though the performance of the living-historians is a product of 1627 and the present in collision (10).

Other important works on culture and representation are Bond and Gilliam's *Social Construction of the Past* (1994), Michael Kammen's *Mystic Chords of Memory* (1991), and Stephen Bann's important *The Inventions of History* (1990).

Battle Reenactments

Since the reenacting trend originally grew out of the muzzle-loading firearms movement, the first books were living-history how-to texts that detailed practical specifics of this avocation and were written by "buckskinners" (reenactors of the mountain man era in the Old West). Sam Fadala's *The Complete Black Powder Handbook* was published in 1979 and is extraordinarily detailed and thorough, probably due to Fadala's training at the University of Arizona, where he earned a Ph.D., according to Jay Anderson (*Living History Sourcebook* 210). Fadala offers a look at the original mountain men, current organizations, rendezvous, a list of pertinent publications, a list of vendors and manufacturers, a glossary, and a guide to the different weapons. A few years later, Ken Grissom came out with his highly regarded *Buckskins and Black Powder: A Mountain Man's Guide to Muzzleloading*. Comprehensive and generously illustrated, this text, according to Anderson, "sets the standard for the field" (*Living History Sourcebook* 210). In more recent years we have Randy D. Smith's *The Black Powder Plainsman: A Beginner's Guide to Muzzleloading and Reenactment on the Great Plains*, published in 1992. Books more closely linked to Civil War reenacting go beyond the details of black powder weaponry, since it involves more of a lifestyle as it is practiced by most hobbyists. R. Lee Hadden produced a more practical guide: *Reliving the Civil War: A Reenactor's Handbook* (1996).

Perhaps the first important scholarly attention to reenacting came from a living-history scholar, Betty Doak Elder. In "War Games: Is History Losing the Battle?" (1981), Elder questions the validity of battle reenactments as a meaningful way of representing historical events, in reference to the celebrations of the American Revolution Bicentennial. Elder's main contribution is a checklist of practices and techniques that would be needed to prevent reenactments from becoming "farb-fests." At this time, reenactment groups were heeding the criticisms of professional historians—some of them reenactors themselves—concerning authenticity and accuracy in the practice of reenacting historical events. Elder's article also points up one of the differences between historical reenacting and living-history outdoor museums and folk parks: the former attracts primarily the lay practitioner; the latter, the professional historian. Still, Elder's article contributed to an increasing awareness among reenactors and a rising pressure among them to keep high and rigid standards of accuracy—not only in dress and weaponry but in drill, tactics, first-person impressions, camp, and even food and music.

The first serious ethnographical study of Civil War reenacting was written by Rory Turner (then of the Folklore Institute of Indiana University), based upon his experiences as a reenactor at the 125th anniversary of the Battle of Gettysburg in 1988—up to that time, the largest battle reenactment ever staged in North America. In "Bloodless Battles: The Civil War Reenacted" (1990), Turner offers a brief history of the reenactment movement in the context of living history and examines the curious grassroots nature of the "hobby," as reenactors call it. He also notes the absence of a single national organization (124). He notes the proliferation of nonmilitary appendages to reenacting, especially the sutlers, or traveling merchants who produce and sell a wide variety of accoutrements and accessories to the living-history soldier. Turner notes the close attention (or even affection) that reenactors pay toward the objects and equipment of performance and that it goes beyond mere fetishism to an expertise "deeply contextualized in knowledge" (126). Further, the objects themselves are contextualized by a "collective aesthetic . . . an aesthetic of painstaking detail and accuracy" and that authenticity becomes a measure of how good a reenactor is at his "impression" (127). Turner focuses on the larger question of why reenactors do what they do and dismisses "pat" explanations such as Civil War reenacting's possible nostalgic appeal to the right-wing reactionary mind.[5] It is "a pleasure structure, a voluntary creation shared by those who for whatever reason feel a resonance with any of the significances" such as personal histories, cultural identity, or merely recreation (130). Turner identifies reenacting as an essentially creative act: "Civil War reenactments are not just symbolic texts that express cultural meanings to be decoded analytically by scholars. They are moments in the life processes of the individuals who create them, moments that form and are formed by the hopes, fears, desires, and needs, of those individuals" (131). He sees the battle as dance and the myriad of characters in it—generals, reporters, gunners, medics, and even those reenacting corpses—as soloists in the ensemble piece. Drills are the rehearsals for those performances (132). But Turner is finally troubled by the residual racism and "easy acceptance of the glory of war" that often seem to be implicit in reenacting the Civil War—that it tends to "perpetuate identities and ideologies rather than to question them" (134–35). This is essentially the same criticism leveled at Williamsburg and other living-history enterprises: whether or not the simulation reinforces some cultural status quo or value rather than challenges those values.

In 1994, Dennis Hall published his "Civil War Reenactors and the Postmodern Sense of History" in the *Journal of American Culture*, a probing look at the rising phenomenon of reenacting in the context of contemporary thought. Hall discusses the popularity of the Civil War itself and then focuses on reenacting, noting that "while a satisfactory demographic analysis has yet to be done, reenacting appears to be a remarkably democratic enterprise with respect to social class, if not race and gender" and that it "appeals to a broad social spectrum" (7). Hall observes, as does Turner, that reenactors are essentially performers and that they perform not just for others but for each other and for themselves (8). There is a particular pride that reenactors have in their own expertise, typically being "down-right learned" in their hobby, but yet they maintain a strict amateur's passion for "the pleasures of the text as lived" (8). Hall reads reenacting not as a "pedagogical exercise" but as a negative reaction to humanity's postmodern predicament—"an exercise in cultural isolation" (8). "Nostalgia, and the popular consciousness of history in general, are manifestations of a sense of powerlessness in the face of rapid changes in the structures with which we make sense of our lives individually and collectively" (9). This search to recover some perceived past glory is what drives the interest in reenacting. Hall identifies the "images and simulacra" of the hobby as fundamental to the attraction of it: that the close replication of the material, tactile cues help create the illusion that the simulated experience is, in David Harvey's words, "indistinguishable from the originals" (qtd. in Hall 10). "In reenacting the imitation of history tends to become the primary reality of history" (10). The reenactor appropriates the visual and tactile tokens of a bygone age and makes them his own, to the point that the history that he imitates is "not so much a reading of history as a writing of it. . . . In his emphasis upon the simulation experience, the reenactor seeks to make, no, to do history rather than understand it" (10).

Two years later, Randal Allred's article, "Catharsis, Revision, and Reenactment: Negotiating the Meaning of the American Civil War" (1996) appeared, also in the *Journal of American Culture*. Drawing from Turner's and Hall's pieces, Allred's essay explores the lasting appeal of the war in the national cultural consciousness, focusing specifically on the phenomenon of reenacting. Allred considers the comments of Robert Penn Warren in *The Legacy of the Civil War* on this same question: how reenacting the war may be a way toward community ownership of the national heritage by way of participation, even though few Americans can remember listening to the stories of anyone who participated in the war, and that most of the nation's people came here after it had ended: "Not that this disqualifies the grandson from experiencing to the full the imaginative appeal of the Civil War. To experience this appeal may be, in fact, the very ritual of being American. To be American is not . . . a matter of blood; it is a matter of an idea—and history is the image of that idea" (qtd. in Allred 1). This quotation seems to speak to the reenactor's experience. Allred offers a description of reenacting as "a culture itself with its own unique traditions, language, and rituals" (1) and goes on to identify a bewildering variety of manifestations—from camp followers to sutlers. He discusses the Civil War reenactor's passion for authenticity. Allred quotes from a number of reenactors themselves, who offer a range of observations on their own passions and reasons for their hobby. In agreement with Turner, Allred observes that often "the realism of the hobby" is what attracts participants—the discomforts and sordid life of a soldier in camp and on campaign (6). This is what creates what Turner calls the "time warp" experience. Allred sees a prime motivation for reenacting as being the desire for "a kind of escape" from the present: "a flight from an age of isolation and fragmentation into an age of community and shared values" (7). But in spite of that, there is also some revision of history going on, at least on a personal level, no matter how assiduously organizers choreograph the battle to simulate the original. "A war that is not even past," to paraphrase Faulkner, "is bound to present speculative possibilities" to the reenactor who "sees the same events unfold before his eyes, yet senses that the power to change the text, to control the narrative, is in his hands" (9–10). Allred, who (like Turner) was a reenactor at the 125th anniversary of Gettysburg, tells several anecdotes that are revealing, including an interview with a Rebel reenactor who had made a pact with a group of others: in the staging of Pickett's Charge on the third day of the event, they would revise the script and break the Union line and win the battle, 125 years later. Ironically, the force of so many muskets firing blanks knocked them to the ground and spoiled the surprise. Allred believes that the events at a battle reenactment of the Civil War make it much like a religious ritual, complete with the act of expiation, sacrifice, and reconciliation—and sometimes even ending in a hymn and prayer. The reenactors are like the guildsmen in a medieval passion play, whose expertise about their roles nearly amounts to priestly authority. The catharsis operates either as purgative or as moral lesson; we are either cleansed or taught by the tragedy (11).

Jim Cullen's *The Civil War in Popular Culture: A Reusable Past* (1995) is one of the most profound commentaries on the impact of the war on American culture. It contains chapters on popular culture and the Civil War, the deification of Lincoln, *Gone with the Wind*, southern rock and roll, glory and the representations of Hollywood, and Civil War reenacting. Well written and dense with absorbing analysis, Cullen's text proceeds on the assumption that the Civil War has come as close as any event to being what Shelby Foote called "the crossroads of our being" (Cullen 2). Cullen notes that reenacting has strong roots in the "sentiments and politics" of our time and that reenacting is experiencing history "as a form of *communion*" (5).

In his chapter on reenacting ("Patriotic Gore"), Cullen focuses on "Jonathan Clarke," the fictional male soldier persona reenacted by a Rhode Island woman. At a large reenactment at Manassas in Virginia in 1992, Cullen makes a number of observations about the blurring of boundaries between reality and representation, including spectators who worried that men falling down were actually hurt (175–76). Cullen points out the differences between Civil War reenactors and other practitioners of living history: reenactors have no affiliation with "local chambers of commerce, the military, or museum administrators" in the same way; they do not get paid to reenact; and, reenacting is "portable"—that is, it is not tied to a site, such as Colonial Williamsburg is. Battle reenacting tends to be scorned by other amateur historians such as those who form discussion roundtables. Cullen also offers an excellent thumbnail history of reenacting, linking its fluctuations with other forms of living history, especially commemorative events such as pageants. By the 1980s, Civil War reenactments were becoming less casual and more "concerned with period detail." He notes the rising interest in authenticity and verisimilitude in identifying "three tiers" of reenactors: "farbs" (those who are inauthentic), "authentics," and "hard-cores," who "frown on anything that compromises accuracy" (186).

Cullen points out the limitations of living history as practiced on the mock battlefield: "Although there is a place in reenactments for death and injury, some important complexities—the chaos, brutality, and uncertainty of wartime, and the disillusionments of its aftermath—are missing. . . . and perhaps have led them to trivialize what has happened" (196). Perhaps reenactment, like science fiction, fills a social need for myth. The great strength of reenactments, adds Cullen, "is that it can give participants a vivid, even visceral, experience of the past on a very personal level" (197). But toward the end of this chapter, Cullen cannot resist expressing his "unease" with reenacting as being perhaps some sort of celebration of white America in its resistance to the rising tide of alternative minority histories (199).

Perhaps the most widely read and acclaimed book on this cultural phenomenon is Tony Horwitz's *Confederates in the Attic: Dispatches from the Unfinished Civil War* in 1998. In an exceptionally readable style, Horwitz proceeds on an odyssey throughout the South to explore the lingering meaning of the Civil War in the minds and hearts of southern Americans. But this experience is framed by his involvement with Robert Lee Hodge (a noted Civil War reenactment authority and author of many articles in the *Camp Chase Gazette*) and a group of reenactors in Virginia. Hodge and his group are self-described "hard-cores" who accept no compromises with authenticity, even declining to participate in battle, since there is no way to plausibly or realistically simulate the violence of battle. Horwitz tells us of his own great-grandfather, a Jewish immigrant from Russia, whose obsession with the Civil War caused him in his young poverty to purchase an expensive book of sketches of the Civil War, and how he himself decorated the entire attic with a mural of Civil War battle. The focal question of the book is this: "Why did this war still obsess so many Americans 130 years after Appomattox? I returned to Poppa Isaac's book. What did that war have to do with him, or with me?" (9). He participates with Hodge and his hard-cores to find out, sharing in the discomforts of the hobby in order to find the source of attraction for what they do. His portrait of reenactors is sympathetic and yet satirical as well, and the commitment of a "hard-core" is difficult to fathom.

Horwitz's odyssey takes him into a number of adventures in eight southern states: a catechism of the United Daughters of the Confederacy, obsessive hobbyists, museums of memorabilia, reactionary racial politics, Charlestonian pride and Atlanta indifference, the Confederate battle flag controversy at South Carolina's capitol, racial murder in Kentucky, an interview with Shelby Foote, a ghostly battlefield walk at Shiloh, Jewish Confederates, racial separation and charter schools in Alabama, and a marathon visiting of battle sites with Hodge called a "Civil Wargasm." Horwitz's own participation in the reenactment of the Battle of the Wilderness uncovers a host of different attitudes and motives for being in a reenactment, from respect for the dead, to being in an era of better manners. Horwitz's conclusion focuses on Robert Penn Warren's speculation that participation in the war is what enables us to feel American.

The same year, Kimberley A. Miller published an article entitled "Gender Comparisons within Reenactment Costume: Theoretical Interpretations" (1998), wherein she explores why people dress in costume. Miller asks whether costuming is for education or to perpetuate the reenactor's fantasy. She challenges the notion that costume dressing for fantasy is secret and private, citing Halloween and Mardi Gras as examples, and says that reenactors may have some of the same motivation to "dress up" in public. She notes the lack of serious scholarly research on reen- acting, except for Turner and Hall. Miller's observations about gender are pro- vocative. Men, she argues, resist the label of "fantasy," even though the imagination is necessary to costuming. Men whom she interviewed said that they dress up for history, the fun of gunplay, and de-individuation—and for the sake of authenticity. Apparently, having and using some arcane expertise have an at- traction for the American male. Women reenactors, on the other hand, embrace fantasy as a reason for the costume. Perhaps the male denial of fantasy is an attempt to reinforce traditional gender roles, Miller observes.

In 1999, an article by Howard Mansfield in *Yankee* magazine, entitled "Pieces of Paper Pinned to Their Coats" appeared. An eloquent piece written as first- person experience, Mansfield's essay is one of the best expressions of the personal side of battle reenacting. Drawing from his observations in the 135th anniversary reenactment of the Battle of Antietam, Mansfield gives us a field-eye view of the action and emotions of a participant:

> In all my dreams I am marching to the drums. Long lines of Union blue stretch over a hill into the morning light. Long marching rows that take a half hour to pass a spot.
>
> Going to see the elephant. That is what many Union boys called going to war. They would see for themselves. . . .
>
> This is a show we put on for ourselves—for each other. Believe in it, have faith, attend to the details, and we can build a better elephant.
>
> This is war without death, just what the peace movement always wanted. Many find reenacting the Civil War disturbing—or silly, like playing trick or treat on the graves of the solemn dead.
>
> Just what are we creating and why?

Mansfield offers this sobering and revealing assessment:

> Americans are said to have no interest in history; last month's news fades into the same background as the Roman Empire. In the evening, walking among fields of tents, I thought it amazing that so many more than 15,000, each at his own expense, each acting as his own museum curator had traveled so far in search of so much.
>
> And what had they come in search of? Honor, valor, glory, fidelity, and honesty. The men who had fought the Civil War were men of conscience and endurance, I was told. They braved so much, endured hardship, and triumphed in pursuit of their ideals. . . . The ethic of that time said that bravery and character were everything. This is the elephant many reenactors have come to see. For them, the battlefield is a meditation.

An assessment just as eloquent but with a darker view of reenacting in general is Philip Beidler's article in *The Virginia Quarterly Review* entitled "Ted Turner et al. at Gettysburg; or, Reenactors in the Attic." Beidler admits up front that, being a native of Gettysburg, he is "no fan of the Civil War industry" and that he resists "any attempt to render war attractive—the Civil War, the Vietnamese war, any war . . . particularly as regards the perverse spectacle called reenactment." He focuses on the film *Gettysburg*, a Ted Turner production based on Michael Shaara's Pulitzer Prize-winning novel *The Killer Angels*. He attacks the "packaging and marketing of the Civil War as part of a larger commodification of cultural desire," of which Turner's film is such a prominent example, and how the reenactors aided in its making. The reenactors, Beidler notes, "were commensurately good. . . . in many ways they were excessively good," or they were too picture-perfect and authentic. "The result was a tableau vivant quality of over-determined detail," with all of the spin-off marketing schemes, from music to coffee-table books that portray battle with little bloodshed: "there is not a disassembled body part in sight." The problem with *Gettysburg*, Beidler argues, is that it is handsomely done, with almost none of the bloodshed and maiming that actually occur in war. With the destructive potential of the .58 caliber minié ball and canister in cannon, the carnage is understated in the film and the picture-perfect reenactor's authenticity. He admits that part of the problem is with our collective conceptions of the war, "for it was, truly, the last pageant war, a war in which bravery and butchery actually co-existed in a way that the culture found psychologically manageable." Beidler asserts that the reenactors focus on this point in "their near religious devotion to authenticity . . . in a world where . . . it was still actually possible to talk about giving one's last full measure of devotion." He cites Turner, Cullen, and Allred in their explanations of the reenacting phenomenon and then responds that reenacting "remains the playacting of an incredible, massed-weaponry, meat-grinder violence that the word carnage just doesn't comprehend." He admits that the Gettysburg story is indeed epic, which is why the entire spectacle is so pernicious.

NOTES

1. Such a tendency may have, in fact, found its first significant manifestation in Louis XIV's creation of a rather idealized peasant village on the grounds of Versailles, where he and his court favorites could "play" at the romanticized simple lives of the common people in rustic clothing and yet return to their silks and pâté de foie gras in the evening.

2. In April 1961, exactly 100 years since Confederate guns opened fire on Fort Sumter, the newly appointed CWCC attempted to meet in Charleston, South Carolina, in order to inaugurate the commemoration of that conflict and of the battle for Fort Sumter itself. A member of the New Jersey delegation, a black woman, was denied a hotel room in color-conscious Charleston, so the meetings were moved to the U.S. Naval base nearby.

> Thereupon, the members of the South Carolina Centennial Commission, almost as if they had read the stage directions from a script written in 1860–1861, seceded from the national Commission. Ultimately, two commemoration meetings were held, one under the auspices of the national Commission at the naval base, and a second meeting at the original headquarters hotel sponsored by "The Confederate States Centennial Conference." (Pressly 8)

This led to added confusion and acrimony, leading the CWCC to adopt a stance of neutrality to most controversial issues, including blocking a proposal to study the war's origins, for fear it would lead to exacerbated sectional acrimony (Fried 126–27).

3. Such was the case with the making of *North and South*, Part Two, a television mini-series, as well as the better-known *Glory* and *Gettysburg*.

4. A reenactor describes just such an experience this way:

> Later, to see all those men marching in unison . . . to be somewhat hypnotized by the thousands of feet crunching into the gravel at the same time . . . to see the mirrored swaying of the shiny silver muskets to the rhythm of the march was all a very powerful experience; but then, that first time I heard the regimental fife and drum corps cut into my consciousness, it stirred me to my very soul. It gave me a feeling of power at being part of a bigger whole that is hard to describe, but exquisite to feel. Later, as a lonely private, I walked the darkened fields of the Shilo [*sic*] reenactment battlefield, hearing the tones of a single harmonica from the left, and saw the flickering flames of a campfire with the surrounding company of men and felt the soft scented breeze of a peaceful night and then heard a dozen male voices singing a familiar song. Then there was not anywhere else that I would rather have been. (Bryan Allred)

5. This is an issue that Tony Horwitz addresses as a central question in his book—that is, what is the imaginative appeal of the Civil War itself for such a broad range of people, including immigrants and others whose ancestors were never involved?

BIBLIOGRAPHY

Books and Articles

Alderson, William T., and Shirley Paine Low. *Interpretation of Historical Sites*. 2nd ed. Nashville, Tenn.: American Association for State and Local History, 1976.

Allred, Bryan. Letter to Randal Allred. April 24, 1994.

Allred, Randal. "Catharsis, Revision, and Reenactment: Negotiating the Meaning of the American Civil War." *Journal of American Culture* 19: 4 (Winter 1996), 1–13.

Anderson, Jay. "Living History." In *A Living History Reader*. Vol. 1: *Museums*. Nashville: American Association for State and Local History, 1991, 3–12.

———. "Living History: Simulating Everyday Life in Living Museums." *American Quarterly* 34 (Fall 1982), 290–306.

———. *The Living History Sourcebook*. Nashville, Tenn.: American Association for State and Local History, 1985.

———. *Time Machines: The World of Living History*. Nashville, Tenn.: American Association for State and Local History, 1984.

———, ed. *A Living History Reader*. Vol. 1: *Museums*. Nashville, Tenn.: American Association for State and Local History, 1991.

Appleby, Joyce, Lynn Hunt, and Margaret Jacob. *Telling the Truth about History*. New York: W. W. Norton, 1994.

Asher, Robert. "Experimental Archaeology." *American Anthropologist* 63 (1961), 793–816.

Bann, Stephen. *The Inventions of History: Essays on the Representation of the Past*. Manchester, England: Manchester University Press, 1990.

Becker, Carl. "Every Man His Own Historian." In *Every Man His Own Historian*. New York: F. S. Crofts, 1935.

Beidler, Philip. "Ted Turner et al. at Gettysburg; or, Reenactors in the Attic." *The Virginia Quarterly Review* 75 (Summer 1999), 488–503.

Boardman, Kathryn. "Revisiting Living History: A Business, an Art, a Pleasure, an Education." On-line posting. The Association for Living History, Farm and Agricultural Museums. February 26, 2001. <http://www.alhfam.org/whitepapers/alhfam.revisit.html>

Bodnar, John. *Bonds of Affection: Americans Define Their Patriotism*. Princeton, N.J.: Princeton University Press, 1996.

———. *Remaking America: Public Memory, Commemoration, and Patriotism in the Twentieth Century*. Princeton, N.J.: Princeton University Press, 1992.

Bond, George Clement, and Angela Gilliam, eds. *Social Construction of the Past: Representation as Power*. London: Routledge, 1994.

Burke, Peter. *History and Social Theory*. Ithaca, N.Y.: Cornell University Press, 1993.

Coles, John. *Archeology by Experiment*. London: Academic Press, 1973.

———. *Experimental Archaeology*. London: Academic Press, 1979.

Cornell, Jared. Letter to Randal Allred. April 22, 1994.

Cullen, Jim. *The Civil War in Popular Culture: A Reusable Past*. Washington, D.C.: Smithsonian Institution, 1995.

Dening, Greg. *Performances*. Chicago: University Chicago Press, 1996.

Elder, Betty Doak. "War Games: Is History Losing the Battle?" *History News* 36:8 (August 1981): 25–28.

Fadala, Sam. *The Complete Black Powder Handbook*. Northfield, Ill.: DBI Books, 1979.

Feverherd, Peter. "Williamsburg: The Past Unchained." *Commonweal* (November 5, 1999), 31.

Fried, Richard M. *The Russians Are Coming! The Russians Are Coming! Pageantry and Patriotism in Cold-War America*. New York: Oxford University Press, 1998.

Glassberg, David. *American Historical Pageantry: The Uses of Tradition in the Early Twentieth Century*. Chapel Hill: University of North Carolina Press, 1990.

Grinder, Alison L., and E. Sue McCoy. *The Good Guide: A Source Book for Interpreters, Docents, and Tour Guides*. Scottsdale, Ariz.: Ironwood Press, 1985.

Grissom, Ken. *Buckskins and Black Powder: A Mountain Man's Guide to Muzzleloading*. Piscataway, N.J.: Winchester Press, 1983.

Hadden, R. Lee. *Reliving the Civil War: A Reenactor's Handbook*. Mechanicsville, Pa.: Stackpole, 1996.

Hall, Dennis. "Civil War Reenactors and the Postmodern Sense of History." *Journal of American Culture* 17: 3 (Fall 1994), 7–11.

Handler, Richard, and Eric Gable. *The New History in an Old Museum: Creating the Past at Colonial Williamsburg*. Durham, N.C.: Duke University Press, 1997.

Horwitz, Tony. *Confederates in the Attic: Dispatches from the Unfinished Civil War*. New York: Pantheon, 1998.

Kammen, Michael G. *Mystic Chords of Memory: The Transformation of Tradition in American Culture*. New York: Alfred Knopf, 1991.

Kirschenblatt-Gimblett, Barbara. *Destination Culture: Tourism, Museums, and Heritage*. Berkeley: University of California Press, 1998.

Leon, Warren, and Margaret Piatt. "Living History Museums." In *History Muse-

ums in the United States: A Critical Assessment, ed. Warren Leon and Roy Rosenzweig. Urbana: University of Illinois Press, 1989, 64–97.

Loomis, Ormond. *Sources on Folk Museums and Living Historical Farms*. Bloomington: Indiana University Press: Folklore Forum, 1977.

Lowenthal, David. *The Past Is a Foreign Country*. Cambridge: Cambridge University Press, 1985.

———. *Possessed by the Past: The Heritage Crusade and the Spoils of History*. New York: Free Press, 1996.

Machlis, Gary E., and Donald R. Field, eds. *On Interpretation: Sociology for Interpreters of Natural and Cultural History*. Rev. ed. Corvallis: Oregon State University Press, 1992.

Mansfield, Howard. "Pieces of Paper Pinned to Their Coats." *Yankee*, 63 (1 September 1999), 78.

Miller, Kimberley A. "Gender Comparisons within Reenactment Costume: Theoretical Interpretations." *Family and Consumer Sciences Research Journal* 27 (September 1998), 35–61.

Milne, Kirsty. "Fighting a Very Civil War." *New Statesman and Society* 20 (August 1993), 12–13.

Pressly, Thomas J. *Americans Interpret Their Civil War*. New York: Free Press/Collier-Macmillan, 1965.

Rath, Frederick L., Jr., and Merrilyn Rogers O'Connell, eds. *Interpretation: A Bibliography on Historical Organization Practices*. Nashville, Tenn.: American Association for State and Local History, 1978.

Reid, Debra. "Research and Living History: Facing the Challenges." On-line posting. The Association for Living History, Farm and Agricultural Museums. February 26, 2001. <http://www.alhfam.org/whitepapers/alhfam.researh.html>

Roth, Stacy F. *Past into Present: Effective Techniques for First-Person Historical Interpretation*. Chapel Hill: University of North Carolina Press, 1998.

Smith, Randy. *The Black Powder Plainsman: A Beginner's Guide to Muzzleloading and Reenactment on the Great Plains*. Bountiful, Utah: Horizon, 1992.

Snow, Stephen Eddy. *Performing the Pilgrims: A Study of Ethnohistorical Role-Playing at Plimoth Plantation*. Jackson: University Press of Mississippi, 1993.

"So What Is Living History? Sounds like an Oxymoron to Me." Living History HELP. On-line posting. The Association for Living History, Farm and Agricultural Museums. February 26, 2001. <http://www.alhfam.org/alhfam.help.html>

Stover, Kate F. "Is It Real History Yet?: An Update on Living History Museums." *Journal of American Culture* 12: 2 (Summer 1989), 13–17.

Susman, Warren I. *Culture as History: The Transformation of American Society in the Twentieth Century*. New York: Pantheon, 1984.

Tilden, Freeman. *Interpreting Our Heritage*. 1957. Chapel Hill: University of North Carolina Press, 1967.

Treviño, Marcella Bush. "Civil War Reenactors." In *St. James Encyclopedia of Popular Culture*, vol. 1, ed. Tom and Sara Pendergast. Detroit: St. James Press, 2000, 521–23.

Turner, Rory. "Bloodless Battles: The Civil War Reenacted." *The Drama Review* 34: 4 (Winter 1990), 123–36.

Vanderstel, David. G. "Humanizing the Past: The Revitalization of the History Museum." *Journal of American Culture* 12: 2 (Summer 1989), 19–25.

Vlach, John Michael. Rev. of *The New History in an Old Museum: Creating the Past at Colonial Williamsburg* by Richard Handler and Eric Gable. *Ethnohistory* 45 (Fall 1998), 806–8.

Wallace, Michael. "Visiting the Past: History Museums in the United States." *Radical History Review* 25 (October 1981), 63–96.

Warren, Robert Penn. *The Legacy of the Civil War*. Cambridge, MA: Harvard University Press, 1983.

Woods, Thomas A. "Museums and the Public Good: Doing History Together." *Journal of American History*, 82 (December 1995), 1111–1115.

Journals

American Civil War. Leesburg, VA, 1988– .

The Artilleryman. Arlignton, MA, 1985– .

Blue and Gray Magazine. Columbus, OH, 1983– .

Camp Chase Gazette. Marietta, OH, 1972– .

The Citizen Companion. Marietta, OH, 1993– .

The Civil War Lady Magazine. Pipeston, MN, 1991– .

Civil War Monitor. Centerville, VA, 1984– .

Civil War News. Arlington, MA, 1989– .

Civil War Times Illustrated. Gettysburg, PA, 1962– .

Living History. Battle Creek, MI, 1955– .

Living History Association Quarterly. Middleboro, MA, 1987– .

Muzzleloading Artilleryman. Winchester, MA, 1979–1985.

The Skirmish Line. Washington, DC, 1955– .

Tournaments Illuminated. Milpitas, CA, 1967– .

MAGAZINES

Dorothy S. Schmidt

More than any other print medium, the magazine represents America. Other nations produce periodicals, but nowhere else is there the multicolored, multivoiced flood of print that inundates Americans weekly, monthly, and quarterly. Numbering in the tens of thousands, with a readership of more than 86 percent of the population, American magazines are not only dazzling in their design and diversity but complex in content and purpose. As consumer products, magazines develop and satisfy the tastes of contemporary Americans; as primary advertising tools of business and industry, magazines help provide the market that supplies the demand for products; and as instruments of entertainment and enlightenment, magazines both create and respond to current social values and the panorama of American culture.

The idea of such periodicals apparently arose almost concurrently in France, England, Germany, and other European countries, but the term *magazine* was first used in English in the early eighteenth century. The *New English Dictionary* cites the *Gentlemen's Magazine*, founded in 1731, as its first example of the word used to describe a collection of articles, fiction, poetry, and "miscellany" gathered into one place as a storehouse or treasure chest. The descriptive term caught on so well that by midcentury several publications included the word *magazine* either in their titles or in subtitles. Today, nearly three centuries later, *magazine* is still the preferred and most commonly used designation for thousands of miscellaneous collections for the general public. Other titles such as *bulletin, journal, quarterly,* and *review* may label more specialized publications, including business, professional, trade, and scholarly periodicals, but these terms are also used for consumer or mass magazines.

Not only content but also the form and frequency of publication have been used as criteria for differentiating between magazines and other periodicals, especially newspapers. While no entirely satisfactory or mutually exclusive categories for periodicals have been established, magazines are usually produced in pamphlet form with a stitched, stapled, or glued cover, rather than as broadsheets or tabloids. As for frequency of publication, magazines traditionally have appeared monthly; but, again, exceptions can be noted, especially in the modern weekly newsmagazines that offer analysis and commentary on current events to augment the news coverage of radio, television, and newspapers.

Expansions of the use of the *magazine* label occurred during the last decades of the twentieth century with the initiation of television magazine programs, for example, *Sixty Minutes*, *Prime Time*, *Dateline*, and *20/20*, which provide viewers with a variety of features, including human interest stories, personality profiles, news analyses, and interpretations of various aspects of American life in a cross-media adaptation of the usual contents of the printed periodical. With the advent of mass computer access, *eJournals* or *e-zines*, both as discrete constructs or replicas of print versions, proliferated on the Internet. Most allow free access, but even these electronic forms may collect a subscription fee from readers who desire the full text and illustrations of the original magazine.

Difficult to define though they may be, magazines hold a unique place in U.S. print media. In form and periodicity, magazines are more durable than newsprint, less formidable than hardbound books, less precipitate than newspapers, yet more timely than books; and magazine content must be designed to attract and hold reader allegiance to ensure either repeated counter purchases or continuing subscriptions.

Although no single magazine has ever claimed the allegiance of the total U.S. reading public, over 170 million persons read magazines regularly, and most read five or six different publications. The perennial world circulation leader has been *Reader's Digest*, but currently the most widely distributed magazine in the United States is *TV Guide*, with a weekly readership approaching the 35 million mark. *TV Guide* contains not only television programming schedules and criticism but lucid articles on current personalities and events as well. The third magazine that shares huge circulation honors with these two is *Modern Maturity*; subscriptions are included with membership in the American Association of Retired Persons, an ever-expanding niche market of over-fifty readers. The continuing popularity of these giants is an ironic refutation of the predicted doom of print media with the advent of electronic media.

Instead, not only have magazines survived, but they have thrived; indeed, many have achieved record circulations in the tens of millions. Other publishers have successfully and profitably identified more limited markets, such as age, sports, hobbies, health, and travel, and produced periodicals specifically for those segments of the mass market. Such targeting benefits advertisers as well. Thus, magazines on the American scene have changed and are still changing, but there seems to be no stemming of the flood. Each calendar year brings hundreds of new magazines addressed to previously untapped topics or markets.

Today thousands of titles, ranging from *Analog* to *Sesame Street Magazine*, from *Scientific American* to *Rolling Stone*, from the *New Yorker* to *Handyman*, and from *Oprah* to *RV World*, tempt readers to indulge relatively narrow interests and tastes, while general magazines such as *Reader's Digest*, *Ladies' Home Journal*, *Atlantic*, *Newsweek*, and *Time* continue to have broad circulations. Increasingly, historians, sociologists, and cultural anthropologists acknowledge the importance of magazines as material artifacts and historical sources far more revealing of the culture of their times than any other single source, thus recognizing, in truth, the magazine's initial and continuing function as a very "storehouse" of information and diversion.

HISTORICAL OUTLINE

The development of magazines was made possible by the invention of printing in 1450. Most examples of the new process were either single flat sheets, appropriately called broadsides, or bound volumes such as Bibles and other treatises. A subsequent development was the printing of several flat sheets folded together without binding as tabloids. Eventually, though, someone decided to put a stitch through the fold to keep the pages from sliding around, and the magazine began its distinctive existence. In large degree, however, form followed content in magazine development so that early English magazines were single-sheet issues, looking almost exactly like their contemporary newspapers but containing comment rather than news.

Magazine content was varied almost from the beginning. Daniel Defoe, credited with starting one of the first magazines in England, in 1710 used the *Review* as a kind of privileged communication among members of his immediate society. A little later Joseph Addison and Richard Steele, first in the *Tatler* and then the *Spectator*, commented on a wide variety of issues then current in London. Essays and short stories originated in the pages of these and other early magazines.

Although printing presses were among the first cargoes to the American colonies, it was not until 1741 that an American magazine, somewhat imitative of its English cousins, was printed and identified as such. If asked, most Americans would probably name the *Saturday Evening Post*, founded by Benjamin Franklin, as the oldest American magazine—a misconception on both counts fostered by the cover claims of that widely known publication. Although purporting to have been established in 1728, the magazine was actually started in 1821, using the offices and press of the defunct *Pennsylvania Gazette*, which, though owned by Franklin, had been founded by someone else and was actually a newspaper, not a magazine. Franklin *almost* printed the first magazine in the colonies, but his *General Magazine, and Historical Chronicle for All the British Plantations in America* lost that premier position to the *American Magazine, or A Monthly View of the Political State of the British Colonies*, issued three days earlier by rival publisher Andrew Bradford. Such are the near misses in historical firsts.

Although neither magazine survived even a full year of publication, other magazines were soon launched. Rogers and Fowle's *American Magazine and Historical Chronicle*, founded in Boston in 1743, lasted three years, thus earning the laurel of magazine historian Frank Luther Mott as the "first really important American magazine." Several other magazines, including another *American Magazine and Monthly Chronicle* by Bradford, the *New American Magazine*, the *Royal American Magazine*, and other variations on the same theme, enjoyed brief lives, but the political foment of the colonies during the next quarter century did not offer a favorable environment for sustained publication. According to Mott, only two American magazines, the *Pennsylvania Magazine*, which employed Thomas Paine, and the *United States Magazine*, were printed during the course of the American Revolution.

Life magazine, 1926. Courtesy of the Library of Congress

The post-Revolutionary period was characterized by a number of other firsts: the first acknowledgment of women's interest in magazines, with the *Gentleman's and Lady's Town and Country Magazine*; the first children's periodical; the first magazine for music lovers, which contained music scores; and the first sectarian magazine, briefly edited by Methodist bishops Coke and Asbury.

Magazine content included political news, essays on various aspects of society, short fiction and sketches, poems, and, not infrequently, polemics. Little advertising, beyond a few classifieds, was sold, and revenue consisted mainly of subscription fees from a limited circulation. Even the distribution of the periodicals was somewhat haphazard and sporadic by modern standards. With early postal regulations seldom clear about the status of periodicals, some earnest postmasters making their own interpretations barred magazines from the mails entirely. But even in adverse environments American magazines flourished because Americans wanted to read them.

The emergence of periodicals dominated by strong editorial figures was one characteristic of the early nineteenth century. James Playsted Wood, in *Magazines in the United States*, writes, "A strong editor, even a strongly wrong-headed editor, has usually meant a strong and influential magazine; whereas intelligent editors of moderate means and no firm opinions have often produced colorless and comparatively ineffective magazines" (33–34). One early example of a strong editor was Joseph Dennie, whose magazine *Port Folio* ran from 1807 to 1821 and served as a model for subsequent literate and urbane publications. Dennie's strength is indicated by the survival of his periodical even while it espoused the unpopular Tory cause. Another editor and publication worthy of note was Charles Brockden Brown and his *Monthly Magazine and American Review*, the first of a series called by Mott "second only to *Port Folio* in importance" (*History*, Vol. 1, 124). Under various titles, Brockden Brown edited the *Literary Magazine* for almost a decade.

The proliferation of magazines during this period included an expansion of magazine content and purpose beyond literature and public opinion. New magazines were directed toward religious groups, the medical profession, women, farmers, and other groups, thus beginning the trend toward specialization, which was somewhat deflected by the mushrooming of the great mass magazines in the first half of the twentieth century but which by the present day has become the mainstream of magazine publishing: the specialized magazine for the special interest group.

One of the most influential women's periodicals of the nineteenth century, indeed, of all time, was *Godey's Lady's Book*. Under the leadership of Sara Josepha Hale, *Godey's* achieved wide circulation during its sixty-eight years of publication. Gowns and other apparel were assiduously copied and sewn from the color fashion plates by dressmakers both amateur and professional. *Godey's*, however, was not merely a fashion book; its contents provided enlightenment for the female mind, and Hale crusaded within its pages for women's right to education in an age that predated woman suffrage in the United States. Within its pages, Edgar Allan Poe described "The Literati of New York," sometimes astutely and sometimes with rather saccharine sanctimony; writers like William Cullen Bryant, Walt Whitman, and Nathaniel Hawthorne were also contributors to this popular magazine.

And there were others. Caroline Kirkland spent six years as editor trying to inject a little frontier freshness and literary quality into the *Union* magazine, which publisher John Sartain viewed primarily as a showcase for his own outstanding engraving talents. The period from 1820 to 1850 saw the births of the *Saturday Evening Post*, *Graham's Magazine*, *Peterson's Magazine*, the *Scientific American*, *North American Review*, *Yale Review*, *Ohio Farmer*, *New York Mirror*, and Horace Greeley's *New-Yorker*.

In addition to these largely acclaimed magazines, huge quantities of print were, unfortunately, summarily dismissed as "trash," both by Mott and by contemporaneous editors. These "penny" magazines and "family libraries" abounded but were often poorly printed, poorly edited collections of pirated or fourth-rate material; however, their very existence testifies to the omnivorous demands of Americans at all levels of sophistication for periodical reading materials, and this was the age in which these demands were answered. Call it the age of expansion, call it America's awakening, or call it the "golden age of periodicals," as Mott did; this country did not see such a burgeoning of print again until after 1900.

The pre–Civil War decade saw the establishment of other familiar names: *Harper's Monthly* (1850), *Country Gentleman* (1853), various regional *Christian Advocates* (1850), *Atlantic Monthly* (1857), and a spate of short-lived university publications. By this time, magazines had progressed in form and appearance far beyond their earlier resemblance to newspapers and had blossomed into hand-colored and embellished, highly illustrated offerings whose engravings were often scissored to grace parlor walls. Although more advertising was being accepted, it was carefully segregated from the editorial and textual materials, and small wonder, for much of it ballyhooed the virtues of everything from laxatives and trusses to cures for baldness, cancer, and impotence—all in the same bottle! The lack of regulation for advertising, either by the magazines themselves or by any publishers' or advertisers' associations, resulted in ads with little or no regard for truth or good taste.

The Civil War interrupted this expansion of magazines, but during the last forty years of the century magazine offerings increased in scope and variety. Popular and enduring titles such as *The Nation, Harper's Bazaar, Scribner's*, and the *American Magazine* began in the 1860s and 1870s, and the breadth of magazine coverage is only hinted at in these titles: *United States Law Review, Instructor, Locomotive, American Brewer, Coal Trade Journal, Popular Science*, and *American Naturalist*. The brief life of *Keepapichinin* (1870–1871) indicates that its subscribers didn't, but the popular humor of *Puck* and *Judge* kept Americans laughing right up to and through the turn of the century. In this period as well the print media's own magazine, *Publishers Weekly*, began its observations of this dynamic industry.

Only technological limitations prevented magazines from becoming the mass circulation giants of the twentieth century. Throughout most of the nineteenth century, magazines were printed on flatbed presses from hand-set type on single pieces of paper, which were hand-fed into the presses. Rarely could a magazine print more than 10,000 impressions, not only because of the time and labor consumed by the process but because type and engravings wore down after repeated impressions. Development in the 1890s of rotary presses, which were capable of printing 10,000 copies an hour on a continuous "web" roll of paper, the development of a cheap wood pulp paper strong enough for this type of printing press, and the use of speedy typesetting machinery removed the barriers to mass production and opened the way for circulations to reach the "magic million."

Not surprisingly, access to such numbers of potential customers drew the attention of industry, and advertising content and revenue grew. The influx of advertising dollars soon matched, then passed sales input. Beginning with almost equal advertising and circulation income in the 1890s, according to U.S. Bureau of the Census manufacturing data, by the late 1920s advertising revenue was three times greater than subscription and sales income.

The shift of emphasis from magazines as the individual voices of single editors or publishers to their use as the major national advertising medium carried both positive and negative results. Magazines became colorful showcases for U.S. technology and progress, with expensive color advertisements brightening their pages and thickening their issues. Throughout the twentieth century, advertising became almost as interesting to magazine readers as editorial content, and rightfully so, for in an economy increasingly dependent on consumerism, it is through such advertising that most Americans become informed about new products, instructed in their uses, and encouraged to purchase everything from toothpaste to Maytag washing machines.

Despite this bounty of advertising dollars, realistic appraisal of magazine content suggests that with economic dependence came loss of editorial freedom and that some of the free-swinging, fresh-air aggressiveness of earlier editors has been compromised by magazines' presence at the table of business and industry. This attitude was angrily espoused by Upton Sinclair in *The Brass Check: A Study of American Journalism*, in which he called the Curtis publications basically an "advertising medium using reading material only to fill the empty spaces between ads." Herbert Schiller in *The Mind Managers* suggested that one influence of the advertising dollar is to make magazine editors more conservative and less likely to broach topics that are controversial enough to offend either readers or advertisers. The pairing of feature articles and huge ads for the company or product featured is a common occurrence in contemporary magazine publishing.

During the 1960s and 1970s, the proliferation of special interest magazines was little less than a quiet revolution in American society and magazine history, as emphasis changed from the collective group to the individual. David Abrahamson, in his pivotal work, *Magazine-Made America: The Cultural Transformation of the Postwar Periodical*, shows the interaction between society's influence on magazines and the magazine's role as molder of social values. With the decline of mass market titles and marketing research enabling advertisers to target specific interest groups, advertising dollars flowed onto the pages, inevitably affecting editorial content.

Fortunately, magazines have not been muzzled entirely, and their investigative reporting has led to exposés and crusades against giant industries such as drug manufacturers, food processors, automakers, big labor, big government, big business, and even big medicine. However, because more and more magazines—in fact the majority of them—are not independent businesses but owned by corporations or conglomerates with widespread holdings and interests, the targets of modern magazines' lances have inevitably been restricted.

Thus, entering the twenty-first century, magazines are consumer products that must be sold to two groups: the magazine readers who purchase the magazine and the businesses who buy the advertising space. Because the latter are the more powerful economically, the editor who fails to meet their needs will witness the death of even a magazine experiencing rising subscriptions and circulation. But the editorial genius who finds a formula for a magazine and is able to adapt it to the rapidly changing American society or to an unchanging segment of that society will have a successful, surviving magazine. Examples of this type of editing and management include the *Reader's Digest, Ladies' Home Journal, Atlantic, Harper's, Time, National Geographic, Scientific American,* and *Playboy*. The editor whose publication gets out of step with change or changes too fast or never develops a distinct identity must preside over its funeral, sometimes twice. Notable examples include *Coronet, Flair, Look, Collier's, Woman's Home Companion, Life, Saturday Evening Post, Ms, Women Sports,* and *George*.

This delicate interrelationship of the reader, the word, and the world of economic and political reality validates the function of magazines as accurate imprints of American culture and necessitates their special study apart from other print media.

REFERENCE WORKS

Research on American magazines in American culture has long been hampered in several ways. First, despite their extended presence as a distinct entity in American publishing, for most of the nineteenth century indexing and statistics for magazines were included under a blanket designation, "periodicals." Therefore, magazine researchers must often categorize and subdivide census data and commentary on historical or economic importance to separate the role of magazines from that of newspapers. This is not an easy division, for, as noted, some early magazines were almost indistinguishable from papers. However, the three criteria of form, content, and periodicity usually serve to make the distinction.

In addition to the identity confusion, magazine study has been most often limited either to discussion of their production as a branch of the craft of journalism or to analysis of their content, as historians and literary critics study certain magazines because some event or author achieved prominence. In the first instance, journalism textbooks examine writing, editing, advertising, layout, and design, with peripheral studies in the economics of publishing and mass communication theory. Another source of professional information comes from associations, organizations, and other groups that report circulation and demographic data.

The focus of attention upon magazines from academic disciplines is even more selective. Whereas most histories of the United States mention Thomas Paine's inflammatory prose, the "muckraking" role of magazines in the early part of the twentieth century, and the radical journals of the 1920s and 1930s, scant attention is given to the continuing role of magazines as reflectors and molders of public opinion and political and social attitudes, and literary criticism has almost uniformly paid more homage to the "books" of American authors than it has to the same writers' works in magazines. Although reaching a vaster audience, magazine writing is commonly dismissed as being of lesser consequence. Even more apparent to the magazine researcher in American popular culture is the qualitative judgment exercised by all three of these approaches in devaluing literally hundreds of magazines as "trash" despite their widespread distribution among the reading public.

Apart from this division of purpose and approach, the sheer monumental bulk of materials confronting the synthesizing scholar has resulted in numerous works examining such small chips off the mountain as individual editors or magazines with brief life spans, but none encompassing the whole. This chapter and bibliography attempt to draw together these disparate strands and point to those references, directories, studies, and sources likely to be most useful to the researcher of magazines in American culture.

Access to periodicals themselves is afforded through a number of standard indexes. Locating the newer editions of such indexes is aided by checking the latest general guides, *American Reference Books Annual* and the *ALA Guide to Reference Books* or the more specialized *Periodical Directories and Bibliographies*, edited by Gary Tarbert. *Ulrich's International Periodicals Directory* is a guide to current domestic and foreign periodicals. Information about early-nineteenth-century periodicals is contained in *Poole's Index to Periodical Literature* for the period 1802–1906. Other guides include the very timely *Working Press of the Nation*, which supplies the address, frequency of publication, circulation, and a short identification of audience for current magazines, as does the *Magazine Industry Market Place (MIMP)* which merged into the *National Directory of Magazines* in 1988. These latter two are useful for the magazine researcher because each magazine's scope and purpose are provided in copy often supplied by the magazine itself. Other more specialized guides may be found in *Periodical Directories and Bibliographies*.

Harper's Weekly, 1876. Courtesy of the Library of Congress

Also descriptive in content is *Magazines for Libraries*, compiled by Bill Katz and Berry G. Richards as a guide for librarians and others. Some 7,850 periodicals considered by the editors to be the best of the 170,000 available are described briefly but cogently in the latest editions of this comprehensive, though not exhaustive, guide.

Several other special guides to publications in education, the humanities, social sciences, and other disciplines are available. For the little magazine, the *International Directory of Little Magazines and Small Presses* almost, but not quite, keeps pace with the rapid births and deaths of more than 4,000 of these fragile, but fascinating, entities. Marion Sader edited the eight-volume *Comprehensive Index to English-Language Little Magazines*, an undertaking flawed only by its being organized alphabetically by proper names of either author or subject, with no topic index. Loos Glazier prepared the useful *Small Press: An Annotated Guide*. For researchers looking at literary periodicals, Daniel Wells prepared *The Literary Index to American Magazines*.

Another group of magazines overlooked in standard guides is the ethnic press. One attempt to remedy the oversight is the *Encyclopedic Directory of Ethnic News-*

papers and Periodicals in the United States, by Lubomyr Wynar, a fairly comprehensive listing. Sandra Ireland lists in database style some 290 entries in *Ethnic Periodicals in Contemporary America*. Of lesser value is Sharon Murphy's *Other Voices: Black, Chicano, and American Indian Press*, which contains more excerpts from periodicals than listings. Additional examples of ethnic directories include Karl J. R. Arndt's *German-American Newspapers and Periodicals 1732–1955*, and another, *A Century of the Swedish-American Press*, by Jonas Oscar Backlund, which reviews the hundred years from 1851 to 1951. Frankie Hutton tabulates *The Early Black Press in America, 1827–1860*, and *The Black Press, U.S.A.*, by Roland E. Wolseley, covers the remarkably active publishing period just before World War I as well as the more recent expansions. *The 1967 Directory of U.S. Negro Newspapers, Magazines and Periodicals in 42 States: The Negro Press—Past, Present and Future*, edited by Frank B. Sawyer, though dated, gives a more complete listing, and Penelope Bullock continues the task of identification in *The Afro-American Periodical Press*.

Although cumbersome to search, the *Reader's Guide to Periodical Literature*, both current issues and the *Nineteenth Century Reader's Guide to Periodical Literature: 1890–1899, with Supplementary Indexing, 1900–1922*, may be used to locate articles examining editors and periodicals from the perspectives of contemporaries and peers. An adjunct to the *Reader's Guide* is *Access*, which serves as a supplementary index to additional periodical titles. Contents of the more scholarly journals may be found through the use of a series of indexes first titled the *International Index*, then the *Social Sciences and Humanities Index*, and currently, the new *Humanities Index*, which surveys 345 magazines, and the even newer (in concept and design) *Social Sciences Index*, which lists articles from 263 periodicals. *America: History and Life*, Part D, indexes articles from more than 3,000 U.S. and foreign periodicals and journals. (Although articles on U.S. magazines are occasionally printed abroad, the difficulties of locating and using the foreign journals usually outweigh their value, since most are rather general in content.) Part A of *America: History and Life*, which is issued annually, contains abstracts of many of the articles; Part B is a book review index; and Part C contains a bibliography of books, articles, and dissertations on American history.

Several bibliographies are journalism-oriented. *Journalist's Bookshelf*, by Roland E. Wolseley, is well annotated, yet here again the viewpoint is largely that of the professional journalist or journalism educator rather than the cultural historian. The "Biography" and "History" sections provide real assistance in identifying major figures and publications. Another frequently listed bibliography, *A Bibliography for the Study of Magazines*, by John H. Schacht, has a fairly comprehensive list of articles on magazines published in the 1950s, and his work is continued by Fred and Nancy Paine in *Magazines: A Bibliography for Their Analysis with Annotations and Study Guides*. Warren C. Price and Calder M. Pickett produced *An Annotated Journalism Bibliography, 1958–1968*, which is useful. The annotations are sufficiently complete and accurate to serve the serious researcher, even though the scattered magazine articles must be located through a numerical entry index providing access to the alphabetized entries.

Sam G. Riley has compiled several specialized groupings of periodicals, including his *Index to Southern Periodicals* and *Corporate Magazines of the United States*. Other bibliographies and current indexes may be found in Paul Vesenji's *An In-*

troduction to Periodical Bibliography, intended primarily as a guide to librarians but useful to magazine scholars as well. Finally, of course, *Dissertation Abstracts International* is the source of the latest scholarly research in the field.

Now that over 50 percent of Americans own computers and more than 30 percent are on-line, electronic research is becoming the norm. While the reader who is intimidated by acronyms and Boolean logic will have some difficulty, for others the availability of far-ranging materials at one's own keyboard is convenient and timesaving. With both academic and commercial search engines and databases, even obscure and out-of-print periodicals are retreivable, some even with full text available. Most libraries subscribe to *Infotrac*, which functions similarly to the *Reader's Guide* for tracking popular periodicals, and on-line versons of most of the standard indexes are also readily accessible. Two annuals providing information for on-line research are *Books and Periodicals Online* and *Fulltext Sources Online*.

RESEARCH COLLECTIONS

Almost every public or university library has a periodicals collection, often with extensive, bound back issues. But almost no library has all of the known periodicals, not even the redoubtable Library of Congress, although it comes close. The *Union List of Serials* provides library locations of magazines in the United States and Canada; it is also helpful for confirming dates of publication and titles and untangling new series/old series confusions. Beginning in 1953, *New Serial Titles* picked up the task. Two directories for locating libraries with special collections or strengths in magazines are Margaret L. Young's *Subject Directory of Special Libraries and Information Centers*, based on her similarly titled *Directory of Special Libraries and Information Centers*.

Special collections of interest to magazine researchers include the collection of nineteenth-century periodicals at the Athenaeum of Philadelphia and a similar grouping at the American Antiquarian Society in Worcester, Massachusetts. Of historical significance is the Edward C. Kimble Collection of Printing and Publishing at the California Historical Society Library in San Francisco. Outstanding collections are found at the Columbia University School of Journalism Library in New York, and the University of Missouri-Columbia Journalism Library has over 3,000 bound periodicals. The University of Minnesota Journalism Library has an extensive pamphlet collection, and the Indiana University Journalism Library has numerous microform and slide holdings. The American Newspaper Publishers Association's library in Washington, D.C., has complete microform files of *Editor & Publisher*, the industry magazine that complements *Publishers Weekly*. Special collections also include the small press offerings found in the Beyond Baroque Foundation Library in Venice, California, and the Marvin Sukon Collection of Little Magazines in the Memorial Library of the University of Wisconsin-Madison. The Popular Culture Library at Bowling Green State University, Ohio, has a fine collection of women's magazines, as well as pulp magazines and other popular forms.

HISTORY AND CRITICISM

Magazine history and criticism for the period from 1741 to 1950 can very nearly be summed up by one man's name, Frank Luther Mott, whose five-volume *A*

History of American Magazines, 1741–1930 is the sole existing attempt of a comprehensive nature. For years it has been the standard source for information on magazines of the past. Unfortunately, Mott died before he could personally extend the work past 1930. This has been left for others to do. Mott's method was to present a chronological overview of a period in each volume and then append detailed individual histories of twenty or more magazines. The thoroughness of his scholarship on those periodicals treated is rarely questioned, but his interpretation of the magazines is almost uniformly journalistic, with few attempts to analyze the audiences for those magazines. The most severe limitation for the popular culture historian is that many magazines receive a citation, a paragraph, or a page, but Mott's selection of "certain important magazines which flourished" in any given period totals only 229, and most of these were definitely midcult and high-cult periodicals. Nevertheless, Mott's *History* is the chart book to which the magazine scholar must repeatedly return.

Mott, who was dean of the University of Missouri School of Journalism for a number of years, also wrote *American Journalism: A History, 1690–1960*, recommended for its treatment of the growth of publishing in America. Theodore Peterson was a student and colleague of Mott, and in 1964 he updated, in somewhat different fashion, the history of magazines to that time. His *Magazines in the Twentieth Century* shows a greater awareness of the interaction between the reading public and the magazine publisher but still leaves a thirty-five-year period (to the present) untabulated. The historian who has made the most notable American culture approach to magazine history is Roland E. Wolseley, in a small volume called *The Changing Magazine*, published in 1973, in which he states his intention to "go beyond the descriptive volumes about magazines which I and others have produced." (Wolseley's other books, all helpful and substantive, include *Understanding Magazines, The Magazine World*, and *The Black Press, U.S.A.*) In this, his most recent book, Wolseley examines the dynamics of magazines as a cultural force in American life while being at the same time tools of American industrialism. He explores some of the perils of conglomerate ownership of magazines but concludes that magazines do have a future in the present electronic age. The book includes a brief annotated bibliography. The other full-scale studies of magazines include Algernon Tassin's early *The Magazine in America* (1916), an informal history of the magazine up to the end of the nineteenth century. James Playsted Wood wrote *Magazines in the United States*, and John W. Tebbel contributed *The American Magazine: A Compact History*. Tebbel continued his magazine research with the coauthorship of Mary Ellen Zuckerman, in *The Magazine in America, 1741–1990*, the most contemporary of the general studies. Tebbel also began a project almost of the magnitude of Mott's undertaking, *A History of Book Publishing in the United States*. Of particular interest to magazine researchers in this series is the creation of periodicals by book publishers as a way of advertising and promoting their other publications.

Earlier histories of magazines in America that treat beginnings include Lyon N. Richardson's *A History of Early American Magazines: 1741–1789*, first published in 1931 and issued in reprint in 1967, and two nineteenth-century works of limited usefulness. Albert H. Smyth, in *The Philadelphia Magazines and Their Contributors, 1741–1850*, gives anecdotal accounts of periodicals and persons in those years. Printed in 1892, the book has no index—a frustration to the modern researcher.

In 1898, William B. Cairns traced the *Development of American Literature: 1815–1833* through periodicals of the time, claiming that American literature developed a distinctive voice and identity through magazines rather than books. Cairns also identifies 137 periodicals not found in *Poole's Index*. John Bakeless, in *Magazine Making*, another older work, provides valuable descriptions of early printing technology and the developments in the craft that made mass magazines possible.

Checklists of American periodicals of the early republic may be found in two scholarly works by Benjamin M. Lewis: *An Introduction to American Magazines: 1800–1810* and *A Register of Editors, Printers, and Publishers of American Magazines: 1741–1810*. Covering the same period, Neal L. Edgar's more recent *A History and Bibliography of American Magazines: 1810–1820* picks up on "literary newspapers," which he claims fall between magazines and newspapers. William Beer's *Checklist of American Magazines 1741–1800* is another guide to those early years when publishers themselves often did not clearly define their product.

Because full-scale histories and interpretations are so limited, specialized studies of segments of the whole become important. One such study, a doctoral dissertation published by the Dutch equivalent of University Microfilms, is an extremely well-researched and documented study of the deaths of the "big four," *Collier's*, *Look*, *Saturday Evening Post*, and *Life*, *The Life Cycle of Magazines*, subtitled *A Historical Study of the Decline and Fall of the General Interest Mass Audience Magazine in the United States during the Period 1946–1972*, in which A. J. van Zuilen, a former director of the New York office of a Dutch publishers' association, uses an integrative, interdisciplinary approach. He includes a lucid explanation of the delicate balances between the public's taste and the advertiser's economic needs that a periodical must maintain to survive. Finally, van Zuilen states that magazines follow cyclical patterns or successions through stages of birth, maturity, decay, and death and that, although individual magazines will continue to follow that cycle, at any given time there will be more magazines born than dying, thus confirming the viability of the medium and the industry as a whole. The book is especially useful for the connections and comparisons drawn between the health of the magazine industry and the growth of electronic media.

House organs, business and association magazines, and others of that type, though far more numerous than standard mass market magazines, have attracted little attention. James L. C. Ford discusses these magazines and their publishers in *Magazines for Millions*. Many of the publications are of extremely high quality, underwritten as they are by the firms for which they are produced. Ford's book is predominantly descriptive and suffers indexing deficiencies. Abigail Fisher Hausdorfer's *House Organ Production* includes a bibliography of periodical articles on house organs. Kathleen Endres and Therese L. Lueck edited *Trade, Industrial, and Professional Periodicals of the United States*, a useful guide to these types of publications.

Several collections of essays give overviews of publishing history. James Woodress edited a Festschrift, *Essays Mostly on Periodical Publishing in America*, which offers nine essays on varied topics, including historic and contemporary magazines. Walter Davenport and James C. Derieux present brief sketches on nineteenth-century magazines and their editors in *Ladies, Gentlemen and Editors*. In *The American Reading Public: What It Reads, Why It Reads*, Roger H. Smith collects a number of essays originally published in *Daedalus* on the state of the print media in the 1960s.

The remainder of magazine histories, for the most part, concentrate on one magazine or magazine group, one editor or publisher, or perhaps one magazine genre. Such works might well be represented by the excellent *The House of Harper* by Henry J. Harper, an important book on nineteenth-century publishing, or by one of the numerous books on the Curtis publishing house, beginning with James Playsted Wood's *The Curtis Magazines*, a compact history of the *Saturday Evening Post* and the other magazines in the group that is so representative of American mass magazines. Joseph Goulden recorded the earlier heydays of the house in *The Curtis Caper*, and one of the best accounts of the failure of that giant is Otto Friedrich's *Decline and Fall*. *George Horace Lorimer and the Saturday Evening Post* by John W. Tebbel covers the glory years of that publication, whose story would not be complete without the memoirs of its foremost artist, *My Adventures as an Illustrator*, by Norman Rockwell. The women's branch of the Curtis triumvirate of *Saturday Evening Post, Country Gentleman*, and *Ladies' Home Journal* is described by Bruce Gould and Beatrice Gould in their *American Story*. The long reign of an earlier editor of the *Ladies' Home Journal*, Edward Bok, son-in-law of Cyrus Curtis but an editorial genius himself, is recounted in his autobiography, *The Americanization of Edward Bok*, and his subsequent biography of Curtis, *The Man from Maine*. In both books, the curious mixture of altruism and business acumen that is the mark of success in publishing prevails. Salme Harju Steinberg in *Reformer in the Marketplace* attests to Bok's skill in working for the betterment of society within the exigencies of a business establishment.

Other early editors and publishers have received attention. In *Success Story: The Life and Times of S. S. McClure* by Peter Lyon, that crusading editor, whose magazine earned the epithet "muckraker" from Teddy Roosevelt, is given an absorbing analysis with a historical perspective lacking in McClure's own *My Autobiography*. That era of publishing is perhaps the best covered of all, but one of the better attempts is Harold S. Wilson's recent *McClure's Magazine and the Muckrakers*. The biographies of some of the principals at the time are also informative, especially Lincoln Steffens' *Autobiography* and Ida M. Tarbell's *All in the Day's Work*.

An editor-publisher of the turn of the century, Frank A. Munsey, was easily the most flamboyant and innovative of the dime magazine publishers. He tells his own history in *The Story of the Founding and Development of the Munsey Publishing House* with an effervescent egotism that cannot be wholly discounted. A later work by George Britt, *Forty Years—Forty Millions: The Career of Frank A. Munsey*, affirms the fact of his publishing genius. Street & Smith, also a pulp publisher, is featured in a well-illustrated and entertaining book by Quentin Reynolds called *Fiction Factory*. Other pulp history is found in *Pulpwood Editor* by Harold Hersey. Backward glances appear in Frank Gruber's *Pulp Jungle*, Peter Haining's edition of *The Fantastic Pulps*, and Tony Goodstone's *The Pulps*. Lastly, Mary Noel's *Villains Galore* examines the popular story weeklies.

Outstanding among the studies of single magazines or publishing houses in addition to the preceding ones are the two volumes by Robert T. Elson on the Luce publishing empire: *Time, Inc.: The Intimate History of a Publishing Enterprise, 1923–1941* and *The World of Time, Inc.: The Intimate History of a Publishing Enterprise, 1941–1960*. Although Elson's works are probably definitive, another writer,

An article in *Collier's* magazine, 1905. Courtesy of the Library of Congress

W. A. Swanberg, had access to much of the same material when he wrote the Pulitzer Prize-winning biography *Luce and His Empire*. John Kobler's entry in Luce illumination is coyly titled *Luce: His Time, Life and Fortune*. The earlier *Life*, a humor magazine whose name Luce appropriated for his periodical, is treated in *Life, the Gentle Satirist* by John Flautz. But in *That Was the Life*, Dora J. Hamblin takes the reader into the exciting world of photojournalism, a genre also explored in the classic *Words and Pictures* by Wilson Hicks and in Margaret Bourke-White's own excellent autobiography, *Portrait of Myself*.

Almost every major popular magazine has had at least one article or book published about it. Helen Damon-Moore in *Magazines for the Millions: Gender and Commerce in the Ladies' Home Journal and the Saturday Evening Post* looks at those two headliners. The casualties especially receive attention as people wonder why the magazines didn't survive. Paul C. Smith, a former publishing executive with Crowell-Collier, wrote in *Personal File* of his attempts to save *Look* and *Collier's*, and part of Theodore H. White's *In Search of History: A Personal Adventure* gives another insider's view of that episode.

Some of the more literary and intellectual periodicals have received more than their share of attention, with numerous essays and works on the *Dial*, *American Mercury*, and *Atlantic* available, despite their limited circulations. Margaret Jones particularly highlighted female writers in *Heretics and Hellraisers: Women Contributors to the Masses, 1911–1917*. Even the diminutive perennial *Reader's Digest*, despite its midcult designation, has had several books written about it. The earliest is a gossipy account by John Bainbridge, called *Little Wonder, or The Reader's Digest and How It Grew*. Continuing the praises of DeWitt and Lucy Wallace and their one-of-a-kind publication is James Playsted Wood's *Of Lasting Interest: The Story of the Reader's Digest* and the pleasant anecdotal account of the phenomenon of Pleasantville, Samuel A. Schreiner Jr.'s *The Condensed World of the Reader's Digest*.

Treatment of women's magazines or women editors is growing with the help of Mary Ellen Zuckerman's *A History of Popular Women's Magazines in the United States, 1792–1995*. Following Mott's format, Kathleen Endres and Therese Lueck edited *Women's Periodicals in the United States: Consumer Magazines*. An earlier English book, *Women's Magazines, 1693–1968*, by Cynthia L. White, concentrates on British periodicals but contains a good section and useful tables on American women's magazines. In *The Lady Persuaders*, Helen Woodward chastises the hypocrisy of the magazines' claiming to be noble organs of public service while actually being governed strictly by advertising interests and economic concerns. In a similar vein, Ellen McCracken examines the symbiosis of overt and covert ads in *Decoding Women's Magazines*. Nancy A. Walker takes a serious look at the role that magazines played in the social conditioning of women in *Shaping Our Mother's World: American Women's Magazines*.

Accounts of early editors include *Our Sister Editors: Sarah J. Hale and the Tradition of Nineteenth Century American Women Editors* by Patricia Okker; Ruth E. Finley's *The Lady of Godey's: S. J. Hale*; and Olive Burt's *First Women's Editor: Sara Josepha Hale*. Hale's long tenure with *Godey's Ladies' Book* set records for quiet crusading and longevity. Margaret Fuller, onetime editor of the *Dial*, is treated by Faith Chippenfield in *In Quest of Love: The Life and Death of Margaret Fuller* in a work as vivid as its subject. Two later editors of competing women's fashion magazines, *Harper's Bazaar* and *Vogue*, tell their experiences in Carmel Snow's *The World of Carmel Snow*, written with Mary Louise Aswell, and Bettina Ballard's *In My Fashion*.

Little magazines have had influence stretching far beyond their circulations. A collection of essays, *The Little Magazine in America: A Modern Documentary History*, edited by Elliott Anderson and Mary Kinze, provides views of a number of "important" little magazines as well as the philosophies of their editors. Reed Whittemore's *Little Magazines* attempts to define them and gives limited examples, whereas Lois Rather gives only a very personal history in *Some "Little" Magazines*. Two books examine the influence of modernism in little magazines—Jayne Marck's *Women Editing Modernism: "Little" Magazines & Literary History* and *The Public Face of Modernism: Little Magazines, Audiences and Reception, 1905–1920* by Mark Morrisson. An excellent treatment of a single little magazine is Paul R. Stewart's *The "Prairie Schooner" Story: A Little Magazine's First 25 Years—1927–1951*. One unusual source of small press and little magazine publication is surveyed in Russell N. Baird's *The Penal Press*, which lists papers and magazines produced inside U.S. prisons.

Another infrequent, but entertaining, area of information and insight on popular magazines is found in popular fiction. Again, uneven quality plagues the lot, but some do provide more than just a good read. The novel by Theodore H. White, *The View from the Fortieth Floor*, is perhaps as close to experiencing the publishing world as a lay reader may come. Clay Blair's *The Board Room: A Novel* is based on his own participation in the life (and death) of the *Saturday Evening Post*. Earlier novels, though dated in style, reveal inner workings of various periods in publishing history. Ralph Ingersoll satirizes a Luce-like couple in *The Great Ones*. Several novels examine the conflict between personal values and job values, including John Brooks' *The Big Wheel* and Matthew Peters' *The Joys She Chose*. Two other novels deal specifically with women in publishing: *Women, Inc.* by Jane Kesner Morris and *Manhattan Solo* by Marjorie Worthington. Anne Rivers Siddons follows the fortunes of a female editor at a fictional 1960s city magazine in *Downtown*, while the mystery *Magazine* by James Mallon features an Irish publisher of a sports magazine. *Slab Rat* by Ted Heller is another mystery set in the offices of a slick New York magazine, but the imaginary publishing settings all carry a note of authenticity since their authors worked for such magazines.

Georgette Carneal in *The Great Day* wrote an early exposé novel of the sleazy world of tabloids and confession magazines, and their latter-day descendants are treated nonfictionally in *The Pious Pornographer* by William Iverson. Charles Beaumont, a contributing editor to *Playboy*, looks back to the media's past in *Remember? Remember?* Also in the exposé mode is Samm Sinclair Baker's *The Permissible Lie*, which reveals the less-than-truthful tactics of advertisers in the mass media.

An area of magazine research that is essential to the understanding of magazines as a cultural force in American life is sociological and demographic data. Knowledge of audience numbers is essential to the advertiser buying space, and some early publishers were not above inflating their circulation figures to command higher advertising fees. Thus, in 1914 the Audit Bureau of Circulation (ABC) was established as an industry self-regulatory agency. Its annual reports contain the sworn circulations of member publications. These figures and data from other sources were contained in the *N.W. Ayer Directory of Publications*, an annual publication, which has now been subsumed into the *Gale Directory of Publications and Broadcast Media*. Charles O. Bennett tells the story of the establishment of the ABC in *Facts without Opinion: First Fifty Years of the Audit Bureau of Circulation*, and Ralph M. Hower chronicles its story in *The History of an Advertising Agency: N. W. Ayer and Son at Work, 1869–1949*.

Modern publishers and advertisers need to know more about reader audiences than merely numbers and location, so surveys, opinion polls, and other demographic profiling have become common. At least twelve agencies in addition to the publisher's own survey departments produce such reports, and these are listed in a pamphlet from the Magazine Publishers Association, *Sources of Information about Magazines*. Interesting examples of such reports include the Magazine Advertising Bureau's *Magazines for Advertising: Their Size, Their Markets, Their Results*; W. R. Simmons' *A Study of the Retention of Advertising in 5 Magazines*; the Association of National Advertisers' *Magazine Circulation and Rate Trends: 1940– 1967*; and the Politz Research studies of readers of *Life, Better Homes and Gardens, American Home*, and others, which detail reader characteristics down to the last pair of shoes purchased. Not surprisingly, the surveys show a close correlation of interests, attitudes, and affluence between audience and magazine, again affirming the value of magazines as mirrors of American society.

Sociologists usually treat magazine reading as one of Americans' many informational and recreational activities, but rarely do they single it out for much emphasis. As a result, no comprehensive study of magazines from that perspective is available, although mention of magazines as a part of the mass media is frequent. There are a number of good articles in journals such as *American Journal of Sociology*, *Sociological Quarterly*, and *Social Forces*. Of particular interest are those articles that examine the impact of advertising found in popular periodicals. Not infrequently, content analysis of magazine fiction reveals pervasive stereotyping that affects and/or reflects widespread social attitudes.

ANTHOLOGIES AND COLLECTIONS

Anthologies and collections, especially those designed for classroom use in communications, literature, and the study of rhetoric, as well as American history "casebooks," routinely use selections from periodicals. Examples would include such titles as *Our Times: The Best from the "Reporter,"* edited by Max Ascoli; Francis William Weeks' *Readings in Communication from "Fortune"*; and *One Hundred Years of the "Nation,"* collected by Henry M. Christman. Some of the anthologies include thematic collections from a number of magazines, Festschrift from individual magazines, or anniversary collections. Of myriad editorship and uncertain quality, the collections yet offer easy access to sometimes hard-to-find material. Nevertheless, for the true flavor of the individual magazines or those of a period, the back files of the periodicals themselves are preferred. Some of the better anthologies are William Wasserstrom's *A Dial Miscellany*; William Phillips and Philip Rahv's *The Partisan Review Anthology*; *The Good Housekeeping Treasury* from that magazine's files; *A Cavalcade of Collier's*, edited by Kenneth McArdle; and *Great Reading from "Life"—A Treasury of the Best Stories and Articles Chosen by the Editors*.

Other collections present a particular point of view or trace a unique influence. The history of women in magazines is found in *Harper's Bazaar: One Hundred Years of the American Female*, edited by Jane Trahey, and in Helen Otis Lamont's *A Diamond of Years: The Best of the "Woman's Home Companion."* Examinations of American culture are offered in collected essays either by a single author or by a group of social critics. Marya Mannes, in her collection of essays from the *Reporter*, *But Will It Sell?* criticizes the rampant materialism and consumer mentality in American culture, while in Arthur M. Weinberg and Lila Weinberg's *The Muckrakers*, the focus is on that era in U.S. history as illustrated in the magazines of the period 1902–1912. John K. M. McCaffery assembled material for *The American Dream: A Half-Century View from American Magazine*, stressing that periodical's emphasis in both editorial and advertising content: the American "success myth."

Other collections also give overviews of particular periods. Cleveland Amory and F. Bradlee's *"Vanity Fair"—Selections from America's Most Memorable Magazine: A Cavalcade of the 1920s and 1930s*, with text and pictures from those decades, rather immodestly claims to be the voice of the sophisticated world of that time. George H. Douglas romps through a bevy of highbrow periodicals in *The Smart Magazines: 50 Years of Literary Revelry and High Jinks at Vanity Fair, the New Yorker, Life, Esquire, and the Smart Set*. In *Adventures of the Mind*, Richard

Thruelson and John Kobler bring together portraits of the 1950s from the pages of the *Saturday Evening Post*. Another fascinating collection is Ray Brosseau's *Looking Forward: Life in the Twentieth Century as Predicted in the Pages of American Magazines from 1895–1905*, wherein the editor finds within the pages of nineteenth-century magazines predictions about life in the later twentieth century. The wide-ranging and scattered emphases of other collections and anthologies prohibit the inclusion of them all, but most are readily accessible.

One further publication type should be mentioned. Occasionally, facsimile editions of early magazines are printed, and these are of great interest, especially if microforms are the researcher's primary exposure to early periodicals. Handling even a facsimile version reaffirms the appeal of popular magazines as attractive creations of art, design, writing, advertising, and unique insight into the America that is and was.

BIBLIOGRAPHY

Books

Abrahamson, David. *Magazine-Made America: The Cultural Transformation of the Postwar Periodical*. Cresskill, N.J.: Hampton Press, 1996.

———, ed. *The American Magazine: Research Perspectives and Prospects*. Ames: Iowa State University Press, 1995.

Access. Syracuse, N.Y.: Gaylord Professional Publications, 1975– . Annual.

ALA Guide to Reference Books. Chicago: ALA, 1996.

America: History and Life. Santa Barbara, Calif.: ABC-Clio, 1964– . Annual.

American Reference Books Annual. Ed. Bohdan S. Wynar. Englewood, Colo.: Libraries Unlimited, 1998– . Annual.

Amory, Cleveland, and F. Bradlee, eds. *"Vanity Fair"—Selections from America's Most Memorable Magazine: A Cavalcade of the 1920s and 1930s*. New York: Viking, 1960.

Anderson, Elliott, and Mary Kinze, eds. *The Little Magazine in America: A Modern Documentary History*. Yonkers, N.Y.: Pushcart Press, 1979.

Arndt, Karl J.R., ed. *German-American Newspapers and Periodicals 1732–1955*. Heidelberg: Quelle and Meyer, 1961.

Ascoli, Max, ed. *Our Times: The Best from the "Reporter."* New York: Farrar, Strauss, 1960.

Association of National Advertisers (ANA). *Magazine Circulation and Rate Trends: 1940–1967*. New York: ANA, 1969.

The Audiences of Five Magazines: Newsweek, Time, U.S. News & World Report, Saturday Evening Post, Life. New York: Newsweek, 1962.

Backlund, Jonas Oscar. *A Century of the Swedish-American Press*. Chicago: Swedish American Newspaper, 1952.

Bainbridge, John. *Little Wonder, or the Reader's Digest and How It Grew*. New York: Reynal, 1945.

Baird, Russell N. *The Penal Press*. Evanston, Ill.: Northwestern University Press, 1967.

Bakeless, John. *Magazine Making*. New York: Viking, 1931.

Baker, Samm Sinclair. *The Permissible Lie*. New York: World, 1968.

Ballard, Bettina. *In My Fashion*. New York: McKay, 1960.

Beaumont, Charles. *Remember? Remember?* New York: Macmillan, 1963.

Beer, William. *Checklist of American Magazines 1741–1800*. Worcester, Maine: American Antiquarian Society, 1923.

Bell, Marion V., and Jean C. Bacon. *Poole's Index Date and Volume Key*. Chicago: Association of College and Reference Libraries, 1957.

Bennett, Charles O. *Facts without Opinion: First Fifty Years of the Audit Bureau of Circulation*. Chicago: ABC, 1965.

Blair, Clay. *The Board Room: A Novel*. New York: Dutton, 1969.

Bok, Edward. *The Americanization of Edward Bok*. New York: Scribner's, 1920.

———. *The Man from Maine*. New York: Scribner's, 1923.

Bourke-White, Margaret. *Portrait of Myself*. New York: Simon and Schuster, 1963.

Boyenton, William H. *Audit Bureau of Circulations*. Chicago: ABC, 1949.

Britt, George. *Forty Years—Forty Millions: The Career of Frank A. Munsey*. New York: Farrar and Rinehart, 1935. Reprint. Port Washington, N.Y.: Kennikat Press, 1972.

Brooks, John. *The Big Wheel*. New York: Harper, 1949.

Brosseau, Ray. *Looking Forward: Life in the Twentieth Century as Predicted in the Pages of American Magazines from 1895–1905*. New York: American Heritage Press, 1970.

Bullock, Penelope L. *The Afro-American Periodical Press*. Baton Rouge: Louisiana State University Press, 1981.

Burt, Olive. *First Women's Editor: Sara Josepha Hale*. New York: Messner, 1960.

Cairns, William B. *Development of American Literature: 1815–1833*. Madison: University of Wisconsin Press, 1898.

Carneal, Georgette. *The Great Day*. New York: Liveright, 1932.

Chielens, Edward E., ed. *American Literary Magazines: The Eighteenth and Nineteenth Centuries*. Westport, Conn.: Greenwood Press, 1986.

———. *American Literary Magazines: The Twentieth Century*. Westport, Conn.: Greenwood Press, 1992.

———. *The Literary Journal in America, 1900–1950*. Detroit: Gale, 1975.

Chippenfield, Faith. *In Quest of Love: The Life and Death of Margaret Fuller*. New York: Coward, 1957.

Christman, Henry M., ed. *One Hundred Years of the "Nation."* New York: Macmillan, 1965.

Cohn, Jan. *Creating America: George Horace Latimer and the Saturday Evening Post*. Pittsburgh: University of Pittsburgh Press, 1989.

Cyganowski, Carol Klimick. *Magazine Editors and Professional Authors in Nineteenth-Century America; The Genteel Tradition and the American Dream*. New York: Garland, 1988.

Damon-Moore, Helen. *Magazines for the Millions: Gender and Commerce in the Ladies' Home Journal and the Saturday Evening Post, 1880–1910*. Albany, N.Y.: SUNY Press, 1994.

Davenport, Walter, and James C. Derieux. *Ladies, Gentlemen and Editors*. Garden City, N.Y: Doubleday, 1960.

Dinan, John A. *Sports in the Pulp Magazines*. Jefferson, N.C.: McFarland, 1998.

Dissertation Abstracts International. Ann Arbor, Mich.: University Microfilms, 1970– .

Douglas, George H. *The Smart Magazines: 50 Years of Literary Revelry and High Jinks at Vanity Fair, the New Yorker, Life, Esquire, and The Smart Set*. Hamden, Conn.: Archon Books, 1991.

Earlham College Women's Programs Office. *The Annotated Guide to Women's Periodicals in the U.S. & Canada*. Richmond, Ind.: T. Mehlman, 1983– .

Edgar, Neal L. *A History and Bibliography of American Magazines: 1810–1820*. Metuchen, N.J.: Scarecrow Press, 1975.

Elson, Robert T. *Time, Inc.: The Intimate History of a Publishing Enterprise, 1923–1941*. New York: Atheneum, 1968.

———. *The World of Time, Inc.: The Intimate History of a Publishing Enterprise, 1941–1960*. New York: Atheneum, 1973.

Endres, Kathleen L., and Therese Lueck, eds. *Women's Periodicals in the United States: Consumer Magazines*. Westport, Conn.: Greenwood Press, 1995.

———. *Trade, Industrial, and Professional Periodicals of the United States*. Westport, Conn.: Greenwood Press, 1994.

Fackler, Mark P., and Charles H. Lippy, eds. *Popular Religious Magazines of the United States*. Westport, Conn.: Greenwood Press, 1995.

Farrell, Tom. *The Working Press of the Nation*. New York: Public Relations Press, Farrell Corporation, 1945– . Annual.

Finley, Ruth E. *The Lady of Godey's: S. J. Hale*, Philadelphia: Lippincott, 1931.

Flautz, John. *Life, the Gentle Satirist*. Bowling Green, Ohio: Bowling Green University Popular Press, 1972.

Foerstel, Herbert N. *Banned in the Media: A Reference Guide to Censorship in the Press, Motion Pictures, Broadcasting, and the Internet*. Westport, Conn.: Greenwood Press, 1998.

Ford, James L. C. *Magazines for Millions*. Carbondale: Southern Illinois University Press, 1969.

Fox, Roy F. *MediaSpeak: Three American Voices*. Westport, Conn.: Praeger, 2000.

Friedrich, Otto. *Decline and Fall*. New York: Harper and Row, 1970.

Gale Directory of Publications and Broadcast Media. 133rd ed. Detroit: Gale. Annual.

Glazener, Nancy. *Reading for Realism: The History of a U.S. Literary Institution, 1859–1910*. Durham, N.C.: Duke University Press, 1997.

Glazier, Loos Pequeno. *Small Press: An Annotated Guide*. Westport, Conn.: Greenwood, 1992.

Goodheart, Eugene. *Pieces of Resistance*. New York: Cambridge University Press, 1987.

Good Housekeeping. *Good Housekeeping Treasury*. New York: Simon and Schuster 1960.

Goodstone, Tony. *The Pulps*. New York: Chelsea House, 1976.

Gould, Bruce, and Beatrice Gould. *American Story*. New York: Harper, 1968.

Goulden, Joseph. *The Curtis Caper*. New York: Putnam, 1965.

Gruber, Frank. *Pulp Jungle*. Los Angeles: Sherbourne, 1967.

Haining, Peter, ed. *The Fantastic Pulps*. New York: St. Martin's Press, 1975.

Hamblin, Dora J. *That Was the Life*. New York: Norton, 1978.

Harper, Henry J. *The House of Harper*. New York: Harper, 1912.

Harper's Bazaar. *Harper's Bazaar: 100 Years of the American Female*. New York: Random House, 1967.

Hausdorfer, Abigail Fisher. *House Organ Production*. Philadelphia: Temple University Press, 1954.

Heller, Ted. *Slab Rat*. New York: Scribner, 2000.

Hersey, Harold. *Pulpwood Editor*. New York: Stokes, 1938. Reprint. Westport, Conn.: Greenwood Press, 1974.

Hicks, Wilson. *Words and Pictures*. New York: Harper, 1952.

Hoerder, Dirk, ed. *The Immigrant Labor Press in North America, 1840s–1970s: An Annotated Bibliography*. Westport, Conn.: Greenwood Press, 1987.

Hower, Ralph M. *The History of an Advertising Agency: N. W. Ayer and Son at Work, 1869–1949*. Cambridge: Harvard University Press, 1949.

Humanities Index. New York: H. W. Wilson, 1974– . Annual.

Husni, Samir. *Guide to New Consumer Magazines*. New York: Oxbridge, 1997– . Annual

Hutton, Frankie. *The Early Black Press in America, 1827–1860*. Westport, Conn.: Greenwood, 1992.

Hutton, Frankie, and Barbara Straus Reed, eds. *Outsiders in 19th-Century Press History: Multicultural Perspectives*. Bowling Green, Ohio: Bowling Green University Popular Press, 1995.

Ingersoll, Ralph. *The Great Ones*. New York: Harcourt, Brace, 1948.

International Directory of Little Magazines and Small Presses. Ed. Len Fulton and Ellen Ferber. Paradise, Calif.: Dustbooks, 1970– . Annual.

International Index. New York: H. W. Wilson, 1907–1965.

Ireland, Sandra L. Jones. *Ethnic Periodicals in Contemporary America: An Annotated Guide*. Westport, Conn.: Greenwood Press, 1990.

Iverson, William. *The Pious Pornographer*. New York: Morrow, 1963.

Janello, Amy, and Brennon Jones. *The American Magazine*. New York: Abrams, 1991.

Jones, Margaret C. *Heretics and Hellraisers: Women Contributors to the Masses, 1911–1917*. Austin: University of Texas Press, 1993.

Katz, Bill, and Berry G. Richards. *Magazines for Libraries*. 10th ed. New York: Bowker, 2000.

Kelly, R. Gordon. *Children's Periodicals of the United States*. Westport, Conn.: Greenwood, 1984.

Kobler, John. *Luce: His Time, Life and Fortune*. Garden City, N.Y.: Doubleday, 1968.

Lamont, Helen Otis, ed. *A Diamond of Years: The Best of the "Woman's Home Companion."* Garden City, N.Y.: Doubleday, 1961.

Lewis, Benjamin M. *An Introduction to American Magazines: 1800–1810*. Ann Arbor: University of Michigan Press, 1961.

———. *A Register of Editors, Printers, and Publishers of American Magazines: 1741–1810*. New York: New York Public Library, 1957.

Life Magazine. *Great Reading from "Life"—A Treasury of the Best Stories and Articles Chosen by the Editors*. New York: Harper, 1960.

Lippy, Charles H. *Religious Periodicals of the United States: Academic and Scholarly Journals*. Westport, Conn.: Greenwood Press, 1986.

Literary Market Place. New York: Bowker, 1940– . Annual.

Lora, Ronald, and William Henry Longton, eds. *The Conservative Press in*

Eighteenth- and Nineteenth-Century America. Westport, Conn.: Greenwood, 1999.

———. *The Conservative Press in Twentieth-Century America*. Westport, Conn.: Greenwood Press, 1999.

Lutz, Catherine, and Jane L. Collins. *Reading National Geographic*. Chicago: University of Chicago Press, 1993.

Lyon, Peter. *Success Story: The Life and Times of S. S. McClure*. New York: Scribner's, 1963.

Magazine Advertising Bureau (MAB). *Magazines for Advertising: Their Size, Their Markets, Their Results*. New York: MAB, 1953.

Magazine Industry Market Place. New Providence, N.J.: R. R. Bowker, 1980–1987.

Magazine Publishers Association (MPA). *Sources of Information about Magazines*. New York: MPA, 1973.

Mallon, James. *Magazine*. Raleigh, N.C.: Pentland Press, 2000.

Mannes, Marya. *But Will It Sell?* New York: Lippincott, 1964.

Marck, Jayne E. *Women Editing Modernism: "Little" Magazines & Literary History*. Lexington: University Press of Kentucky, 1995.

McArdle, Kenneth, ed. *A Cavalcade of Collier's*. New York: Barnes, 1959.

McCaffery, John K. M., ed. *The American Dream: A Half-Century View from American Magazine*. Garden City, N.Y.: Doubleday, 1964.

McClure, S. S. *My Autobiography*. New York: Ungar, 1914, 1963.

McCracken, Ellen. *Decoding Women's Magazines*. London: Macmillan, 1993.

McKerns, Joseph P. *Biographical Dictionary of American Journalism*. Westport, Conn.: Greenwood Press, 1989.

Morris, Jane Kesner. *Women, Inc*. New York: Holt, 1946.

Morrisson, Mark. *The Public Face of Modernism: Little Magazines, Audiences and Reception, 1905–1920*. Madison; University of Wisconsin Press, 2000.

Mott, Frank Luther. *American Journalism: A History, 1690–1960*. 3rd ed. New York: Macmillan, 1962.

———. *A History of American Magazines, 1741–1930*. 5 vols. Cambridge: Harvard University Press/Belknap Press, 1957–1968.

Mueller, Carolyn J., ed. *Periodicals of the Midwest & West: An Annotated Survey*. Ann Arbor, Mich.: Pierian Press, 1986.

Munsey, Frank A. *The Story of the Founding and Development of the Munsey Publishing House*. New York: Munsey, 1907.

Murphy, Sharon. *Other Voices: Black, Chicano, and American Indian Press*. Dayton, Ohio: Pflaum/Standard, 1974.

National Directory of Magazines. New York: Oxbridge Communications, 1987–1998.

National Research Bureau. *Working Press of the Nation*. Vol. 11. Chicago: NRB, 1979.

New Serial Titles. New Providence, N.J.: R. R. Bowker, 1950–1970.

Nineteenth Century Reader's Guide to Periodical Literature: 1890–1899, with Supplementary Indexing, 1900–1922. 2 vols. New York: H. W. Wilson, 1944.

Noel, Mary. *Villains Galore*. New York: Macmillan, 1954.

Norris, James D. *Advertising and the Transformation of American Society, 1865–1920*. Westport, Conn.: Greenwood Press, 1990.

Nourie, Alan, and Barbara Nourie, eds. *American Mass-Market Magazines*. Westport, Conn.: Greenwood Press, 1990.

Okker, Patricia. *Our Sister Editors: Sarah J. Hale and the Tradition of Nineteenth Century American Women Editors*. Athens: University of Georgia Press, 1995.

Paine, Fred K., and Nancy E. Paine. *Magazines: A Bibliography for Their Analysis with Annotations and Study Guide*. Metuchen, N.J.: Scarecrow Press, 1987.

Periodical Directories and Bibliographies. Farmington Hills, Mich.: Gale, 1986.

Peters, Matthew. *The Joys She Chose*. New York: Dell, 1954.

Peterson, Theodore. *Magazines in the Twentieth Century*. Urbana: University of Illinois Press, 1964.

Phillips, William, and Philip Rahv, eds. *The Partisan Review Anthology*. New York: Holt, Rinehart, and Winston, 1962.

Politz Research (PRI). *An Audience Study of the American Home Magazine*. New York: PRI, 1957.

——. *A Study of the Accumulative Audience of "Life."* New York: Time, 1950.

——. *A 12-Months Study of Better Homes and Gardens Readers*. Des Moines: Meredith, 1956.

Poole's Index to Periodical Literature, 1802–1881. Rev. ed. Boston: Houghton-Mifflin, 1891. Annual supplements, 1882–1906.

Price, Kenneth M., and Susan Belasco Smith. *Periodical Literature in Nineteenth-Century America*. Charlottesville: University Press of Virginia, 1995.

Price, Warren C., and Calder M. Pickett. *An Annotated Journalism Bibliography, 1958–1968*. Minneapolis: University of Minnesota Press, 1970.

Rather, Lois. *Some "Little" Magazines*. Oakland, Calif.: Rather Press, 1971.

Reader's Guide to Periodical Literature. New York: H. W. Wilson, 1900–   . Annual.

Reed, David. *The Popular Magazine in Britain and the United States, 1880–1960*. London: British Library, 1997.

Reynolds, Quentin. *Fiction Factory*. New York: Random House, 1955.

Richardson, Lyon N. *A History of Early American Magazines: 1741–1789*. New York: Nelson, 1931. Reprint. Chicago: Octagon, 1967.

Riley, Sam G., ed. *Corporate Magazines of the United States*. Westport, Conn.: Greenwood Press, 1992.

——. *Index to City and Regional Magazines of the United States*. New York: Greenwood Press, 1989.

——. *Index to Southern Periodicals*. Westport, Conn.: Greenwood Press, 1986.

——. *Magazines of the American South*. Westport, Conn.: Greenwood Press, 1986.

Riley, Sam G., and Gary W. Selnow, eds. *Regional Interest Magazines of the United States*. Westport, Conn.: Greenwood Press, 1991.

Roberts, Nancy. *American Peace Writers, Editors and Periodicals*. Westport, Conn.: Greenwood Press, 1991.

Rockwell, Norman. *My Adventures as an Illustrator*. Garden City, N.Y.: Doubleday, 1960.

Sader, Marion, ed. *Comprehensive Index to English-Language Little Magazines, 1890–1970*. 8 vols. Millwood, N.Y.: Kraus-Thomson, 1976.

Sawyer, Frank B., ed. *1967 Directory of U.S. Negro Newspapers, Magazines and Pe-*

riodicals in 42 States: The Negro Press—Past, Present and Future. New York: U.S. Negro World, 1968.

Schacht, John H. *A Bibliography for the Study of Magazines*. Urbana: University of Illinois Press, 1966.

Schiller, Herbert. *The Mind Managers*. Boston: Beacon Press, 1973.

Schneirov, Matthew. *The Dream of a New Social Order: Popular Magazines in America, 1893–1914*. New York: Columbia University Press, 1994.

Schreiner, Samuel A., Jr. *The Condensed World of the Reader's Digest*. New York: Stein and Day, 1977.

Server, Lee. *Danger Is My Business: An Illustrated History of the Fabulous Pulp Magazines*. San Francisco: Chronicle Books, 1993.

Siddons, Anne Rivers. *Downtown*. Boston: G. K. Hall, 1994.

Simon, Rita James. *The Ambivalent Welcome: Print Media, Public Opinion, and Immigration*. Westport, Conn.: Praeger, 1993.

Sinclair, Upton. *The Brass Check: A Study of American Journalism*. Pasadena, Calif.: Upton Sinclair, 1920.

Sloan, David E. E., ed. *American Humor Periodicals and Comic Periodicals*. Westport, Conn.: Greenwood Press, 1987.

Smith, Paul C. *Personal File*. New York: Appleton, 1964.

Smith, Roger H., ed. *The American Reading Public: What It Reads, Why It Reads*. New York: Bowker, 1963.

Smyth, Albert H. *The Philadelphia Magazines and Their Contributors, 1741–1850*. Philadelphia: R.M. Lindsay, 1892. Reprint. Detroit: Gale, 1970.

Snow, Carmel, with Mary Louise Aswell. *The World of Carmel Snow*. New York: McGraw-Hill, 1962.

Social Sciences and Humanities Index. Vols. 19–61. New York: H. W. Wilson, 1965–1974. Annual.

Social Sciences Index. New York: H. W. Wilson, 1974– . Annual.

Spragens, William C. *Electronic Magazines: Soft News Programs on Network Television*. Westport, Conn.: Praeger, 1995.

Steffens, Lincoln. *Autobiography*. New York: Harcourt, Brace, 1968.

Steinberg, Salme Harju. *Reformer in the Marketplace*. Baton Rouge: Louisiana State University Press, 1979.

Stewart, Paul R. *The "Prairie Schooner" Story: A Little Magazine's First 25 Years—1927–1951*. Lincoln: University of Nebraska Press, 1955.

Swanberg, W. A. *Luce and His Empire*. New York: Scribner's, 1972.

Tarbell, Ida M. *All in the Day's Work*. New York: Macmillan, 1939.

Tassin, Algernon. *The Magazine in America*. New York: Dodd, Mead, 1916.

Tebbel, John W. *The American Magazine: A Compact History*. New York: Hawthorn Books, 1969.

———. *George Horace Lorimer and the Saturday Evening Post*. Garden City, N.Y.: Doubleday, 1948.

———. *A History of Book Publishing in the United States*. 3 vols. New York: Bowker, 1975–1978.

Tebbel, John, and Mary E. Zuckerman. *The Magazine in America, 1741–1990*. New York: Oxford University Press, 1991.

Thruelson, Richard, and John Kobler, eds. *Adventures of the Mind*. New York: Knopf, 1959.

Trahey, Jane. *Harper's Bazaar: One Hundred Years of the American Female*. New York: Random House, 1967.

Ulrich's International Periodicals Directory. New York: Bowker, 1932– . Annual.

Union List of Serials in Libraries of the United States and Canada. 3rd ed. New York: H. W. Wilson, 1966.

Unsworth, Michael E. *Military Periodicals*. Westport, Conn.: Greenwood Press, 1990.

U.S. Department of Commerce. *Historical Statistics: Colonial Times to 1970*. Part 2. Washington, D.C.: U.S. Department of Commerce, Bureau of the Census, 1975.

Vesenji, Paul. *An Introduction to Periodical Bibliography*. Ann Arbor, Mich.: Pierian Press, 1974.

W. R. Simmons & Associates Research. *A Study of the Retention of Advertising in 5 Magazines*. New York: W. R. Simmons, 1965.

Walker, Nancy A. *Shaping Our Mother's World: American Women's Magazines*. Jackson: University of Mississippi, 2000.

Wasserstrom, William, ed. *A Dial Miscellany*. Syracuse, N.Y.: Syracuse University Press, 1963.

Weeks, Francis William, ed. *Readings in Communication from "Fortune."* New York: Holt, 1961.

Weinberg, Arthur M., and Lila Weinberg, eds. *The Muckrakers: The Era in Journalism That Moved America to Reform—The Most Significant Magazine Articles of 1902–1912*. New York: Simon and Schuster, 1961.

Wells, Daniel A. *The Literary Index to American Magazines*. Westport, Conn.: Greenwood Press, 1996.

White, Cynthia L. *Women's Magazines, 1693–1968*. London: Michael Joseph, 1970.

White, Theodore H. *The Changing Magazine*. New York: Hastings House, 1973.

———. *In Search of History: A Personal Adventure*. New York: Harper and Row, 1978.

———. *The View from the Fortieth Floor*. New York: Sloane, 1960.

Whittemore, Reed. *Little Magazines*. Minneapolis: University of Minnesota Press, 1963.

Wilson, Harold S. *McClure's Magazine and the Muckrakers*. Princeton, N.J.: Princeton University Press, 1970.

Wolseley, Roland E. *The Black Press, U.S.A.* Ames: Iowa State University Press, 1971.

———. *The Changing Magazine*. New York: Hastings House, 1973.

———. *Journalist's Bookshelf*. 7th ed. Philadelphia: Chilton, 1961.

———. *The Magazine World*. New York: Prentice-Hall, 1951.

———. *Understanding Magazines*. 2nd ed. Ames: Iowa State University Press, 1969.

Wood, James Playsted. *The Curtis Magazines*. New York: Ronald Press, 1971.

———. *Magazines in the United States*. 3rd ed. New York: Ronald Press, 1956.

———. *Of Lasting Interest: The Story of the Reader's Digest*. Garden City, N.Y.: Doubleday, 1958. Reprint. Westport, Conn.: Greenwood Press, 1975.

Woodress, James, ed. *Essays Mostly on Periodical Publishing in America*. Durham, N.C.: Duke University Press, 1973.

Woodward, Helen. *The Lady Persuaders*. New York: Obolensky, 1960.

Working Press of the Nation. New Providence, N.J.: R. R. Bowker, 1990– . Annual.

Worthington, Marjorie. *Manhattan Solo*. New York: Knopf, 1937.

Wynar, Lubomyr. *Encyclopedic Directory of Ethnic Newspapers and Periodicals in the United States*. Littleton, Colo.: Libraries Unlimited, 1972.

Young, Margaret L., et al., eds. *Directory of Special Libraries and Information Centers*. 5th ed. Detroit: Gale Research, 1977.

———. *Subject Directory of Special Libraries and Information Centers*. 4th ed. Detroit: Gale Research, 1976.

Zuckerman, Mary Ellen. *A History of Popular Women's Magazines in the United States, 1792–1995*. Westport, Conn.: Greenwood, 1998.

Zuilen, Antoon J. van. *The Life Cycle of Magazines: A Historical Study of the Decline and Fall of the General Interest Mass Audience Magazine in the United States during the Period 1946–1972*. Uithoorn, Netherlands: Graduate Press, 1977.

Periodicals

American Brewer. New York, 1868– .

American Journal of Sociology. Chicago, 1895– .

American Magazine. New York (Webster, ed.), 1787–1788.

The American Magazine. New York (Leslie's), 1876–1956.

American Magazine, or *A Monthly View of the Political State of the British Colonies*. Philadelphia, January–March 1741.

The American Magazine and Historical Chronicle. Boston, September 1743–December 1746.

American Magazine and Monthly Chronicle. Philadelphia, October 1757–October 1758.

American Mercury. New York, January 1924– .

American Naturalist. Boston, 1867–(Philadelphia, 1878–1898).

Analog. New York, 1963– .

Atlantic Monthly. Boston, November 1857– .

Better Homes & Gardens. Des Moines, July 1922– .

Christian Advocate. New York, 1826– .

Christian Advocate. Philadelphia, January 1823–December 1834.

Coal Trade Journal. New York, 1869– .

Collier's. New York, April 28, 1888–January 4, 1957.

Coronet. Chicago, 1936–1961.

Country Gentleman. Philadelphia, January 6, 1853–1955.

The Dial. Chicago and New York, May 1880–July 1929.

Editor & Publisher. New York, June 29, 1901– .

The Family Handyman. St. Paul, 1950– .

Flair. New York, February 1950–January 1951.

Fortune. New York, 1930– .

General Magazine, and *Historical Chronicle, for All the British Plantations in America*. Philadelphia, January–June 1741.

Gentleman's Magazine. (Cave's) London, 1731–1907.

Gentlemen and Lady's Town and Country Magazine. Boston, May–December 1784.

Godey's Lady's Book. Philadelphia, July 1830–August 1898.

Graham's Magazine. Philadelphia, January 1826–December 1858.

Harper's Bazaar. New York, 1867– .

Harper's Monthly. New York, June 1850– .

The Instructor. Dansville, N.Y., 1891– .

Journal of American Culture. Bowling Green, Ohio, 1978– .

Judge. New York, October 29, 1881–January 1939.

Keepapichinin. New York, 1870–1871.

Ladies' Home Journal. Philadelphia, December 1883– .

Life. New York, 1936–1972.

The Literary Magazine, and American Register. Philadelphia, October 1803–December 1807.

Locomotive. Hartford, Conn., 1867– .

Look. Des Moines, Iowa, 1937–1971.

McCall's Magazine. Dayton, Ohio, September 1873– .

Monthly Magazine and American Review. New York, April 1799–December 1800.

The Nation. New York, July 6, 1865– .

National Geographic. Washington, D.C., October 1888– .

New American Magazine. Woodbridge, N.J., 1757–1760.

New York Mirror. New York, August 2, 1823–1857(?).

New Yorker. New York, 1925– .

New-Yorker. New York (Greeley, ed.), March 22, 1834–1841.

North American Review. Boston, May 1815– .

Ohio Farmer. Cleveland, 1852– .

Pennsylvania Magazine. Philadelphia, 1775–1776.

Peterson's Magazine. Philadelphia, January 1842–April 1898.

Playboy. Chicago, 1953– .

Popular Science Monthly. New York, May 1872– .

The Port Folio. Philadelphia, January 1801–December 1827.

Publishers Weekly. New York, January 18, 1872– .

Puck. New York, March 1877–September 1918.

Reader's Digest. Pleasantville, N.Y., 1922– .

The Review. London (Defoe, ed.), February 1704–July 1712.

Rolling Stone. San Francisco, 1967– .

Royal American Magazine. Boston, January 1774–March 1775.

Saturday Evening Post. Philadelphia, August 4, 1821– .

Scientific American. New York, August 1845– .

Scribner's. New York, January 1887–May 1939.

Sesame Street Magazine. New York, 1970– .

Social Forces. Chapel Hill, N.C., 1922– .

Sociological Quarterly. Carbondale, Ill., 1960–

The Spectator. London, March 1711–December 1714.

The Tatler. London, April 1709–January 1711.

Time. New York, March 3, 1923– .

TV Guide. Philadelphia, 1953– .

United States Law Review. St. Louis and New York, 1866– .

United States Magazine. Philadelphia, January–December 1779.

Vogue. New York, December 17, 1892– .

Woman's Home Companion. Cleveland and New York, January (?) 1874–January
    1957.
Women Sports. San Mateo, Calif., 1974–1979.
Yale Review. Cambridge, Mass., 1892–   .

MAGIC AND MAGICIANS

Steven S. Tigner

Magic is a performing art that aims at playing on a spectator's sense of wonder, either by apparently doing what is actually impossible or by actually doing what is apparently impossible, from the spectator's point of view. A famous instance of magic in the first mode is found in the earliest substantial account known of a conjuring performance: the tale of Dedi's (or Djedi's) appearance before Khufu (Cheops, builder of the Great Pyramid) around 2475 B.C., as recorded on the Westcar papyrus. Here Dedi "decapitates" and "restores" the head of a waterfowl, among other things.[1] He does not actually do these things; he only appears to. An equally well-known instance of magic in the second mode is recounted in the *Memoirs* of the father of modern magic, Jean Eugène Robert-Houdin: a performance of the "light/heavy box" before Arab chieftains in North Africa on October 28, 1856. A box, which at one moment can be lifted with ease, at another becomes impossible to budge. This really happens; it does not merely appear to happen. The trick relies on the power of a concealed electromagnet, the properties of which were then not widely known.[2] Familiar twentieth-century examples of the same two types include the sawing-in-two illusion and the needle-through-balloon trick, respectively.

Magic and magicians have flourished in American popular culture over the past quarter century as never before. Today they are familiar in virtually every variety of television programming and "stage" show (from Broadway theater to the street, bar, and laundromat) and have been featured in every literary genre published in any print, mechanical, or electronic medium. Magic themes and personalities are employed widely in advertising. Magical entertainment is enjoyed at every level of society, and magical acts are included among the most prominent touring and resident companies of variety entertainers. Its therapeutic uses in hospitals and nursing homes are today touted as much as its educational benefits were a century ago. Public and private museums and libraries feature both permanent and temporary exhibitions of magic illusions, apparatus, books, posters, artifacts, and ephemera.

All this activity is fed by a thriving international subculture of magicians, with its own organizations and economy. There are magazines, manufacturers, and meetings, clubs, conventions, schools, and all manner of services, dealers and agents.

Much of the publishing in magic today continues to be of the insider variety. As a result, some of the most important works in the field cannot be found in any public institution, including the Library of Congress. Perhaps more than in any other subject area, researchers on magic and magicians must rely on private sources and collections.

HISTORICAL OUTLINE

A few brief accounts of the indigenous magic of Native American peoples are recorded by European conquistadors, explorers, and missionaries in documents dating from the period of contact. Later accounts of travelers and more recent studies of anthropologists and other systematic inquirers have helped fill in the picture. Feats recounted in such sources cover a broad range, from a sixteenth-century Spanish missionary's account of seeing a tiny figure rise and dance in the hand of a Toltec medicine man performing in the Tianquiztli marketplace in New Spain, to several reports and studies dealing with the ritual mystery of the shaking tent.[3]

With other forms of idle amusement, magic was banned in the British colonies. Indeed, the earliest indication of magical activity in colonial America is the record of a show in the Boston area that did not happen because on December 4, 1687, a Judge Sewall and a committee of townspeople persuaded tavern keeper Captain John Wing that it was not lawful for him to allow it in his establishment. Unfortunately, we do not know the name of the magician who thus failed to make history.

The most significant record of magic in the first half of the eighteenth century occurs in a series of five weekly advertisements appearing from March 18 through April 15, 1734, in the *New-York Weekly Journal*, for "the famous German Artist" Joseph Broome, "who is to perform the Wonders of the World by Dexterity of Hand" at "the House of Charles Sleigh, in Duke Street. . . . 1s., 9d. & 6d. is the price for admittance. He begins at 7 o'clock in the Evening."

Private homes, taverns, and halls were the common places of magical performance in early America; reliance on sleight of hand rather than elaborate apparatus was the rule; and the lure of "European" performers was commonly invoked in advertisement (often enough with truth). The most prominent traveling magicians to have left significant traces over several years in several colonies (and Jamaica) by advertising in the local papers were the "Noted" Mr. Bayly (from 1767 to 1783) and the "Celebrated" Hymen Saunders (from 1770 to 1786), both British. Other sleight of hand artists were about, of course. George Washington "went to see slight of hand performed" in Alexandria on September 19, 1769, as his diary attests.

The year 1787 marks three firsts in magic in the United States: the first recorded performance of the bullet-catching trick (by John Brenon, while balancing himself on a slack wire); the first recorded performance of magic by a woman (by Mrs. John Brenon, with "dexterity of hand"); and the first of nearly three decades of pioneering performances by the Italian magician Signor (Senor, Seignior, Signior) Falconi.

Falconi appeared in theaters as well as other establishments and advertised "Natural Philosophical Experiments" using more apparatus than his magical precursors and contemporaries. He featured such mechanical marvels as "a Head of Solid Gold, of the size of a walnut, shut up Hermetically, in a Chrystal Vessel, and which will answer by Signs, every Question," and "An Automaton, Representing an Indian, armed with a Bow and Arrow," that shot arrows into a board several feet away, hitting numbers on the board corresponding with numbers either openly or secretly selected by members of the audience.

"Automata" featured in magic shows and exhibitions were of two sorts, corresponding to the two sorts of magical feats noted earlier. Some mechanisms actually did what they appeared to do; others did not. Both sorts are described in the works of Hero of Alexandria in the first century A.D., and his sources go back at least to the third century B.C. The most famous "automaton" of them all was, like Falconi's Indian, a piece of apparatus designed to conceal or disguise the control of its human operator. This was the great chess-playing automaton constructed by Baron Wolfgang von Kempelen in 1769. Benjamin Franklin, then ambassador to France, was defeated by it in 1783. Its first performance in America was not till 1826, at which time it was in the hands of Johann Nepomuk Maelzel. A decade later the young Edgar Allan Poe published an essay attempting an analysis of its operation. The device eventually ended up in the Chinese Museum in Philadelphia, where it was destroyed by fire in 1854.

The last decade of the eighteenth century marked not only the height of Signor Falconi's career but also the beginning of publishing on magic in America. The first account of how to perform magic to be printed on an American press was the long article entitled "Legerdemain, or Sleight of Hand," in volume 9 of Thomas Dobson's pirate edition of the *Encyclopaedia Britannica*. Dobson, a Philadelphia printer, dropped *Britannica* from the title, called it "The First American Edition," and issued it in parts over the years 1790–1797. Volume 9 appeared in 1793 (though 1797, the completion date, appears on the title page, which was added later).[4]

The first magic book to be published in America belongs to a series of works on magic founded on Reginald Scot's pioneering treatment of "the conueiances of Legierdemaine and juggling" in Booke 13 of *The Discoverie of Witchcraft* (1584). It was Henry Dean's *Hocus Pocus; or, The Whole Art of Legerdemain, in Perfection*, printed by Mathew Carey in Philadelphia (1795). This was copied from the eleventh edition (ca. 1790) of a work that had first appeared in London in 1722. Still later editions were printed in New York and Boston.

Jacob Meyer is generally credited with being the first professional magician born in America (1734), though his performing career was carried out entirely in Europe, where he usually appeared under the stage name Jacob Philadelphia, after the place of his birth.

The first American-born magician to win fame as a performer in his own country was Richard Potter. Potter's mother was a black slave named Dinah (or Dinnah), attached to the Frankland household of Hopkinton, Massachusetts. The

Houdini and the water torture cell, ca. 1913. Courtesy of the Library of Congress

father is not known, though chronological considerations rule out Sir Charles Frankland, who is sometimes named as the leading candidate. Sir Charles had been dead for fifteen years by the time Richard Potter was born in 1783. The young Potter attended school in Hopkinton but shipped as a cabin boy to England at age ten and there joined a circus. He returned to Boston in 1801, quite possibly as an assistant to Scottish magician and ventriloquist John Rannie. At any rate, when Rannie left America in 1811, Potter opened his own show, which toured mainly, though not exclusively, within the New England area. He had married Sally Harris of Roxbury in 1808 and in 1814 bought farmland in Andover, New Hampshire, and built his home there. Potter Place, as it became known, was also the site of many of his entertainments. Later he was buried there, under a headstone inscribed: "In memory of Richard Potter, the Celebrated Ventriloquist who died Sept 20, 1835, aged 52."

Like Rannie before him, Potter combined the visual illusions of magic with the vocal illusions of ventriloquism and polyphony, the latter art "consisting of imitations of the voices and cries of animated nature" (to quote Mr. Love, a British contemporary practitioner of the art). In keeping with the trends in advertising and public interest, Potter, like Falconi, billed himself as providing "philosophical amusements," "scientific entertainments," and "mysterious experiments." "Mr. Potter will perform the part of the anti-combustible Man Salamander and will pass a red hot bar of iron over his tongue, draw it through his hands repeatedly, and afterwards bend it into various shapes with his naked feet," says one billing. "He will also perform a variety of pleasing magical deceptions."

The wide range of public interests to which magical entertainers were catering is reflected in the publications of the time, too. The first work to contain magic that was actually written in America was William Frederick Pinchbeck's *The Expositor*, published in Boston in 1805. The full title continues: *or, Many Mysteries Unravelled. Delineated in a Series of Letters, between a Friend and His Correspondent. Comprising the Learned Pig, Invisible Lady and Accoustic Temple, Philosophical Swan, Penetrating Spy Glasses, Optical and Magnetic, and Various Other Curiosities on Similar Principles: Also, a Few of the Most Wonderful Feats as Performed by the Art of Legerdemain: With Some Reflections on Ventriloquism*. Pinchbeck's advertisements proclaimed that his Learned Pig had drawn "unbounded applause" from President John Adams when he performed his pick-a-card tricks in Washington.

The same range of interests was reflected in publications aimed at the family home entertainment market. Typical of the period is a series of American reprints, beginning in 1821, of various editions of a British work titled *Endless Amusement: A Collection of Upwards of 400 Entertaining and Astonishing Experiments*. "Among a variety of other Subjects, are amusements in Arithmetic, Mechanics, Hydraulics . . . All the Popular Tricks and Changes of the Cards, &c., &c., &c., The whole so clearly explained as to be within the reach of the most limited capacity."

The generation of American-born magicians following Richard Potter included not only (for a short time) Potter's own son, Richard, but such leading figures as Jonathan Harrington, Wyman the Wizard (John W. Wyman Jr.), and Professor Young (William Henry Young), who held their own over long careers in competition with the leading lights of Europe, who still dominated the scene. The most significant of the Europeans of the period were Monsieur Adrien (Adrian, Adrean), Herr Alexander (Johann Friedrich Alexander Heimburgher), Andrew Macallister, and Signor Antonio Blitz.

Wyman the Wizard was the first American-born performer to stage a full-evening show. He was also among the first magicians to introduce the "gift show" (door prizes, etc.) and to include spirit-medium effects in his program. Like Potter before him and his contemporary Harrington, he combined magic with ventriloquism and other entertainments. Wyman performed at the White House a total of six times, for Presidents Van Buren, Fillmore, and Lincoln.

Among the foreign-born performers, Antonio Blitz was perhaps the best known in his time and is certainly the best known to us, owing to his autobiographical memoirs, *Fifty Years in the Magic Circle*. Blitz's show traveled from Canada to the Caribbean and featured not only magic and ventriloquism but plate spinning and trained canaries. Bullet catching was featured in the program for a while as well. Yet, like many others before and since, Blitz found that "it became attended with so much danger, that I found it necessary, for self-protection, to abandon it." He was also much imitated. "In later years," he complains in his memoirs, the imitators "proved an incalculable annoyance, there being not less than thirteen people travelling the country using my name and profession, circulating a verbatim copy of my handbill and advertisement—not only assuming to be the *original* Blitz, but in many instances claiming to be a son or nephew."[5] The "incalculable annoyance" in all this was not simply moral but financial as well. Blitz accumulated hundreds of letters demanding payment and threatening suit for the unpaid bills of these impostors.

The first genuine international star of magic to play in America was Scottish-born stage actor and magician "Professor" John Henry Anderson: "The Great Wizard of the North" (i.e., Scotland). Already well established in the British Isles and on the continent as a master of the spectacular full-evening stage show, Anderson arrived in New York in 1851. He continued to mingle his skills as a legitimate stage actor—his favorite part the title role in *Rob Roy*—with those of a magician. He charged twice the price of Blitz for his magic performances (fifty cents for adults, as opposed to Blitz's twenty-five) and gave America its first substantial taste of several promotional as well as magical innovations. He staged charity benefit performances and held contests of wit resulting in such publications as *The Wizard's Book of Conundrums* and *The Ladies Budget of Wit*. He published and sold such items as *Professor Anderson's Note-Book; or, Recollections of His Continental Tour* (of which various different forms survive) and *The Fashionable Science of Parlor Magic*: "Being a Series of the Newest Tricks of Deception, arranged for Amateurs and Lovers of the Art to which is added An Exposure of the Practice made use of by Professional Card Players, Blacklegs and Gamblers." American printings begin with the "84th" English edition (ca. 1851) and run to the "250th" edition, which appeared ca. 1864. There was sheet music, too, selling for twenty-five cents: "The Bottle Polka," "The Mystic Polka," and "The Inexhaustable Waltz: Composed and arranged for the Piano Forte expressly for Professor Anderson's Grand Drawing Room Entertainments, by Mons. Kneringer, 1st Prize Merit Pianist from the Conservatoire Royal de Paris." This was hype such as America had never seen before.

Three points ought to be made about Professor Anderson's magical repertoire. First, several of his more notable effects, such as the aerial suspension of his son and the inexhaustible bottle, had been introduced to European audiences by Robert-Houdin just a few years before. Second, Anderson's including the exposure of gambler's tricks and cheats in his trick books was an early attempt both to distinguish the legitimate deceptions of "the fashionable science" of magical entertainment from the illegitimate deceptions of "professional card players, blacklegs and gamblers" and to portray the magician as specially qualified to render public service in exposing the tricks of fraudulent deceivers. Third, carrying this role into a new area, Anderson, like Wyman, pioneered in taking on "the pernicious and fatal delusion" of "the great spirit rapping humbug" by turning an expose of table rapping and other "manifestations" into a popular stage act.

Anderson returned to England in 1853. Earlier in his career, in Glasgow in 1846, Anderson had lost everything in a theater fire. It happened again at Covent Garden in 1856. Both times he was wiped out in the process of struggling to build a career in legitimate theater. Both times he turned to magic to rebuild his financial base. This time his world tour took him to Australia, from whence he arrived at San Francisco in 1859, providing that city with the grandest magical spectacle it had ever seen. The year 1860 found him again in New York, by way of Panama.

A southern tour as far as Richmond was cut short owing, as Anderson claimed, to the fact that "no Wizards of the 'North' were wanted in that section of the Union." Yet, as Charles Pecor reveals, "An examination of the *Richmond Daily Whig* for this period . . . gives no indication of any difficulty encountered by Anderson in that city."[6] Anderson's fortunes dwindled nonetheless. Whatever he made in a tour of the Midwest and Canada was lost in the theatrical failure in New York of "The Wizard's Tempest," a spectacular magical and political burlesque of Shakespeare's *Tempest*. He sailed for England in 1862, heavily in debt and leaving behind his wife and three children. He went into bankruptcy in 1866. The Great Wizard of the North died in 1874 and was buried not far from where he had been born, in Aberdeen, a few months short of his sixtieth birthday.

Anderson's younger contemporary, Robert Heller (William Henry Ridout Palmer), whose father was organist at Faversham Parish Church in Kent, England, was formally trained as a keyboard artist at the Royal Academy of Music. He began his magical career in 1851, when, posing as a Frenchman, he put together a show in open and deliberate imitation of Robert-Houdin. In the fall of the following year he brought the show to America and played in New York and Philadelphia through most of 1853. In January 1854 Heller went on tour as a pianist with the Germania Musical Society, eventually landing in Washington, where he settled down, married into fashionable society, and took a post as a church organist. But in 1861 he was on the road again with a new show combining magic and music. The combination was brought to perfection in 1864, when Heller placed himself under the management of Edward Hingston, who earlier had managed both Professor Anderson and popular humorist Artemus Ward. Heller commenced what was "the longest run by a magical entertainer in America in a single locale"[7] until the Siegfried and Roy show in Las Vegas and Le Grand David in Beverly, Massachusetts, both of which are still running today, long after surpassing Heller's run of about 368 performances in the French Theatre on Broadway.

Heller's most enduring magical feat was his evolving version of the second-sight trick (describing objects while blindfolded), which he had first copied from Robert-Houdin. Among his popular musical features was what by all accounts must have been a hysterically funny imitation of a young girl practicing her music lesson at the piano. In concert with Wyman, Anderson, and eventually most performers of the time, he included feats duplicating (or even improving upon) the tricks of the spiritualist.

Heller left San Francisco in 1869 for a tour around the world, returning to America in 1878. On November 28, 1878, following a brief illness during a run of several weeks in Philadelphia, he died. Heller's personal cultivation, classical musical talent, and sophisticated wit had endeared him to America's social elite to an extent that no previous magical performer had known. That, ultimately, was perhaps his most pioneering contribution to the history of magic in America.

In that pioneering capacity he was well accompanied by Carl (Compars) Herrmann, whose claims to having appeared before, and been decorated by, the crowned heads of Europe were in fact true. Carl Herrmann, perhaps accompanied and assisted by his younger brother, Alexander, first appeared in the United States in 1861. What set him apart from other performers up to that time, and what he himself emphasized in advertisements, was that he performed on an essentially bare stage, without the spectacle and clutter of ornate apparatus. He produced rabbits, bowls of goldfish, and showers of coins, scaled throw-out cards into the audience, performed the linking rings, and such like. But he also did bullet catching, second sight, and, with an expressly educational aim, spiritualist exposures. Carl Herrmann appeared before U.S. audiences in the early, middle, and late 1860s. On his final American tour, which ended in the spring of 1870 in San Francisco, he was accompanied by his brother, Alexander.

Alexander Herrmann, "Herrmann the Great" or "the Great Herrmann," began his own performances as a magician in the United States in 1874, the year that John Henry Anderson died and the year that Houdini was born. If we need a chronological marker for the beginning of America's golden age of magic, this is it. In 1875 Alexander Herrmann married Adelaide Scarcez and the following year became a naturalized citizen. When he died twenty years later in 1896, he was traveling in his own private railway car, just one measure of the level of extravagant living that had by then become possible for a stage magician.

At the beginning of his career, Herrmann the Great, like his brother, relied more on his manipulative skills and stage presence than on bulky or ornate apparatus. Adelaide was his assistant. Like his brother, his mainstays were producing bowls of goldfish and presenting various small apparatus effects such as the linking rings in addition to performing a variety of feats with coins and cards. He occasionally did a relatively safe bullet-catching routine employing up to seven assistants (six "soldiers" and a "sergeant"). His effects were not new, but his polished presence, audacity, and great skill set a new standard. The Great Herrmann became America's quintessential magician.

Following Alexander's death, Leon Herrmann, a nephew, carried on the show with Adelaide for three seasons. They then parted, but both continued to perform: Leon until his death in 1909, and Adelaide, "Queen of Magic," until she retired at age seventy-five in 1928. By the time Adelaide took over the show, the Herrmanns had acquired a good deal of the larger apparatus and lavish stage sets characteristic of the age. Some went with Leon; some she sold; and she added other pieces to it over the course of her three decades as star of her own illusion show. Adelaide's nephew, Felix Kretchman, also performed under the Herrmann name until 1937.

The Great Herrmann's chief American rival and successor, Harry Kellar (Heinrich/Henry Keller), was born in Erie, Pennsylvania, in 1849. His formative years were spent as an assistant to the Fakir of Ava (I. Harris Hughes) and John Henry Anderson Jr. After a brief period on his own (as the Great Harcourt, among other things), he became an assistant to the Davenport Brothers and Fay. After a few years Kellar and Fay went off on their own, taking a show to Central and South America. They lost their apparatus in a shipwreck on the way to England. Fay returned to the United States and rejoined the Davenport Brothers. Kellar's savings were compromised by a bank failure in New York. After rebuilding his show in England, Kellar returned to Central America, joined with Ferdinand and Louis Guder, and later Al Hayman and still later Dave Hayman to form the Royal Illusionists. They worked the Pacific coast as far north as San Francisco and then headed for Australia in 1876. They worked their way around the world, and, after suffering many casualties, the remnants landed in New York at the end of 1878. After a brief tour Kellar headed for South America and worked his way around the world a second time in the opposite direction. He returned to North America in 1884 and never left the continent thereafter, playing largely within the confines of the United States.

Kellar's greatest successes were as an illusionist: producing, vanishing, levitating, transforming, and transposing live human beings in a variety of different dramatic settings. Most of his illusions were, to use the polite phrase, "patterned after" the work of other illusionists (mainly British). Following the death of Alexander Herrmann in 1896, Kellar reigned supreme as America's premier magician until 1908, when he formally turned his show over to the young Howard Thurston and retired to Los Angeles. There he died in 1922.

In 1898 the Chinese conjuror Chee Ling Qua, who performed under the stage name Ching Ling Foo, arrived in the United States to appear at a major exposition in Omaha. While Oriental conjuring had occasionally been seen in the United States before Ching Ling Foo's appearance, it was this occasion that inspired the Oriental strain of magical performance that has since become a permanent part of American conjuring. Almost immediately magicians were performing effects "patterned after" Ching Ling Foo, as they still are today. A trademark effect was the production of a very large bowl of water from virtually nowhere. Perhaps the most frequently imitated feat, for which many methods have been developed, is Ching's torn and restored rice paper (tissue) trick; and the "Foo can" remains a standard prop.

Foremost among the imitators were the Great Lafayette (Siegmund Neuberger), who included a Ching-like Chinese magician among his various stage personae, and William Ellsworth Robinson, sometime illusion-builder for Kellar and for Alexander, Adelaide, and Leon Herrmann, who achieved his greatest performing success as "Chung Ling Soo," both in this country and abroad. Chung Ling Soo is remembered today primarily as the most prominent of the dozen or so magicians who have died performing bullet-catching feats. That was in 1918.

Thurston was in his late thirties and already the veteran of a highly successful world tour with a full evening show when he accepted the mantle from Kellar in 1908. His subsequent career lived up fully to Kellar's expectations, and Thurston remained king of American big-show magicians until his death in 1936. He himself played primarily in the major theaters of the East and Midwest, though beginning in 1923 he sent out supplementary road companies to cover smaller theaters and to travel into other parts of the country.

Thurston's first road company was headed by Danish-born Harry August Jansen, on whom Thurston bestowed the stage name "Dante." Jansen was a seasoned showman who more than a decade earlier had set out on a successful world tour himself and in the early 1920s had headlined with one of Horace Goldin's "Sawing a Woman in Half" vaudeville units. The "Thurston Presents Dante" show was a clear success, and Jansen kept the "Dante" name for the remainder of his performing career. Following the death of Thurston, Dante's claim to being Thurston's successor as America's greatest, world-touring, big-show magician was probably warranted. His great "Sim Sala Bim" show was playing in Berlin in August 1939, when the war forced his hasty departure and eventual return to the United States. In 1942 he played himself in the Laurel & Hardy film *A-Haunting We Will* Go. After the war he returned to Europe, playing there until 1949, when he came home for good. He died at his home in California in 1955, aged seventy-one.

Thurston's chief headlining contemporary showman was Harry Houdini. As a performer, Houdini's forte lay in feats of escape coupled with feats of self-promotion, and with these he toured the world. But he was also a pioneer aviator; an early producer of silent films; a great collector of historical materials related to magic and spiritualism; a long-term, promotionally active president of the Society of American Magicians; an investigator of spiritualist fraud; and, with significant editorial and research assistance, the writer of some significant books on magic, magic history, and the investigation of spiritualists. Much more has been written by and about Houdini than about any other figure in the history of American magic.

Dante's chief performing rival in this country was Blackstone. Both Dante and Blackstone were rising and competitive stars during the heydays of Thurston and Houdini. Houdini died in 1926, Thurston ten years later, after movies and the Great Depression had forced a general downscaling in the live theater business. While Dante had toured the world, Blackstone played almost exclusively within the United States and Canada. Born Henry ("Harry") Boughton in Chicago in 1885, he performed under various names during his early twenties but eventually teamed up with his younger brother, Peter ("Pete") in 1910, when they billed themselves as "Harry Bouton & Co. Presenting Straight and Crooked Magic." With some apparatus acquired from the Great Albini show following Albini's death in 1913 and with a quantity of advertising paper acquired from the printer for the financially troubled magician Frederik in 1915, Harry and Peter Bouton listed themselves as "manager" and "stage manager" for the "Frederik the Great" show through 1917. World War I rendered that stage name less desirable, and the switch to "Blackstone the Magician" (reportedly inspired by a sign for Blackstone Cigars) was effected in 1918. Over the next several decades, the name Blackstone became thoroughly established as a name to conjure with in American popular culture. It lives on today in the second-generation Harry Blackstone, magician, who continues to incorporate in his own stage shows such effects as the dancing handkerchief and the vanishing bird cage that became classics in his father's hands.

Just beneath this upper crust of top-ranked big-show performers of the first half of the twentieth century were myriad others: the big shows that did not endure or that were more successful abroad than in the States; the smaller shows that played concomitantly smaller theaters, movie houses, lodge halls, school auditoriums, and other meeting places anywhere they could be found; the vaudeville and variety specialists; the circus and carnival magicians; the society performers, and so on. Many of these were highly influential in the development of new feats and new styles of performance.

Some outstanding illusionists found it more profitable to play the world than to try to compete on a sustained basis with the likes of Kellar, Thurston, or Blackstone within the confines of the United States. Servais Le Roy, Horace Goldin, Carter the Great, the Great Raymond, Nicola, and David Bamberg fall at least roughly into this category.

Many magicians simply preferred doing the sort of show that could be worked alone or with a single partner. T. Nelson Downs, Nate Leipzig, Max Malim, Al Baker, Dunninger, Dai Vernon, and Cardini, to name some prominent examples born before 1900, left indelible marks on the profession in the twentieth century.

Dunninger pioneered in broadcast media magic and is the only magician ever to have become a national sensation on radio. He may also have made some pioneering appearances during the very earliest days of television.

With the advent of television came new performing possibilities for all sorts of magical performers, though the immediate postwar decade in which television came of age marked a relatively low period in public interest in magic. Mark Wilson must be credited with the pioneering development of the first national television series, and Milbourne Christopher with bringing the magic "special" to the tube.

Starting with a local *Time for Magic* children's series aired in Dallas in 1954, Mark Wilson grew in popularity over the next six years till he went national with *The Magic Land of Allakazam* on Saturday morning CBS-TV in 1960, a show that was to run five years (the final three on ABC-TV). His book *The Mark Wilson Course in Magic* (1975) includes further historical comment.

On May 27, 1957, Milbourne Christopher hosted the world's first ninety-minute television magic spectacular, "The Festival of Magic," featuring a number of international performers in addition to Christopher himself. Three years later he successfully resurrected the full-evening illusion show in New York. No such spectacle had enjoyed an extended run in the Big Apple since Dante played there two decades before. Some further details on Christopher's career are included in *Milbourne Christopher's Magic Book* (1977).

As important as these milestones were in reviving popular interest in magic in America, none came close to the extraordinary effect created by Doug Henning's smash hit on Broadway, *The Magic Show*, which opened on May 28, 1975. That show's four-and-a-half-year run marked the onset of a new wave of popular interest in magic that is still with us today. Since that time Henning has starred in two other Broadway shows and eight television specials and has toured internationally with a full-evening magic and illusion show. The slightly more youthful David Copperfield has created his own brand of magic spectacle and has to date staged nine television specials in addition to maintaining a full schedule with his touring road show. Harry Blackstone has had his share of success on Broadway as well and has appeared repeatedly on television, in leading entertainment centers, and with his own touring road show. Siegfried and Roy have been top headliners in Las Vegas for a decade, with major television productions to boot. And then there is the phenomenon on Cabot Street in Beverly, Massachusetts: Le Grand David and His Own Spectacular Magic Company, the largest and longest-running resident magic show in history. Formed in 1976, the company of several dozen elaborately costumed performers, entertaining in their own beautifully restored Cabot Street Cinema Theatre (now supplemented with a second show in a second restored theater, the Larcom), is still going strong after more than a 1,000 performances throughout more than a decade of full matinee and evening shows on weekends and holidays. See the Le Grand David company's 289-page exhaustive bibliography, *Marco the Magic's Production of Le Grand David and His Own Spectacular Magic Company BIBLIOHISTORY: The First Ten Years, 1976–1986* (1988).

This brief historical review has necessarily concentrated on selected pioneering performers and a few of the most widely known stage and television personae in American magic. The historical facets of the remaining sections of this chapter, touching on the roles of other important persons, institutions, and phenomena in the evolution of conjuring in the United States, constitute an essential supplement to the perspectives afforded by this limited review.

REFERENCE WORKS

What American popular usage calls a "magician" academic libraries refer to as a "conjurer" or "conjuror." (Both spellings have secure precedent in English for all senses of the word.) Thus the *Subject Guide to Books in Print* (the quickest source of current bibliography for magic books from public presses) follows the *Library of Congress Subject Headings* in stipulating s.v. "Conjuring" : "Here are entered works of modern (parlor) magic, legerdemain, prestidigitation, etc. Works dealing with occult science (supernatural arts) are entered under the heading Magic."

In the Library of Congress classification system works on parlor magic and tricks are cataloged under "GV" (Recreation) 1541–61, at the end of the subsection on indoor games and amusements. Melvil Dewey's decimal classification system, still in use in many libraries, also catalogs the subject near the end of its subsection on indoor games and amusements, at 793.8, but follows American popular usage in calling it "Magic."

Encyclopedias published in America (*Americana, Funk and Wagnalls, World Book,* etc.) generally follow American popular usage rather than the dominant Library of Congress classification system by including their treatments of the topic in the "M" volume (s.v. "Magic," or "Magic, Stage," "Magician," etc.). Recent editions of the *Encyclopaedia Britannica,* on the other hand, enter theirs under "Conjuring."

The most recent general reference work on the subject is a very substantial contribution by Earle J. Coleman, aptly titled *Magic: A Reference Guide.* The best widely accessible general bibliography of magic is Robert Gill's *Magic as a Performing Art: A Bibliography of Conjuring,* covering "the modern, the readily available, the commonplace and the utilitarian" among magic books in English published during the period 1935–1975. Gill is not Procrustean about the beginning date, however, so a number of earlier classics sensibly appear among the book's 1,066 fully annotated entries. Pages xvii-xxii discuss the major magic bibliographic works to 1975. These include several works of James B. Findlay, *Magical Bibliographies: A Guide* and his *Collectors Annuals* for 1949–1954, plus the great *Ninth Collectors Annual of* 1975, cataloging the Findlay library; *The Paul Fleming Book Reviews* volumes of 1944 and 1946; the 1952 Magic Circle *Catalogue of the Reference Library and the Lending Library*; the 1920 *Bibliography of Conjuring and Kindred Deceptions* by Sidney W. Clarke and Adolphe Blind; two works of Trevor H. Hall, *A Bibliography of Books on Conjuring in English from 1580 to 1850* and *Old Conjuring Books*; Edgar Heyl's *Conjuring Books, 1580 to 1850*; Harry Price's *Short-Title Catalogue* of 1929, with a 1935 *Supplement*; Ellis Stanyon's turn-of-the-century *Bibliography of Conjuring* and *Bibliography of Conjuring and Kindred Arts*; and the *Checklist of the Older Books on Conjuring in the Library of Roland Winder as at December 1966.*

The best comprehensive bibliography of early magic works in English is Raymond Toole-Stott's *A Bibliography of English Conjuring, 1581–1876,* supplemented two years later with *A Bibliography of English Conjuring, 1569–1876,* comprising a total of 1,414 full bibliophilic entries. The second volume includes four pages of "Errata and Corrigenda" for the first volume, plus an index to the whole. Since each surviving issue and edition of each work examined by Toole-Stott receives a separate entry in this bibliography, the actual number of titles covered is considerably smaller. The bulk of them are British imprints. About 215 magic titles appearing under American imprint for the first time are included, beginning in the year 1795. Of these, the majority were published in the final decade of the period covered. The bibliography's 1876 terminus, coinciding with the U.S. centennial, celebrates the appearance of Professor Hoffmann's *Modern Magic, a Practical Treatise on the Art of Conjuring*, a work that "marked the borderline between the old and new conjuring" (Toole-Stott), "arguably the most influential magic book ever published" (Gill). Since this work also happily appears in Gill's bibliography, there is a sense in which these two bibliographies together cover the first 181 years of magic-book publishing in America.

The Bowker bibliography *Performing Arts Books 1876–1981* has about 130 entries that fall between the 1876 terminus of Toole-Stott and the 1935 formal beginning of Gill's coverage, plus works published after Gill's 1975 cutoff date through 1981. The main heading under which these works are listed is "Conjuring," with thirteen subsections, though many relevant titles appear rather under "Magic" and its several subsections.

There are seventy-five entries on magic in Don Wilmeth's admirably comprehensive annotated bibliography, *American and English Popular Entertainment: A Guide to Information Sources*, volume 7 of Gale's Performing Arts Information Guide Series. Of special interest to magic historians is Geoffrey Lamb's "A Bibliography of Magical History: Books in English Relating to Conjuring History, 1580–1980," which appeared serially in *The Magic Circular* (1983–1985).

For biographical dictionary material on prominent magicians, the most useful guide is the second edition of the *Performing Arts Biography Master Index: A Consolidated Guide to Over 270,000 Biographical Sketches of Persons Living and Dead, As They Appear in Over 100 of the Principal Biographical Dictionaries Devoted to the Performing Arts*, edited by Barbara McNeil and Miranda Herbert. The first significant (though also idiosyncratic) biographical dictionary of magicians was Will Goldston's *Who's Who in Magic*, a work included later as part of his *Tricks That Mystify*.

Richard J. Weibel compiled "An Annotated Bibliography of Conjuring Psychology," which first appeared in the *Journal of Magic History* and was then reprinted in his *Conjuring Psychology*. To this bibliography should now be added the valuable review and bibliography in Chapter 2 of Earle J. Coleman's *Magic: A Reference Guide*. For bibliography and discussion of other aspects of psychology and magic, see John Fisher's *Body Magic*.

William Doerflinger's "comprehensive guide to the wonderful world of magic," *The Magic Catalogue*, provides a useful resource for information to 1977. In addition to a general account of the history of magic and surveys of magic tricks in several categories, the book contains sections on antique magic and catalogs, museums of magic, magicians' societies, magic conventions, magic dealers, a directory of dealers and catalogs, courses in magic, magazines for magicians, and an excellent selected bibliography. The bibliography is reprinted in Albo, Page, and Burger's *More Classic Magic with Apparatus*. A less comprehensive, but similar, survey of magic in the 1950s may be found in Will Dexter's *Everybody's Book of Magic*, later reprinted as *Famous Magic Secrets*. A more recent volume of this ilk is *Bill Severn's Guide to Magic as a Hobby*.

Jack Potter's *The Master Index to Magic in Print*, published in fourteen large, loose-leaf volumes from 1967 to 1975, covers virtually every magic feat, sleight, gimmick, or trick discussed in most magic literature in English to 1964. Sid Lorraine says of his *Latest Reference File*: "To the best of my knowledge, this is the most comprehensive and up-to-date compilation, of its kind, ever produced." With 1985 revisions, he is surely correct. The *File* is a twenty-page, double-column list of names and addresses in thirty-nine categories. A pointedly commercial venture along "yellow pages" lines was the *Magic Directory, 1982–83* by Monson Productions. An international edition of *Yellow Magic Pages* (now *International Magic Yellow Pages*) continues to be published periodically by Wittus Witt in West Germany.

Various magical organizations such as the London-based Magic Circle and the Chicago-centered Magic Collectors Association have from time to time published directories of members. The most comprehensive directories of magicians have been produced by the Canadian dean of magic organizers, Len Vintus. The latest edition of the Canada and United States section of his *Magicians of the World Directory* appeared in 1978. Of historical interest is the *Who's Who in Magic*, published by Will Goldston in London in 1934.

The definitive guide to relevant periodicals is *A Bibliography of Conjuring Periodicals in English: 1791–1983*, by James B. Alfredson and George L. Daily Jr., with an introduction by F. William Kuethe. This succeeds the same authors' pioneering work, *A Short Title Check List of Conjuring Periodicals in English*, and includes a section on comic books. Further information on comic book magicians will be found in the *Magic Collectors Information Consortium*, No. 1 (April 1986). No. 6 of the series contains a bibliography of the mystery fiction of magic writer Clayton Rawson.

There are three significant general dictionaries in the field. Henry Hay's *Cyclopedia of Magic*, though now more than a generation out of date, is still valuable and in print. Geoffrey Lamb's *Illustrated Magic Dictionary*, though more recent, is unfortunately no longer in print at this writing. A somewhat eccentric dictionary by one who in his heyday contributed much to the American magic scene is John McArdle's *International Dictionary of Magitain*. T. A. Waters' *Encyclopedia of Magic and Magicians* (1988) has most recently set a new standard in the field. Programs and reviews of great magic shows have been collected by Max Holden in *Programmes of Famous Magicians*, by Arnold Furst in *Famous Magicians of the World* and *Great Magic Shows*, and by Tony Taylor in *Spotlight on 101 Great Magic Acts*. A "Bibliohistory" of Le Grand David & His Own Spectacular Magic Company covering the years 1976–1980 appeared in the *Journal of Magic History*.

The great pioneering bibliography on memory and mnemonics is Morris N. Young's *Bibliography of Memory*. A pioneering work on magicians' advertising art is J. B. Findlay's *International Guide to Posters and Playbills*. The best annotated collection of poster art (to 1975) is *100 Years of Magic Posters* by Charles and Regina Reynolds. There is also a significant annotated collection by Mario Carrandi Jr., included as "Chapter Seven: Magic Posters," in Albo, Page, and Burger's *More Classic Magic with Apparatus*, Classic Magic volume 3.

An early series of reference lists of magic lecture notes was J. Gary Bontjes's "A Checklist of Magic Lecture Notes" (1962–1974). F. William Kuethe produced *A Conjuring Bibliography of Forcing Items* in 1962 and, more recently, the leading reference work on magicians' coins and tokens: *Magicians' Tokens and Related Items: An Illustrated Check-List, with Estimates of Values and Rarities.* To these should now be added his more recent Albo Classic Magic Supplement, *Forcing Books and Book Tests*, and his chapter entitled "Tokens and Coins" in the Albo Classic Magic volume 5. Kuethe's great predecessor was J. B. Findlay, whose *Conjurers, Coins and Medals* led the way.

The best reference work on magic sets is the quarterly periodical *A.B.C. of Magic Sets*, published in West Germany by Hans-Günter Witt ("Wittus Witt") since 1980. It is international in scope and is now happily supplemented by Witt's *Zauberkästen*, the 132-page hardbound catalog of his great magic set exhibition in the Stadtmuseum Düsseldorf (August 26-October 11, 1987). The leading reference work on magic audio recordings is also a periodical, *Magic Sounds*, published in Mexico by Craige Snader ("Alex Redans") since 1973. In 1981 it became *Magic Sounds and Sights*, when video recordings were added. Larry Thornton of Calgary has published a *Video Magic Index* of more than 500 videotapes to 1984.

For still photographs of American magicians there is nothing to compare with the Irving Desfor Photographic Library, now housed in the American Museum of Magic and painstakingly cataloged by historian and designer Joanne Joys. The nearly 500-page illustrated catalog "Photomagic: The Irving Desfor Collection 1938–1978," compiled by Joanne Joys and completed in camera-ready form, still awaits a publisher. In the meantime there remains in print a volume titled *Great Magicians in Great Moments: A Photo Album by Irving Desfor*, based on the same collection.

Magicians have long used pseudonyms as writers and performers. While completeness is out of the question, Peter Warlock's *Pseudonyms* identifies well over 1,000 historical and contemporary magicians and magic writers by their stage and pen names. ("Peter Warlock" is Alec Bell.)

A major compiler of reference lists and indexes related to magic is Samuel H. (Sam) Sharpe. These have formed the basis of the following reference publications, among others: *Encyclopedia of Suspensions and Levitations*, edited by Bruce Armstrong with a chronology by S. H. Sharpe; *Oriental Conjuring and Magic* by Will Ayling, from an index by S. H. Sharpe; and S. H. Sharpe, *Conjurers' Optical Secrets*, *The Magic Play*, and *Words on Wonder*.

RESEARCH COLLECTIONS

Most of the major research collections in the United States that are related to magic and magicians are in private hands. The chief exceptions are the magic collections in the Library of Congress, in the Humanities Research Center at the University of Texas at Austin, in the library of the University of California, Berkeley, and in the New York Public Library.

The most notable magic items in the Library of Congress are largely, though not exclusively, contained within the Houdini and the McManus-Young Collections, housed in the Rare Book and Special Collections Division. Many items in the Houdini and the McManus-Young Collections that were not retained by the Library of Congress went toward forming the core of the magic collection in the Humanities Research Center at the University of Texas at Austin. Another significant portion went to the University of California, Berkeley.

Houdini at the grave of John Henry Anderson, Wizard of the North, Aberdeen, Scotland. Courtesy of the Library of Congress

The New York Public Library's singular magic holdings are in the Society of American Magicians Library, housed in the library's Theatre Collection. The Herbert Downs Memorial Library, also associated with the Society of American Magicians, is housed in the S.A.M. Magic Hall of Fame (1500 N. Vine Street, Hollywood, Calif. 90028). The S.A.M. Film and Tape Library is under the care of Pete Petrashek, 3409 South 89th St., Omaha, Nebr. 68124.

The Carl Waring Jones Collection is located in the Rare Book Division of the Princeton University Library. There are also substantial, though not comprehensive, holdings in the theater and rare book collections of Harvard and Yale, as well as in the Boston and Cleveland public libraries, and various historical rarities are at the Folger Shakespeare Library in Washington, D.C., and the Huntington Library in San Marino, California. Many of the larger public libraries have respectable holdings in magic, and these should, of course, not be overlooked as places to begin research in the field. For ancillary material on English witchcraft, the most comprehensive collection in America is the Cornell Witchcraft Collection in the Cornell University Libraries' Department of Rare Books, located in the Olin Library.

The best-known private collections have private institutional associations. That of Robert and Elaine Lund in the American Museum of Magic is outstanding.

This author is much indebted to the Lunds and their collection. Like all other private collections, it is accessible by appointment only (P.O. Box 5, Marshall, Mich. 49068). David Price's *Magic: A Pictorial History of Conjurers in the Theater* gives an accurate picture of the scope and character of the unique resources of the Egyptian Hall Museum of David and Virginia Price (1954 Old Hickory Blvd., Brentwood, Tenn. 37027).

The Mulholland Library of Conjuring and the Allied Arts, for many years at the Players Club in New York, is now in Los Angeles with Ricky Jay as curator (10100 Santa Monica Blvd., 5th floor, Los Angeles, Calif. 90067). The Magic Castle in Hollywood is no doubt the most widely known magic institution in America. Among its manifold attractions are a large library and film collection, open to members and special guests (Academy of Magical Arts, 7001 Franklin Ave., Hollywood, Calif. 90028). The Houdini Magical Hall of Fame is a commercial enterprise that offers illusion displays, apparatus, and other memorabilia to the paying public. Its historical core is derived largely from the Dunninger collection (4983 Clifton Hill, Niagara Falls, Ontario, Canada).

A few of the most distinguished private libraries are not associated with any institution or publishing or commercial venture, and further particulars cannot be given here. However, there is one convenient identifying characteristic of those persons who possess the best research libraries and collections: they are likely to be members of the Magic Collectors Association (MCA). Hence the best advice to a researcher fresh to the field is to locate the closest member of that association. The Executive Secretary of the MCA is Walter Gydesen (19 Logan Street, New Britain, Conn. 06051). There is now a New England Magic Collectors Association as well, for whom the contact person is Edward Hill, P.O. Box 30, Harmony, R.Is. 02829. A discussion of several of the major conjuring collections may be found in Chapter 1 of Robert J. Albo's *Further Classic Magic with Apparatus*, volume 4.

HISTORY AND CRITICISM

The most influential account of the nature, general principles, and definition of the topic is contained in several introductory sections of J. E. Robert-Houdin's *The Secrets of Conjuring and Magic*. There will be found the father of modern magic's oft-quoted dictum: "A conjuror . . . is an actor playing the part of a magician."

The first significant general history of magic in English was Thomas Frost's *Lives of the Conjurers*, published in London in 1874. The first such work by an American, with an American emphasis, was H. J. Burlingame's *Leaves from Conjurers' Scrap Books*, published in 1891. William Godwin's earlier *Lives of the Necromancers* had covered some of the same ground, as had P. T. Barnum's *Humbugs of the World*. But neither focused on the subject of magic and magicians with anything like the clarity or perspective of Frost or Burlingame. Albert A. Hopkins came along with *Magic, Stage Illusions and Scientific Diversions, Including Trick Photography* in 1897. This work was remarkable for the large number of its illustrations and for the historical introduction and bibliography contributed by Henry Ridgeley Evans. The bibliography was the most extensive ever compiled in the field at the time. All of the preceding works are still in print.

Major general works on magic history by Americans in the twentieth century begin with Henry Ridgeley Evans' *The Old and the New Magic* and *History of Conjuring and Magic*. In 1935 John Mulholland wrote a short pioneering history of magic titled *John Mulholland's Story of Magic*, which was based largely on primary materials in his own growing collection of books, ephemera, prints, and photographs. The same pattern was iterated on a larger scale by Milbourne Christopher, first with *Panorama of Magic* and then resoundingly with *The Illustrated History of Magic*. Edward Claflin, with Jeff Sheridan, followed with *Street Magic: An Illustrated History of Wandering Magicians and Their Conjuring Arts*. The largest volume of this genre to date is David Price's *Magic: A Pictorial History of Conjurers in the Theater*, based on the major collections of the Egyptian Hall Museum of Nashville, Tennessee. While its special strengths were not in the history of American magic, British magic historian Sidney W. Clarke's *The Annals of Conjuring*, which appeared serially in *The Magic Wand*, 1924–1928, was the most authoritative comprehensive history of magic of its time. It did not become generally available in book form until 1984. The story of Sidney W. Clarke himself is engagingly and authoritatively told by Edwin A. Dawes in *The Barrister in the Circle*.

An important work for the early history of magic in America is Charles J. Pecor's 1977 doctoral dissertation, published under the title *The Magician and the American Stage 1752–1874*. An extremely rich source for the researcher is a facsimile printing of a manuscript originally commissioned by Houdini. Published in 1983 as *Houdini's History of Magic in Boston 1792–1915*, it presents the results of H. J. Moulton's combing the archives of the Boston Public Library for every newspaper reference to a magician to be found there to the year 1915.

Because it is neither widely known nor taken into account by writers on the history of magic, it is worth repeating here an important cautionary note by magic historian, museum proprietor, and professional journalist Robert Lund regarding the reliability of newspaper accounts of magicians:

> Until . . . the 1930s or thereabouts, the person who sold ads for the theatrical page of a paper frequently doubled as a "critic." . . . Wearing both hats simultaneously, a critic wasn't likely to do much criticizing. There was nothing objective about his comments. They were almost always favorable. With few exceptions, the only unfavorable comments were directed at non-advertisers. . . . Performers and theatre owners . . . were often promised a flattering notice as an inducement to advertise. A paid ad entitled the advertiser to . . . a certain amount of space in the news columns . . . written by the performers themselves or by the owners of the theatres or halls where the entertainment took place.[8]

Caveat lector.

Two general works by leading British magic historian Edwin A. Dawes bear American as well as British imprints: *The Great Illusionists* and, with Arthur Setterington, *The Encyclopedia of Magic*. Both titles are misleading, the former because the book deals with many figures who were neither great nor illusionists; the latter because it is not an encyclopedia either in form or in content. Dawes' own titles (rejected for commercial reasons by the publishers) were, respectively, *The Pursuit of Illusion* and *The Book of Magic*.

Biographical works of various kinds have played a significant role in the history of magic in America. On all counts the most influential such work was Lascelles Wraxall's English translation of Jean Eugène Robert-Houdin's *Confidences d'un prestidigitateur*, first published in 1859 under the title *Memoirs of Robert-Houdin: Ambassador, Author, and Conjurer* and later as *King of Conjurers*. It was this work that finally inspired the young Hungarian-born immigrant Erich Weiss (Erik Weisz) to enter upon his career in magic in 1891. He wanted to be "like Robert-Houdin," and his friend and first performing partner, Jack Hayman (Jacob Hyman), was responsible for misinforming him that by adding an *i* to his hero's last name it would mean just that. Hence, at age seventeen, Erich Weiss became "Houdini," a name that gained such prominence over the next thirty years that it remains the most widely recognized name in American magic. In American popular culture today Houdini's own story has largely supplanted the inspirational function that Robert-Houdin's *Memoirs* retains in France. That Houdini himself vigorously strove for that result there can be no doubt. But so did many others. Only Houdini was successful.

Stung by the refusal of the widow of Robert-Houdin's son Emile to receive him in 1901, Houdini launched a literary vendetta against his former hero in the form of a book, *The Unmasking of Robert-Houdin*, published seven years later. While the book did not achieve its aim, it remains of considerable historical interest as the first sustained attempt to mine Houdini's large and growing collection for historical information. Its errors and oversights became the subject of two extensive rebuttals. The first was Maurice Sardina's *Les Erreurs de Harry Houdini*, translated and edited by Victor Farelli as *Where Houdini Was Wrong*. The second was Jean Hugard's *Houdini's "Unmasking" : Fact vs Fiction*. Both Robert-Houdin's *Memoirs* and Houdini's *Unmasking* continue to receive occasional critical attention in the literature.

While Robert-Houdin's own *Memoirs* remains the most important account of his career, others have appeared in English. William Manning, a boyhood friend of Robert-Houdin's eldest son, gave us *Recollections of Robert-Houdin*, while Henry Ridgeley Evans wrote an abbreviated account under the title *A Master of Modern Magic: The Life and Adventures of Robert-Houdin*. A later biography of Robert-Houdin for young readers has been written by I. G. Edmonds under the title *The Magic Man: The Life of Robert-Houdin*. Both Robert-Houdin and Houdini are included among the same author's *The Magic Makers: Magic and the Men Who Made It*. The most recent, serious, fact-filled study is Samuel H. Sharpe's *Salutations to Robert-Houdin*.

There is no universally acknowledged definitive account of Houdini's life, though Milbourne Christopher's *Houdini: The Untold Story* comes close. Some others favor William Lindsay Gresham's *Houdini, the Man Who Walked through Walls*. The first full biography was Harold Kellock's *Houdini, His Life-Story*. Done with the cooperation of Houdini's widow, Beatrice, it probably comes as close as any to the romanticized version of his life that Houdini himself would have favored being published. These three rate being called "major" biographies, though all fall short of being definitive. It must not go unnoted that from 1900 to 1922 Houdini himself oversaw the production of various editions of his self-promotional account, *The Adventurous Life of a Versatile Artist*.

Soon after the appearance of Kellock's biography, Will Goldston published *Sensational Tales of Mystery Men*, which included a good deal of less flattering material about Houdini. Unfortunately, the book is marred by enough demonstrable errors that one must always hedge its authority with qualifiers. No such cautions are needed for Walter B. Gibson's *Houdini's Escapes*, an authoritative account by magic's most prolific author and sometime secretary to Houdini. A number of Gibson's books over the years included accounts of Houdini and his magic. The last, appearing nearly a half century after the first, was *The Original Houdini Scrapbook*. J. C. Cannell's *The Secrets of Houdini* appeared next. Both Gibson's *Houdini's Escapes* and Cannell's *Secrets of Houdini* achieved instant notoriety and remain in print today. Following Cannell's account came *Houdini and Conan Doyle* by B.M.L. Ernst and Hereward Carrington. Ernst had been a long-standing friend of Houdini's and was his lawyer. The book is based on the correspondence between Houdini and Doyle, largely over spiritualism. A number of derivative biographies appeared over the years, several for the juvenile market. There were *The Great Houdini, Magician Extraordinary* by Beryl Williams and her husband, Samuel Epstein; Lace Kendall's *Houdini: Master of Escape*; Robert Kraske's *Harry Houdini, Master of Magic*; John Ernst's *Escape King: The Story of Harry Houdini*; Anne Edwards' *The Great Houdini*; Gyles Brandreth and John Morley's *The Magic of Houdini: The Man and His Magic*; Florence Meiman White's *Escape! The Life of Harry Houdini*; David Warren's *The Great Escaper*; and Raymund Fitzsimons's *Death and the Magician: The Mystery of Houdini*. Some recent works have included material based in part on original research efforts. Milbourne Christopher extended his own prior study with *Houdini: A Pictorial Life*. Bernard C. Meyer had a crack at psychobiography with *Houdini: A Mind in Chains*. More satisfyingly creative is Lynn Sukenick's *Houdini*, a small collection of poems in the distinguished Yes! Capra Chapbook series, containing such exquisite lines as "In the din did Houdini nod." James Randi (James Randall Zwinge) and B. R. Sugar produced *Houdini: His Life and Art*, and Doug Henning and Charles Reynolds did *Houdini—His Legend and His Magic*. Of particular note as well is Lawrence Arcuri's *Houdini Birth Research Committee Report* to the National Committee of the Society of American Magicians. While Houdini always claimed his boyhood home of Appleton, Wisconsin, as his birthplace, and April 6, 1874, as his birth date—claims accepted by several biographers—the fact is that he was born on March 24, 1874, in Budapest, Hungary. This report assembles the evidence.

The year 1811 marks the publication of the first known autobiography of a magician in America: *The Life, Adventures and Unparalleled Sufferings of Andrew Oehler*, a substantial volume of 226 pages. In 1833 there appeared another substantial autobiographical account by a straight-playing mentalist, that is, one who entertained by displaying genuinely remarkable mental powers: *A Memoir of Zerah Colburn*. The following year George Smith's booklet *Memoirs and Anecdotes of Mr. Love, the Polyphonist* appeared in London, to be reprinted in Boston in 1850. John Henry Anderson issued a lot of paper over his spectacular career. On several occasions in midcentury he issued booklet collections of autobiographical anecdotes under the title *Professor Anderson's Note-Book*. Several versions survive. In 1858 appeared the substantial autobiography of Jonathan H. Green, *The Reformed Gambler*, a trickster who played and then exposed (first in 1844 with *Gambling Unmasked* then more extensively in 1847 with *Gambling Unmarked!*) the other side of the street.

In 1859, the year in which Robert-Houdin's *Memoirs* first appeared in English,

Luke P. Rand published a fabulous, sixty-page *Sketch of the History of the Davenport Boys*. There followed a similar account by Orrin Abbott in 1864 under the title *The Davenport Brothers*. The brothers published their own extensive self-promotional account in 1869 under the title *The World Renowned Spiritual Mediums: Their Biography, and Adventures in Europe and America*.

George W. Kirbye, "professionally known as a Ventriloquist, Magician, Equilibrist and Athlete," produced his slim *Autobiography* in 1861. The first of Carl Herrmann's promotional pamphlets in America, with biographical sketch, appeared in the same year, as *Herrmann, First Prestidigitateur*. An augmented version appeared five years later under the title *Herrmann and Ancient and Modern Magic, with a Biographical Sketch of the Great Prestidigitateur*.

A landmark autobiography by Signor (Antonio) Blitz, dedicated "To My American Friends and Patrons," appeared in 1871 under the title *Fifty Years in the Magic Circle*. Written from memory rather than notes and hence peppered with minor factual errors as well as some larger, deliberate ones, the work nonetheless provides one of the fullest and most winsome accounts of magic in mid-nineteenth-century America by one of its most imitated practitioners. Blitz's first "highly diverting combination of Eccentric and Amusing Anecdotes" had been published twenty years earlier under the title *The Vagaries of a Ventriloquist*.

The year 1871 also saw the private publication of John Wyman's *Jokes and Anecdotes of Wyman, the Magician and Ventriloquist* and a pamphlet titled *Biographical Sketch of Simmons* by Dr. H. S. Lynn. Hugh Simmons was a thirty-five-year-old British-born illusionist who also performed as Washington Simmons, Professor Simmons, and Dr. H. S. Lynn. Under the last name he published in 1873 a more substantial autobiographical booklet titled *The Adventures of the Strange Man*, reprinted in 1882 under the title *Travels and Adventures of Dr. Lynn*. E. P. Hingston records a highly entertaining encounter in Salt Lake City with an unnamed conjurer who must be Dr. Lynn in *The Genial Showman, Being Reminiscences of the Life of Artemus Ward*, published in 1870. Artemus Ward—President Lincoln's favorite humorist, by some accounts—was in reality Charles Farrar Browne.

E. P. Hingston not only managed Artemus Ward but brought Robert Heller (William Henry Palmer) great success with a similar mode of presentation. A biographical sketch of Heller by Henry Ridgeley Evans is part of a compilation of Heller's music put together by H. L. Clapham in 1932 under the title *Melody Magic*. Today there is Frank Koval's *Robert Heller: Music and Mystery*. Thanks to the efforts of James Hagy we now have a fine monograph on Robert Heller's contemporary, William Henry Young ("Professor Young"), *The One Young* (1986).

Henry (Heinrich) Keller became Harry Kellar partly (and unsuccessfully) to avoid the charge that Keller was an imitation of Heller. In 1886, before he had won the premier position in American magic, Kellar's "autobiography," titled *A Magician's Tour Up and Down and Round about the Earth*, was published. The embellishments of this work became such an embarrassment to Kellar that he later bought up what copies he could to remove them from circulation.

The first significant biographical treatment of Alexander Herrmann appeared in Thomas Telemachus Timayenis' *A History of the Art of Magic, Containing Anecdotes, Explanation of Tricks, and a Sketch of the Life of Alexander Herrmann*. This was later expanded in scope and rewritten by W. E. Goemann as *A History of the*

Art of Magic, Containing Anecdotes, Explanation of Tricks and a Sketch of the Life of the Three Herrmanns, Carl, Alexander and Leon. In 1897 H. J. Burlingame produced *Herrmann the Magician: His Life, His Secrets*, which has since been reprinted both as *Herrmann the Great* and as *Magician's Handbook*. In 1979 came I. G. Edmonds' *The Magic Brothers, Carl and Alexander Herrmann*.

A few other biographical works relating to largely nineteenth-century figures are worth mentioning in transition to the next century. "Stuart Cumberland" (Charles Garner), a highly successful mentalist of the John Randall Brown and Washington Irving Bishop school of "muscle-reading," wrote several engaging works about his life and skills as a performer and exposer of spiritualist fraud. These include *A Thought-Reader's Thoughts, People I Have Read, That Other World*, and *Spiritualism—The Inside Truth*. British magician and world traveler "Charles Bertram" (James Bassett) included the United States in his itinerary and left us with two fine accounts: *Isn't It Wonderful?* and *A Magician in Many Lands*.

Lulu Hurst (The Georgia Wonder), as the subtitle explains, "writes her autobiography, and for the First Time Explains and Demonstrates the Great Secret of her Marvellous Power." Published in 1897, it recounts her remarkable career as a teenage wonder woman in the mid-1880s. The act that Lulu Hurst created was later copied and developed by other women, most notably Annie Abbott. John Fisher includes a number of their feats in *Body Magic*.

Shortly after the Civil War, Professor E. Cooper Taylor took an ambitious show through much of the western frontier. The definitive account has yet to be written, but we have a nice start in *A Few Moments in the Career of Prof. E. Cooper Taylor 1852–1927* by E. Cooper Taylor III.

Danish-born "Julius Zancig" (Julius Jensen) developed an extraordinarily successful "telepathy" (second sight) act in 1899 with his first wife, Agnes. They told their own story to 1907 in *Two Minds with but a Single Thought*. Following Agnes' death in 1916, Julius shared "single thoughts" with Paul Vucci (later "Paul Rosini"), David Bamberg (later "Fu Manchu"), and a second wife, "Agnes" (really named Ada), until his death in 1929. Light on the same period is shed by Frank "The Mystifier" Nightingale in the historical section of his *Magic for Magicians*.

Paul Vucci had taken his stage name, Paul Rosini, from another of his employers, "Carl Rosini" (John Rosen), whose story is told by Robert E. Olson in *Carl Rosini: His Life and Magic*. David Bamberg ("Fu Manchu") is, with Robert Albo and Eric Lewis, an author of *The Oriental Magic of the Bambergs*, a lavishly produced tribute to, and review of, this six-generation family of magicians, appropriately giving greatest emphasis to David's father, Tobias David Bamberg ("Okito"). Tobias David Bamberg usually went by the name "Theo" (Theodore) and, as Theodore Bamberg, with Robert Parish, had earlier written *Okito on Magic: Reminiscences and Selected Tricks*. David Bamberg's nearly lost autobiography has finally been published by David Meyer as *Illusion Show: A Life in Magic*.

David P. Abbott was a professional magician for only a short while in his youth, though his later invention of "spirit painting" contributed to many great illusion shows, including Thurston's, and he baffled innumerable houseguests with his famous talking tea kettle. His *Behind the Scenes with the Mediums* is a classic, and *The Marvellous Creations of Joseffy* remains our best source on that Austrian-born magician. Most remarkable of all, perhaps, is *David P. Abbott's Book of Mysteries*, published more than forty years after his death.

"Chung Ling Soo" (William Ellsworth Robinson) died in a bullet-catching accident in 1918. The best account of his life and death is by "Will Dexter" (William T. Pritchard), *The Riddle of Chung Ling Soo*. Val Andrews' *Gift from the Gods: The Story of Chung Ling Soo, Marvelous Chinese Conjurer* is notable largely for its splendid illustrations. His death is among those discussed in Ben Robinson et al., *Twelve Have Died*, as well as in Gary R. Frank's recent booklet, *Chung Ling Soo: The Man behind the Legend!*

Over a twenty-year career cut short in 1916 by a pioneering brain tumor operation that eventually left him blind, "Karl Germain" (Karl Mattmueller) rose to become a leading performer on the Lyceum and Chautauqua circuits. Germain died in 1959, and his story is touchingly told by Stuart Cramer in *The Secrets of Karl Germain* and *Germain the Wizard and His Legerdemain*. *The Life and Mysteries of the Celebrated Dr. "Q"* by "C. Alexander" is in fact the autobiography of Claude Conlin, a celebrated mentalist who also performed as "Alexander, the Man Who Knows." He died in 1954. Of the same ilk but of much more recent vintage is *The Amazing World of Kreskin*, by himself (George J. Kresge). An embellished (and perhaps better-timed) autobiography of San Francisco–born "Carl Hertz" (Leib Morgenstern) appeared in 1924, the year he died. Titled *A Modern Mystery Merchant*, it was published in England, where he enjoyed his greatest success.

Howard Thurston's *My Life of Magic* (ghosted by J. N. Hilliard and Walter Gibson) appeared in 1929. In 1938, two years after Thurston's death, his friend Thomas C. Worthington produced a brief *Recollections of Howard Thurston, Conjurer, Illusionist, and Author*. In 1981 appeared Robert E. Olson's biographical tribute, *The World's Greatest Magician: A Tribute to Howard Thurston*. Helping to fill out the picture are a 475-page facsimile *Thurston-Dante Letter Set*, compiled by Phil Temple in 1981, and the *Thurston Scrapbook, Being the Text of the MS. Titled "My Magic Husband Thurston the Great" by Grace Thurston* (Howard's first wife), first issued in 1985.

A satisfactory, full-length biography of "Dante" (Harry A. Jansen) has yet to be written, though Val Andrews' *Goodnight, Mister Dante* provides an interesting anecdotal account.

We are not in a much better position with Dante's chief rival, Harry Blackstone. Neil Foster edited a fifty-two-page pictorial souvenir titled *The Great Blackstone: World's Greatest Magician and His "Show of 1001 Wonders,"* Robert Lund compiled *Blackstone . . . And Now a Word from Our Sponsor*, a collection of Blackstone endorsements of commercial products, and now there is *The Blackstone Book of Magic and Illusion*, by Harry Blackstone Jr., with Charles and Regina Reynolds, but Daniel Waldron has yet to publish what will be the definitive account.

Horace Goldin's *It's Fun to Be Fooled* is a classic personal memoir sweeping the twentieth century up to the mid-1930s. Mike Caveney has recently produced *The Great Leon: Vaudeville Headliner*, and William V. Rauscher has given us *Monarch of Magic: The Story of Servais LeRoy*. There are valuable accounts of Leipzig and Malini, based largely on the recollections of Dai Vernon but written up by Lewis Ganson. These appeared as *Dai Vernon's Tribute to Nate Leipziq* by Lewis Ganson and *Malini and His Magic* by Dai Vernon, edited by Lewis Ganson. The story of Dai Vernon himself is not yet complete, but Lewis Ganson's *The Dai Vernon Book of Magic* includes biographical material up to the mid-1950s. Of the same period is John Scarne's *The Amazing World of John Scarne: A Personal History*. An illuminating look at one of magic's more controversial figures is Ed Levy's compilation, *Richard Himber: The Man and His Magic*. Gene Gordon gave us a fascinating and highly informative memoir in *Gene Gordon's Magical Legacy*. William V. Rauscher's *Marco the Magi: Wise Man of Magic* profiles the founder and leader of the Le Grand David company. Of still more recent vintage are Lee Grabel's *The Magic and Illusions of Lee Grabel* and David Charvet's *Jack Gwynne: The Man, His Mind, and His Royal Family of Magic*.

There are colorful accounts of the tent-show magicians Augustus P. Rapp and Willard the Wizard in *The Life and Times of Augustus Rapp* by Rapp himself and in *Willard the Wizard* by Bev Bergeron.

The first attempt at a comprehensive history of black magicians in America is Jim Magus' "A History of Blacks in Magic," published serially in *The Linking Ring* in 1983–1984. Other survey pieces in this area of growing historical interest are an unsigned article titled "Magicians: Dozen Negroes Practice Hocus-pocus Art in Tradition of Vaudeville Heyday," which appeared in *Ebony* magazine in 1949, and Robert Lund's reports in *Abracadabra* in 1963.

A satisfactory survey of women in magic, both as performers and as assistants, has yet to be written. The closest work of that sort to date is *Those Beautiful Dames*, compiled by Frances Marshall. Slightly earlier is a chapter on "Women in Magic" in *Bill Severn's Guide to Magic as a Hobby*. Frances Marshall's most recent account of her own story is *My First Fifty Years*. *Backstage with Magigals*, a Magigals Club newsletter and bulletin of general interest, has been in progress since December 1952, though copies are scarce. The stories of several female performers on the flaming fringe of magic are entertainingly told by Ricky Jay in *Learned Pigs and Fireproof Women*.

Interesting perspectives on some of the twentieth century's great stage performers are offered by works written by or about their assistants and illusion builders. Guy Jarrett, who built illusions for Broadway shows as well as for such magicians as T. Nelson Downs, gives us particularly colorful commentary on the magic of his day in *Guy Jarrett's 1936 Magic and Stagecraft*. Over a long career George Boston worked for several American stage magicians, including Howard Thurston. His story is told in *Inside Magic*. An unfortunately inaccurate account of Edmund Spreer, David Bamberg's "chief assistant, performer, builder, and idea man, confidant and friend," is attempted by Robert E. Olson in *Illusion Builder to Fu Manchu*. The Australian performer turned major American magic manufacturer Percy Abbott gives his reminiscences in *A Lifetime in Magic*. A leading builder of illusions for the greatest stage performers of the twentieth century was the Thayer Magical Manufacturing Company. An enormous amount of magic is contained in the instruction sheets that Thayer produced for the apparatus and supplies in which he dealt. These have now been collected and published in Glenn Gravatt's four-volume *Thayer Catalog Instruction Sheets*. In 1933 two of Floyd Thayer's employees, Carl and Emmet Owen, bought out Thayer Manufacturing and formed the company that today continues under the name Owen Magic Supreme. Les and Gertrude Smith have been the proprietors since 1963. The story of Carl Owen and the Thayer Manufacturing Company is told in Richard Buffum's *Keep the Wheels Turning*. More recently, in *The Brema Brasses*, Buffum has given us the story of America's premier manufacturer of brass apparatus during the first half of the twentieth century. John McKinven, a keen investigator and painstaking restorer,

David Copperfield and "tornado of fire," New York, 2001. © Reuters NewMedia Inc./CORBIS

gave us *Roltair: Genius of Illusions*. The most recent book featuring the work of an outstanding contemporary illusion builder and restorer is *The Mystery of Psycho* by John Gaughan and Jim Steinmeyer. John Gaughan was a builder for Owen Magic Supreme before setting up his own very distinguished shop.

The single most important book on illusions to appear in the third quarter of the twentieth century was not by a craftsman assistant or manufacturer, but by an especially ingenious and creative performer, Robert Harbin. Harbin invented the Zig-Zag Girl Illusion, one of the most popular of all time. Its construction was revealed to the profession in 1970 in *The Magic of Robert Harbin*. A few years later stage presentations and building plans for more than 100 illusions, including such time-tested feats as the substitution trunk, the buzz saw, and the thin model sawing-in-two, were compiled by Byron G. Wels in *The Great Illusions of Magic*.

American magicians have had running battles with purported mediums, psychics, spiritualists, and the like from the beginning of spiritualism in the middle of the nineteenth century right down to the present day. Limitations of space preclude more than a sampling here. Some of the more significant volumes not already mentioned are these. The indispensable account of the origins of spiritualism remains E. W. Capron's *Modern Spiritualism: Its Facts and Fanaticisms, Its Consistencies and Contradictions*, and the most notorious, first-generation inside debunking job was Reuben Briggs Davenport's *The Deathblow to Spiritualism: Being the True Story of the Fox Sisters, as Revealed by Authority of Margaret Fox Kane and Catherine Fox Jencken*. Two early exposés of spiritualist fraud by the magicians J. N. Maskelyne and Herr Dobler are included in James Webb's anthology, *The Mediums and the Conjurors*. In the next generation Houdini produced *Miracle Mongers and Their Methods* and *A Magician among the Spirits*. In the next decade John Mulholland wrote his now classic *Beware Familiar Spirits*. In more recent times Robert Nelson has cast some light in this corner with his autobiographical *The Last Book of Nelson*, and the prolific Milbourne Christopher has given us *ESP, Seers and Psychics; Mediums, Mystics and the Occult*; and *Search for the Soul*. James "The Amazing" Randi wrote *The Magic of Uri Geller*, with a follow-up *The Truth about Uri Geller* and a more general contemporary survey, *Flim-Flam!* A genuinely confessional and fascinating account, *The Psychic Mafia* by M. Lamar Keene, "Prince of Spiritualists," may be compared with the fictional, though highly illuminating and entertaining, *Confessions of a Psychic* and *Further Confessions of a Psychic* by Uriah Fuller (Martin Gardner). William V. Rauscher provides his own characteristic perspective in *ESP or Trickery? The Problem of Mentalism within the World of Magic*.

Several times during the course of the twentieth century various magic authorities published lists of the purportedly best or greatest books in magic, but none can compare with that which appeared in the foreword to Albo, Page, and Burger's *More Classic Magic with Apparatus*. The difference is that Albo's list was empirically constructed on the basis of an international survey of 635 magic bibliophiles, 370 of whom lived in the United States or Canada. An astonishing aspect of this survey was the extremely sharp cutoff point in the list of books it generated. Every book on the "winners" list was nominated by 40 percent or more of the magic bibliophiles surveyed, while the next runner-up received only 15 percent support. There are thirty-nine books (or sets) on the list, the last two being tied for thirty-eighth place. Here is the list:

1. John Northern Hilliard, *Greater Magic*.
2. J. B. Bobo, *Modern Coin Magic*.
3. Harlan Tarbell, *The Tarbell Course in Magic*. 7 vols.
4. Robert J. Albo et al., *The Oriental Magic of the Bambergs*.
5. Professor Hoffmann, *Modern Magic, More Magic, and Later Magic*.
6. Nevil Maskelyne and David Devant, *Our Magic*.
7. Lewis Ganson, *The Dai Vernon Book of Magic*.
8. Camille Gaultier, *Magic without Apparatus*, translated by Jean Hugard.
9. George Starke et al., eds., *Stars of Magic*.
10. T. Nelson Downs, *The Art of Magic*.
11. Harold R. Rice, *Rice's Encyclopedia of Silk Magic*, 3 vols.
12. Milbourne Christopher, *The Illustrated History of Magic*.
13. Jean Eugéne Robert-Houdin, *The Secrets of Conjuring and Magic*, translated by Professor Hoffmann.
14. S. W. Erdnase, *The Expert at the Card Table*.
15. Robert Harbin, *The Magic of Robert Harbin*.
16. Tony Corinda, *Thirteen Steps to Mentalism*.
17. Will Goldston, *The Locked Books*, 3 vols.
18. Jean Hugard and Frederick Braue, *Expert Card Technique*.
19. Robert J. Albo et al., *Classic Magic with Apparatus*.
20. Dariel Fitzkee, *Magic by Misdirection*.
21. Harry Lorayne, *Close-Up Card Magic*.
22. C. Lang Neil, *The Modern Conjurer and Drawing-Room Entertainer*.
23. Frances Marshall et al., *The Success Book*, 4 vols.
24. John Booth, *The John Booth Classics*.
25. Carl Willmann, *Die moderne Salon-Magie*.
26. Friedrich Wilhelm Conradi, *Démonstrations Mystérieuses*.

27. Edwin T. Sachs, *Sleight of Hand.*

28. Henry Hatton and Adrian Plate, *Magicians' Tricks.*

29. Sidney W. Clarke, *The Annals of Conjuring.*

30. C. Alexander, *The Life and Mysteries of the Celebrated Dr. "Q."*

31. Henry Ridgely Evans, *The Old and the New Magic.*

32. Walter Brown Gibson and Morris N. Young, *Houdini on Magic.*

33. Harry Houdini, *The Unmasking of Robert-Houdin.*

34. Jules Dhotel, *Magic with Small Apparatus*, translated by Paul Fleming.

35. Ian Adair, *Encyclopedia of Dove Magic*, 5 vols.

36. Albert A. Hopkins, comp. and ed., *Magic, Stage Illusions and Scientific Diversions, including Trick Photography.*

37. Ottokar Fischer, *Illustrated Magic*, translated by Fulton Oursler and J. B. Mussey.

38. Ottokar Fischer, *J. N. Hofzinser's Card Conjuring*, translated by S. H. Sharpe.

39. Karl Fulves, *The Best of Slydini . . . and More.*

A number of excellent works published since the above survey was conducted are dealt with elsewhere in this chapter. A highly recommended longer list of selected works in magic is found in William Doerflinger's *The Magic Catalogue.* The most lengthy narrative review of how-to books to date is Chapter 3 ("The Creation of Illusion: Manuals on the Execution of Magic") in Earle Coleman's *Magic: A Reference Guide.*

The life of magic in American popular culture is fed not only with books, but with apparatus and supplies, with organizations, magazines, and manufacturers. There is no really satisfactory history of magic manufacturers and dealers in the United States, though there are flawed reviews in the chapter entitled "Laboratories of Legerdemain" in H. R. Evans' *History of Conjuring and Magic* and in Robert J. Albo's "Magic Craftsmen Past and Present," in *Classic Magic with Apparatus.* The most venerable general dealers in magic (manufacturing and publishing, wholesale and retail) in the United States today are Abbott's Magic Mfg. Co., Colon, Mich. 49040; Magic, Inc., 5082 N. Lincoln Ave., Chicago, Ill. 60625; Owen Magic Supreme, 734 No. McKeever Ave., Azusa, Calif. 91702; and Louis Tannen, Inc., 6 W. 32nd St. 4th Fl., New York 10001. Each of these has broadly served the magic subculture in the United States for several decades, and they all publish substantial catalogs. There are a multitude of specialty houses and smaller general dealers, many of whom are members of the Magic Dealers Association (Hank Lee, 125 Lincoln Street, Boston 02205), and a number of whom advertise in the major magic magazines (see later).

Two long-standing magic book publishers outside the United States are major suppliers to U.S. magicians. These are Micky Hades International, P.O. Box 1414, Station M, Calgary, Alberta T2P 2L6, Canada; and Supreme Magic Company, Ltd., 64, High Street, Bideford, Devon, England.

The chief long-standing general organizations of magicians in the United States are the Society of American Magicians (S.A.M., Lock Drawer 789-G, Lynn, Mass. 01903) and the International Brotherhood of Magicians (I.B.M., P.O. Box 227, Kenton, Ohio 43326). Membership in both is international and tied to local member organizations where possible. (S.A.M. has local "Assemblies"; I.B.M. has local "Rings.") Both organizations publish monthly magazines for members only: *M-U-M* for S.A.M., and *The Linking Ring* for I.B.M.

Another general international organization with substantial membership in the United States is the Magic Circle (84 Chenies Mews, London WC1 6HX, England), which boasts "the longest continuous running magic periodical in magic's history," *The Magic Circular*.

Abbott's Magic Manufacturing Company publishes *The New Tops*, and Tannen's publishes *The Magic Manuscript*, both monthly magazines of general interest. The leading and longest-standing independent monthly magazine of magic is *Genii, The International Conjuror's Magazine* (P.O. Box 36068, Los Angeles 90036).

There are hundreds of other magic periodicals. A survey of entries in the Alfredson and Daily *Bibliography of Conjuring Periodicals in English: 1791–1983* reveals that about 175 *new* magic periodicals were begun in the United States in the decade of the 1970s. Most survived only a few issues. Among the most recent new periodicals, Stan Allen's *Inside Magic* (P.O. Box 963, Los Alamitos, Calif. 90720), started in 1985, is doing a superb job of covering current events in the world of magic and magicians.

There are several large annual conventions of magicians in the United States. The Society of American Magicians and the International Brotherhood of Magicians hold conventions in the summer at various sites around the country. Abbott's Magic Manufacturing Company holds its annual "Abbott Magic Get-Together" at home base in Colon, Michigan, in August. Tannen's annual Magic Jubilee is held in the fall at various resort locations north of New York City. The Magic Collectors Association holds its annual convention in Chicago in the spring. The Stevens Magic Emporium (3238 East Douglas, Wichita, Kans. 67208) coordinates an annual Desert Magic Seminar convention in Las Vegas. There are numerous regional conventions as well. For a sociological study of magic as an occupation, see Robert A. Stebbins' *The Magician*.

ANTHOLOGIES AND REPRINTS

For commercial publishing and reprinting books on magic and conjuring there is no rival to Dover Publications. Write to the publisher for the current catalog. Magico Magazine, P.O. Box 156, New York 10002, is exclusively devoted to publishing and reprinting books on magic and conjuring and is responsible for providing the current generation with such historical classics as Houdini's *The Unmasking of Robert-Houdin* and Sidney W. Clarke's *The Annals of Conjuring*. The Gambler's Book Club/GBC Press, P.O. Box 4115, Las Vegas, Nev. 89106, has reprinted such classics as Erdnase's *The Expert at the Card Table* and Maskelyne's classic exposé of gambling cheats, *Sharps and Flats*.

Walter J. Johnson, Inc., 355 Chestnut Street, Norwood, N.J. 07648, is the U.S. publisher for the English Experience series of facsimile reprints of books originally published in England between 1475 and 1640, including such conjuring landmarks as Reginald Scot's *The Discoverie of Witchcraft* and Samuel Rid's *The Art of Jugling or Legerdemaine*. John McArdle issued a small facsimile reprinting of the 1614 edition in 1952. The Imprint Society of Barre, Massachusetts, has also published a reprint of *The Art of Jugling or Legerdemaine*, 1612 edition, in modern type and spelling, in Arthur F. Kinney's volume, *Rogues, Vagabonds, and Sturdy Beggars.* They also reprinted E.P. Hingston's 1870 classic, *The Genial Showman.*

Two reprint series from Arno Press, now an imprint of Ayer Company Publishers, Inc., P.O. Box 958, Salem, N.H. 03079, include volumes of value to conjuring researchers. The Occult series reprints Reuben Briggs Davenport's *The Death-Blow to Spiritualism*, for example, and includes series editor James Webb's original Arno Press anthology, *The Mediums and the Conjurors.* The series Perspectives in Psychical Research includes Stuart Cumberland's *A Thought-Reader's Thoughts* and John Mulholland's *Beware Familiar Spirits.*

Meyerbooks, P.O. Box 427, Glenwood, Ill. 60425, produces some excellent reprints, anthologies, and original works, including H. J. Moulton's *Houdini's History of Magic in Boston 1792–1915*, David Meyer's *Legerdemain, or Sleight of Hand* and *The Wizard Exposed*. Abracadabra Press, P.O. Box 334, Balboa Island, Calif. 92662, has published Richard Buffum's *The Brema Brasses* and has begun a series of monographs with Thomas A. Sawyer's *Stanley Collins: Society Entertainer and Magic Collector.*

Thomas A. Sawyer, 12502 Red Hill Ave., Santa Ana, Calif. 92705, publishes material related to Professor Hoffmann. *Professor Hoffmann: A Study* by J. B. Findlay and Sawyer has been followed by Sawyer's *Professor Hoffmann: A Bibliography*, *The Hoffmann Collector: The First Ten Years*, and other works. Magical Publications, 572 Prospect Blvd., Pasadena, Calif. 91103, began a Magical Pro-Files series in 1986 with Peter Warlock's *Walter Jeans Illusioneer*. Mike Caveney's *The Great Leon: Vaudeville Headliner* continues the series.

The most venerable of reprint series in America was the Fleming Magic Classic Series, which began in 1945 with Camille Gaultier's *Magic without Apparatus* and continued with Sach's *Sleight-of-Hand* and Maskelyne and Devant's *Our Magic* the next year and more thereafter. The stock and reprint rights went from Fleming to Lloyd Jones' Magic Ltd. thereafter. Following the death of Lloyd Jones, the stock of Magic Ltd. was bought out by Lee Jacobs Productions, P.O. Box 362, Pomeroy, Ohio 45769, which is also the leading reprint publisher of magic posters.

Anthologies, collections, and annuals abound in American magic. Several have been noted elsewhere in this chapter, and there would be little point in attempting a comprehensive list here. The range is indicated by listing a selection of "encyclopedias," however. There are Ian Adair's *Encyclopedia of Dove Magic*, Jack Chanin's *Encyclopedia of Sleeving*, Keith Clark's *Encyclopedia of Cigarette Tricks*, Joseph Dunninger's *Dunninger's Complete Encyclopedia of Magic*, Frank Garcia's *The Encyclopedia of Sponge Ball Magic*, Martin Gardner's *Encyclopedia of Impromptu Magic*, *Walter Gibsons Encyclopedia of Magic and Conjuring*, Henry Hay's *Cyclopedia of Magic*, Jean Hugard's *Encyclopedia of Card Tricks*, Burling Hull's *The Encyclopedic Dictionary of Mentalism*, Stewart James' *Abbott's Encyclopedia of Rope Tricks*, Harold R. Rice's *Rice's Encyclopedia of Silk Magic*, and T. A. Waters' *The Encyclopedia of Magic and Magicians.*

Magicians and magic have played a significant role in popular fiction in America, especially in mystery stories and novels. There is no better place to begin exploring this aspect of magic in American popular culture than with two splendid anthologies: Otto Penzler's *Whodunit? Houdini? Thirteen Tales of Magic, Murder, Mystery*, and *Sleight of Crime: Fifteen Classic Tales of Murder, Mayhem, and Magic*, collected by Cedric E. Clute Jr. and Nicholas Lewin. The latter ends usefully with "More

Magical Mysteries: A Reader's Guide to Longer Works of Larcenous Legerdemain." Among the pieces included in those anthologies are works by major magic writers Walter B. Gibson (writing under his own name as well as that of Maxwell Grant) and Clayton Rawson. Two volumes of Maxwell Grant's tales from the 1930s, *Norgil the Magician* and *Norgil: More Tales of Prestigitection* have been collected and reprinted by the Mysterious Press. Clayton Rawson's classic tales of the Great Merlini (1938–1942) were reprinted by Collier Books in 1962.

A reprint of a series of episodes of Lee Falk and Phil Davis' Mandrake the Magician, the comic strip character and senior contemporary of Norgil and Merlini, was produced by Nostalgia Press in 1970. *Mandrake* continues its long run today—with Fred Fredericks as the current illustrator—and "Mandrake" in comic book form, in Spanish, Portuguese, and French, continues to flourish in Latin America and Western Europe.

The history of Tannen's "Stars of Magic," probably the slickest instructional series in the history of American conjuring, is symptomatic of current trends. It began in 1945 as an expensive sequence of high-quality individual lessons delivered on quality coated paper, with crisp photographs accompanying lean, but lucid, prose instructions. The complete series, bought serially over the decade to 1954, cost a grand total of ninety-four dollars. In 1955 Tannen began selling the complete set in a spring binder for twenty-five dollars. In 1961 the set was bound in book form and the price finally reduced to fifteen dollars. A new and similar series was begun a few years later, but by the mid-1980s Tannen's "Stars of Magic" lessons had switched from print to videotape. By the close of 1986, the current tape was being offered for a delivered price of seventy-two dollars. The best current over-the-counter instruction in magic has always been expensive. That is not likely to change. But a ten-dollars used copy of the 1961 *Stars of Magic* reprint is an almost unbeatable value if one's aspiration is simply to prepare to play as a performing artist upon a spectator's sense of wonder.

NOTES

1. English translations may be found in William Kelly Simpson, ed., *The Literature of Ancient Egypt: An Anthology of Stories, Instructions, and Poetry*, new ed. (New Haven, Conn.: Yale University Press, 1972), and in Miriam Lichtheim, *Ancient Egyptian Literature: A Book of Readings*, vol. 1 (Berkeley: University of California Press, 1973).

2. Jean Eugéne Robert-Houdin, *Memoirs of Robert-Houdin*, trans. Lascelles Wraxall, with a new introduction and notes by Milbourne Christopher (New York: Dover, 1964), Chapter 20, "Travels in Algeria."

3. Milbourne Christopher, *The Illustrated History of Magic* (New York: T. Y. Crowell, 1973), Chapter 5; and E. T. Kirby, *Ur-Drama, the Origins of Theatre* (New York: New York University Press, 1975), contain the two most useful accounts of Native American magic. See also John Mulholland, *Quicker Than the Eye* (1932).

4. See *Legerdemain, or Sleight of Hand: A Facsirnile Reproduction with Plates from the Third Edition (1797) of the Encyclopaedia Britannica*, with an essay on its origins and a guide to its appearances in all editions by David Meyer (Glenwood, Ill.: Meyerbooks, 1986).

5. Antonio Blitz, *Fifty Years in the Magic Circle* (Hartford, Conn.: A. B. Belknapp and Bliss, 1871), 140ff.

6. Charles Pecor, *The Magician on the American Stage 1752–1874* (Washington, D.C.: Emerson and West, 1977), 207.

7. Ibid., 230.

8. Albert F. Munroe and Robcrt Lund, "Magic in Detroit, 1837–1887," *Journal of Magic History* 11 (April 1980), 6.

BIBLIOGRAPHY

Books and Articles

Current addresses for the major magic publishers are given elsewhere in this chapter. Current addresses for private and specialty publishers are provided within this bibliography.

Abbott, David P. *Behind the Scenes with the Mediums*. Chicago: Open Court, 1907.

———. *David P. Abbott's Book of Mysteries*. Omaha, Nebr. 68101: Modern Litho, P.O. Box 369, 1977.

———. *The Marvellous Creations of Joseffy*. Chicago: Open Court, 1908.

Abbott, Orrin. *The Davenport Brothers: Their History, Travels and Manifestations*. New York: Privately printed, 1864.

Abbott, Percy A. *A Lifetime in Magic*. Colon, Mich.: Abbott Magic Mfg., 1960.

Adair, Ian H. *Encyclopedia of Dove Magic*. 5 vols. Bideford, England: Supreme, 1968–1987.

Albo, Robert J., Eric Lewis, and David Bamberg. *The Oriental Magic of the Bambergs*. Classic Magic, Vol. 1. San Francisco: San Francisco Book, 1973.

Albo, Robert J., Patrick Page, and Marvin Burger. *Classic Magic Index*. Classic Magic, Vol. 7. [Oakland, Calif. 946091]: Privately printed [418–30th St.], 1986.

———. *Classic Magic with Apparatus*. Classic Magic, Vol. 2. Piedmont, Calif.: Privately printed, 1976.

———. *Final Classic Magic with Apparatus*. Classic Magic, Vol. 6. N.p.: Privately printed, 1986.

———. *Further Classic Magic with Apparatus*. Classic Magic, Vol. 4. N.p.: Privately printed, 1982.

———. *More Classic Magic with Apparatus*. Classic Magic, Vol. 3. Piedmont, Calif.: Privately printed, 1978.

———. *Still Further Classic Magic with Apparatus*. Classic Magic, Vol. 5. N.p.: Privately printed, 1985.

Alexander, C. (C. Alexander Conlin). *The Life and Mysteries of the Celebrated Dr. "Q."* Los Angeles: Alexander, 1921.

Alfredson, James B., and George L. Daily Jr. A *Bibliography of Conjuring Periodicals in English: 1791–1983*. Intro. F. William Kuethe. York, Pa. 17402: Magicana for Collectors, 3320 Spondin Drive, 1986.

———. A *Short Title Check List of Conjuring Periodicals in English*. York, Pa.: Privately printed, 1976.

Anderson, John Henry. "The Bottle Polka. Composed and Arranged for the Piano Forte, for Professor Anderson's Grand Soirees Mysterieuses by Mons. Kneringer." New York: S. C. Jollie, 1851.

———. *The Fashionable Science of Parlor Magic: Being a Series of the Newest Tricks of Deception, Arranged for Amateurs and Lovers of the Art to Which Is Added an Exposure of the Practice Made Use of by Professional Card Players, Blacklegs and Gamblers*. 84th ed. "Temple of Magic" [Philadelphia]: "The Great Wizard of the North" [Brown, Printer, 1851].

———. "The Inexhaustable, [*sic*] Waltz. Composed and arranged for the Piano Forte expressly for Professor Anderson's Grand Drawing Room Entertainments, by Mons. Kneringer, 1st Prize Merit Pianist from the Conservatoire Royal de Paris." New York: S.C. Jollie, 1851.

———. *The Ladies Budget of Wit. Conundrums Sent in to Compete for the Valuable Service of Silver . . . Presented by Professor Anderson . . . on His Great Conundrum Night . . . Metropolitan Hall. Feb. 6th, 1852.* New York: Baker, Godwin, 1852.

———. "The Mystic Polka. Composed expressly for Professor Anderson's Grand Soirees Mysterieuses." New York: S.C. Jollie, 1852.

———. *Professor Anderson's Note-Book; or, Recollections of His Continental Tour.* [Philadelphia: Brown, Printer, 1851, etc.]

———. *The Wizard's Book of Conundrums, Containing over One Thousand Original and Spirited Riddles, Contributed by the Wits of New York and Vicinity, and Offered in Competition for the Celebrated Prizes Given by Professor Anderson at Metropolitan Hall Feb. 6 1852.* New York: T. W. Strong, 1852.

Andrews, Val. *Gift from the Gods: The Story of Chung Ling Soo, Marvelous Chinese Conjurer.* Alcester, England: Goodliffe, 1981.

———. *Goodnight, Mister Dante. A Bibliography of Harry A. Jansen ("Dante the Magician") 1883–1995.* Alcester, England: Goodliffe, 1978.

Arcuri, Lawrence. *The Houdini Birth Research Committee Report.* New York: Magico Magazine, 1980.

Armstrong, Bruce, ed. *Encyclopedia of Suspensions and Levitations.* With a Chronology by S. H. Sharpe. Calgary, Canada: Micky Hades, 1976.

Ayling, Will, and S. H. Sharpe. *Oriental Conjuring and Magic.* Bideford, England: Supreme, 1981.

Bamberg, David. *Illusion Show: A Life in Magic.* Glenwood, Ill.: David Meyer Magic Books, 1988.

Bamberg, Theodore (Okito). *Quality Magic.* London: Will Goldston, 1921. Reprinted with new introduction and index. Mexico D.F. 03020, Mexico: Craige Snader, Apartado 12–655, 1986.

Bamberg, Theodore, and Robert Parrish. *Okito on Magic: Reminiscences and Selected Tricks.* 2nd ed. Chicago: Edward Drane, 1968.

Barnouw, Erik. *The Magician and the Cinema.* New York: Oxford University Press, 1981.

Barnum, P. T. *The Humbugs of the World. An Account of Humbugs, Delusions, Impositions, Quackeries, Deceits and Deceivers Generally, in All Ages.* New York: Carleton, 1865.

———. *The Life of P. T. Bannon.* New York: Redfield, 1854. Many later editions.

———. *Struggles and Triumphs; or, Forty Years' Recollections.* (This is the same work as *The Life of P. T. Barnum* except for revisions and additions.) New York: J. B. Burr, 1869. Many later editions, the best being the Bryan edition, New York: Alfred A. Knopf, 1927.

Bergeron, Bev. *Willard the Wizard.* Orlando, Fla. 32805: Lake Crane Publications, 7013 Delora Dr., 1979.

Bertram, Charles (James Bassett). *Isn't It Wonderful? A History of Magic and Mystery, Together with His Reminiscences*. London: Swan Sonnenschein, 1896.

———. *A Magician in Many Lands*. New York: E. P. Dutton, 1911.

"Bibliohistory: Marco the Magi's Production of Le Grand David & His Own Spectacular Magic Company." *Journal of Magic History* 2 (December 1980), 165–95.

Blackstone, Harry, Jr., with Charles and Regina Reynolds. *The Blackstone Book of Magic and Illusion*. Foreword by Ray Bradbury. New York: Newmarket Press, 1985.

Blitz, Antonio. *Fifty Years in the Magic Circle*. Hartford, Conn: A. B. Belknapp and Bliss, 1871.

———. *The Vagaries of a Ventriloquist: Being a Highly Diverting Combination of Eccentric and Amusing Anecdotes, Illustrating the Astonishing Effects Produced by the Remarkable Faculty of Ventriloquism, as Practised by Signor Blitz, Now Exhibiting Nightly, Together with His Learned Canary Birds, Natural Magic, &c. at the Lecture Room, Chinese Museum*. Philadelphia: U. States Power Book and Job Printing Office, 1851.

Bobo, J. B. *Modern Coin Magic*. Minneapolis: Carl Waring Jones, 1952. Reprint. New York: Dover, 1982.

———. *The New Modern Coin Magic*. 2nd enl. ed. Chicago: Magic, 1966.

Bontjes, J. Gary. "A Checklist of Magic Lecture Notes." Supplement to *The Magic Cauldron*, No. 27; with Second, Third, and Fourth Checklists in Nos. 32 (1969), 41 (1971), and 54 (1974). Glen Burnie, Md. 21061: F. William Kuethe, 700 Glenview Ave., S.W., 1968.

Booth, John. *The John Booth Classics*, comprising *A Conjurer's Reminiscences, Forging Ahead in Magic* (1939), and *Marvels of Mystery* (1941). Bideford, England: Supreme, 1975.

———. "The Memoirs of a Magician's Ghost: The Autobiography of John Booth." *The Linking Ring*, May 1963, and continuing monthly to the present.

———. *Psychic Paradoxes*. Buffalo, N.Y.: Prometheus Books, 1986.

———. *Wonders of Magic*. Los Alamitos, Calif. 90720: Ridgeway Press, 12032 Montecito Road, 1986.

Boston, George L., with Robert Parrish. *Inside Magic*. New York: Beechurst Press, 1947.

Brandreth, Gyles, and John Morley. *The Magic of Houdini: The Man and His Magic*. London: Pelham Books, 1978.

Buffum, Richard. *The Brema Brasses*. Balboa Island, Calif. 92662: Abracadabra Press, P.O. Box 334, 1981.

———. *Keep the Wheels Turning*. Azusa, Calif. 91702: Owen Magic Supreme, 734 No. McKeever Ave., 1978.

Burlingame, H. J. *Around the World with a Magician and a Juggler*. Chicago: Clyde, 1891.

———. *Herrmann the Magician: His Life, His Secrets*. Chicago: Laird and Lee, 1897; also published as *Herrmann the Great* and *Magician's Handbook: Tricks and Secrets of the World's Greatest Magician, Herrmann the Great*. Chicago: Wilcox and Follet, 1942.

———. *History of Magic and Magicians*. Chicago: Chas. L. Burlingame, 1895.

————. *Leaves from Conjurers' Scrap Books; or, Modern Magicians and Their Works*. Chicago: Donohue, Henneberry, 1891. Reprint. Detroit: Singing Tree Press, 1971.

Cannell, J. C. *The Secrets of Houdini*. London: Hutchinson, 1931. Reprint. New York: Dover, 1973.

Capron, E. W. *Modern Spiritualism: Its Facts and Fanaticisms, Its Consistencies and Contradictions*. Boston, 1855. Reprint. New York: Arno Press, 1976.

Carrington, Hereward. *Side-Shows and Animal Tricks*. Kansas City: The Sphinx, 1913.

Caveney, Mike. *The Great Leon: Vaudeville Headliner*. Magical Pro-Files series. Pasadena, Calif. 91103: Magical Publications, 572 Prospect Blvd., 1987.

Chanin, Jack. *Encyclopedia of Sleeving*. Philadelphia: Privately printed, 1948.

Charvet, David. *Jack Gwynne: The Man, His Mind, and His Royal Fancily of Magic*. Brush Prairie, Wash. 98606: Charvet Studios, P.O. Box 210, 1987.

Christopher, Milbourne. *ESP, Seers and Psychics*. New York: Crowell, 1970.

————. *Houdini: A Pictorial Life*. New York: Crowell, 1976.

————. *Houdini: The Untold Story*. New York: Crowell, 1969. Reprinted with selections from Houdini's letters and private papers. New York: Pocket Books, 1970.

————. *The Illustrated History of Magic*. New York: Crowell, 1973.

————. *Mediums, Mystics, and the Occult*. New York: Crowell, 1975.

————. *Milbourne Christopher's Magic Book*. New York: Crowell, 1977. Bergenfield, N.J.: New American Library, 1979.

————. *Panorama of Magic*. New York: Dover, 1962.

————. *Search for the Soul*. New York: Crowell, 1979.

Clalin, Edward, with Jeff Sheridan. *Street Magic. Art Illustrated History of Wandering Magicians and Their Conjuring Arts*. New York: Doubleday, 1977.

Clapham, H. L., comp. *Melody Magic*. With a biographical sketch of the composer William Henry Palmer ("Robert Heller"), by H. R. Evans. Washington, D.C.: H. L. Clapham, 1932.

Clark, Hyla M. *The World's Greatest Magic*. New York: Crown, 1976.

Clark, Keith. *Encyclopedia of Cigarette Tricks*. Ed. Bruce Elliott. 2nd ed. New York: Tannen, 1952.

Clarke, Sidney W. *The Annals of Conjuring*. London: George Johnson, 1929. Originally published serially in *The Magic Wand*, 1924–1928. Reprinted with comprehensive index by Robert Lund. New York: Magico Magazine, 1984.

Clarke, Sidney W. and Adolphe Blind. *The Bibliography of Conjuring and Kindred Deceptions*. London: George Johnson, 1920.

Clute, Cedric E., Jr., and Nicholas Lewin, eds. *Sleight of Crime: Fifteen Classic Tales of Murder, Mayhem and Magic*. Chicago: Regnery, 1977.

Colburn, Zerah. *A Memoir of Zerah Colburn; Written by Himself. Containing an Account of the First Discovery of His Remarkable Powers; His Travels in America and Residence in Europe; A History of the Various Plans Devised for His Patronage; His return to This Country, and the Causes Which Led Him to His Present Profession; with His Peculiar Methods of Calculation*. Springfield, Mass.: G. and C. Merriam, 1933.

Coleman, Earle J. *Magic: A Reference Guide*. Westport, Corm.: Greenwood Press, 1987.

Conradi, Friedrich Wilhelm. *Démonstrations mystérieuses*. Magische Bibliothek Bd. 4. Berlin: Horster, 1904.

Corinda, Tony (Thomas William Simpson). *Thirteen Steps to Mentalism*. Harry Clarke, 1960. Reprint. New York: Tannen, 1968.

Cramer, Stuart. *Germain the Wizard and His Legerdemain*. Goleta, Calif.: Buffum, 1966.

———. *The Secrets of Karl Germain*. Cleveland: Mr. Merriweather and Co., 1962.

Cumberland, Stuart (Charles Garner). *People I Have Read*. London: Pearson, 1905.

———. *Spiritualism—The Inside Truth*. London: Odhams, 1919.

———. *That Other World*. London: Grant Richards, 1918.

———. *A Thought-Reader's Thoughts: Being the Impressions and Confessions of Stuart Cumberland*. London, 1888. Reprint. New York: Arno Press, 1975.

Davenport, Reuben Briggs. *The Death-Blow to Spiritualism: Being the True Story of the Fox Sisters, as Revealed by Authority of Margaret Fox Kane and Catherine Fox Jencken*. New York, 1888. Reprint. New York: Arno Press, 1976.

Davenport Brothers. *The World Renowned Spiritual Mediums: Their Biography, and Adventures in Europe and America. Truth Is Stranger than Fiction*. Boston: William White, 1869.

Dawes, Edwin A. *The Barrister in the Circle*. London: Magic Circle, 1983.

———. *The Great Illusionists*. Secaucus, N.J.: Chartwell Books, 1979.

Dawes, Edwin A., and Arthur Setterington. *The Encyclopedia of Magic*. New York: Gallery Books, 1986.

Dean, Henry. *The Whole Art of Legerdemain; or, Hocus Pocus in Perfection*. London, 1722. 1st American ed. *Hocus Pocus; or, The Whole Art of Legerdemain, in Perfection: By Which the Meanest Capacity May Perform the Whole without the Help of a Teacher. . . .* Philadelphia: Mathew Carey, 1795.

Desfor, Irving. *Great Magicians in Great Moments: A Photo Album by Irving Desfor*. Pomeroy, Ohio: Lee Jacobs Productions, 1983.

Dexter, Will (William Thomas Pritchard). *Everybody's Book of Magic*. London: Arco, 1956. Reprinted as *Famous Magic Secrets*, 1965.

———. *The Riddle of Chung Ling Soo* [William Ellsworth Robinson]. London: Arco, 1955. Reprint. Bideford, England: Supreme, 1973.

———. *This Is Magic: Secrets of the Conjurer's Craft*. London: Arco, 1958. Reprint. New York: Citadel Press, n.d.

Dhotel, Jules. *Magic with Small Apparatus*. Trans. from French by Paul Fleming. Berkeley Heights, N.J.: Fleming, 1947.

Doerflinger, William. *The Magic Catalogue: A Guide to the Wonderful World of Magic*. New York: E. P. Dutton, 1977.

Dornfeld, Werner C. (Dorny). *Trix and Chatter. A Novelty-serio-comic-magic-ologue*. Chicago: Arthur P. Felsman, 1921.

Downs, T[homas] Nelson. *The Art of Magic*. Ed. John Northern Hilliard. Buffalo, N.Y.: Downs-Edward, 1909. Reprinted with a new introduction by Charles R. Reynolds. New York: Dover, 1980.

Dunninger, Joseph. *Dunninger's Complete Encyclopedia of Magic*. New York: Lyle Stuart, 1967.

———. *Dunninger's Secrets*. As told to Walter Gibson. Secaucus N.J.: Lyle Stuart, 1974.

———. *Houdini's Spirit Exposés and Dunninger's Psychical Investigations: Spirit Ex-*

posés from Houdini's Own Manuscripts, Records, and Photographs. Ed. J. H. Kraus. New York: Experimenter, 1928.

———. *Inside the Medium's Cabinet.* New York: David Kemp, 1935.

———. *100 Houdini Tricks You Can Do.* New York: Arco, 1954. Reissued 1975.

Edmonds, I. G. *The Magic Brothers, Carl and Alexander Herrmann.* New York: Elsevier/Nelson Books, 1979.

———. *The Magic Makers: Magic and the Men Who Made It.* Nashville, Tenn.: T. Nelson, 1976.

———. *The Magic Man: The Life of Robert-Houdin.* Nashville, Tenn.: T. Nelson, 1972.

Edwards, Anne. *The Great Houdini.* New York: Putnam, 1977.

Endless Amusement: A Collection of Upwards of 400 Entertaining and Astonishing Experiments. London: 1818. 1st American (2nd) ed. Philadelphia: M. Carey and Sons, 1821.

Erdnase, S. W. (E. S. Andrews). *The Expert at the Card Table.* Las Vegas: Gambler's Book Club, 1967. Originally published under the title *Artifice, Ruse and Subterfuge at the Card Table.* Wilmette, Ill.: Frederick Drake, 1902.

Ernst, Bernard M. L., and Hereward Carrington. *Houdini and Conan Doyle: The Story of a Strange Friendship.* New York: Boni, 1932.

Ernst, John. *Escape King: The Story of Harry Houdini.* Englewood Cliffs, N.J.: Prentice-Hall, 1975.

Evans, Henry Ridgeley. *Adventures in Magic.* New York: Leo Rullman, 1921.

———. *Edgar Allen Poe and Baron von Kempelen's Chess-Playing Automaton.* Kenton, Ohio: International Brotherhood of Magicians, 1939.

———. *History of Conjuring and Magic.* Rev. ed. Kenton, Ohio: William W. Durbin, 1930.

———. *Hours with Ghosts.* Chicago: Laird and Lee, 1897.

———. *Magic and Its Professors.* New York: Routledge, 1902.

———. *A Master of Modern Magic: The Life and Adventures of Robert-Houdin.* New York: Macoy, 1932.

———. *The Old and the New Magic.* 2nd ed. Chicago: Open Court, 1909.

———. *Some Rare Old Books on Conjuring and Magic of the Sixteenth, the Seventeenth and the Eighteenth Century.* Kenton, Ohio: International Brotherhood of Magicians, 1943.

Falk, Lee, and Phil Davis. *Mandrake the Magician: Mandrake in Hollywood.* Franklin Square, N.Y.: Nostalgia Press, 1970.

Findlay, J. B. *Collectors Annuals.* Shanklin, Isle of Wight: Privately printed, 1949–1954. *Ninth Collectors Annual,* 1975.

———. *Conjurers, Coins and Medals.* Shanklin, Isle of Wight: Privately printed, 1964.

———. *International Guide to Posters and Playbills.* Shanklin, Isle of Wight: Privately printed, 1972.

———. *Magical Bibliographies: A Guide.* Shanklin, Isle of Wight: Privately printed, 1953.

Findlay, J. B., and Thomas A. Sawyer. *Professor Hoffmann: A Study.* Santa Ana, Calif. 92701: Privately printed, 521 S. Lyon Street, No. 105, 1977.

Fischer, Ottokar. *Illustrated Magic.* Trans. and ed. Fulton Oursler and J. B. Mussey;

intro. Fulton Oursler. New York: Macmillan, 1931. A translation of *Das Wunderbuch der Zauberkunst.* Stuttgart: Perthes, 1929.

————. *J. N. Hofzinser's Card Conjuring.* Trans. and ed. with notes by S. H. Sharpe. London: Magic Wand, 1931. A translation of *J. N. Hofzinser Kartenkünste.* Vienna and Leipzig: Jahoda and Siegel, 1910.

————. *The Magic of J. N. Hofzinser.* Trans. Richard Hatch. Omaha, Nebr. 68102: Walter B. Graham, 1612 California Street, 1986. A translation of *Johann Nepomuk Hofzinser Zauberkünste.* Berlin: Marvelli, 1942.

Fisher, John. *Body Magic.* Briarcliff Manor, N.Y.: Stein and Day, 1979.

Fitzkee, Dariel (Dariel Fitzroy). *Magic by Misdirection.* St. Rafael, Calif.: St. Raphael House, 1945. Reprint. Oakland, Calif: Magic, 1978.

Fitzsimons, Raymund. *Death and the Magician: The Mystery of Houdini.* New York: Atheneum, 1981.

Fleming, Paul (Paul Fleming Gemmill). *The Paul Fleming Book Reviews.* 3 vols. Berkeley Heights, N.J.: Fleming Book Co., 1944, 1946; Oakland, Calif.: Magic, 1979.

Foster, Neil. *The Great Blackstone: World's Greatest Magician and His "Show of 1001 Wonders."* Colon, Mich.: Abbott's Magic Mfg., 1970.

Frank, Gary R. *Chung Ling Soo: The Man behind the Legend!* Calgary, Canada: Micky Hades, 1987.

Frost, Thomas. *The Lives of the Conjurers.* London: Tinsley Brothers, 1874. Reprint. Detroit: Singing Tree Press, 1970; Ann Arbor: Plutarch Press, 1971 [facsimile of 1881 ed.]; New York: Gordon Press, n. d.; New York: Magico Magazine, 1986.

Fuller, Uriah (Martin Gardner). *Confessions of a Psychic.* Teaneck, N.J. 07666: Karl Fulves, Box 433, 1975.

————. *Further Confessions of a Psychic.* Teaneck, N.J.: Karl Fulves, 1980.

Fulves, Karl. *The Best of Slydini . . . and More.* New York: Tannen, 1976.

Furst, Arnold. *Famous Magicians of the World.* Oakland, Calif: Magic, 1957.

————. *Great Magic Shows.* Los Angeles: Genii, 1968.

Ganson, Lewis. *The Dai Vernon Book of Magic.* London: Harry Stanley, 1957; Bideford, England: Supreme, 1971.

————. *Dai Vernon's Tribute to Nate Leipzig.* London: Harry Stanley, 1963. Reprinted as *The Leipzig Book.* Bideford, England: Supreme, 1971.

Garcia, Frank. *Encyclopedia of Sponge Ball Magic.* New York: Privately printed, 1976.

Gardner, Martin. *Encyclopedia of Impromptu Magic.* Chicago: Magic, 1978.

Gaughan, John, and Jim Steinmeyer. *The Mystery of Psycho.* Pasadena, Calif. 91103: Magical Publications, 572 Prospect Blvd., 1987.

Gaultier, Camille. *Magic without Apparatus.* Trans. Jean Hugard. 2nd ed. Oakland, Calif.: Magic, 1980.

Gibson, Walter Brown. *Houdini's Escapes.* New York: Harcourt, Brace, 1930.

————. *Houdini's Escapes and Magic: Prepared from Houdini's Private Notebooks and Memoranda with the Assistance of Beatrice Houdini, Widow of Houdini, and Bernard M. L. Ernst, President of the Parent Assembly of the Society of American Magicians.* New York: Blue Ribbon Books, 1932. Reprinted with an introduction by Milbourne Christopher. New York: Funk and Wagnalls, 1976.

————. *The Original Houdini Scrapbook.* New York: Corwin/Sterling, 1976.

———. *Walter Gibson's Encyclopedia of Magic and Conjuring*. New York: Drake, 1976.

Gibson, Walter Brown, and Morris N. Young. *Houdini on Magic*. New York: Dover, 1953.

Gill, Robert. *Magic as a Performing Art: A Bibliography of Conjuring*. New York: R. R. Bowker, 1976.

Godwin, William. *Lives of the Necromancers; or, An Account of the Most Eminent Persons in Successive Ages, Who Have Claimed for Themselves, or to Whom Has Been Imputed by Others, the Exercise of Magical Power*. 2nd ed. New York: Harper and Brothers, 1847.

Goemann, W. E. *A History of the Art of Magic, Containing Anecdotes, Explanation of Tricks and a Sketch of the Life of the Three Herrmanns, Carl, Alexander and Leon*, by T. T. Timayenis. Rewritten by W. E. Goemann. New York: Minerva, 1901.

Goldin, Horace. *It's Fun to Be Fooled*. London: Stanley Paul, 1937.

Goldston, Will. *The Locked Books*. 3 vols. *Exclusive Magical Secrets; More Exclusive Magical Secrets*; and *Further Magical Secrets*. London: Magician, 1912–1927. *Exclusive Magical Secrets* reprinted New York: Dover, 1977.

———. *Sensational Tales of Mystery Men*. London: Goldston, 1929.

———. *Tricks That Mystify*. London: Will Goldston, (1934).

———. *Who's Who in Magic*. London: Will Goldston, 1934.

Gordon, Gene. *Gene Gordon's Magical Legacy*. Lilburn, Ga. 30093: David Ginn, 4387 St. Michaels Drive, 1980.

Grabel, Lee. *The Magic and Illusions of Lee Grabel*. Palo Alto, Calif. 94302: Enchantus Productions, c/o Ormond McGill, P.O. Box 1103, 1986.

Grant, Maxwell (Walter B. Gibson). *Norgil: More Tales of Prestigitection*. New York: Mysterious Press, 1979.

———. *Norgil the Magician*. New York: Mysterious Press, 1977.

Gravatt, Glenn. *Thayer Catalog Instruction Sheets*. 4 vols. Ed. Theron Fox. Oakland, Calif.: Magic, 1979–1981.

Green, Jonathan H. *Gambling Unmarked! or, The Personal Experience of J. H. Green, The Reformed Gambler: Designed as a Warning to the Young Men of This Country*. Philadelphia: G.B. Zieber, 1847.

———. *Gambling Unmasked: or, the Personal Experience of the Reformed Gambler, J. H. Green, designed as a Warning to the Young Men of This Country*. New York: Burgess, Stringer, 1844.

———. *The Reformed Gambler: or, The History of the Later Years of the Life of Jonathan H. Green (the "Reformed Gambler") to Which Is Added a Complete and Full Exposition of the Game of Thimbles; Diamond Cut Diamond or the Gentleman's Game . . .* Philadelphia: T. B. Peterson and Brothers, 1858.

Gresham, William Lindsay. *Houdini, the Man Who Walked Through Walls*. New York: Holt, Rinehart, and Winston, 1959. Reprint. Macfadden-Bartell, 1961.

Hagy, James. *The One Young*. Shaker Heights, Ohio 44120: Privately Printed, 17019 Fernwood Road, 1986.

Hall, Trevor H. *A Bibliography of Books on Conjuring in English from 1580 to 1850*. Minneapolis: Carl Waring Jones, 1957.

———. *Old Conjuring Books, a Bibliographical and Historical Study.* London: Duckworth, 1972.

Hanson, Herman, and John U. Zweers. *The Magic Man.* Cincinnati: Haines House of Cards, 1974.

Harbin, Robert (Ned Williams). *The Magic of Robert Harbin.* Ed. Peter Warlock (Alec Bell). N.p.: Privately printed, 1970.

Hatton, Henry, and Adrian Plate. *Magicians' Tricks: How They Are Done.* New York: Century, 1910.

Hay, Henry (June Barrows Mussey), ed. *Cyclopedia of Magic.* Philadelphia: McKay, 1949. Reprint. New York: Dover, 1975.

Henning, Doug, with Charles Reynolds. *Houdini—His Legend and His Magic.* New York: Times Books, 1977.

Hermann, Carl. *Herrmann and Ancient and Modern Magic with a Biographical Sketch of the Great Prestidigitateur. A Collection of Anecdotes and Notices of the Press, and a Collection of Amusing Trials and Experiments in Parlor Magic by Professor Herrmann.* New York: Privately printed, 1866.

———. *Hermann, First Prestidigitateur for the Great European Theatres. . . .* New York: Wynkoop, Hallenbeck, and Thomas, 1861.

Hertz, Carl. *A Modern Mystery Merchant: The Trials, Tricks, and Travels of Carl Hertz, the Famous American: Illusionist.* London: Hutchinson, 1924.

Heyl, Edgar. *Conjuring Books, 1580 to 1850.* Baltimore: Privately printed, 1963.

Hill, Edward. *Magic Collectors Information Consortium,* No. 1. Harmony, R.I. 02829: MCIC, P.O. Box 30, 1986.

Hilliard, John Northern. *Greater Magic.* Minneapolis: Carl Waring Jones, 1938.

Hingston, Edward P[eron]. *The Genial Showman, Being the Reminiscences of the Life of Artemus Ward* [Charles Farrar Browne]. New York: Harper and Brothers, 1870. Reprinted with an introduction by Walter Muir Whitehill. Barre, Mass.: Imprint Society, 1971.

Hoffmann, Professor (Angelo John Lewis). *Later Magic.* New York: E. P. Dutton, 1904. Reprint. New York: Dover, 1979.

———. *Modern Magic: A Practical Treatise on the Art of Conjuring.* London: George Routledge and Sons, 1876. Reprinted with a new introduction by Charles Reynolds. New York, 1978.

———. *More Magic.* London: Routledge, 1890.

Holden, Max. *Programmes of Famous Magicians.* New York: Privately printed, 1937. Reprint. Chicago: Magic, 1968.

Hopkins, Albert A., comp. and ed. *Magic, Stage Illusions and Scientific Diversions, including Trick Photography.* With an introduction and bibliography by Henry Ridgely Evans. New York: Munn, 1897. Many reprint editions: Benjamin Blom; Arno Press; Dover; Peter Smith.

Houdini, Harry (Erich Weiss). *The Adventurous Life of a Versatile Artist.* New York: Clarence Wright, 1900–1922. Numerous editions, 16 to 64 pp.

———. *Houdini, Souvenir Program.* New York: Al. Greenstone, 1925. Facsimile reprint. Pomeroy, Ohio: Lee Jacobs, 1979.

———. *A Magician among the Spirits.* New York: Harper and Row, 1924. Reprint. New York: Arno Press, 1972.

———. *The Marvelous Adventures of Houdini, the Justly Celebrated Elusive American.* Brooklyn: Privately printed, 1917.

———. *Miracle Mongers and Their Methods*. New York: E. P. Dutton, 1920. Reprinted with Foreword by the Amazing Randi. Buffalo, N.Y.: Prometheus Books, 1981.

———. *The Unmasking of Robert-Houdin*. New York: Publishers Printing, 1908. *Together with a Treatise on Handcuff Secrets*. London: George Routledge and Sons, 1909. Reprint. New York: Magico Magazine, [1978].

Hugard, Jean (John Gerard Rodney Boyce). *Houdini's "Unmasking": Fact vs Fiction*. With an Introduction and Supplementary Chapter by Milbourne Christopher. Printed in book form, with a title page date 1957, as part of *Hugard's Magic Monthly*, June 1957–January 1959.

———, ed. *Encyclopedia of Card Tricks*. New York: Max Holden, 1937. Reprint. New York: Dover, 1974.

Hugard, Jean, and Frederick Braue. *Expert Card Technique*. 3rd ed. London: Faber, 1950.

Hull, Burling "Volta." *The Edison of Magic and His Incredible Creations*. With a biography by Samuel Patrick Smith. Tavares, Fla. 32778: Samuel and Lee Smith, P.O. Box 769, 1977.

———. *The Encyclopedic Dictionary of Mentalism*. 2 vols. 3rd ed. Calgary, Canada: Micky Hades, 1973.

Hurst, Lulu (The Georgia Wonder). *Lulu Hurst (The Georgia Wonder) Writes Her Autobiography, and for the First Time Explains and Demonstrates the Great Secret of her Marvellous Power*. Rome, Ga.: Lulu Hurst Book, 1897.

James, Stewart, comp. *Abbott's Encyclopedia of Rope Tricks*. Vol. 1: Colon, Mich.: Abbott's Magic Mfg., 1941. Reprint. New York: Dover, 1975. Vol. 2: Colon, Mich.: Abbott's Magic Mfg, 1962.

Jarrett, Guy. *Guy Jarrett's 1936 Jarrett Magic and Stagecraft, Technical*. With additional material by Jim Steinmeyer. Chicago: Magic, 1981.

Jay, Ricky. *Learned Pigs and Fireproof Women*. New York: Villard Books, 1986.

Joys, Joanne. "Photomagic: The Irving Desfor Collection 1938–1978." Unpublished page proofs, 484 pages.

Keene, M. Lamar. *The Psychic Mafia*. As told to Allen Spraggett. New York: Dell, 1976.

Kellar, Harry. *A Magician's Tour Up and Down and Round About the Earth. Being the Life and Adventures of the American Nostradamus, Harry Kellar*. Ed. by His Faithful "Familiar", "Satan", Junior. Chicago: R. R. Donnelley and Sons, 1886. Reprint. New York: Magico Magazine, 1984.

Kellock, Harold. *Houdini, His Life-Story. By Harold Kellock from the Recollections and Documents of Beatrice Houdini*. New York: Harcourt, Brace, 1928.

Kendall, Lace. *Houdini: Master of Escape*. Philadelphia: Macrae Smith, 1960.

Kinney, Arthur F. *Rogues, Vagabonds, and Sturdy Beggars*. Barre, Mass.: Imprint Society, 1973.

Kirby, E. T. *Ur-Drama: The Origins of Theatre*. New York: New York University Press, 1975.

Kirbye, George W. *Autobiography, or a Sketch of the Life and Adventures of George W. Kirbye, Professionally Known as a Ventriloquist, Magician, Equilibrist and Athlete. Giving Full Details of the Extraordinary Career and Romantic History from His Birth until the Present Time*. N. p.: Privately printed, [ca. 1861].

Koval, Frank. *Robert Heller: Music and Mystery*. Chadderton, Oldham OL9 9QX, England: Privately printed, 26 Thatch Leach, 1985.

Kraske, Robert. *Harry Houdini, Master of Magic*. Champaign, Ill.: Garrard, 1973.

Kreskin (George J. Kresge). *The Amazing World of Kreskin*. New York: Random House, 1973.

Kuethe, F. William, Jr. "A Conjuring Bibliography of Forcing Items." Supplements to *The Magic Cauldron*, February and March 1962, June 1965.

———. *Forcing Books and Book Tests*. Albo Classic Magic Supplement. Oakland, Calif. 94609: Classic Magic, 418 30th St., 1987.

———. "Magicians' Tokens and Related Items: An Illustrated Check-List, with Estimates of Values and Rarities." *TAMS Journal* 18 (October 1978), Part 2.

———. "Tokens and Coins." In *Still Further Classic Magic with Apparatus*, by Robert Albo, ed. Vol. 5 (N.p.: Privately printed, 1985).

Lamb, Geoffrey. "A Bibliography of Magical History: Books in English Relating to Conjuring History, 1580–1980." Published serially in *The Magic Circular* 77 (August 1983) through 79 (May 1985).

———. *Illustrated Magic Dictionary*. New York: Elsevier/Nelson Books, 1979.

Le Grand David (company). *Marco the Magi's Production of Le Grand David and His Own Spectacular Magic Company BIBLIOHISTORY: The First Ten Years, 1976–1986*. Beverly, Mass. 01915: White Horse Productions, 286 Cabot Street, 1988.

Levy, Ed, ed. *Richard Himber: The Man and His Magic*. New York: Magico Magazine, 1980.

Lorayne, Harry. *Close-Up Card Magic*. Ed. Louis Tannen with intro. Dai Vernon. New York: Tannen, 1962.

Lorraine, Sid. *Sid Lorraine's Latest Reference File*. Toronto, Canada M4C 3C8: Privately printed, 781 Coxwell Avenue, 1985.

Lund, Robert. *Blackstone . . . And Now a Word from Our Sponsor*. Southfield, Mich.: Woefully out of Tune with the Times Press, 1971.

———. "Robert Lund Reports" [on black magicians]. *Abracadabra*, 35 (June 1, 1963), 323; 35 (June 8, 1963), 346–47; 35 (June 15, 1963), 359.

Lynn, H. S. (Hugh Simmons). *The Adventures of the Strange Man. With a Supplement showing "How It's Done."* London: Egyptian Hall, 1882.

———. *Biographical Sketch of Simmons, the Miraculous Illusionist from the Opera Houses and Theatres of London, the Cities and Courts of Continental Europe, Australia and China, and the Courts of the Tycoon of Mikadi of Japan, Whose Astonishing Illusions Are Performed Entirely without Apparatus or Confederates, Now on a Tour through the United States Previous to his Departure for Europe. . . .* Boston: J. H. and F. F. Farwell Printing Office, [ca. 1871].

McArdle, John. *International Dictionary of Magitain*. Newtown, Conn.: Privately printed, 1963.

McKinven, John A. *Roltair: Genius of Illusions*. Lake Forest, Ill. 60045: Privately printed, 306 Rose Terrace, 1980.

McNeil, Barbara, and Miranda Herbert eds. *Performing Arts Biography Master Index: A Consolidated Guide to Over 270,000 Biographical Sketches of Persons Living and Dead, As They Appear in Over 100 of the Principal Biographical*

Dictionaries Devoted to the Performing Arts. 2nd ed. Detroit: Gale Research, 1982.

Magic Circle. *A Catalogue of the Reference Library and the Lending Library.* Comp. Colin Donister. London: Magic Circle, 1952.

Magic Directory, 1982–1983. Madison, Wis.: Monson Productions, 1982.

"Magicians: Dozen Negroes Practice Hocus-Pocus Art in Tradition of Vaudeville Heyday." *Ebony* (December 1949), 72–76.

Magus, Jim. "A History of Blacks in Magic." Published serially in *The Linking Ring,* 63 (August 1983) through 64 (June 1984).

Manning, William. *Recollections of Robert-Houdin.* London: Chiswick Press, 1891.

Marshall, Frances. *My First Fifty Years.* Chicago: Magic, 1981.

———, comp. *Those Beautiful Dames.* Chicago: Magic, 1984.

Marshall, Frances, and Jay Marshall (and a panel of experts). *The Success Book.* 4 vols. Chicago: Magic, 1973–1984.

Maskelyne, John Nevil. *"Sharps and Flats," a Complete Revelation of the Secrets of Cheating at Games of Chance and Skill.* London: Longmans, Green, 1894. Reprint. Las Vegas: Gambler's Book Club, 1971.

Maskelyne, Nevil. *Maskelyne on the Performance of Magic.* Reprint of Part I ("The Art of Magic") of *Our Magic,* 1911 ed. [see next entry]. New York: Dover, 1976.

Maskelyne, Nevil, and David Devant (David Wighton). *Our Magic.* 2nd ed. Berkeley Heights, N.J.: Fleming, 1946. Reprint. Bideford, England: Supreme, 1971.

Meyer, Bernard C. *Houdini: A Mind in Chains.* New York: E. P. Dutton, 1976.

Meyer, David. *Legerdemain, or Sleight of Hand.* Facsimile reproduction with plates from the 3rd ed. (1797) of the *Encyclopaedia Britannica,* with an essay on its origins and guide to its appearances in all editions. Glenwood, Ill. 60425: Meyerbooks, P.O. Box 427, 1986.

———, comp. *The Wizard Exposed.* Intro. and bibliographic notes by Edwin A. Dawes. Glenwood, Ill.: Meyerbooks, 1987.

Moulton, H. J. *Houdini's History of Magic in Boston 1792–1915.* Glenwood, Ill.: Meyerbooks, 1983.

Mulholland, John. *Beware Familiar Spirits.* 1938. Reprint. New York: Arno Press, 1975. Reprinted with an introduction by Martin Gardner. New York: Scribner's, 1979.

———. *John Mulholland's Story of Magic.* New York: Loring and Mussey, 1935.

———. *Quicker Than the Eye. The Magic and Magicians of the World.* Indianapolis: Bobbs-Merrill, 1932.

Munroe, Albert F., and Robert Lund. "Magic in Detroit, 1837–1887." *Journal of Magic History* 2 (April 1980), 3–16.

Neil, C[harles] Lang. *The Modern Conjurer and Drawing-Room Entertainer.* 3rd ed. London: C. Arthur Pearson, 1922.

Nelson, Robert. *The Last Book of Nelson.* Kernersville, N.C. 27284: Nelson Enterprises, 470 Forest Lake Circle, 1970.

Nightingale, The Mystifier (Frank). *Magic for Magicians.* Los Angeles, Calif.: Knight, 1964.

Oehler, Andrew. *The Life, Adventures and Unparalleled Sufferings of Andrew Oehler Containing the Account of His Travels through France, Italy, the East and West*

Indies, and Part of the United States; His Imprisonment in France, Germany and Spain; and the Latitude, Soil, Climate, Productions, Manners and Customs of the Different Countries. Written by Himself. Trenton, N.J.: D. Fenton, 1811.

Olson, Robert E. *Carl Rosini: His Life and Magic.* Chicago: Magic, 1966.

———. *Illusion Builder to Fu Manchu.* Charlotte, N.C. 28205: Morris Costumes, 3108 Monroe Road, 1986.

———. *The World's Greatest Magician: A Tribute to Howard Thurston.* Calgary, Canada: Micky Hades, 1981.

Pecor, Charles J. *The Magician on the American Stage 1752–1874.* Washington, D.C.: Emerson and West, 1977.

Penzler, Otto, ed. *Whodunit? Houdini? Thirteen Tales of Magic, Murder, Mystery.* New York: Harper and Row, 1976.

Performing Arts Books 1876–1981. Including an International Index of Current Serial Publications. New York: R. R. Bowker, 1981.

Pinchbeck, William. *The Expositor; or, Many Mysteries Unravelled. Delineated in a Series of Letters, between a Friend and His Correspondent. Comprising the Learned Pig, Invisible Lady and Accoustic Temple, Philosophical Swan, Penetrating Spy Glasses, Optical and Magnetic, and Various Other Curiosities on Similar Principles: Also, a Few of the Most Wonderful Feats as Performed by the Art of Legerdemain: With Some Reflections on Ventriloquism.* Boston: Privately printed, 1805.

Potter, Jack. *The Master Index to Magic in Print.* 14 vols. Calgary, Canada: Micky Hades, 1967–75.

Price, David. *Magic: A Pictorial History of Conjurers in the Theater.* New York: Cornwall Books, 1985.

Price, Harry. *Short-Title Catalogue of Works on Psychical Research . . . Legerdemain and Other Methods of Deception . . . from C. 1450–1929.* London: National Laboratory of Psychical Research, 1929. *Supplement, 1472–Present Day.* London: University of London Council for Psychical Investigation, 1935.

Rand, Luke P. *A Sketch of the History of the Davenport Boys, Their Mediumship, Journeyings, and the Manifestations, and Tests Given in their Presence by the Spirits, A Full Account of the Arrest and Trials of L. P. Rand and the Davenport Mediums, at Mexico, and at Phoenix—Their Incarceration, and the Deliverance of L. P. Rand from His Prison by the Angels . . .* Oswego, N.Y.: T. P. Ottaway, 1859.

Randi, The Amazing (James Randall Zwinge). *Flim-Flam!* New York: Lippincott and Crowell, 1980. Reprint. Buffalo: Prometheus Books, 1982.

———. *The Magic of Uri Geller.* New York: Ballantine Books, 1975.

———. *The Truth about Uri Geller.* Rev. ed. Buffalo, N.Y.: Prometheus Books, 1982.

Randi, the Amazing (James Randall Zwinge), and Bert Randolph Sugar. *Houdini: His Life and Art.* New York: Grosset and Dunlap, 1976.

Rapp, Augustus. *The Life and Times of Augustus Rapp the Small Town Showman.* Chicago: Jay Marshall for Ireland Magic, 1959.

Rauscher, William V. *ESP or Trickery? The Problem of Mentalism within the World of Magic.* Woodbury, N.J. 08096: Privately printed, 62 Delaware St., 1984.

———. *Marco the Magi: Wise Man of Magic.* Woodbury, N.J.: Privately printed, 1984.

————. *Monarch of Magic: The Story of Servais LeRoy*. Woodbury, N.J.: Privately printed, 1984.

————. *The Wand: In Story and Symbol*. Woodbury, N.J.: Privately printed, 1984.

Rawson, Clayton. *Death from a Top Hat* (1938); *The Footprints on the Ceiling* (1939); *The Headless Lady* (1940); *No Coffin for the Corpse* (1942). Reprint. New York: Collier Books, 1962–1963.

Reynolds, Charles, and Regina Reynolds. *100 Years of Magic Posters*. New York: Darien House, 1975.

Rice, Harold R. *Rice's Encyclopedia of Silk Magic*. 3 vols. Cincinnati: Silk King Studios, 1948–1962.

R[id], S[amuel]. *The Art of Jugling or Legerdemaine. Wherein Is Deciphered, All the Conveyances of Legerdemaine and Jugling, How They Are Effected, & Wherin They Chiefly Consist.* . . . London, 1612. Facsimile reprint. Norwood, N.J.: Walter J. Johnson, 1974. Facsimile reprint of 1614 ed. New York: John McArdle, 1952.

Robert-Houdin, Jean Eugène. *King of Conjurers: Memoirs of Robert-Houdin*. A translation of *Confidences d'un prestidigitateur* (Blois, 1858) by Lascelles Wraxall (1859). With a new introduction and notes by Milbourne Christopher. New York: Dover, 1964.

————. *The Secrets of Conjuring and Magic*. Trans. Professor Hoffmann (Angelo John Lewis). New York: George Routledge and Sons, 1878.

Robinson, Ben, with Larry White. *Twelve Have Died*. Ed. E. A. Dawes and J. N. Booth. Watertown, Mass. 02172: Magic Art Book Co., 137 Spring St., 1986.

Sachs, Edwin T. *Sleight-of-Hand*. 5th ed. Ed. Paul Fleming. Berkeley Heights, N.J.: Fleming Book Co., 1953. Reprint. New York: Dover, 1980.

Sardina, Maurice. *Where Houdini Was Wrong*. Trans. and ed. with notes by Victor Farelli. London: George Armstrong, 1950.

Sawyer, Thomas A. *The Hoffmann Collector: The First Ten Years*. Santa Ana, Calif.: Privately printed, 1986.

————. *Professor Hoffmann: A Bibliography*. Santa Ana, Calif.: Privately printed, 1983.

————. *Stanley Collins: Society Entertainer and Magic Collector*. Balboa Island, Calif.: Abracadabra Press, 1984.

Scarne, John (Orlando Scarnecchia). *The Amazing World of John Scarne: A Personal History*. New York: Crown, 1957.

Scot, Reginald. *The Discoverie of Witchcraft*. London, 1584. Facsimile reprint, English Experience series No. 299. Norwood, N.J. 07648: Walter J. Johnson, 355 Chestnut Street, 1971. Modern reprint. New York: Dover, 1972.

Severn, William. *Bill Severn's Guide to Magic as a Hobby*. New York: David McKay, 1979.

Sharpe, Samuel H. *Conjurers' Optical Secrets*. Calgary, Canada: Micky Hades, 1986.

————. *Introducing Houdini versus Robert-Houdin: The Whole Truth*. Reighton, England: Privately printed, 1955.

————. *The Magic Play*. Chicago: Magic, 1976.

————. *Salutations to Robert-Houdin*. Calgary, Canada: Micky Hades, 1983.

————. *Words on Wonder*. Southfield, Mich. 48034: Wonder Publications, 23500 Coventry Woods Lane, 1984.

Shevlin, Clay H. *Historians' Guide to Conjuring*. San Leandro, Calif. 94578: Conjuring Historical Society, P.O. Box 3186, 1981.

Smith, George. *Memoirs and Anecdotes of Mr. Love, the Polyphonist: to Which Is Added an Explanation of the Phenomenon of Polyphony . . . Principally Selected and Abridged from the Octavo Volume Published in London in 1834. . . .* Boston: Privately printed, 1850.

Stanyon, Ellis. "A Bibliography of Conjuring." Published serially in *Magic* 1 (October 1901) through 4 (October 1903), and 10 (December 1909) through 11 (April 1911).

―――. *A Bibliography of Conjuring and Kindred Arts*. London: Privately printed, 1899. Reprinted in C. Lang Neil, *The Modern Conjurer and Drawing-Room Entertainer*. London: C. Arthur Pearson, 1903; and 2nd ed., 1911 (omitted from 3rd ed., 1922).

Starke, George, et al., eds. *Stars of Magic*. New York: Louis Tannen, 1961.

Stebbins, Robert A. *The Magician*. Toronto: Irwin, 1984.

Sukenick, Lynn. *Houdini. Yes!* Capra Chapbook series, No. 14. Santa Barbara, Calif.: Capra Press, 1973.

Tannen, Louis, ed. *Stars of Magic*. New York: Tannen, 1961.

Tarbell, Harlan. *The Tarbell Course in Magic*. 7 vols. New York: Tanners, 1941–1972.

Taylor, E. Cooper, III. *A Few Moments in the Career of Prof. E. Cooper Taylor 1852–1927*. Rev. ed. Tuckahoe, N.Y. 10707: Privately printed, 95 Lake Avenue, 1977.

Taylor, Tony. *Spotlight on 101 Great Magic Acts*. Calgary, Canada: Micky Hades, 1964.

Temple, Phil, comp. *Thurston-Dante Letter Set*. San Rafael, Calif. 94913: Privately printed, P.O. Box 12855, 1981.

Thornton, Larry. *Video Magic Index*. Calgary, Alberta T2B OS3, Canada: Privately printed, 3036–29 A. St., S.E., 1984.

Thurston, Grace. *Thurston Scrapbook, Being the Text of the MS. Titled "My Magic Husband Thurston the Great" by Grace Thurston*. Novato, Calif. 94947: Phil Temple, 1041 Third St., No. 4, 1985.

Thurston, Howard. *My Life of Magic*. Philadelphia: Dorrance, 1929.

Timayenis, T[homas] T[elemachus]. *A History of the Art of Magic, Containing Anecdotes, Explanation of Tricks, and a Sketch of the Life of Alexander Herrmann*. New York: J. J. Little, 1888.

Toole-Stott, Raymond. *A Bibliography of English Conjuring, 1581–1876*. Derby DE1 1LZ, England: Harpur and Sons of Derby, Rowditch Printing Works, 1976.

―――. *A Bibliography of English Conjuring, 1569–1876*. Vol. 2. Derby, England: Harpur and Sons of Derby, 1978.

Vernon, Dai. *Malini and His Magic*. Ed. Lewis Ganson. London: Harry Stanley, 1963. Reprint. Bideford, England: Supreme, 1973.

Vintus, Len. *Magicians of the World. Directory: Canada and U.S.A. Section*. Winnipeg, Man., Canada R2C 2M2: Privately printed, 604 Bond Street, 1978.

Warlock, Peter (Alec Bell). *Pseudonyms*. Wallington, Surrey SM6 9RH, England: Privately printed, 24 Wordsworth Road, 1980.

————. *Walter Jeans Illusioneer*. Magical Pro-Files series. Pasadena, Calif. 91103: Magical Publications, 572 Prospect Blvd., 1986.

Warren, David. *The Great Escaper*. Milwaukee: Raintree, 1979.

Waters, T. A. *The Encyclopedia of Magic and Magicians*. New York: Facts on File, 1988.

Webb, James, ed. *The Mediums and the Conjurers*. Reprint of *Modern Spiritualism*, by J. N. Maskelyne, first published in 1876 by F. Warne, London; of *Exposé of the Davenport Brothers*, by Herr Dobler, first printed in 1869 by D. and J. Allen, Belfast; and of *Spirit-Mediums and Conjurors*, by G. Sexton, first published in 1873 by J. Burns, London. New York: Arno Press, 1976.

Weibel, Richard J. *Conjuring Psychology*. New York: Magico Magazine, 1980.

Wels, Byron G. *The Great Illusions of Magic*. 2 vols. New York: Tannen, 1977.

White, Florence Meiman. *Escape! The Life of Harry Houdini*. New York: J. Messner, 1979.

Williams, Beryl, and Samuel Epstein. *The Great Houdini, Magician Extraordinary*. New York: J. Messner, 1950.

Willmann, Carl. *Die moderne Salon-Magie*. 2nd ed. Hamburg: Bartl, 1926.

Wilmeth, Don B. *American and English Popular Entertainment: A Guide to Information Sources*. Detroit: Gale Research, 1980.

Wilson, Mark. *Mark Wilson Course in Magic*. North Hollywood, Calif.: Mark Wilson Course in Magic, 1975.

Winder, Roland. *Checklist of the Older Books on Conjuring in the Library of Roland Winder as at December 1966*. Leeds, England: Privately printed, 1966.

Witt, Wittus (Hans-Günter Witt). *International Magic Yellow Pages*. 5th ed. 1987. Haus Vogelsang, Moylandstr. 23, Postfach 13 07 49, D—4150 Krefeld 1, West Germany.

————. *Zauberkästen*. Munich: Hugendubel Verlag, 1987.

Worthington, Thomas C. *Recollections of Howard Thurston, Conjurer, Illusionist, and Author*. Intro. H. R. Evans. Baltimore: Privately printed, 1938.

Wyman, John. *Jokes and Anecdotes of Wyman, the Magician and Ventriloquist*. Burlington, N.J.: Privately printed, 1871.

Young, Morris N. *Bibliography of Memory*. Philadelphia: Chilton, 1961.

Zancig, Julius (Julius Jensen). *Two Minds with but a Single Thought*. N.p.: Paul Naumann, 1907.

Periodicals

A.B.C. of Magic Sets. Düsseldorf, 1980– .

Abracadabra. Birmingham, England, 1946– .

Backstage with Magigals. Chicago, 1952– .

Genii. Los Angeles, 1936– .

The Hoffman Collector. Santa Ana, Calif., 1974– .

Inside Magic. Los Alamitos, Calif., 1985– .

Journal of Magic History. Toledo, Ohio, 1979– .

The Linking Ring. Winnipeg, 1922– .

Magic. London, 1900–1920.

The Magic Cauldron. Glen Burnie, Md., 1962–1977; New Series, 1977– .

The Magic Circular. London, 1906– .

Magic Collectors Information Consortium. Harmony, R.I., 1986– .
The Magic Manuscript. Newport Beach, Calif., 1979– .
Magicoal. New York, 1950–52; New Series, Milwaukee, 1959– .
Magic Sounds. Mexico City, 1973–1981.
Magic Sounds and Sights. Mexico City, 1981– .
The Magic Wand. London, 1910–1957.
M-U-M. New York, 1911–1927; New Series, New York, 1951– .
The New Tops. Colon, Mich., 1961– .

MEDICINE AND PHYSICIANS

Anne Hudson Jones

The aura of power surrounding medicine and its practitioners has made physicians favorite subjects of dramatists, satirists, novelists, and other artists from ancient times to the present. Traditionally, physicians have been portrayed as quacks or demigods, reflecting society's ambivalent attitude toward their special status. Although the presentation of medicine and the physician in American popular culture has a rich European heritage, artists have modified and added to that heritage in response both to medicine's extraordinary development in the past century and to America's own changing social concerns.

The importance in the real world of popular portrayals of medicine and the physician can be demonstrated by reactions to such television shows as *Medic*, *Marcus Welby, M.D.*, and *Quincy, M.E.* In 1955 *Medic* was receiving so many letters from its viewers about various diseases and medical problems that to answer all of them, the Los Angeles County Medical Association began forwarding the letters to the medical associations of the correspondents' respective states.[1] At the height of its popularity, *Marcus Welby, M.D.* elicited approximately 5,000 letters a week from people who wrote Welby to ask for his help in dealing with their ills.[2] Not only the lay public responded to the show: Robert Young was invited to address many medical groups, among them the American Academy of Family Physicians and the graduating class of the University of Michigan Medical School. The show received more than thirty awards from medical groups, including one from the American Medical Association (AMA) for special achievement.[3] A more recent example of the impact such shows can have is the March 4, 1981, *Quincy, M.E.* episode about Tourette's syndrome, which is widely credited with having helped pass orphan drug legislation in this country.[4]

Physicians have been interested in, and concerned about, their public image at least since 1955, when the AMA set up the Physicians Advisory Committee (PAC) on Television, Radio and Motion Pictures to help maintain medical accuracy in public programming and to protect the image of the practicing physician.[5] In the early 1960s the Joint Committee on Mental Illness and Health recommended that American psychiatrists carefully consider their public image. One result of that recommendation was an article analyzing depictions of psychiatrists in popular fiction, which concluded that psychiatrists should indeed be concerned about their unfavorable portrayals.[6]

Despite the acknowledged importance popular beliefs about medicine and popular images of physicians have for both patients and practitioners, there has as yet been surprisingly little systematic study of medicine and the physician in American popular culture. Few book-length studies exist, but there are many articles, in widely scattered journals, about one aspect or another of the presentation of medicine and the physician in American literature, cartoons, medicine shows, film, radio, and television. This chapter provides a brief historical summary of those presentations and surveys the scholarly work done to date.

HISTORIC OUTLINE

In Western culture, medicine and the physician have been subjects of literature since ancient times. Early Greek and Roman dramatists, epigrammatists, and satirists frequently aimed barbs at physicians. The first works of prose fiction were popular romances and Milesian tales, which included physicians as minor characters.[7] In later British and European literature the physician became a stock character, ridiculed or portrayed as a quack. Chaucer's *Canterbury Tales*, Boccaccio's *Decameron*, and the commedia dell'arte provide early examples; the famous physicians in Moliére's plays follow.[8] The physician as a character taken seriously and portrayed sympathetically, however, did not begin to emerge until the nineteenth century, in the novels of Balzac's *Human Comedy*,[9] in Zola's *Doctor Pascal*, and in George Eliot's *Middlemarch*. This changed presentation of physicians in fiction seems to have resulted from advances in scientific knowledge, which gave physicians greater professional stature. British and European literature is rich in its use of the physician and medical themes and has supplied the material for several book-length studies.[10]

It is easier to trace the history of presentations of medicine and the physician in American literature than it is to decide which of those presentations constitute popular rather than high culture. In nineteenth-century American literature, for example, Nathaniel Hawthorne presents physician-scientists in many of his stories and novels, and Herman Melville satirizes surgeons in several of his works. Later in the century, the physician was portrayed sympathetically in novels of two physician-writers, Oliver Wendell Holmes and S. Weir Mitchell. Fictional women physicians appeared as major characters for the first time in the 1880s in novels by William Dean Howells, Sarah Orne Jewett, and Elizabeth Stuart Phelps Ward. Certainly the best-known physician-scientist of American literature is Sinclair Lewis' Martin Arrowsmith, who appeared in *Arrowsmith* in 1925. Throughout American literature, physician characters appear frequently and in works of such varied writers as Henry James, Ellen Glasgow, James Gould Cozzens, Robert Penn Warren, John Steinbeck, Katherine Anne Porter, Carson McCullers, William Carlos Williams, William Faulkner, and Walker Percy, to name only a few.

Among works of American popular literature dealing with medicine and the physician, none have had more long-lasting effects than the Dr. Kildare stories,

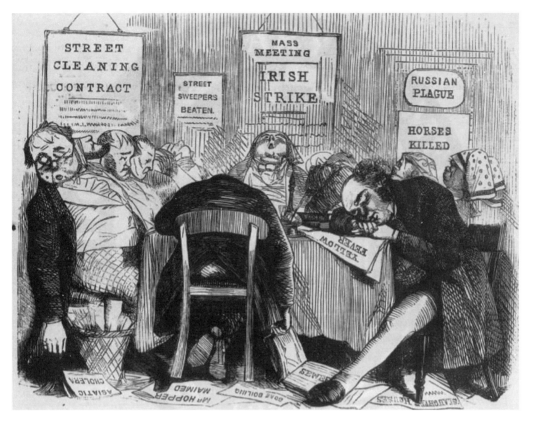

Cartoon of the New York City Board of Health that appeared in the August 5, 1865, issue of *Harper's Weekly*. Courtesy of the National Library of Medicine

written between 1936 and 1943 by Frederick Faust, under the pseudonym Max Brand. Sixteen movies, a weekly radio program, and two television series have been based on these books. Frank Slaughter's series of novels, many about physicians and medicine, now number more than fifty and have sold more than 50 million copies worldwide. His *Women in White* was the basis for a four-part television drama in 1979. Richard Hooker's *M*A*S*H* novels came out in the 1960s, and Robin Cook's first and best-known medical thriller, *Coma*, appeared in 1977. Cook's output continued with such titles as *Brain, Fever, Godplayer, Mindbend*, and *Outbreak*. Billed as a medical *Catch-22*, Samuel Shem's *The House of God*, published in 1978, is still an underground classic on medical school campuses. Two popular genres, detective fiction and science fiction, use physicians in fairly predictable ways. Physicians' training in observation and diagnosis makes them naturals for detective work. Television's *Quincy, M.E.* is another version of the physician-detective, whose line began with Sir Arthur Conan Doyle's Sherlock Holmes, modeled on the surgeon Dr. Joseph Bell, and Dr. Watson. In science fiction, the role of the physician has usually been combined with that of the research scientist, producing almost a stock character, familiar from the time of Mary Shelley's *Frankenstein* in 1816.

With the development of psychiatry and the spread of its influence in American culture, the psychiatrist has become a favorite character in literature and appears with increasing frequency beginning in the 1930s, in works by "standard" authors such as F. Scott Fitzgerald, Eugene O'Neill, Tennessee Williams, and Arthur Miller, as well as in works by "popular" authors such as Mary Jane Ward, Theodore Isaac Rubin, and Elliott Baker. At least one recognizable subgenre of popular fiction has resulted, derived from a combination of the novel, autobiography, and psychological case history. The outstanding example of this subgenre is Joanne Greenberg's *I Never Promised You a Rose Garden*, published under the pseudonym Hannah Green in 1964. Metaphors of madness and hospital settings, especially mental asylums, abound in modern popular literature. The institutional environment serves as a microcosm of society as a whole, and the insane are often depicted as being more sane than their medical keepers. Ken Kesey's *One Flew over the Cuckoo's Nest*, published in 1962, is one of the best-known examples. Our fascination with psychiatrists continues: they have appeared as important characters in a number of recent Broadway plays, for example *Equus* (1974), *Whose Life Is It Anyway?* (1979), *Nuts* (1980), *Duet for One* (1981), and *Agnes of God* (1982).

Other recent plays on Broadway reflect a new popular concern with prolonged illness and death and dying. In one year, 1979, Brian Clark's *Whose Life Is It Anyway?*, Bernard Pomerance's *The Elephant Man*, Arthur Kopit's *Wings*, and Steve Carter's *Nevis Mountain Dew* were all playing on Broadway, and Michael Cristofer's *The Shadow Box* was touring the country. Like Sam Shepard's *Inacoma*, based on the Karen Quinlan case, all these plays are responses to possibilities created by sophisticated medical technology. Larry Kramer's *The Normal Heart* and William M. Hoffman's *As Is* were the first plays about AIDS to be produced on Broadway, both in 1985. There will probably be others, as long as the epidemic continues unabated.

European medical caricature dates back to the Renaissance, but medical caricature did not develop in the United States until the Civil War period. The first medical cartoon published in this country has been identified as "The Quarantine Question," which appeared in *Harper's Weekly* in 1858. Medical cartoons were published in the 1880s in early American magazines such as *Puck* and *Life*, and gradually they began to appear routinely in most major American newspapers and magazines. The best-known newspaper comic strip featuring a physician as its main character is *Rex Morgan, M.D.* Written by a psychiatrist, Dr. Nicholas Dallis, under the pseudonym Dal Curtis, and drawn by Marvin Bradley and Frank Edgington, *Rex Morgan, M.D.* has run continuously since its first appearance, on May 2, 1948, until the present. Comic books have featured few practicing physicians as heroes, although some use scientist-physicians, such as Dr. Andrew Bryant, Dr. Hugo Strange, and Dr. X.

Medicine shows, which originated as a form of entertainment designed to help quacks and street hawkers sell their patent medicine wares, also have a long European heritage, dating back to medieval times. They flourished in this country from the eighteenth century until they were virtually closed down by legislation in the twentieth century. The real heyday of medical show impresarios such as William Avery Rockefeller, "Nevada Ned" Oliver, John E. Healy, "Texas Charley" Bigelow, and John Austen Hamlin was the nineteenth century, but some, such as Dudley J. LeBlanc, the promoter of Hadacol and the Hadacol Caravans, were well known even as late as the 1950s.

Literally hundreds of physician characters appeared in American films during the twentieth century, but with the exception of the psychiatrists among them they have been little studied. Of major importance is the series of sixteen Dr. Kildare and Dr. Gillespie films, which appeared in the 1930s and 1940s. The first was *Interns Can't Take Money* in 1937, followed in 1938 by *Young Dr. Kildare*, which introduced the famous Lew Ayres (Dr. Kildare) and Lionel Barrymore (Dr. Gillespie) team. Ayres and Barrymore made nine films together, ending with *Dr. Kildare's Victory* in 1941. After Ayres left the series, Barrymore made another six films as Dr. Gillespie, with a variety of young interns (and actors) vying to become his assistant. The final film of the series was *Dark Delusion* in 1947. In the 1950s a radio show was based on the films, and two television series followed in the 1960s. The movie *M*A*S*H* had equally great success in 1970, inspiring a television series that lasted eleven seasons—longer than any other medical series in the history of television. But by far the most important physician characters in American films are the psychiatrists, who began appearing in minor roles as early as 1906 in the comedy *Dr. Dippy's Sanitarium*. However, only a few films from the early decades of this century depict psychiatric treatment seriously; they include D. W. Griffith's *The Restoration* in 1909; *The Cabinet of Dr. Caligari*, made in Germany in 1919 and distributed in the United States in 1921; and *Private Worlds* in 1935.

By the 1940s there was a boom in psychological films. *Lady in the Dark* appeared in 1944, *Spellbound* in 1945, *The Dark Mirror* in 1946, *Nightmare Alley* in 1947, and *The Snake Pit* in 1948. Notable psychological films of the 1950s and 1960s include *Harvey* in 1950, *The Cobweb* in 1955, *The Three Faces of Eve* in 1957, *Splendor in the Grass* in 1961, both *David and Lisa* and *Freud* in 1962, *A Fine Madness* in 1966, and both *Marat/Sade* and *Titicut Follies* in 1967. The indisputable hit of the 1970s crop of psychological films was *One Flew over the Cuckoo's Nest*, whose antipsychiatric story found a most receptive audience in 1975. It was followed by *Annie Hall*, *Equus*, and *I Never Promised You a Rose Garden*, all three in 1977; *An Unmarried Woman* in 1978; and *The Bell Jar* in 1979. The pace did not slow in the 1980s, with *Ordinary People* in 1980, *Whose Life Is It, Anyway?* in 1981, both *Frances* and *I'm Dancing as Fast as 1 Can* in 1982, *Zelig* in 1983, *Agnes of God* in 1985, and *Hannah and Her Sisters* in 1986.

Radio serials began in the 1920s. Many used physicians as characters, and by the 1930s several were featuring physicians as the main characters of their own series. One of the earliest daytime network serials to do so was *Peggy's Doctor*, which began in 1934 and was discontinued in 1935. *Dr. Christian* ran from 1937 until 1953, *Doc Barclay's Daughters* from 1939 to 1940, *The Doctor's Wife* from 1952 through 1956, and *The Affairs of Dr. Gentry* from 1957 through 1959. The longest running was *Young Dr. Malone*, which began in 1939 and continued through 1960. At least two of radio's daytime network serials featured women physicians: *Joyce Jordan, Girl Interne* (later *Joyce Jordan, M.D.*), which ran from 1938 through 1948 on CBS and was then revived by ABC for the 1951–1952 season; and *The Life and Loves of Dr. Susan*, which ran only one year, 1939. A spin-off from the earlier Dr. Kildare films was a weekly radio program in the 1950s, *Young Dr. Kildare*. As intriguing as these radio programs sound to students of popular culture, very few of them have been preserved in either tape or script form.

The most important medium in American popular culture for the presentation of physicians and medical themes is television. Beginning in the early 1960s, television's daytime network serials picked up where radio left off. Both *General Hospital* and *The Doctors* began in 1963, and *Days of Our Lives* began in 1965. Other 1960s daytime television serials—but not network serials—presenting physicians and medical themes were *Young Dr. Malone, Dr. Hudson's Secret Journal*, and *The Nurses*.

Far more impressive than the daytime medical serials have been the primetime medical shows. From 1952 through 1986 there were approximately forty of these using physicians as main characters and medical themes as the main subject material. Among the first were *City Hospital*, from 1952 to 1953; *Doc Corkle* in 1952; *The Doctor*, from 1952 to 1953; and *Medic*, from 1954 to 1956. The most successful of the early shows were *Ben Casey* and *Dr. Kildare*, both beginning in 1961 and running through 1966. They are the classics of the first-generation doctor shows, and their format, an old mentor and a young man, was imitated by many other shows attempting to cash in on their success.

Unlike the movies, which have featured so many psychiatrists, television has favored physicians who are general practitioners or surgeons. But in the early 1960s there were two short-lived television series about psychiatrists: *Breaking Point*, in the 1963–1964 season, and *The Eleventh Hour*, which lasted two seasons, from 1962 to 1964. By far the most successful of the second-generation medical series, however, was *Marcus Welby, M.D.*, which ran from 1969 through 1976 and ranked among the top ten shows in the Nielsen ratings for the first three of those seasons. *Medical Center*, which also began in 1969 and ended in 1976, was not far behind *Welby* in the Nielsen ratings for three of its first four seasons. Another successful medical series that began in 1969 was *The New Doctors*, one of three segments making up the dramatic series *The Bold Ones*.

Ushering in the third generation of doctor shows was the most successful medical series of all time, *M*A*S*H*, which premiered in 1972 and ran for eleven seasons, ending with a two-and-a-half-hour special in 1983. *M*A*S*H* won awards every season it was on the air, and after it closed, there was an exhibit featuring the show at the Smithsonian Institution in 1984. Although no other doctor show during these years was in the same class with *M*A*S*H*, there were several others of note. *Emergency!*, which began the same year as *M*A*S*H*, lasted for six seasons, and *Quincy, M.E.* ran for seven seasons, from 1976 through 1983. Of interest because it featured a woman physician, Julie Farr, was *Having Babies*, which lasted only five weeks in 1978.

Trapper John, M.D., which started in 1979, and the short-lived *After-M*A*S*H*, which started in 1983, were both spin-offs from *M*A*S*H*. But the indisputable hit of the fourth-generation television doctor shows is *St. Elsewhere*, which began in 1982. Despite its initial low ratings, the series received critical acclaim and was kept on the air until it garnered broader audience support and more respectable ratings. Another show of interest, because it featured a woman physician, was *Kay O'Brien*, about a second-year female surgical resident. It had a brief run, beginning in 1986, but did not last the whole season. The enormous success of such television shows as *ER* and *Chicago Hope* during the 1990s suggests that physicians and medical professionals will remain an important presence in American popular culture during the twenty-first century.

Factual medical shows providing information about medicine to the general public have not met with much success. Among the best of the attempts have been

Medix, *Today's Health*, and *Feeling Good*. Another kind of show, factual but with dramatic intent, was *Lifeline*, based on activities of real-life physicians involved in life-and-death situations. It premiered in 1978 but did not last a complete season despite the astronomical sums spent filming each episode. Since 1978 the episodes from *Lifeline* have been rerun several times on PBS stations.

REFERENCE WORKS

There are no reference works or bibliographies specifically designed to bring together information about medicine and the physician in American popular culture. A secondary bibliography, *Medicine and the Arts*, was compiled and published by the National Library of Medicine in 1986, in conjunction with a special colloquium, "Medicine and the Arts: Two Faces of Humanity," held at the library on April 22, 1986. Not limited to either American or popular culture, this bibliography covers medical themes in art and literature, as well as the physician as artist, and comprises 306 items published in English since 1980. It is intended as a starting point for further research.

For literature, four bibliographies offer some guidance, although two of them list primary works, not secondary studies. The earliest of these is an article by Evelyn Rivers Wilbanks, "The Physician in the American Novel, 1870–1955," which lists more than 400 novels with physicians as the main character. The usefulness of the bibliography is limited by Wilbanks's arbitrary, albeit necessary, decision to use only the form and not the quality of the works for her selection. She admits that she has not read all of the books on her list, and she attempts no classification of them as standard literature, popular culture, or trash. Despite its deficiencies, the list is useful simply because it is the only one there is. The other primary bibliography is *Literature and Medicine: Topics, Titles and Notes* by Joanne Trautmann and Carol Pollard, with 1,312 entries. Trautmann and Pollard's aim was to provide an annotated listing of literary works that could be used by people teaching humanities in a medical school. They use two organizational schemas: a chronological listing, with each entry accompanied by a short plot summary; and a topic list, organizing works under such categories as abortion, alcoholism, doctors, medical ethics, plague, science fiction, surgery, and women as healers and patients. Trautmann and Pollard insist that they included only "first-rate" literary works or works of special interest because of their medical topics or themes. In 1982 a revised edition of the bibliography appeared, with 84 additional entries.

Jon Erlen's "Medicine in Literature: Theses—A Survey of Secondary Sources" is a bibliography of fifty-five English-language Ph.D. dissertations and master's theses published since 1950 about medical themes in literature. The fourth bibliography for literature and medicine is a secondary bibliography limited to only one area of medicine: Norman Kiell's *Psychoanalysis, Psychology and Literature: A Bibliography*. Kiell makes no claim to exhaustiveness but has followed a principle of selection that includes "articles, monographs, or books which deal with literary writing from a psychological point of view."[11] Kiell has also edited the only reference work for medical caricatures and cartoons: *Psychiatry and Psychology in the Visual Arts and Aesthetics: A Bibliography*, divided into twenty-one subject categories, of which caricatures and cartoons is one.

There is no reference work for medicine shows or for medicine and the phy-

Cast of the television show "M*A*S*H." Kobal Collection/CBS-TV

sician in films, radio, or television. For films, however, two general reference guides are helpful: *The American Film Institute Catalog of Motion Pictures Produced in the United States: Feature Films 1921–1930*, edited by Kenneth W. Munden, and *The American Film Institute Catalog of Motion Pictures: Feature Films 1961–1970*, edited by Richard P. Krafsur. These two volumes are the first products of the American Film Institute's continuing project to catalog all films produced since the beginning of the motion picture industry. The 1920s and the 1960s catalogs include a volume of entries summarizing each film, as well as subject and credit indexes. Because the subject index includes such categories as medicine men, physicians, psychiatrists, quacks, and surgeons, the catalogs are valuable resources for research on medicine and the physician in American films. For radio, two general guides are of some help: Frank Buxton and Bill Owen's *The Big Broadcast 1920–1950* (a new edition of their older work, *Radio's Golden Age*) and John Dunning's *Tune In Yesterday: The Ultimate Encyclopedia of Old-Time Radio 1925–1976*. For television, a useful general reference work is Tim Brooks and Earle Marsh's *The Complete Directory to Prime Time Network TV Shows, 1946-Present*. This work's limitation is indicated by its title: it covers only prime-time shows. As supplements to it, Vincent Terrace's *Encyclopedia of Television*, in three volumes, and *Les Brown's*

Encyclopedia of Television are useful because they give information about daytime programs.

The increased interest in medicine and the physician in popular culture in the past few years may mean that there will eventually be better reference tools available, but now it is much easier to point to what is lacking than to what exists.

RESEARCH COLLECTIONS

There are no research collections designed to support scholarly inquiry into medicine and the physician in American popular culture. Although many medical school libraries have collections of prints and caricatures, they include international as well as American items, and few collections are fully cataloged. Even the National Library of Medicine cannot say for certain what percentage of its prints and caricatures is American rather than international. At least four medical school libraries have or had a Weinstein Collection of fiction by and about physicians. These collections have been established by donations from B. Bernard or Eva Evelyn Weinstein. The University of Miami's Weinstein Collection includes approximately 600 books, but there is no published list of the titles; the University of Mississippi Medical Center's Rowland Medical Library has 300 titles in its Weinstein Collection, as does the Tulane University Medical Library; the University of North Carolina's Health Affairs Library has dispersed its Weinstein Collection because of space shortage. In addition to the three remaining Weinstein Collections, there are two other small collections of some interest. The first is at the University of Cincinnati, where the Health Sciences Library has begun a collection of literary works by or about physicians. The second is at the Medical College of Pennsylvania, where the Archives and Special Collections on Women in Medicine has more than 500 books on women in medicine, including some fiction with women physicians as characters; however, there is no separate listing of the fictional works.

Until there is a cohesive collection of materials on medicine and the physician in American popular culture, scholars working in this field will have to use more general research collections, film archives, and popular culture collections.

HISTORY AND CRITICISM

The only book-length studies of images of general physicians in American literature are four unpublished dissertations completed between 1963 and 1976. Of these, the two earlier ones are more interesting. In the first, "The Physician-Scientist as Character in Nineteenth-Century American Literature," Lois Elizabeth DeBakey examines the scientific milieu of the nineteenth century and novels by Nathaniel Hawthorne, Herman Melville, Oliver Wendell Holmes, S. Weir Mitchell, William Dean Howells, and Sarah Orne Jewett to determine how closely literary depictions of the physician-scientist accord with the historical reality of the medical profession. Her work provides a good, solid introduction to the relationship between literature and medicine in the nineteenth-century United States. The second, Carolyn Brimley Norris' "The Image of the Physician in Modern American Literature," is longer and more complex than DeBakey's. Norris establishes two major categories of physicians—the priest and the Pan—and organizes the works she examines accordingly. Her priest-doctors include characters from F. Scott Fitzgerald, Robert Penn Warren, John Steinbeck, Katherine Anne Porter, Henry James, William Faulkner, and Lloyd C. Douglas. Her Pan-doctors are from Ellen Glasgow and James Gould Cozzens. In addition, Norris devotes one chapter to the black American doctor, one to Sinclair Lewis, and one to the economic doctor; one of her three appendixes is a discussion of priest and Pan physicians on television, Drs. Kildare and Ben Casey, respectively. Norris' categories and discussions are intriguing, and chronologically her study starts where DeBakey's stops. The two later dissertations, Alex John Cameron's "The Image of the Physician in the American Novel: 1859 to 1925" and David Edward Stooke's "The Portrait of the Physician in Selected Prose Fiction of Nineteenth-Century American Authors," cover basically the same literature DeBakey does but are shorter and less sophisticated than DeBakey's or Norris' studies.

In addition to the unpublished dissertations, there are many published articles about physicians in American literature. In one titled "Images of Women Doctors in Popular Fiction: Comparison of the 19th and 20th Centuries," Mary Roth Walsh discusses the three nineteenth-century novels by William Dean Howells, Sarah Orne Jewett, and Elizabeth Stuart Phelps Ward that use women physicians as main characters and compares those early presentations of women physicians with the few that exist in popular twentieth-century fiction. She does not attempt any real literary analysis of the works, however. In "The Doctor as Scapegoat: A Study in Ambivalence," Nancy Y. Hoffman analyzes physician characters of Sherwood Anderson, Sinclair Lewis, John Steinbeck, F. Scott Fitzgerald, Carson McCullers, and Joseph Heller to show how society makes scapegoats of them. "Literature and Medicine," a cover article in *MD Medical Newsmagazine*, offers a brief historical survey of the relationship between the two disciplines from Homer to Gerald Green. Many articles about literary images of physicians, physician-writers, and medical themes in literature have appeared in the first five volumes of the annual journal *Literature and Medicine*.

The categories of scientist and physician overlap, and articles about scientists in fiction sometimes include discussion of works whose main character is a physician-scientist. Thomas D. Clareson's "The Scientist as Hero in American Science-Fiction, 1880–1920" offers a short discussion of Edward Bellamy's *Dr. Heidenhoff's Process*. In "The Scientist in Contemporary Fiction," Bently Glass includes discussion of Sinclair Lewis' *Arrowsmith*, as does Jay Tepperman in his article "The Research Scientist in Modern Fiction." Charles E. Rosenberg's "Martin Arrowsmith: The Scientist as Hero" provides valuable background information about the people and events that influenced Lewis in his creation of the novel.

The psychiatrist in American literature has evoked almost as much critical response as have all the other kinds of physicians combined—and this despite the fact that psychiatry did not emerge as a separate medical specialty until the twentieth century. Three unpublished dissertations focus on the psychiatrist in American fiction. The first, Herbert Jordan Guthmann's "The Characterization of the Psychiatrist in American Fiction, 1859–1965," surveys literary depictions of mental healers and psychiatrists from the novels of Oliver Wendell Holmes and S. Weir Mitchell through those of Joseph Heller and Thomas Pynchon. Not surprisingly, Guthmann concludes that in more recent fiction psychiatrists are portrayed far less favorably than they were in earlier works. The second, Philip Henry Bufithis'

"The Artist's Fight for Art: The Psychiatrist Figure in the Fiction of Major Contemporary American Novelists," examines the conflict between the psychiatrist and artist figures in works of eight novelists: Vladimir Nabokov, William S. Burroughs, Saul Bellow, J.D. Salinger, Norman Mailer, John Barth, James Purdy, and Ken Kesey. The third, Carol Krusen Scholz's "They Share the Suffering: The Psychoanalyst in American Fiction between 1920 and 1940," offers biographical criticism of five writers—Ludwig Lewisohn, Conrad Aiken, F. Scott Fitzgerald, Waldo Frank, and Vardis Fisher—who use psychoanalysts as characters in their novels.

Several psychiatrists have themselves published analyses of popular presentations of psychiatrists. In "Saturday's Psychiatrist," Harry A. Wilmer reports on his informal survey of all seventy-plus references made to psychiatry by book and play reviewers in 1953 issues of *Saturday Review*. Another psychiatrist, Robert Plank, published a brief and disappointing article called "Portraits of Fictitious Psychiatrists," in which he discusses psychiatrist characters in several obscure works of science fiction. In contrast, Charles Winick's article, "The Psychiatrist in Fiction," is one of the best available. It is of special interest because it was written as a result of the Joint Committee on Mental Illness and Health's recommendation that American psychiatrists "do something about the public 'image' of the psychiatrist."[12] Winick's concern is not with the literary quality or merit of works but with their popularity, as judged by their sales and their ripple effects in movie, play, and television adaptations. This makes the article an especially important resource for students of popular culture. In a much shorter article, "Psychiatrists Portrayed in Fiction," published just a year after Winick's, another psychiatrist, Marjorie C. Meehan, offers her analyses of fictional psychiatrists as villains, noble characters, magicians, spiritual guides, unfeeling scientists, useless nonentities, and complex individuals. Winick's and Meehan's articles make an interesting pair because in her discussion Meehan disagrees with several of Winick's conclusions.

Three critics argue that the popularity of psychiatric themes in fiction has resulted in new subgenres or formulas for the modern novel. Anthony Hopkins, in his article "Physical Models and Spiritual States: Institutional Environments in Modern Fiction," argues that a sizable group of fictional works has the same pattern, based on use of a limited environment, often a hospital or mental institution, as a sustained symbol for society as a whole. Examples of such fiction are Elliott Baker's *A Fine Madness* and Ken Kesey's *One Flew over the Cuckoo's Nest*, both published in the early 1960s. More convincing is an excellent article by Kary K. and Gary K. Wolfe, "Metaphors of Madness: Popular Psychological Narratives," which traces the development of a new subgenre based on a combination of the novel, memoirs, autobiography, and the psychological case history. The outstanding work of this subgenre is Joanne Greenberg's *I Never Promised You a Rose Garden*, published in 1964 under the pseudonym Hannah Green. The Wolfes discuss representative movies and television shows as well as fiction.

Images of physicians in American drama have also been studied. Three works focus specifically on the image of the psychiatrist. One is W. David Sievers' 1955 book, *Freud on Broadway: A History of Psychoanalysis and the American Drama*, which is useful, but limited and by now dated. Sievers explores the backgrounds of psychological drama, discusses the first Freudian plays, and then alternates between chapters dealing with specific decades and chapters dealing with specific playwrights. Eugene O'Neill, Philip Barry, Tennessee Williams, and Arthur Miller get special attention; the chronological coverage ends with "War and Post-War Neurosis." Another 1955 study of images of psychiatrists in drama, Harry A. Wilmer's article "Psychiatrist on Broadway," is actually more central for the study of popular culture. Wilmer examines the psychiatrist figures in eighteen dramas that played on Broadway between the 1930s and 1955. All eighteen were popular hits; several won the Pulitzer Prize; several won the New York Drama Critics Circle Award; and three had more than 800 performances each. They include, for example, George Axelrod's *The Seven Year Itch* and Tennessee Williams' *A Streetcar Named Desire*. My own article from 1985, "Psychiatrists on Broadway, 1974–1982," examines the characterizations of psychiatrists in five more recent plays: *Equus, Whose Life Is It Anyway?, Nuts, Duet for One*, and *Agnes of God*.

An older study of the relationship between drama and medicine in general is George W. Corner's "Medicine in the Modern Drama." Many of the plays Corner discusses are British or Scottish, but they became part of American popular culture when they played on the New York stage. Corner discusses specifically two American plays, Sidney Howard's *Yellow Jack*, about Walter Reed's work against yellow fever, and Sydney Kingsley's *Men in White*, a study of the hospital doctor. A more recent article by Mel Gussow, "The Time of the Wounded Hero," provides an interesting historical contrast to Corner's article. Gussow discusses the past season's several successful plays dealing with deformity, disability, serious illness, and prolonged dying. Ironically, the technological progress of medicine has shifted the dramatic focus from the doctor to the patient, who is the new hero.

The best article on the history of American medical caricature is Chauncey D. Leake's "Medical Caricature in the United States." Leake traces the development of medical caricature in this country and speculates about why it was so slow. The article includes reproductions of the first American cartoons about physicians, taken from both private collectors and public sources. A second article, Wolfgang Born's "The Nature and History of Medical Caricature," is of some interest for its discussion of European caricature, but its history of American caricature is largely derivative of Leake's. The most interesting article about medical caricatures is "The Psychiatrist in Caricature: An Analysis of Unconscious Attitudes toward Psychiatry," by Frederick C. Redlich, himself a psychiatrist. Redlich examined thirty cartoons, representing the work of twenty artists, which were originally published in magazines such as the *New Yorker*, the *Saturday Evening Post*, and *Collier's*. Redlich's analysis is fascinating, and his article has become a classic. The best-known newspaper comic strip featuring a physician, "Rex Morgan, M.D.," has failed to capture the imagination of critics and commentators the way so many other strips have; there are virtually no critical studies or commentaries about it. One article of historical interest is Melinda Wagner's "Psychiatrist at the Drawing Board." Wagner discusses the origin of the strip, written by Dr. Nicholas Dallis, a psychiatrist, and drawn by Marvin Bradley and Frank Edgington. There is some mention of the kinds of episodes chosen for the strip and of the strip's readership.

The best histories of the patent medicine industry in this country are two books by James Harvey Young, *The Toadstool Millionaires: A Social History of Patent Medicines in America before Federal Regulation* and *The Medical Messiahs: A Social History of Health Quackery in Twentieth-Century America*. The former includes a chapter entitled "Medicine Show"; the latter, a chapter called "Medicine Show Impresario," which is about Dudley LeBlanc and the Hadacol craze. In addition, Young has published several other articles about patent medicine and popular culture. One is "The Patent Medicine Boom" in *The History of Popular Culture*, edited by Norman F. Cantor and Michael S. Werthman. There Young correlates the increase in Americans' taste for "bitters" during the second half of the nineteenth century with the rise of the temperance movement. In "From Hooper to Hohensee: Some Highlights of American Patent Medicine Promotion," Young traces the history of patent medicine advertising and reproduces some of the early advertisements. An article from the *Journal of Popular Culture*, Jerry C. Brigham and Karlie K. Kenyon's "Hadacol: The Last Great Medicine Show," is related to this aspect of medicine and popular culture. But the outstanding history of medicine shows remains Brooks McNamara's *Step Right Up*.

The only work dealing with images of general physicians in American film is Jack Spears' invaluable article "The Doctor on the Screen," which is included in his 1971 anthology of essays titled *Hollywood: The Golden Era*. In the article, Spears surveys screen presentations of doctors, nurses, and hospitals, from the peep shows at the turn of the century, such as *The Doctor's Favorite Patient* and *The Downward Path*, to the 1969–1970 television series *Marcus Welby, M.D.*, *The Bold Ones*, and *Medical Center*. Spears does more cataloging than critical reviewing, but the comments he does make are helpful. He organizes his article chronologically by subcategories, such as the country doctor; the comic doctor; the western doctor; the military doctor; the woman doctor; medical students, interns, and residents; medical history; and medical ethics. Philip A. and Beatrice J. Kalisch have published a useful article about the 1930s and 1940s series of Dr. Kildare and Dr. Gillespie films, which provides plot summaries, analyses of the images of physicians and nurses, and stills from some of the films.

All the remaining scholarship has been done on psychiatrists and film. Most articles strike a common theme: Hollywood's disappointing oversimplification and sensationalism of psychiatry. One of the earliest, Franklin Fearing's 1946 article "The Screen Discovers Psychiatry," is a good example. Fearing discusses how and why psychiatry should be used in films and then points out how *Spellbound* and *Love Letters* fall short. The next year another article by Fearing, "Psychology and the Films," was accompanied by Lawrence S. Kubie's "Psychiatry and the Films." A psychiatrist himself, Kubie deplores the infantile level Hollywood has maintained in its depiction of psychiatry in films. He uses *Harvey*, *Shock*, *Spellbound*, and *The Seventh Veil* to demonstrate his points, and he concludes with suggestions about ways Hollywood could portray psychiatry responsibly in its films. In the companion article, Fearing begins by surveying the stereotyped psychiatrists of the movies: the all-wise father psychiatrist; the insane psychiatrist; the criminal psychiatrist; the seductive female psychiatrist; and the philosophical-whimsical psychiatrist. Then he comments on Kubie's article and calls for research on the effects of films on their audiences. These three articles give a good sense of how psychiatry and psychology were being used in films of the 1940s and of how such films were popularly received.

Two articles from the 1950s indicate that Fearing's and Kubie's criticisms were little heeded in Hollywood. In "Movie Psychiatrics," Martin S. Dworkin contrasts the use of psychiatry in Hollywood films like *Crossfire* and *Blind Alley* with its use in the documentary film *The Lonely Night*, made by Irving Jacoby of Affiliated Films for the Mental Health Film Board. Dworkin's discussion is instructive. The second article from the 1950s is Norman N. Holland's "Psychiatry in Pselluloid." Humorous in intent, the article nevertheless makes good points about Hollywood's failings with psychiatrists in film.

Leslie Y. Rabkin, a clinical psychologist, has added two helpful articles to the literature about psychiatrists in film. The first, "The Movies' First Psychiatrist," is about D. W. Griffith's 1909 film, *The Restoration*, which Rabkin considers the first cinematic presentation of psychiatric treatment. The second, "The Celluloid Couch: Psychiatrists in American Films," is organized chronologically and discusses the changes in film presentations of psychiatrists from decade to decade throughout the twentieth century. Rabkin's concluding classification of movie psychiatrists seems oversimplistic—too neatly Freudian—but Rabkin's report of his historical research provides a good basis for further studies. Another interesting article is Irving Schneider's "Images of the Mind: Psychiatry in the Commercial Film." Schneider, a psychiatrist, asserts that the history of film and the history of psychiatry have many parallels, thus producing an almost natural interest of the one field in the other. He then surveys presentations of psychiatry and psychiatrists in American film throughout this century and finally concludes that psychiatry, films, and consumers have grown up together. In a later article, "The Psychiatrist in the Movies: The First Fifty Years," Schneider says that movie psychiatrists can be categorized as Dr. Dippy, Dr. Evil, or Dr. Marvelous.

Two other articles about psychotherapy and psychotherapists in film deserve brief mention. Milton Eber and James McG. O'Brien's "Psychotherapy in the Movies" uses the films *Ordinary People* (1980), *Lady in the Dark* (1944), and *Spellbound* (1945) to demonstrate a simplistic forty-year-old formula used by filmmakers to portray psychotherapy. Laurel Samuels, in "Female Psychotherapists as Portrayed in Film, Fiction and Nonfiction," identifies female psychotherapists in forty-one films, twenty-one novels, and seven popular works of nonfiction and asks why these female psychotherapists are portrayed in such sexist and unprofessional ways.

Little has been written about radio or television medical serials outside the context of more general histories of the serials. Two books, Raymond William Stedman's *The Serials: Suspense and Drama by Installment* and Madeleine Edmondson and David Rounds' *The Soaps: Daytime Serials of Radio and TV*, offer discussion of both radio and television "hospital" operas as part of their general history of soap opera serials. Mary B. Cassata's chapter "The Soap Opera," in Brian G. Rose's *TV Genres: A Handbook and Reference Guide*, provides a helpful introductory overview and survey of research.

The first substantial critical article about prime-time medical dramas on television is a chapter titled "Doctors and Lawyers: Counselors and Confessors" in Horace Newcomb's book *TV: The Most Popular Art*. In his chapter, Newcomb traces the evolution of the doctor and lawyer shows on television and compares the formula of the first-generation shows with that of the second. He uses *Ben Casey* and *Dr. Kildare* as examples of first-generation doctor shows; their formula depends largely on the interaction of an older male mentor with a younger pupil. Newcomb chooses *Marcus Welby, M.D.* as the best example of a second-generation doctor show; its formula has changed significantly from that of the earlier shows

Scene from the film *The Elephant Man*, 1980. Kobal Collection/Paramount

and depends partially on Robert Young's previous success in *Father Knows Best*. Welby ministers to the physical and emotional needs of an extended family that includes his assistants, his patients, and the television public. Newcomb's analysis of the doctor shows is excellent and has been said to have "pioneered the study of the medical (and legal) genre on television."[13]

The second substantial critical work is Michael R. Real's chapter "Marcus Welby and the Medical Genre," which is included in his book *Mass-Mediated Culture*. Real spends only the very first part of his chapter on fictional medical dramas; in the rest, he deals with documentary medical shows, commercials and health, television's potential, and the question of priorities. The broader scope of Real's chapter makes it useful in ways Newcomb's was not intended to be. David Thorburn's essay "Television Melodrama," included in Horace Newcomb's anthology *Television: The Critical View*, offers some critical discussion of the hospital opera, and especially of *Medical Center*. A more recent and very helpful resource is Robert S. Alley's "Medical Melodrama," in Rose's *TV Genres: A Handbook and Reference Guide*. Alley provides an overview, a summary of development from *Medic* to *St. Elsewhere*, and a discussion of themes and issues. Based on his interviews of David Victor, the producer of *Dr. Kildare* and *Marcus Welby, M.D.*, and Frank Glicksman, one of the producers of *Medical Center* and *Trapper John, M.D.*, Alley supplies fascinating background information unavailable elsewhere.

Several articles from the 1960s and early 1970s are interesting reflections of the medical community's response to its depiction on television. In "Advice on Medical Accuracy in the Entertainment Media," Dudley M. Cobb Jr. explains the formation and function of the AMA's Physicians Committee on Television, Radio and Motion Pictures. In 1965 *Television Quarterly* published an interesting pair of articles about the *Ben Casey* show. The first, "Rx for TV Doctors," is by a physician, Murdock Head, who criticizes television doctor shows not just because of the unrealistic images of physicians they project but also because of their possible effects on millions of viewers. He thinks that television medical shows can interfere with the physician-patient relationship in real life. Matthew Rapf and Wilton Schiller, the producers of *Ben Casey*, answer Head's criticisms in their article, "Let's Not Offend Anyone." They insist that most charges leveled at *Ben Casey* by medical critics are contradictory. For example, some complain that the show is too grim; others complain that it is not grim enough to be realistic because Casey never loses a patient. They conclude that many medical critics probably do not watch the show regularly. Of most interest are Rapf and Schiller's statements about how they are mindful of the public good in writing the show. In contrast to medical critics of earlier doctor shows, Michael J. Halberstam has few complaints in his article "An M.D. Reviews Dr. Welby of TV." Clearly the formula for the second-generation doctor shows is more acceptable to medical palates than was the formula for the first.

Although physicians on television are more likely to be general practitioners than psychiatrists, an article by Robert Sklar, "Prime-Time Psychology," offers an analysis of television's general presentation of psychiatry. Sklar says that some viewers enjoy seeing psychiatrists ridiculed in stereotyped images, but many viewers still regard psychiatrists as helpers and healers. He attributes to this second attitude of the viewing public the increase in psychiatrists presented favorably in dramatic specials such as "Sybil" and "A Last Cry for Help."

Although not scholarly, the articles in *TV Guide* nonetheless provide helpful information about medical shows on television, and some *TV Guide* articles even offer serious analyses of shows. An example is Richard Gehman's "Caseyitis," which explains the popular appeal of *Ben Casey* as a result of its "*high-minded violence.*" Another, Leslie Raddatz's "Let's Play 'Father Image,'" describes the father image formula that seems an important element in the success of medical shows such as *Ben Casey*, *The Eleventh Hour*, *Breaking Point*, and *Dr. Kildare*. A second article by Raddatz, "The Destiny of 'The Bold Ones,'" explains how the show uses real physicians and nurses as actors whenever possible. "There's a Doctor in the House" outlines the relationship between those who produce the television shows and the AMA's advisory committee. Bill Davidson's "Medical Center" presents four ways the medical show of 1971 was different from the medical show of 1961.

Several other *TV Guide* articles deserve mention. "Through the Years with Dr. Kildare" is a historical retrospective of Dr. Kildare's presence in American popular culture from the 1930s to the 1970s. Otto Wahl's article "TV Myths about Mental Illness" lists six frequent myths about mental illness that television programs propagate. Although basically a personality profile, Bill Davidson's "Jack Klugman of 'Quincy'" explains how Klugman's personal experience with a physician convinced him that he wanted to play in a doctor show. A useful analysis of factual medical shows such as *House Call, Health Field, Feeling Fine, Ounce of Prevention*, and *Today's Health* is provided by Marshall Goldberg's "A Doctor Examines TV's Health Shows." In addition to surveying the shows, Goldberg suggests some of the reasons factual medical shows attract so few viewers compared to fictional medical shows. Sally Bedell's "Behind the Scenes at 'Lifeline' " is a fascinating account of the filming of an episode in that shortlived series.

David Johnston's *TV Guide* article "Teamwork 'M*A*S*H'-Style" mentions some of the important changes that occurred in that show in its first eight years on television. They seem to correspond to changes in the general public's attitudes toward physicians during that period of time. Eventually, *M*A*S*H* got a book of its own, David S. Reiss' "*M*A*S*H*": *The Exclusive, Inside Story of T.V.'s Most Popular Show*, which documents the history of the series, gives episode-by-episode summaries of all eleven seasons, and lists the many distinguished awards and nominations that *M*A*S*H* received, season by season.

ANTHOLOGIES AND REPRINTS

To date there are very few anthologies or reprints of popular culture materials about medicine and the physician. The best is William H. Helfand's *Medicine and Pharmacy in American Political Prints (1765–1870)*, which reproduces from such publications as *Harper's Weekly, Yankee Doodle*, and the *New York Illustrated News* political caricatures that are based on medical and pharmaceutical images. Organized topically, the book's chapters intersperse commentary among the reprints. The other anthologies of medical cartoons are not scholarly in intent. They include Austin Smith's *Dear Patient: A Collection of Cartoons concerning Doctors and Their Patients; More Cartoon Classics from Medical Economics*; and William N. Jeffers' *Antidepressants: Third in a Series of Cartoon Classics from Medical Economics*.

One anthology of literature is especially important for students of popular culture: *Great Science Fiction about Doctors*, edited by Edward Groff Conklin and Noah D. Fabricant. Four other anthologies, designed as textbooks, bring together literary materials with medical themes: Alan Abraham Stone and Sue Smart Stone's *The Abnormal Personality through Literature*; Sandra Galdieri Wilcox and Marilyn Sutton's *Understanding Death and Dying: An Interdisciplinary Approach*; Joseph Ceccio's *Medicine in Literature*; and Norman Cousins' *The Physician in Literature*.

NOTES

1. Robert S. Alley, "Medical Melodrama," in *TV Genres: A Handbook and Reference Guide*, ed. Brian G. Rose (Westport, Conn.: Greenwood Press, 1985), 74.

2. Michael R. Real, "Marcus Welby and the Medical Genre," in *Mass-Mediated Culture* (Englewood Cliffs, NJ.: Prentice-Hall, 1977), 121.

3. Michael J. Halberstarn, "An M.D. Reviews Dr. Welby of TV," *New York Times Magazine*, January 16, 1972, 35.

4. Anne Hudson Jones, "*Quincy* and Orphan Drug Legislation," *Institute for the Medical Humanities Chronicle* 5 (Fall 1987), 2; Abbey S. Meyers, "Working toward Passage of the Orphan Drug Act: An Example of Determination," *American Medical Writers Association Journal* 3 (March 1988), 4–6.

5. "There's a Doctor in the House," *TV Guide* 18 (April 18, 1970), 41–42.

6. Charles Winick, "The Psychiatrist in Fiction," *Journal of Nervous and Mental Disease* 136 (1963), 43.

7. Darrell W. Amundsen, "Romanticizing the Ancient Medical Profession: The Characterization of the Physician in the Graeco-Roman Novel," *Bulletin of the History of Medicine* 48 (Fall 1974), 320–37; Darrell W. Amundsen, "Images of Physicians in Classical Times," *Journal of Popular Culture* 11 (Winter 1977), 642–55.

8. John H. Dirckx, "The Quack in Literature," *Pharos* 31 (January 1976), 2–7.

9. F.N.L. Poynter, "Doctors in *The Human Comedy*," *Journal of the American Medical Association* 204 (April 1, 1968), 105–8.

10. Examples are Saul Nathaniel Brody, *The Disease of the Soul: Leprosy in Medieval Literature* (Ithaca, N.Y.: Cornell University Press, 1974); Christine E. Petersen, *The Doctor in French Drama 1770–1775* (New York: AMS Press, 1966); Herbert Silvette, *The Doctor on the Stage: Medicine and Medical Men in Seventeenth-Century England* (Knoxville: University of Tennessee Press, 1967); Gian-Paolo Biasin, *Literary Diseases: Theme and Metaphor in the Italian Novel* (Austin: University of Texas Press, 1975); Susan Sontag, *Illness as Metaphor* (New York: Farrar, Straus, and Giroux, 1977); and E. R. Peschel, ed., *Medicine and Literature* (New York: Neale Watson Academic, 1980), which also includes a few essays about American literature.

11. Norman Kiell, ed., *Psychoanalysis, Psychology and Literature: A Bibliography* (Madison: University of Wisconsin Press, 1963), 3.

12. Charles Winick, "The Psychiatrist in Fiction," *Journal of Nervous and Mental Disease* 136 (1963), 43.

13. Real, "Marcus Welby and the Medical Genre," 121.

BIBLIOGRAPHY

Books and Articles

Alley, Robert S. "Medical Melodrama." In *TV Genres: A Handbook and Reference Guide*. Ed. Brian G. Rose. Westport, Conn.: Greenwood Press, 1985, 73–89.

Bedell, Sally. "Behind the Scenes at 'Lifeline.'" *TV Guide* 26 (October 7, 1978), 26–31.

Born, Wolfgang. "The Nature and History of Medical Caricature." *Ciba Symposia* 6 (November 1944), 1910–24.

Brigham, Jerry C., and Karlie K. Kenyon. "Hadacol: The Last Great Medicine Show." *Journal of Popular Culture* 10 (Winter 1976), 520–33.

Brooks, Tim, and Earle Marsh. *The Complete Directory to Prime Time Network TV Shows, 1946-Present*. Rev. ed. New York: Ballantine Books, 1981.

Brown, Les. *Les Brown's Encyclopedia of Television*. New York: Zoetrope, 1982.

Bufithis, Philip Henry. "The Artist's Fight for Art: The Psychiatrist Figure in the Fiction of Major Contemporary American Novelists." Ph.D. diss., University of Pennsylvania, 1967.

Buxton, Frank, and Bill Owen. *The Big Broadcast 1920–1950*. New York: Viking, 1966.

Cameron, Alex John. "The Image of the Physician in the American Novel: 1859 to 1925." Ph.D. diss., University of Notre Dame, 1973.

Cassata, Mary B. "The Soap Opera." In *TV Genres: A Handbook and Reference Guide*, ed. Brian G. Rose. Westport, Conn.: Greenwood Press, 1985, 131–49.

Ceccio, Joseph. *Medicine in Literature*. New York: Longman, 1978.

Clareson, Thomas D. "The Scientist as Hero in American Science-Fiction, 1880–1920." *Extrapolation* 7 (1965), 18–28.

Cobb, Dudley M., Jr. "Advice on Medical Accuracy in the Entertainment Media." *Western Medicine* 7 (November 1966), 313–16.

Conklin, Edward Groff, and Noah D. Fabricant, eds. *Great Science Fiction about Doctors*. New York: Collier Books, 1963.

Corner, George W., IV. "Medicine in the Modern Drama." *Annals of Medical History*, n.s. 10 (July 1938), 309–17.

Cousins, Norman, ed. *The Physician in Literature*. Philadelphia: Saunders Press, 1982.

Davidson, Bill. "Jack Klugman of 'Quincy.' " *TV Guide* 25 (March 26, 1977), 29–34.

———. "Medical Center." *TV Guide* 19 (July 17, 1971), 12–16.

DeBakey, Lois Elizabeth. "The Physician-Scientist as Character in Nineteenth-Century American Literature." Ph.D. diss., Tulane University, 1963.

Dunning, John. *Time In Yesterday: The Ultimate Encyclopedia of Old-Time Radio 1925–1976*. Englewood Cliffs, N.J.: Prentice-Hall, 1976.

Dworkin, Martin S. "Movie Psychiatrics." *Antioch Review* 14 (December 1954), 484–91.

Eber, Milton, and James McG. O'Brien. "Psychotherapy in the Movies." *Psychotherapy: Theory, Research and Practice* 19 (Spring 1982), 116–20.

Edmondson, Madeleine, and David Rounds. *The Soaps: Daytime Serials of Radio and TV*. New York: Stein and Day, 1973.

Erlen, Jon. "Medicine in Literature: Theses—A Survey of Secondary Sources." *The Watermark: Newsletter of the Association of Librarians in the History of the Health Sciences* 7 (Summer 1983), 1–3.

Fearing, Franklin. "Psychology and the Films." *Hollywood Quarterly* 2 (January 1947), 118–21.

———. "The Screen Discovers Psychiatry." *Hollywood Quarterly* 1 (January 1946), 154–58.

Gehman, Richard. "Caseyitis." In *TV Guide: The First 25 Years*. Ed. Jay S. Harris. New York: Simon and Schuster, 1978, 63–65.

Glass, Bentley. "The Scientist in Contemporary Fiction." *Scientific Monthly* 85 (December 1957), 288–93.

Goldberg, Marshall. "A Doctor Examines TV's Health Shows." *TV Guide* 25 (May 14, 1977), 4–8.

Gussow, Mel. "The Time of the Wounded Hero." *New York Times*, April 15, 1979, sec. 2: 1, 30.

Guthmann, Herbert Jordan. "The Characterization of the Psychiatrist in American Fiction, 1859–1965." Ph.D. diss., University of Southern California, 1969.

Halberstam, Michael J. "An M.D. Reviews Dr. Welby of TV." *New York Times Magazine*, January 16, 1972, 12–13, 30, 32, 34–35, 37.

Head, Murdock. "Rx for TV Doctors." *Television Quarterly* 4 (Spring 1965), 28–33.

Helfand, William H. *Medicine and Pharmacy in American Political Prints (1765–*

1870). Madison, Wis.: American Institute of the History of Pharmacy, 1978.

Hoffman, Nancy Y. "The Doctor as Scapegoat: A Study in Ambivalence." *Journal of the American Medical Association* 220 (April 3, 1972), 58–61.

Holland, Norman N. "Psychiatry in Pselluloid." *Atlantic* 203 (February 1959), 105–7.

Hopkins, Anthony. "Physical Models and Spiritual States: Institutional Environments in Modern Fiction." *Journal of Popular Culture* 6 (Fall 1972), 383–92.

Jeffers, William N. *Antidepressants: Third in a Series of Cartoon Classics from Medical Economics*. Oradell, N.J.: Medical Economics, 1972.

Johnston, David. "Teamwork 'M*A*S*H'-Style." *TV Guide* 28 (January 5, 1980), 22–26.

Jones, Anne Hudson. "Psychiatrists on Broadway, 1974–1982." *Literature and Medicine*, 4 (1985), 128–40.

Kalisch, Philip A., and Beatrice J. Kalisch. "When Americans Called for Dr. Kildare: Images of Physicians and Nurses in the Dr. Kildare and Dr. Gillespie Movies, 1937–1947." *Medical Heritage*, 1 (September/October 1985), 348–63.

Kiell, Norman, ed. *Psychiatry and Psychology in the Visual Arts and Aesthetics: A Bibliography*. Madison: University of Wisconsin Press, 1965.

———. *Psychoanalysis, Psychology and Literature: A Bibliography*. Madison: University of Wisconsin Press, 1963.

Krafsur, Richard P., ed. *The American Film Institute Catalog of Motion Pictures: Feature Films 1961–1970*. New York: R. R. Bowker, 1976.

Kubie, Lawrence S. "Psychiatry and the Films." *Hollywood Quarterly* 2 (January 1947), 113–17.

Leake, Chauncey D. "Medical Caricature in the United States." *Bulletin of the Society of Medical History of Chicago*, 4 (April 1928), 1–29.

"Literature and Medicine." *MD Medical Newsmagazine* 6 (August 1962), 115–19.

Literature and Medicine. Vols. 1–3. Albany: State University of New York Press; 1982–84. Vols. 4– . Baltimore: Johns Hopkins University Press; 1985– . (See especially Vol. 2: *Images of Healers*; Vol. 3: *The Physician Writer*; and Vol. 4: *Psychiatry and Literature*.)

McNamara, Brooks. *Step Right Up*. Garden City, N.Y.: Doubleday, 1976.

Meehan, Marjorie C. "Psychiatrists Portrayed in Fiction." *Journal of the American Medical Association* 188 (April 20, 1964), 255–58.

More Cartoon Classics from Medical Economics. Oradell, N.J.: Medical Economics Book Division, 1966.

Munden, Kenneth W., ed. *The American Film Institute Catalog of Motion Pictures Produced in the United States: Feature Films 1921–1930*. New York: R. R. Bowker, 1971.

National Library of Medicine. *Medicine and the Arts*. Specialized Bibliography Series 1986–82. April 1986. Bethesda, Md.: National Library of Medicine, 1986.

Newcomb, Horace. "Doctors and Lawyers: Counselors and Confessors." In *TV The Most Popular Art*. Garden City, N.Y.: Doubleday/Anchor, 1974, 110–34.

Norris, Carolyn Brimley. "The Image of the Physician in Modern American Literature." Ph.D. diss., University of Maryland, 1969.

Plank, Robert. "Portraits of Fictitious Psychiatrists." *American Imago* 13 (Fall 1956), 259–68.

Rabkin, Leslie Y. "The Celluloid Couch: Psychiatrists in American Films." *Psychocultural Review* 3 (Spring 1979), 73–89.

———. "The Movies' First Psychiatrist." *American Journal of Psychiatry* 124 (October 1967), 545–47.

Raddatz, Leslie. "The Destiny of 'The Bold Ones.' " *TV Guide* 17 (October 25, 1969), 40–46.

———. "Let's Play 'Father Image.' " *TV Guide* 12 (May 23, 1964), 24–27.

Rapf, Matthew, and Wilton Schiller. "Let's Not Offend Anyone." *Television Quarterly* 4 (Spring 1965), 34–37.

Real, Michael R. "Marcus Welby and the Medical Genre." In *Mass-Mediated Culture*. Englewood Cliffs, N.J.: Prentice-Hall, 1977, 118–39.

Redlich, Frederick C. "The Psychiatrist in Caricature: An Analysis of Unconscious Attitudes toward Psychiatry." *American Journal of Orthopsychiatry* 20 (July 1950), 560–71.

Reiss, David S. *M*A*S*H": The Exclusive, Inside Story of T.V.'s Most Popular Show*. Indianapolis/New York: Bobbs-Merrill, 1980. Updated 1983.

Rosenberg, Charles E. "Martin Arrowsmith: The Scientist as Hero." *American Quarterly* 15 (Fall 1963), 447–58.

Samuels, Laurel. "Female Psychotherapists as Portrayed in Film, Fiction and Nonfiction." *Journal of the American Academy of Psychoanalysis* 13 (July 1985), 367–78.

Schneider, Irving. "Images of the Mind: Psychiatry in the Commercial Film." *American Journal of Psychiatry* 134 (June 1977), 613–20.

———. "The Psychiatrist in the Movies: The First Fifty Years." In *Psychoanalytic Study of Literature*, ed. J. Reppen and M. Charney. Hillsdale, N.J.: Analytic Press, 1985, 53–67.

Scholz, Carol Krusen. "They Share the Suffering: The Psychoanalyst in American Fiction between 1920 and 1940." Ph.D. diss., University of Pennsylvania, 1977.

Sievers, W. David. *Freud on Broadway: A History of Psychoanalysis and the American Drama*. New York: Hermitage House, 1955.

Sklar, Robert. "Prime-Time Psychology." *American Film* 4 (March 1979), 59–63.

Smith, Austin, ed. *Dear Patient: A Collection of Cartoons concerning Doctors and Their Patients*. New York: Physicians Publications, 1957.

Spears, Jack. "The Doctor on the Screen." In *Hollywood: The Golden Era*. New York: Barnes, 1971, 314–32.

Stedman, Raymond William. *The Serials: Suspense and Drama by Installment*. Norman: University of Oklahoma Press, 1971.

Stone, Alan Abraham, and Sue Smart Stone, eds. *The Abnormal Personality through Literature*. Englewood Cliffs, N.J.: Prentice-Hall, 1966.

Stooke, David Edward. "The Portrait of the Physician in Selected Prose Fiction of Nineteenth-Century American Authors." Ph.D. diss., George Peabody College for Teachers, 1976.

Tepperman, Jay. "The Research Scientist in Modern Fiction." *Perspectives in Biology and Medicine* 3 (Summer 1960), 547–59.

Terrace, Vincent. *Encyclopedia of Television*. Rev. ed. 3 vols. New York: Zoetrope, 1985, 1986.

"There's a Doctor in the House." *TV Guide* 18 (April 18, 1970), 41–44.

Thorburn, David. "Television Melodrama." In *Television: The Critical View*, ed. Horace Newcomb, 2nd ed. New York: Oxford University Press, 1979, 536–53.

"Through the Years with Dr. Kildare." *TV Guide* 21 (January 20, 1973), 15–18.

Trautmann, Joanne, and Carol Pollard. *Literature and Medicine: Topics, Titles and Notes*. Rev. ed. Pittsburgh: University of Pittsburgh Press, 1982.

Wagner, Melinda. "Psychiatrist at the Drawing Board." *Today's Health* 41 (August 1963), 14–17, 58–60, 63.

Wahl, Otto. "TV Myths about Mental Illness." *TV Guide* 24 (March 13, 1976), 4–8.

Walsh, Mary Roth. "Images of Women Doctors in Popular Fiction: Comparison of the 19th and 20th Centuries." *Journal of American Culture* 1 (Summer 1978), 276–84.

Wilbanks, Evelyn Rivers. "The Physician in the American Novel, 1870–1955." *Bulletin of Bibliography* 22 (September–December 1958), 164–68.

Wilcox, Sandra Galdieri, and Marilyn Sutton. *Understanding Death and Dying: An Interdisciplinary Approach*. Port Washington, N.Y.: Alfred, 1977.

Wilmer, Harry A. "Psychiatrist on Broadway." *American Imago* 12 (Summer 1955), 157–78.

———. "Saturday's Psychiatrist." *American Imago* 12 (Summer 1955), 179–86.

Winick, Charles. "The Psychiatrist in Fiction." *Journal of Nervous and Mental Disease* 136 (1963), 43–57.

Wolfe, Kary K., and Gary K. Wolfe. "Metaphors of Madness: Popular Psychological Narratives." *Journal of Popular Culture* 9 (Spring 1976), 895–907.

Young, James Harvey. "From Hooper to Hohensee: Some Highlights of American Patent Medicine Promotion." *Journal of the American Medical Association* 204 (April 1, 1968), 100–104.

———. *The Medical Messiahs: A Social History of Health Quackery in Twentieth-Century America*. Princeton, N.J.: Princeton University Press, 1967.

———. "The Patent Medicine Boom." In *The History of Popular Culture*, ed. Norman F. Cantor and Michael S. Werthman. New York: Macmillan, 1968, 477–79.

———. *The Toadstool Millionaires: A Social History of Patent Medicines in America before Federal Regulation*. Princeton, N.J.: Princeton University Press, 1961.

MUSEUMS AND COLLECTING

Dennis Hall

Collecting is a very common, if not universal, human predilection, and the museum is its most conspicuous, although not exclusive, institutional result. The study of the one, as a consequence, invariably implicates the study of the other, although until the last decade of the twentieth century, the greatest attention fell onto the study of collectors and museums rather than to the process of collecting itself, which has resided in the shadows of implication in the study of museums, great and small.

The museum has come a long way from the academic building at Alexandria, from the scholar's study in Oxford and Paris, from the hoard of valuables, from the Enlightenment collection or cabinet of curiosities, from the bourgeois resort for pleasure and learning, to what it now takes to be the site of indeterminacy, ephemerality, fragmentation, and contention characteristic of that cluster of post-modern institutions that we, at the dawn of the twenty-first century, call "museums," without much concern about the consistency of our usage. While many would like to think of the homes of the muses as secure models of taxonomical order and venues for refined entertainment, teaching, and learning, since time out of mind museums have commonly been chaotic and their contents as likely dingy as elegant.

"Museum" is a noun that once evoked (and in some circles still does) a sense of the narrowly distributed culture of the elite, a term that signed practices of preservation and delectation observed in spaces set apart from ordinary use. In their early history, museums were distinctly private places that held personal collections, and only later did they become accessible as rigidly controlled public spaces. By the end of the eighteenth century, however, museums in the West opened up; increasingly, they became venues of fashionable and sometimes robust aesthetic pleasure and entertainment. In English-speaking environments in the nineteenth century, particularly in America, the museum expanded the audience that it sought to entice but narrowed its focus. Victorian earnestness hallowed the museum, making it a very quiet place devoted to learning—often to instrumental knowledge—and to moral rearmament of the middling and increasingly the working classes. The *Oxford English Dictionary*—itself a monument to the Victorian passion for preservation and improvement—reveals this orientation when it defines a museum as "a repository for the preservation and exhibition of objects illustrative of antiquities, natural history, fine and industrial art or some particular branch of any of these subjects, either generally or with reference to a definite region or period" (M 781).

In American practice even greater emphasis fell upon useful knowledge. While never a solidly fixed phenomenon, the power of the museum as a force in American culture has been profound, and its role in American popular culture has been extensive, even if the character of that function has been diffuse and difficult to assess. We tend to know what museums are without bothering or being able to define them, just as we tend to acknowledge their importance without knowing with any precision how or why they are salient agents in our lives. The history of American museums is, in large measure, a collection of arguments over not so much what museums are but what museums ought to do, that is, what ought to be collected, preserved, and exhibited, and by whom.

For a very long time—and this notion extends powerfully into the present—the status of an object was taken to reside outside the museum itself. The object's rarity, its capacity to elicit pleasure, its instructive qualities were assumed to reside either in the object itself (e.g., an illuminated manuscript, *The Book of Kells*) or in the object's associations (e.g., a pistol, the gun that Booth used to shoot Lincoln). The museum, under this dispensation, is thought to mediate between the object and the museum visitor, to communicate the significance of the object to the viewer, however contentious that may be. From the outset of museums' catering to the public, objections were raised against museums on philosophical grounds; to take objects, especially works of art, out of the lived-in life space that created and sustained them and to put them into museums meant, in effect, to destroy them.

Beginning in the nineteenth century and into the present, however, the museum as a practical matter increasingly confirmed a status upon the objects and by extension upon their creators, whether known or anonymous. To be collected, to be preserved, and to be exhibited—and so, too, to be described, analyzed, categorized, and cataloged, essential tropes in this realm—are to be afforded significance; to be so treated publicly is to be afforded status, to be certified, by whatever authority, great and small, as salient. This effect is especially powerful in the United States because of our relatively short history and, until the last quarter of the twentieth century, our relative cultural isolation from Europe and beyond.

Within the last twenty years, American museums have been increasingly taken as the sites of the social construction of cultural realities, as sites of interesting, sometimes crucial discursive practices and related power struggles. Museums are commonly seen as an important battlefield in the culture wars of the late twentieth and early twenty-first centuries. The nature and extent of that conflict, however, are difficult to assess, for the skirmishes are fought at particular museums, each with its own character and interests.

The difficulties and opportunities for study of American museums are in large measure the result of their profusion and aggressively democratic spirit. In the

Smithsonian Museum of Natural History, Washington, DC. Courtesy of the Library of Congress

late twentieth century all things became targets of acquisitiveness, the accumulation of commodities in profusion being a mark of the culture of postcapitalism. That profusion is reflected in the sheer number of entities that might legitimately be characterized as a museum; 15,000 is a conservative estimate. Their variety is astounding; the standard list of the American Association of Museums includes aquariums, arboretums, and botanical gardens, art museums of all kinds, children's museums, general museums, historical sites and houses, historical museums, natural history museums, nature centers, planetariums, science and technology museums, specialized museums, and zoos. The number of specialized museums, especially those unable or unwilling to join one of the major associations and those dealing with the more ephemeral objects of human attention, may put the total number of museums and their detailed taxonomy beyond human comprehension. Museums, broadly understood, are more popular than ever and constitute a significant element of American popular culture.

American museums have always been more sensitive to the needs and interests of the public than have their European counterparts, but as museums have become increasingly dependent upon the patronage of their publics and less obliged to wealthy benefactors, they are democratized as never before. The distinctions, for example, among high and low and folk art have been dissolving since the 1960s and are sustained only in a few enclaves. Museums, reverting to an earlier form more characteristic of the seventeenth and early eighteenth centuries than of the nineteenth and early twentieth centuries, are becoming elaborate cabinets of curiosities. Museums, indeed, provide the clearest evidence of postmodernism's collapse of the distinctions among high culture and mass or popular culture and what was once a clearly distinct folk culture. Moreover, with the profusion and diffusion of mass material culture, collecting cultural artifacts, once the prerogative of the wealthy or penchant of those willing to make an eccentric sacrifice, has become increasingly common. Every man and woman may garner his or her own collection, may make of his or her space a museum. As a consequence, museums and collecting are increasingly of interest to students of popular culture.

The museum is now less clearly an agent of social and cultural control, telling people what to think and how to think, than an agent of mediation or popular entertainment, dealing in what is now known as "infotainment" or "edutainment" and dealing with it in a manner often noisy and boisterous, sometimes providing a cultural carnival and sites of resistance. Both museums as institutions and collecting as a cultural practice are devices for communal and individual definition.

HISTORICAL OUTLINE

The history of the museum as a cultural institution is long, venerable, and complex, almost dauntingly so. Fortunately, the study of museums has been blessed by the career of Alma S. Wittlin, who in 1949 published *The Museum: Its History and Its Tasks in Education*, substantially revised in 1970 as *Museums: In Search of a Useable Future*. While not universally accepted, Wittlin's work is invariably consulted and cited; she provides an orientation to the history of museums of use to anyone embarking upon this subject. While definitions of museums abound, each bearing the load of the theoretical interests of its author, Wittlin's is more serviceable than many. "The word Museum," she writes,

> echoes a multiplicity of meanings rooted in history. . . . The following qualities are inherent in them: inspirational values; an encyclopedic approach to learning and inquiry; privacy and secrecy; rarity and costliness; features related to storage and hiding of things. . . . Museums provide information and stimulation by means of objects, in distinction from libraries and classrooms, where experiences are generated by symbols, by the written or spoken word. . . . It is generally considered that museums fulfill three main functions. They serve as *depositories* devoted to the preservation and conservation of objects of particular value—treasured for their association with events and personalities of history, for their significance in representing human excellence in terms of scientific ingeniousness or of artistic achievement, and for providing samples of the natural environment or objects related to human ways of living at different time and in different societies. They are *centers of research* and *educational agencies*. Some institutions are mainly or exclusively devoted to a single function; others endeavor to serve two of them or all three. (*Museums: In Search of a Useable Future* 1)

Here we have most of the issues at stake in a study of any museum, from the British Museum or the Louvre or the American Philosophical Society in the nineteenth century, to the Guggenheim or the Smithsonian or the Rock and Roll Hall of Fame and Museum or the Oklahoma Route 66 Museum in the present. Moreover, they are the issues at stake in the study of the vast number of privately held collections, many of which will one day become institutionalized as museums.

Wittlin also provides a functional analysis of what she calls the "Preludes to

Public Museums," an account of those collections and other museological impulses, from antiquity to the emergence of the museum as we now commonly know it in the last quarter of the eighteenth century and in the nineteenth century based upon the uses and gratifications of these essentially private depositories: economic hoard collections, social prestige collections, magic collections, collections as expressions of group loyalties, collections as means of stimulating curiosity and inquiry, collections as means of emotional experience. Clearly, a given collection may serve several ends; a reliquary holding a local saint's bones, for example, might meet the needs of hoarding treasure, magic, group solidarity, and emotional experience. This functional analysis may also usefully be applied to contemporary museums catering to popular culture as well as the more traditionally defined, both nonprofit and proprietary, as, for example, the Newseum (Arlington, Virginia), the Sarasota Classic Car Museum, or the National Rifle Association's National Firearms Museum (Fairfax, Virginia).

Museums did not begin the slow and difficult process of emerging from the private cabinets of curiosities into the public institutions that we know today until the eighteenth century. The museum as we know it is a product of the Enlightenment, its passionate curiosity, and its interest in instrumental knowledge. The historiography and sociology of knowledge in this period enjoyed an explosion in the closing years of the 1990s; many of these works do not deal directly with museums but prove very useful to an understanding of the contexts in which the modern museum arose, particularly the desire for encyclopedic comprehensiveness and the struggles with taxonomy: Foster Stockwell's *A History of Information Storage and Retrieval*, Bill Katz's *Cuneiform to Computer: A History of Reference Sources*, and Daniel Headrick's *When Information Came of Age: Technologies of Knowledge in the Age of Revolution, 1700–1850*. In his chapter on "Classifying Knowledge" in *A Social History of Knowledge from Gutenberg to Diderot*, Peter Burke views the taxonomy of museum collections as a piece with this era's concern with the order of dictionaries, encyclopedias, libraries, and the curricula:

> No wonder then that the apparently irresistible rise of museums in this period has been explained not only as an indicator of the expansion of curiosity but as an attempt to manage a "crisis of knowledge" following the flood of new objects into Eurpoe from the New World and elsewhere—alligators, armadillos, feathered head-dresses, newly discovered Egyptian mummies, Chinese porcelain—objects which resisted attempts to fit them into traditional categories. (109)

The history of the museum in France is tied to, and reflected in, the development of the Louvre, established in 1793 by the French Republic based upon the confiscation of the private collections of the Bourbon kings, to which were soon added objects collected by Napoleon's armies. So, too, the history of the museum in England is tied to, and reflected in, that development of the British Museum, founded in 1753 by an act of Parliament, responding to a bequest of Sir Hans Sloane and open to the public in 1759. It would be well into the nineteenth century when that public access to the British Museum would become anything like contemporary practice. It would grow through a mix of public and private support from the proceeds of Industrial Revolution and empire, into one of the world's premier institutions. Edward Miller provides a full and fascinating account of the British Museum's development in *That Noble Cabinet: A History of the British Museum*.

The development of the museum in the United States, as a practical matter, began in Philadelphia, setting the dominant pattern for museum development in the rest of the nation, even to this day. "The vitality with which the new nation's social and political life was charged," Herbert and Marjorie Katz suggest, "characterized our cultural development as well. An inspired citizen of a mind to turn a private passion into a public interest would work at his self-appointed task until he succeeded. Such a man was Charles Wilson Peale of Philadelphia. An artist by profession and a naturalist by inclination, Peale was determined to do something about the fact that there was no place where Philadelphians could come either to see his fine portraits of contemporaries or to view his growing natural history collection" (2). Unlike most of his British counterparts, Peale made his collection genuinely accessible and on a democratic basis, but when the collection outgrew his house, he and the collection in 1794 moved in with the American Philosophical Society. Much of the material from the Lewis and Clark expedition entered this collection. The same pattern was to be repeated by others in Philadelphia, in New York, in Boston, and as far west as Ohio in the first quarter of the century, a story told in Katz and Katz, *Museums, U.S.A.* The evolution of the Smithsonian Institution into America's national museum was a slow and convoluted process, taking Congress eight years of debate to pass legislation accepting James Smithson's bequest (the entire estate of an English scientist who never visited America) and its terms and many more years for the Smithsonian's mission to evolve.

Wittlin describes three general patterns of reformation taking place after the initial settlement of public museums in roughly the first half of the nineteenth century in the period up to 1914, in the period between the wars, and in the period 1945 to the present. The first of these is marked by the attempt to impose order on what were commonly chaotic accumulations of objects, by the development of "national" institutions, and by specialization either of distinct sections within larger institutions or of the development of separate museums—art museums, ethnological museums, natural history museums, and the like. Steven Conn's *Museums and American Intellectual Life, 1876–1926*, in chapters on various specialty museums in nineteenth-century America from Charles Wilson Peale to the international exhibitions marking the American sesquicentennial, seeks to ground them in nineteenth-century intellectual history so as to understand better the Victorian fascination with "stuff" and the energetic building of institutions of all kinds. Related to this concern with stuff has been the explosion of interest in material culture reflected in Marvin Harris' publication in 1979 of *Cultural Materialism: The Struggle for a Science of Culture* and in the initial publication of the *Journal of Material Culture* in 1995. See also *Objects and Others: Essays on Museums and Material Culture*.

The second pattern is marked by the attempt, most conspicuously but certainly not exclusively in Russian and the fascist states, to employ the museum as an instrument of nationalism and state propaganda. The third pattern is marked by processes of rebuilding, first, by repairing the physical damage done by the war and second, by returning expropriated objects, a process that had been extended to apply to expropriations having taken place well before World Wars I and II;

The Jade room, Metropolitan Museum of Art, New York. Courtesy of the Library of Congress

and third, by reconstructing the mission of institutions called museums. Many of these processes took place under the aegis of the United Nations Educational, Scientific, and Cultural Organization (UNESCO)'s Museum Section and the International Council of Museums (ICOM).

Increasingly, the history of museums has become the vehicle for critical argument and theoretical development (see later); a characteristic exercise in the move in this direction in historical studies is Joel J. Orosz's very readable *Curators and Culture: The Museum Movement in America, 1740–1870*, which argues for an American compromise between the museum as popular resort and the museum as the resort of scholars—a middle ground between a relatively open and relatively closed cultural arena, preservation, and status, on the one hand, and education and egalitarianism, on the other hand.

REFERENCE WORKS

Students of the museum are blessed with two comprehensive research tools, the compilers of which are candidates for bibliographical sainthood. These two works are the first stop in one's search, and that is well before switching on the computer to begin rifling the Web, for they orient one to the nature and taxonomy of the resources available on museums and so make one a more efficient and better user of other devices.

The Museum: A Reference Guide is edited by Michael Steven Shapiro with the help of Louis Ward Kemp. A part of the Greenwood Press bibliographical series, this book is to the study of museums what *The Handbook of American Popular Culture* seeks to be to the study of American popular culture. It is a collection of eleven bibliographical essays by as many different hands, most of them museum professionals: "The Natural History Museum," "The Art Museum," "The Museum of Science and Technology," "The History Museum," "The Folk Museum," "Museum Collections," "Museum Education," "Museum Exhibition," "The Public and the Museum," "Biography and the Museum," and "Professionalism and the Museum." Each essay provides a historical outline, a survey of sources, and a bibliographic checklist. There is one index to names for the whole work. Also noteworthy are three appendixes. Appendix A is an international list of museum directories with its own subject index. This list is unavoidably selective; for example, there are only four automobile museums listed; given the extent and growth and distribution and rapid change of the museum phenomenon, this list, while useful, needs be supplemented with Web searches. Appendix B is devoted to "Museum Archives and Special Collections." This guide to eighteen U.S archives is a major access tool to archival material and provides addresses and phone numbers and hours (all of which should now be checked on the Web) and a general description of holdings in the realms of museology and collecting. Appendix C is a list of "Museum-Related Periodicals." This book's tilt is toward the United States.

Peter Woodhead and Geoffrey Stansfield's *Keyguide to Information Sources in Museum Studies* tilts toward Britain and somewhat less toward Europe and so complements Shapiro's book, particularly useful in light of the explosion in museum studies in Britain, especially among the red-brick social scientists. A crucial reference tool in three parts, its extremely detailed table of contents and the very detailed index to subjects as well as names make it easy to use. Part One is an overview of museum studies and its literature, a collection of succinct bibliographical essays on how and where to find printed information. Part Two is an annotated bibliographical list of sources of information; examples include bibliographies of museum studies literature, guides to periodicals in museum studies, a list of museum studies periodicals, guides to theses, and an annotated list of monographs (important works categorically organized, including a collection of guides to museums by continent and county). Part Three is an annotated list of sixty-nine selected museum organizations. While published in Britain and clearly international in scope, it seems to cover American work well, but one gets a clear sense that relatively little work has been done in America and by Americans.

It is well to keep in mind that these books do not deal with the World Wide Web or with proprietary or oddball museums at all well; indeed, some of the very stuff of popular culture study is dealt with not at all. All the same, these are essential tools and taken together are the first stop on the bibliographic trek.

Museology is a field teeming with handbooks, perhaps a reflection of a felt need for guidance in a realm relatively new to academic specialty in which many of the practitioners were trained primarily in other realms and a reflection of the sponsorship of groups like the International Council of Museums, the American Association of Museums, and the American Association of State and Local History, all of which are concerned about defining and maintaining standards, from preservation to presentation, from fund-raising to marketing, from taxonomy to ethics.

Typical of such books is Edward P. Alexander's *Museums in Motion: An Introduction to the History and Functions of Museums*, a textbookish volume probably used in museology courses but full and clear, with direct discussions of what a museum is, with accounts of art, natural history, science, and technology; of history museums along with botanical gardens and zoos; of the museum as collection, as conservation, as research, as exhibition, as interpretation, and as cultural and social center; of museums as a profession (publications, accreditation, study, and credentials); and of museum ethics. *Museums in Motion* reflects the disposition (bias is too strong a word) of its publisher, the American Association of State and Local History, and as such may be of greater use to the student of popular culture than some of the others.

Gary Edson and David Dean's *The Handbook for Museums* performs essentially the same function, claiming that it "provides essential information for people working in the museum world" (i), and the foreword declares, "The publication [1994] of this handbook is without a question a major milestone in the history of museum management" (xi). Addressed to the professional, it is intended as both a textbook for students and a reference tool for practitioners, covering such matters as interpretation and communication and the ever-present topics of professionalism and ethics. Many charts and graphs fill the pages, as do boxes of technical notes about humidity and security. This handbook also provides boilerplate document forms for catalogs, accession records, and a host of other necessary paper. Chapter 19 is a "Glossary of Museum Related Terms," most useful to those of us not in the trade, especially when time comes to write about museum-related subjects.

Of greatest interest to students of popular culture in books of this kind are the sections on interpretations and communities, which often reveal the unstated premises and issues at stake in museum practices, and on ethics, with lists of prohibitions providing more insight into the temptations and sins of museum practice than lists of exhortations provide into the virtues and good works of museums. More detailed discussions illustrated in particular applications appear in *The Ethics of Collecting Cultural Property*, essays, largely from an archaeological perspective, by eighteen different hands with useful bibliography and appendixes. Also in this vein is Alison Grinder and E. Sue McCoy's *The Good Guide: A Sourcebook for Interpreters, Docents, and Tour Guides*, a how-to book for volunteer and staff tour guides and interpreters. Its contents are applicable across a wide range of settings and are useful to the student of museums interested in the analysis of specific guide practices (or if one finds oneself in the role of guide sometime).

For a wide variety of materials on museums, from the fairly general to the very specific, the researcher needs routinely to consult three organizations, at least initially accessible through the World Wide Web: the International Council of Museums (ICOM) (http://www.icom.org), the American Association of Museums (AAM) (http://aam-us.org), and the Smithsonian Institution (http://www.si.edu). All three of these organizations publish a lot of material, in the case of ICOM and AAM much of it dealing with highly technical matters, marketing, and development but some of it general and critical, of more immediate interest to a student of cultural studies. The Smithsonian, particularly, sponsors a wide variety of development projects and many critical and theoretical discussions, exercising its role as the U.S. national museum, including what amounts to a national Center for Museum Studies (http://museumstudies.si.edu/), and so it provides a stimulus to theoretical development and a model of museum practices. As a consequence, it was a lightning rod for controversy in the culture wars of the last two decades of the twentieth century and remains so today. The degree to which the Smithsonian is a bellwether is open to debate, but in any event, no student of museums as an American popular culture phenomenon may overlook current developments at this constantly evolving institution.

The American Association of Museums is something like a trade association and as such reveals current fears and trends; it is very concerned about marketing, membership development, community building, endowment growth, and the like. While a very large group, it is well to remember that not all, not nearly all, museums in the United States are members. AAM publishes *The Official Museum Directory* (30th ed., 2000, available on the Web and in research libraries in the much handier paper format), which is a very useful reference tool, allowing one to get a sense of the scope and diversity of the museum phenomenon in America and clearly demonstrating its popularity, remarkable in extent and character given that the museum is not a mass-mediated cultural exercise in the common understanding of that expression. This directory provides access information to "museums" broadly understood: "Aquariums," "Arboretums/Botanical Gardens," "Art," "Children's," "General," "Historical Sites/Houses," "History," "Natural History," "Nature Centers," "Planetariums," "Science/Technology," "Specialized" [read "miscellaneous"], and "Zoos." It is organized by state, then alphabetically by name with indexes to personnel, institutions by category, institutions by collections, and museums and institutions on the Web.

AAM's embrace of the Web reflects a rapidly growing reality in museum practice. One may, for example, pursue specific lines of inquiry and discussion by subscribing to the Museum Discussion List: Museum-L@Home.Ease.Lsoft.Com (archived at http://home.ease.lsoft.com/archives/museum-l.html). Closer to the core of the museum as a popular culture phenomenon in the new millennium, however, is the specter of the virtual museum. A great deal of Web-based activity surrounds museums, as a brief visit to the Virtual Libraries museum pages (http://www.icom.org/vlmp) sponsored by ICOM demonstrates. Almost every museum making a claim to that status has a Web site, ranging from a page or two to tens, even hundreds of pages, assembled with varying degrees of skill. A distinction is emerging between museum Web pages and a virtual museum. "A virtual museum," Jamie McKenzie writes,

> is an organized collection of electronic artifacts and information resources—virtually anything can be digitized. The collection may include paintings, drawings, photographs, diagrams, graphs, recordings, video segments, newspaper articles, transcripts of interviews, numerical databases, and a host of other items which may be saved on the virtual museum's file server. It may also offer pointers [links] to great resources around the world relevant to the museum's main focus. ("Building a Virtual Museum Community").

He goes on to make a distinction between a learning museum, which provides resources sufficient to invite repeat visits and enable substantial investigation and exploration, and a marketing museum, which is fundamentally a communications device aimed at increasing the number of visitors to the original physical museum or promoting museum shop sales. Interesting difficulties arise when a museum Web site sponsors both a marketing and a learning museum; the Smithsonian, the British Museum, and the Louvre are, to my mind, characteristic examples. To get a sense of the phenomenon, however, go down the less traveled (?) roads, mapped by ICOM's Museums of the USA (http://www.museumca.org/usa/) or Museums on the Web (http://www.people.Virginia.EDU/~lha5w/museum/). There are lots of pretty pictures (most of them protected from downloading) and a great deal of cacophony. There is much discussion of (and fretting about) "virtual museums," especially the increasing number that exists and operates only in cyberspace. To get a sense of the discourse in this realm, consult *The Virtual and the Real: Media in the Museum*, edited by Selma Thomas and Ann Mintz, a collection of eleven essays by fourteen different hands, and Suzanne Keene's *Digital Collections: Museums and the Information Age*. Much extended, serious analysis of the virtual museum as a cultural phenomenon remains to be done. Abundantly clear here are the opportunities for further popular culture study.

A considerable presence in cyberspace as well as in real time and space is the phenomenon described in Lynne Arany and Archie Hobson's travel guide to *Little Museums*. Such places as the California Surf Museum, the Delta Blues Museum, the International UFO Museum and Research Center, the Muscle Car Ranch, the Museum of Bad Art, the New Orleans Historic Voodoo Museum, and the Vacuum Cleaner Museum are collectively and, in some cases, individually drawing large crowds. Most of these have Web pages; see Unusual Museums of the Internet (http://www.unusualmuseums.org.). The museological impulse—the attractions and satisfactions of the structure and functions of the museum that Wittlin describes—has a very long reach; indeed, museums engage people almost apart from the objects of their attention. As a practical matter, museums of this kind have been studied not at all as cultural phenomenon.

RESEARCH COLLECTIONS

In view of the museum's function to preserve, it is surprising that museums are commonly an archival nightmare. Michael Steven Shapiro in *The Museum: A Reference Guide* describes this situation and the concerted effort to ameliorate it beginning in the mid-1970s in the *Guide*'s Appendix B, "Museum Archives and Special Collections," which includes a selective list of "prominent" holders of research materials: American Museum of Natural History (New York), Archives of American Art (Smithsonian, Washington, D.C.), Baltimore Museum of Art, Cleveland Museum of Natural History, Corcoran Gallery of Art (New York), Detroit Institute of Arts, Fogg Art Museum (Cambridge, Massachusetts), Franklin Institute Science Museum (Philadelphia), Isabella Stewart Gardner Museum (Boston), Metropolitan Museum of Art (New York), Museum of Comparative Zoology (Cambridge, Massachusetts), Museum of Science and Natural History (St. Louis), Museum Reference Center (Smithsonian, Washington, D.C.), Philadelphia Museum of Art, St. Louis Art Museum, Smithsonian Institution Archives (Washington, D.C.), University [of Pennsylvania] Museum (Philadelphia). The appendix concludes with a "Bibliographic Checklist" of works essential to working with and in museum archives.

Also useful is the list of manuscript collections in the selected bibliography to Joel Orosz's *Curators and Culture: The Museum Movement in America, 1740–1870.*

Clearly, the major player in this effort to bring order to research into the museum as such is the Smithsonian Institution; a description of its holdings and services is available at its Web site, and the Archives has its own pages (http://www.si.edu/archives/about.htm). Given the proliferation of museums, it is always useful to consult the National Union Catalog of Manuscript Collections (NUCMC), now conveniently accessible on-line at http://www.loc.gov/coll/nucmc/nucmc.html, and its Directory of Archival and Manuscript Repositories in the United States (http://www.loc.gov/coll/nucmc/other.html).

Most popular culture museums and collections are defined either by medium or by genre; there are very few general collections or archives. The most notable, of course, is the Popular Culture Library at Bowling Green State University, Bowling Green, Ohio (on the Web at http://www.bgsu.edu/colleges/library/pcl/pcl.html), but even this collection's bias is toward printed matter. For archival material on the collection, preservation, and exhibiting of popular culture, one needs to go to the Smithsonian.

THEORY AND CRITICISM

The 1970s and 1980s marked a resurgence of critical interest in museums, particularly their role in social and cultural formation, the result of general interest in what was known as the New Historicism; in the study of material culture; and in the theoretical work of Michel Foucault and Pierre Bourdieu. The museum has become an increasingly interesting object of inquiry as a site of cultural and social formation. As Genevieve Bell points out, "[C]urrent academic research tends to fall into one of 4 categories: 1. Commentaries on particular exhibits, 2. Analysis of museums as powerful social institutions, 3. Handbook & Instructional guides for running museums, 4. Analysis of museum visitors." In keeping with the penchants of postmodern culture and criticism, these interests are often fragmented and increasingly overlap.

The University of Leicester grew into an important center of the British explosion of museum studies in the 1990s, sponsoring and publishing a wide variety of studies informed by critical theory and the practices and dispositions of red-brick social science, which lend themselves well to popular culture studies. A good introduction to this orientation is Eilean Hooper-Greenhill's *Museums and the Shaping of Knowledge*, a very well-documented history of museums of the newer sort that, informed by the theory of Michel Foucault, seeks to examine the museum's role in the "discursive" practices of a given era and to understand museums as sites of epistemological disruption as well as consensus building. The book is required reading for the contemporary student of museums.

Particularly in the American experience, the museum as an institution has been at the center of the struggle for cultural democracy and so a valent in any account, for good or ill, of popular culture. Lawrence Levine's *Highbrow/Lowbrow: The Emergence of Cultural Hierarchies in America* is a useful orienting device. While

Peabody Museum of Natural History, Yale University, New Haven, Connecticut. Courtesy of the Library of Congress

American culture has always been divided along economic, racial, and class lines, Levine argues that in the nineteenth century, especially the first half of it, Americans, in addition to whatever specific cultures they were part of, shared a public culture less hierarchically organized, less fragmented into relatively rigid adjectival boxes than their descendants were to experience a century later. Museums played an important role in the "sacralization" of culture, in the identification of order and hierarchy and culture as opposed to immigrants and urban life and industrialization.

Museums also play an important role in developing a sense of self and community and a sense of past and present and future and defining the relationships among them. As Robert Hewison describes the phenomenon,

> The impulse to preserve the past is part of the impulse to preserve the self. Without knowing where we have been, it is difficult to know where we are going. The past is the foundation of the individual and collective identity; objects from the past are the source of significance as cultural symbols. Continuity between past and present creates a sense of sequence out of aleatory chaos and, since change is inevitable, a stable system of ordered meaning enables us to cope with both innovation and decay. The nostalgic impulse

is an important agency in adjustment to crisis; it is a social emollient and reinforces national identity when confidence is weakened or threatened. (47)

In times of social, political, and cultural turmoil, then, museums become more important and their conduct more hotly contested.

David Harvey, commenting on the 1960s axiom to "think globally and act locally," succinctly defines the dilemma facing museums operating in the condition of postmodernity and the issues that engage their critics:

> The assertion of any place-bound identity has to rest at some point, on the motivational power of tradition. It is difficult, however, to maintain any sense of historical continuity in the face of all the flux and ephemerality of flexible accumulation [of late capitalism]. The irony is that such tradition is now often preserved by being commodified and marketed as such. The search for roots ends up at worst being produced and marketed as an image, as a simulacrum or pastiche (imitation communities constructed to evoke images of some folksy past, the fabric of traditional working-class communities being taken over by an urban gentry). . . . At best, historical tradition is reorganized as a museum culture, not necessarily of high modernist art, but of local history, of local production, of how things once upon a time were made, sold, consumed, and integrated into a long-lost and often romanticized daily life (one from which all trace of oppressive social relations may be expunged). Through the preservation of a partially illusory past it becomes possible to signify something of local identity and perhaps to do it profitably. (303)

Indeed, "living history" and the "new social history" are controversial subjects, particularly among historians who work in museums and other public outreach programs and historians who work in the academy and environs. The issues are complex but clearly relevant to an understanding of museums and popular culture. The most efficient orientation to this realm is to consult Randal Allred's essay on "Living History and Battlefield Reenactments" in this collection; the special issue of the *Journal of American Culture* (12: 2, Summer 1989), edited by James W. Miller et al., "Museums and the Academic"; Jay Anderson's *Time Machines: The World of Living History*; and Thomas Schelereth's *Material Culture Studies in America*. Robert Hewison's *The Heritage Industry* and Barbara Kirshenblatt-Gimblett's *Destination Culture: Tourism, Museums and Heritage* provide trenchant analyses of these complex issues.

The interest in the museum as a social and cultural institution inexorably leads to an interest in the museum visitor. In addition to numerous attendance and demographic studies, anthropological methods have become increasingly common approaches, particularly useful to popular culture studies. For example, John H. Falk in *The Museum Experience* examines "the way the public uses museums" (1), employing what he calls the "interactive experience model," derived from the overlap of three contexts—the physical, the social, and the personal—before the visit, during the visit, after the visit, and the visit remembered. A short, but very useful, annotated bibliography is rich in items dealing with psychological and sociological studies relevant to such an audience analysis. Eilean Hooper-Greenhill's

Museums and Their Visitors deals with theory and practice from the museum professional's point of view.

Carol Duncan in *Civilizing Rituals: Inside Public Art Museums*, for another take on this concern, suggests that the museum visit is a kind of ritual and that museums are environments structured around specific ritual scenarios. Catherine Bell's *Ritual Theory, Ritual Practice* helps orient one new to this kind of analysis. So, too, Genevieve Bell approaches museums in terms of the cultural ecology of museums. Many commentators on museums now address institutional kinship lines, the effects of physical environments upon human interaction, the drawing and blurring of boundaries, and similar anthropological concerns.

Many technical books and articles appearing under the head of museum marketing may prove of use to the student of popular culture, but a useful first stop in this line of inquiry is Neil Harris' *Cultural Excursions: Marketing Appetites and Cultural Tastes in Modern America*, a collection of seventeen essays published elsewhere, the first seven of which deal with the rise of the museum in public consciousness via blockbuster exhibitions and international tourist culture, among other agents. Harris is often credited with starting in the United States in the 1960s the more serious study of museums and the concern about the museum's role in shaping public values. This concern endures, as, for example, in Alberta Arthurs' "Making Change: Museums and Public Life," and is contextualized in studies surrounding the concept of civic culture and civil religion, as, for example, in *The Civic Culture Revisited: An Analytic Study*. Editors Ivan Karp, Christine Mullen Kreamer, and Steven Lavine take this notion of "civil culture" as the organizing principle of their most useful collection of essays by seventeen different hands, *Museums and Communities: The Politics of Public Culture*, which deals with questions of cultural authority and the struggle to control it; especially useful for framing consideration of museums is Ivan Karp's introductory essay to Part One, "On Civil Society and Social Identity" (19–33).

In turn, these interests inexorably lead to an interest in particular museums and exhibits—the devil residing in the details. Michael Belcher's *Exhibitions in Museums*, addressed to the museum professional, is pretty technical but useful for understanding the premises of exhibition practice; see especially the sections on "The Exhibition Environment" and "The Museum Visitor and Exhibition Effectiveness."

A useful place to begin the practice of "reading" museums and exhibitions as texts is Sharon Macdonald and Gordon Fyfe's *Theorizing Museums*, a collection of well-documented essays by ten different hands on such topics as the museum and globalization, the museum and contested historical interpretations (e.g., the *Enola Gay* exhibition at Smithsonian), ethnographic exhibitions, feminist perspectives on museums, theoretical analysis of the visiting process ("Decoding the Visitor's Gaze"), and similar topics suggested by the reading practices of critical theory. A central concern is borders, boundaries, and the whole theoretical business surrounding taxonomy and classification, typically illustrated in specific applications. Especially useful as an overview is Sharon Macdonald's introduction, "Theorizing Museums" (1–18). This collection is of singular value to students of popular culture because it offers models of reading practices transferable to other museums or exhibits.

Another such collection is *Exhibiting Dilemmas: Issues of Representation at the*

Smithsonian, edited by Amy Henderson and Adrienne L. Kaeppler. "Exhibiting Dilemmas is about how exhibition issues are being played out at the Smithsonian Institution" (1), understood in terms of the ideological and semiotic content of exhibits, and so it is a collection of examples of critical theory's moves on museums: the *Enola Gay* controversy in 1995, "The West as America" exhibit in 1991 at the National Museum of American Art, and the Hope Diamond exhibit, among others. As Susan A. Crane's collection *Museums and Memory* demonstrates, the forging and distorting of memory and the whole thorny question of "authenticity," in which processes museums play an important role, are an increasingly hot concern in museum studies. Crane's "Introduction" provides a useful descriptive summary of the contents, allowing one efficiently to choose from the theoretically sophisticated, yet readable, offerings.

Popular culture, as such, as an explicitly marked category, has yet to develop a large body of serious critical museum studies. Descriptive journalistic accounts of little or distinctly idiosyncratic museums abound, and some accounts of popular museums as business enterprises appear from time to time, but serious critical analysis of museums as a popular cultural phenomenon are rare. This situation is, in large measure, the result of the erosion of the distinction between high, middle, and low culture. Nearly all museums are now engaged in popular culture and are part of the popular culture phenomenon; the terms "museum" and "popular culture" are nearly coextensive, and so to deal with a museum is to deal with popular culture.

In 1981, however, when Fred E. H. Schroder edited and the Bowling Green State University Popular Press published *Twentieth-Century Popular Culture in Museums and Libraries*, the divide between mass-mediated culture and the cultural artifacts likely to show up in all but roadside museums was much greater, much more distinct than in 2002. The Guggenheim Museum's "Art of the Motorcycle" exhibit was then unthinkable. These essays by sixteen different authors show their age and reflect the time in which they were written, revealing a self-consciousness and defensiveness about popular culture studies surviving into the early 1980s. In large measure, these essays constitute an argument for the systematic preservation of the popular cultural artifacts, particularly the mass-produced, electronically mediated, disposable, and commercialized products of entertainment, communication, and transportation—an argument that has carried. "Popular culture is twentieth-century American culture," Schroder rightly notes in the Introduction (7). That point is now much more commonly acknowledged and even accepted. The objects of popular culture are now much more eagerly and systematically collected, principally by individuals but increasingly by public museums, and so is repeated a pattern stretching back at least as far as the eighteenth century.

A major first step toward this serious analysis, however, is Kevin Moore's *Museums and Popular Culture*, another in the University of Leicester series on Contemporary Issues in Museum Culture, edited by Susan M. Pearce and Elaine Heumann Gurian. The work claims, somewhat disingenuously in my view, to be a "relatively straightforward analysis of the representations of popular culture in museums" (vii). Informed by the work of Susan Pearce, particularly her views on collecting and on the study of material culture, Moore provides a sophisticated and useful account of a good many thorny issues, for example, the differences between popular culture objects in a museum and a popular culture museum, the place of working-class culture, authenticity, exhibitions of objects that are neither art nor social history—noting that "the most significant collections of material culture relating to popular culture are not in museums but in private hands" (84)—the role of museum displays that consciously or inadvertently explore the spurious (91), and the role of real things, real people, and real places, among others. Chapter 6 models a method of object study in its treatment of a football used in the World Cup final at Wembly in 1966. *Museums and Popular Culture* is to date the best book on this subject and the issues for museums, arising from the disintegration of dominant cultural hierarchies. It is not a collection of ready formulations; rather, it is a collection of suggestive observations on how the concepts and practices of "popular culture" and "museum" engage one another.

COLLECTING

For the student of American popular culture, Moore's most fertile observation may be that "the most significant collections of material culture relating to popular culture are not in museums but in private hands" (84), for, in the condition of postmodernity, everyone is increasingly his or her own museum curator, ably assisted by *The Antiques Road Show* and like television offerings, eBay and like Internet auction sites, and the profusion of Web sites devoted to the collection of nearly every imaginable object. Whether people engage in collecting more now than in the immediate or remote past is a matter of dispute, but what collecting is done is now more conspicuous than ever before. The processes and meanings of collecting are just emerging as an object of scholarly and critical attention. The anthropologist James Clifford, citing the work of Jean Baudrillard and Susan Stewart, concludes:

> Stewart's work brings collecting and display sharply into view as crucial processes of Western identity formation. Gathered artifacts—whether they find their way into curio cabinets, private living rooms, museums of ethnography, folklore, or fine art—function within a developing capitalist "system of objects." By virtue of this system a world of *value* is created and a meaningful deployment and circulation of artifacts maintained. For Baudrillard collected objects create a structured environment that substitutes its own temporality for the "real time" of historical and productive processes: "The environment of private objects and their possession—of which collections are an extreme manifestation—is a dimension of our life that is both essential and imaginary. As essential as dreams." (Clifford 54)

Scholarship on collecting is often indirect, the concern arising as a tangent to other interests, as, for example, in Russell Belk's extensive work on collecting, most notably *Collecting in a Consumer Society*, arising out of more comprehensive studies of consumer behavior; in psychological studies like Werner Muensterberger's *Collecting: An Unruly Passion: Psychological Perspectives*; in more general studies of "material culture," for example, Arjun Appadurai's collection of essays on *The Social Life of Things*; or in Michael Thompson's *Rubbish Theory: The Creation and*

Destruction of Value. While Phyllis Mauch Messenger's *The Ethics of Collecting Cultural Property* is very much focused on issues facing professional anthropologists, ethical concerns provide very useful interpretive perspectives. Perhaps the most striking and provocative study that links collecting and museums and cultural history is Barbara Benedict's *Curiosity: A Cultural History of Early Modern Inquiry*, the best book on collecting that is not explicitly about collecting.

As any visit to the World Wide Web, driven by plugging in the word "collecting" or the name of an object commonly or even uncommonly collected, demonstrates, collecting and collectors are ubiquitous. The auction Web site eBay, "the world's online marketplace," has made one of the primary instruments of collecting available to unprecedented numbers of people, many of whom have had little or no prior access to an auction market of any kind. The idea, if not always the social or economic fact, that value might be determined in a marketplace rather than in the estimates of an authority has had a powerful stimulus to collecting. There are very many collecting periodicals focused upon particular objects and upon current prices, which are out of date as soon as they are published, are intermittently and most commonly privately preserved, and seem to be diminishing somewhat with the action in cyberspace. It is almost impossible to get a systematic handle on these materials. Two places to begin, however, are *The Guide to United States Popular Culture*, which, while it has no entry on collecting per se, has many entries on the objects of collectors' desire, and, as its long title suggests, *The Encyclopedia of Ephemera: A Guide to the Fragmentary Documents of Everyday Life for the Collector, Curator, and Historian* by Maurice Richards.

A most useful "reader" on collecting that will orient one to the study of the process is a collection of twelve essays, *The Cultures of Collecting*, edited by John Elsner and Roger Cardinal, which includes among other very useful items a translation of Jean Baudrillard's "The System of Collecting" and Mieke Bal's "Telling Objects: A Narrative Perspective on Collecting."

The premier scholar in this realm is Susan M. Pearce, whose *Museums, Objects, and Collections: A Cultural Study, On Collecting: An Investigation into Collecting in the European Tradition*, and *Collecting in Contemporary Practice* are foundational studies. Anyone engaging in the study of collecting needs first to consult the first book. First, its bibliography is the best single source for studies on collecting, particularly the more recent ones informed by critical theory and the practices of cultural studies. Second, its opening chapter, "Collecting Culture," amounts to a handbook, providing definitions and outlining basic considerations. "The contemporary collecting of objects," Pearce points out, "can be seen to be permeated with social characteristics which may be described as postmodern" (14). *Collecting in Contemporary Practice* marks the shifting paradigms from studies of collections, to studies of the processes of collecting. This book reports and interprets the results of the Contemporary Collecting in Britain Survey, with accounts of who collects what, the roles of collecting in work and play, in buying and giving, in families and homes, and among men and women, motives and meanings, and the contemporary practice of collecting. While a compelling (some might find it intimidating) account, Pearce's study is not the last word on collecting; rather, it is an important first word in a new and sophisticated analysis of collecting as a cultural practice, which sees it as neither psychological aberration nor blind consumption.

BIBLIOGRAPHY

Museums

Alexander, Edward P. *Museums in Motion: An Introduction to the History and Functions of Museums*. Nashville, Tenn.: American Association for State and Local History, 1979.

Anderson, Jay. *A Living History Reader*. Vol. 1: *Museums*. Nashville, Tenn.: American Association for State and Local History, 1991.

———. *The Living History Source Book*. Nashville, Tenn.: American Association for State and Local History, 1985.

Arany, Lynne, and Archie Hobson. *Little Museums*. New York: Holt/Owl, 1998.

Arthurs, Alberta. "Making Change: Museums and Public Life." In *The Politics of Culture: Policy Perspectives for Individuals, Institutions, and Communities*, ed. Gigi Bradford, Michael Gary, and Glenn Wallach. New York: New Press, 2000, 208–17.

Belcher, Michael. *Exhibitions in Museums*. Washington, D.C.: Smithsonian Institution Press, 1993.

Bell, Catherine. *Ritual Theory, Ritual Practice*. New York: Oxford University Press, 1992.

Bell, Genevieve. "The Museum as Cultural Ecology: A Study." Intel Architectural Labs, April 1998. (http://developer.intel.com/ial/about/museumwhitepaper.htm).

Bourdieu, Pierre. *Distinction: A Social Critique of the Judgement of Taste*. Cambridge: Harvard University Press, 1984.

———. *The Field of Cultural Production: Essays on Art and Literature*. Ed. Randal Johnson. New York: Columbia University Press, 1993.

Burke, Peter. *A Social History of Knowledge from Gutenberg to Diderot*. Malden, Mass.: Blackwell, 2000.

The Civic Culture Revisited: An Analytic Study. Ed. Gabriel A. Almond and Sidney Verba. Boston: Little, Brown, 1980.

Conn, Steven. *Museums and American Intellectual Life, 1876–1926*. Chicago: University of Chicago Press, 1998.

The Cultures of Collecting. Ed. John Elsner and Roger Cardinal. Cambridge: Harvard University Press, 1994.

Duncan, Carol. *Civilizing Rituals: Inside Public Art Museums*. London: Routledge, 1995.

Edson, Gary, and David Dean. *The Handbook for Museums*. New York: Routledge, 1994.

The Ethics of Collecting Cultural Property. 2nd ed. Ed. Phyllis Mauch Messenger. Albuquerque: University of New Mexico Press, 1999.

Exhibiting Cultures: The Poetics and Politics of Museum Display. Ed. Ivan Karp and Steven D. Lavine. Washington, D.C.: Smithsonian, 1991.

Exhibiting Dilemmas: Issues of Representation at the Smithsonian. Ed. Amy Henderson and Adrienne L. Kaeppler. Washington, D.C.: Smithsonian Institution Press, 1997.

Falk, John H. *The Museum Experience*. Washington, D.C.: Whalesback Books, 1992.

Foucault, Michel. *The Archeology of Knowledge*. New York: Pantheon, 1972.

Grinder, Alison, and E. Sue McCoy. *The Good Guide: A Sourcebook for Interpreters, Docents, and Tour Guides*. Scottsdale, Ariz.: Ironwood Press, 1985.

Harris, Marvin. *Cultural Materialism: The Struggle for a Science of Culture*. New York: Vintage, 1979.

Harris, Neil. *Cultural Excursions: Marketing Appetites and Cultural Tastes in Modern America*. Chicago: University of Chicago Press, 1990.

Harvey, David. *The Culture of Postmodernity: An Enquiry into the Origins of Cultural Change*, 1980. Cambridge, Mass.: Basil Blackwell, 1989.

Headrick, Daniel R. *When Information Came of Age: Technologies of Knowledge in the Age of Revolution, 1700–1850*. New York: Oxford University Press, 2000.

Hewison, Robert. *The Heritage Industry: Britain in a Climate of Decline*. London: Methuen, 1987.

Hooper-Greenhill, Eilean. *Museums and the Shaping of Knowledge*. New York: Routledge, 1992.

———. *Museums and Their Visitors*. New York: Routledge, 1994.

Interpretation: A Bibliography on Historical Organization Practices. Ed. Frederick L. Rath Jr. and Merrilyn Rogers O'Connell. Nashville, Tenn.: American Association for State and Local History, 1978.

Katz, Bill. *Cuneiform to Computer: A History of Reference Sources*. Lanham, Md.: Scarecrow, 1998.

Katz, Herbert and Marjorie Katz. *Museums, U.S.A.: A History and Guide*. Garden City, N.Y.: Doubleday, 1965.

Keene, Suzanne. *Digital Collections: Museums and the Information Age*. Oxford: Butterworth/Heinemann, 1998.

Kirshenblatt-Gemblett, Barbara. *Destination Culture: Tourism, Museums and Heritage*. Berkeley: University of California Press, 1998.

Levine, Lawrence. *Highbrow/Lowbrow: The Emergence of Cultural Hierarchies in America*. Cambridge: Harvard University Press, 1988.

Maleuvre, Didier. *Museum Memories: History, Technology, Art*. Stanford, Calif.: Stanford University Press, 1999.

McKenzie, Jamie. "Building a Virtual Museum Community." Paper delivered at the Museums and the Web Conference, Getty Information Institute, Los Angeles, March 16–19, 1997. http://www.fno.org/museum/museweb.html

———. "Virtual Museums: Full of Sound and Fury Signifying . . ." http://www.fno.org/museum/muse/html

Miller, Edward. *That Noble Cabinet: A History of the British Museum*. Athens: Ohio University Press, 1974.

Moore, Kevin. *Museums and Popular Culture*. London: Cassell, 1997.

The Museum: A Reference Guide. Ed. Michael Steven Shapiro with Louis Ward Kemp. Westport, Conn.: Greenwood Press, 1990.

"Museums and the Academy." Ed. James W. Miller, Thomas A. Woods, and Kurt E. Leichtle. Special issue of *Journal of American Culture* 12: 2 (Summer 1989).

Museums and Communities: The Politics of Public Culture. Ed. Ivan Karp, Christine Mullen Kreamer, and Steven D. Lavine. Washington, D.C.: Smithsonian Institution Press in cooperation with American Association of Museums, 1992.

Museums and Memory. Ed. Susan A. Crane. Stanford, Calif. : Stanford University Press, 2000.

Objects and Others: Essays on Museums and Material Culture. Ed. George W. Stocking Jr. Madison: University of Wisconsin Press, 1985.

The Official Museum Directory. 30th ed. Ed. Karen Chassie et al. Washington, D.C.: American Association of Museums, 2000. Available on-line at http://www.aam-us.org

Orosz, Joel J. *Curators and Culture: The Museum Movement in America, 1740–1870*. Tuscaloosa: University of Alabama Press, 1990.

Pearce, Susan M. *Museums, Objects, and Collections: A Cultural Study*. Leicester: Leicester University Press, 1992.

———. *On Collecting: An Investigation into Collecting in the European Tradition*. London: Routledge, 1995.

Stockwell, Foster. *A History of Information Storage and Retrieval*. Jefferson, N.C.: McFarland, 2001.

Theorizing Museums. Ed. Sharon Macdonald and Gordon Fyfe. Oxford and Cambridge, Mass.: Blackwell/Sociological Review, 1996.

Thinking about Exhibitions. Ed. Ressa Greenberg, Bruce Fergeson, and Sandy Nairne. London: Routledge, 1996.

Twentieth-Century Popular Culture in Museums and Libraries. Ed. Fred E. H. Schroder. Bowling Green, Ohio: Bowling Green State University Popular Press, 1981.

The Virtual and the Real: Media in the Museum. Ed. Selma Thomas and Ann Mintz. Washington, D.C.: American Association of Museums, 1998.

Wittlin, Alma S. *Museums: In Search of a Useable Future*. Cambridge: MIT Press, 1970.

Woodhead, Peter and Geoffrey Stansfield. *Keyguide to Information Sources in Museum Studies*. 2nd ed. London: Mansell, 1994.

Collecting

Baudrillard, Jean. *Selected Writings*. Stanford, Calif.: Stanford University Press, 1988.

Belk, Russell. *Collecting in a Consumer Society*. London: Routledge, 1995.

Benedict, Barbara M. *Curiosity: A Cultural History of Early Modern Inquiry*. Chicago: University of Chicago Press, 2001.

Clifford, James. "On Collecting Art and Culture." In *The Cultural Studies Reader*, ed. Simon During. New York: Routledge, 1993, 49–73.

Crane, Susan A. *Collecting and Historical Consciousness in Early Nineteenth-Century Germany*. Ithaca, N.Y.: Cornell University Press, 2000.

The Cultures of Collecting. Ed. John Elsner and Roger Cardinal. Cambridge: Harvard University Press, 1994.

The Ethics of Collecting Cultural Property. 2nd ed. Albuquerque: University of New Mexico Press, 1999.

The Guide to United States Popular Culture. Ed. Ray B. Browne and Pat Browne. Bowling Green, Ohio: Popular Press, 2001.

Muensterberger, Werner. *Collecting: An Unruly Passion: Psychological Perspectives*. Princeton, N.J.: Princeton University Press, 1994.

Objects of Special Devotion: Fetishes and Fetishism in Popular Culture. Ed. Ray B. Browne. Bowling Green, Ohio: Popular Press, 1980.

On Collecting, Collectors, and Collections. Ed. Robert L. Brown. Brimfield, Mass.: Brimfield, [1999?].

Pearce, Susan M. *Collecting in Contemporary Practice*. Walnut Creek, Calif.: Sage, 1998.

————. *Experiencing Material Culture in the Western World*. London: Leicester University Press, 1997

Richards, Maurice. *The Encyclopedia of Ephemera*. New York: Routledge, 2000.

Rigby, Douglas and Elizabeth. *Lock, Stock and Barrel: The Story of Collecting*. Philadelphia: J. B. Lippincott, 1944.

The Social Life of Things. Ed. Arjun Appadurai. Cambridge: Cambridge University Press, 1986.

Stewart, Susan. *On Longing: Narratives of the Miniature, the Gigantic, the Souvenir, the Collections*. Baltimore: Johns Hopkins University Press, 1984.

Thompson, Michael. *Rubbish Theory: The Creation and Destruction of Value*. Oxford: Oxford University Press, 1979.

Periodicals

An OCLC (Online Catalog Library of Congress) search of the keywords "museum" and "periodicals" yields a list of slightly over 5,000 items; for "collecting" and "periodicals," 3,000, the vast majority of which focus on describing and pricing objects collected. The following list is highly selective of the more general kind of periodicals, principally dealing with museums.

AIC Newsletter. Washington, D.C.: American Institute for Conservation of Historic and Artistic Works. (1976–   ).

American Association of Zoological Parks and Aquariums Newsletter. Wheeling, W.Va.: American Association of Zoological Parks and Aquariums. (1960–   ).

ARTnews. New York: ARTnews Associates. (1902–   ).

ASTC Newsletter. Washington, D.C.: Association of Science-Technology Centers. Bimonthly newsletter (1973–   ).

AVISO [formerly *Bulletin*]. Washington, D.C.: American Association of Museums. Monthly newsletter (1975 [as *AVISO–*   ).

Council for Museum Anthropology Newsletter. Flagstaff, Ariz.: Council for Museum Anthropology. (1977–   ).

Curator. New York: American Museum of Natural History. (1958–   ).

Ephemera News. Westport, Conn.: Ephemera Society of America. (1982–   ).

Historic Preservation. Washington, D.C.: National Trust for Historic Preservation. (1949–   ).

History News. Nashville, Tenn.: American Association for State and Local History. (1946–   ).

History News Dispatch. Nashville, Tenn.: American Association for State and Local History. (1986–   ).

International Journal of Museum Management and Curatorship. Guildford, England: Butterworth Scientific. (1982–   ).

Journal of Material Culture. Thousand Oaks, Calif.: Sage. (1995–   ).

Journal of Museum Education [formerly *Roundtable Reports*]. Rockville, Md.: Museum Education Roundtable. (1976–).

Muse. Ottawa, Canada: Canadian Museums Association. (1966–).

Museum. Paris: United Nations Educational, Scientific and Cultural Organization. (1949–).

Museum News. Washington, D.C.: American Association of Museums. (1923–).

Museum Studies Journal. San Francisco: Center for Museum Studies, John F. Kennedy University. (1983–1988).

Museums Journal. London, England: Museums Association. (1901–).

Preservation News. Washington, D.C.: National Trust for Historic Preservation. (1961–).

Science Museum News. Pittsburgh: Association of Science Museum Directors. (1976–).

Technology & Conservation of Art, Architecture, and Antiquities: The Magazine for Analysis/Preservation/Restoration/Protection/Documentation. Boston: Technology Organization. (1977–).

Some Useful Web Sites

To plug "museum" or "collecting" into a good search engine produces a plethora of sites, for few, if any, objects of human attention have no communities of collectors or museums. These provide opportunities for study or occasions for chaos, depending upon one's orientation.

American Association of Museums. http://www.aam-us.org

American Culture Studies Resources in BGSU [Bowling Green State University] Libraries: Finding Archives and Manuscript Repositories. http://www.bgsu.edu/colleges/library/infosrv/lue/amcultst/acsarchives.html

The Collectors Link. http://www.thecollectorslink.com/

International Council of Museums. http://www.icom.org/

Popular Culture at the American Studies Group Yellow Pages at the University of Virginia (AS@UVA). http://xroads.virginia.edu/~YP/yppop.html

Popular Culture Library at Bowling Green State University (Ohio). http://www.bgsu.edu/colleges/library/pcl/pcl.html

Museum Computer Network: Museum Sites Online. http://www.mcn.edu/sitesonline.htm

Museum Discussion List (Listserv) and Archives. http://home.ease.lsoft.com/archives/museum-l.html

Museums on the Web. http://www.people.Virginia.EDU/~lha5w/museum/

Museumstuff.com. http://www.museumstuff.com/

Smithsonian Institution. http://www.si.edu/

Unusual Museums of the Internet. http://www.unusualmuseums.org/

Virtual Library museums pages. http://www.icom.org/vlmp/

MUSIC

George Plasketes

"It has become commonplace to say that popular music is an index to the life and history of a nation . . . the extent to which the manners, customs, and current events of every generation have been given expression in popular songs, particularly in the United States. Such songs have reflected the changing character of our people. Every period of American history has had its own characteristic songs," wrote Sigmund Spaeth in his *History of Popular Music in America*, published in 1948. More than fifty years later, the author's words ring louder and truer in American popular culture.

Simply stated, popular music is a cultural giant. Music has grown to be a multibillion-dollar business, a financial fact that in itself signifies a cultural phenomenon worthy of serious scholarly attention. Yet, like other mass-mediated popular art forms such as film and television, music has struggled for academic acceptance. Just as art and commerce often collide, academics and commerce also represent an uneasy intersection. In the essay "The Academic at the Crossroads of Commerce," Rob Bowman (1997) writes that the lingering attitude within academics that "money somehow sullies one's work . . . that it cannot be rigorous, scholarly, serious . . . has greatly impeded the introduction and subsequent integration of popular music studies within the academy."

During the past thirty years, music has managed to gradually establish a credible place for itself as a legitimate area of critical inquiry. "If there really is such a 'discipline' as popular music studies, it probably began, not coincidentally, at about the same time this journal [*Popular Music and Society*] did—1971," writes Gary Burns, editor of the music quarterly since 1994, when its founder, sociologist R. Serge Denisoff, died. Denisoff's pioneering efforts in 1971, along with those of popular culture patriarch Ray Browne, whose Popular Press journals offer outlets for nontraditional, academic writings on every aspect of popular culture, provided significant impetus for the acceptance of popular music as a serious scholarly endeavor. (Reflections on the study of poplar music's evolution/revolution abound in the essays in *Popular Music and Society*'s twenty-fifth anniversary issue, 21: 1 [Spring 1997].)

Since the early 1970s, the body of literature devoted to music's meanings, messages, and marketplace has expanded dramatically in writings that are vast and varied, scholarly and journalistic, theoretical and anecdotal, objectively detached and passionately involved. Further evidence of music's scholarly surge can be seen in the increasing number of resources, archival collections, and regional, national, and international associations and conferences devoted to music-related topics. In addition, the ranks of university presses with music and culture series are growing steadily. Temple University, the University of Chicago, Wesleyan University, and Vanderbilt University, in association with the Country Music Foundation, are among the recent publishers to expand their catalogs into music, joining other university presses such as Harvard, Duke, and Mississippi, among many others. *The Chronicle of Higher Education* (May 1, 1998) further recognized the growing emphasis on music studies in an article, "More Scholars Focus on Popular Music as a Key to Examining Culture and History."

As a maturing, emerging field of critical inquiry, popular music may be more appropriately characterized as an "interdiscipline" rather than a discipline. As a complex cultural text, music invites, if not embraces, a broad range of approaches and methodologies, including history, philosophy, sociology, literature, ethnography, mythology, genre, music, art, performance, technology, journalism, psychology, communications, film, mass media, cultural studies, African American studies, women's studies, religion, business and economics, politics, folklore, and American studies.

HISTORICAL OUTLINE

"How much history can be transmitted by pressure on a guitar string?" wonders the late Robert Palmer in *Deep Blues*. The question resonates as meditation, prefacing the music critic's phrases that follow—"the thought of generations, the history of every human being." The question may be as provocative a one-liner as any expressed in criticism, regardless of subject. Palmer's thought might be reverently expanded beyond a riff or chord to include a song, sound, melody, voice, lyric, chorus, artist, composer, event, place, persona, or image—any of the many ways by which music marks our individual and collective timelines.

Music's rich heritage can be conveniently chronicled according to eras and the significant people, developments, and events that shaped its evolution into a popular art form and contemporary $12 billion industry (nearly double the volume of film in 1998) within the multimedia marketplace that is the core of American popular culture.

Before America established its own signature sound, music was inherited and borrowed from European and African traditions. The audience during music's eighteenth-century infancy was initially colonists. Colonial music imported from England to the New World consisted of ballads, opera, folk, more "sophisticated" compositions of *art music*. Since the number of musical performers was limited, composers, lyricists, and publishers were more prominent. The earliest forms of "popular music" were distributed in printed *broadsides*, sheet music, and songbooks. The term "popular" was relative. Promotion was not a priority to many publishers.

Many viewed themselves as part of the cultural establishment rather than merchants peddling a popular entertainment product. With no radio, phonograph, or machinery for "plugging" or merchandising music, success meant a few hundred people buying a song on sheet music or a few thousand more hearing it sung. Perhaps the earliest song that could be considered American folk music is "Springfield Mountain," a ballad about a young man who dies from a rattlesnake bite in 1761.

The British influence remained through the rebellious years of the Revolution. In the late 1770s, the marching tune "Yankee Doodle," with its numerous musical and verbal antecedents, became recognized as America's first popular song. In 1814, Francis Scott Key contributed "The Star Spangled Banner," which possessed similar historical significance and permanence in the American music catalog. The list of "national" tunes continually grew to include Julia Ward Howe's "Battle Hymn of the Republic" (1862) and John Philip Sousa's "The Stars and Stripes Forever" (1897), among others.

As slaves brought rhythms from West Africa, other musical influences were integrated into Euro-American colonial culture. One of the more interesting early African American entertainment encounters was the blackface minstrel. With the banjo as a primary instrument of accompaniment, "Negro minstrels" such as George Washington Dixon, who popularized "The Coal Black Rose" in 1827, were actually white men "masquerading" as black singers. This mode of performance foreshadowed not only the black influences and interactions that would characterize American music but the exploitation by whites of black musical forms.

Numerous means of musical dissemination developed. In addition to minstrel shows, musical groups and families such as the Hutchinsons began to tour the country near the mid-1800s, exposing the songs of their programs. Circuses, county fairs, and medicine shows provided outlets for song plugging or promoting. Amateur nights and sing-alongs in theaters were precursors to the contemporary karaoke scene. *Buskers* in saloons and dives contributed with widely varying materials. More elaborate productions followed, including plays by Harrigan and Hart and traveling shows like *A Trip to Beautiful*. Music halls and opera houses established by Tony Pastor, Koster and Bial, and Weber and Fields proved suitable venues for musicals, productions, and comic operas by creators such as Gilbert and Sullivan.

A distinctive American sound began to emerge in the songs of Stephen Foster. Foster's compositions combined elements of traditional folk music, minstrel mimicry, and black church music. Before he died at age thirty-seven in 1864, Foster wrote nearly 200 songs. "Oh! Susanna," "Old Folks at Home," "Jeannie with the Light Brown Hair," "Beautiful Dreamer," "My Old Kentucky Home," and "Camptown Races" are among Foster's tunes that have endured as American standards.

Thomas Edison's invention of the "talking machine" in 1877 set the stage for the mass distribution and promotion of music. The Graphophone improved upon Edison's phonograph by using a wax cylinder rather than tin foil. Emile Berliner then developed the gramophone, which was marketed for home use by the Victor Talking Machine Company. Initially, the high cost of the new communication medium meant that only the elite could afford the machine. When Columbia Phonograph Company introduced the two-sided disc turning at 78 rpm in 1905, recorded music was ready to enter the marketplace. The limited range, fidelity, and quality of early recording technology forced record manufacturers to focus initially on brass bands and booming voices. The recordings of opera star Enrico Caruso helped popularize the new entertainment machine.

The modern popular music business had begun to take shape. In the 1890s, music merchants clustered in New York, many of them on 28th Street, which became known as Tin Pan Alley, named because of the sound of the rinky-tink pianos being played in offices up and down the street. These music writing factories produced new songs for the public to buy, play, and sing at home. Songs were constantly fine-tuned with music and lyrics designed to capture trends, fads, and shifts in public interest. Between 1900 and 1910, there were nearly 100 songs that each sold over 1 million copies of sheet music. To increase the widespread appeal, songs were simplified in both form and style. Instead of emphasizing many verses that told a long, complicated story, new songs stressed simple lyrics, a punchy message, and a catchy chorus that was repeated over and over, making the songs easy to remember.

Between the 1890s and the first two decades of the twentieth century, there was a rapid spread of more complex music rhythmically rooted in African American traditions and Euro-American melodies. Ragtime's foot-tapping syncopation struck the right chord during the dawning of a new American age under the optimistic leadership of Teddy Roosevelt. New dances, many with animal names such as turkey trot, monkey glide, camel walk, and kangaroo dip, spread and created a sensation with their close body contact. In 1913, Americans were introduced to the first of what would be many Latin fads in music and dance—the tango, which sparked excitement and controversy with its exotic rhythms and erotic movements.

Other important contributors of the period included W. C. Handy, Irving Berlin, George M. Cohan, and Victor Herbert. In 1914, the American Society of Composers, Authors, and Publishers (ASCAP) was established as a music licensing company that would collect and distribute royalties to songwriters. A second guild, Broadcast Music Incorporated (BMI), was not formed until 1940.

By the time the Roaring Twenties rolled around, the Victorian morality that had guided the culture was replaced by more carefree attitudes and new moral codes. Signs of the times included shimmy dances such as the Charleston, short "flapper" dresses, and the introduction of the automobile. Electrical phonographs replaced hand-cranked machines. Prohibition sparked illegal drinking, often at speakeasies. The jukebox was a popular source of cheap music at these establishments. Brassy, raucous Dixieland jazz from southern black bars and bordellos was prevalent. The music of the jazz age, which included Cole Porter and Billie Holliday, blues songs, and suggestive titles and lyrics, provoked a great deal of criticism of its social effects on youth and morals. The industry began to recognize potential profits from targeting music to specific groups in the market. For example, the blues of Bessie Smith appealed to black audiences, while the country music of Jimmie Rodgers was popular among rural whites. When sales of jazz and blues recordings slowed in the mainstream, the industry hired white artists to record black music. This process, known as "covering," became a common practice among recording artists and continues today, even though it is often criticized for being commercially and artistically exploitative.

Performance of "Pirates of Penzance" at a national music camp in Interlochen, Michigan, 1942. Courtesy of the Library of Congress

Although many hit songs were written for, and introduced in, stage and film musicals, the major media for exposing songs were radio and recordings. The first commercial station, KDKA, began broadcasting in Pittsburgh in 1920. Radio's repeated performances fixed songs in people's minds, while programs such as *Lucky Strike's Your Hit Parade* and *Kraft Music Hall* showcased crooners such as Rudy Vallee, Hoagy Carmichael, and Bing Crosby, while Duke Ellington and Louis Armstrong were among the most popular black performers.

In 1927, Les Paul created the first electric guitar, an instrument that would shape sound for generations to come. That same year, music found a new vehicle on the silver screen as *The Jazz Singer*, featuring Al Jolson, became the first film sound track. As record sales reached 100 million, sheet music sales dwindled. One form of music with widespread appeal was swing, a white variation of blues and jazz that did not reflect the raw emotions and experience of African American culture. Popularized in the mid-1930s by Big Band leaders such as Benny Goodman, Count Basie, Artie Shaw, Jimmy and Tommy Dorsey, Harry James, and Glenn Miller, swing helped keep the suffering recording industry alive during the Great Depression.

While swing and dances such as the jitterbug were not exclusively teenage-oriented, there were signs of an emerging youth culture by the 1940s, a trend that crystallized with the bobby-soxers' reaction to teen idol Frank Sinatra. Peggy Lee, Perry Como, Doris Day, Mel Torme, and Vic Damone were among other popular vocalists. In 1942 Bing Crosby recorded "White Christmas," which would become the best selling record ever.

After World War II, the development of specialized music markets accelerated, alongside significant technological advances such as 45 rpm singles, 33 ⅓ rpm long-playing albums, and portable magnetic tape equipment. The number of record companies grew from 11 to nearly 200, and the industry expanded beyond its New York base to cities across the country.

A greater diversity of artists and styles of music marked the era: Rodgers and Hammerstein musicals such as *Oklahoma!* (1943) and *South Pacific* (1949); Hank Williams (country); Miles Davis (jazz); the Weavers (traditional folk); Fats Domino (rhythm and blues); and the unusual instrumental adaptations of Mitch Miller, who produced twenty-two hits for Columbia Records between 1948 and 1952.

The arrival of television and the birth of rock and roll emerged together with a new youth culture in the 1950s. Rhythm and blues combined with the backbeat and twang of rockabilly and catchy pop to form a new sound. White artists and promoters continued to appropriate or adapt black music. Disc jockeys such as Cleveland, Ohio's, Alan Freed, who is widely credited with coining the term "rock and roll," featured this new music repeatedly on top forty radio formats. Bill Haley and the Comets were among the first to break through with "Rock around the Clock," which was featured in the teen rebellion film *Blackboard Jungle*. Chuck Berry, Fats Domino, Buddy Holly, Jerry Lee Lewis, Little Richard and, of course, Elvis Presley shook, rattled, and rolled as pioneers of this dynamic form of expression that thrilled screaming youth audiences, shocked mainstream middle-America, and forever changed music and popular culture.

The adult market in the 1950s featured Frank Sinatra, Dinah Shore, Nat King Cole, the Kingston Trio, Johnny Mathis, Liberace, Perry Como, and musicals such as *My Fair Lady* and *West Side Story*. On television numerous variety shows, like *The Lawrence Welk Show* and *American Bandstand*, were weekly showcases for teen and adult music and performers.

Rock and roll blossomed on numerous levels during the 1960s—economically, socially, politically, and culturally. The music industry, recognizing the marketability of different styles of music and new emerging audiences, became established in the commercial entertainment marketplace. Music was central to the youth "experience," its identities, ideologies, and activities. Increasingly, sophisticated song lyrics became magnified and meaningful, from personal ballads to counter-culture anthems for protest and change amid the turbulent political and social backdrop of the times.

The folk scene, particularly in clubs and hip places such as Greenwich Village, began to take shape early in the decade. Bob Dylan and Simon and Garfunkel were among the artists who defined the literate lyricism of the acoustic movement. The Beatles added European elements of melody. In the mid-1960s, Beatlemania swept the country; the British Invasion had begun. Among the bands to follow the Fab Four were the Rolling Stones, the Who, Kinks, Dave Clark Five, and Herman's Hermits. A variety of styles began to emerge, from the psychedelic rock of the Doors, to the swamp sounds of Creedence Clearwater Revival, to the jangling folk rock harmonies of the Byrds, to the sha-las and doo-langs of the "girl group" sound that included Dusty Springfield, Leslie Gore, the Shirelles, Chiffons, and Shangri-Las. Out of Detroit, Motown's soulful sound featured Marvin Gaye, Smokey Robinson, Stevie Wonder, the Supremes, Four Tops, Temptations, and many others. The Beach Boys and instrumental groups such as the Ventures and Safaris pioneered surf music, while farther up the California coast in San Francisco, hippies and flower children grooved, tripped, and jammed to the Grateful Dead's blend of country, blues, and folk rock and the surrealistic sounds of the Jefferson Airplane. The festival scene, from Newport Folk and Monterey Pop, to the "peace, love, and harmony" at Max Yasgur's farm at Woodstock in 1969, helped music's visibility and commercial viability. While Top 40 radio thrived with a variety of hit singles, "underground" and FM stations also began to spring up, providing exposure for album-oriented rock.

Much of the romantic idealism that characterized youth culture of the 1960s ended tragically in 1969 at Altamont, the site of a free Rolling Stones concert. As Mick Jagger sang "Sympathy for the Devil," Hell's Angels, who were hired as security for the show, were unable to control the rowdy crowd, and an eighteen-year-old black youth, Meredith Hunter, was stabbed to death. The promise of rock music as a foundation for a new culture fragmented further when two of its most electrifying stars, Jimi Hendrix and Janis Joplin, died of drug overdoses.

However, the music and its culture were well enough established to survive. Early in the 1970s, record producer Jon Landau proclaimed, "I have seen the future of rock and roll and it is Bruce Springsteen." "The Boss," as he was referred to, fulfilled the Landau prophecy with the subtle masterpiece *The Wild, the Innocent and the E-Street Shuffle* (1973), followed by a bombastic breakthrough *Born to Run* (1975) and *Darkness on the Edge of Town* (1978). The Springsteen phenomenon spread beyond the rock culture to the mainstream as the New Jersey artist appeared on the covers of *Time* and *Newsweek*.

Beyond Bruce, there were the softer sounds of singer-songwriters along the country/rock and folk/rock axis. Joni Mitchell, Cat Stevens, James Taylor, Carly Simon, Linda Ronstadt, Bonnie Raitt, the Eagles, and Crosby, Stills, Nash, and Young were among the significant artists in this genre. Carole King's *Tapestry* (1971) remains a classic and until Alanis Morrisette's *Jagged Little Pill* (1995) was the best selling album by a female artist.

Perhaps as much as anything, disco defined the decade. Its rhythmic dance beat, fashion, club scene—the most famous being Studio 54—and performers such as Donna Summer and the Village People represented a culture unto itself. The sound track to *Saturday Night Fever* (1977), featuring the Bee Gees hit "Stayin' Alive," became one of the best selling records of all time.

Despite such successes, the record industry slumped financially. Shifting buying patterns caused by disco's popularity, rises in oil prices (vinyl used in records was a petroleum by-product), and home taping on cassettes contributed to declining sales.

As the industry struggled, a new youth subculture and antiestablishment music, known as punk, emerged and widened the scope of rock. Edgy bands such as the Sex Pistols and the Clash denounced the establishment's control of mass culture and lashed out against consumer society. Punk evolved into New Wave of the 1980s with bands such as the Police, Talking Heads, Blondie, Devo, the Cars, the B-52s, and Duran Duran.

In 1981, the Buggles' "Video Killed the Radio Star" announced the arrival of the all-music cable channel, MTV. Music video represented a new form of expression that changed the way the industry and audiences looked at music, figuratively and literally. Images, lots of them, became paramount, almost supplanting the significance of the music itself. Commercial considerations, marketing and music strategies, fashion and style, attitudes, film, television (the series *Miami Vice* was pitched simply as "MTV Cops"), and the arts were all shaped by music video. Megastars such as Madonna, Prince, Michael Jackson, and Springsteen dominated the charts with multimillion-selling albums. Jackson's *Thriller* (1982) remains the best-selling album of all time, while Springsteen's *Born in the U.S.A.* (1984) is among the top three. Multimedia synergy between music, film, and television became the industrial mode of operation and cultural consumption in response to the "I want my MTV" youth slogan of the Reagan years.

Music channels became commonplace on cable's niche landscape. VH-1, TNN (the Nashville Network), CMT (Country Music Television) followed MTV. Live benefit concerts such as Live Aid and Farm Aid helped raise money and social consciousness.

As technological developments accelerated along with economic imperatives, music became increasingly more mobile, miniature, and specialized. By 1988, compact disc sales surpassed vinyl sales, signaling the phase-out of the spinning black artifacts as a format for recorded music. With the exception of a subculture of collectors, club deejays, and rappers who used records for "scratching," the 45 single and 33 ⅓ album were about to follow a similar path of obsolescence, or cultural progress, as the 78 rpm and eight-track tape did previously.

Increased specialization continued into niche culture of the 1990s. Pop, rock, classic rock, jazz, folk, punk, New Wave, alternative, modern, classical, grunge, heavy metal, blues, soul, country, world, reggae, funk, chunk, rap, hip-hop, swing, lounge, New Age, women's music, and variations, hybrids, and fragments in between were among the genres and subgenres within the retail racks and rotations of the music marketplace, from huge labels and chains such as Virgin and Tower Records, to the independents.

Technology's effect on music production and distribution was increasingly dramatic as the new century approached. High-tech electronic and engineering techniques conveniently and efficiently mix and produce quality sound without actual instruments or musicians. The synergistic cross-promotion of musical product between television, film, video, and radio expanded to include the CD-ROM packages and the Internet via MP3 technology, a bootlegger-turned-downloader's cyberdream come true. Major music companies such as Universal and Sony were the first to test digital music and sell directly to consumers via downloading in 1999. Music from virtually every era was remastered and reissued in multidisc anthologies, box set retrospectives, or their enhanced original packages. As the dimensions of popular music expanded, media coverage on all levels—print, broadcast, cable, and Internet—also increased.

Some of the important trends and marks on the decade's timeline included Kurt Cobain and Nirvana, who defined the grunge scene early in the 1990s. Alternative eventually became absorbed into the mainstream following Cobain's death in 1994. The "women's movement" gathered strength via Lilith Fair and the edgy "g-r-r-l" sound of artists such as Alanis Morrisette, whose *Jagged Little Pill* (1995) became one of the biggest selling records of all time, surpassing Carole King's classic *Tapestry* in the female singer-songwriter category. Artists from earlier eras aged gracefully rather than resembling roaming rock dinosaurs. Bob Dylan, Neil Young, the Rolling Stones, and James Taylor were among the "elders" who aged gracefully and grungefully, continuing to be influential, productive, and popular with new recordings and sold-out tours. Country remained popular with megastars such as Garth Brooks. Marilyn Manson replaced MTV's Beavis and Butthead as the whipping boy blamed for every societal ill. Sound track sales soared, and swing's "jump and jive" sound and steps were revived. Hip-hop, teen pop, and assembly-line-packaged boy group crooners (Backstreet Boys, 'N Sync, 98 Degrees, Five) and female phenoms Britney Spears and Christina Aguilera dominated the decade's end. Some of the most significant music developments of the decade went beyond the creative realm and the charts to the corporate world. In 1998, Seagram's $10.4 acquisition of Polygram gave the company roughly one-quarter of the $11.4 billion recording market. As a result, once-mighty labels such as A & M and Geffen lost identities and employees. The overall industry emphasis shifted from artist development, nurturing, and enduring acts, to instant hit gratification and the commercial imperative. Such disposability and commercialism reflected collective consciousness of the 1990s. At the dawning of a new era, popular music has grown and adapted into a multifaceted form that keeps pace with the rapid technological, economic, artistic, and sociopolitical changes of American popular culture. In the words of Colin Larkin, "Popular music now has age on its side" (1992).

REFERENCE WORKS

The breadth of popular music—its history, artists, and songs—is too overwhelming for any single reference source, volume, or comprehensive study, whether general or specific. Likewise, the approaches to music as a subject can be divided into often-intersecting categories of investigation, writing, and cataloging that are further subdivided into scholarship, journalism, criticism, history, library archiving, collecting, and even fandom. As popular music and its many dimensions have become an established area of interdisciplinary study, reference tools and resources such as bibliographies, encyclopedic volumes, chart compendiums, collections, histories, music guides, and on-line locations for genres, songs, artists, record companies, eras, and music culture and activities have steadily expanded.

During the past twenty years, several publishing houses have established themselves as outlets for music studies. Greenwood Press (Westport, Connecticut), Scarecrow Press (Metuchen, New Jersey), and Haworth Press (Binghamton, New York) represent an impressive triad of publishers that devote a significant portion of their catalogs to music resource materials.

The two leading academic music quarterlies provide annual music reference listings. Cambridge University Press' *Popular Music* has published "Booklists" for nearly twenty years. In 1998, Robert Pruter began to compile an annual bibliography of music articles from journals, trade, and popular periodicals in the Popular Press' (Bowling Green, Ohio) *Popular Music and Society*. The more specialized *Music Reference Services Quarterly*, published by Haworth Press, is particularly useful to music reference librarians. The scope of the journal articles is practical, historical, and theoretical. Topics include administrative aspects of archiving, collection development, preservation, censorship, on-line services for music libraries, subject heading codes, popular songwriting, composers, choreographers, and deaths of musicians.

One of the most current and comprehensive compilations is Gary Haggerty's *A Guide to Popular Music Reference Books* (1995). The annotated collection cites more than 400 titles, including bibliographies, biographies, yearbooks, discographies, guides, almanacs, encyclopedias, glossaries, and dictionaries of a remarkably wide range of musical styles and genres.

Another recent volume, Jeffrey N. Gatten's *Rock Music Scholarship: An Interdisciplinary Bibliography* (1995), emphasizes the diversity and intersections of fields of music study. The nearly 1,000 annotated entries include journal articles, chapters, books, dissertations, films, and videos, representing areas such as communication, education, ethnomusicology, history, literature, art, music, politics, psychology, religion, and sociology.

Mark W. Booth, B. Lee Cooper, and Frank W. Hoffman are among a fraternity of authors who have accumulated significant bodies of work as music resource specialists. Booth's *American Popular Music: A Reference Guide* (1983) is essential and as good a starting place as any for any pre-1980s music research. The book is very thorough and well organized, a fine example of how reference guides should be structured. Booth spans the generals and specifics of American popular music, offers commentary, and frames the survey with comprehensive bibliographies and discographies. Areas include songs, records, sheet music, record collecting, technology, social interpretation, biography, history, careers, the music business, and virtually every genre and era. Booth's "Music" chapter in the second edition of the *Handbook of American Popular Culture* (1989) is an updated, scaled-down version of his book.

Cooper is one of the most prolific researchers in the field, particularly in the area of popular songs, lyrics, and themes. In addition to regularly contributing discographic and bibliographic review essays to *Popular Music and Society*, the music obsessive (a catchall for scholar, critic, fan, journalist, historian) has authored, compiled, and collaborated on a staggering number of works. Students will find that any work with Cooper's signature will be thorough and include exhaustive bibliographic and discographic listings as well as valuable reference, cross-reference, and subreference materials that will expedite research and reveal new sources.

Two of Cooper's earliest books emphasize theoretical and methodological connections between music resources and teaching: *Images of American Society in Popular Music: A Guide to Reflective Thinking* (1982) and *The Popular Music Handbook: A Resource Guide for Teachers, Librarians, and Media Specialists*. Both books contain extensive music bibliographies, discographies, and cross-reference sources. The perspectives and materials presented remain relevant. Cooper provides a more current spin and sources in his essay "Teaching with Popular Music Resources: A Bibliography of Interdisciplinary Instructional Approaches" (1998).

Cooper has not veered far from the lyric and resource path. *A Resource Guide to Themes in Contemporary American Song Lyrics, 1950–1985* (1986) and *Popular Music Perspectives: Ideas, Themes, and Patterns in Contemporary Lyrics* (1991) continue to provide a structural and conceptual framework for his research.

Most recently, Cooper and Wayne S. Haney have compiled *Rock Music in American Popular Culture: Rock 'n' Roll Resources* (1995, 1997, 1999). The three (and counting) volumes are an engaging, information-overload archive of essays, critical commentaries, lists, book and record reviews, biographical sketches, and resource materials, framed by song lyric relations with sociocultural elements and themes. Each edition features at least twenty topics, alphabetically arranged. A sampling of subjects includes baseball, Christmas carols, dance crazes, food images, nursery rhymes, and work experiences (vol. 1); cars, cigarettes, disc jockeys, Halloween, legends, marriage, railroads, and war (vol. 2); child performers, death, hoaxes, military activities, novelty recordings, tobacco, and western images (vol. 3). Of note is the introduction in volume 3, which concludes with the authors' " 'Hot 100' Popular Music Books of 1971–1995: Key References For Rock Researchers." (Though more era- and genre-specific, the duo's *Rockabilly: A Bibliographic Resource Guide* [1990] is a fine resource.)

Another Cooper collaborator is librarian/historian Hoffman, whose immense *The Literature of Rock, 1954–1978* (1981) represents some of the pioneering efforts in locating music material in print. Cooper joined Hoffman for the subsequent compilations: *Rock II, 1979–1983* (two volumes) (1986) and *III, 1984–1990* (1995).

British scholar David Horn's The *Literature of American Music in Books and Folk Music Collections: A Fully Annotated Bibliography* (1977; revised with Richard Jackson in 1988), is a spectacular compilation covering nearly 3,000 book-length studies on all genres of America music from the colonial years through the mid-1970s. Guy A. Marco updates Horn's format with *Literature of American Music III, 1983–1992* (1996) and the author-centered *Checklist of Writings on American Music, 1640–1992* (1996), which indexes all monographs cited in the three *Literature of American Music* volumes.

Roger D. Kinkle's *The Complete Encyclopedia of Popular Music and Jazz, 1900–1950* (1974), a massive volume of writer and performer works, bios, indexes, and lists; D.W. Krummel et al. *Resources of American Music History: A Directory of Source Materials from Colonial Times to World War II* (1981); and Paul Taylor's *Popular Music since 1955* (1985) further expand the bibliographic holdings.

The difficulties of cataloging early American music are reflected in the sparse bibliographic sources from the era. Surveys by Sonneck and Upton (1945, 1964), Wolfe (1964), Hixon (1970), and Wolf (1963) are good starting places.

Other collections are more specialized, from Hart, Eagles, and Howorth's bibliographic guide to the blues (1989), to Carolyn Wood's *The Literature of Rock and Roll: A Special Collection* (1991), to Edie Meadows' *Jazz Reference and Research Materials* (1981).

Some of the best collections on black music include Dominique-Rene De Lerma's (1981, 1982, 1984) four-volume compilation on black music that includes reference materials, Afro-American idioms, geographical studies, and theory, education, and related studies; JoAnn Skoronski's *Black Music in America* (1981); and Kimberly R. Vann's annotated guide, which features forty years of black music articles from *Ebony Magazine* beginning in 1945 (1990). A similar approach to magazine content can be found Jeffery Gatten's *Rolling Stone Index* (1993), a twenty-five year chronicle of a popular culture periodical. Gatten's (1995) interdisciplinary bibliography on rock music scholarship is also a fine reference source.

Numerous bibliographies are more academically oriented. James Heintze (1985) and Rita Mead (1974) list master's theses and doctoral dissertations in music studies. Equally scholarly in scope are George H. Lewis' "The Sociology of Popular Music: A Selected and Annotated Bibliography" (1977) and Gilbert Rodman's "Everyday I Write the Book: A Bibliography of (Mostly) Academic Work on Rock and Pop Music" (1990, 1992). *Popular Music and Society* published a highly useful index of articles that appeared in that quarterly music journal's 25-year history in Volume 22 for Spring 1997.

Though variously arranged, popular song inventories provide useful categories and "discographies," or listings of records, composers, and songs. These indexes date back to the collection published by Minnie E. Sears in 1926. Notable continuations include Michael Gray's *Bibliography of Discographies* (1983) and indexes compiled by De Charms and Breed (1966), Leigh (1964), and Havlice (1975). David Ewen, who has authored numerous biographical and critical music resources and histories, integrates commentary into song groupings in *American Popular Songs from the Revolutionary War to Present* (1966). James Fuld uses a similar biographical and historical approach in his song reference works (1955, 1971). Other notable indexes include Nat Shapiro's ten-volume *Popular Music: An Annotated Index of American Popular Songs* (1986), Julius Mattfeld's *Variety Music Cavalcade, 1620–1969* (1971), and the *Stecheson Classified Song Directory* (1961) and its *Supplement* (1978), which groups songs by lyrical subject.

Casual browsing of the music section of any bookstore chain or book Web site reveals the immense expansion of the music reference sources during the 1990s. Music/record guides, encyclopedias, chart compendiums, and other reference books spanning eras, artists, and genres are widely available and routinely revised and updated.

The distinctions between music guides, surveys, and encyclopedias have become considerably blurred. Publishers and compilers continually modify their approaches. The end result complements biography and discography with geomusicological and historical perspectives.

Record guides packed with capsule reviews have been widely, if not exclusively, recognized for their benefit to consumers. However, the comprehensive and critical composition of recent guides has helped establish such volumes as important reference sources. Three series distinguish themselves from the rest of the pack: *MusicHound*, *The Rough Guide*, and *All Music Guide*. These series are highly valuable reference sources that totally eclipse the scope and depth of earlier record review mainstream anthologies such as those published by *Rolling Stone* (Marsh and Swenson 1979, 1983; DeCurtis and Henke 1992). Not only are the collections well researched and thorough—almost to the point of being exhaustive, ranging from 500 pages to 1,400—but the contributors complement the familiar formulas, discographies, cross-references, record ratings, dates, labels, and consumer guidance ("What to Buy," "What to Buy Next," "Worth Searching For," "What to Avoid"), with insightful critical, biographical, musicological, and historical commentaries on the artists, their bodies of works, and musical styles and genres.

Though reference-enhanced, these handbooks also maintain their browsing quality for casual consumers. Each publication contains its own signature elements, a range that includes photographs and illustrations; full-length CD samplers; fascinating sidebars on various subgenres, instruments, terms, and festivals; Web site, mail-order, catalog, magazine, and fanzine directories; geographical charts and music maps; essential recordings for various stylistic genres; and essays on tangential topics such as bootlegs, reissues, cassette culture, producers, session musicians, and labels.

Visible Ink's *MusicHound* series has become the most ubiquitous and indispensable of these reference collections. Entries in their *Essential Album Guide* catalog include *Folk* (Walters and Mansfield), *Country* (Graff and Mansfield), *Rock* (Graff and Durcholz), *R & B* (Graff, du Lac, and McFarlin), *Jazz* (Holtje and Lee), *Blues* (Rucker and Schuller), *Lounge* (Knopper), and *Swing* (Knopper). *Soundtracks* (Deutsch) is under the *VideoHound* banner.

The notable omission of World Music from the *MusicHound* catalog may be intentional considering that *World Music: The Rough Guide* (Broughton, 1994) runs to 700 pages. This volume may stand as one of *the* most exhaustive and fascinating assemblages of reference materials in any musical genre (there is also a separate volume on reggae). Like the All Music Guide series (Erlewine, Bogdanov, and Woostra, 1995, 1996, 1997), the Rough Guide has published opera, classical, jazz, and even a travel guide, *Music USA* (Unterberger, 1999).

Penguin and Blackwell publish some worthwhile record surveys as well, including *The Penguin Guide to Jazz* (Oliver, 1994), *The Blackwell Guides to Blues Records* (Oliver, 1989) and *Chicago Soul* (Pruter, 1993).

Some precursors have maintained a sense of resourceful timelessness as record guides. *Christgau's Record Guide: The 80s* (1990) features 3,000 records reviewed and graded by one of America's leading rock critics, Robert Christgau. This follow-up to his guide to 1970s albums is culled from the critic's *Village Voice* writings. Christgau's judgments are incisive, knowledgeable, and amusing. While his views may be an acquired taste to some, Christgau colleague and cultural critic Greil Marcus says, "The entries . . . read like tiny novels . . . [with an] endless capacity for surprise."

For music outside the mainstream—post-1975 punk, alternative, and New Wave—*The Trouser Press Record Guide* (1997), is an indispensable source. Editor Ira A. Robbins and his legion of contributors provide some of the more insightful commentaries found in any guides. The scope extends from the obvious Athens and Austin hubs, to the international and underground scenes. The reviewers are particularly adept at cataloging rarities, EPs, imports, and unreleased cassettes. The earlier four editions, which date back to 1983, are worth seeking out since entries vary from volume to volume.

There are also some unconventional approaches to record guides. Most of these may be somewhat arbitrary in content and less inclusive. Don't be fooled by the novel nature of their premises, either. These books are valuable as supplementary resources, and they contain thoughtful, entertaining commentaries. In *Stranded* (1979), Greil Marcus recruits twenty leading music writers to choose one album that they would take to a desert island. Jimmy Guterman and Owen O'Donnell's *The Worst Rock 'n' Roll Records of All Time* (1991) blends smart and smart-ass perspectives on singles, albums, and performers whom "fans love to hate." *Listen to This!* (Reder and Baxter, 1999) is based on recommendations by musicians rather than critics. More than 100 artists offer their favorite artists, albums, and songs. The anecdotal volume is a fun, browser-friendly variation of record guides, complete with appropriate cross-references, discographies, biographical information, and critical commentary.

Britney Spears. © Painet

Musician Marshall Crenshaw's *Hollywood Rock* (1994) integrates different elements, especially fun, into the standard guide formula. Categories include movies about rock and roll, musicals with rock scores, movies with rock stars as actors, rockumentaries, and movies with influential rock sound tracks. Though intentionally not as voluminous as other guides, the reviews are well written and recognize many obscure films. In addition to requisite production and casting information, each review highlights scenes, songs, lines, and cameos and rates each film in three categories: music, attitude, and fun.

In addition to music guides, there is an encyclopedia-like reference source for virtually every musical genre: American garage, psychedelic, and hippie rock (Joynson); country (McCloud; Stambler and Grelun); blues (Herzhaft; Santelli); Cajun and zydeco (Nyhan, Rollins, and Babb); rock (Pareles and Romanowski; Miller; Nite; Romanowski and George-Warren); the rock and roll hall of fame (Talevski). Garland's gorgeous music encyclopedia series, which will reach ten volumes, includes Africa (Stone), Southeast Asia (Miller and Williams), and Australia and the Pacific Islands (Laeppler and Love). Likewise, there are a limited number of encyclopedia-like volumes devoted to megastars such as the Beatles and Elvis Presley, whose careers, recordings, and films span several decades. Patsy Guy Hammontree's groundbreaking reference source on Elvis (1985) is part of Greenwood Press' impressive Bio-Bibliography series. Worth and Tamerius (1990),

Stern and Stern (1987), and Banney (1987) are among the many who have contributed to the Elvis reference library. In addition, Plasketes' *Images of Elvis Presley in American Culture, 1977–1992: The Mystery Terrain* (1997) is a post-Presley critical cultural chronicle that surveys images, references, and representations of the King in music, art, literature, television, film, religion, theater, sports, and politics from 1977 through 1997.

Colin Larkin's *The Guinness Encyclopedia of Popular Music* (1992) is a more traditional format. The massive, four-volume set contains 14,500 entries. This A to Z collection may embody the fullest representation of popular music genres, styles, and artists in one reference book. *The Penguin Encyclopedia of Popular Music*, edited by Donald Clarke (1989), is similar in structure and scope.

There are two benchmark sources for chart data tabulations, those published by the *Billboard* conglomerate and Joel Whitburn's Record Research company. *Billboard*'s breadth ranges from Top 40 and Hot 100 chart compendiums from any era such as *The Billboard Book of One Hit Wonders* (Jancik), to the more esoteric *The Billboard Guide to Progressive Music* (Bradley Smith). All are fascinating reads for fan and scholar alike. Among the vast number of works in the Whitburn canon are compilations of top albums and album tracks, top hits and singles in country, pop, rhythm and blues, easy listening, and "bubbling under" singles and albums that just missed the charts.

A vital, but often overlooked, reference source is the multidisc box set. Expensive but hard to resist for fan, collector, or scholar, the box set may be an audio version of the coffee-table book. Though it has long been a feature of the music industry, the box set has evolved into a music marketplace phenomenon with the evolution of the CD format. Hundreds of musical artists, eras, and styles have been anthologized in these lavish packages. In 1993 alone over 150 boxed set retrospectives were issued in the United States and abroad. Not only are these multirecord artifacts excellent aural journeys packed with b-sides, rarities, demos, and remastered recordings, but they provide extensive historical, biographical, and discographical contexts.

HISTORY AND CRITICISM

Historical narratives of popular music may be most accessible according to musical genres. For many years, standard music histories that were broad-based were the norm. It was not until the mid-1950s that historians began to recognize and include "popular music" in standard historical accounts. In 1966, Gilbert Chase placed popular music within the vast music timeline with *American Music: From the Pilgrims to the Present*. Charles Hamm's *Yesterdays: Popular Song in America* (1979) and David Ewen's *All the Years of American Popular Music* (1977) remain two of the best-documented chronicles of popular music. The narrative in Donald Clarke's *The Rise and Fall of Popular Music* (1995) spans the Renaissance to rock, while Ian Whitcomb's *After the Ball* (1986) covers pop from rag to rock.

Histories of popular music tend to be specialized, with narratives categorized by particular eras, styles, genres, and even regions. Biography, with modes ranging from the unauthorized, to scholarly inquiries, to movie, video, and cable network productions, has continually expanded and become an increasingly popular historical form. In addition, essays with critical/historical perspectives are common-place in music anthologies.

A sampling, by subject, of some of the notable specialized histories include Broadway and Tin Pan Alley composers (Wilder, 1972); jazz and theater (Mellers, 1965); radio deejays of the 1950s and 1960s (Smith, 1989); American singing groups from 1940 to 1990 (Warner, 1992); country music (Carr, 1979; Green, 1976; Malone, 1985; Kingsbury and the Country Music Foundation, 1994; Ellison, 1995; Tosches, 1977); gospel (Cusic, 1993); rhythm and blues (Shaw, 1978); blue-grass (Rosenberg, 1985); the 1950s (Shaw, 1974); the 1960s (Pichaske, 1989); the American South (Booth, 1991); swing (Stowe, 1994; Erenberg, 1998); bebop (DeVeaux, 1997); alternative (Lavine and Blashill, 1996).

Rock chronicles abound and are diverse in their approaches. The first compre-hensive rock history, Charlie Gillett's *The Sound of the City* (1970), remains the most acclaimed. Gillett focuses on the musical form, its cross-fertilization and undercurrents rather than star status of popular historical accounts. Carl Belz's *The Story of Rock* (1972), Jonathan Eisen's two editions of *The Age of Rock* (1969, 1970), and Nik Cohn's *Rock from the Beginning* (1969) are also enduring early rock perspectives.

The rock histories published by *Rolling Stone* (Miller, 1980; Ward, Stokes, and Tucker, 1986; DeCurtis and Henke, 1992), though journalistic-leaning, are cred-ible, critical, and informative profiles of eras, musical styles, and artists. The mag-azine's numerous interview anthologies (Herbst, 1981; Loder, 1989) and compilations (Fong-Torres, 1974, 1976, and 1999) are also valuable historical re-sources. Other broad-based histories range from the British (Hatch and Milward, 1989), to Robert Palmer's (1995) "unruly" history, which was the accompanying text for the Public Television documentary series. Archivist Michael Ochs (1984) provides a photographic view of the first two decades of rock and roll. Luke Crampton and Dafyyd Rees combine the historical and encyclopedia formats into the massive (1,000 pages) *VH-1's Rock Star Encyclopedia* (1999).

Nick Tosches, one of the most respected music critics of the rock era, profiles twenty-five pioneers of rock and roll from its earliest forms in rhythm and blues and country and western from 1945 until its birth in the mid-1950s in *Unsung Heroes* (1984). Dave DiMartino's (1994) singer-songwriter compilation is an *A to Zevon* of performers and composers.

An increasing number of histories explore "the women's movement" in music. Charlotte Greig's *Will You Still Love Me Tomorrow?* (1989) examines the girl groups of the 1950s. Gillian Gaar's historical narrative in *She's a Rebel* (1992) demystifies the male-dominated industry and traces the empowerment of women over four decades. *Trouble Girls* (O'Dair, 1997) is a fairly typical *Rolling Stone* publication with pop appeal, including a preface by Yoko Ono. The collection features female artist portraits and profiles by women photographers and writers. Organized by decade and categories such as pioneers, sparrows, and rebels, the volume is both useful and engaging.

Several histories approach rock from sociocultural, organizational, or political perspectives. Chapple and Garofalo's *Rock and Roll Is Here to Pay* (1977), along with Stokes' *Starmaking Machinery* (1977) remain two of the most important in-dustrial inquiries. Record executive Joe Smith's *Off the Record* (1988), a 430-page oral history of the music industry, is another insightful entertainment organization study. Don Cusic's *Music in the Market* (1995) examines the triad of market, artists, and consumers. David Sanjek's *Pennies from Heaven* (1996) is a broader treatment of the popular music business in the twentieth century.

One of the most prolific record industry scholars is the late R. Serge Denisoff, who combined journalistic methods with sociological theory in numerous areas of popular music. *Solid Gold* (1975), *Tarnished Gold* (1986), and *Inside MTV* (1987) constitute a comprehensive music industry trilogy. *Risky Business: Rock in Film* (1991) by Denisoff and William Romanowski is an equally in-depth account of music-video-film symbiosis, while *True Disbelievers* (1995) with George Plasketes chronicles the Elvis fanaticism movement. *Great Day Coming* (1971) and *Sing A Song of Social Significance* (1972) are the best of Denisoff's sociopolitical writings. A bibliography of Denisoff's works, compiled by Linda Vazquez and William Schurk, appears in *Popular Music and Society* 21: 1 (Spring 1997).

Simon Frith, Richard A. Peterson, and George Lewis are among other sociological critics whose interactive analysis of commercial music production, artists, and audiences has a lasting impact. All three have been publishing works for three decades. Their diverse, collective body of work is highly recommended. Frith's most important work remains *Sound Effects: Youth, Leisure and the Politics of Rock and Roll* (1981), a model analysis of culture and industry conspiring to create music. *Music for Pleasure* (1988) and *Performing Rites* (1996) examine the sociology and value of popular music. Many of Peterson's contributions are productions of culture studies, including his *Creating Country Music: Fabricating Authenticity* (1997). Lewis is a prolific, engaging writer whose music commentaries range from social protest in black popular music (1973) to country music lyrics (1976). His bibliography on "The Sociology of Popular Music" (1979) is among his many notable articles that have been published in a variety of journals. Lewis' regular contributions to *Popular Music and Society* as audio review editor are particularly noteworthy. Lewis' critical commentaries covering a wide range of recordings and artists transcend conventional reviews with their insight, scope, and style.

Jim Curtis' *Rock Eras* and Herb Hendler's *Year by Year in the Rock Era* (1987) span the mid-1950s until the mid-1980s. Less interpretive than Curtis or Paul Friedlander's (1996) social perspective, Hendler's history does not contain narrative but carefully assembled fragments of influential news, statistical information, artists, hits, events, trivia, fads, trends, and lifestyles. The cumulative result is a highly useful cultural chronicle that is also convenient to browse. In *Music in the Air* (1982), Philip Eberly examines how technology and the mass media, particularly radio, have contributed to popular music's development and changing tastes, beginning in the early 1920s up to the pre-MTV era in the early 1980s. Philip Ennis' distinctive *The Seventh Stream* (1992) weaves facts, figures, and dates into a historical web of artistic, commercial, and sociopolitical trends.

Chronicles of black musical traditions are wide-ranging. Eileen Southern provides a scholarly general overview in *Music of Black Americans: A History* (1983). Dena Epstein (1977) looks at pre–Civil War folk roots and spirituals. Samuel A. Floyd's *The Power of Black Music* (1995) is an interpretive history tracing roots from Africa to the United States. Courlander (1963) explores rural folk traditions, while Robert Toll's *Blacking Up* (1974) is a study of the minstrel show. Ragtime's diverse entries include broad-based studies such as Edward Berlin's *Ragtime: A*

Musical and Cultural History (1980) and *They All Played Ragtime* (Blesh and Janis, 1950). Waldo (1976) focuses on ragtime's mid-twentieth-century revivals; Schafer and Riedel (1973) examine classic ragtime and different strands of the form; and Jasen and Tichenor treat folk ragtime in *Rags and Ragtime: A Musical History* (1978).

Book-length treatments of rap and hip-hop are slowly accumulating, the most recent being Alan Light's *Vibe History of Hip Hop* (1999), which includes a CD compilation of essential hip-hop music. One of the best analyses of the popular 1990s forms can be found in *Black Noise: Rap Music and Black Culture in Contemporary America* (1993) by Tricia Rose. Judy McCoy's (1992) rap reference guide is also a useful resource that focuses on the music in the 1980s.

One of the richest reference sources for the blues is Sheldon Harris' *Blues Who's Who* (1979). Paul Oliver's *The Story of the Blues* (1969) is a good general history. Inner-city accounts include Charles Keil's *Urban Blues* (1966), Gerri Hirshey's *Nowhere to Run: The Story of Soul Music* (1984), and Robert Pruter's *Chicago Soul* (1966) and *Doowop: The Chicago Scene* (1996). William Ferris' *Blues from the Delta* (1978) and Robert Palmer's *Deep Blues* (1981) are detailed accounts of the blues cradle in the Mississippi Delta.

Peter Guralnick ranks among the premier music historians. His roots writings are rich, critical chronicles gleaned from firsthand interviews. In *Sweet Soul Music* (1986), Guralnick covers the evolution of southern-based soul during the 1960s, focusing on artists such as James Brown, Otis Redding, Solomon Burke, and Aretha Franklin, as well as the Stax/Volt/Atlantic labels and Muscle Shoals studio. *Feel Like Going Home* (1971) and *Lost Highways* (1989) include intimate portraits of early rock and blues artists, including Jerry Lee Lewis, Howlin' Wolf, Muddy Waters, Charlie Rich, and the owners of Sun and Chess records. Guralnick's two volumes on the life of Elvis Presley, *Last Train to Memphis* (1994) and *Careless Love: The Unmaking of Elvis Presley* (1999), are the deepest biographical works on Presley, with Jerry Hopkin's *Elvis* (1971) and Dave Marsh (1992) earning honorable mentions.

Like Guralnick, longtimers Greil Marcus and Dave Marsh have established a significant critical canon. *Fortunate Son* (1985), a collection of Marsh's works, is an important journalistic view of American popular music. In addition to editing *Rolling Stone* record guides, Marsh's notable works include biographies of Bruce Springsteen (1987) and Elvis (1992); a book-length musicological study of the song "Louie, Louie" (1993); fragments in *The First Rock and Roll Confidential* (1985); and lists with extensive commentary in *The Heart of Rock and Soul: The 1001 Greatest Singles Ever Made* (1989).

Marcus is arguably the most penetrating cultural critic around. *Mystery Train: Images of America in Rock 'n' Roll Music* (1976), which examines the music and mythologies of Robert Johnson, Randy Newman, Sly and the Family Stone, the Band, and Elvis, remains one of the most important works on popular music ever written. Marcus has also been a punk chronicler, with *Lipstick Traces: A Secret History of the 20th Century* (1989), and an Elvis observer with *Dead Elvis: A Chronicle of a Cultural Obsession* (1991). Marcus' regular contributions in the magazine columns such as *Art Forum* and *Interview* are also worth seeking out.

Since the world music explosion in the American music marketplace in the late 1980s with recordings such as Paul Simon's *Graceland*, there have been an increasing number of books devoted to world roots. Broughton's *World Music: The Rough Guide* may offer the most efficient access to a comprehensive bibliography of world music literature. Timothy Taylor's *Global Pop* (1997) provides an overview of the world music marketplace. In addition, the Temple Press Music, Mass Media and Culture series features numerous world music titles. *Reggae Routes* (Chang and Chen, 1998), *Carribean Currents* (Manuel, Bilby, and Largey, 1995), and *The Brazilian Sound* (McGowan and Pessanha, 1998) highlight rumba, reggae, samba, and bossa nova, among other exotic forms. Views of the music of the Dominica including Deborah Hernandez's *Bachata* (1995) and Paul Austerlitz's *Merengue* (1997) provide separate social histories of Dominican popular music and identity.

Nonprint materials such as audio, video, and film are often overlooked as rich resources of musical heritage. A few examples include National Public Radio's *Sound and Spirit*, a weekly, one-hour geomusicultural journey that threads history, culture, and spirituality with a musical theme or topic. Transcripts and playlists are available, as are videos of some of the music-related television productions from PBS. Bill Moyers' musicological documentary on the hymn "Amazing Grace" and Ken Burns' epic chronicle on jazz are but two examples. Documentary filmmaker Les Blank's *American Voices* series, distributed by Flower Films, is an equally rich celebration of ethnomusical diversity. His subjects include the musical traditions and rituals of Appalachia, Louisiana (Cajun, zydeco, Mardi Gras), Texas-Mexico, Polynesia, Serbia, Africa, Cuba, the blues, and Lightnin' Hopkins. The catalog of multimedia sources for music is constantly expanding, along with the number of productions and programs devoted to music and its heritage dimensions on cable networks and other program outlets. Check your local listings and on-line resources regularly.

ANTHOLOGIES AND REPRINTS

While the Internet is rapidly becoming a listening room unto itself, libraries at all levels—local, community, public, regional, or those affiliated with educational institutions—continue to expand their collections of music-related materials, from books, magazines, and print sources, to sound recordings. Locating sources, identifying holdings, and availability through interlibrary loan programs are more accessible and convenient than ever. Individual library directories and on-line sites usually contain index categories and inventories, often with brief summaries of the holdings.

The number of libraries with large record collections remains limited. The largest archive of recorded music is located at the Library of Congress in Washington, D.C. Its Music and Recorded Sound Division houses a record collection that numbers in the millions. In addition, the library's American Folklife Center features an archive of Folk Song. Nearby, the Smithsonian also features a Folkways Archive.

Among the extensive collection that is part of the New York Public Library is the Rodgers and Hammerstein Archive, located at the Performing Arts Research Center in Lincoln Center. In addition to recorded music, the holdings include sheet music, songbooks, and other musical artifacts. Also in Manhattan is the Bernard A. and Morris N. Young Library of Early American Popular Music.

Several universities have established significant music archives. In addition to being the center for popular culture studies, Bowling Green State University in Ohio has an impressive audio center that began in 1967. The center's founder and director, William Schurk, is an enthusiastic music collector, scholar, obsessive, and locator of the most obscure tunes or artists. Other representative collections can be found in the libraries at the University of Oregon, Brown University in Providence, Rhode Island, the University of Florida's Belknap Collection for the Performing Arts, the UCLA Archive for Popular American Music, and the Eastman Music School Sibley Music Library at the University of Rochester. The largest collections for specific musical genres and styles are often within the regions they are indigenous to or associated with. For example, Nashville has the Country Music Foundation Library. Tulane University features the William Hogan Archives of New Orleans Jazz. (Other jazz collections are at the Free Library in Philadelphia and Rutgers Institute of Jazz Studies in Newark, New Jersey.) New York's Public Library Lincoln Center Branch houses extensive Broadway musical materials, including a Billy Rose Theater Collection. In Los Angeles, the Institute of the American Musical, originally located in New York, also has an extensive collection of books and records. The Center for the Study of Southern Culture in Oxford, Mississippi, a short drive from the Delta, is an incredible blues archive. Its director, William Ferris, is a leading blues authority and author. The Rock and Roll Hall of Fame and Museum in Cleveland not only embodies an excellent rock reference locale but features an Education Department, which sponsors programs, seminars, field trips, conferences, and workshops for all ages. Director Robert Santelli and his staff also publish a quarterly newsletter, *Backbeat*, and provide lesson plans for music education.

Anthologies that assemble essays on various aspects of music are valuable as both critical and reference sources. The catalog of such collections in music has expanded significantly during the past fifteen years. Scholarly anthologies exclusive to an academic audience are somewhat outnumbered by music readers with broad crossover appeal to popular audiences. This, in part, may be a reflection of popular music's struggle for academic credibility as a discipline. But as music studies and courses devoted to music and culture become a part of program curricula and as interdisciplinary studies emerge, such anthologies are increasingly published and adopted for teaching purposes.

Among the more theoretical approaches are the anthologies *Popular Music and Communication* (Lull, 1987), which emphasizes communication perspectives, and *Mapping the Beat* (Swiss, Sloop, and Herman, 1997), which features essays in three sections: (1) "Noise, Performance, and the Politics of Sound"; (2) "History, Technology, and Policy"; and (3) "Sound, Location, and Movement in the Spaces of Popular Music." *America's Musical Pulse* (Bindas, 1992) is an expansive collection of essays that survey politics, class, economics, race, gender, and the social contexts of music. Each essay also includes valuable bibliographic sources specific to the subject being discussed.

Timothy E. Scheurer, author of *Born in the USA: The Myth of America from Colonial Times to the Present* (1991), compiles essays in two volumes of *American Popular Music* (1989, 1991), which span from the nineteenth century and Tin Pan Alley, to the age of rock.

The forementioned Simon Frith has edited a number of vital music anthologies. *Facing the Music* (1988) is a compact reader with essays on teen identity, commodity, video, politics of crossover, and hit radio. The expansive *On Record* (1990), edited by Frith and Andrew Goodwin, includes music writings on semiotics, musicology, sex, the music business, star studies, the creative process, subcultures, and cultural studies. Frith's *Sound and Vision* (1993), edited with Goodwin and Lawrence Grossberg, is a music video reader. The cultural scope of Anthony DeCutis' *Present Tense* (1992) is similar to the Frith-edited anthologies.

The Penguin Book of Rock and Roll Writing (Heylin, 1992) is a massive volume with popular appeal. The book features nine sections devoted to diverse rock writings on aesthetics, style, eras, stars, themes, criticism, experience, money, and casualties in styles ranging from criticism to fictional satires and from short stories to journalism. Among the impressive list of contributors are Jon Landau, Nik Cohn, Charlie Gillett, Greil Marcus, Simon Frith, Lester Bangs, Tom Wolfe, Tama Janowitz, and Patti Smith. These eighty previously published pieces provide a composite of contemporary music criticism and thought and how they have evolved. Nick Kent's *The Dark Stuff* (1994) is a less ambitious collection of rock writings from 1972 to 1995.

The evolution of music journalism and criticism is also evident in a number of "best of" compilations that feature writings (reviews, essays, interviews) by music critics and journalists. Among the stable of important critics whose works have been assembled into collections are Dave Marsh (1985), Ben Fong-Torres (1999), Robert Christgau (1999), Anthony DeCurtis (1998), Kurt Loder (1990), and the late Lester Bangs in *Psychotic Reactions and Carburetor Dung* (1988). Marcus' *In the Fascist Bathroom* (1993) is a collection of primarily punk pieces compiled from his columns in *Artforum*, *New West*, *Rolling Stone*, and *Village Voice* between 1977 and 1992.

Many anthologies are more specialized. Bill Flanagan (1987), Paul Zollo (1991), and Jenny Boyd (1992) have assembled impressive collections of interviews with songwriters and musicians about the creative process. George Lewis' *All That Glitters* (1993) and Cecilia Tichi's *High Lonesome* (1994) and *Reading Country Music* (1998) are among the most diverse, comprehensive collections of country music commentary.

Elvis anthologies begin with Jac Tharpe's *Elvis: Images and Fancies* (1979), then jump to the 1990s with readers edited by Kevin Quain (1992), Ebersole and Peabody (1994), and Chadwick's *In Search of Elvis* (1997), which is largely culled from a conference on Elvis in Oxford, Mississippi, in 1995. In 1994, EducArts, a nonprofit organization dedicated to interdisciplinary education, sponsored *Icons of Popular Culture I: Elvis and Marilyn*. An accompanying art exhibition catalog and collection of essays from the conference followed (DePaoli, 1994). Such symposiums are becoming more commonplace, the most recent symposium devoted to Frank Sinatra. In addition, the Rock and Roll Hall of Fame in Cleveland annually sponsors educational programs devoted to artists, eras, and genres.

In addition, the music quarterly *Popular Music and Society* frequently publishes special issues devoted to a particular topic. Instruments, technology, the Beatles, teaching music, and the Columbine school shootings are among recent special forums published.

BIBLIOGRAPHY

Books and Articles

Auserlitz, Paul. *Merengue: Dominican Music and Dominican Identity*. Philadelphia: Temple University Press, 1997.

Bangs, Lester. *Psychotic Reactions and Carburetor Dung*. Ed. Greil Marcus. New York: Knopf, 1988.

Banney, Howard F. *Return to Sender: The First Complete Discography of Elvis Tribute and Novelty Recording, 1956–1986*. Ann Arbor, Mich.: Pierian Press, 1987.

Belz, Carl. *The Story of Rock*. New York: Oxford University Press, 1972.

Berlin, Eward A. *Ragtime: A Musical and Cultural History*. Berkeley: University of California Press, 1980.

Bindas, Kenneth J., ed. *America's Musical Pulse: Popular Music in Twentieth-Century Society*. Westport, Conn.: Greenwood Press, 1992.

Blesh, Rudi, and Harriet Janis. *They All Played Ragtime*. New York: Knopf, 1950.

Booth, Mark W. *American Popular Music: A Reference Guide*. Westport, Conn.: Greenwood Press, 1983.

———. "Music." In *Handbook of American Popular Culture*. 2nd ed. Ed. M. Thomas Inge. Westport, Conn.: Greenwood Press, 1989, 771–90.

Booth, Stanley. *Rhythm Oil: A Journey Through the Music of American South*. New York: Pantheon, 1991.

Bowman, Rob. "The Academic at the Crossroads of Commerce." *Popular Music & Society* 21: 1 (Spring 1977), 5–10.

Boyd, Jenny. *Musicians in Tune: 75 Contemporary Musicians Discuss the Creative Process*. New York: Fireside, 1992.

Broughton, Simon, ed. *World Music: The Rough Guide*. London: Penguin, 1994.

Burns, Gary. "*Popular Music and Society* and the Evolving Discipline of Popular Music Studies." *Popular Music and Society* 21: 1 (Spring 1997), 123–132.

Burns, Ken. *Jazz: A Film by Ken Burns*. Boston: PBS Home Video, 2000.

Carr, Patrick, ed. *The Illustrated History of Country Music, by the Editors of Country Music Magazine*. New York: Doubleday, 1979.

Chadwick, Vernon, ed. *In Search of Elvis: Music, Race, Art, Religion*. Boulder, Colo.: Westview, 1997.

Chapple, Steve, and Rebee Garofalo. *Rock and Roll is Here to Pay: The History and Politics of the Music Industry*. Chicago: Nelson-Hall, 1977.

Chang, Kevin O'Brien, and Wayne Chen. *Reggae Routes*. Philadelphia, Penn.: Temple University Press, 1998.

Chase, Gilbert. *America's Music: From the Pilgrims to the Present*. New York: McGraw-Hill, 1966. Reprint. Westport, Conn.: Greenwood Press, 1981.

Christgau, Robert. *Any Old Way You Choose It: Rock and Other Pop Music, 1967–1973*. Baltimore: Penguin Books, 1973.

———. *Christgau's Record Guide: Rock Albums of the 70's*. New York: DaCapo, 1981.

———. *Christgau's Record Guide: The 80's*. New York: Pantheon, 1990.

———. *Growin' Up All Wrong: 75 Great Rock and Pop Artists from Vaudeville to Techno*. Cambridge: Harvard University Press, 1999.

Clarke, Donald. *The Rise and Fall of Popular Music: A Narrative History from the Renaissance to Rock 'n' Roll*. New York: St. Martin's, 1995.

Clarke, Donald, ed. *The Penguin Encyclopedia of Popular Music*. New York: Viking, 1989.

Cohn, Nik. *Rock from the Beginning*. New York: Pocket, 1969.

Cooper, B. Lee. *Images of American Society in Popular Music: A Guide to Reflective Teaching*. Chicago: Nelson Hall, 1982.

———. *The Popular Music Handbook: A Resource Guide for Teachers, Librarians, and Media Specialists*. Littleton, Colo.: Libraries Unlimited, 1984.

———. *Popular Music Perspectives: Ideas, Themes, and Patterns in Contemporary Lyrics*. Bowling Green, Ohio: Popular Press, 1991.

———. *A Resource Guide to Themes in Contemporary American Song Lyrics, 1950–1985*. Westport, Conn.: Greenwood Press, 1986.

———. "Teaching with Popular Music Resources: A Bibliography of Interdisciplinary Instructional Approaches." *Popular Music and Society* 22: 2 (Summer 1998), 85–115.

Cooper, B. Lee, and Wayne S. Haney. *Rock Music in American Popular Culture: Rock 'n' Roll Resources*. Binghamton, N.Y.: Haworth Press, 1995.

———. *Rock Music in American Popular Culture II: More Rock 'n' Roll Resources*. Binghamton, N.Y.: The Haworth Press, Inc., 1997.

———. *Rock Music in American Popular Culture III: More Rock 'n' Roll Resources*. Binghamton, NY: Haworth Press, 1999.

———. *Rockabilly: A Bibliographic Resource Guide*. Metuchen, N.J.: Scarecrow Press, 1990.

Courlander, Harold. *Negro Folk Music, USA*. New York: Columbia University Press, 1963.

Crampton, Luke, and Dafyyd Rees. *VH-1's Rock Star Encyclopedia*. New York: DK, 1999.

Crenshaw, Marshall. *Hollywood Rock: A Guide to Rock 'n' Roll Movies*. New York: HarperPerennial, 1994.

Curtis, Jim. *Rock Eras: Interpretations of Music and Society, 1954–1984*. Bowling Green, Ohio: Popular Press, 1986.

Cusic, Don. *Music in the Market*. Bowling Green, Ohio: The Popular Press, 1995.

———. *The Sound of Light: A History of Gospel Music*. Bowling Green, Ohio: The Popular Press, 1993.

DeCharms, Desiree, and Paul F. Breed. *Songs in Collections: An Index*. Detroit: Information Service, 1966.

DeCurtis, Anthony. *Rockin' My Life Away: Writing About Music and Other Matters*. Raleigh, N.C.: Duke University Press, 1998.

DeCurtis, Anthony, ed. *Present Tense: Rock and Roll Culture*. Durham, N.C.: Duke University Press, 1992.

DeCurtis, Anthony, and James Henke, with Holly George-Warren, eds. *The Rolling Stone Illustrated History of Rock and Roll*. Rev. ed. New York: Random House, 1992.

De Lerma, Dominique-Rene. *Bibliography of Black Music*. 4 vols. Westport, Conn.: Greenwood Press, 1981–1984.

Denisoff, R. Serge. *Great Day Coming: Folk Music and the American Left*. Urbana: University of Illinois Press, 1971.

——. *Inside MTV*. New Brunswick, N.J.: Transaction, 1987.

——. *Sing a Song of Social Significance*. Bowling Green, Ohio: Popular Press, 1972.

——. *Solid Gold: The Popular Recording Industry*. New Brunswick, N.J.: Transaction, 1975.

——. *Tarnished Gold: The Record Industry Revisited*. New Brunswick, N.J.: Transaction, 1986.

Denisoff, R. Serge, and George Plasketes. *True Disbelievers: The Elvis Contagion*. New Brunswick, N.J.: Transaction, 1995.

Denisoff, R. Serge, and William Romanowski. *Risky Business: Rock in Film*. New Brunswick, N.J.: Transaction, 1991.

DePaoli, Geri, ed. *Elvis + Marilyn: 2 × Immortal*. New York: Rizzoli, 1994.

Deutsch, Didier C., ed. *VideoHound's Soundtracks: Music from the Movies, Broadway and Television*. Detroit: Visible Ink, 1999.

DeVeaux, Scott. *The Birth of BeBop: A Social and Musical History*. Berkeley: University of California Press, 1997.

Di Martino, Dave. *Singer Songwriters: Pop Music's Performers-Composers from A to Zevon*. New York: Billboard Books, 1994.

Eberly, Philip K. *Music in the Air: America's Changing Tastes in Popular Music, 1920–1980*. New York: Hastings House, 1982.

Ebersole, Lucinda, and Richard Peabody, eds. *Mondo Elvis*. New York: St. Martin's 1994.

Eisen, Jonathan. *The Age of Rock: Sounds of the American Cultural Revolution*. New York: Vintage, 1969.

——. *The Age of Rock 2: Sights and Sounds of the American Cultural Revolution*. New York: Vintage, 1970.

Ellison, Curtis W. *Country Music Culture: From Hard Times to Heaven*. Jackson, Miss.: The University Press of Mississippi, 1995.

Ennis, Philip H. *The Seventh Stream: The Emergence of Rock 'n' roll in American Popular Music*. Hanover, N.H.: Wesleyan University Press, 1992.

Epstein, Dena. *Sinful Tunes and Spirituals: Black Folk Music to the Civil War*. Urbana: University of Illinois Press, 1977.

Erenberg, Lewis A. *Swingin' the Dream: Big Band Jazz and the Rebirth of American Culture*. Chicago: University of Chicago Press, 1998.

Erlewine, Michael, Vladimir Bogdanov, and Chris Woostra, eds. *All Music Guide to Rock*. San Francisco: Miller Freeman, 1995, 1996, 1997.

Erlewine, Michael, and Cub Koda, eds. *All Music Guide to the Blues*. San Francisco: Miller-Freeman, 1996.

Ewen, David. *All the Years of American Popular Music*. Englewood Cliffs, N.J.: Prentice-Hall, 1977.

——. *American Popular Songs from the Revolutionary War to the Present*. New York: Random House, 1966.

Ferris, William. *Blues from the Delta*. Garden City, N.Y.: Anchor/Doubleday, 1978.

Flanagan, Bill. *Written in My Soul: Rock's Greatest Songwriters Talk about Creating Their Music*. Chicago: Contemporary Books, 1987.

Floyd, Samuel L. *The Power of Black Music: Interpreting Its History from Africa to the United States*. New York: Oxford University Press, 1995.

Fong-Torres, Ben. *Not Fade Away: A Backstage Pass to 20 Years of Rock and Roll*. San Francisco: Miller-Freeman, 1999.

Fong-Torres, Ben, ed. *The Rolling Stone Rock and Roll Reader*. New York: Putnam, 1974.

———. *What's the Sound: The Contemporary Music Scene from the Pages of Rolling Stone*. Garden City, N.J.: Doubleday Anchor Books, 1976.

Friedlander, Paul. *Rock and Roll: A Social History*. Boulder, Colo.: Westview Press, 1996.

Frith, Simon. *Music for Pleasure: Essays in the Sociology of Pop*. New York: Routledge, 1988.

———. *Performing Rites: On the Value of Popular Music*. Cambridge: Harvard University Press, 1996.

———. *Sound Effects: Youth, Leisure and the Politics of Rock and Roll*. New York: Pantheon, 1981.

Frith, Simon, ed. *Facing the Music*. New York: Pantheon, 1988.

Frith, Simon, and Andrew Goodwin, eds. *On Record: Rock, Pop, and the Written Word*. New York: Pantheon, 1990.

Frith, Simon, Andrew Goodwin, and Lawrence Grossberg, eds. *Sound and Vision: The Music Video Reader*. New York: Routledge, 1993.

Fuld, James J. *American Popular Music 1875–1950*. Philadelphia: Musical Americana, 1955, 1956, 1971.

———. *Book of World Famous Music: Classical, Popular and Folk*. New York: Crown, 1971.

Gaar, Gillian G. *She's a Rebel: The History of Women in Rock and Roll*. Seattle: Seal Press, 1992.

Gatten, Jeffery N. *Rock Music Scholarship: An Interdisciplinary Bibliography*. Westport, Conn.: Greenwood Press, 1995.

———. *The Rolling Stone Index: Twenty-Five Years of Popular Culture, 1967–1991*. Ann Arbor, Mich.: Popular Culture, Ink., 1993.

Gillett, Charles. *The Sound of the City: The Rise of Rock and Roll*. New York: Outerbridge and Dienstfrey, 1970.

Graff, Gary, Josh Fredom duLac and Jim McFarlin, eds. *MusicHound R & B: The Essential Album Guide*. Detroit: Visible Ink Press, 1996.

Graff, Gary, and Daniel Durcholz. *MusicHound Rock: The Essential Album Guide*. Detroit: Visible Ink, 1996.

Graff, Gary, and Brian Mansfield. *MusicHound Country: The Essential Album Guide*. Detroit: Visible Ink, 1998.

Gray, Michael H. *Bibliography of Discographies*. Vol. 1: *Popular Music*. New York: Bowker, 1983.

———. *Bibliography of Discographies—Volume II: Popular Music*. New York: R.R. Bowker Company, 1983.

Green, Douglas B. *Country Roots: The Origins of Country Music*. New York: Hawthorn Books, 1976.

Greig, Charlotte. *Will You Still Love Me Tomorrow? Girl Groups from the '50s On*. London: Virago Press, 1989.

Guralnick, Peter. *Careless Love: The Unmaking of Elvis Presley*. Boston: Little, Brown, 1999.

————. *Feel Like Going Home: Portraits in Blues and Rock and Roll*. New York: Outerbridge and Dienstfrey, 1971.

————. *Last Train to Memphis: The Rise of Elvis Presley*. Boston: Little, Brown, 1994.

————. *Lost Highways: Journeys and Arrivals of American Musicians*. New York: Harper and Row, 1989.

————. *Sweet Soul Music: Rhythm and Blues and the Southern Dream of Freedom*. New York: Harper and Row, 1986.

Guterman, Jimmy, and Owen O'Donnell. *The Worst Rock n' Roll Records of All Time*. New York: Citadel Press, 1991.

Haggerty, Gary. *A Guide to Popular Music Reference Books: An Annotated Bibliography*. Westport, Conn.: Greenwood Press, 1995.

Hamm, Charles. *Yesterdays: Popular Song in America*. New York: W. W. Norton, 1979.

Hammontree, Patsy Guy. *Elvis Presley: A Bio-Bibliography*. Westport, Conn.: Greenwood Press, 1985.

Harris, Sheldon. *Blues Who's Who: A Biographical Dictionary of Blues Singers*. New Rochelle, N.Y.: Arlington House, 1979.

Hart, Mary L., Brenda M. Eagles, and Lisa N. Howorth. *The Blues: A Bibliographic Guide*. New York: Garland, 1989.

Hatch, David, and Stephen Milward. *From Blues to Rock: An Analytical History of Pop Music*. Manchester, England: Manchester University Press, 1989.

Havlice, Patricia Pate. *Popular Song Index*. Metuchen, N.J.: Scarecrow Press, 1975.

Heintze, James. *American Music Studies: A Classified Bibliography of Master's Theses*. Detroit: Information Coordinators, 1985.

Hendler, Herb. *Year by Year in the Rock Era*. New York: Praege, 1987.

Herbst, Peter, ed. *The Rolling Stone Interviews: Talking with the Legends of Rock and Roll, 1967–1980*. New York: St. Martin's Press, 1981.

Hernandez, Deborah Pacini. *Bachata: A Social History of Dominican Popular Music*. Philadelphia: Temple University Press, 1995.

Herzhaft, Gerard. *Encyclopedia of the Blues*. Fayetteville: University of Arkansas Press, 1997.

Heylin, Clinton, ed. *The Penguin Book of Rock and Roll Writing*. London: Penguin, 1992.

Hirshey, Gerri. *Nowhere to Run: The Story of Soul Music*. New York: Penguin, 1984.

Hixon, Donald L. *Music in Early America: A Bibliography of Music in Evans*. Metuchen, N.J.: Scarecrow Press, 1970.

Hoffman, Frank. *The Literature of Rock, 1954–1978*. Metuchen, N.J.: Scarecrow Press, 1981.

Hoffman, Frank, and B. Lee Cooper. *The Literature of Rock II: Including an Exhaustive Survey of the Literature from 1979–1983 and Incorporating Supplementary Material from 1954–1978 Not Covered in the First Volume*. Metuchen, N.J.: Scarecrow Press, 1986.

————. *The Literature of Rock III, 1984–1990*. Metuchen, N.J.: Scarecrow Press, 1995.

Holtje, Steve, and Nancy Ann Lee eds. *MusicHound Jazz: The Essential Album Guide*. Detroit: Visible Ink, 1998.

Hopkins, Jerry. *Elvis*. New York: Simon and Schuster, 1971.

————. *Elvis: The Final Years*. New York: St. Martin's Press, 1980.

Horn, David. *The Literature of American Music in Books and Folk Music Collections: A Fully Annotated Bibliography*. Metchen, N.J.: Scarecrow Press, 1977. Revised with Richard Jackson in 1988.

Jancik, Wayne. *The Billboard Book of One Hit Wonders*. New York: Billboard, 1998.

Jasen, David, and Trebor Jay Tichenor. *Rags and Ragtime: A Musical History*. New York: Seabury Press, 1978.

Joynson, Vernon. *Fuzz, Acid and Flowers—A Comprehensive Guide to American Garage, Psychedelic and Hippie Rock (1964–1975)*. London: Borderline Productions, 1998.

Keil, Charles. *Urban Blues*. Chicago: University of Chicago Press, 1966.

Kent, Nick. *The Dark Stuff: Selected Writings on Rock Music*. London: Penguin, 1994.

Kingsbury, Paul, and the Country Music Foundation, eds. *Country: The Music and the Musicians—From the Beginnings to the 90's*. New York: Abbeville, 1994.

Kinkle, Roger D. *The Complete Encyclopedia of Popular Music and Jazz, 1900–1950*. 4 vols. New Rochelle, N.Y.: Arlington House, 1974.

Knopper, Steve. *MusicHound Swing! The Essential Album Guide*. Detroit: Visible Ink, 1999.

Knopper, Steve, ed. *MusicHound Lounge: The Essential Album Guide to Martini Music and Easy Listening*. Detroit: Visible Ink, 1999.

Krummel, D.W., Jean Geil, Dris J. Dyen, and Deane L. Root. *Resources of American Music History: A Directory of Source Materials from Colonial Times to World War II*. Urbana IL: University of Illinois Press, 1981.

Laeppler, Adrienne L., and J. W. Love. *The Garland Encyclopedia of World Music: Australia and the Pacific Islands*. Levittown, Pa.: Garland, 1998.

Larkin, Colin, ed. *The Guinness Encyclopedia of Popular Music*. Middlesex, England: Guinness, 1992.

Lavine, Michael, and Pat Blashill. *Noise from the Underground: A Secret History of Alternative Rock*. New York: Fireside/Simon and Schuster, 1996.

Leigh, Robert. *Index to Song Books: A Title Index to over 11,000 Copies of Almost 6,800 Song Books Published Between 1933 and 1962*. Stockton, Calif.: Robert Leigh, 1964.

Lewis, George H. "Country Music Lyrics." *Journal of Communication*, 26 (Autumn 1976), 37–40.

————. "Social Protest and Self Awareness in Black Popular Music." *Popular Music and Society*. Volume 2:4 (1973), 327–333.

————. "The Sociology of Popular Music: A Selected and Annotated Bibliography." *Popular Music and Society*. 1979, 57–68.

Lewis, George, ed. *All That Glitters: Country Music in America*. Bowling Green, Ohio: Popular Press, 1993.

Light, Alan, ed. *Vibe History of Hip Hop*. New York: Three Rivers Press, 1999.

Loder, Kurt. *Bat Chain Puller: Rock & Roll in the Age of Celebrity*. New York: St. Martin's Press, 1990.

————. *The Rolling Stone Interviews, the 1980s*. New York: St. Martin's Press, 1989.

Lull, James, ed. *Popular Music and Communication*. Newbury Park, Calif.: Sage, 1987.

Malone, Bill. *Country Music, USA*. Rev ed. Austin: University of Texas Press, 1985.

Manuel, Peter L., Kenneth M. Bilby, and Michael D. Largey. *Caribbean Currents*. Philadelphia, Penn.: Temple University Press, 1995.

Marco, Guy A. *Checklist of Writings on American Music, 1640–1992*. Lanham, Md.: Scarecrow Press, 1996.

———. *Literature of American Music III, 1983–1992*. Lanham, Md.: Scarecrow Press. 1996.

Marcus, Greil. *Dead Elvis: A Chronicle of a Cultural Obsession*. New York: Doubleday, 1991.

———. *In the Fascist Bathroom: Punk in Pop Music, 1977–1992*. Cambridge: Harvard University Press, 1993.

Marcus, Greil. *Lipstick Traces: A Secret History of the 20th Century*. Cambridge: Harvard University Press, 1989.

———. *Mystery Train: Images of America in Rock 'n' Roll Music*. New York: Dutton, 1976.

Marcus, Greil, ed. *Stranded: Rock and Roll for a Desert Island*. NewYork: Alfred A. Knopf, 1979.

Marsh, Dave. *Elvis*. (2nd ed.) New York: Thunder's Mouth Press, 1992.

———. *The First Rock and Roll Confidential*. New York: Pantheon, 1985.

———. *Fortunate Son*. New York: Random House, 1985.

———. *Glory Days: Bruce Springsteen in the 1980s*. New York: Pantheon, 1987.

———. *The Heart of Rock and Soul: The 1001 Greatest Singles Ever Made*. New York: Plume, 1989.

———. *Louie, Louie*. New York: Hyperion, 1993.

Marsh, Dave, and John Swenson, eds. *The Rolling Stone Record Guide*. New York: Random House/Rolling Stone, 1979.

———. *The New Rolling Stone Record Guide*. New York: Random House/Rolling Stone, 1983.

Mattfeld, Julius. *Variety Music Cavalcade, 1620–1969: A Chronology of Vocal and Instrumental Music Popular in the United States*. 3rd ed. Englewood Cliffs, N.J.: Prentice-Hall, 1971.

McCloud, Barry. *Definitive Country—The Ultimate Encyclopedia of Country Music and Its Performers*. New York: Perigee Books, 1998.

McCoy, Judy. *Rap in the 1980s: A Reference Guide*. Metuchen, N.J.: Scarecrow, 1992.

McGowan, Chris, and Ricardo Pessanha. *The Brazilian Sound: Samba, Bossa Nova and the Popular Music of Brazil*. Philadelphia: Temple University Press, 1998.

Mead, Rita H. *Doctoral Dissertations In American Music: A Classified Bibliography*. Brooklyn, N.Y.: Institute for Studies in American Music, 1974.

Meadows, Eddie. S. *Jazz Reference and Research Materials*. New York: Garland, 1981.

Mellers, Wilfred. *Music in a New Found Land: Themes and Developments in the History of American Music*. New York: Knopf, 1965.

Miller, Jim, ed. *The Rolling Stone Illustrated History of Rock and Roll, 1950–1980*. Rev. ed. New York: Rolling Stone Press, 1980.

Miller, Terry E., and Sean Williams. *The Garland Encyclopedia of World Music: Southeast Asia*. Levittown, Pa: Garland, 1998.

"More Scholars Focus on Popular Music as a Key to Examining Culture and History." *The Chronicle of Higher Education* (May 1, 1998), A16-A22.

Moyers, Bill. *The Bill Moyers Collection: Amazing Grace*. New York: Films for the Humanities, 1992. (Documentary film)

Nite, Norm N. *Rock On: The Illustrated Encyclopedia of Rock and Roll*. 3 vols. New York: Harper and Row, 1982, 1985.

Nyhan, Pat, Brian Rollins, and David Babb. *Let the Good Times Roll: A Guide to Cajun and Zydeco Music*. Ville Platte, La.: Upbeat Books, 1998.

Ochs, Michael. *Rock Archives: A Photographic Journal through the First Two Decades of Rock and Roll*. New York: Doubleday, 1984.

O'Dair, Barbara, ed. *Trouble Girls: The Rolling Stone Book of Women in Rock*. New York: Random House, 1997.

Oliver, Paul. *The Blackwell Guide to Blues Records*. Cambridge, Mass.: Basil Blackwell, 1989.

———. *The Story of the Blues*. Philadelphia: Chilton, 1969.

———. *The Penguin Guide to Jazz*. New York: Penguin, 1994.

Palmer. Robert. *Deep Blues*. New York: Viking, 1981.

———. *Rock and Roll: An Unruly History*. New York: Harmony, 1995.

Pareles, Jon, and Patricia Romanowski, eds. *The Rolling Stone Encyclopedia of Rock and Roll*. New York: Rolling Stone/Summit, 1983.

Peterson, Richard A. *Creating Country Music: Fabricating Authenticity*. Chicago: University of Chicago Press, 1997.

Pichaske, David R. *A Generation in Motion: Popular Music and Culture in the Sixties*. Granite Falls, Minn.: Ellis Press, 1989.

Plasketes, George. *Images of Elvis Presley in American Culture 1977–1992: The Mystery Terrain*. Binghamton, N.Y.: Haworth, 1997.

Pruter, Robert. *The Blackwell Guide to Soul Recordings*. Oxford, England: Blackwell Ltd., 1993.

———. *Chicago Soul*. Urbana: University of Illinois Press, 1991.

———. *Doowop: The Chicago* Scene. Urbana: University of Illinois Press, 1996.

Quain, Kevin, ed. *The Elvis Reader: Texts and Sources on the King of Rock and Roll*. San Francisco, Calif.: San Francisco Chronicle, 1992.

Reder, Alan and John Baxter. *Listen to This!* New York: Hyperion, 1999.

Robbins, Ira A. ed. *The Trouser Press Record Guide: 90's Rock*. 5th ed. New York: Fireside/Simon and Schuster, 1997.

Rodman, Gilbert B. "Everyday I Write the Book: A Bibliography of (Mostly) Academic Work on Rock and Pop Music." *Tracking: Popular Music Studies* 2 (Spring 1990), 17–50. Rev. ed. 1992.

Romanowski, Patricia and Holly George-Warren, eds. *The New Rolling Stone Encyclopedia of Rock*. New York: Fireside/Rolling Stone, 1995.

Rose, Tricia. *Black Noise: Rap Music and Black Culture in Contemporary America*. Middletown, Conn.: Wesleyan University Press, 1993.

Rosenberg, Neil. *Bluegrass: A History*. Urbana: University of Illinois Press, 1985.

Rucker, Leland, and Tim Schuller, eds. *MusicHound Blues: The Essential Album Guide*. Detroit: Visible Ink, 1997.

Sanjek, David. *Pennies from Heaven: The American Popular Music Business in the Twentieth Century*. New York: DaCapo, 1996.

Santelli, Robert. *The Big Book of the Blues: A Biographical Encyclopedia*. New York: Penguin, 1993.

Schafer, William, J., and Johannes Riedel. *The Art of Ragtime: Form and Meaning of an Original Black American Art*. Baton Rouge: Louisiana State University Press, 1973.

Scheuer, Timothy E. *Born in the USA: The Myth of America from Colonial Times to the Present*. Jackson: University of Mississippi Press, 1991.

Scheuer, Timothy E., ed. *American Popular Music* Vol. 1: *The 19th Century and Tin Pan Alley*. Bowling Green, Ohio: Popular Press, 1989.

———. *American Popular Music*. Vol. 2: *The Age of Rock*. Bowling Green, Ohio: Popular Press, 1991.

Shapiro, Nat. *Popular Music: An Annotated Index of American Popular Songs*. 10 vols. Detroit: Gale Research, 1986.

Shapiro, Nat, and Bruce Pollack, eds. *Popular Music, 1920–1979: A Revised Cumulation*. 3 vols. Detroit: Gale Research, 1985.

Shaw, Arnold. *Honkers and Shouters: The Golden Age of Rhythm and Blues*. New York: Collier, 1978.

———. *The Rockin' '50's: The Decade That Transformed the Pop Music Scene*. New York: Hawthorn, 1974.

Skoronski, JoAnn. *Black Music in America: A Bibliography*. Metuchen, N.J.: Scarecrow, 1981.

Smith, Bradley. *The Billboard Guide to Progressive Music*. Menomonee Falls, Wis.: Billboard Books, 1997.

Smith, Joe. *Off the Record: An Oral History of Popular Music*. New York: Warner, 1988.

Smith, Wes. *The Pied Pipers of Rock and Roll: Radio Deejays of the 50's and 60's*. Marietta, Ga.: Longstreet Press, 1989.

Sonneck, Oscar G. T. and William Treat Upton. *Bibliography of Early American Secular Music (Eighteenth Century)*. Washington, D.C.: Library of Congress, Music Divison, 1945. Reprint. New York: DaCapo Press, 1964.

Southern, Eileen. *Music of Black Americans: A History*. New York: W.W. Norton, 1983.

Spaeth, Sigmund. *The History of Popular Music in America*. New York: Random House, 1948.

Stambler, Irwin. *The Encyclopedia of Pop, Rock and Soul*. New York: St. Martin's, 1989.

Stambler, Irwin, and Grelun Landon. *Country Music: The Encyclopedia*. New York: St. Martin's, 1998.

Stecheson, Anthony, and Anne Stecheson. *Stecheson Classified Song Directory*. Hollywood, Calif.: Music Industry Press, 1961. *Supplement*, 1978.

Stern, Jane, and Michael Stern. *Elvis World*. New York: Knopf, 1987.

Stokes, Geoffrey. *Starmaking Machinery: Inside the Music Business of Rock and Roll*. New York: Vintage, 1977.

Stone, Ruth M., ed. *The Garland Encyclopedia of World Music: Africa*. Levittown, Pa.: Garland, 1997.

Stowe, David W. *Swing Changes: Big-Band Jazz in New Deal America*. Cambridge: Harvard University Press, 1994.

Swiss, Thomas, John L. Sloop, and Andrew Herman, eds. *Mapping the Beat: Popular Music and Contemporary Thought.* Walden, Mass.: Blackwell, 1997.

Talevski, Nick. *The Unofficial Encyclopedia of the Rock and Roll Hall of Fame.* Westport, Conn.: Greenwood Press, 1998.

Taylor, Paul. *Popular Music since 1955: A Critical Guide to Literature.* New York: Mansell, 1985.

Taylor, Timothy T. *Global Pop: World Music/World Markets.* New York: Routledge, 1997.

Tharpe, Jac, ed. *Elvis: Images and Fancies.* Jackson: University of Mississippi Press, 1979.

Tichi, Cecilia. *High Lonesome: The American Culture of Country Music.* Chapel Hill: University of North Carolina Press, 1994.

Tichi, Cecilia, ed. *Reading Country Music: Steel Guitars, Opry Stars, and Honky Tonk Bars.* Durham, N.C.: Duke University Press, 1998.

Toll, Robert. *Blacking Up: The Minstrel Show in Nineteenth-Century America.* New York: Oxford University Press, 1974.

Tosches, Nick. *Country: Living Legends and Dying Metaphors in America's Biggest Music.* New York: Stein and Day, 1977.

———. *Unsung Heroes of Rock and Roll: The Birth of Rock and Roll in the Dark and Wild Years before Elvis.* New York: Charles Scribner's Sons, 1984.

Unterberger, Richie. *Music USA: The Rough Guide.* London: Penguin/Rough Guide, 1999.

Vann, Kimberly R. *Black Music in Ebony: An Annotated Guide to the Articles on Music in Ebony Magazine.* Chicago: Center for Black Music Research, 1990.

Vazquez, Linda, and William Schurk, comps. "Bibliography of Books, Book Chapters, and Articles by R. Serge Denisoff." *Popular Music and Society* 21: 1 (Spring 1997), 141–146.

Waldo, Terry. *This is Ragtime.* New York: Hawthorn Books, 1976.

Walters, Neal and Brian Mansfield. *MusicHound Folk: The Essential Album Guide.* Detroit: Visible Ink, 1997.

Ward, Ed, Geoffrey Stokes, and Ken Tucker. *Rock of Ages: The Rolling Stone History of Rock and Roll.* New York: Rolling Stone/Summit, 1986.

Warner, Jay. *The Billboard Book of American Singing Groups: A History, 1940–1990.* New York: Billboard, 1992.

Whitburn, Joel, comp. *Billboard Book of Top 40 Hits, 1955 to Present.* New York: Watson-Guptill, 1983.

———. *Bubbling under Singles and Albums.* Menomonee Falls, Wis: Record Research, 1998.

———. *Pop Hits, 1940–1954.* Menomonee Falls, Wis.: Record Research, 1994.

———. *Top Country Albums, 1964–1997.* Menomonee Falls, Wis.: Record Research, 1997.

———. *Top 40 Country Hits, 1944–1993.* Menomonee Falls, Wis.: Record Research, 1994.

———. *Top Pop Album Tracks, 1955–1992.* Menomonee Falls, Wis.: Record Research, 1993.

———. *Top Pop Albums, 1955–1992.* Menomonee Falls, Wis.: Record Research, 1993.

———. *Top Pop Singles.* Menomonee Falls, Wis.: Record Research, 1994.

————. *Top Rhythm and Blues Singles, 1942–1988*. Menomonee Falls, Wis.: Record Research, 1988.

Whitcomb, Ian. *After the Ball: Pop Music from Rag to Rock*. New York: Limelight Editions, 1986.

Wilder, Alec. *American Popular Song: The Great Innovators, 1900–1950*. New York: Oxford University Press, 1972.

Wolf, Edwin, II. *American Song Sheets, Slip Ballads and Poetical Broadsides, 1850–1870*. New York: Krause Reprint, 1963.

Wolfe, Richard J. *Secular Music in America, 1801–1825: A Bibliography*. 3 vols. New York: New York Public Library, 1964.

Wood, Carolyn. *The Literature of Rock and Roll: A Special Collection*. Cambridge, Mass.: Charles Wood, 1991.

Worth, Fred L., and Steven D. Tamerius, comps. *Elvis: His Life from A to Z*. New York: Wings Books, 1990.

Zollo, Paul. *Songwriters on Songwriting*. Cincinnati: Writers Digest, 1991.

Periodicals

American Music. Champaign, Ill., 1983– .

Billboard. Los Angeles, 1894– .

Black Perspectives in Music. Cambria Heights, N.Y., 1973– .

Cash Box. New York, 1942– .

JEMF Quarterly. Los Angeles, 1965– .

Journal of Country Music. Nashville, Tenn., 1970– .

Music Reference Services Quarterly. Binghamton, N.Y.: 1990– .

Notes: The Quarterly Journal of the Music Library Association. Ann Arbor, Mich., 1934– .

Popular Music. Cambridge, England, 1987– .

Popular Music and Society. Bowling Green, Ohio, 1976– .

Rolling Stone. San Francisco, 1967– .

Spin. New York, 1985– .

NEW AGE MOVEMENTS

Joel D. Rudinger

Few areas of American popular culture elicit as strong an emotional response as the matrix of ideas that constitute the human potential New Age movement. It is held by some to be a cult and mistaken by others as a religion, by some as blasphemy against the Christian religion and by others as selfish, ego-stroking, do-good hedonism. Misunderstanding abounds. Yet by those who embrace its basic ideas, it is seen as the key and last hope for the salvation of the human race in a world struggling with technology, religious bigotry and hate, media violence, suburban chaos, racism, cultural confusion, worldwide genocide, rampant materialism, and two generations of parents who are lost and foundering in their own moral and spiritual vacuity.

The New Age movement emerged in the 1960s as a combination of apocalyptic Christianity and pagan divination. As the 1960s generation matured into the 1980s and 1990s, the New Age movement was clearly an emotional and political issue. People chose sides. When there were blame and anger to be placed, they fell on the doorstep of the New Agers, who tended to be quietly private in their practices.

While many New Age practitioners hold strong convictions, they are not out to convert unbelievers. If one is to take responsibility for his or her own behavior, and that includes self-healing on the psychic as well as the physical plane, then one who does not practice the habits of self-improvement is the loser for that and no other reason. "When the student is ready, the teacher will appear" is a belief that is the basis for tolerance for others' lack of understanding. The tenets of the New Age philosophy are meant to honor the integrity of all human beings and to allow them to realize their greatest potential of body, mind, and spirit in their own time and at their own speed.

The physical body, the mental body, and the spiritual, or etheric, body are the trinity of New Age practitioners, and that is part of the source of the tension between them and those who have not accepted their values and practices. In general, one can say that the philosophy of the New Ager is that god is not a person or an entity to be personified. Rather, that which is called god is Universal Energy, and because all things exist within, and are a part of, the Universal Energy, people share the same powers that created the universe and everything in it. It is a basic New Age understanding that humankind is divine, and the source of humankind's global distemper is that people have forgotten this simple fact. The drive of the New Ager is to embrace this idea of personal divinity, and everything that is done is an attempt to reenter this state of consciousness.

The term "New Age movement" is an informal and vague designation for a school of thought that encompasses a wide range of separate groups and ideas. It is probably more precise to speak of New Age movements, that is, a plurality of interests and perspectives, seemingly unrelated to each other. These movements describe literally hundreds of groups, organizations, teachers, techniques, products, writings, and programs that popularize Hindu, Buddhist, and other Eastern-oriented religions and philosophic concepts by blending those concepts with familiar Western ideas. Douglas R. Groothius, in *Confronting the New Age*, speaks of the New Age movement as "an umbrella term referring to a variety of people, organizations, events, practices, and ideas. Sociologically speaking, it is not a centrally organized movement with one human leader. . . . It is a constellation of like-minded people and groups all desiring a spiritual and social change that will usher in a New Age of self-actualization."

Although the New Age movement began in the early 1960s, with many key historical figures and movements that set the stage for its inception, the word "New" referred to the belief that the human race and the earth itself were on the verge of a new era of human history. It was a philosophy looking forward to a time of better energy and increased awareness of the world both within and around us. The dawning of the age of Aquarius (1962) and the approaching new millennium in 2001 created a widely popular interest in the movement.

The unifying characteristics common to most groups within this movement include the following. All is Oneness, one reality, one energy; everything is god/goddess or divine and, therefore, all human beings are divine. Human cognition must change so that people can know their divinity. Humanity's problem is not sin but ignorance because humans have simply "forgotten" that they are divine. As an extension of the creative Universal Energy that is the first and continuing cause of all things, humankind is basically good and, by accessing one's full potential, one can take control over oneself and be one's own savior. Finally, we have all reincarnated, lived before multiple times, and will yet live multiple lives in the future in a cycle of rebirth and spiritual purification and learning. Values tend to be relative; that is, there are no absolute values and no absolute truths. What is true for one occasion may not be true for another. A new world is coming, one of enlightenment, peace, and love.

Gary Zukav, author of *The Dancing Wu Li Masters* and *The Seat of the Soul*, has, as his premise in *The Seat of the Soul*, that in the past, people depended upon their five physical senses for their evolution. The physically rooted senses have led to a bestial Darwinian survival of the fittest and, on a cultural level, to what Herbert Spencer called social Darwinism. Humans have perceived themselves at the top of an evolutionary chain, and yet they still fight and destroy each other for power and control. The physical senses, which are limited and external, are the cause of human conflict, says Zukav. Knowing this, the New Ager can put a different spin

Various methods of divination are displayed on a fortune teller's table. © Painet

on the saying "What got me to where I am today will not get me where I need to go tomorrow." Zukav points to great teachers in the history of humankind (e.g., Jesus, Buddha, Krishna, Mohammed), who have gone beyond the limitations of the five senses, people whom he calls "multisensory." What supersedes the five senses is another kind of power that he sees as Love, love "of life in every form [in which] it appears, a power that does not judge what it encounters, a power that perceives meaningfulness and purpose in the smallest detail upon the Earth" (1989). The great teachers, he says, realize that one's soul is immortal, beyond body, beyond personality. "When the energy of the soul is recognized, acknowledged, and valued, it begins to infuse the life of the personality. When the personality comes fully to serve the energy of its soul, that is authentic empowerment," and that is the real goal and purpose of the new evolutionary process. New Agers, likewise, see the future evolution of humans as psychic; no longer is it merely biological and physical. The biological process is not the evolutionary process that will save the earth and humankind in the future. Now, say New Agers, is the time for a change in attitude and awareness of our greater potential, and this precisely is the defining concept that marks a change from the middle of the twentieth century and beyond.

Because of its basic positive approach to the self and human potential, and because New Age ideas exist in many different forms, expressed by so many different interest groups, they have had massive exposure to every facet of American life, from business, art, politics, religion, education, domestic life, to the practice of medicine. One can find influences of New Age thinking everywhere in every aspect of American culture. As time goes on in the new millennium, this area of American popular culture will become more defined as it becomes the focus for scholarship and academic analysis. For now, it is like standing in the eye of a hurricane trying to identify and describe a conglomeration of whirling artifacts. It is expected that soon studies of the New Age movement in all its many facets will begin to show up in scholarly publications and attain its proper respect as the tremendously important psychosociohistorical phenomenon that it is.

HISTORICAL OUTLINE

The New Age movement is an international social movement that emerged in the Western world in the late 1960s. From the 1970s and into the 1990s, it was an important new force in American popular culture. Even now, it is a movement that is continuing to redefine itself.

A number of scholarly sources look back in time to detect the embryonic signs of the New Age movement. If one sees the movement not as a wholly new phenomenon but as one that has had its seeds in earlier philosophies, then one can view it as a persistent tradition that has shadowed and paralleled Christianity for hundreds of years. As the occult was subdued and diminished by religious skeptics, the new science of the eighteenth and nineteenth centuries gave the metaphysical and supernatural a new idiom with which to express itself.

The predecessors to the New Age movement fully accepted the science of cause and effect as a method of expanding their own religious beliefs. Partially responsible for the growth in the New Age movement is its direct relationship to the explosion of popular scientific interest and its rational vocabulary. At the same time, the further that science began to divorce nature and the world from the individual, the more the human potential movement expanded as a psychic safety valve. Sigmund Freud discovered and articulated the id and the ego, thus beginning a concept of a person as more than a collective being but as a unique and passionate individual. As the idea took hold in the United States in the early 1920s, coupled with a rise of pre-depression prosperity and a middle class beginning to experience the Horatio Alger American Dream, the concept of human potential evolved on a conscious level and on a scale heretofore unseen. In a country relatively devoid of inherited social roles, personal achievement and social enhancement seemed possible. Entrepreneurship created new wealth and new dreams. The educational and political emancipation of women further liberalized the imagination of American culture.

Simultaneously, Christian literalism (fundamentalism) was beginning to crack as scientific evidence of Darwinian evolution began to challenge the biblical theory of creationism in the courts and in the classrooms. The political structure of democracy, also, allowed the fertile imagination to flourish. Large tracts of western land still lay open for development. The expanse of the frontier became a part of American thought. To the bright, thoughtful, and optimistic, potentiality abounded everywhere.

Swedish scientist, mystic, and religious philosopher Emanuel Swedenborg (1688–1772) advocated the existence and importance of the dream-accessed spiritual world, which he saw as having greater meaning than the familiar, physical, sensual world. He analyzed the relation between the material and the spiritual worlds in his treatment of the law of correspondences. Everything in the material world he saw as an extension, or likeness, of something in the spiritual world, a concept that is currently studied as aspect theory.

Franz Anton Mesmer (1733–1815), father of hypnotism, theorized the existence of a "universal magnetic fluid" and explained it in the language of science. His conclusions reformulated old concepts of magical power or "sacred spiritual energy." Today his studies have become restructured into the contemporary ideas of animal magnetism, astral light, and psychic energy. Psychic healers in the 1980s and 1990s attested to their witnessing this psychic energy and, further, saw it in the form of an auric flow of colors, waves of energy, and impulses surrounding living bodies.

The transcendental movement in the early nineteenth century, articulated best by Ralph Waldo Emerson (1803–1882), introduced to the Western world Asian perspectives that were new and significant. Emerson integrated Eastern metaphysics with popular American values, such as the drive to self-improve, individualism, and personal responsibility. Poet Walt Whitman (1819–1892) expressed these ideas poetically to the American people in his anthems *Song of Myself* and *Leaves of Grass*.

Bringing together the key ideas of Swedenborg, Mesmer, Emerson, and others involved in expanding human potential in the middle of the nineteenth century, spiritualism articulated in scientific language the structure of the universe as a whole. Spiritualism also maintained that, despite traditional Christian faith, it could scientifically demonstrate the continuance of human beings after their passing. Mediums claimed to converse with souls of the departed. In *The Spirit Land*, by S. B. Emmons (1858), the preface begins: "This volume is intended as an antidote to a species of errors that have been rife in every age of the Christian church." A schism was evident. Christian fundamentalists vehemently rejected the spiritualist embrace of the supernatural and natural law as opposed to God's biblical doctrines.

Natural law and Darwin's theory of evolution—particularly, that ontogeny recapitulates phylogeny—became credible to the scientific community as experimentation and observation verified many of the spiritualist beliefs. Spiritualism spread across North America. The metaphysical and occult communities diversified according to small group interests. Christian Science, while rejecting many of the concepts of spiritualism, nevertheless focused on healing. Their practice and application of metaphysical science produced more than mere anecdotal results.

Madame Helena Petrovna Blavatsky (1831–1891), in New York City in 1875, founded the Theosophical Society. The society created and nurtured a number of ideas that would become the bedrock of the New Age movement. Reincarnation, astrology, channeling, yoga, Atlantis (the lost warrior nation), and Lemuria (the lost nation of artists and philosophers) are among them. Blavatsky's *Isis Unveiled* (1877) discusses the Theosophical Society's beliefs. The society had three key objectives: (1) first and foremost, to create a Universal Brotherhood of Humanity (the Great White Brotherhood), which would exist without distinction of race, sex, creed, caste, or color; (2) to encourage the study of comparative religion,

Madame Helena Petrovna Blavatsky. Courtesy of the Library of Congress

philosophy, and science; and (3) to investigate the unexplained laws of nature and humans' latent powers. Writers and artists attracted to these quests incorporated them into their works and thereby carried these ideals to a larger public.

By the beginning of the twentieth century, major components of all the metaphysical traditions began to divide, but theosophy in particular splintered into literally hundreds of new occult and metaphysical organizations. Astrological interest became popular. Similarly, Hinduism and Buddhism, channeled into Western society by the theosophists, have become integrated throughout North America. Edgar Cayce (1877–1945) was a follower of theosophy. His trance medium experiences with reincarnation ultimately led to a Virginia Beach research institute and dozens of books, which have flowed out to influence millions of readers worldwide.

These developments led to the metaphysical fairs and psychic hot lines on television and the Internet and to the thousands of Unitarian and Unity churches that sponsor workshops, seminars, and lectures on New Age subjects, such as Dr. Deepak Chopra's *The Seven Spiritual Laws of Success*, quantum physics, reiki healing, tai chi, herbal and aroma therapies, chanting and meditation, biofeedback, and more. In short, the thousands of splinter groups that fall under the umbrella of New Age are intellectually involved in, and continue to search for, the three principles of the Theosophical Society created a scant 125 years ago.

REFERENCE WORKS

Because the subject area of New Age is so broadly defined—ranging from angelology to witchcraft, from auras to gemology—reference works in this realm tend to be correspondingly diverse. Compounding the problem of a lack of scholarly definition and focus is the fact that New Age studies have been anathema to most university scholars, the one most important group that most often makes inroads into new areas of knowledge. Perhaps because academe, as a whole, has kept New Age studies at arm's length, the description of the New Age movement has been left in the hands of nonscholars and people guided by motives other than achieving tenure. The New Age movement, then, is in the hands of practitioners with emotional ties to their studies. For this reason, the New Age movement enjoys a special place in the study of American popular culture, because it is still "free-ranging" in all areas of America. As Fox Mulder says in the New Age-inspired television series *X Files*, "the Truth is [still] out there." It is safe to say that the mosaic of the big picture is still in pieces and has yet to be assembled.

Some of the New Age references listed here are scholarly and are reinforced with both practical experience and good research. Others, however, are based upon imagination and creative insight. For the student of New Age ideas, however, they all represent a part of the New Age movement's perception and approach to itself and are, therefore, of value historically, sociologically, and informationally. Some of the following resources have brief descriptions, and some have none. The value of each resource is relative and different for different readers, depending upon their purpose.

The most comprehensive listing of New Age topics, including selected biographies and bibliographies, can be found in the *New Age Encyclopedia* by J. Gordon Melton, Jerome Clark, and Aidan A. Kelly. This is a reference guide to the beliefs, concepts, terms, people, and organizations that make up the new global movement toward spiritual development, health and healing, higher consciousness, and related subjects. There are 334 entries, most with substantial essays, including one on the historical development of the New Age. An appendix lists U.S. educational institutions offering a B.A. in this area, as well as schools with lesser programs. The index is extensive. This publication is an excellent place to begin any investigative study into New Age ideas. The second edition was published in 2001.

Angels A to Z, edited by James R. Lewis, Evelyn Dorothy Oliver, and Kelle S. Sisung, has 300 entries discussing angels across religious traditions, including New Age thought. Angels in various religions (Christianity, Islam, Hinduism) are treated. There is coverage of guardian angels and fallen angels and biblical figures associated with angels. Angels in art, architecture, film, television, and music, as well as literature about angels, from Dante to today's New Age writers, are included. Angels are also discussed in terms of the occult and metaphysics, with entries on unidentified flying objects (UFOs), fairies, and witches. There are brief bibliographies at the ends of entries including far-ranging sources.

The Astrology Encyclopedia by James R. Lewis offers basic information about astrology. There are 780 alphabetically arranged entries "intended to help today's students of astrology better understand the heavenly influences." The focus is strongest on natal astrology, which deals with individual personalities. Entries ranging in length from one sentence to more than fifteen pages include dozens of historical and contemporary astrologers, hundreds of astronomical bodies, and technical terms of astrology and astronomy. Interesting for the casual reader are longer entries such as astrotherapy, Chinese astrology, history of astrology in America, and history of Western astrology. Many of the longer entries have appended lists of sources, and many of the biographical entries are followed by a list of selected writings. See also the *Larousse Encyclopedia of Astrology*, edited by Jean-Louis Brau, Helen Weaver, and Allen Edmands.

Cunningham's Encyclopedia of Crystal, Gem, and Metal Magic by Scott Cunningham is an exhaustive encyclopedia about the magical properties of gems and precious metals. The author provides a succinct history of the uses of each stone, its folklore, the deities that it represents, and its magical uses. This work includes an annotated bibliography.

Cunningham's Encyclopedia of Magical Herbs is also by Scott Cunningham. Beginning herbalists should find this encyclopedia useful. Besides the practical nature of the book, it is filled with historical, mythological, and magical information and contains a cross-reference of folk names.

The Element Illustrated Encyclopedia of Mind, Body, Spirit, and Earth is by Joanna Crosse. Children's questions about the wider universe are not easily answered by conventional encyclopedias. This full-color reference book stimulates discussion on the type of metaphysical and mystical subjects that children and their families are talking about and takes readers on a comprehensive journey through the world's mysteries, marvels, and unexplained phenomena.

Encyclopedia of Angels, by Rosemary Ellen Guiley, is richly illustrated with medieval, Renaissance, and contemporary paintings, prints, drawings, and photographs. This encyclopedia contains the history and development of angelologies and the importance of angels to the major religions of the world. The book traces the path of angels across such diverse subjects as mysticism, mythology, folklore, magic, visions of the Virgin Mary, out-of-body experiences, extraterrestrials, psychology, and philosophy.

The Encyclopedia of Dreams: Symbols & Interpretations, by Rosemary Ellen Guiley, is two books in one. Part One lays the foundation for dream interpretation, explaining the importance of dreams and how they work. Part Two lists 600 alphabetical and cross-referenced entries on the most common subconscious symbols and what they mean.

The Encyclopedia of Ghosts and Spirits, by Rosemary Ellen Guiley, has some 400 alphabetically arranged entries, varying in length from a couple of paragraphs to several pages, and describes a wide range of beliefs, folklore, and strange phenomena. It includes an index and has references and cross-references.

Encyclopedia of New Age Beliefs, by John Ankerberg and John Weldon, is an excellent resource on the New Age for the Christian apologist addressing the New Age movement or simply a curious seeker of truth.

Since its publication in 1920, An *Encyclopedia of Occultism*, by Lewis Spence, has remained the supreme arbiter in all matters of dispute concerning the occult. It contains 2,500 entries and articles summarizing the entire history of the subject.

Encyclopedia of Occultism and Parapsychology by J. Gordon Melton and Leslie A.

Shepard is a synthesis of two one-volume works: Nancy Fodor's *Encyclopedia of Psychic Science* and Spence's *Encyclopedia of Occultism*. It also has revisions and additional up-to-date information and includes articles about modern occult magicians and critics of the paranormal.

The Encyclopedia of Palmistry, by Edward D. C. Campbell, offers a complete resource to understanding the mysteries hidden in the patterns and lines of the hands. The book includes information about the geography of the hand, identifying palm and fingerprints, the significance of hand and finger shapes, and more. Also useful is the *Encyclopedia of Signs, Omens, and Superstitions* by Zolar.

The Encyclopedia of the Paranormal, edited by Gordon Stein, with an introduction by Carl Sagan, defines the paranormal as that which cannot be currently explained by scientific means. It includes a wide range of ninety subject entries written objectively in lively, critical, short essay form by contributors from the fields of science, theology, philosophy, magic, history, and general academic scholarship. It reflects research in psychokinesis, astrology, alchemy, reincarnation, and even the Bermuda Triangle. Notable people involved with paranormal phenomena are examined as well as historical or "religious" movements, such as New Age thinking and theosophy. Carl Sagan, in his foreword, says, "I wish [this book] were on the shelves of every newspaper editorial desk and every television newsroom, to encourage more skeptical backbone in reporting . . . and in school libraries so that children would have some counterbalance to the many paranormal and mystical claims in our society" (Stein 1996).

The Encyclopedia of Witches and Witchcraft, by Rosemary Ellen Guiley, contains some 400 entries from witchcraft's early pagan heritage to the present. Emphasis is placed on the periods of witch persecutions, including the Inquisition and the Salem witch trials in the America of 1692.

Harper's Encyclopedia of Mystical & Paranormal Experience, by Rosemary Ellen Guiley and Marion Zimmer Bradley contains entries applicable to 1994 trends in spiritual thinking. Most helpful are comments and observations on native New Age spirituality.

The Roots of Consciousness: The Classic Encyclopedia of Consciousness Studies, by Jeffrey Mishlove illustrated with 100 photos and illustrations, explores the idea that telepathy, clairvoyance, precognition, psychokinesis, astral projection, and other such powers are latent within everyone. Throughout the text, Mishlove presents the viewpoints of both believers and nonbelievers as a further means of introducing the language and concepts of psychic functioning. The reader will find clear presentations of a wide variety of phenomena long relegated to the realm of the "supernatural" and of new theories now unifying these phenomena with leading physicists' understandings of the universe.

The UFO Book: Encyclopedia of the Extraterrestrial is by Jerome Clark, the former editor of the UFO magazine *Fate* and former vice president of the J. Allen Hyneck Center for UFO Studies as well as the editor of its quarterly publication, *The International UFO Reporter*. He has published several books and a three-volume *UFO Encyclopedia* encompassing every conceivable aspect of UFOs. *The UFO Book* is an abridgment of the much larger, three-volume encyclopedia published in 1998. *The UFO Book* is clear, in-depth, cross-referenced, and user-friendly. It includes a historical overview of UFO phenomena, an overview of the roots of its terminology, and information regarding resources in print in other media. Every

Ralph Waldo Emerson. Courtesy of the Library of Congress

subject, whether a discussion of a specific topic or a specific incident, is organized alphabetically and clearly cross-referenced. One hundred photographs and drawings illustrate the allegedly real and proven bogus evidence, helping readers decide for themselves whether or not extraterrestrials exist.

Wicca A to Z: A Modern Witch's Encyclopedia, by Gerina Dunwich, focuses on every aspect of Wicca and the "magickal" arts, from abracadabra to zoomorphism. It explains the different traditions, sabbats, and rituals of the Wiccan spiritual path, as well as Wiccan jargon, folklore, amulets, and talismans and the numerous herbs and gemstones associated with witchcraft.

Witches: An Encyclopedia of Paganism and Magic, by Michael Jordan, offers a complete assessment of modern paganism and magic as practiced by witches, druids, feminists, and others who believe that conventional religion has little relevance in the twenty-first century. Presented alphabetically, fully cross-referenced, and illustrated, *Witches* covers all the key figures and practices of paganism in the contemporary Western world, dispelling the myths that have long cloaked the subject. Many entries are supplemented with candid interviews with four prominent pagans, whose observations lend an insight into the workings of their collective faith.

Encyclopedia of Afterlife Beliefs and Phenomena, by James R. Lewis and Rudolph

Steiner, has a foreword by Raymond A. Moody, author of *Life after Life* and other works about near-death experiences, which makes plain this work's perspective. It is written from the believer's point of view. This is not to say that the skeptic or person with a particular religious view will not find useful information. The approximately 250 articles are in dictionary format and range from a few lines to several pages, each with a list of sources. Mircea Eliade's *Encyclopedia of Religion* is used heavily in articles on religious topics. There is an appendix listing related organizations and an index. Within articles, cross-references refer to terms that have their own separate articles. The essays are uneven in their coverage. Topics range from the very broad to the obscure, including the raelian movement (a flying-saucer religion). There are biographies of many people in the psychic and near-death-experience fields, including Edgar Cayce, Elisabeth Kubler-Ross, and William Crookes.

Harper's Encyclopedia of Mystical and Paranormal Experience, by Rosemary Ellen Guiley and Marion Zimmer Bradley, is a major source in the understanding of the mystical experience. In *The Illustrated Encyclopedia of Divination: A Practical Guide to the Systems That Can Reveal Your Destiny*, by Stephen Karcher, the author presents divination as a legitimate way for human beings to connect and interact with the nonphysical worlds of soul and spirit. As head of an international association for the divinatory arts and creator of the Eranos Foundation's I Ching Project, he clearly understands divination's psychological and spiritual value. It is a broad survey of hundreds of types of divination throughout the world, described in a single paragraph or up to half a dozen pages each. Included are esoteric examples of obscure divination—such as a Hermetic oracle of bibliomancy and a Santeria method employing coconut shells. The book has a glossary, index, and bibliography.

Wheels of Life: A User's Guide to the Chakra System, by Anodea Judith, offers a Western approach to the chakra system. This comprehensive guide addresses the development of the physical, emotional, mental, spiritual, and political aspects of human life. Using a multidimensional approach that combines theoretical understanding and practical exercises, the author shows how each of the levels of consciousness represented by the chakras is necessary for a complete life.

A Chakra & Kundalini Workbook: Psycho-Spiritual Techniques for Health, Rejuvenation, Psychic Powers and Spiritual Realization, by John Mumford, compiles material from a lifetime of teaching. Mumford, who was classically trained in India and as a physician, has merged a Western medical approach with Indian traditional philosophy and practice. The text contains many new afterimage visualization techniques and unique meditation methods. This is, in every sense, a "workbook." Mumford provides exact, step-by-step guidance to the progressive mind-body exercises. In the final section there is a Tantric ritual that demonstrates how there are "levers" with which one can transform the everyday moment into one of transcendence.

Energies of Transformation: A Guide to the Kundalini Process, by Bonnie L. Greenwell, is a comprehensive self-help book to help people understand and integrate the life-transforming experience of Kundalini awakening. It describes seven categories of phenomena related to Kundalini, provides Eastern and Western perspectives of the experience, includes twenty-three case histories, and gives practical guidance for people who are in a "Kundalini process."

RESEARCH COLLECTIONS

Because historical interest in New Age concerns is so recent, and because it has not been emphasized academically as an area of study, solid research collections are few. Other than for the Bangor Theological Seminary's Moulton Library's collection, on which there are little organized data, the largest and best organized collection is the American Religions Collection at the University of California at Santa Barbara. The collection contains the largest publicly accessible selection of New Age books and periodicals in North America, as well as a growing file of archival and ephemeral material. Anyone interested in working in this area would do well to consult this collection.

HISTORY AND CRITICISM

An introductory historical overview of the New Age movement can be found in Melton et al.'s *New Age Encyclopedia*. A more recent scholarly approach is Michael York's *Emerging Network: A Sociology of the New Age and Neo-Pagan Movements*. This text outlines the American background for current New Age ideas and moves to a discussion of the spokespersons of the New Age, including Marilyn Ferguson and her *Aquarian Conspiracy*, Ram Dass, Werner Erhard, Edgar Cayce, Alice Bailey, Ruth Montgomery, Shirley MacLaine, and Jose Arguelles. While this book has a double focus, the comparisons between New Age and neopaganism are interesting. The text includes survey profiles of selected groups as well as a quasi-anthropological field report of some esoteric practices. Also included in the general discussion is a critical review of Helen Schucman's influential channeled and anonymously published work, *A Course in Miracles*.

BIBLIOGRAPHY

Alper, Frank. *Exploring Atlantis*. 3 vols. Farmingdale, N.Y.: Coleman, 1982.
Altman, Nathaniel. *Eating for Life*. Wheaton, Ill.: Theosophical Publishing House, 1977.
Amber, Reuben. *Color Therapy*. New York: ASI, 1980.
Ankerberg, John, and John Weldon. *Encyclopedia of New Age Beliefs*. Eugene, Oreg.: Harvest House, 1996.
Bach, Marcus. *The Chiropractic Story*. Marina del Rey, Calif.: DeVores, 1968.
Baer, Randall, and Vicki Baer. *Windows of Light*. San Francisco: Harper and Row, 1984.
Bagnall, O. *Origins and Properties of the Human Aura*. New York: University Books, 1970.
Barnett, Libby, and Maggie Chambers. *Reiki Energy Medicine: Bringing Healing Touch into Home, Hospital, and Hospice*. Rochester, N.Y.: Healing Arts Press, 1996.
Baughman, John. *The New Age*. Eugene, Ore.: Inner Space Travel Agency, 1997.
Bergon, Anika, and Vladimir Tuchack. *Zone Therapy*. New York: Pinnacle Books, 1974.
Berkeley Holistic Health Center. *The Holistic Health Handbook*. Berkeley, Calif.: And/Or Press, 1978.

Blavatsky, Helena P. *Isis Unveiled*. 2 vols. New York: J. W. Bouton, 1877.

Brau, Jean-Louis, Helen Weaver, and Allen Edmands, eds. *Larousse Encyclopedia of Astrology*. New York: New American Library, 1980.

Brennen, Barbara Ann. *Hands of Light: A Guide to Healing through the Human Energy Field*. New York: Bantam Books, 1987.

Brown, Michael F. *The Channeling Zone: American Spirituality in an Anxious Age*. Cambridge: Harvard University Press, 1997.

Bruyere, Rosalyn. *Wheels of Light*. Glendale, Calif.: Healing Light Center, 1987.

Bry, Adelaide. *Visualization: Directing the Movies of Your Mind*. New York: Barnes and Noble Books, 1979.

Campbell, Edward D. C. *The Encyclopedia of Palmistry*. Encino, Calif.: Perigee, 1966.

Carter, Mildred. *Helping Yourself with Foot Reflexology*. West Nyack, N.Y.: Parker, 1969.

Cater, Mary Ellen. *My Years with Edgar Cayce*. New York: Harper and Row, 1972.

Cayce, Edgar. *Auras*. Virginia Beach, Va.: ARE Press, 1945.

———. *Edgar Cayce on Atlantis*. New York: Paperback Library, 1968

Cayce, Hugh Lynn. *Venture Inward*. New York: Harper and Row, 1964.

Chandler, Russell. *Understanding the New Age*. Dallas, Tex.: Word, 1998.

Chopra, Deepak. *Ageless Body, Timeless Mind: The Quantum Alternative to Growing Old*. New York: Harmony Books, 1993.

———. *The Seven Spiritual Laws of Success: A Practical Guide to the Fulfillment of Your Dreams*. San Rafael, Calif.: Amber-Allen, 1993.

Church, Connie. *Crystal Love*. New York: Villard Books, 1988.

Clark, Jerome. *The UFO Book: Encyclopedia of the Extraterrestrial*. Detroit: Visible Ink Press, 1998.

———. *The UFO Encyclopedia*. 3 vols. Detroit: Visible Ink Press, 1998.

Clark, Linda. *Health, Youth and Beauty through Color Breathing*. Millbrae, Calif.: Celestial Arts, 1976.

Corbett, Cynthia. *Power Trips*. Santa Fe: Timewindow, 1988.

A Course in Miracles. 2nd ed. Combined vol. New York: Penguin Group, 1996.

Crosse, Joanna. *The Element Illustrated Encyclopedia of Mind, Body, Spirit and Earth*. Boston: Shaftesbury Element Children's Books, 1998.

Cunningham, Scott. *Cunningham's Encyclopedia of Crystal, Gem, and Metal Magic*. St. Paul: Llewellyn, 1988.

———. *Cunningham's Encyclopedia of Magical Herbs*. 2nd ed. St. Paul: Llewellyn, 2000.

———. *Magic Herbalism: The Secret of the Wise*. St. Paul: Llewellyn, 1996.

Curran, Douglas. *In Advance of the Landing: Folk Concepts of Outer Space*. New York: Abbeville Press, 1985.

Day, Harvey. *Encyclopedia of Natural Health and Healing*. Santa Barbara, Calif.: Woodbridge Press, 1979.

Denning, Melita, and Osborne Phillips. *The Llewellyn Practical Guide to Creative Visualization: The Dynamic Way to Success, Love, Plenty and Spiritual Power*. 2nd ed. St. Paul: Llewellyn, 1985.

———. *The Magick of the Tarot*. St. Paul: Llewellyn, 1987.

Dintenfass, Julius. *Chiropractic: A Modern Way to Health*. New York: Pyramid Books, 1970.

DiOrio, Ralph A. *The Healing Power of Affirmation*. Garden City: N.Y.: Doubleday, 1985.

Dunwich, Gerina. *Wicca A to Z: A Modern Witch's Encyclopedia*. Secaucus, N.J.: Carol Publishing Group, 1997.

Eby, Edwin Harold. *A Concordance of Walt Whitman's* Leaves of Grass *and Selected Prose Writings*. New York: Greenwood Press, 1998.

Eliade, Mircea, ed. *Encyclopedia of Religion*. New York: Macmillan, 1993.

Emmons, S. B. *The Spirit Land*. Philadelphia: J. W. Bradley, 1858.

Family Guide to Natural Medicine: How to Stay Healthy the Natural Way. Pleasantville, N.Y.: Reader's Digest Association, 1993.

Ferguson, Marilyn. *The Aquarian Conspiracy*. Los Angeles: J. P. Tarcher, 1980.

Fiore, Dr. Edith. *The Unquiet Dead: A Psychologist Treats Spirit Possession*. New York: Ballantine Books, 1987.

Fisichella, Anthony. *Metaphysics: The Science of Life*. St. Paul: Llewellyn, 1987.

Fodor, Nancy. *Encyclopedia of Psychic Science*. New Hyde Park, N.Y.: University Books, 1966.

Freeman, James Dillet. *Prayer: The Master Key*. Unity Village, Mo.: Unity Press, 1975.

Garfield, Patricia. *Creative Dreaming*. New York: Simon and Schuster, 1974.

Garten, M. O. *The Health Secrets of a Naturopathic Doctor*. West Nyack, N.Y.: Parker, 1967.

Gawain, Shatki. *Creative Visualization*. Mill Valley, Calif.: Whatever, 1979.

———. *Living in the Light: A Guide to Personal and Planetary Transformation*. San Rafael, Calif.: New World Library, 1986.

Geis, Larry, Alta P. Kelley, and Aidan A. Kelly. *The New Healers*. Berkeley, Calif.: And/Or Press, 1980.

Gittelson, Bernard. *Biorhythm: A Personal Science*. New York: Warner Books, 1976.

Greenwell, Bonnie L. *Energies of Transformation: A Guide to the Kundalini Process*. London, England: Shakti Press, 1995.

Greer, Mary K. *Tarot Constellations: Patterns of Personal Destiny*. North Hollywood, Calif.: Newcastle, 1987.

Groothius, Douglas R. *Confronting the New Age*. Downers Grove, Ill.: InterVarsity Press, 1988.

———. *Unmasking the New Age*. Downers Grove, Ill.: InterVarsity Press, 1986.

Grossi, Ralph. *Reliving Reincarnation through Hypnosis*. Norris, Tenn.: Exposition Press, 1975.

Grupta, Yogi. *Yoga and Long Life*. New York: Dodd, Mead, 1958.

Guiley, Rosemary Ellen. *Encyclopedia of Angels*. New York: Facts on File, 1996.

———. *The Encyclopedia of Dreams: Symbols & Interpretations*. New York: Crossroad, 1993.

———. *The Encyclopedia of Ghosts and Spirits*. New York: Facts on File, 1992.

———. *The Encyclopedia of Witches and Witchcraft*. New York: Facts on File, 1989.

Guiley, Rosemary Ellen, and Marion Zimmer Bradley. *Harper's Encyclopedia of Mystical and Paranormal Experience*. San Francisco: Harper, 1991.

Haberly, Helen. *Reiki: Hawayo Takata's Story*. Olney, Md.: Archdigm, 1990.

Hall, Dorothy. *Iridology*. New Caanan, Conn.: Keats, 1981.

Harner, Michael. *The Way of the Shaman: A Guide to Power and Healing*. San Franscisco: Harper and Row, 1980.

Heline, Corinne. *Color and Music in the New Age*. La Canada, Calif.: New Age Press, 1964.

Hittleman, Richard. *Guide to Yoga Meditation*. New York: Bantam Books, 1969.

Hofer, Jack. *Total Massage*. New York: Grosset and Dunlap, 1976.

Horan, Paula. *Empowerment through Reiki: The Path to Personal and Global Transformation*. Wilmot, Wis.: Lotus Light, 1992.

Hulke, Malcome. *An Encyclopedia of Alternative Medicine and Self-Help*. New York: Schocken Books, 1979.

Inglis, Brian. *The Case for Unorthodox Medicine*. New York: Berkley Books, 1969.

Jackson, Adam J. *Alternative Health—Iridology: A Guide to Iris Analysis and Preventative Health Care*. London: Macdonald Optima, 1992.

Jackson, Richard. *Holistic Massage*. New York: Sterling, 1980.

Jensen, Bernard. *The Science and Practice of Iridology*. Provo, Utah: BiWorld, 1952.

Jordan, Michael. *Witches: An Encyclopedia of Paganism and Magic*. London: Kyle Cathie, 1996.

Judith, Anodea. *Wheels of Life: A User's Guide to the Chakra System*. Detroit: Llewellyn, 1987.

Kaatz, William, and Melanie Branon. *Channeling: The Intuitive Connection*. San Francisco: Harper and Row, 1987.

Karcher, Stephen. *The Illustrated Encyclopedia of Divination: A Practical Guide to the Systems That Can Reveal Your Destiny*. Rockport, Mass.: Element, 1997.

Keeney, Bradford. *Shaking Out the Spirits: A Psychotherapist's Entry into the Healing Mysteries of Global Shamanism*. Barrytown, N.Y.: Station Hill Press, 1994.

Kunz, Dora, ed. *Spiritual Aspects of the Healing Arts*. Wheaton, Ill.: Theosophical Publishing House, 1985.

Lad, Vasant. *Ayurveda: The Science of Self Healing: A Practical Guide*. Wilmot, Wis.: Lotus Press, 1984.

Leadbeater, C. W. *The Chakras: A Monograph*. Wheaton, Ill.: Theosophical Publishing House, 1972.

Leonard, Jim, and Phil Laut. *Rebirthing: The Science of Enjoying All Your Life*. Cincinnati, Ohio: Trinity, 1983.

Lewis, James R. *The Astrology Encyclopedia*. Detroit: Gale Research, 1994.

Lewis, James R., Evelyn Dorothy Oliver, and Kelle S. Sisung, ed. *Angels A to Z*. Detroit: Gale Research, 1995.

Lewis, James R., and Rudolph Steiner. *Encyclopedia of Afterlife Beliefs and Phenomena*. Detroit: Gale Research, 1994.

Lidell, Lucy. *The Sivananda Companion to Yoga*. New York: Simon and Schuster, 1984.

Lovelock, James. *Gaia: A New Look at Life on Earth*. New York: Oxford University Press, 1979.

Luce, Gay Gaer. *Biological Rhythms in Psychiatry and Medicine*. Chevy Chase, Md.: National Institute of Mental Health, 1970.

Melton, J. Gordon, Jerome Clark, and Aidan A. Kelly, eds. *New Age Encyclopedia*. Detroit: Gale Research, 1990.

Melton, J. Gordon, and Leslie A. Shepard. *Encyclopedia of Occultism and Parapsychology*. 4th ed. 2 vols. Detroit: Gale Research, 1996.

Miller, Roberta DeLong. *Psychic Massage*. New York: Harper and Row, 1975.

Mishlove, Jeffrey. *The Roots of Consciousness: The Classic Encyclopedia of Consciousness Studies*. Tulsa: Council Oak Books, 1993.

Montgomery, Ruth. *Strangers among Us: Enlightened Beings from a World to Come*. New York: Coward, McCann, and Geoghegan, 1979.

Moody, Raymond A. *Life after Life*. Philadelphia, Pa.: Stackpole, 1975.

Mumford, John. *A Chakra & Kundalini Workbook: Psycho-Spiritual Techniques for Health, Rejuvenation, Psychic Powers and Spiritual Realization*. St. Paul: Llewellyn, 1994.

Neimark, Anne E. *With This Gift*. New York: William Morrow, 1978.

Netherton, Morris, and Nancy Schiffrin. *Past Lives Therapy*. New York: Morrow, 1978.

Orr, Leonard, and Sondra Ray. *Rebirthing in the New Age*. Millbrae, Calif.: Celestial Arts, 1977.

Parker, William R., and Elaine St. John. *Prayer Can Change Your Life*. New York: Cornerstone Library, 1974.

Parrioh-Harra, Carol W. *Messengers of Hope*. Marina del Rey, Calif.: Devorss, 1983.

Pathak, R. R. *Therapeutic Guide to Ayurvedic Medicine*. Nagpur, India: Baldyanath, 1970.

Ram Dass, Baba. *Be Here Now*. Christobal, N. Mex.: Lama Foundation, 1971.

———. *Journey of Awakening*. New York: Bantam Books, 1978.

———. *The Miracle of Love*. New York: E. P. Dutton, 1979.

Raphael, Katrina. *Crystal Healing*. New York: Aurora Press, 1987.

Reisser, Paul C., Terri K. Reisser, and John Weldon. *New Age Medicine*. Downers Grove, Ill.: InterVarsity Press, 1987.

Sabin, Katherine C. *ESP and Dream Analysis*. Chicago: Henry Regnery, 1974.

Scott, Gini Graham. *The Shaman Warrior*. Phoenix, Ariz.: Falcon Press, 1988.

Smith, Bradford. *Meditation*. Philadelphia: J. P. Lippincott, 1963.

Spence, Lewis. *An Encyclopedia of Occultism*. 1920. New York: Citadel Press, 1993.

Sprangler, David. *Emergence: The Rebirth of the Sacred*. New York: Dell, 1984.

Stead, Christine. *The Power of Holistic Aromatherapy*. Poole, England: Javelin Books, 1986.

Stein, Diane. *Essential Reiki: A Complete Guide to an Ancient Healing Art*. Freedom, Calif.: Crossing Press, 1995.

Stein, Gordon, ed. *The Encyclopedia of the Paranormal*. Amherst, N.Y.: Promethean Press, 1996.

Stevenson, Ian. *Twenty Cases Suggestive of Reincarnation*. 2nd ed. Charlottesville: University Press of Virginia, 1974.

Sutpen, Richard. *Past Lives, Future Loves*. New York: Pocket Books, 1978.

———. *Sedona: Psychic Energy Vortexes*. Malibu, Calif.: Valley of the Sun, 1986.

Tart, Charles. *Altered States of Consciousness*. Garden City, N.Y.: Anchor, 1969.

Tisserand, Robert. *Aromatherapy*. Rochester, N.Y.: Destiny Books, 1977.

Trall, Russell T. *The Scientific Basis for Vegetarianism*. St. Catherines, Ontario, Canada: Provoker Press, 1970.

Trevelyn, George. *A Vision of the Aquarian Age*. Walpole, N.H.: Stillpoint, 1984.

Troeger, Thomas H. *Meditation: Escape to Reality*. Philadelphia: Westminster Press, 1977.

Udupa, K. N., and R. H. Singh. *Science and Philosophy of Indian Medicine*. Nagpur, India: Baldyanath, 1978.

Walker, Barbara. *The Secrets of the Tarot: Origin, History, and Symbolism*. San Francisco: Harper and Row, 1984.

Wambach, Helen. *Reliving Past Lives: The Evidence under Hypnosis*. New York: Harper and Row, 1978.

Weil, Andrew. *8 Weeks to Optimal Health: A Proven Program for Taking Full Advantage of Your Body's Natural Healing Power*. New York: Alfred A. Knopf, 1998.

———. *The Marriage of the Sun and the Moon: The Quest for Unity in Consciousness*. Boston: Houghton Mifflin, 1972.

———. *Spontaneous Healing: How to Discover and Enhance Your Body's Natural Ability to Maintain and Heal Itself*. New York: Alfred A. Knopf, 1995.

Weschke, Carl Llewellyn, and Stan Baker. *The Truth about 20th Century Astrology*. St. Paul, Minn.: Llewellyn, 1989.

White, George Starr. *A Lecture Course of Physicians on Natural Methods in Diagnosis and Treatment*. Los Angeles: Phillips Printing, 1918.

Whitman, Walt. *Song of Myself*. Ed. Stephen Mitchell. Boston: Shambala, 1998.

Yogi, Marharishi Mahesh. *The Science of Being and the Art of Living*. New York: Signet, 1963.

York, Michael. *Emerging Network: A Sociology of the New Age and Neo-Pagan Movements*. Lanham, Md.: Rowman and Littlefield, 1995.

Zolar. *Encyclopedia of Signs, Omens, and Superstitions*. New York: Carol Publishing Group, 1995.

Zukav, Gary. *The Dancing Wu Li Masters: An Overview of the New Physics*. New York: Bantam Books, 1979.

———. *The Seat of the Soul*. New York: Simon and Schuster, 1989.

NEWSPAPERS

Agnes Hooper Gottlieb,
Amy Kiste Nyberg, and
Richard Schwarzlose

The American newspaper: to paraphrase Mark Twain, reports of its death are greatly exaggerated. For the last half of the twentieth century, doomsayers predicted that the death of newspapers was imminent. They were wrong. Newspapers changed much in character and content during the past century, and we can anticipate even more radical changes to accommodate new technologies in the future. But the fact remains that newspapers have been with us for three centuries and will continue, for the foreseeable future, to be a major source of information and social culture. Not only are newspapers fascinating records of times past, but they provide fertile ground for historical study. Despite the maxim that newspapers provide a first draft of history, historians have been reluctant to rely upon newspapers as primary source material for events gone by.

More recently, however, newspapers have become a rich source of study in and of themselves. The burgeoning field of communication research has focused especially on the newspaper as a cultural artifact of American society. Millions of Americans turn to newspapers—from the penny-saver circulated for free in small towns, to the economic powerhouse of the *Wall Street Journal*—for news and information every day. As the oldest form of mass communication, the newspaper also is an integral component of American popular culture. Research into newspapers has been both complicated and liberated in recent years by the emergence of the Internet—complicated because newspapers are forging ahead into the new medium and liberated because the Internet has provided an avenue to archival and library sources that was unimaginable a decade ago.

HISTORICAL OUTLINE

Salacious gossip about the French court and an item critical of Indian allies proved to be the undoing of *Public Occurrences Both Foreign and Domestic*, the first attempt to publish a newspaper in the colonies. Massachusetts authorities shut it down after the first issue appeared in 1690. Its editor, Benjamin Harris, a Boston bookseller who had fled London after running afoul of the law there, published his paper in violation of colonial laws requiring all publications to first obtain a license. While such licensing laws had been phased out in 1695 in England, they remained in force in the colonies until 1730.

The colonial newspaper was a direct descendant of the English press, which in turn traces its roots to the news sheets, or corantos, that initially were collections of foreign news items. The first English-language coranto was published in Amsterdam in 1620. The monarchy and the church strictly regulated printing in England from the time of the introduction of the first printing press there in 1476, but once licensing restrictions eased, the English newspaper thrived. London saw the publication of its first daily newspaper in 1702.

The first successful colonial newspaper was John Campbell's *Boston News-Letter*. Campbell, as postmaster of Boston, was in a unique position to gather information for his publication from letters and foreign newspapers that passed through his office and because of his access to official government information. He also had a strong information network in place already, since he had produced a handwritten newsletter carrying primarily business news for several years prior. The paper, which began publication in 1704, was quite tame in comparison with that published by Harris and carried the phrase "Published by Authority" prominently below the nameplate. Since a rich oral tradition of news exchange in such varied venues as the church and the local pub made local reports mostly unnecessary, much of the material to appear in this newspaper was reprinted from English and foreign newspapers, catering to a desire for news from "back home," even if the news was months late. The *News-Letter* lasted for seventy-two years.

The *New England Courant*, begun in 1721, was published by James Franklin, whose younger brother, Benjamin, later would become the most successful of the colonial printers. The *Courant* was the voice of leaders of the Anglican Church, a minority presence in Puritan New England. From the beginning, the purpose of the newspaper was to stir up controversy, and many historians point to the *Courant* as the founder of the "crusading" tradition in American newspapers. Its first crusade was rather misguided—an editorial campaign against the smallpox vaccination (simply because it was favored by the Reverend Cotton Mather and the Puritan clergy), but the newspaper quickly expanded its criticism to the government. Franklin landed in jail for several weeks in 1722 (because the publisher was responsible for the content of the newspaper, regardless of who actually wrote the articles). When he was forbidden to print by the court in 1723, he circumvented the order by putting seventeen-year-old Benjamin's name in the masthead. The paper was short-lived, folding in 1726 after failing to become economically viable.

Boston, as the intellectual center of the colonies, gave birth to the American newspaper, but journalism soon expanded to other colonial cities. Early newspapers included the *American Mercury*, published in Philadelphia in 1719 by Andrew Bradford; and its rival, the *Pennsylvania Gazette*, started in 1728 and purchased in 1729 by Benjamin Franklin, who would retire from active management of the paper at age forty-two to pursue other interests. In New York, John Peter Zenger published the *New York Weekly Journal*. His crusade against the corrupt colonial governor landed him in jail, and his trial introduced the concept of truth as a defense against libel and suggested that the proper role of the newspaper was as

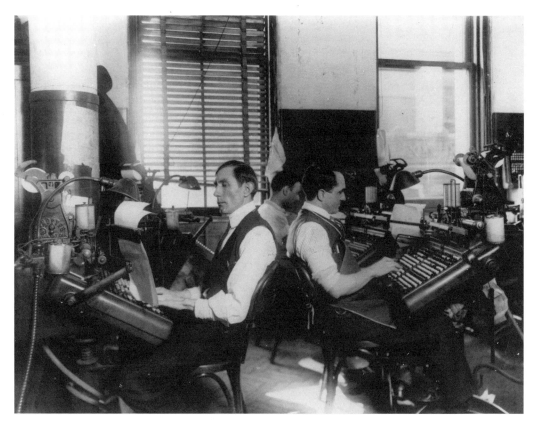

Linotype composition, *New York World*. Courtesy of the Library of Congress

a watchdog on government (although no laws were changed at the time). Other colonies that established newspapers, in order of appearance, included Maryland, Rhode Island, South Carolina, North Carolina, Connecticut, New Hampshire, Georgia, New Jersey, Vermont, and Delaware. Historians point to a number of factors that led to the growth of newspapers in the latter half of the eighteenth century, including increasing population, wealth, industry, commerce, improved communication, and a more tolerant attitude toward publishers.

Despite initial claims of neutrality, printers soon became embroiled in the Revolutionary War, and newspapers supported either the English or the revolutionaries' point of view. The best known of the Tory printers was James Rivington, who published the *New York Gazetteer* and who was forced to flee to England for a time when attacked by a Patriot mob in 1775, returning later as the "King's printer." On the other side, the leading Patriot newspaper was the *Boston Gazette*, supported by radical Sam Adams and others. The most famous of the Revolutionary War writers was not a printer at all but pamphleteer Thomas Paine, whose *Common Sense* was widely reprinted in newspapers. The main function of newspapers during the Revolutionary War was not reportage—in fact, much of what appeared in papers was based largely on rumors and secondhand accounts, and it was often weeks later that accounts of battles appeared in print. Instead, newspapers served as vehicles to rally people to the Patriot (or Tory) point of view.

The Revolutionary War enhanced the status of printers and expanded their role. The newspapers that emerged from the war would take an active part in the creation of the new republic and the partisan politics that accompanied it.

The cornerstone of press freedom in America, the First Amendment, was created at the end of the Revolution. Its inclusion in the Bill of Rights as drafted by James Madison recognized the importance of the press in keeping the citizenry of the new nation informed. The states ratified the Bill of Rights in 1791. Although the Founding Fathers envisioned the First Amendment primarily as a prohibition against prior restraint, or licensing, that narrow interpretation of press freedom gradually expanded to encompass more broadly the role of the press as a watchdog on government. In the early days of the nation, however, the First Amendment provided little protection for editors of newspapers in opposition to the ruling Federalists.

The defining characteristics of the party press, as it came to be known, were its support by, and allegiance to, the political factions of the time. It was a time of tremendous growth for newspapers, up from 38 in 1780 to 101 in 1790, a decade that saw the birth of the daily newspaper. The editors of these newspapers were members of political parties, which they supported in print, and their news reflected their party loyalties. Newspapers were rewarded with lucrative government printing contracts. The leading Federalist paper was the *Gazette of the United States*, published in the nation's capital beginning in 1789. It was supported by Alexander Hamilton and published by John Fenno. The opposition newspaper was the *National Gazette*, supported by anti-Federalist Thomas Jefferson and edited by Philip Freneau beginning in 1791. When Jefferson left President Washington's cabinet in 1793, however, the financial support for the paper dwindled, and it closed up shop that year. The independently founded *Aurora* in Philadelphia, edited by Benjamin Franklin Bache in 1790, also was a strong anti-Federalist voice and remained as the leading Republican newspaper after the demise of the *Gazette*. The passage of the Alien and Sedition Acts of 1798 during the Adams administration was used to suppress the opposition press, and while only a few indictments resulted, the law had a chilling effect on press freedom.

Historians credit the *National Intelligencer*, first published in 1800, with establishing new standards for political reporting. The triweekly newspaper offered detailed accounts of proceedings in both the Senate and the House, and it was an important source of news from the nation's new capital, Washington, D.C., for newspapers around the country. Reporters had access to the House of Representatives from the beginning, but the Senate excluded reporters until 1795 and refused them access to the floor of the Senate until 1802. It wasn't until the 1820s that the out-of-town newspapers began sending their own correspondents to Washington. Their dispatches came in the form of letters, written under pseudonyms to protect them from the wrath of politicians unhappy with their coverage.

The election of Thomas Jefferson in 1800 ended the rule of the Federalists, who had controlled national government since the inception of the new nation, but it didn't end the partisan press. It's important to recognize, however, that the party press was not the only type of newspaper in the new nation. Westward expansion led to the development of the so-called frontier press. By 1800, there were twenty-one newspapers west of the Appalachian Mountains. Legal printing sustained newspapers in these communities. Editors became "boosters" of their villages as a way to draw settlers, and they used their columns to press for improvements that would ensure the survival of the new settlements. Content was contributed, in large part, by newspaper readers themselves. The abolitionist and black presses had their roots in the early nineteenth century. William Lloyd Garrison published *The Liberator* in Boston from 1831 to 1865, and the first newspaper edited by blacks, *Freedom's Journal*, appeared in New York in 1827. A small mercantile press flourished as well, carrying business, financial, and shipping news. The labor press was born with the publication of the *Journeyman Mechanic's Advocate* in Philadelphia, reporting on the workingman and the labor movement ignored by the mainstream press. The *Cherokee Phoenix*, the first Native American newspaper, was published in Georgia from 1828 to 1832. Foreign-language newspapers in German and French were part of the landscape even before the nineteenth century. The first German-language newspaper was *Philadelphische Zeitung*, started in 1732, and the first French-language newspaper was *Courrier de Boston*, begun in 1789. For the most part, however, readership of newspapers in America was confined to a small group of political and economic elites. The cost of newspapers, at six cents per copy, was beyond the reach of most audiences.

Developments in technology, coupled with the rise of an educated middle class during the period of Jacksonian democracy, led to the next major period of journalism history, the penny press, so named because newspapers sold for a penny. Distinguishing characteristics of the penny press included the following: (1) its price; (2) the shifting of financial support from political parties to advertising and the increasing importance of the newspaper publisher as businessman rather than party patriot; (3) the expansion of sales from subscription only to include street sales; and (4) content that decreased its emphasis on political views to redefine news more broadly as reportage on a range of topics. The first successful penny newspaper was Benjamin Day's *New York Sun*, published in 1833. Other successful penny newspapers of the period included James Gordon Bennett's *New York Herald*, 1835, which became the most successful newspaper in the nation until displaced by the papers of Joseph Pulitzer and William Randolph Hearst in the 1880s; Horace Greeley's *New York Tribune*, 1841; and the *New York Times*, established by Henry J. Raymond in 1851.

The influence of the penny press reached far beyond New York. In Philadelphia, the *Public Ledger*, established in 1836, modeled itself after Day's newspaper. One partner in that venture struck out on his own to found the *Baltimore Sun* in 1837. Both newspaper owners forged an agreement with the *Herald* to exchange news, and the Baltimore paper also established a Washington bureau that became well respected.

Whether this period heralded a true "revolution" in newspapers has sparked a lively debate among journalism historians, but most find within the penny press the foundation of modern American newspapers. Many of the elements familiar to newspapers today found their way into the penny press, including sports reporting, the rise of the "human interest" story, and reporting on the lives of everyday people who came into contact with the police and the courts. At the same time, the staples of economic and political news were retained, leading one historian to label the period a time of both continuity and change. News was no longer confined to reporting on the public activities of the political and economic elite. News was redefined to include a wide range of activities that reflected changing social, political, and economic conditions. The success of the penny newspapers, coupled with the shift in content, challenged established editors and led to condemnation of the upstarts as "sensationalistic." In 1840, newspaper editors and prominent community leaders organized an attack on Bennett's *Herald*, urging readers to boycott the newspaper and the advertisers who supported it. Bennett countered by stepping up coverage of churches and religious events, as well as toning down some of the more offensive coverage, and the protest was short-lived.

During the penny press era, one of the lasting influences was the emergence of news as a commodity. Earlier newspapers had often simply reprinted articles from other publications, and editors relied on submissions by unpaid contributors. By the 1830s, however, timeliness became a factor in the newspaper business, spurred by a number of technological developments, including the telegraph, which made obtaining news in a timely manner possible. A study of the press between 1830 and 1860 reveals that the time between an event and its coverage in newspapers declined considerably. The increasing competition for news also led to the development of reporters, hired professionals actively engaged in seeking out and writing news for publication. The earliest reporters were the Washington correspondents who covered the nation's capital beginning in the 1820s. In fact, Bennett served as the Washington correspondent for a leading New York newspaper before founding the *Herald*. In 1844, the introduction of the telegraph added a new dimension to information dissemination. Newspapers in smaller towns could now compete with the big-city newspapers, and "telegraphic" news became a common newspaper feature. The roots of the Associated Press, the nation's largest cooperative news-gathering organization, are found in this period, when several New York newspapers banded together to pay for boats that would meet ships in the harbor before they docked. They got a jump on other New York newspapers and also sold the news to out-of-town newspapers.

Advertising had always been a part of American newspapers, but the growing circulation of penny newspapers, which made them an increasingly attractive medium to advertisers, and increased reliance by newspapers on advertising revenue cemented the relationship. In the 1840s, agents began to represent the various newspapers, acting as space brokers, and were the forerunners of the modern advertising agency.

Increasing tensions among states in the North, South, and West, which led to the Civil War, posed a new set of problems for the press as free press issues collided with the government's need to control information in a time of war. War news dominated newspapers in both North and South, and initially there was little organized government censorship. In the North, when a strictly voluntary censorship program proved unworkable, the job of censoring the press was given over to the Department of War under the direction of Edwin Stanton. The government imposed control of the telegraph lines, as well as a system of review in the field, and that brought some order to war reporting. In the South, much of the war news was provided by the Press Association of the Confederate States, which served the forty-three surviving daily newspapers in the South, as well as the hundreds of smaller weekly newspapers. The association worked with the Confederate military to establish censorship guidelines. Shortages of materials and manpower plagued the southern papers to a much greater degree than those in the North, and the war took its toll on southern newspapers. By the end of the war, only twenty southern daily newspapers remained.

The Civil War was the first war to be thoroughly documented by photographers. More than 1,500 photographers recorded images of the Civil War, but Mathew Brady and his assistants are the best known of the time. Their photographs did not appear in newspapers, since the technology for photographic reproduction was a decade away, but some newspapers did convert the images to line drawings for reproduction.

The impact of the Civil War on journalism, historians suggest, was twofold. First, the war whetted the public's appetite for timely news. Most newspapers devoted a major portion of their resources to war coverage, and readers began to expect currency in news reporting. Second, the Civil War influenced the writing style of reporters, who shifted from a narrative prose style to a more concise recounting of events organized in what modern-day journalists label the "inverted pyramid" for its emphasis on summarizing the most important details at the beginning of the news story.

The history of newspapers after the Civil War is very much intertwined with technological advancements. Steady improvements in printing, paper production, photography, and telegraphy translated directly into more sophisticated newspapers. The original "byline," for example, was a "By Telegraph" line that appeared in news stories during the Civil War. Although newspapers were not directly affected by the invention of the telephone or electric light, the telephone allowed for easier access to sources, and the lightbulb permitted newspaper reading in the evening, an advancement that helped proliferate afternoon newspapers. The trend away from morning newspapers actually began with an increased reliance on telegraph news, which made it possible to communicate breaking news stories to the reading public. Many morning newspapers began publishing later editions and finally established separate evening editions that were sister papers with a different name and often different staffs. By 1890, about two-thirds of the daily newspapers were published in the afternoon, a trend that reversed itself seven decades later when the reading habits of American people were changed again—this time by television.

Photography in newspapers had lagged during the Civil War because of an inability to reproduce halftones. As early as the 1850s, it was possible to reproduce photos on flatbed newspaper presses, but the curved stereotype presses standard on most American newspapers posed a problem. Although some newspapers, like the *New York Daily Graphic*, pioneered the use of photographic illustrations, it wasn't until the 1890s that photographs began appearing regularly in most newspapers.

The thirty-five-year period after the Civil War and the end of the century saw an explosion in newspapers and their circulations. The penny press era had faded, although some of the original penny papers, like the *Baltimore Sun*, the *Chicago Tribune*, the *New York Times*, the *New York Herald*, the New York *Tribune*, the *Philadelphia Bulletin*, and the *Washington Star*, metamorphosed into modern newspapers. But, beyond transformation, this was a period of tremendous growth in which many of the mighty newspapers of the twentieth century can trace their roots, including the *San Francisco Chronicle*, 1865; *Atlanta Constitution*, 1868; *Boston Globe*, 1872; *Chicago Daily News* and *Dallas Times-Herald*, 1876; *Washington Post*,

1877; and *Los Angeles Times*, 1881. The *Wall Street Journal* also began publishing in 1889.

Newspapers in New York, Chicago, Philadelphia, and Boston all had circulations above 100,000 by 1892. Tops in circulation was Joseph Pulitzer's *New York World*, which championed a "New Journalism." Journalism historian Frank Luther Mott described in great detail the characteristics of Pulitzer's New Journalism, which had a profound effect on newspapers throughout the United States. The *World* was a big newspaper, often as many as sixteen pages, and cost only two cents. It used prominent headlines and was a leader in illustrations, making it an easy paper to read. It was guilty of blatant self-promotion and sponsored games and contests to involve readers. It provided solid coverage of important news, interspersed with sensationalism. Pulitzer had an affinity for crusades, like his fund to build a pedestal for the Statue of Liberty, and was responsible for the original stunt journalism that sent Nellie Bly into an insane asylum in 1888 and later on a jaunt around the world. All of these traits became standard for most newspapers; some, like stunt journalism, faded with the decade, while others, like layout and photography, are evident in newspapers even today.

During the 1890s "yellow journalism" reared its ugly head. Used even today to describe the seamiest side of lurid, sensational, overexaggerated reporting, yellow journalism was coined as an outgrowth of the circulation wars between Pulitzer's *World* and William Randolph Hearst's *New York Morning Journal*. Hearst's newspaper was oversensational, preoccupied with sexual exploits, and not above overstating the truth. The term "yellow journalism" stems from the "Yellow Kid" comic that first appeared in the *World* until the artist, Richard F. Outcault, was hired away to the *Journal*. Both papers continued with their own version of the Kid, and the figure of the bald, toothless imp in an oversized yellow shirt came to symbolize the decline of journalistic standards. While the public in theory lamented the deplorable direction that newspapers were taking, circulations soared, showing that the reading public enjoyed the entertainment that newspapers were providing.

In contrast to the irresponsible nature of yellow journalism, the turn of the century also saw the creation of "muckraking," a journalistic style with loftier goals. The term was coined by none other than then-President Theodore Roosevelt, who derogatorily compared the reforming reporters to the man with the muck rake in the popular book *Pilgrim's Progress*. So intent was this man in the muck that he never lifted his rake or stopped his toil even when the crown of heaven was offered. While Roosevelt used the term scornfully, muckrakers wore the title like a mantle that protected them from criticism. Muckraking flourished during the Progressive Era as magazines and newspapers exposed political and economic wrongdoing. In tandem with this, women reporters in the first decade of the twentieth century often were assigned to write socially responsible articles that exposed urban problems and led to civic reforms. This writing, dubbed municipal housekeeping journalism, exposed the dangers of industrial progress and city living and led to the establishment of juvenile courts, homogenized milk, safer schools, and other reforms.

The black press also prospered after the Civil War. Well-known black newspapers like *New York Age*, the *Philadelphia Tribune*, and the *Afro-American* of Baltimore were established. Foremost in the group was the *Chicago Defender*, founded by Robert S. Abbott in 1905. He established a national circulation base for his newspaper, which was highly critical of the racism and slights of mainstream newspapers. By 1915, it had a circulation of 230,000 and has been at least partially credited with triggering the great northern migration of blacks out of the rural and racist South.

The 1920s saw the proliferation of tabloid journalism. Although tabloid as a term simply means that a newspaper is a smaller half-sheet of paper, the tabloids as a group have been denigrated as more sensational and less serious than standard-size newspapers. Chief among the tabloids was the *New York Daily News*, founded in 1919 by Joseph Medill Patterson and Colonel Robert Rutherford McCormick, cousins who cooked up the idea in France during service in World War I. The *Daily News* was a hit with subway riders, who loved its compact size and heavy reliance on photos. By 1924, the *Daily News'* 750,000 circulation made it the largest newspaper in the United States. Imitators followed.

Throughout the first four decades of the twentieth century, the field of journalism became more professionalized, and its rituals became more routinized. Reporters began talking about "objectivity" as a goal for news stories, and journalism schools began teaching the rules of journalism to aspiring reporters. Even during the lean years of the Great Depression, many newspapers remained solid, profitable businesses, although advertising revenues fell, and newspaper profits dipped. The number of newspapers fell from 1,942 in 1930 to 1,744 at the end of World War II. No longer the only source for news and information—a fact that was made glaringly apparent when Americans sat glued to their radios for battle information during the war—newspapers suffered from the competition afforded by radio and the pull of another popular entertainment medium, the movies.

After World War II, the black press experienced the apex of its influence. Several newspapers, especially the *Chicago Defender*, the *Pittsburgh Courier*, and the *Afro-American* of Baltimore, had national circulation bases. But, from a circulation of 257,000 at the end of the war, the *Chicago Defender* shrank to a circulation of 33,000 by 1970. In fact, during the civil rights movement, smaller, community-based black newspapers prospered while the national ones declined.

The 1950s saw the rise of television, a medium that swiftly changed the leisure and reading habits of Americans. No longer were Americans interested in putting up their feet after work and settling in with an evening newspaper. The effect on afternoon newspapers was pervasive. In 1950, evening newspapers outnumbered morning ones by three to one. One by one, however, afternoon newspapers folded. Many of the twenty-five major metropolitan dailies that folded between 1950 and 1978 were afternoon papers. Also apparent during this time was the tendency of morning newspapers to swallow up or incorporate their afternoon counterpart into one single newspaper. Thirty-two mergers of this kind occurred between 1978 and 1983. By that time, only twenty-nine cities had competing daily newspapers, and New York topped the list with three, the *Daily News*, the *New York Post*, and the *New York Times*. By 1997, the number of evening papers had shrunk to 816, and many of those were newspapers that published all-day editions. The total number of daily newspapers in 1997 was 1,509. City newspapers shrank or disappeared altogether, thwarted by shifts in population and reading habits and difficulty in circulating to outlying areas because of heavy traffic. At the same time, however, a rise in suburban living saw a new marketing opportunity for midsize newspapers. By 1983, more than 2,000 suburban newspapers flourished, about 500 of them daily. In New York, Long Island's *Newsday*, founded in 1940, was a prime example of this trend.

During the 1960s, newspapers, too, were affected by the political unrest and social upheaval. Underground newspapers that represented the liberal, hippie generation flourished, while newspapers outside the mainstream, including I. F. Stone's *Weekly* and the *Catholic Worker*, enjoyed great success. Alternative writing styles, like the new "New Journalism," promoted journalism as story. Writers such as Tom Wolfe and Truman Capote became known as the style's foremost practitioners.

Contemporary newspapers moved away from family-run businesses and toward ownership by newspaper chains. By 1997, Gannett Co. led the field with eighty-seven daily newspapers, many of them in suburban areas, and a total circulation that topped 5.9 million. Knight-Ridder was a distant second in readership with thirty-three newspapers and a 3.9 million circulation base. Other prominent chains were Newhouse Newspapers (twenty-three papers), Dow Jones (twenty), Thomson Newspapers (sixty-two), and the *New York Times* (twenty).

Although wire service news was a staple throughout the century, the intense competitive rivalry between the Associated Press (AP) and United Press International (UPI) gradually waned. AP, the news cooperative, thrived, while the for-profit UPI limped along and changed hands repeatedly. During this same period, however, specialized news wires, like the New York Times News Service, the Gannett news wire, and Dow Jones, supplemented news from the AP, while the British Reuters also gained ground.

The final decades of the twentieth century saw a steady decline in the percentages of newspaper readers. The Newspaper Association of America statistics showed that in 1970, 77.6 percent of adults reported reading a weekday newspaper, compared to only 58.7 percent in 1997. Sunday newspaper readership also declined, but not as dramatically. In 1970, 72.3 percent of adults said that they read a Sunday newspaper while 68.5 percent said the same in 1997. Although readership percentages did indeed decline during these years, rumors of the death of the industry were vastly exaggerated. In fact, circulations for Sunday newspapers increased by 14 million in the final fifty years of the century, and the number of Sunday newspapers increased from 549 in 1950 to 903 in 1997. Total circulations for daily newspapers fluctuated during that same time period from a 1987 high of 62.8 million, and, although a downward trend has been observed since then, the fact is that circulations in 1997 were still 3 million higher than in 1950.

So, too, did daily newspapers remain in control of the biggest chunks of advertising dollars. In 1997, the National Association of Advertisers (NAA) reported that daily newspapers received 22.1 percent of all the money spent on advertising. That compared to 19.9 percent spent on regular television (but with 2.8 percent of the pie handed to cable television, television as a whole actually nosed out newspapers from first place) and 19.8 percent spent on direct mail. The industry, however, announced plans to launch a five-year drive to keep newspaper readers and to lure back those who had drifted away. While the reasons that people read newspapers changed dramatically from the beginning of the century, when it was the sole source of information, to the end, when it competed against numerous electronic rivals, the fact remained that about 112 million Americans read a newspaper every day.

The largest newspapers in the country actually have remained stable for the last two decades, with the exception of the emergence of the Gannett Co.'s national newspaper, *USA Today*, as a formidable force. In fact, the story of newspapers for the last two decades of the century is very much intertwined with the impact and influence of *USA Today*. When it first appeared in 1982, *USA Today* pioneered the use of color, graphics, and a shorter, crisper news format, characteristics that were at first disdained but slowly embraced by newspapers throughout the world. *USA Today* was scornfully referred to as "McPaper" by newspaper critics and dismissed as fast-food journalism. As the century and, indeed, the millennium ended, however, even the Grey Old Lady of Newspapers, the *New York Times*, had begun using color photography and introduced a breezier, feature style to its front page.

First in circulation at the end of the century was the *Wall Street Journal* with 1.77 million. Rounding out the top ten were *USA Today*, 1.71 million; the *New York Times*, 1.07 million; *Los Angeles Times*, 1.05 million; the *Washington Post*, 775,900; the *New York Daily News*, 721,300; the *Chicago Tribune*, 653,600; *Newsday*, 569,000; *Houston Chronicle*, 549,100; and *Chicago Sun-Times*, 484,400. It's interesting to note that *Newsday*, a suburban newspaper without a city base, ranked in the top ten.

Another important trend was the impact of the computer and the Internet on newspapers. By 1998, more than 750 newspapers in North America offered on-line services, including Web sites and electronic newspapers. Important among these emerging service technologies was consumer reliance on on-line classified advertising. Although it is impossible to predict the ultimate effect of on-line technologies on newspaper reading, it is clear that, rather than trying to squelch the competition (as the newspaper industry did during the early days of radio), newspapers have embraced the technology. Ninety-eight of the top 100 newspapers by circulation in the United States offered on-line services by 1998.

While weekly newspapers declined in numbers during recent years, circulations grew. In 1960, there were 8,174 weekly newspapers in the United States with an average circulation of 2,566 and a total circulation figure of 20.97 million. By 1997, the number of weekly newspapers had shrunk to 7,214, but their circulations had soared to an average individual total of 9,763 and a total circulation of 70.43 million. More people were reading fewer newspapers.

REFERENCE WORKS

Journalism research has been transformed in recent years by Internet technology and increasingly sophisticated library databases that index and sort newspaper articles by publication, topic, and authors. In fact, it is impossible to predict how newspaper research ultimately will be conducted. Still, researchers approaching a study of the newspaper from traditional sources encounter a reasonably well organized and manageable literature and a rapidly improving availability of newspaper files. (This section discusses newspaper checklists and indexes, among other subjects; see Research Collections for the leading newspaper collections.)

The literature about newspapers, being relatively small, has been gathered in several useful bibliographies and continues to be classified and thoughtfully discussed. Most recently, Christopher H. Sterling et al. compiled *Mass Communications Research Resources: An Annotated Guide*, published in 1998. Sterling breaks down his entries into general bibliographies with separate sections for biographical information, print media, and other highly specific categories. He also provides a nice section on sources for government statistics. Jo A. Cates' 1997 second edition of *Journalism: A Guide to the Reference Literature* annotates about 1,000 different books and sources. Lucy Shelton Caswell's *Guide to Sources in American Journalism History* (1989) and W. David Sloan's *American Journalism History* (1989) were part of a Greenwood Press series in Bibliographies and Indexes in Mass Media and Communications. Sloan separated the more than 2,500 books and scholarly articles by time period but also provided a useful topical index that makes it relatively easy to track down articles by subject or name. Taken together, Sloan's and Caswell's books provide an excellent source of articles, conference papers, and bibliographies that update and expand upon older sources. Warren C. Price's *The Literature of Journalism: An Annotated Bibliography* contains 3,147 well-annotated entries up to 1958. Price arranged his material under fifty-two subject headings and provided a complete subject and author index. Price was working on a supplement to this work at the time of this death in 1967. This task was taken over by Calder M. Pickett and completed under the title *An Annotated Journalism Bibliography, 1958–1968*, with Pickett sharing editorship with Price. Although arranged alphabetically by author (rather than subject) and having briefer annotations, this update contains 2,172 tittles (some pre-1958) and has an extensive subject index.

Another attempt at a general survey of the literature about newspapers is Richard A. Schwarzlose's *Newspapers: A Reference Guide*, published in 1987, which discusses about 1,650 books, monographs, and periodicals that deal with newspapers. Utilizing the bibliographic essay format, which allows titles to be discussed in the context of each other, the *Guide* has separated the chapters on history, biography, anthology, newspaper production and staffing, press and society, press law, press technology, and references.

The eighth edition of *The Journalist's Bookshelf: An Annotated and Selected Bibliography of United States Print Journalism*, by Ronald E. Wolseley, is now out of print but still available in libraries. It was published in 1986 with 2,247 titles, divided into forty-four subject categories. Wolseley introduced *Bookshelf* in 1939, and for the latest edition he was joined by his wife, Isabel Wolseley. Focusing on print journalism and offering brief descriptive annotations, *Bookshelf* includes sections on the literature about high school journalism as well as fiction in its various forms about journalism.

Eleanor Blum's *Basic Books in the Mass Media* also is out of print, but her list of 1,179 books is worth tracking down because it concentrates on reference titles and introduces researchers to basic sources about the media. It is extensively annotated. Blum and Frances Goins Wilhoit worked together on the follow-up *Mass Media Bibliography: An Annotated Guide to Books and Journals for Research and Reference* (1990).

To update older bibliographies or to keep track of the new literature about newspapers, the reader can consult several periodicals and journals. *Journalism History*, *American Journalism Review*, and *Journalism Quarterly* are three scholarly

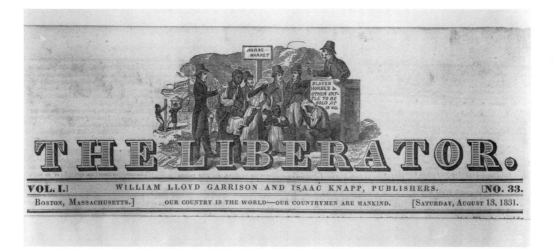

Masthead for *The Liberator*, 1831. Courtesy of the Library of Congress

quarterly journals that review books on newspapers. Also helpful in their areas of specialization are the book reviews of *American Journalism Review*; the bimonthly *Columbia Journalism Review*, for current affairs and commentary; *Public Opinion Quarterly*, for public opinion and media effects; and *Journal of Communication*, for books on social, cultural, and political aspects of communication.

The monthly *Communication Booknotes: Recent Titles in Telecommunications, Information and Media*, created by Christopher H. Sterling in 1969, recently was reorganized as *Communication Booknotes Quarterly*. Under both formats, *Booknotes* provides chatty, informed introductions to new books, giving special emphasis to telecommunication, international communication, new technologies, and information processing. Of special note is *Booknotes'* interest in electronic publications, although newspaper literature does get brief notice in it.

Internet sources abound in biographical areas of newspaper research. Most libraries offer biographical index sources on their Internet menu, and researchers should be aware that electronic research in this area has now become a mandatory step in the research process. In addition to this venue, several bibliographies focus on specialized areas of newspapers. John A. Lent's *Women and Mass Communication in the 1990s* (1999) picks up where the 1991 *Women and Mass Communications: An International Annotated Bibliography* left off.

Ralph E. McCoy has produced two volumes of bibliography on the literature about press freedom. The first volume, *Freedom of the Press: An Annotated Bibliography*, lists 8,000 books, pamphlets, journal articles, and films on press freedom. Many of the annotations are miniessays. In 1979 McCoy produced a ten-year supplement, *Freedom of the Press: A Bibliocyclopedia, Ten-Year Supplement (1967–1977)*, which contains 6,500 entries.

The black press has received considerable attention since the 1960s. George H. Hill selected 4,069 books, monographs, theses, and articles in journals, magazines, and newspapers in *Black Media in America: A Resource Guide*, a 333-page volume published in 1984. Hill's annotations are descriptive. Two decades of literature on blacks' multidimensional relationship with the mass media is the subject of

Blacks and Media: A Selected, Annotated Bibliography, 1962–1982, compiled by J. William Snorgrass and Gloria T. Woody and published in 1985. The book, which is out of print, lists over 400 books and articles, under four headings: print media, broadcast media, advertising and public relations, and film and theater.

Communications and Society: A Bibliography on Communications Technologies and Their Social Impact, compiled in 1983 by Benjamin F. Shearer and Marilyn Huxford, includes 2,732 pamphlets, journal articles, and dissertations as sources on technology's various relationships with media. The book's entries are not annotated. Carl L. Cannon's 1924 *Journalism: A Bibliography* organizes and describes the heart of the New York Public Library's massive and unmatched nineteenth- and early twentieth-century holdings on journalism. Extensively cross-referenced, the bibliography includes several hundred books, pamphlets, and magazine articles and has subject headings on many obscure and lesser aspects of journalism. Gale Research has reprinted Cannon's valuable bibliography.

Researchers utilize newspaper files for a variety of reasons, but they often need help identifying and locating the newspapers that can help them in finding stories on specific news events. Many sources can give the names of newspapers published at different times in various locations. Colonial printer Isaiah Thomas' *The History of Printing in America* still provides worthwhile information nearly 200 years after its publication. Clarence S. Brigham compiled the two-volume *History and Bibliography of American Newspapers, 1690–1820*, which lists 2,120 newspapers published in the colonies and United States during our first 130 years. Each entry sketches the paper's history and gives dates of its publication and locations of its files. The reader should rely on the 1962 reprint of this title because it contains revisions. Winifred Gregory compiled the nearly 800-page *American Newspapers, 1821–1936: A Union List of Files Available in the United States and Canada*, which lists all known papers during the book's 115-year period, their publication dates, and locations of files.

Newspaper annuals provide a year-by-year checklist of existing newspapers. *The American Newspaper Directory*, published from 1869 to 1908 by the George P. Rowell advertising agency, lists newspapers of all publication frequencies and provides basic information about the papers. *Rowell's Directory* was absorbed by a rival annual, *N. W. Ayer's American Newspaper Annual*, founded in 1880. Ayer's annual has had several names over the years: *American Newspaper Annual and Directory* from 1910 to 1929, *Ayer Directory of Newspapers and Periodicals* from 1930 to 1972, and *Ayer Directory of Publications* from 1973 to 1982, but in 1983 the *IMS Directory of Publications* took over the annual. Now, the 2002 *Gale Directory of Publications and Broadcast Media* provides the most complete listing of newspapers in its 4,500 pages. The more compact and cheaper *Hoover's Guide to Media Companies* (1996) and *Peterson's Media Companies 2000* (1999) provide other sources.

The annual that concentrates on daily newspapers is the *International Year Book*, published by *Editor & Publisher*, the weekly trade publication of newspapering. Beginning in 1921 as the *International Year Book Number* of *Editor & Publisher*, usually appearing in January, the *Year Book* became a separately published annual in 1959. It provides valuable circulation, advertising, personnel, and technical information on all daily newspapers and gives brief entries on weekly, ethnic, and college papers.

Some specialized checklist and finding guides are described by their titles: Lubomyr R. Wynar and Anna T. Wynar's *Encyclopedic Directory of Ethnic Newspapers and Periodicals in the United States*, in its second edition in 1976, but now out of print; *Native American Periodicals and Newspapers, 1828–1982: Bibliography, Publishing Record, and Holdings*, edited by James P. Danky and compiled by Maureen E. Hady; Danky's *Undergrounds: A Union List of Alternative Periodicals in Libraries of the United States and Canada*, published in 1974; and the *1999 National Hispanic Media Directory, Part One: U.S. Media Companies*.

Having identified the desired newspaper, the researcher next turns to the task of locating copies of the paper. Brigham and Gregory list files for papers from 1690 to 1936, but most of the files that they list are of original bound paper copies. Deteriorating newsprint and space shortages by the late 1940s necessitated the conversion of newspaper files to microforms (such as microfilm and microfiche), making many more newspapers available to a researcher through the interlibrary loan system. Recognizing these trends, the U.S. Library of Congress began reporting the microform holding of libraries throughout the country in 1948. It is in this area that researchers must delve into the Library of Congress home page, where newspapers and periodicals are cataloged and indexed. In hard copy, the library's most recent reports date back more than a decade to *Newspapers in Microform: United States, 1948–1983* and *Newspapers in Microform: Foreign Countries, 1948–1983*. The years in the subtitles are for the reports submitted by libraries; the newspapers listed represent the whole of newspaper history.

Many libraries and historical societies now list their newspaper microfilm holdings on their home page. Therefore, it is imperative when doing research that requires access to old newspapers to complete an on-line search before any legwork is begun. Any search engine, such as Yahoo! or Alta Vista, lists thousands of newspapers that are available by microfilm. Some of these collections also can be accessed through interlibrary loan.

Meanwhile, several private corporations have done extensive microfilming of old and current newspapers for sale to libraries. Microfilming Corporation of America (MCA) has produced full runs of many American colonial and Revolutionary newspapers published between 1763 and 1783. Thomas W. Jodziewicz's *Birth of America: The Year in Review 1763–1783: A Chronological Guide and Index to the Contemporary Colonial Press*, now out of print, indexes the contents of this MCA microfilm collection. Readex Microprint has put all the pre-1821 newspapers listed in Brigham on microcards in a series titled "Early American Newspapers, 1704–1820." Bell and Howell produced current runs of several leading U.S. metropolitan newspapers.

Researchers occasionally need to locate newspaper coverage of specific news events. If the event is of national or regional significance and occurred in the past twenty years, finding coverage is relatively easy through a Lexis-Nexis on-line search. Earlier events pose more of a challenge but can be researched simply by pinpointing the date of the event by a search of *Reader's Guide to Periodicals* and then searching the newspaper back issues for that time period. In addition, Anita Cheek Milner's three excellent volumes of *Newspaper Indexes: A Location and Subject Guide for Researchers* introduce the scholar to many indexes, some of them obscure, available in libraries, newspapers, and historical and genealogical societies.

Published in 1977, 1979, and 1982, these three volumes do not duplicate information.

Significant indexes of early newspapers are Lester J. Cappon and Stella F. Duff's *Virginia Gazette Index, 1736–1780*, a two-volume guide to this Williamsburg weekly; the semiannual index to *Niles' Weekly Register*, an early news compendium published in Baltimore from 1811 to 1849; Donald M. Jacobs' *Antebellum Black Newspapers*, indexing the four earliest black papers between 1827 and 1841; and John W. Blassingame, Mae G. Henderson, and Jessica M. Dunn's *Antislavery Newspapers and Periodicals*, covering numerous abolitionist and black papers between 1817 and 1871.

The *New York Times Index*, covering the paper from its founding in 1851 to the present, is familiar to many researchers and in recent years provides excellent descriptions of the paper's contents. Because the paper fell below its present standards for news coverage from 1870 to 1900, the researcher should also consult the *New York Daily Tribune Index*, thirty-one annual index volumes covering 1876 to 1907, a period when the *Tribune* was one of the nation's most important newspapers. These indexes are available in some libraries on microfilm.

Bell and Howell's *Newspaper Index* provides printed indexes of many major circulation dailies, including the *Los Angeles Times*, *New Orleans Times-Picayune* and the *States-Item*, *Detroit News*, *Houston Post*, *San Francisco Chronicle*, *Denver Post*, *St. Louis Post-Dispatch*, *Boston Globe*, *Christian Science Monitor*, and *USA Today*. Other papers have participated at times since this project began in 1972. Bell and Howell also has published the *Index to Black Newspapers*, including the *New York Amsterdam News*, *Atlanta Daily World*, *Baltimore Afro American*, *Chicago American Muslim Journal*, *Chicago Defender*, *Cleveland Call & Post*, *Norfolk Journal & Guide*, *Los Angeles Sentinel*, and *Detroit Chronicle*.

Printed indexes, appearing monthly and cumulating only quarterly or annually, allow such slow access to newspapers that some entrepreneurs in 1979 formed Information Access Company, which offers the InfoTrac index of newspapers and periodicals. Since 1995, the company's Gale Group also publishes the on-line or CD-ROM version of the National Newspaper Index of the *New York Times*, *Wall Street Journal*, *Christian Science Monitor*, *Los Angeles Times*, and *Washington Post*. Prior to this, the service provided microfilmed indexing of the newspaper.

Printed and microfilmed indexes, however, have absolutely been overshadowed by on-line indexes, accessible through computer terminals and updated daily. If one can access index databases, one can bypass the indexes and go directly to full texts of newspaper stories stored in databases. Aimed at journalists but useful to all researchers, the 1997 update of *Search Strategies in Mass Communication* by Jean Ward and Kathleen A. Hansen describes all modern data sources, including databases, and how to use them.

Finally, the Internet is also the best way to learn the names, addresses, and telephone numbers of the editors, reporters, and correspondents of the nation's newspapers. Newspapers usually give individual reporters and editors their own E-mail address, which they publish in the newspaper and on their home page. Meanwhile, the hard-copy annual *Working Press of the Nation* assists publicists, government and corporate information officers, and freelancers in contacting newspaper people.

RESEARCH COLLECTIONS

Because newspapers may be either sources or subjects of research, this section briefly surveys major collections of U.S. newspapers and major resource holdings about newspapers.

Once again, the traditional newspaper collections have been superseded by Internet possibilities. Most newspapers in the United States have established Web pages that provide at least some of the news product on-line. These newspapers often offer access to complete news files for a fee or to subscribers. On-line search sites can help locate news archives. For example, the U.S. News Archives on the Web (http://metalab.unc.edu/slanews/internet/archives.html) shows links that are available to news archives on the Web. Of course, a primary stop for a newspaper researcher should also be the Web site for the Newspaper and Current Periodical Reading Room at the Library of Congress (http://lcweb.loc.gov/rr/news/about. html). The Library of Congress provides links to various news archives and on-line newspaper sources. The library is also home to the nation's largest collection of newspapers, with more than 850,000 unbound issues, 75,000 bound volumes, and hundreds of thousands of microfilm reels. The library regularly receives 1,420 newspaper titles, 350 from the United States and 1,070 from foreign countries. The library provides an on-line service that describes the newspapers that it regularly receives as well as a "Chronological Index of Newspapers" from 1801 to 1967.

The nation's second largest newspaper collection belongs to the State Historical Society of Wisconsin in Madison. The library no longer publishes its *Periodicals and Newspapers Acquired by the State Historical Society of Wisconsin Library*, but a listing of the society's holdings can be accessed from its Web site (http://www. shsw.wisc.edu/library/collect.html). This is a national collection of newspapers, with emphasis on colonial and early American newspapers west of the Appalachians, labor newspapers, underground newspapers and Native American and African American newspapers and periodicals.

Another major newspaper collection is at the American Antiquarian Society in Worcester, Massachusetts, which has the largest and most complete collection of pre-1821 American newspapers in the country. The collection formed the basis of Clarence S. Brigham's *History and Bibliography of American Newspapers*, noted earlier, which remains the best guide to this collection.

A very large collection of rare and obscure newspapers is kept at the Center for Research Libraries (CRL) in Chicago. Founded in 1949, the center is sponsored by over sixty universities and has about 8,000 volumes of older U.S. newspapers and sixty-six current microfilm subscriptions to U.S. papers. It also holds about 4,000 microforms of 500 American foreign language newspapers, 6,000 volumes of foreign papers, and 114 current foreign newspapers listed in the "CRLCatalog," an on-line catalog that is accessed through the Web (http://wwwcrl.chicago.edu). Another large newspaper collection is at the University of Illinois Library at Urbana, which has 40,000 microfilm reels of newspapers of all kinds and subscribes to 125 papers in hard copy and 100 papers on microfilm.

Other university libraries offer unique and specialized newspaper collections: Yale has many British and colonial America papers; Rutgers emphasizes papers of the Middle Atlantic states up to 1820; Georgia has 1,600 Confederate newspapers;

Columbia emphasizes Russian and East European papers; Indiana has about 1,000 issues of California gold rush newspapers; California at Berkeley and Reuther Library at Wayne State University have large labor newspaper collections; libraries at the Hoover Institute of Stanford, UCLA, and Connecticut have extensive underground newspaper collections; and Northwestern offers strong African, underground, and women's newspaper collections.

Further assistance in identifying and locating newspaper files is promised through the United States Newspaper Program, a centralized effort to identify, inventory, preserve, and report the newspaper holdings of many libraries across the country. Begun in 1983 and funded by the National Endowment for the Humanities, the project is building an inventory of file holdings and locations for 30,000 U.S. newspapers from throughout our history (which is about 10 percent of the estimated total newspaper titles appearing since 1960). The inventory is maintained by the Online Computer Library Center (OCLC) database, accessible to researchers around the nation.

One other way of researching newspapers' files is in the newspapers' own libraries or "morgues," as they are called in the business. Newspapers have in recent years created and maintained computer records of their articles, supplemented by actual copies of the daily newspapers. Newspapers that allow the public to use these morgues were listed in *Newspaper Libraries in the U.S. and Canada*, edited by Elizabeth L. Anderson in 1980 in a second edition and in *Newspaper Libraries: A Bibliography, 1933–1985*, by Celia Wall.

Morgues of a few defunct newspapers are preserved in libraries, for example, *Boston Herald* at Boston University, *Philadelphia Bulletin* at Temple University, *Philadelphia Public Ledger* at the Philadelphia Free Library, *New York Sun* at the New York Public Library, *Brooklyn Eagle* at the Brooklyn Public Library, the *Newark Evening News* at the Newark (New Jersey) Public Library, and the *New York Herald Tribune* at the Queensborough Public Library.

Manuscript collections of newspaper people fall into two groups. One group consists of a few nineteenth-century personalities whose personal papers in most cases reflect other, usually political or literary interests as well as newspapering. Heavy concentrations of such collections are in the Library of Congress, Columbia University Library, and the Newberry Library and in the libraries at Syracuse University, California at Berkeley, Yale, and Emory, among other depositories. This group represents publishers and editors almost exclusively.

The other group consists largely of twentieth-century newspeople, many of whom are not distinguished beyond news work. The group represents a broad cross-section of the newspaper industry, such as publishers, editors, reporters, labor leaders, political cartoonists, and foreign correspondents. Several depositories actively seek the papers of active and retired journalists. Two aggressive collections with significant holdings on twentieth-century journalists are the Twentieth Century Archive at Boston University and the Archive of Contemporary History of the American Heritage Center at the University of Wyoming in Laramie.

Meanwhile, the Mass Communications History Collections of the State Historical Society of Wisconsin has specialized in the papers of journalists since 1955. The center's guide to its holdings, *Sources for Mass Communications, Film, and Theater Research: A Guide*, was last published in 1981, but up-to-date searching is possible through the society's Web site (http://shsw.wisc.edu).

Aside from the cluster of manuscript collections previously noted, the researcher will find small caches of personal papers on newspapering tucked away in many lesser libraries and societies across the country. Philip M. Hamer's *A Guide to Archives and Manuscripts in the United States*, published in 1961, surveys 1,300 depositories, mentioning more than 7,600 of the most noteworthy collections, some involving journalists.

The most comprehensive bound listing of manuscript collections is the Library of Congress' *National Union Catalog of Manuscript Collections* (NUCMC), which was introduced in 1962 and ceased publication in 1993. The most effective way now to search the collections is to use the Library of Congress Manuscript Division home page (http://lcweb.loc.gov/rr/mss/), which is much quicker and more efficient than searching the hard-copy, multivolume NUCMC.

Journalists also are popular subjects for oral history interviews. *The Oral History Collection of Columbia University* should be perused, but again a more up-to-date search can be conducted on the Web (http://www.columbia.edu/cu/libraries/indiv/oral/). Another interesting source for searching collections is the Oral History Association Web site (http://omega.dickinson.edu/organizations/oha/), which contains a list of collections and sites around the country.

HISTORY AND CRITICISM

The historical literature about newspapers has a decidedly journalistic and approving slant to it. Steeped in names, dates, places, "firsts," political labels, gossip, and fragments of fact, some newspaper histories even have a promotional tone about them. Meanwhile, criticism of newspapers has been steady and generally vigorous since World War I, although political criticism far outstrips commentary about news reporting.

The best general histories of newspapers are college textbooks. *The Press and America: An Interpretive History of the Mass Media*, by Edwin Emery and Michael Emery, a father–son team, was begun in 1954 and is now in its eighth edition. Emphasizing newspapers in their media and political settings, the book provides a wealth of names and dates but is most valuable for its extensive, up-to-date bibliography. An older text, *American Journalism: A History, 1690–1960*, by Frank Luther Mott, was last updated in 1962 before Mott's death. Its "history as a chronicle" approach makes this book's emphasis on names, dates, and places a valuable resource for students and teachers. A more recent entry in the field of journalism history textbooks is *The Media in America: A History*, by William David Sloan and James D. Startt, first published in 1989 and now in its fourth edition. Each chapter was written by a specialist in that particular period of journalism history. Another excellent history is *Voices of a Nation: A History of Mass Media in the United States*, by Jean Folkerts and Dwight L. Teeter Jr. The third edition was published in 1998 and has a stronger focus on contemporary media history than some of the earlier texts.

More recently, Rodger Streitmatter's *Mightier than the Sword: How the News Media Have Shaped American History* provides an interesting, topical approach to this unwieldy topic. A brief, but excellent, social history of newspapers, focusing on the origins of objectivity, is Michael Schudson's *Discovering the News: A Social History of American Newspapers*. A more general history of news is provided by Mitchell Stephens in *History of News from the Drum to the Satellite*, published in 1988, focusing on the content of news. Sociologist Alfred McClung Lee published *The Daily Newspaper in America: The Evolution of a Social Instrument*, in 1937. Although needing updating, this book delves into aspects of history of newspapering not touched by later historians. Several older histories also require attention. Isaiah Thomas, publisher of the *Massachusetts Spy* in Worchester and founder of the American Antiquarian Society (AAS), contributed the first history in 1810, *The History of Printing in America, with a Biography of Printers and an Account of Newspapers*. An authoritative record of seventeenth-century newspaper publishing, this book was revised in 1874 by a committee and in 1970 by Marcus A. McCorison, director of the AAS. A detailed older history of the press, *History of Journalism in the United States*, useful for the period up to 1800, was published in 1920 by George H. Payne. Frederic Hudson, managing editor of the *New York Herald* from the early 1840s to 1866, produced *Journalism in the United States from 1690 to 1872*, which is voluminous, generally accurate, and focused on New York City's penny press movement. Willard Grosvenor Bleyer's 1927 *Main Currents in the History of American Journalism* combines the great-man, progressive, and New York City emphases of earlier books into a single, comprehensive narrative that is accurate, balanced, and well written.

There are many histories of journalism's various periods, areas, and specializations, and a few are noted here as more useful or comprehensive than the rest. For colonial and Revolutionary newspapering, see Clarence S. Brigham's *Journals and Journeymen: A Contribution to the History of Early American Newspapers*, containing fifteen delightful and informed sketches on newspaper topics; Elizabeth C. Cook's *Literary Influences in Colonial Newspapers, 1704–1750*, a 1912 analysis of newspaper content; Arthur M. Schlesinger's *Prelude to Independence: The Newspaper War on Britain, 1764–1776*, describing newspapers' role in fomenting Revolutionary unrest; Bernard Bailyn and John B. Hench's *The Press and the American Revolution*, a collection of essays offering new evidence and perspectives on the Revolution; and Jeffrey Smith's *Printers and Press Freedom: The Ideology of Early American Journalism*, a review of the concept of press freedom as developed in the colonies (1988).

In *The Press, Politics and Patronage: The American Government's Use of Newspapers, 1789–1875*, Culver H. Smith outlines the relationship between press and government that characterized the first period of our national history. Thomas C. Leonard's *The Power of the Press: The Birth of American Political Reporting* describes in compelling detail landmark episodes of political discourse in press coverage between 1721 and 1906. Barbara Cloud illuminates little-studied economic aspects of the frontier press in *The Business of Newspapers on the Western Frontier*, published in 1992.

New York Times staffer Augustus Maverick's *Henry J. Raymond and the New York Press, for Thirty Years: Progress in American Journalism from 1840 to 1870*, although largely an appreciative biography of Raymond, gives good glimpses of New York City's journalism, its practitioners, and its performance during thirty years. In *Objectivity and the News: The Public and the Rise of Commercial Journalism*, Dan Schiller argues that the penny press and other commercial journalism fostered objectivity before the Civil War. David T. Z. Mindich also tackles the weighty subject of objectivity and its origins in his 1998 *Just the Facts: How "Objectivity" Came to Define American Journalism*. The transition from party to penny press is examined in Gerald Baldasty's *The Commercialization of News in the Nineteenth Century*, published in 1992.

J. Cutler Andrew's *The North Reports the Civil War* and *The South Reports the Civil War* provide the authoritative overviews of journalism in the war; Emmet Crozier's *Yankee Reporters* describes the activities of ten Civil War correspondents; and Louis M. Starr's *Bohemian Brigade: Civil War Newsmen in Action* examines censorship and news coverage from the viewpoint of leading managing editors. James Horan's 1955 biography, *Mathew Brady: Historian with a Camera*, includes more than 400 illustrations.

Richard Schwarzlose's two-volume study, *The Nation's Newsbrokers*, covering 1865 to 1920, is the definitive work on the period. Sidney Kobe's *The Yellow Press and the Gilded Age of Journalism* is an illustrated survey of leading papers and personalities between 1865 and 1900, and Allen Churchill's *Park Row* sketches New York City newspapering from 1883, when Joseph Pulitzer bought the *New York World*, to 1931, when the *World* disappeared in a merger. Emmet Crozier's *American Reporters on the Western Front, 1914–1918* describes the lives and activities of World War I correspondents and the conditions that they faced.

Catherine L. Covert and John D. Stevens' *Mass Media between the Wars: Perceptions of Cultural Tension, 1918–1941* is a collection of essays on the significant changes in media content and activity in the interwar period. Simon Michael Bessie's *Jazz Journalism: The Story of the Tabloid Newspapers* concentrates on New York City's bout with tabloid sensationalism in the 1920s, and John J. McPhaul's *Deadlines and Monkeyshines: The Fabled World of Chicago Journalism* reveals Chicago's rowdy journalism after World War I. Daniel G. Hallin's *The "Uncensored War": The Media and Vietnam* is the best of several attempts to understand journalism's role in that unpopular war. John Fialka provides a lively rundown of high and low points in press coverage in *Hotel Warriors: Covering the Gulf War* (1992). Bradley Greenberg and Walter Gantz edit a collection of different aspects of the Gulf War in *Desert Storm and the Mass Media* (1993).

The Dissident Press: Alternative Journalism in American History, by Lauren Kessler, introduces the journalism of blacks, feminists, immigrants, political radicals, utopians, and war resisters. A more recent collection is *Outsiders in 19th Century Press History*, edited by Frankie Hutton and Barbara Straus Reed (1995). Roland E. Wolseley's 1971 *The Black Press, U.S.A.*, a useful overview, has been updated in a 1990 edition. *The Origins of the Black Press: New York 1827–1847* by Burnell Tripp (1992) is a good source on the early black press. *Issues and Trends in Afro-American Journalism*, edited in 1980 by James S. Tinney and Justine J. Rector, emphasizes history in a selection of essays and articles.

Robert E. Park's *The Immigrant Press and Its Control*, although published in 1922, persists because of its focus on the foreign-language journalism at a time of large immigration. *The Ethnic Press in the United States: A Historical Analysis and Handbook*, edited by Sally M. Miller, is an excellent collection of twenty-seven historical sketches of ethnic press systems. Each essay includes bibliographies of books and articles on the press systems.

Rodger Streitmatter's *Unspeakable: The Rise of the Gay and Lesbian Press in Amer-*

ica is both a social history and critical analysis of the topic and one of the most recent comprehensive surveys.

David Armstrong's *A Trumpet to Arms: Alternative Media in America* is a sympathetic and well-researched exposition of the activities and contributions of a broad range of dissident newspapers in American history. *The Underground Press in America*, by Robert J. Glessing, and *The Paper Revolutionaries: The Rise of the Underground Press*, by Laurence Leamer, are valuable and evenhanded examinations of journalism's role in the youth revolution of the 1960s. The history of Native American journalism is told in James E. Murphy and Sharon M. Murphy's *Let My People Know: American Indian Journalism, 1828–1978*, while John M. Coward's 1999 book, *The Newspaper Indian: Native American Identity in the Press, 1820–1890*, discusses the representations of Native Americans in newspapers.

Among many histories of individual newspapers, a few stand out: Allan Nevins' *The Evening Post: A Century of Journalism*; Frank M. O'Brien's *The Story of the Sun, New York: 1833–1928*; *The Sunpapers of Baltimore*, by Gerald W. Johnson, Frank R. Kent, H. L. Mencken, and Hamilton Owens; *The New York Tribune Since the Civil War*, by Harry W. Baehr Jr.; Richard Kluger's *The Paper: The Life and Death of the New York Herald Tribune*; Meyer Berger's *The Story of the New York Times, 1951–1951*; Gay Talese's *The Kingdom and the Power*, also about the *New York Times*; Howard Bray's *The Pillars of the Post: The Making of a News Empire in Washington*; Marshall Bergers' *The Life and Times of Los Angeles: A Newspaper, a Daily and a City*; Kevin Michael McAuliffe's *The Great American Newspaper: The Rise and Fall of the Village Voice*; Peter Prichard's *The Making of McPaper: The Inside Story of USA Today*; and David Halberstam's *The Powers That Be*, which examines the power of the *Los Angeles Times* and the *Washington Post*, along with Time and the Columbia Broadcasting System.

Space limitations prevent a full description of journalism's largest body of literature, the biographies and memoirs of newspaper people. Consult the bibliographies mentioned earlier or a library catalog to find works about specific individuals. A few biographical aids and some specialized collections, however, should be noted here. Alan E. Abram's *Journalist Biographies Master Index*, published in 1979, contains 90,000 references to journalists' biographical material located in 200 biographical and historical sources.

The *Dictionary of Literary Biography* includes four volumes subtitled *American Newspaper Journalists*. Edited by Perry J. Ashley, these four volumes contain nearly 250 in-depth biographies of publishers, editors, and correspondents. Forty-four excellent sketches, most of them living journalists and first appearing in the *Saturday Evening Post* between 1928 and 1946, are evenly divided between *Post Biographies of Famous Journalists* (1942) and *More Post Biographies: Articles of Enduring Interest About Famous Journalists and Journals and Other Subjects Journalistic* (1947).

Two recent biographical collections of high-profile groups in journalism are John C. Behrens' *The Typewriter Guerillas: Closeups of 20 Top Investigative Reporters*, which appeared in 1977, and Barbara Belford's *Brilliant Bylines: A Biographical Anthology of Notable Newspaper Women in America*, which combines short biographies of, and samples of journalism by, twenty-four newspaperwomen, stretching from antebellum America to the present. An important study that focuses on writers and editors, rather than owners and publishers, from a labor history perspective

William Randolph Hearst. Courtesy of the Library of Congress

is Hanno Hardt and Bonnie Brennan's collection of essays in *Newsworkers: Toward a History of the Rank and File*, covering 1850 through the 1930s, published in 1995.

From a topical perspective, one finds several serviceable histories of newspaper activity. F. B. Marbut's *News from the Capital: The Story of Washington Reporting* is well researched but much too brief. *The Press and the Presidency: From George Washington to Ronald Reagan*, by John Tebbel and Sarah Miles Watts, is for the general reading audience and is handicapped only by a pro-press approach. Press freedom history is sketched through selections and introductory essays by Leonard W. Levy in *Freedom of the Press from Zenger to Jefferson: Early American Libertarian Theories* and by Harold L. Nelson in *Freedom of the Press from Hamilton to the Warren Court*.

In *Goodbye, Gutenberg: The Newspaper Revolution of the 1980s*, Anthony Smith describes the history of newspaper technology and the technological revolution set in motion in this decade. The new media technology and its promise for reframenting the marketplace and reasserting the identities of minorities in media content are the topic of *Minorities and Media: Diversity and the End of Mass Com-*

munication by Clint C. Wilson II and Felix Gutierrez. In *Understanding the New Technologies of the Mass Media*, George Whitehouse's basic textbook gives an inclusive survey up through the mid-1980s (1986).

Ishbel Ross treats the history of women in the media from a 1930s viewpoint in *Ladies of the Press: The Story of Women in Journalism by an Insider*, while Marion Marzolf brings a 1970s revisionist perspective to the topic in *Up from the Footnotes: A History of Women Journalists*. Maurine Beasley and Sheila Gibbons revised and expanded their 1977 classic *Taking Their Place: A Documentary History of Women in Journalism* with a second edition in 1993. Gender issues from the 1850s to the present are covered in Nan Robertson's *The Girls in the Balcony: Women, Men and the New York Times* (1992).

Among many criticisms and appraisals of newspapers, a few are classic either for their arguments or for their style. William Salisbury's *The Career of a Journalist*, published in 1908, exposes newspaper practices and policies by one who was a reporter. Hamilton Holt's 1909 *Commercialism and Journalism* is the first organized attack on sensationalism and advertising pressures in newspapers. Will Irwin's series for *Collier's* in 1911 surveys and criticizes every aspect of newspapering, using the muckraking style of the day. The series was reprinted in 1969 as *The American Newspaper*, edited by Clifford F. Weigle and David G. Clark. An excellent, in-depth report on the debate over newspaper performance is Marion Marzolf's 1991 work, *Civilizing Voices: American Press Criticism 1880–1950*.

Another muckraker, Upton Sinclair, produced a scathing attack on newspapers in *The Brass Check: A Study of American Journalism* in 1919. Silas Bent's *Ballyhoo: The Voice of the Press* picked up in 1927 where Sinclair had left off, attacking the excesses of sensationalism in metropolitan newspapers. *Freedom of the Press*, published in 1935 by George Seldes, takes on the press in terms of corrupting influences on news, irresistible power in news handling, and Big Press versus the individual. It is a blistering indictment.

A. J. Liebling, press critic for the *New Yorker*, generated three volumes of insightful and witty criticism of the post–World War II press: *The Wayward Pressman* in 1947; *Mink and the Red Herring: The Wayward Pressman's Casebook*, two years later; and *The Press*, editions of which were issued in 1961, 1964, and 1975. Meanwhile, Oswald Garrison Villard, a former newspaper publisher and the industry's ranking liberal, produced *The Disappearing Daily: Chapters in American Newspaper Evolution* in 1944, an appraisal that pointed an accusing finger at specific bad guys in the business.

Ben H. Bagdikian's *The Effete Conspiracy and Other Crimes by the Press*, published in 1972, is a pivotal discussion of media problems at a time when many, including President Nixon, were attacking the media, primarily for being too liberal. Bagdikian asserted here, however, that the media are too conservative. Bagdikian's *Media Monopoly* has become the standard for studies of corporate influence on publishing and the adverse affects of conglomerates. The fifth edition was published in 1995. John Hohenberg's *A Crisis for the American Press*, published in 1978, discusses the erosion of press freedom, journalists' lack of commitment, and the public's indifference to principles of free speech. Former National News Council chairman Norman E. Issacs in *Unintended Gates: The Mismanaged Press* (1986) blames editors and publishers primarily for the press' faults. The *Washington Post*'s national correspondent David S. Broder critically examines and analyzes his own and colleagues' performance in *Behind the Front Page: A Candid Look at How the News Is Made*. In *Read All about It: The Corporate Takeover of America's Newspapers*, former *Chicago Tribune* editor James Squires condemns intrusion into editorial practices and fears the demise of newspapers (1993).

The preceding criticism deals primarily with newspaper politics—their partisanship and susceptibility to economic pressures. Gradually, however, criticism of the press as a literary entity has begun to emerge. Walter Lippmann in *Public Opinion*, the 1922 classic, defined the fundamental nature of news and the impact of news upon the pictures in people's heads. Gaye Tuchman's *Making News: A Study in the Construction of Reality* (1978) deals with the forces and values defining facts and framing events for public consumption.

Tuchman, along with Arlene Kaplan Daniels and James Benet, edited the now-classic *Hearth and Home: Images of Women in the Mass Media* (1978), one of the first studies of media treatment of women. Todd Gitlin's *The Whole World is Watching: Mass Media in the Making and Unmaking of the New Left* traces the changing coverage of the Students for a Democratic Society and how coverage affected the movement.

In *Manufacturing the News* (1980) Mark Fishman examines the beat system and other news-gathering techniques that influence the view of reality presented in the news columns. Seven essays in *Reading the News* (1987) explore the limitations and emphases of the news report, relying on the who-what-when-where-why-and-how newswriting formula as their organizing theme. The book, edited by Robert Karl Manoff and Michael Schudson, is useful because of its simple and direct approach to criticism of the news report. Edward Herman and Noam Chomsky present a compelling study that shows how outside influences shape news judgment in *Manufacturing Consent: The Political Economy of the Mass Media* (1988).

William Grider provides a scathing review of recent media coverage in *Who Will Tell the People: The Betrayal of American Democracy* (1992), and Jim Willis takes a detailed look at agenda-setting and self-censorship in the news business with *The Shadow World: Life between the News Media and Reality* (1991). Project Censored, started in 1976, is centered at Sonoma State University, California, and each year publishes a compilation of the top stories that mainstream media failed to report, titled *News That Didn't Make the News*.

Finally, an indispensable glimpse at the people who produce the news report in the newspapers and other media is provided in *The American Journalist: A Portrait of U.S. News People and Their Work*, published in 1986 by David H. Weaver and G. Cleveland Wilhoit. The authors compare this new survey of attitudes, education, and perspectives on work with earlier survey findings.

In the periodical press, criticism of newspapers may be found in *Columbia Journalism Review*; *AJR: American Journalism Review* (prior to 1983, it was published as *WJR: Washington Journalism Review*); *Quill*, the publication of the Society of Professional Journalists, Sigma Delta Chi; the *Bulletin of the American Society of Newspaper Editors*; the *AIM Report* of the conservative Accuracy in Media watchdog group; and the *Nieman Reports*, a quarterly journal of the Nieman fellowship program for journalists at Harvard University.

Research on media history, politics, and practices is found in *Journalism Quarterly*, journal of the American Association for Education in Journalism and Mass Communication; *Newspaper Research Journal*, published at Memphis State University; *Journalism History*, published at University of Nevada, Las Vegas; *American Journalism Review*, published by the American Journalism Historians Association; *Journal of Communication*, published by the Annenberg School of Communications and the International Communication Association; *Journal of Popular Culture*, journal of the Popular Culture Association; *Public Opinion Quarterly*, journal of the American Association for Public Opinion Research; and *Mass Comm Review*, published at Temple University; *Communication Abstracts* is a quarterly that indexes and arranges abstracts of new articles on all aspects of mass communication.

ANTHOLOGIES AND REPRINTS

Some contend that most of what appears in newspaper columns does not qualify as collectible writing. Newswriting, after all, is a functional, not a fine, enterprise; a desirable quality of newswriting to those in the business is its failure to call attention to itself or to its author. Not surprisingly, therefore, little hard news reporting has been reborn in anthologies, and most of the newspaper writing that has been collected owes its reincarnation either to the startling events that it records or to the style of its writing. The books mentioned in this section give the erroneous impression that rewards and collectibility are and ought to be reserved for those who manage to break away from hard news reporting. The reader, of course, can sample hard news reporting by delving into the burgeoning newspaper files.

Efforts to collect American newspaper literature over the industry's 300-year history include Calder M. Pickett's 1977 *Voices of the Past: Key Documents in the History of American Journalism*, which begins with sixteenth-century news accounts and carries forward to the resignation of President Nixon in 1974. The 250 selections, while emphasizing newspaper accounts, include some magazine and broadcast copy. An anthology by Louis L. Snyder and Richard M. Morris, *A Treasury of Great Reporting: "Literature under Pressure" from the Sixteenth Century to Our Own Time*, first appeared in 1949 and was updated in 1962. The collection features eye-catching and sensational news events. Norman Sims put together a collection of "modern" literary journalism in *Literary Journalism in the 20th Century* (1990). Editors Kevin Kerrane and Ben Yagoda compiled an anthology of literary journalism that covers a range both historically and topically in *The Art of Fact* (1997). Also noteworthy is Thomas Connery's collection of essays analyzing writers from Mark Twain to Truman Capote, *A Sourcebook of American Literary Journalism* (1992).

American Press Opinion: Washington to Coolidge, edited by Allan Nevins, is an excellent and thoughtful anthology of some of the best editorials and editorialists in American newspapering. Stephen Hess and Milton Kaplan's *The Ungentlemanly Art: A History of American Political Cartoons*, reaching a second edition in 1975, covers the ground from 1747 to the mid-1970s. Focusing narrowly on newspaper comics, *The Smithsonian Collection of Newspaper Comics* (1977), edited by Bill Blackbeard and Martin Williams, begins in 1896 with the "Yellow Kid" and includes almost 100 different panels and strips.

Martin E. Dann includes articles, editorials, advertisements, and cartoons from the black press during its first two-thirds of a century in *The Black Press, 1827–1890: The Quest for National Identity*. *Twentieth Century Reporting at Its Best* (1964), edited by Bryce W. Rucker, contains fifty-five stories from twenty-five newspapers and three wire services up to the 1960s, selected as examples of outstanding writing rather than rapid reporting. W. David Sloan, Cheryl Wray, and C. Joanne Sloan updated *Great Editorials*, publishing a second edition in 1997 that collects a wide range of editorials, arranged chronologically, with an excellent introduction to each author's work. A companion collection of seventy stories, titled *Masterpieces of Reporting*, edited by W. David Sloan and Cheryl Wray, also was published in 1997. Two additional volumes are planned.

A sampling of the work of war correspondents from the American Revolution to the Gulf War is found in Nathaniel Lande's *Dispatches from the Front: A History of the American War Correspondent* (1998).

Collecting winners of Pulitzer Prizes, the pinnacle of newspaper awards, has been a favorite undertaking. John Hohenberg has edited two such anthologies: *The Pulitzer Prize Story: News Stories, Editorials, Cartoons, and Pictures from the Pulitzer Prize Collection at Columbia University*, covering 1917 to 1958, and *The Pulitzer Prize Story II: Award-Winning News Stories, Columns, Editorials, Cartoons, and News Pictures, 1959–1980*.

Other Pulitzer anthologies are W. David Sloan's *Pulitzer Prize Editorials: America's Best Editorial Writing, 1917–1979*; *Pulitzer Prize Cartoons: The Men and Their Masterpieces* by Dick Spencer III, the second edition of which covers 1922 to 1953; Gerald W. Johnson's *The Lines Are Drawn: American Life since the First World War as Reflected in the Pulitzer Prize Cartoons*, published in 1958; and Sheryle Leekley and John Leekley's *Moments: The Pulitzer Prize Photographs*, including in its second edition both spot news and feature photos up through 1982.

W. David Sloan, along with Valerie McCrary and Johanna Cleary, produced *The Best of Pulitzer Prize News Writing*, a significant anthology that is unusual because of its emphasis on the prize's hard news categories. The collection includes seventy-one prize-winning articles from 1917 through the 1970s, selected for their outstanding writing style and arranged under writing headings: narrative, investigative, profile, descriptive, and analytical.

Anthologies of single writers, columnists, and cartoonists are too numerous and diverse to attempt to sample here. The reader is advised to consult the bibliographies listed earlier or a library catalog for the newsperson or newspaper of interest.

Journalists adore reproductions of their newspaper pages. They celebrate newspaper anniversaries by shrinking and reprinting old front pages, and they adorn the pages of their trade publications with miniature reproductions of newspapers. To both the casual reader and the researcher, these reproductions offer glimpses of historical styles of news selection and placement, the relationship between news and advertising, and the use of headlines, graphics, and other typographical devices, all of which are as much a part of the cultural experience of reading the newspaper as are the subjects, styles, and slants of newswriting.

The leading general collection of page reproductions is *America's Front Page News, 1690–1970*, edited by Michael C. Emery, R. Smith Schuneman, and Edwin Emery. Pages are selected for their historical representations and for the significance of the news that they reported. Some collections by newspapers of their own pages are *125 Years of Famous Pages from the New York Times, 1851–1976*;

Keeping Posted: One Hundred Years of News from the Washington Post; and *Front Page: 100 Years of the Los Angeles Times, 1881–1981.*

BIBLIOGRAPHY

Books and Articles

Abrams, Alan E., ed. *Journalist Biographies Master Index*. Detroit: Gale Research, 1979.

Anderson, Elizabeth L., ed. *Newspaper Libraries in the U.S. and Canada*. New York: Special Libraries Association, 1980. 1st ed. Entitled *Directory of Newspaper Libraries in U.S. and Canada*, edited in 1976 by Grace D. Parch.

Andrews, J. Cutler. *The North Reports the Civil War*. Pittsburgh: University of Pittsburgh Press, 1995.

———. *The South Reports the Civil War*. Princeton, N.J.: Princeton University Press, 1970.

Armstrong, David. *A Trumpet to Arms: Alternative Media in America*. Los Angeles: J. P Tarcher, 1981.

Ash, Lee, and William G. Miller, comps. *Subject Collections: A Guide to Special Book Collections and Subject Emphases as Reported by University, College, Public, and Special Libraries and Museums in the United States and Canada*. 6th ed. New York: R. R. Bowker, 1985.

Baehr, Harry W., Jr. *The New York Tribune since the Civil War*. New York: Dodd, Mead, 1936.

Bagdikian, Ben H. *The Effete Conspiracy and Other Crimes by the Press*. New York: Harper and Row, 1972.

———. *Media Monopoly*. 5th ed. Boston: Beacon Press, 1995.

Bailyn, Bernard, and John B. Hench, eds. *The Press and the American Revolution*. Worcester, Mass.: American Antiquarian Society, 1980.

Baldasty, Gerald. *The Commercialization of the News in the Nineteenth Century*. Madison: University of Wisconsin Press, 1992.

Beasley, Maurine and Sheila Gibbons. *Taking Their Place: A Documentary History of Women in Journalism*. 2nd ed. Lanham, Md.: American University Press, 1993.

Behrens, John C. *The Typewriter Guerillas: Closeups of 20 Top Investigative Reporters*. Chicago: Nelson-Hall, 1977.

Belford, Barbara. *Brilliant Bylines: A Biographical Anthology of Notable Newspaper Women in America*. New York: Columbia University Press, 1986.

Bent, Silas. *Ballyhoo: The Voices of the Press*. New York: Boni and Liveright, 1927.

Berger, Meyer. *The Story of the New York Times, 1851–1951*. New York: Simon and Schuster, 1951.

Bergers, Marshall. *The Life and Times of Los Angeles: A Newspaper, a Daily and a City*. New York: Atheneum, 1984.

Bessie, Simon Michael. *Jazz Journalism: The Story of the Tabloid Newspapers*. New York: E. Dutton, 1938.

Blackbeard, Bill, and Martin Williams, eds. *The Smithsonian Collection of Newspaper Comics*. Washington, D.C.: Smithsonian Institution Press, 1977.

Bleyer, Willard Grosvenor. *Main Currents in the History of American Journalism*. Boston: Houghton Mifflin, 1927.

Blum, Eleanor. *Basic Books in the Mass Media*. 3rd ed. Urbana: University of Illinois Press, 1980. 1st ed., entitled *Reference Books in the Mass Media*, 1962.

Blum, Eleanor, and Frances Goins Wilhoit. *Mass Media Bibliography: An Annotated Guide to Books and Journals for Research and Reference*. Urbana: University of Illinois Press, 1990.

Bray, Howard. *The Pillars of the Post: The Making of a News Empire in Washington*. New York: W. W. Norton, 1980.

Brigham, Clarence S. *History and Bibliography of American Newspapers, 1690–1824*. 2 vols. Hamden, Conn.: Archon Books, 1947, 1962.

———. *Journals and Journeymen: A Contribution to the History of Early American Newspapers*. Philadelphia: University of Pennsylvania Press, 1950.

Broder, David S. *Behind the Front Page: A Candid Look at How the News Is Made*. New York: Simon and Schuster, 1987.

Cannon, Carl L., comp. *Journalism: A Bibliography*. New York: New York Public Library, 1924. Reprint. Detroit: Gale Research, 1967.

Caswell, Lucy S. *Guide to Sources in American Journalism History*. Westport, Conn.: Greenwood, 1989.

Cates, Jo A. *Journalism: A Guide to the Reference Literature*. Englewood, Colo.: Libraries Unlimited, 1997.

Churchill, Allen. *Park Row*. New York: Rinehart, 1958.

Cloud, Barbara. *The Business of Newspapers on the Western Frontier*. Reno: University of Nevada Press, 1992.

Connery, Thomas. *A Sourcebook of American Literary Journalism*. Westport, Conn.: Greenwood, 1992.

Cook, Elizabeth C. *Literary Influences in Colonial Newspapers, 1704–1750*. New York: Columbia University Press, 1912.

Covert, Catherine L. and John D. Stevens, eds. *Mass Media between the Wars: Perceptions of Cultural Tension, 1918–1941*. Syracuse, N.Y.: Syracuse University Press, 1984.

Coward, John M. *The Newspaper Indian: Native American Identity in the Press, 1820–1890*. Urbana: University of Illinois Press, 1999.

Crozier, Emmet. *American Reporters on the Western Front, 1914–1918*. New York: Oxford University Press, 1959.

———. *Yankee Reporters, 1861–65*. New York: Oxford University Press, 1956.

Danky, James P. *Undergrounds: A Union List of Alternative Periodicals in Libraries of the United States and Canada*. Madison: State Historical Society of Wisconsin, 1974.

Danky, James P., ed., and Maureen E. Hady, comp. *Native American Periodicals and Newspapers, 1828–1982: Bibliography, Publishing Record, and Holdings*. Westport, Conn: Greenwood Press, 1984.

Dann, Martin E., ed. *The Black Press, 1827–1890: The Quest for National Identity*. New York: Putnam, 1971.

Dictionary of Literary Biography, American Newspaper Journalists. Ed. Perry J. Ashley. Vols. 23, 25, 43. Detroit: Gale Research, 1983–1985.

Emery, Edwin, and Michael Emery. *The Press and America: An Interpretive History of the Mass Media*. 8th ed. Boston: Allyn and Bacon, 1996.

Emery, Michael C., R. Smith Schuneman, and Edwin Emery, eds. *America's Front Page News, 1690–1970*. New York: Doubleday, 1970.

Fialka, John. *Hotel Warriors: Covering the Gulf War*. Washington, D.C.: Woodrow Wilson Press Center, 1992.

Fishman, Mark. *Manufacturing the News*. Austin: University of Texas Press, 1980.

Folkerts, Jean, Dwight L. Teeter, and Keith Kincaid. *Voices of a Nation: A History of Mass Media in the United States*. 4th ed. Boston: Allyn and Bacon, 2002.

Gale Directory of Publications and Broadcast Media. Detroit: Gale, 2002.

Gitlin, Todd. *The Whole World Is Watching: Mass Media in the Making and Un-making of the New Left*. Berkeley: University of California Press, 1980.

Glessing, Robert J. *The Underground Press in America*. Bloomington: Indiana University Press, 1970.

Greenberg, Bradley, and Walter Gantz. *Desert Storm and the Mass Media*. Cresskill, N.J.: Hampton Press, 1993.

Gregory, Winifred, ed. *American Newspapers, 1821–1936: A Union List of Files Available in the United States and Canada*. New York: H. W. Wilson, 1937.

Grider, William. *Who Will Tell the People: The Betrayal of American Democracy*. New York: Simon and Schuster, 1992.

Halberstam, David. *The Powers That Be*. New York: Alfred A. Knopf, 1979.

Hallin, Daniel G. *The "Uncensored War": The Media and Vietnam*. New York: Oxford University Press, 1986.

Hamer, Philip M., ed. *A Guide to Archives and Manuscripts in the United States*. New Haven, Conn.: Yale University Press, 1961.

Hardt, Hanno, and Bonnie Brennan, eds. *Newsworkers: Toward a History of the Rank and File*. Minneapolis: University of Minnesota Press, 1995.

Herman, Edward, and Noam Chomsky. *Manufacturing Consent: The Political Economy of the Mass Media*. New York: Pantheon, 1988.

Hess, Stephen, and Milton Kaplan. *The Ungentlemanly Art: A History of American Political Cartoons*. 2nd ed. New York: Macmillan, 1975.

Hill, George H. *Black Media in America: A Resource Guide*. Boston: G. K. Hall, 1984.

Hohenberg, John. *A Crisis for the American Press*. New York: Columbia University Press, 1978.

———, ed. *The Pulitzer Prize Story: News Stories, Editorials, Cartoons, and Pictures from the Pulitzer Prize Collection at Columbia University*. New York: Columbia University Press, 1959.

———. *The Pulitzer Prize Story II: Award–Winning News Stories, Columns, Editorials, Cartoons, and News Pictures, 1959–1980*. New York: Columbia University Press, 1980.

Holt, Hamilton. *Commercialism and Journalism*. Boston: Houghton Mifflin, 1909.

Hoover's Guide to Media Companies. Austin, Texas: Hoover's Business Press, 1996.

Horan, James. *Mathew Brady: Historian with a Camera*. New York: Crown, 1955.

Hudson, Frederic. *Journalism in the United States from 1690 to 1872*. New York: Harper, 1873.

Hutton, Frankie, and Barbara Straus Reed, eds. *Outsiders in 19th Century Press History*. Bowling Green, Ohio: Bowling Green University Press, 1995.

Irwin, Will[iam Henry]. *The American Newspaper*. Ed. Clifford F. Weigle and David G. Clark. Ames: Iowa State University Press, 1969.

Isaacs, Norman E. *Untended Gates: The Mismanaged Press*. New York: Columbia University Press, 1986.

Johnson, Gerald W. *The Lines Are Drawn: American Life since the First World War as Reflected in the Pulitzer Prize Cartoons*. Philadelphia: J. B. Lippincott, 1958.

Johnson, Gerald W., Frank R. Kent, H. L. Mencken, and Hamilton Owens. *The Sunpapers of Baltimore*. New York: Alfred A. Knopf, 1937.

Kerrane, Kevin, and Ben Yagoda. *The Art of Fact: A Historical Anthology of Literary Journalism*. New York: Scribner, 1997.

Kessler, Lauren. *The Dissident Press: Alternative Journalism in American History*. Beverly Hills, Calif.: Sage, 1984.

Kluger, Richard. *The Paper: The Life and Death of the New York Herald Tribune*. New York: Knopf, 1986.

Kobe, Sidney. *The Yellow Press and the Gilded Age of Journalism*. Tallahassee: Florida State University Press, 1964.

Lande, Nathaniel. *Dispatches from the Front: A History of the American War Correspondent*. New York: Oxford University Press, 1998.

Leamer, Laurence. *The Paper Revolutionaries: The Rise of the Underground Press*. New York: Simon and Schuster, 1972.

Lee, Alfred McClung. *The Daily Newspaper in America: The Evolution of a Social Instrument*. New York: Macmillan, 1937.

Leekley, Sheryle, and John Leekley. *Moments: The Pulitzer Prize Photographs*. 2nd ed. New York: Oxford University Press, 1986.

Lent, John A. *Women and Mass Communications in the 1990s*. Westport, Conn.: Greenwood, 1999.

———. *Women and Mass Communications: An International Annotated Bibliography*. Westport, Conn.: Greenwood, 1991.

Leonard, Thomas C. *The Power of the Press: The Birth of American Political Reporting*. New York: Oxford University Press, 1982.

Levy, Leonard W., ed. *Freedom of the Press from Zenger to Jefferson: Early American Libertarian Theories*. Indianapolis: Bobbs-Merrill, 1966.

Liebling, A[bbot] J[oseph]. *Mink and Red Herring: The Wayward Pressman's Casebook*. Garden City, N.Y.: Doubleday, 1949.

———. *The Press*. Comp. Jean Stafford. 3rd ed. New York: Ballantine, 1975.

———. *The Wayward Pressman*. Garden City, N.Y.: Doubleday, 1947.

Lippmann, Walter. *Public Opinion*. New York: Harcourt, Brace, 1922.

Los Angeles Times. *Front Page: 100 Years of the Los Angeles Times, 1881–1981*. Ed. Digby Diechl. New York: Scribner's, 1978.

Manoff, Robert Karl, and Michael Schudson, eds. *Reading the News*. New York: Pantheon, 1987.

Marbut, F[rederick] B. *News from the Capital: The Story of Washington Reporting*. Carbondale: Southern Illinois University Press, 1971.

Marzolf, Marion. *Civilizing Voices: American Press Criticism, 1880–1950*. New York: Longman, 1991.

———. *Up from the Footnotes: A History of Women Journalists*. New York: Hastings House, 1977.

Mass Communications History Center, State Historical Society of Wisconsin.

Sources for Mass Communications, Films, and Theater Research: A Guide. Madison: State Historical Society of Wisconsin, 1982.

Maverick, Augustus. *Henry J. Raymond and the New York Press, for Thirty Years: Progress in American Journalism from 1840 to 1870.* Hartford, Conn.: A. S. Hale, 1870.

McAuliffe, Kevin Michael. *The Great American Newspaper: The Rise and Fall of the Village Voice.* New York: Scribner's, 1978.

McCoy, Ralph E. *Freedom of the Press: A Bibliocyclopedia, Ten-Year Supplement (1967–1977).* Carbondale: Southern Illinois University Press, 1979.

———. *Freedom of the Press: An Annotated Bibliography.* Carbondale: Southern Illinois University Press, 1968.

McPhaul, John J. *Deadlines and Monkeyshines: The Fabled World of Chicago Journalism.* Englewood Cliffs, N.J.: Prentice-Hall, 1962.

Miller, Sally M., ed. *The Ethnic Press in the United States: A Historical Analysis and Handbook.* Westport, Conn.: Greenwood Press, 1987.

Milner, Anita Cheek, ed. *Newspaper Indexes: A Location and Subject Guide for Researchers.* 3 vols. Metuchen, N.J.: Scarecrow Press, 1977, 1979, 1982.

Mindich, David T. Z. *Just the Facts: How "Objectivity" Came to Define American Journalism.* New York: New York University Press, 1998.

More Post Biographies: Articles of Enduring Interest about Famous Journalists and Journals and Other Subjects Journalistic. Athens: University of Georgia Press, 1947.

Mott, Frank Luther. *American Journalism: A History, 1690–1960.* 3rd ed. New York: Macmillan, 1962.

Murphy, James E., and Sharon M. Murphy. *Let My People Know: American Indian Journalism, 1828–1978.* Norman: University of Oklahoma Press, 1981.

National Hispanic Media Directory, Part One: U.S. Media Companies. Carlsbad, Calif.: WPR Publishing, 1999.

Nelson, Harold L., ed. *Freedom of the Press from Hamilton to the Warren Court.* Indianapolis: Bobbs-Merrill, 1967.

Nevins, Allan. *The Evening Post: A Century of Journalism.* New York: Boni and Liveright, 1922.

———, ed. *American Press Opinion: Washington to Coolidge.* New York: Heath, 1928.

New York Times. *125 Years of Famous Pages from the New York Times, 1851–1976.* Ed. Herbert J. Cohen. New York: Arno, 1976.

Newspapers in Microform: Foreign Countries, 1948–1983. Washington, D.C.: Library of Congress, 1984.

Newspapers in Microform: United States, 1948–1983. Washington, D.C.: Library of Congress, 1984.

O'Brien, Frank M. *The Story of the Sun, New York: 1833–1928.* 2nd ed. New York: D. Appleton, 1928.

Park, Robert E. *The Immigrant Press and Its Control.* New York: Harper, 1922.

Payne, George H. *History of Journalism in the United States.* New York: Appleton-Century-Crofts, 1920.

Peterson's Media Companies. Princeton, N.J.: Peterson's, 1999.

Pickett, Calder M., ed. *Voices of the Past: Key Documents in the History of American Journalism.* Columbus, Ohio: Grid, 1977.

Post Biographies of Famous Journalists. Athens: University of Georgia Press, 1942.

Price, Warren C. *The Literature of Journalism: An Annotated Bibliography*. Minneapolis: University of Minnesota Press, 1977.

Price, Warren C., and Calder M. Pickett. *An Annotated Journalism Bibliography, 1958–1968*. Minneapolis: University of Minnesota Press, 1970.

Prichard, Peter. *The Making of McPaper: The Inside Story of USA Today*. Kansas City, Kans.: Andrews McMeel and Parker, 1987.

Project Censored. *News That Didn't Make the News*. New York: Seven Stories Press.

Robertson, Nan. *The Girls in the Balcony: Women, Men and the New York Times*. New York: Random House, 1992.

Ross, Ishbel. *Ladies of the Press: The Story of Women in Journalism by an Insider*. New York: Harper, 1936.

Rucker, Bryce W., ed. *Twentieth Century Reporting at Its Best*. Ames: Iowa State University Press, 1964.

Salisbury, William. *The Career of a Journalist*. New York: B. W. Dodge, 1908.

Saturday Evening Post. *More Post Biographies: Articles of Enduring Interest about Famous Journalists and Journals and Other Subjects Journalistic*. Ed. John E. Drewry. Athens: University of Georgia Press, 1947.

———. *Post Biographies of Famous Journalists*. Ed. John E. Drewry. Athens: University of Georgia Press, 1942.

Schiller, Dan. *Objectivity and the News: The Public and the Rise of Commercial Journalism*. Philadelphia: University of Pennsylvania Press, 1981.

Schlesinger, Arthur M. *Prelude to Independence: The Newspaper War on Britain, 1764–1776*. New York: Alfred A. Knopf, 1958.

Schudson, Michael. *Discovering the News: A Social History of American Newspapers*. New York: Basic Books, 1978.

Schwarzlose, Richard A. *The Nation's Newsbrokers*. Vol. 1: *The Formative Years, From Pretelegraphy to 1865*. Vol. 2: *The Rush to Institution, from 1965 to 1920*. Evanston, Ill.: Northwestern University Press, 1989–1990.

———. *Newspapers: A Reference Guide*. Westport, Conn.: Greenwood Press, 1987.

Seldes, George. *Freedom of the Press*. Indianapolis: Bobbs-Merrill, 1935.

Shearer, Benjamin F., and Marilyn Huxford, comps. *Communications and Society: A Bibliography on Communications Technologies and Their Social Impact*. Westport, Conn.: Greenwood Press, 1983.

Sims, Norman. *Literary Journalism in the 20th Century*. New York: Oxford University Press, 1990.

Sinclair, Upton. *The Brass Check: A Study of American Journalism*. Pasadena, Calif.: Privately printed, 1919.

Sloan, W. David. *American Journalism History*. Westport, Conn: Greenwood, 1989.

Sloan, W. David, ed. *Pulitzer Prize Editorials: America's Best Editorial Writing, 1917–1979*. Ames: Iowa State University Press, 1980.

Sloan, W. David, Valarie McCrary, and Johanna Cleary. *The Best of Pulitzer Prize News Writing*. Columbus, Ohio: Publishing Horizons, 1986.

Sloan, W. David, and James D. Startt. *The Media in America: A History*. Northport, Ala.: Vision Press, 1999.

Sloan, W. David, and Cheryl Wray. *Masterpieces of Reporting*. Vol. 1. Northport, Ala.: Vision Press, 1997.

Sloan, W. David, Cheryl Wray, and C. Joanne Sloan. *Great Editorials*. 2nd ed. Northport, Ala.: Vision Press, 1997.

Smith, Anthony. *Goodbye, Guttenberg: The Newspaper Revolution of the 1980s*. New York: Oxford University Press, 1980.

Smith, Culver H. *The Press, Politics, and Patronage: The American Government's Use of Newspapers, 1789–1875*. Athens: University of Georgia Press, 1977.

Smith, Jeffrey. *Printers and Press Freedom: The Ideology of Early American Journalism*. New York: Oxford University Press, 1988.

Snorgrass, J. William, and Gloria T. Woody, comps. *Blacks and Media: A Selected, Annotated Bibliography, 1962–1982*. Tallahassee: University Presses of Florida, 1985.

Snyder, Louis L., and Richard B. Morris, eds. *A Treasury of Great Reporting: "Literature Under Pressure" from the Sixteenth Century to Our Own Time*. 2nd ed. New York: Simon and Schuster, 1962.

Spencer, Dick, III. *Pulitzer Prize Cartoons: The Men and Their Masterpieces*. 2nd ed. Ames: Iowa State College Press, 1953.

Squires, James. *Read All about It: The Corporate Takeover of America's Newspapers*. New York: Times Books, 1993.

Starr, Louis M. *Bohemian Brigade: Civil War Newsmen in Action*. New York: Alfred A. Knopf, 1954.

State Historical Society of Wisconsin. *Periodicals and Newspapers Acquired by the State Historical Society of Wisconsin Library*. Ed. James P. Danky and Clifford W. Bass. Madison: State Historical Society of Wisconsin, 1983–1989.

Stephens, Mitchell. *History of News from the Drum to the Satellite*. New York: Viking, 1988.

Sterling, Christopher H. et al. *Mass Communications Research Resources: An Annotated Guide*. Mahwah, N.J.: Erlbaum, 1998.

Streitmatter, Rodger. *Mightier than the Sword: How the News Media Have Shaped American History*. Boulder, Colo.: Westview Press, 1997.

———. *Unspeakable: The Rise of the Gay and Lesbian Press in America*. Boston: Faber and Faber, 1995.

Talese, Gay. *The Kingdom and the Power*. New York: World, 1969.

Tebbel, John, and Sarah Miles Watts. *The Press and the Presidency: From George Washington to Ronald Reagan*. New York: Oxford University Press, 1985.

Thomas, Isaiah. *The History of Printing in America with a Biography of Printers and an Account of Newspapers*. Albany, N.Y.: J. Munsell, 1810, 1874. Abridged ed., edited by Marcus A. McCorison, in 1970.

Tinney, James S., and Justine J. Rector, eds. *Issues and Trends in Afro-American Journalism*. Lanham, Md.: University Press of America, 1980.

Tripp, Burnell. *The Origins of the Black Press: New York 1827–1847*. Northport, Ala.: Vision Press, 1992.

Tuchman, Gaye. *Making News: A Study in the Construction of Reality*. New York: Free Press, 1978.

Tuchman, Gaye, Arlene Kaplan Daniels, and James Benet, eds. *Hearth and Home: Images of Women in the Mass Media*. New York: Oxford University Press, 1978.

U.S. Library of Congress. *Newspapers in Microform: Foreign Countries, 1948–1983*. Washington, D.C.: Library of Congress, 1984.

———. *Newspapers in Microform: United States, 1948–1983*. 2 vols. Washington, D.C.: Library of Congress, 1984.

Villard, Oswald Garrison. *The Disappearing Daily: Chapters in American Newspaper Evolution*. New York: Alfred A. Knopf, 1944.

Wall, Celia. *Newspaper Libraries: A Bibliography, 1933–1985*. Washington, D.C.: Special Libraries, 1986.

Ward, Jean, and Kathleen A. Hansen. *Search Strategies in Mass Communication*. 3rd ed. New York: Longman, 1997.

Washington Post. *Keeping Posted: One Hundred Years of News from the Washington Post*. Ed. Laura Longley Babb. Washington, D.C.: Washington Post, 1977.

Weaver, David H., and G. Cleveland Wilhoit. *The American Journalist: A Portrait of U.S. News People and Their Work*. Bloomington: Indiana University Press, 1986.

Whitehouse, George. *Understanding the New Technologies of the Mass Media*. Englewood Cliffs, N.J.: Prentice-Hall, 1986.

Willis, Jim. *The Shadow World: Life between the News Media and Reality*. New York: Praeger, 1991.

Wilson, Clint C., II, and Felix Gutierrez. *Minorities and Media: Diversity and the End of Mass Communication*. Beverly Hills, Calif.: Sage, 1985.

Wolseley, Roland E. *The Black Press, U.S.A.* 2nd ed. Ames: Iowa State University Press, 1990.

Wolseley, Ronald E., and Isabel Wolseley. *The Journalist's Bookshelf: An Annotated and Selected Bibliography of United States Print Journalism*. 8th ed. Indianapolis: R. J. Berg, 1986.

Wynar, Lubomyr R., and Anna T. Wynar. *Encyclopedic Directory of Ethnic Newspapers and Periodicals in the United States*. 2nd ed. Littleton, Colo.: Libraries Unlimited, 1976.

Newspaper Indexes and Text Services

Blassingame, John W., Mae G. Henderson, and Jessica M. Dunn, eds. *Antislavery Newspapers and Periodicals*. 5 vols. Boston: G. K. Hall, 1980–1984.

Bylines. New York: United Media Enterprises, current. Daily, on-line.

Cappon, Lester J., and Stella F. Duff. *Virginia Gazette Index, 1736–1780*. 2 vols. Williamsburg, Va.: Institute of Early American History and Culture, 1950.

Index to Black Newspapers. Wooster, Ohio: Bell and Howell, 1977– . Quarterly.

Jacobs, Donald M., ed. *Antebellum Black Newspapers*. Westport, Conn.: Greenwood Press, 1976.

Jodziewicz, Thomas W. *Birth of America: The Year in Review, 1763–1783: A Chronological Guide and Index to the Contemporary Colonial Press*. Glen Rock, N.J.: Microfilming Corporation of America, 1976.

National Newspaper Index. Belmont, Calif.: Information Access, 1979– . Monthly, microfilm, and on-line.

Newspaper Index. Wooster, Ohio: Bell and Howell, 1971– . Monthly.

New York Daily Tribune Index. New York: The Tribune, 1876–1907.

New York Times Index. First Series, 15 vols., 1851–1912; Second Series, 68 vols.,

1913–1929; Third Series, 1930– . New York: R. R. Bowker and New York Times. Semimonthly.

New York Times Obituaries Index. Vol. 1, 1858–1968; Vol. 2, 1969–1978. New York: New York Times, 1970–1980.

NEXIS Service. Dayton: Mead Data Central, varies with source. Daily, on-line.

Niles' Weekly Register. "Index." Baltimore, 1811–1849. Semiannual.

Online Computer Library Center. Dublin, Ohio: Library of Congress and participating libraries. Continuously, on-line.

VU/TEXT Information Services. Philadelphia: Knight-Ridder, varies with source. Daily, on-line.

Periodicals and Annuals

Aim Report. Washington, D.C., 1969– .

American Journalism Review. College Park, Md., 1993– .

American Newspaper Directory. New York, 1869–1908.

Ayer Directory of Publications (title varies). Philadelphia, 1880–1982. Renamed *IMS Directory of Publications* in 1983.

Bulletin. Reston, Va., 1941– .

Center for Research Libraries. *Catalog.* Chicago, 1982– .

Columbia Journalism Review. New York, 1962– .

Communication Abstracts. Beverly Hills, Calif., 1978– .

Communication Booknotes: Recent Titles in Telecommunications, Information and Media. Washington, D.C., 1969– .

Hudson's Washington News Media Contacts Directory. Washington, D.C.: 1968– .

International Year Book. New York: Editor & Publisher, 1959– . Continuation of annual *International Year Book Number* of *Editor & Publisher*, 1921–1958.

Journal of Communication. Philadelphia, 1951– .

Journal of Popular Culture. Bowling Green, Ohio, 1967– .

Journalism History. Las Vegas, Nev., 1974– .

Journalism Quarterly. Urbana, Ill., 1924– .

Mass Comm Review. San Jose, Calif., 1973– .

Newspaper Research Journal. Memphis, 1979– .

Nieman Reports. Cambridge, Mass. 1947– .

Public Opinion Quarterly. Chicago, 1937– .

Quill, Chicago, 1912– .

U.S. Library of Congress. *National Union Catalog of Manuscript Collections.* Ann Arbor, Mich.: J. W. Edwards, 1962; Hamden, Conn.: Shoe String Press, 1964; Washington, D.C.: Library of Congress, 1965–1993.

WJR: Washington Journalism Review. Washington, D.C., 1977–1982.

Working Press of the Nation. 5 vols. Chicago: National Research Bureau, 1945– . Annual.

Johannes Gutenberg's printing press. Courtesy of the Library of Congress

Benjamin Franklin's printing shop. Painting by Jean Leon Gerome, 1910. Courtesy of the Library of Congress

Newspaper boy for *The Evening Star*, Washington, D.C. Courtesy of the Library of Congress

Two men reading into a microphone for a radio show. Courtesy of the Denver Public Library

The set of the NBC morning show *Today*, 1961. Courtesy of the Library of Congress

War comes to the livingroom, 1968. Courtesy of the Library of Congress

Newstand in Boston. © Painet

Television production studio. © Painet

PHOTOGRAPHY

Richard N. Masteller

Photography has enjoyed popularity in America since 1839, when news of its first widely successful form, the daguerreotype, reached American shores from France. Since these early days, a multitude of photographic formats have entered and passed from the scene, recording it for posterity, shrinking the world while expanding its horizons, and feeding contradictory human desires for scientific information, romantic escapism, and comfortable home truths. Contemporary considerations of the photographic image stress its status as a surrogate reality; the image, could we but learn to read it, might reveal the social construction of reality inherent in the mind of its maker, in the minds of its depicted subjects, perhaps even in the minds of its viewers.

While the field of "fine art" or "creative" photography has profited from sustained critical attention, the intractable billions of images produced by less accomplished photographers have proved difficult to reduce to patterns of order or significance, and "popular" photography has thus suffered from comparative neglect. Nevertheless, researchers with a large variety of tools from a wide variety of disciplines have been gathering the riches and attempting to assess the cultural significance of popular photography. This chapter surveys some of the results and suggests a framework for approaching photography as an artifact of popular culture.

To be considered in the province of popular culture, photography must at least involve a large number of people. It may be useful to divide popular photography into three categories: photography of the people, by the people, and for the people. In its earliest years, the making of photographs by large numbers of people was impossible. Most were without the necessary technical knowledge and financial resources, and the medium itself was experimental and unpredictable. Yet beginning with the daguerreotype and continuing in subsequent forms such as the tintype and the *carte de visite*, the photograph drew thousands of people to portrait studios, whether elaborate establishments on Broadway in New York City in the

1850s or temporary quarters set up by itinerant photographers in hotel rooms across America. The legacy of this entrepreneurial spirit lives today in the portable landscapes and floodlights of the nearby K-Mart. One category of popular photography is, therefore, practiced by commercial photographers: it is photography of the people.

The second category—photography by the people—designates those who take their own photographs but who are relatively untrained photographers. These are the snapshooters, the holiday or vacation practitioners, those who are interested primarily in recording an event or perhaps in capturing a "pretty" picture. Although the outer limits of this group include more serious amateur photographers who join camera clubs and perhaps develop their own films and photographs, the largest number of people in this category is likely to have somebody else (or the camera itself in contemporary "instant" and digital photography) complete the photograph that they have taken. In essence, photography by the people designates the work of largely untutored record makers.

Photography for the people is the third category of popular photography. It designates the realm of imagery produced for advertising and information transmission of all kinds, whether in books, magazines, and newspapers, on political posters or bubble gum cards, or for television, movie, and computer screens. This is clearly an enormous area for research, but it is one that must concern us least here, in part because it borders on areas explored by other analysts of popular culture and in part because large numbers of people, although exposed to it, do not have the same direct involvement in the production of imagery as they do in the other two categories of popular photography.

Photography as an artifact of popular culture, then, is most directly photography of the people or by the people: large numbers are exposed to it or engage in it. But unlike photography for the people, such as that taken by photojournalists, photography of or by the people is not translated into another visual medium for broad public consumption; and unlike creative photography (photography despite the people?), popular photographers have less artistic and technical training; less concern with social, philosophical, or ideological ramifications of the photographic act; and less desire to produce images for isolated aesthetic contemplation.

HISTORICAL OUTLINE

Although the world's first photograph, which was the result of an eight-hour exposure, has been dated to 1827, the first technique to receive worldwide acclaim was named by and for its inventor, Louis J. M. Daguerre. As early as 1837, Daguerre produced a permanent image on a daguerreotype, a thin, copper plate that he silvered, sensitized to light, exposed in a camera obscura, and developed in mercury vapor. The technical details of his process were made public at a joint meeting of the French Academy of Sciences and the Academy of Fine Arts on August 19, 1839; within five months, over thirty editions of Daguerre's manual had appeared, and newspapers had spread the details throughout Europe, to Russia, and to the United States.

These newspaper accounts, as well as memoirs, letters, and cartoons, reveal that the public at large was enamored of the "mirror with a memory," especially as refinements in the early 1840s shortened exposure time and improved image quality. Although landscapes and cityscapes were common, portraiture was the most prevalent subject matter of daguerreotypes. In 1849, *Godey's Lady's Book* suggested that daguerreotypists were "limning faces at a rate that promises soon to make every man's house a Daguerreian Gallery." Such galleries, often quite elaborate, opened in major American cities; there were eighty-six in New York City in 1853. In smaller towns and villages, itinerant daguerreotypists also found eager sitters. To protect the delicate images from tarnish and abrasion, daguerreotypes were most often covered with a brass mat and glass and inserted in elaborately tooled leather cases, padded with silk or velvet. But they were also placed in brooches, medallions, and watch cases. Depending on size and competition, daguerreotype portraits ranged from twenty-five cents to perhaps fifty dollars; the average price usually fluctuated from about two dollars to seven or eight dollars. In 1863, the *New York Herald Tribune* estimated that approximately 3 million American daguerreotypes were being produced annually.

Photography of the people soon benefited from additional inventions. Every daguerreotype was unique; although daguerreotype copies of daguerreotypes were made, the mass production of photographic images had to await not only a negative-positive system of picture making but also a sufficiently detailed image to rival the precision of the daguerreotype. In France in 1850, L. D. Blanquart-Evrard announced his process of printing photographs on thin paper coated with albumen. In England in 1851, Frederick Scott Archer made negatives composed of light-sensitive collodion on glass, obtaining a more precise image more quickly than had previous negative processes. Ambrotypes on glass, dating from about 1854, and melainotypes or ferrotypes (later called tintypes), dating from 1856, were based on Archer's collodion process. Until near the end of the century, however, the albumen paper print made from a collodion negative was the dominant process in photography.

Predicated on the replicability and mass production inherent in the negative-positive process, the *carte de visite* rose in popularity as the daguerreotype waned. *Cartes de visite*, patented in France by Disdéri in 1854, were small albumen portraits about 4 by 2½ inches, pasted on cards about 1/16-inch thick. A camera fitted with multiple lenses enabled usually eight exposures to be made on the same negative. At the beginning of the 1860s, "cardomania" skyrocketed. In England, 70,000 portraits of the Prince Consort sold in the week following his death. In America during January 1861, the E. and H. T. Anthony Company, the largest photographic company in the nineteenth century, made 1,000 portraits a day of Major Robert Anderson, a central figure in the attack on Fort Sumter. Images of other soldiers and of poets, musicians, and entertainers were supplied to meet an insatiable demand. After Lincoln's assassination, photomontage *cartes* appeared of George Washington welcoming Lincoln into heaven. More mundane figures also appeared in *cartes*. An advertisement in Leslie's on January 7, 1860, offered "Your Photograph on a Visiting Card: 25 Copies for One Dollar." Thus, one could trade with friends and mail cards to distant relatives, especially during the Civil War. Schoolchildren today continue the same ritual that Disdéri first popularized.

The birth of the family album can be dated to about 1860, when the photographic industry began to produce albums with specially cutout pages for the insertion of *cartes*. At first they were only slightly larger than *cartes*, but albums became more elaborate as picture formats changed. By 1870, the E. and H. T.

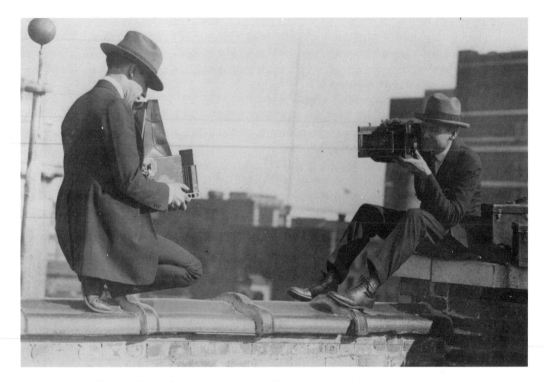

Two photographers in the early 1900s. Courtesy of the Library of Congress

Anthony Company listed nearly 500 album styles. Some were simple; many were lavish: several inches thick, leather-bound, gilt-edged, sometimes inlaid with mother-of-pearl, and usually fitted with heavy, engraved metal clasps. Modeled on medieval breviaries, such designs reflect the preciousness attached to photographs of the people.

The albumen print made at a photographer's studio remained the dominant form of photography of the people throughout the last four decades of the nineteenth century, but a variety of merchandising tactics gave the appearance of innovation. Although artificial, painted backdrops were used in England prior to 1851, they were relatively rare in America during the 1840s and 1850s. During the second half of the 1860s they became increasingly prevalent, especially in the studios of such entrepreneurs and self-promoters as Napoleon Sarony, famous for his theatrical photographs, and José Mora. In the comfort of the studio one could sit in front of a Greek temple or stand before a sylvan scene. Elaborate accessories proliferated—artificial rocks, rustic fences, plaster Grecian urns. In 1870, Mora's studio utilized 50 painted backgrounds—soon to grow to 150. His clientele of socialites and celebrities could choose among "plains and mountains, tropic luxuriance and polar wastes," Egypt, or Siberia. Matching the proliferation of backgrounds was a proliferation of image sizes. The "cabinet" size, about 4 by 6 inches, became popular in America about 1867. It brought new considerations about retouching negatives and posing sitters because poor technique and less "photogenic" subjects were more apparent in its larger size. "Boudoir" prints, "promenade" prints, and "imperial" prints followed in the 1870s—all enterprising tactics to foster photography of the people.

Photography by the people can be dated, with some plausibility, to the rise of amateur exchange clubs in the 1850s in England and America. These small groups of people had sufficient funds and sufficient technical training to make their own images of friends and surroundings. But the flowering of photography as practiced by the masses of people is more practically dated to 1888, when George Eastman announced his Kodak camera with the slogan, "You Push the Button, We Do the Rest." The Kodak was easily portable; it could be held in one's hand and weighed only 1½ pounds. It was bought already loaded with a roll of film that would take 100 circular photographs 2½ inches in diameter. When the roll was fully exposed, the camera was returned to the factory, where it was unloaded, reloaded with fresh film, and returned to the owner along with the prints that had been developed from the previous film. As Eastman wrote in the owner's manual, "Photography is thus brought within the reach of every human being who desires to preserve a record of what he sees. Such a photographic note book . . . enables the fortunate possessor to go back by the light of his own fireside to scenes which would otherwise fade from the memory and be lost."

The Kodak camera, together with its first roll of film, cost twenty-five dollars; processing the exposed film and loading new film cost another ten dollars. By October 1889, the company was receiving sixty to seventy-five Kodaks and processing 6,000–7,000 negatives a day. By early 1900, thirty-five different Kodak cameras had been marketed. One of them, the "Brownie," was introduced especially for children to use; it cost one dollar and took six pictures on a roll of film that cost fifty cents to buy and develop. Over 100,000 were sold within a year in England and America. Numerous variations of its basic design kept it the most popular roll-film box camera, and it survived in one form or another essentially until the advent of the Instamatic camera in 1963.

In the twentieth century, photography of the people continued despite the enormous increase in photography by the people and despite the attack by fine-art photographers on studio portraiture at the turn of the century. The Photo-Secession Exhibition in 1902 and the opening of the Little Galleries of the Photo-Secession in 1905 were the culmination of a decade of increasing antagonism between those who desired to establish photography as an art form, those who practiced photography less seriously as a hobby in the Kodak manner, and those whose commercial aims were paramount. There is not sufficient space here to detail their various battles. While the creative photographers whom Alfred Steiglitz chose to welcome to the Photo-Secession evolved into a small circle of confidants, photographers of the people continued to hold to commercially successful conventions of portraiture. Although softly focused imagery replaced the excessive artificial backdrops of the late 1800s, studios continued to aim for revelations of "character" and continued to produce formal family portraits, which reasserted solidarity and continuity in the face of social change. At the same time, studios cultivated their role in recording rites of passage: birthdays of children, graduations, weddings, and anniversaries. Meanwhile, hobbyists continued to look to burgeoning periodicals of amateur photography, such as *American Photography*, *Photo Era*, and *Photo-Beacon*, for advice on taking pictures. As snapshooters, they continued to indulge in an entertaining, increasingly convenient hobby.

The diverse innovations of twentieth-century photographic technology attempted to cater to these contradictory aims. We note only the most important of these innovations.

The Leica camera was first marketed in 1925 and fully refined by 1932. Offered as a camera for professional photojournalists and serious amateurs, its innovative, compact design provided freedom of movement, while its 35mm negative and excellent lens produced detailed images. As a relatively expensive camera, it created a market somewhere between the largest number of casual snapshooters and professional photographers. While the inexpensive box camera evolved over the years into the Instamatic, the efficient design of the Leica spurred other manufacturers to produce the Contax, the Exakta, the Nikon, and other less expensive 35mm cameras such as the Argus C-3, and photography by the people spread further across the spectrum of economic and social classes.

Color photography had its first widely celebrated success in 1907, when the Lumière brothers (Auguste Marie, Louis Nicolas, and Louis Jean) marketed their Autochrome process, which produced a unique positive transparency, as did Kodachrome film, first marketed in 1935. In 1941, Kodacolor film appeared; this negative film allowed any number of positives to be made.

The industry's desire to increase photography by the people has not only spurred the invention of various color processes but has also led to increasingly simplified, automatic cameras. Photoelectric exposure meters were marketed in the early 1930s and incorporated into some cameras in 1938. Today, a wide range of fully automatic cameras has given new significance to the original Kodak slogan, "You Push the Button, We Do the Rest."

One of the most startling innovations in popular photography occurred despite Kodak's dominance in the marketplace. In 1947, Dr. Edwin Land announced the invention of his instant-picture process, and a year later the first Polaroid-Land camera went on sale. In 1956, the 1-millionth Polaroid camera was sold. Polaroid's series of innovations, such as shorter development times, instant color film (1963), development outside the camera (1972), and automatic, ultrasonic focusing (1978), have all helped to make photography by the people easier and, some would say, as dramatic as the original daguerreotype process.

Photography by the people today reflects the same fascination with technical innovations and the same desire for effortless records and revelations that accompanied the rise of popular photography in the nineteenth century. Two phenomena—the contemporary disposable camera and the advent of digital imaging—can perhaps illustrate the links between these centuries, as well as provide a dubious measure of how far we have come. The original disposable camera, such as Fuji Corporation's "Quicksnap" or Kodak's "Fling," was marketed in the 1970s as an ideal, carefree substitute for expensive equipment when taking photographs on sandy beaches, around salt water, or on ski slopes or rafting trips. Consumers bought the cardboard and plastic camera with film already loaded, as was the case with the original Kodak in 1888. After the roll was exposed, both camera and film were taken to a photo processor. A century ago, Kodak returned 100 prints, as well as the original camera loaded with a new roll of film. Today, prints are returned, but the camera is discarded. One simply buys another disposable camera already loaded with film at the convenience store checkout line.

If we can now dispose of cameras, the most recent innovations allow us to dispose of film as well. With the advent of computer chips, scanners, ink jet and laser printers, and electronic storage media, people can now store and manipulate digital imagery without waiting for film to be processed or prints to be returned. They can choose to print an image that they can hold in their hands, or they can choose to store an intangible image electronically. As equipment for digital imaging becomes less expensive, more people will be able to alter the color palette of an image, to combine components from different times and places in one image, or to erase undesirable elements of an image, in effect creating their own versions of reality to a degree previously impossible. Whether people are lured by the possibility of reshaping reality or whether they continue the more conventional desire of their nineteenth-century forebears simply to record it, photography shows no signs of diminishing in importance as a phenomenon of popular culture.[1]

REFERENCE WORKS

Beyond the scope of this chapter is the host of Internet Web sites pertaining to photography and photographic history that are being created by museums, archives, and professional and amateur photographers and photohistorians. Given the ease of data collection and manipulation that computer technology allows, researchers can navigate list-oriented sites efficiently, searching for the names of particular photographers, for example, or studios. They can have at their fingertips a host of texts and images (although beholding the real thing is still preferable). Readers are urged to investigate such Web sites as they think about photography as a phenomenon of popular culture, even as they continue to consult the standard reference works. These standard works typically attempt to survey the history of the medium and thus reflect the diversity of its practitioners and functions. Students of popular photography must thus read selectively within the following four texts. Although these might better be listed under the section History and Criticism in this chapter, they appear here because they are well-illustrated introductions to the evidence that critical analysis can shape into culturally illuminating studies of the medium's popularity.

The second edition of Helmut and Alison Gernsheim's *The History of Photography from the Camera Obscura to the Beginning of the Modern Era* is out of print, but larger libraries should have copies. Written by the eminent collectors who assembled the Gernsheim Collection at the University of Texas, the text is organized chronologically by technical advances in the history of the medium. The major divisions of the text treat photography's prehistory, its invention, the early years, the collodion period, and the gelatin period. The text has a British orientation, and coverage ends about 1914, but, of the four core histories, it is the most complete in its coverage of the science and mechanics of photography. It supplies some helpful data that allow one to begin to theorize about the popular influence of the medium, and chapters on "The Popularization of Photography," "The *Carte-de-visite* Period," and "Push-button Photography" aid students of photography as popular culture. It also has a wealth of esoteric names and details not readily available elsewhere. This one-volume work was subsequently split into two volumes: *The Origins of Photography* appeared in 1982; *The Rise of Photography: 1850–1880, the Age of Collodion*, appeared in 1987.

Beaumont Newhall's *The History of Photography from 1839 to the Present* remains a classic. Sometimes referred to as the dean of photohistorians, Newhall began his career as an art historian. The seeds of his *History* were sown in the first exhibition of photography to be held at the Museum of Modern Art in New York, an exhibition that Newhall organized in 1937. The current edition begins with the prehistory of photography and ends with a few images from the 1970s. For studying photography as a popular phenomenon, the greatest limitation of the text is its predominant focus on "creative" photography; perhaps less obvious is a preference for a purist, unmanipulated photography that was seen as "modern" in the 1930s and 1940s. Nevertheless, the book is essential. Individual chapters consider the daguerreotype; "portraits for the million" (ambrotypes, tintypes); and documentary photography during and after the Civil War, at the turn of the century, and in the 1930s. The facts surrounding the rise of photojournalism and brief discussions of *Life*, *Look*, and the advent of the photo-essay are also included. The book thus provides a stage from which to begin a consideration of the influence of photography on popular culture.

The third indispensable history is Robert Taft's *Photography and the American Scene: A Social History, 1839–1889*. Like the Gernsheim and Newhall texts, Taft organizes his chapters by chronology and by process. Unlike the Gernsheims and Newhall, however, Taft's focus is exclusively American, and he is less concerned with "artistic" images. Although his fictional scenarios of social interaction are sometimes quaint ("How many a bashful beau has had his pangs of embarrassment eased by the relieving words, 'Let's look at the pictures in the album!' "), they are grounded in almost 500 footnotes gathered from a wide range of primary sources, including American photographic and nonphotographic periodicals. Taft has good discussions of the rise of amateur photographic exchange clubs, of family albums, of western expeditionary photography before and after the Civil War, and of the entrance of photography via the halftone screen into newspapers and cultural organs such as *Harper's Monthly* and *The Century*. Completed in 1938, his text is dated in some respects, but it remains an indispensable resource and guide to original material. Of the four histories, Taft's comes closest to "a social history."

The fourth important historical survey is Naomi Rosenblum's *A World History of Photography*. Updating and internationalizing Gernsheim and Newhall, her audacious endeavor results in a massive compendium of images and names. Although her predominant orientation remains fine art photography, she ranges—of interest here—from instances of popular photography in the last century, to travel photographs, to discussions of studio work, down to recent examples of digital imaging. Rosenblum responds to the power of the single image, but she also considers the social applications of photography and notes its relation to other national and international social and cultural changes. A valuable bibliography lists other bibliographies and encyclopedias; general, American, and international histories; critical studies and anthologies of essays; and works devoted to a wide range of individual photographers.

One additional historical survey warrants listing as a reference source. William Welling's *Photography in America: The Formative Years 1839–1900* repeats some of the material in Newhall and Taft and has little analysis of photography's social or cultural ramifications. But the book is distinguished by the extensive number of carefully documented facsimile reprints of excerpts and illustrations from early journals, guides, and newspaper notices demonstrating the appeal of photography in America. It is thus a convenient compendium for the person without access to original nineteenth-century materials.

Before plunging into indexes for research in popular photography, one should consult two older, but still useful, bibliographical essays of primary sources and secondary aids. Marsha Peters and Bernard Mergen in " 'Doing the Rest': The Uses of Photographs in American Studies" direct their essay toward historians and American studies scholars, raise initial questions, and suggest ways of approaching the rich photographic evidence pervading our past and present society. Thomas Schlereth's "Mirrors of the Past: Historical Photography and American History" surveys sources, approaches, and problems, with some attention to popular photography.

One particular CD-ROM also opens the door for fundamental research: *Photographers on Disc: An International Index of Photographers, Exhibitions, and Collections*, prepared by the George Eastman House, provides in a single, searchable, electronic source some 80,000 listings of photographers, photographic manufacturers, and publishers; 3,500 exhibition histories from 1839 to 1996; almost 600 institutional records from museums, libraries, archives, and historical societies; and some 2,000 bibliographical citations.

Other conventional reference works include the following. Laurent Roosens and Luc Salu's three-volume *History of Photography: A Bibliography of Books* compiles some 16,000 nineteenth- and twentieth-century publications grouped under some 3,000 wide-ranging subject headings and subheadings. Helmut Gernsheim's *Incunabula of British Photographic Literature* lists over 600 works (books and periodicals) that were illustrated with original photographs and another 350 works pertaining to British photographic literature from 1839 to 1875. Gernsheim includes many reproductions; a list of photographic journals, almanacs, and annuals; and citations to "important essays on photography" in the period. At the University of Texas, Roy Flukinger has compiled the 400-page *Windows of Light: A Bibliography of the Serials Collection within the Gernsheim and Photography Collections of the Harry Ransom Humanities Research Center*. Library catalogs also point to resources: the New York Public Library has published *Photographica: A Subject Catalog of Books on Photography*, which reproduces nearly 8,000 catalog cards of books, periodicals, exhibition catalogs, and related materials under about 120 subject headings pertaining to still photography and allied topics. *A Library Catalog of the International Museum of Photography at George Eastman House* is a compilation (also available in microfilm or microfiche) of catalog cards for over 30,000 volumes in the research library of this preeminent photography museum.

Several indexes guide researchers to articles. Beaumont Newhall's "Photography" in Bernard Karpel's *Arts in America: A Bibliography* provides over 900 annotated entries to books, catalogs, and articles. Almost 600 of these refer to creative photographers, but one also finds selected titles covering other aspects of the broad field of photography, as well as a convenient, annotated list of historical and contemporary periodicals in the field. *Photographic Literature: An International Bibliographic Guide to General and Specialized Literature on Photographic Processes*, compiled by Albert Boni, cites essays from the nineteenth century to 1970, but it is slanted toward technical aspects of the medium. Focusing on the first four decades of the medium, William S. Johnson's *Nineteenth-Century Photography: An Annotated Bibliography, 1839–1879* lists alphabetically thousands of photographers or writers on photography as it cites nearly 21,000 books and articles published from 1839 to 1990. Johnson surveyed both general-interest periodicals and specialist journals on photography for this project. In addition to the main alphabetical list, he includes briefer sections organized by country and year and by application (such as "exhibitions," "societies," or "stereographic photography"). Of more modest scope, but with helpful annotations, is Robert S. Sennett's *Photographers and Photography to 1900: An Annotated Bibliography*.

Other broader, obvious reference tools—the *Art Index*, *RILA (International Repertory of the Literature of Art)*, the *Reader's Guide to Periodical Literature*, the *Social Science Index*, and the *Humanities Index*—may be helpful for particular subject headings, such as "photography clubs and societies." An index that attempts to cover the spectrum of modern art, including photography, is *Artbibliographies Modern*. It began in 1971 with the title *LOMA 1969 (Literature of Modern Art 1969)* and assumed its subsequent title with volume 2. With volume 4 it began abstracting some of the articles and books that it cites. Readers can consult the individual volumes or turn instead to *Photography*, a 1982 compilation of 3,200 annotated entries on photography that originally appeared between 1972 (volume 4) and 1979 (volume 11) in *Artbibliographies Modern*. *Art Design Photo*, begun in 1974 and edited by Alexander Davis, continues the format of unabstracted citations begun in *LOMA 1969*; it surveys a wider range of periodicals than does *Artbibliographies Modern*. William S. Johnson has also compiled several annual indexes to articles. First published as *An Index to Articles on Photography, 1977*, his volumes for 1979, 1980, and 1981 are titled *International Photography Index*. Although the creative aspects of the medium predominate, these useful indexes include sections on photography and society, history, criticism, and organizations; and succinct notes about the contents of articles drawn from over 100 American and foreign periodicals.

Other reference tools aid more particular concerns. William Welling's *Collector's Guide to Nineteenth-Century Photographs* not only illustrates kinds of photographs but also lists nineteenth-century photographic journals and late nineteenth-century photographic societies and their officers. He also briefly discusses major, present-day repositories. William Culp Darrah's books *Stereo Views: A History of Stereographs in America and Their Collection* and *The World of Stereographs* are essential starting points for any study of the immensely popular stereograph, the double photograph that appeared three-dimensional in a stereoscope. The first book includes a history of the invention, development, and merchandising of the format; lists of stereographers; information for identifying and classifying the myriad number of views; and brief discussions of popular views. His second book expands the first; it contains 300 illustrations, lists of 3,500 stereographers in North America and 4,200 in other parts of the world, and brief discussions of eighty subjects that appeared frequently in stereograph cards. Critical analysis is minimal, but, as reference guides, Darrah's books help chart the vast domain of stereographs. Darrah's *Cartes de Visite in Nineteenth Century Photography* resembles his stereograph volumes. He surveys the history and diversity of *cartes*, including business arrangements and economics, and he provides a "subject guide" and selection of images ranging from "advertising" to "zoology." Lou McCullough's *Card Photographs: A Guide to Their History and Value* contains a nice selection of images within chapters on *cartes de visite*, cabinet photographs, stereographs, photographic postcards, and other image sizes.

Several texts directed toward collectors interested in cameras and other photographica can serve as useful reference tools. One of the better guides is George Gilbert's *Collecting Photographica: The Images and Equipment of the First Hundred Years of Photography*. Gilbert includes photographs of early equipment, original prices, and a selection of ads from the popular press. He also reproduces examples of other photographica spawned by the rise of amateur photography; the Montgomery Ward catalog of 1900, for example, contained an ad for photo belt buckles, photo watch charms, and photo garter belts ("It is now quite a fad for the ladies to wear the picture of a favored one on her garter"). Adding to the book's utility are appendixes of important dates, guides to dating equipment, and a detailed chart outlining "A Brief History of Most Eastman and Kodak Cameras, 1887–1939." Restricting itself to camera equipment, *A Century of Cameras from the Collection of the International Museum of Photography at George Eastman House*, written by Eaton S. Lothrop Jr., includes photographs of such items as the book camera, the watch camera, and the concealed vest camera. The book features 151 items ranging from the 1839 Giroux Daguerreotype camera to the 1942 Leica, a brief technical description for each, and a citation to an original advertisement appearing in amateur photographic or popular magazines.

Researchers may find useful some extremely diverse encyclopedias, biographical dictionaries, and other lists in the field of photography. Edward L. Wilson was the editor and publisher of the influential periodical *The Philadelphia Photographer*. In 1894 he published *Wilson's Cyclopaedic Photography: A Complete Handbook of the Terms, Processes, Formulae and Appliances Available in Photography, Arranged in Cyclopaedic Form for Ready Reference*. The volume quotes a large number of authorities on a variety of topics and is especially informative on practices of studio photography. Published in 1911 and reprinted in 1973, *Cassell's Cyclopaedia of Photography*, edited by Bernard E. Jones, also provides descriptions of techniques, processes, and formulas, as well as biographical entries and historical sketches of photographic societies. The *International Center of Photography Encyclopedia of Photography* attempts a similar range of information leading into our contemporary period.

Richard Rudisill's "Directories of Photographers: An Annotated World Bibliography" in *Photographers: A Sourcebook for Historical Research*, edited by Peter Palmquist, reflects the ongoing efforts of a host of amateur sleuths, museum curators, and photographic historians who have attempted simply to establish fundamental information about photographers—names, life dates, locations. Rudisill's annotations help the researcher select from brief articles to thousand-page compendiums of photographers at work from the dawn of photography to the present all over the world. This project evolved from Rudisill's publication in 1973 of *Photographers of the New Mexico Territory: 1854–1912*, wherein one finds reference, for example, to I. W. Tabor, a major studio photographer in San Francisco from 1864 to 1905 who supplied wholesale views from all over the West to firms back East. H. P. Stultz, on the other hand, is described as "primarily a man open to financial possibilities rather than a photographer." About mid-1885 he acquired a view camera to make and sell photographs of public and private buildings, this only one of several entrepreneurial activities that included his establishing a company to manufacture hairdressing from soap root.

Photographers at Taft Presidential Inauguration, 1909. Courtesy of the Library of Congress

Researchers interested in women photographers may begin with Naomi Rosenblum's *A History of Women Photographers*, which resembles her *World History of Photography* in its copious images and useful discussions. Among its bibliographies is one focused on "women and photography." Peter Palmquist's many publications include *A Bibliography of Writings by and about Women in Photography, 1850–1950* and his two-volume *Shadowcatchers: A Directory of Women in California Photography*, volume 1 devoted to practitioners before 1901, volume 2 continuing to 1920. Numerous illustrations accompany the useful information and documentation that Palmquist provides. See also Palmquist's *Camera Fiends and Kodak Girls: Fifty Selections by and about Women in Photography, 1840–1930* and *Camera Fiends and Kodak Girls II: Sixty Selections by and about Women in Photography, 1855–1965*. Working with census data, business directories, and other sources, including the imprints on *cartes de visite*, William Culp Darrah's "Nineteenth-Century Women Photographers" in *Shadow and Substance: Essays on the History of Photography in Honor of Heinz K. Henisch*, edited by Kathleen Collins, provides statistics for both American and European studio practitioners and ventures some conclusions about the prevalence of women studio photographers. See also Martha Kreisel's *American Women Photographers: A Selected and Annotated Bibliography*, which compiles over 1,000 citations for over 600 photographers from the 1880s to the present.

African American photographers are the subject of *Black Photographers, 1840–1940: An Illustrated Bio-bibliography* by Deborah Willis-Thomas. From her base at the Schomberg Center for Research in Black Culture at the New York Public Library, she profiles sixty-five people in a variety of photographic roles, includes a general bibliography of blacks in photography, and lists major public and private collections. Also consult her subsequent volume: *An Illustrated Bio-bibliography of Black Photographers, 1940–1988*.

City directories can also provide mundane, but occasionally useful, information. As long ago as 1958 the Chicago Historical Society published *Chicago Photographers 1847 through 1900 as Listed in Chicago City Directories*. In 1985 Ronald Polito compiled a revised edition of *A Directory of Boston Photographers: 1840–1900*, based on Boston business directories. His list of 890 studio photographers indicates the presence of advertisements in the directories and includes a list of photographic activity by year, which enables one to see the increasing numbers of photographers as the nineteenth century progressed. Categories within the *Directory* list women photographers, dealers, copyists, and album manufacturers. Evidence of the value of city directories is most apparent in a recent (and ongoing) compendium. *Craig's Daguerreian Registry*, by John S. Craig, is the most comprehensive guide to daguerreotypists and members of allied professions at work in the United States from 1839 to 1860. Based on some twenty-five years of research in over 1,600 city directories and in hundreds of books and articles, the three-volume *Registry* includes biographical and historical sketches when this information is known. An Internet on-line version allows one to navigate quickly among the various names.

Such sources may help to document the perilous and peripatetic journeys of commercial firms and individuals as they tried to create and cater to the public fascination with photography in the nineteenth century. Scholars interested in present-day business statistics should consult the various issues of the *Wolfman Report on the Photographic Industry in the United States* and the *Wolfman Report on the Photographic and Imaging Industry in the United States*. There, for example, one can learn that disposable personal income rose 184 percent from 1950 to 1968, while public spending for picture-making rose 641 percent. In 1975, according to the *Report*, American amateur photographers took approximately 6.7 billion photographs; since 1980, they are estimated to have taken over 10 billion photographs a year.

RESEARCH COLLECTIONS

Guides exist for locating significant fine art photographs, but it is much more difficult to conceive, prepare, and publish aids for the broader range of photographs of interest to students of popular culture. What follows are a brief discussion of major national resources and some general suggestions for tapping photographic materials probably available wherever scholars may be located. Researchers are reminded again, moreover, to investigate the Web sites of the Library of Congress, the Smithsonian Institution, the International Museum of Photography at George Eastman House, the California Museum of Photography, the New York Public Library, and other institutions.

Ernest H. Robl's *Pictures Sources, No. 4* is a guide to 980 collections. Although it is not restricted to photographs, it has useful summaries of holdings in major collections, a note on access and reproduction policies, and indexes arranged by collection, geographical location, and subject matter. Concerned only with photography, the *Index to American Photographic Collections*, edited by Andrew Eskind, lists almost 600 collections by state, including major museums, public libraries, newspaper and magazine archives, and historical societies; some 65,000 photographers appear in a photographer's index.

Washington, D.C., houses major repositories of photography, many of which are noted in Shirley Green's *Pictorial Resources in the Washington, D.C. Area*. The two most comprehensive are the Smithsonian Institution's Division of Photographic History in the National Museum of American History and the Prints and Photographs Division of the Library of Congress. The former houses a History of Photography Collection, consisting of some 500,000 pictorial items ranging from daguerreotypes to modern color prints. The latter is one of the most comprehensive resources in the country. Here are such collections as the Civil War photographs of Mathew Brady and his associates; the 120,000 glass-plate negatives of the George Bain Collection, which constitutes the major portion of the first important news picture agency in the United States; and the 270,000 negatives and 150,000 photographs gathered by the Historical Section of the Farm Security Administration from 1935 to 1943. Paul Vanderbilt's *Guide to the Special Collections of Prints and Photographs in the Library of Congress* is an out-of-print guide to these holdings, arranged alphabetically by collection and including brief descriptions of their contents. See also *Library of Congress Prints and Photographs: An Illustrated Guide*.

New York City is another major repository. The Museum of the City of New York has extensive collections, as does the New York Public Library. As noted earlier, the latter has published *Photographica: A Subject Catalog of Books on Photography*. At the other end of the state, in Rochester, the International Museum of Photography at George Eastman House continues its pioneering role as one of the oldest museums in the United States devoted exclusively to photography. The museum maintains an international collection of about 500,000 images, including extensive holdings of daguerreotypes, *cartes de visite*, stereographs, and studio photographs; a comprehensive collection of photographic equipment; and about 45,000 historical and contemporary books and periodicals, including many rare volumes from the nineteenth century. As noted earlier, a *Library Catalog of the International Museum of Photography at George Eastman House* is available.

The Gernsheim Collection of about 150,000 images and 6,000 books and periodicals is a unit within the Photography Collection of the Harry Ransom Humanities Research Center at the University of Texas in Austin. Like the collection at the International Museum of Photography at George Eastman House, the Gernsheim Collection spans the history of the medium. International in scope and with a British emphasis, it is especially rich in nineteenth-century items. Selected images from the collection and brief comments about their aesthetic virtues appear in Roy Flukinger's *The Formative Decades: Photography in Great Britain, 1839–1920*. Recall as well his *Windows of Light*, the guide to the serials in this collection, mentioned earlier. Students of photography as popular culture may find relevant images in the *New York Journal American* photo morgue, containing some 1 million items; the Smithers collection focusing on the Big Bend area of Texas from about 1915 to the 1950s; the studio photographs of Jno Trlica, a Czech photographer active around Granger, Texas, from the 1920s to the 1950s; or the E. O. Goldbeck panorama collection, some reproductions from which appear in *The Panoramic Photography of Eugene O. Goldbeck*, edited by Clyde W. Burleson and E. Jessica

Hickman. These constitute only some of the approximately 4 million images at the University of Texas.

Especially important for scholars of photography as popular culture are two archives of *cartes de visite* and stereographs. William Culp Darrah's collection of 57,000 *cartes*, filed alphabetically by country or state and illustrating the work of over 21,000 photographers, is housed in the Special Collections Department of Pattee Library at Pennsylvania State University in State College, Pennsylvania. The California Museum of Photography at the University of California, Riverside, holds the Keystone-Mast Collection of over 350,000 stereographic negatives and prints representing the archive of the Keystone View Company. Active from 1892 through the 1930s, Keystone commissioned stereo views for education and home entertainment and also purchased negatives from competitors such as Underwood and Underwood, B. W. Kilburn, H. C. White, the Universal Photo Art Company, and the American Stereoscopic Company. The presence of the Keystone-Mast archive at the California Museum of Photography makes it perhaps the best place to study the history of stereographic photography and its role in American cultural history. Two other discrete collections in the museum are the University Print Collections of some 10,000 photographs spanning the history of photography and the Bingham Collection of photographic apparatus, numbering over 4,000 items.

Other important materials lie scattered throughout the United States in state and local historical societies and in university archives. For example, the New York State Historical Association in Cooperstown houses some 55,000 images. The University of Washington in Seattle has about 200,000 images covering the period from 1860 to 1930 in Washington Territory, Alaska, and Canada. The Appalachian Oral History Project at Alice Lloyd College in Pippa Passes, Kentucky, includes a Photographic Archive dedicated to collecting and copying old photographs depicting the history, culture, folklife, and family relationships in central Appalachia from 1880 to the present. The Bancroft Library of the University of Calfornia in Berkeley contains over 1 million picture items. One can begin to approach these and other resources by consulting the *Directory of Genealogical and Historical Societies in the United States and Canada*, edited by Dina C. Carson; or Andrea Hinding's *Women's History Sources: A Guide to Archives and Manuscript Collections in the United States*, the index to which lists photograph collections, photographers, and related terms; or the *Union Guide to Photograph Collections of the Pacific Northwest*, published by the Oregon Historical Society; or Andrew Eskind's *Index to American Photographic Collections*, mentioned earlier.

Some museums and historical societies have published guides or finding aids to their own collections. Books treating a photographer or studio within the holdings of an institution can also suggest its potential. Harvard University Library's *Photographs at Harvard and Radcliffe: A Directory* lists and briefly describes various collections of over 2 million photographs. The Photography Archive at Harvard's Carpenter Center for Visual Arts, for example, contains 20,000 negatives and 2,000 prints in its "Social History of America" collection, mainly from professional photographic studios throughout America from 1910 to the present. Michael Lesy's controversial *Wisconsin Death Trip* is based on the Charles Van Schaick Collection in the State Historical Society of Wisconsin; his *Real Life: Louisville in the Twenties* draws on the commercial photographs of Caulfield and Shook housed in the Photographic Archives of the University of Louisville. Ann Novotny's *Alice's*

World: The Life and Photography of an American Original, Alice Austen, 1866–1952 selects from several thousand negatives in the Staten Island Historical Society. The Montana Historical Society has released two books based on over 23,000 photographs by F. Jay Haynes and his son: *F. Jay Haynes Photographer* and, edited by Edward W. Nolan, *Northern Pacific Views: The Railroad Photography of F. Jay Haynes, 1876–1905.*

Scholars interested in comparing Canadian and American photographic images and practices need to know about the National Photography Collection, a center for research in the history of amateur and professional photography within the Public Archives Canada in Ottawa. One of the fruits of a systematic, long-term project begun in 1977 at the collection, Lilly Koltun's *Private Realms of Light: Amateur Photography in Canada, 1839–1940* presents about 200 images from various Canadian archives; she appends biographical sketches and a good bibliography. The *Guide to Canadian Photographic Archives*, edited by Christopher Seifried for the Public Archives Canada, contains over 8,500 entries reported by over 100 archives.

These examples point to the fact that national archives, state and local historical societies, and university collections are treasure troves of neglected resources because large numbers of photographs and family photograph albums eventually find their way to such repositories. Nevertheless, the scholar who hopes to study photography as an artifact of popular culture might best start at home, not just in the local historical society. Arrangements can sometimes be made with local camera stores to survey long-unclaimed photographs, and members of local camera clubs are usually happy to share their hobby with whoever will listen and look. Finally, scholars should not overlook the homes of their friends or their own dens, closets, and attics.

HISTORY AND CRITICISM

The last two decades have witnessed astute analyses of the role of the museum and the marketplace in establishing and maintaining the value of particular photographers at the expense of other ways of thinking about photography. Accompanying these critiques have been frequent demands for an analysis of imagery grounded in the context of its making and its reception. As a result, some writers have turned from celebrations of artistic genius to ask questions about the conception, execution, and reception of these purportedly fine art photographs, and other writers have begun to examine the role of imagery once treated lightly as merely vernacular or amateur work. Nevertheless, beginning researchers should still consult older texts in order to witness the growth of photography as a cultural practice. Included in the ensuing discussion, then, are some of these older works; while often anecdotal and unsystematic, they record the growth of the medium as seen by some of its participants as it was becoming popular. There follows a discussion of texts focusing on particular photographic formats or processes. Popular appeal and dissemination were, after all, tied to these technical aspects of the medium. The flaw in texts organized around processes or formats is that larger social and cultural implications are frequently subordinated or ignored. This section concludes with recent, more theoretical works that provide models for addressing these larger implications.

Besides the standard historical surveys and references—Gernsheim, Newhall, Taft, and Rosenblum, and Welling's *Photography in America*—older histories can be useful. Erich Stenger's *The History of Photography: Its Relation to Civilization and Practice*, translated by Edward Epstean, is primarily technical and oriented toward European, particularly German photography, but Stenger includes anecdotal sections on amateur photography, the role of the *carte de viste*, the advent of identification and criminal photography, and a compendium of photographic references appearing in popular, nonphotographic literature. John Werge's *The Evolution of Photography* is more a primary than a secondary source. It is a meandering reminiscence of Werge's impressions and reactions to the enterprise of photography in the nineteenth century and of his visits to exhibitions, salons, and studios in England and in America. The second part of the book reprints some of his eclectic articles that first appeared in photographic journals of his day. W. Jerome Harrison's *A History of Photography Written as a Practical Guide and an Introduction to Its Latest Developments* and Gaston Tissandier's *A History and Handbook of Photography* are each oriented more toward technical and scientific discussions than toward photography as a popular phenomenon. But they are useful as evidence of the widespread fascination with scientific experimentation and technique that inextricably accompanied the advent and progress of photography. The third part of Tissandier's text, moreover, "The Applications of Photography," examines various social uses. He anticipates telegraphic communication of photographs and suggests that photographs of criminals be displayed in public places as "it would thus be possible to make the arrest of malefactors, upon whom the police are unable to lay their hands, more easy. It would be the same with dead bodies which had not been claimed by anyone."

Other useful, older works suggest the growing popularity of the medium in the nineteenth century. The printing history of John Towler's *The Silver Sunbeam* recommends it to students of popular culture. There were four editions of 1,000 copies each from January through November 1864, plus other editions in 1866, 1869, 1870, 1873, and, finally, the ninth edition in 1879. It was sold in England and America, and Spanish translations appeared in 1876, 1884, and 1890. Rather than revisions, each edition included supplements on the latest techniques; the first edition of 351 pages had grown to 599 pages by the ninth edition. The 1969 reprint of the first edition includes advertisements and is worth perusal by scholars who are seeking insights into the scientific methods that had to be mastered to practice photography before the advent of dry plates and the Kodak camera.

Besides such scientifically oriented manuals, books were published to help the commercial photographer succeed. Marcus Aurelius Root's *The Camera and the Pencil or the Heliographic Art* was written by a successful Philadelphia daguerreotypist. The book attempts to establish his profession as a fine art, mixing chapters of advice on putting clients at ease and on coloring photographs with chapters invoking Plato, Cicero, Joshua Reynolds, Edmund Burke, and John Ruskin on the varieties of the beautiful. As such, it demonstrates the early pretensions of this popular art to a fine art status. H. J. Rodgers' *Twenty-Three Years under a Skylight, or Life and Experiences of a Photographer* is a rather lightweight manual designed primarily to aid portrait photographers in solving the problems of posing and costume, but Rodgers' text is also interesting for its simplistic, popular considerations of physiognomy and phrenology as they relate to portraiture. James F.

Ryder's *Voigtlander and I: In Pursuit of Shadow Catching. A Story of Fifty-Two Years' Companionship with a Camera* is a rambling reminiscence by a successful photographer in New York state and later in Cleveland, whose career began in the daguerreotype era and lasted until the turn of the century.

General histories and reminiscences have diminished as critics have come to focus on the problematic diversity and influence of the medium. Two recent works manifest this sharpened critical awareness. Mary Warner Marien in *Photography and Its Critics: A Cultural History, 1839–1900* analyzes early discussions of photography in order to explore nineteenth-century concepts of modernity, technology, knowledge, and social change. *Photography in Nineteenth-Century America* is a collection of essays and splendid images edited by Martha Sandweiss to accompany an exhibition of the same name at the Amon Carter Museum. Among the essays are Alan Trachtenberg's "Photography: The Emergence of a Keyword," Sarah Greenough's " 'Of Charming Glens, Graceful Glades, and Frowning Cliffs': The Economic Incentives, Social Inducements, and Aesthetic Issues of American Pictorial Photography, 1880–1902," and Peter Bacon Hales' "American Views and the Romance of Modernization."

Still, there are recent, more general works that continue in a style resembling the historical survey, with the virtue of beginning to address the social implications of popular photography. Heinz Henisch's *Positive Pleasures: Early Photography and Humor* is a compendium of examples drawn from cartoons, literature, music, fashion, advertising, and politics, underscoring the diffusion of the photographic phenomenon in the nineteenth century. It amplifies a chapter from Heinz and Bridget Henisch's *The Photographic Experience 1839–1914: Images and Attitudes*, which should be consulted for its useful bibliographies and many illustrations as the authors touch on the varied relationships between photography and painting, book publishing, and journalism, among other topics. Concentrating on French society, Michel F. Braive's *The Era of the Photograph: A Social History* lacks full documentation, but it is useful both because it cites contemporary accounts of how, for example, family albums or *cartes de visite* fostered group entertainment and because it attempts to relate the varieties of photographs to their social contexts. It also includes black-and-white reproductions of numerous lithographs demonstrating the popularity of the invention. Pierre Bourdieu's *Photography: A Middle-Brow Art* is a more systematic analysis of the social functions of photography for amateur and professional photographers of different classes. Based on surveys and interview data (included in the original 1965 French edition but omitted in the 1990 translation), Bourdieu argues that photography as a cultural practice necessarily reflects the social norms and values of its practitioners. Jean-Luc Daval's *Photography: History of an Art* is a coffee-table book emphasizing the art of photography, but its excellent images reproduce less familiar works along with icons in the history of the medium, and it includes some discussion of popularization and social effects. William F. Robinson's *A Certain Slant of Light: The First Hundred Years of New England Photography* is more tightly focused and less sumptuous than Daval's survey. Although it concentrates on "forceful, innovative, and often beautiful images," the merits of the book are its restricted locale, its integration of the images of famous photographers (Walker Evans, Jack Delano, Marion Post Wolcott) with imagery from studios and serious amateurs, and its good discussions of landscape photography (the Kilburn brothers), late-nineteenth-century portraiture, and amateur clubs and their journals, among other topics. Robinson includes frequent citations from original sources and complete documentation. Alan Thomas' *Time in a Frame: Photography and the Nineteenth-Century Mind* has a British orientation. The value of the book lies in its cogent speculations about the effect of photographic imagery on the people viewing it and in Thomas' attempts to "read" images in socially meaningful ways. With studio photography, he carefully traces the importance of "fashionable display" among the upper classes and its echo among the lower classes. Discussing family albums, he stresses the importance of both the image sequence and the images themselves. The occasional tension between "actuality" (the real elements depicted in the portrait) and "arrangement" (e.g., of costume and pose) is for Thomas a rich source of visual information leading to social and psychological insights about the persons portrayed. Such insights must be offered cautiously, but Thomas' arguments are worth considering because they go beyond merely reiterating photography's popularity to venture some cultural observations based on that popularity.

Having examined these texts, one can profitably turn to studies of particular processes. A technical guide to many of these is William Crawford's *The Keepers of Light: A History & Working Guide to Early Photographic Processes*. Several studies of daguerreotypes are helpful. Helmut and Alison Gernsheim's *L.J.M. Daguerre: The History of the Diorama and the Daguerreotype* is a well-documented introduction to its subjects, tracing developments in France, America, Britain, and Germany. Beaumont Newhall's *The Daguerreotype in America* follows the method of his *History*: he establishes origins, traces technical developments, and identifies practitioners. Separate chapters consider the thirty-seven daguerreotype galleries operating on Broadway in 1853 and the itinerant daguerreotypists traveling by wagon through small towns and rural regions. Good reproductions of daguerreotypes and brief biographical sketches of daguerreotypists are included. Another well-illustrated and detailed history is Floyd Rinhart and Marion Rinhart's *The American Daguerreotype*. It includes biographical sketches of some 2,000 professional and amateur daguerreotypists and others related to the art. Richard Rudisill's *Mirror Image: The Influence of the Daguerreotype on American Society* adds an important dimension to these studies by relating the popularity of the daguerreotype to its social and cultural function. Rudisill suggests that the daguerreotype affected life in the United States in three ways: it encouraged cultural nationalism, promulgating affective images that reinforced notions of an American character; it furthered the transition from an agrarian to a technological society, in that the image was produced with a fascinating mechanical and scientific instrument; and it reinforced faith in the truth and spiritual insight that one gained from carefully perceiving the works of God in nature. Rudisill's book includes excellent reproductions, numerous quotations from a wide range of original sources, and a still-useful annotated bibliography. William F. Stapp's *Robert Cornelius: Portraits from the Dawn of Photography* is a well-produced monograph that accompanied an exhibition at the Smithsonian Institution's National Portrait Gallery of works by the man whom Stapp identifies as having made the first American portrait photographs. Besides excellent reproductions, the book includes seven appendixes reprinting descriptions of the daguerreotype process as it was announced to the world in the journals and newspapers of late 1839. *The Daguerreotype: A Sesquicentennial Celebration*, edited by John Wood, includes among its essays and images

Alan Trachtenberg's "Mirror in the Marketplace: American Responses to the Daguerreotype, 1839–1851." Trachtenberg argues that the exuberant rhetoric surrounding popular responses to the daguerreotype was accompanied by some "discordant notes" suggesting, among other things, cultural uneasiness over private identity and public "image." Wood also edited *America and the Daguerreotype*, a collection of well-reproduced images and eight essays that include discussions of landscape, postmortem images, and occupational daguerreotypes, among other topics. *Secrets of the Dark Chamber: The Art of the American Daguerreotype*, an exhibition catalog prepared by Merry A. Foresta and John Wood, not only reproduces excellent images but reprints almost forty nineteenth-century texts on the daguerreotype that appeared in the popular and photographic press. *Silver & Gold: Cased Images of the California Gold Rush*, edited by Drew Heath Johnson and Marcia Eymann, is an extended example of the American daguerreotype doing particularly important cultural work. Floyd and Marion Rinhart's *American Miniature Case Art* illustrates and identifies the variety of often elaborate cases made to hold daguerreotypes.

Cartes de visite always appear briefly in histories of photography, and William Culp Darrah's *Cartes de Visite in Nineteenth Century Photography*, noted under Reference Works, is a compendium of primarily American images. But Anne McCauley's *A.A.E. Disdéri and the Carte de Visite Portrait Photograph* is the first extensive study of its inventor and of the economics, aesthetics, and popularity of this small card photograph. Although she confines her study to France and Disdéri, she plausibly suggests that his strategies for self-promotion and success were typical of hundreds of other people who tried to earn a living producing and marketing photographs to growing middle and leisure classes, and she speculates that the *carte* "represents an early step toward the simplification of complex personalities into immediately graspable and choreographed performers whose faces rather than actions win elections and whose makeup rather than morals gains public approbation." Max Kozloff, in "Nadar and the Republic of Mind," also touches on the politics of the *carte de visite* in a growing mass society:

> Like the Gatling gun of 1862, its aim was [to] decrease the ratio of effort to output by mechanizing the product. Poses could be standardized, droves of assistants could be hired, and sales volume could be increased.... Whether directly or not, most portraits registered the bonding of people to their community, if only because innumerable clues were given to show their place within its hierarchies. ... (This state of affairs did not hamper individualism, but it certainly categorized it.)

Readers should consult Kozloff's other wide-ranging and provocative essays on photography, collected in *Photography and Fascination*, in *The Privileged Eye*, and in *Lone Visions, Crowded Frames*.

Scholars interested in stereography might begin with Oliver Wendell Holmes' three articles in the *Atlantic Monthly*: "The Stereoscope and the Stereograph," "Sun-Painting and Sun-Sculpture; With a Stereoscopic Trip across the Atlantic," and "Doings of the Sunbeam." The third article makes incidental reference to the stereograph, but the first two helped popularize the format, as did Holmes' contribution toward designing a convenient, handheld viewer. As noted in the section on "Reference Works," William Culp Darrah's *Stereo Views* and *The World of Stereographs* are essential guides. *Points of View: The Stereograph in America: A Cultural History*, edited by Edward W. Earle, raises the kinds of social and cultural questions that many discussions of photography ignore. The illustrated anthology includes essays on ethnic portrayals in stereographs, on the stereograph as a commodity, and on the use of stereographs in visual education in the schools. A chronology of stereography is incorporated in a chronology of other socially and culturally significant events.

The burgeoning of amateur photography that occurred with the invention of Kodak cameras provides rich material for sociological and cultural studies. One should first consult the Gernsheim, Newhall, and Taft histories and George Gilbert's *Collecting Photographica*. Beaumont Newhall's "How George Eastman Invented the Kodak Camera" is an informative essay. But the most detailed analysis of the development of the popular photographic industry is Reese Jenkins' *Images and Enterprise: Technology and the American Photographic Industry, 1839–1925*. Using Eastman Kodak Company as a case study, Jenkins explores the industrialization that made photography popular. His is the only book—among the many dealing with technical advances in photography—that relates such advances to theoretical models of industrial and technological change familiar to economic historians. In *Anthony the Man, the Company, the Cameras: An American Photographic Pioneer* William Marder and Estelle Marder, with the help of editing by Robert G. Duncan, have produced a book very different from Jenkins' by collecting voluminous information from 1840 to 1983 on the major photographic supplier and distributor of equipment and photographic views in the nineteenth century: Edward Anthony, the E. and H. T. Anthony Company, and their twentieth-century successors, Ansco and GAF. A useful reference tool, if short on cultural analysis, the book includes profuse illustrations, advertisements, chronologies, and reprints of three Anthony catalogs from 1854 and 1862. Eaton Lothrop's "Personality Cameras" is a briefer, humorous look at some of the merchandising tactics of firms like Kodak and Ansco. Lothrop discusses and illustrates cameras that tied into children's storybook or cartoon heroes, beginning with the Brownie and followed by such variations as the Donald Duck camera, the Hopalong Cassidy camera, the Brenda Starr Cub Reporter camera, the Charlie-Tuna camera (available in 1972 for $4.95 and three labels from a can of Star-Kist tuna), and the Mick-a-matic camera, which came in the shape of Mickey Mouse's head and was large enough to cover one's face when it was held up to take a photograph.

What amateurs, in fact, did with their equipment is considerably more difficult to study systematically. Moreover, the very ambiguity of the term "amateur" complicates matters, for at times it has referred to weekend snapshooters, to those whose avocation led them to develop and print their own work in makeshift darkrooms, to more or less devoted members of photographic societies and camera clubs, and to those who may have taken an initial weekend hobby and developed it with such facility that they found themselves elevated to the ranks of "fine art" photographers. The sheer number of "amateurs" with these various motivations, the glut of snapshots, and the deprecation of vernacular imagery in much writing about photography can daunt both novice and experienced researchers. Nevertheless, some studies of family albums and snapshots have raised important questions and provide models for further research.

A catalog that accompanied an exhibition of artifacts and photographs at the State Historical Society of Wisconsin, George Talbot's *At Home: Domestic Life in the Post-Centennial Era, 1876–1920*, recognizes the importance of situating these vernacular images in their social and cultural context. Talbot draws distinctions among, for example, a midwestern merchant prince who could afford elaborate studio portraits and a handsome commissioned album, a struggling homesteader who could afford only a view of his family taken in front of his home by a traveling photographer, and a poor urban laborer who could afford only a cheap tintype taken by a street photographer. Talbot suggests that such photographs, whatever their class origin, functioned as family keepsakes, demonstrating what people were proud of, what they thought interesting, and what they wanted to show others.

Studio portraiture first filled the pages of family albums, and it needs more exploration than it has received. Bevis Hillier's *Victorian Studio Photographs* is a book of images and biographical sketches of famous people drawn from the files of a British studio. It has brief introductions describing the typical Victorian studio and discussing portrait photographers as descendants of portrait painters. Ben L. Bassham's *The Theatrical Photographs of Napoleon Sarony* introduces a good selection of images with an essay detailing the business practices and successful self-promotion strategies of Sarony. Estelle Jussim's "From the Studio to the Snapshot: An Immigrant Photographer of the 1920s" is important because she pays attention to the social context of a Russian immigrant photographer and because she attempts to relate photographic format and style to cultural changes. Drawing on Erving Goffman's work, Jussim suggests that the studio portrait creates an idealized self as a stay against flux and chaos; the photographer's task is "the establishment of a suitable stage upon which the self [can] act out its delusional systems, its ideal." The snapshot portrait, however, reflects a loss of faith in this ideal: it captures only "a shard of the whole personality . . . an accidental recording of a gesture." *Wedding*, by Barbara P. Norfleet, selects seven professional studios across the country, ranging from the late nineteenth century to the mid-1960s, and reproduces candid and formal wedding photographs, along with unfortunately brief excerpts from interviews with photographers. Norfleet's book avoids intensive analysis, but its images and interviews support Jussim's argument about idealized portraiture. Said one photographer: "I also know what to avoid and what to bring out in the work—what they like and what they don't like. I'll get a divorced mother and dad in the same group for a picture when the couple said I could never do it."

Outside the studios, nineteenth-century itinerant photographers also sought to make images of the people. Alan B. Newman's *New England Reflections, 1882–1907: Photographs by the Howes Brothers* reflects the photo boom of the late 1970s in its occasionally inappropriate art-world captions ("Apron, geometry, and light" identifies an elderly woman in a chair on a porch). But Gerald McFarland's introduction, "The World of the Howes Brothers," draws on family records and letters to present a detailed, thoroughly illuminating account of the working methods of the brothers, sometime studio operators but more frequently itinerant photographers, whose 21,000 glass negatives are in the Ashfield, Massachusetts, Historical Society. The 200 images reproduced in the book show households of all classes, factory workers, shopkeepers, quarry workers, and delivery men. Images by a quite different itinerant photographer appear in John Carter's *Solomon D. Butcher: Photo-*

graphing the American Dream, based on archives in the Nebraska State Historical Society. As Peter Hales has suggested in "A Prairie Home Companion," Carter and the Historical Society deserve commendation for resisting the temptation to treat Butcher's work either as transparent windows on the past or as newly discovered icons for aesthetic contemplation. Butcher's photographs render such encomiums difficult. He was an indifferent printer, and he occasionally etched his negatives to "correct" and—one can only conclude—to play with the views that he had taken. By including some of Butcher's recollections of the situations in which photographs were taken, Carter helps one understand that the photographic act was a collaboration, a compromise between what was possible and what was desired. Thus, Mrs. Hilton had her parlor organ and family photographed in front of the cattle pen not only because lighting conditions were better than inside her home, not only because she wished to suggest her abilities as an organist, but also because she wanted to hide her family's failure to move from a sod house to a frame house. Jay Ruby in "The Wheelman and the Snapshooter or, the Industrialization of the Picturesque" discusses less serious itinerant photographers, namely, those who wed the turn-of-the-century bicycle craze with the Kodak craze.

While the work of studio and itinerant photographers filled the first albums, present-day albums also contain snapshots taken by amateurs. The variety of approaches for analyzing these images reflects not only their ubiquity but also concerns about the very definition of the artifact itself. What isn't a snapshot? What is a family photograph? Some orientation is provided by David Jacobs in "Domestic Snapshots: Toward a Grammar of Motives." An astute analysis and useful bibliography appear in Patricia Holland's " 'Sweet It Is to Scan . . . ': Personal Photographs and Popular Photography." Holland surveys leisure and domestic uses of photography and examines the role of the family album, images of the working class, the influence of Kodak's mass marketing, and the role of women as photographers and as keepers of the photograph album. Also consult the work Holland coedited with Jo Spence, *Family Snaps: The Meanings of Domestic Photography*. *The Familial Gaze*, edited by Marianne Hirsch, is based on an exhibition and conference at Dartmouth College; the volume includes twenty-two essays by various photographers, artists, curators, literary theorists, and historians who examine family photographs from a variety of perspectives, exploring the power of the image to shape personal memory and self-conception.

In "The Family Photo Album as a Form of Folklore," Amy Kotkin reports some results of her work with the Smithsonian Institution's Family Folklore Program. She underscores the importance of interviewing the people who are most closely connected with the images and suggests that family photographs function on three levels: viewed over time, they serve as the basis for family legends and thus family continuity; as part of material culture, their similarities in pose and setting suggest widely shared familial values; finally, they show evidence of becoming part of the rituals that they record and in that sense help to create the very family life that they depict. Kotkin concludes with a list of questions important for analyzing family albums: who takes the photographs, who arranges the album, where is it kept, and how often and under what circumstances is it viewed?

Steven J. Zeitlin, Kotkin, and Holly Cutting Baker followed up some of these questions in *A Celebration of American Family Folklore*. Again working through the

Family Folklore Program of the Smithsonian's Festival of American Folklife, they incorporate family photographs throughout their discussions of the forms of family lore; reproduce transcripts of "family stories" organized according to such topics as "heroes," "rogues," "survivors," "courtship" and "family feuds"; and include discussions of family photography and family albums.

More methodologically provocative are works that examine collections of snapshots taken by many amateurs. Michael Lesy finds the theories of Freud and Jung helpful. Examples of his method have appeared in *Afterimage* as "Snapshots: Psychological Documents, Frozen Dreams" and "Fame and Fortune: A Snapshot Chronicle" and in *Time Frames: The Meaning of Family Pictures*, which reproduces images with transcriptions from oral interviews. Julia Hirsch in *Family Photographs: Content, Meaning, and Effect* situates family photographs within the heritage of Renaissance painting. Her ideas are thought-provoking, if impressionistic, but she severely restricts her definition of family photographs to those that include at least two people with a blood tie, thereby excluding many of the images found in family albums. Exploring a wider definition of the family photograph and its effect on self-definition in our late, post-Holocaust world is Marianne Hirsch's *Family Frames: Photography, Narrative, and Postmemory*.

The Snapshot Photograph: The Rise of Popular Photography, 1888–1939 by Brian Coe and Paul Gates concerns the Kodak camera in Britain. Initial chapters discuss, too briefly, the social background of popular photography and distinguish it from professional photography and advanced amateur photography. Unsubstantiated is the assertion that naive, untutored snapshooters captured more truthful depictions of the "character" of their subjects than did other kinds of photographers. Subsequent chapters give a detailed history of Kodak cameras popular in England. The book does not deliver the social analysis that its title implies, but its selection of snapshots gathered under such categories as "Leisure," "The Seaside," and "Interiors" may be useful. See also Graham King's informal, but thoughtful and well-illustrated, discussion in *Say "Cheese"! Looking at Snapshots in a New Way*. King includes chapters on the history of the snapshot, its qualities, and its typical subjects. *The Snapshot*, edited by Jonathan Green, consists of brief headnotes written by creative photographers, followed by a selection of their images demonstrating that they can master, or at least mimic, the snapshot style. The essay by Steven Halpern, "Souvenirs of Experience: The Victorian Studio Portrait and the Twentieth-Century Snapshot," redeems the book—again because of his sensitive evocation of the contexts and implications surrounding formal, materialistic Victorian portraiture and informal, experiential snapshots. Gisèle Freund's *Photography and Society*, originally published in France in 1974, is concerned with the social, political, and commercial contexts of documentary photography and photojournalism, but the updated 1980 translation also includes a chapter on amateur photography.

Current scholarship has demonstrated increasing success in tracing the functions of popular photographs within the processes of daily life. Celebrations of individual genius and the aesthetic image continue, but several works are trying with new sophistication to assess collective practices. Grounded in fields as diverse as information theory, cultural anthropology, intellectual or social history, American studies, women's studies, and cultural studies, recent work suggests that research into popular photography will continue to yield illuminating insights into the culture that it represents.

In *Prints and Visual Communication*, William M. Ivins Jr. had asserted that photographs provided an important new way of reporting on reality because they were without the syntax of mediation that had characterized previous information transferral systems. Important as his study was, this view was a misconception about the transparency of the photographic medium, and much subsequent work has been devoted to correcting his assumptions and extending the implications of the corrections. See especially Estelle Jussim's *Visual Communication and the Graphic Arts: Photographic Technologies in the Nineteenth Century*, an extensive examination of the effect of photomechanical processes on the transmission of graphic images. Jussim's focus on other graphic arts concerns photography for the people. But for one studying photography as popular culture, the import of works using information theory is their insistence that no photograph or its reproduction is an unmediated "window" on the world: to presume so is to be a victim of the medium, rather than an analyst of it. Briefer, but equally illuminating, discussions of this issue are Joel Snyder and Neil Allen's "Photography, Vision and Representation" and Allan Sekula's "On the Invention of Photographic Meaning."

Armed with these warnings, recent researchers have indicated even in their titles the wider social and cultural emphasis that they seek. Grace Seiberling's *Amateurs, Photography, and the Mid-Victorian Imagination* examines in detail the photographic societies and exchange clubs often mentioned in the standard histories. She distinguishes the small band of British landed gentry and upper-middle-class "amateur" photographers in the early 1850s from both commercial entrepreneurs and snapshot hobbyists of later years. Contrasting sharply with American entrepreneurial daguerreotypists, Seiberling's British amateurs undertook photography because they had the education, economic means, and leisure to do so; it was one of many different activities appealing to those who appreciated art and science, were curious about the natural world, and desired to pursue their interests with others of like mind. Seiberling finds precedents for photographic societies and exchange clubs in other amateur organizations that fostered the pursuit of knowledge in Victorian England, and she provides ample evidence of the social nature of the endeavor. It was deemed important enough in the Photographic Society Club, for example, to specify in their rules that members "meet and dine together five times during the year. One of which dinners shall take place in some Country locality favourable to Photographic Pursuits." Seiberling reproduces a selection of the photographs that were included in exchange club albums and provides a comprehensive bibliography of photograph collections and primary and secondary sources for further research.

Also reflecting the wider and finer net being cast by contemporary scholars is Peter Bacon Hales' *Silver Cities: The Photography of American Urbanization, 1839–1915*. Hales seeks recurrent patterns of depiction and "webs of significance" among a wide variety of commercial and amateur images. Examining his photographers and their productions as reflectors, transformers, and transmitters of their culture, Hales moves from images produced in the "developmental period" of photography and urbanization (1839–1870), to "grand-style" celebrations of monumental public buildings and majestic boulevards (1870–1893), arguing that this "grand style gave the authority of fact to what was, and would remain, an unrealized ideal." The extent of the gap between image and reality helped inspire, according to Hales, a third programmatic use of the camera in the hands of reformers, particularly Jacob Riis. While Hales' concern with the dissemination of the image brings his book close to one boundary of this chapter—photography for the people, rather than of or by the people—no student of photography as a popular phenomenon should overlook this well-produced, well-written, and provocative volume.

Another recent essay attempting to situate photographic practice in a cultural context is Patricia Zimmerman's "Filming Adventures in Beauty: Pictorialism, Amateur Cinematography, and the Filmic Pleasures of the Nuclear Family from 1897 to 1923." Although concerned primarily with cinematography rather than still photographs, Zimmerman thoughtfully surveys prescriptive literature in popular and photographic books and journals to suggest that nostalgic "pictorialist" tenets encouraged amateur still and motion picture photographers to turn from the world of industrial capitalism and urban growth toward an idealization of nature and natural forms, toward more personal, subjective experiences, and toward depictions of family life largely divorced from the social and political contexts in which such life was embedded. Despite this nostalgic emphasis, Zimmerman also reports that making home movies was seen as a vehicle for introducing the industrial "scientific management" movement of the Progressive Era into the home. As with "time and motion" studies of efficiency in the workplace, home movies, too, could be analyzed, some writers asserted, to improve the dynamics of family life. Certainly, one must be wary of the gap between prescription and practice, but Zimmerman appears to have found yet another example of photography's influence in the wider culture.

One of the most important disciplines for bridging the gap between prescription and practice is anthropology. Although they are no longer published, back issues of *Studies in the Anthropology of Visual Communication* and its successor, *Studies in Visual Communication*, might well be consulted. A guide to using the camera in field study, John Collier Jr. and Malcolm Collier's *Visual Anthropology: Photography as a Research Method* provides suggestions for approaching photographic evidence that apply equally well to analyzing popular photography. Richard Chalfen in *Snapshot Versions of Life* applies descriptive ethnographic methods to explore the "home mode of visual communication." He divides the process of film communication into five kinds of events for systematic investigation—planning events, shooting events both on-camera and behind-camera, editing events, and exhibition events. He then examines the components of each event—the participants, settings, topics, message forms, and codes—in order to understand the photographic artifact as an expressive medium, as visual communication, and as a social activity. Chalfen's distinctive research procedures may perhaps lead to new understanding, especially when researchers begin to draw inferences from their detailed charting of data and venture into the cultural interpretations that Chalfen resists in this book. Readers might also consult his "The Sociovidistic Wisdom of Abby and Ann: Toward an Etiquette of Home Mode Photography" and two other essays with an anthropological flavor by Christopher Musello, "Family Photography" and "Studying the Home Mode: An Exploration of Family Photography and Visual Communication."

Scholars in American studies are also contributing to current knowledge. Peter

Hales' book has already been recommended. Alan Trachtenberg's "Introduction: Photographs as Symbolic History" in *The American Image: Photographs from the National Archives, 1860–1960* raises pertinent questions and demonstrates the importance of sensitive response to the form, content, and context of the image, as does his *Reading American Photographs: Images as History: Mathew Brady to Walker Evans*. "Western Views in Eastern Parlors: The Contribution of the Stereograph Photographer to the Conquest of the West" by Richard N. Masteller also stresses the importance of context. He grounds the work of E. O. Beaman, an eastern photographer who participated in John Wesley Powell's survey of the Colorado River in 1871–1872, in relevant diaries of the journey and argues that the stereograph format simultaneously promoted and trivialized western scenery, thereby fostering a complex response of awe, arrogance, and indifference toward the land. In a special issue of the *Journal of American Culture* (4 [Spring 1981]) devoted to photography, Ralph Bogardus and David Jacobs also situate the snapshot and family photograph within a functional context of production and use. See Bogardus' "Their '*Carte de visite* to Posterity': A Family's Snapshots as Autobiography and Art" and Jacobs' "Domestic Snapshots: Toward a Grammar of Motives." The value of William Stott's *Documentary Expression and Thirties America* includes its ability to relate Farm Security Administration photography to other modes of expression and analysis prevalent in the 1930s. James Guimond's *American Photography and the American Dream*, while also focusing on documentary (and other) photographers, seeks to understand their images in relation to both liberal and conservative versions of the American Dream. All these works are models of research and analysis based on the assumption that photographs are embedded in a social and cultural matrix; the matrix is as much the subject of study as the photographs themselves.

The scholarly interest in women's studies and women's issues has also led to fruitful considerations of popular photography. Carole Glauber's *Witch of Kodakery: The Photography of Myra Albert Wiggins, 1869–1956* recovers one woman's career as she moved from amateur status to an award-winning member of Alfred Stieglitz's Photo-Secession group. Although her images included staged "Dutch genre" scenes with titles such as "Family Cares" or "The Babe," Glauber suggests that Wiggins embodied the ideal of the "new woman" of her day, that photography was a vehicle for her self-expression and independence. Other women whose names may be more familiar also initially found outlets for their creativity as amateur photographers. C. Jane Gover in *The Positive Image: Women Photographers in Turn of the Century America* examines Gertrude Käsebier, Alice Austen, Frances Benjamin Johnston, and others who sought personal fulfillment through photography while still connected to a traditional domestic environment. In a thoughtful and provocative analysis, Judith Fryer Davidov in *Women's Camera Work: Self/Body/Other in American Visual Culture* examines a network of female photographers to remind us that photographs construct versions of history and versions of self, in part by depicting the "other," particularly Native Americans, African Americans, Asian Americans, and the migrant poor.

Some of the most provocative writing about photography's cultural impact appears in Susan Sontag's *On Photography*. An earlier manifestation of some of her ideas appears in Walter Benjamin's "The Work of Art in the Age of Mechanical Reproduction" and in Marshall McLuhan's "The Photograph: The Brothel-without-Walls" in his book *Understanding Media: The Extensions of Man*. Benjamin worried that the capacity for unlimited photographic reproduction would destroy the "aura" surrounding the unique work of art, an "aura" that he defined as "the unique phenomenon of a distance, however close at hand." Further, the mass-produced photograph had political as well as aesthetic consequences, such mass reproduction helping to create a mass society. McLuhan agreed, suggesting not only that photographs created a sense of accelerated transience in the world, abolishing both space and time, but that they also wiped out national frontiers and cultural barriers. Sontag's analyses take these ideas much further. Aphoristic, meditative, paradoxical, she is deeply troubled by the acquisitive, aggressive act of photography and argues that we are both victims and victimizers in a cave of shadows that we have ourselves created: "A way of certifying experience, taking photographs is also a way of refusing it—by limiting experience to a search for the photogenic, by converting experience into an image and souvenir." Focusing on photography not only as an artifact of popular culture but also as an artifact of Western culture, her analyses are disturbing perhaps because she has come so close to penetrating our surrogate selves.

Finally, students of photography as a cultural phenomenon should grapple with the important arguments, essays, and photo works of critics and photographers who are trying to reveal and cast off the visual and ideological blinders through which they suggest most of us view photographs. To select only one example, consider Allan Sekula's approach toward Leslie Shedden, the proprietor of the biggest and only successful photographic studio in Glace Bay, and Shedden's archive of commissioned mining photographs. In "Photography between Labour and Capital," Sekula engages in a historical analysis of the imagery of labor and of photography's role in adjusting human beings to industrial life. Many names familiar in standard photographic histories appear—Daguerre, Root, Holmes—but so do the names of Herbert Hoover and Frederick Winslow Taylor, the proponent of scientific management, for Sekula wants to "try to understand something of the relationship between photographic culture and economic life." The essays in *The Contest of Meaning: Critical Histories of Photography*, edited by Richard Bolton, ask such questions as: "What are the social consequences of aesthetic practice? How does photography construct sexual difference? How is photography used to promote class and national interests? What are the politics of photographic truth?" Similar provocative and difficult cultural questions are explored in A. D. Coleman's *Depth of Field: Essays on Photography, Mass Media, and Lens Culture*; Jennifer Green-Lewis' *Framing the Victorians: Photography and the Culture of Realism*; Max Kozloff's *Lone Visions, Crowded Frames: Essays on Photography*; Suren Lalvani's *Photography, Vision, and the Production of Modern Bodies*; Celia Lury's *Prosthetic Culture: Photography, Memory and Identity*; John Pultz's *The Body and the Lens: Photography 1839 to the Present*; Abigail Solomon-Godeau's *Photography at the Dock: Essays on Photographic History, Institutions, and Practices*; and John Tagg's *The Burden of Representation: Essays on Photographies and Histories*. The critical enterprise in all these works and in journals such as *October* is to situate the photographic act within the matrix of culture in order to consider the ways in which photography affects fundamental elements both of that culture and of our consciousness.

ANTHOLOGIES AND REPRINTS

There are no reprints devoted solely to photography as a popular culture phenomenon. *Photographers on Photography*, edited by Nathan Lyons, draws its thirty-nine essays from the ranks of twenty-three professional and creative photographers. Although it does not treat photography as a phenomenon of popular culture, it is a useful compendium of issues thoughtfully addressed. Beaumont Newhall's *Photography: Essays and Images* reprints fifty-four essays, excerpts, and news articles from 1760 to 1971, together with numerous images. Although most pertain to creative photographers and to photography as a fine art, a few more popular accounts are included, such as an enthusiastic discussion by Alexander Black of amateur dry-plate photography in *The Century Magazine* in 1887. Seventy-five informative and diverse selections in Vicki Goldberg's *Photography in Print: Writings from 1816 to the Present* range from Alfred Stieglitz to Weegee, Lewis Carroll to Roland Barthes, James Thurber to Susan Sontag. Goldberg reprints several of the works mentioned in this essay (Holmes, Kozloff, Sekula; excerpts from Benjamin, Ivins, Root, and Rudisill). The virtue of the twenty essays in *Reading into Photography: Selected Essays, 1959–1980*, edited by Thomas F. Barrow, Shelley Armitage, and William E. Tydeman, is their focus on contemporary, theoretical issues of the role of photography. Snyder and Allen's essay, "Photography, Vision and Representation," is among those reprinted. A more recent anthology, *Illuminations: Women Writing on Photography from the 1850s to the Present*, edited by Liz Heron and Val Williams, makes easily available a wide array of feminist, postmodern, and postcolonial approaches to photographs and photographic criticism by writers such as Rosalind Krauss and Lucy Lippard, as well as excerpts from more traditional perspectives.

In 1973, Arno Press issued the Literature of Photography series, sixty-two out-of-print nineteenth- and twentieth-century books, manuals, and treatises covering the spectrum of scientific, technical, and artistic aspects of photography both in America and abroad. While many of the works are technically oriented, this emphasis reflects the mixture of scientific experimentation, ingenuity, and fascination that accompanied the development of photography in the nineteenth century; in addition, a few titles (cited in the section History and Criticism) are important for tracing photography's professionalization and popularization. In 1979, Arno issued Sources of Modern Photography, a companion series of fifty-one titles. These and other Arno Press titles are now available from Ayer Company Publishers, North Stratford, N.H., 03590.

Finally, Primary Source Media, a member of the Gale Group, 12 Lunar Drive, Woodbridge, Conn. 06525, has drawn on the holdings of the International Museum of Photography at George Eastman House to publish a History of Photography microfilm series of 2,100 monographs and pamphlet titles and approximately 125 periodicals covering the history, technology, and aesthetics of photography both in America and abroad. Utilizing a refined microfilm image capable of conveying the nuances of the original photographs that were often tipped into nineteenth-century periodicals, the series is relatively expensive, but it makes available to larger libraries important items that exist in only a few national and international collections.

NOTE

1. Many of the details in this brief outline have been derived from Beaumont Newhall's *The History of Photography from 1839 to the Present* and from Robert Taft's *Photography and the American Scene: A Social History, 1839–1889*, both of which are discussed in the following section.

BIBLIOGRAPHY

Books and Articles

Artbibliographies Modern. Santa Barbara, Calif.: American Bibliographical Center and Clio Press, 1973– .

Barrow, Thomas F., Shelley Armitage, and William E. Tydeman, eds. *Reading into Photography: Selected Essays, 1959–1980*. Albuquerque: University of New Mexico Press, 1982.

Bassham, Ben L. *The Theatrical Photographs of Napoleon Sarony*. Kent, Ohio: Kent State University Press, 1978.

Benjamin, Walter. "The Work of Art in the Age of Mechanical Reproduction." In *Illuminations*. New York: Schocken, 1969, 217–51.

Bogardus, Ralph F. "Their '*Carte de visite* to Posterity': A Family's Snapshots as Autobiography and Art." *Journal of American Culture* 4 (Spring 1981), 114–33.

Bolton, Richard, ed. *The Contest of Meaning: Critical Histories of Photography*. Cambridge: MIT Press, 1989.

Boni, Albert, ed. *Photographic Literature: An International Bibliographic Guide to General and Specialized Literature on Photographic Processes*. Mansfield Center, Conn.: Martino, 1996.

Bourdieu, Pierre. *Photography: A Middle-Brow Art*. Trans. Shaun Whiteside. Stanford, Calif.: Stanford University Press, 1990.

Braive, Michel F. *The Era of the Photograph: A Social History*. Trans. David Britt. London: Thames and Hudson, 1966.

Burleson, Clyde W., and E. Jessica Hickman, eds. *The Panoramic Photography of Eugene O. Goldbeck*. Austin: University of Texas Press, 1986.

Carson, Dina C., ed. *Directory of Genealogical and Historical Societies in the United States and Canada*. Niwot, Colo.: Iron Gate, 1998.

Carter, John E. *Solomon D. Butcher: Photographing the American Dream*. Lincoln: University of Nebraska Press, 1985.

Chalfen, Richard. *Snapshot Versions of Life*. Bowling Green, Ohio: Bowling Green State University Popular Press, 1987.

———. "The Sociovidistic Wisdom of Abby and Ann: Toward an Etiquette of Home Mode Photography." *Journal of American Culture* 7 (Spring/Summer 1984), 22–31.

Chicago Historical Society. *Chicago Photographers 1847 through 1900 as Listed in Chicago City Directories*. Chicago: Chicago Historical Society Print Department, 1958.

Coe, Brian, and Paul Gates. *The Snapshot Photograph: The Rise of Popular Photography, 1888–1939*. London: Ash and Grant, 1977.

Coleman, A. D. *Depth of Field: Essays on Photography, Mass Media, and Lens Culture.* Albuquerque: University of New Mexico Press, 1998.

Collier, John, Jr., and Malcolm Collier. *Visual Anthropology: Photography as a Research Method.* Rev. and expanded ed. Albuquerque: University of New Mexico Press, 1986.

Collins, Kathleen, ed. *Shadow and Substance: Essays on the History of Photography in Honor of Heinz K. Henisch.* Bloomfield Hills, Mich.: Amorphous Institute Press, 1990.

Craig, John S. *Craig's Daguerreian Registry.* 3 vols. Torrington, Conn.: John S. Craig, 1994, 1996.

Crawford, William. *The Keepers of Light: A History & Working Guide to Early Photographic Processes.* Dobbs Ferry, N.Y.: Morgan and Morgan, 1979.

Darrah, William Culp. *Cartes de Visite in Nineteenth Century Photography.* Gettysburg, Pa.: William C. Darrah, 1981.

———. "Nineteenth-Century Women Photographers." In *Shadow and Substance: Essays on the History of Photography in Honor of Heinz K. Henisch,* ed. Kathleen Collins. Bloomfield Hills, Mich.: Amorphous Institute Press, 1990, 89–103.

———. *Stereo Views: A History of Stereographs in America and Their Collection.* Gettysburg, Pa.: Times and News, 1964.

———. *The World of Stereographs.* 1977. Reprint. Nashville, Tenn.: Land Yacht Press, 1997.

Daval, Jean-Luc. *Photography: History of an Art.* New York: Rizzoli, 1982.

Davidov, Judith Fryer. *Women's Camera Work: Self/Body/Other in American Visual Culture.* Durham, N.C.: Duke University Press, 1998.

Davis, Alexander, ed. *Art Design Photo.* London: Idea Books, 1974– .

Earle, Edward W., ed. *Points of View: The Stereograph in America: A Cultural History.* Rochester, N.Y.: Visual Studies Workshop Press, 1979.

Eskind, Andrew H., ed. *Index to American Photographic Collections.* 3rd enlarged ed. New York: G. K. Hall, 1995.

Flukinger, Roy. *The Formative Decades: Photography in Great Britain, 1839–1920.* Austin: University of Texas Press, 1985.

———. *Windows of Light: A Bibliography of the Serials Collection within the Gernsheim and Photography Collections of the Harry Ransom Humanities Research Center.* Austin: University of Texas Harry Ransom Humanities Research Center, 1994.

Foresta, Merry A., and John Wood. *Secrets of the Dark Chamber: The Art of the American Daguerreotype.* Washington, D.C.: National Museum of American Art and Smithsonian Institution Press, 1995.

Freund, Gisèle. *Photography and Society.* Boston: David Godine, 1980.

Gernsheim, Helmut. *Incunabula of British Photographic Literature. A Bibliography of British Photographic Literature 1839–75 and British Books Illustrated with Original Photographs.* London and Berkeley, Calif.: Scholar Press in association with Derbyshire College of Higher Education, 1984.

———. *The Origins of Photography.* 3rd rev. ed. New York: Thames and Hudson, 1982.

———. *The Rise of Photography: 1850–1880, the Age of Collodion.* 3rd rev. ed. New York: Thames and Hudson, 1987.

Gernsheim, Helmut, and Alison Gernsheim. *The History of Photography from the Camera Obscura to the Beginning of the Modern Era.* 2nd ed. New York: McGraw-Hill, 1969.

———. *L.J.M. Daguerre: The History of the Diorama and the Daguerreotype.* 2nd rev. ed. New York: Dover, 1968.

Gilbert, George. *Collecting Photographica: The Images and Equipment of the First Hundred Years of Photography.* New York: Hawthorne Books, 1976.

Glauber, Carole. *Witch of Kodakery: The Photography of Myra Albert Wiggins, 1869–1956.* Pullman: Washington State University Press, 1997.

Goldberg, Vicki, ed. *Photography in Print: Writings from 1816 to the Present.* 1981. Reprint. Albuquerque: University of New Mexico Press, 1988.

Gover, C. Jane. *The Positive Image: Women Photographers in Turn of the Century America.* Albany: State University of New York Press, 1988.

Green, Jonathan, ed. *The Snapshot.* Millerton, N.Y.: Aperture, 1974. Originally published as a special issue of *Aperture* 19: 1 (1974).

Green, Shirley. *Pictorial Resources in the Washington, D.C. Area.* Washington, D.C.: Library of Congress, 1976.

Green-Lewis, Jennifer. *Framing the Victorians: Photography and the Culture of Realism.* Ithaca, N.Y.: Cornell University Press, 1996.

Greenough, Sarah. " 'Of Charming Glens, Graceful Glades, and Frowning Cliffs': The Economic Incentives, Social Inducements, and Aesthetic Issues of American Pictorial Photography, 1880–1902." In *Photography in Nineteenth-Century America,* ed. Martha Sandweiss. Fort Worth, Tex.: Amon Carter Museum, New York: Harry N. Abrams, 1991, 258–81.

Guide to Canadian Photographic Archives. Ed. Christopher Seifried. Ottawa: Public Archives Canada, 1984.

Guimond, James. *American Photography and the American Dream.* Chapel Hill: University of North Carolina Press, 1991.

Hales, Peter B. "American Views and the Romance of Modernization." In *Photography in Nineteenth-Century America,* ed. Martha Sandweiss. Fort Worth, Tex.: Amon Carter Museum; New York: Harry N. Abrams, 1991, 204–57.

———. "A Prairie Home Companion." Review of *Solomon D. Butcher: Photographing the American Dream,* by John E. Carter. *Afterimage* 14 (February 1987), 16.

———. *Silver Cities: The Photography of American Urbanization, 1839–1915.* Philadelphia: Temple University Press, 1984.

Halpern, Steven. "Souvenirs of Experience: The Victorian Studio Portrait and the Twentieth-Century Snapshot." In *The Snapshot,* ed. Jonathan Green. Millerton, N.Y.: Aperture, 1974, 64–67.

Harrison, W. Jerome. *A History of Photography Written as a Practical Guide and an Introduction to Its Latest Developments.* 1887. Reprint. New York: Arno Press, 1973.

Harvard University Library. *Photographs at Harvard and Radcliffe: A Directory.* Cambridge: Harvard University Library, 1984.

Henisch, Heinz. *Positive Pleasures: Early Photography and Humor.* University Park: Pennsylvania State University Press, 1998.

Henisch, Heinz, and Bridget Henisch. *The Photographic Experience 1839–1914: Im-*

ages and Attitudes. University Park: Pennsylvania State University Press, 1994.

Heron, Liz, and Val Williams, eds. *Illuminations: Women Writing on Photography from the 1850s to the Present.* Durham, N.C.: Duke University Press, 1996.

Hillier, Bevis. *Victorian Studio Photographs.* Boston: David Godine, 1975.

Hinding, Andrea, ed. *Women's History Sources: A Guide to Archives and Manuscript Collections in the United States.* 2 vols. New York: Bowker, 1979.

Hirsch, Julia. *Family Photographs: Content, Meaning, and Effect.* New York: Oxford University Press, 1981.

Hirsch, Marianne, ed. *The Familial Gaze.* Hanover: University Press of New England, 1999.

————. *Family Frames: Photography, Narrative, and Postmemory.* Cambridge: Harvard University Press, 1997.

Holland, Patricia. " 'Sweet It Is to Scan . . . ' Personal Photographs and Popular Photography." In *Photography: A Critical Introduction,* ed. Liz Wells. New York: Routledge, 1997.

Holmes, Oliver Wendell. "Doings of the Sunbeam." *Atlantic Monthly* 12 (July 1863), 1–15.

————. "The Stereoscope and the Stereograph." *Atlantic Monthly* 3 (June 1859), 738–48.

————. "Sun-Painting and Sun-Sculpture; With a Stereoscopic Trip across the Atlantic." *Atlantic Monthly* 8 (July 1861), 13–29.

International Center of Photography Encyclopedia of Photography. New York: Crown, 1984.

International Museum of Photography at George Eastman House. *Library Catalog of the International Museum of Photography at George Eastman House.* New York: Macmillan Library Reference, 1987.

Ivins, William M., Jr. *Prints and Visual Communication.* 1953. Reprint. New York: Da Capo, 1969.

Jacobs, David L. "Domestic Snapshots: Toward a Grammar of Motives." *Journal of American Culture* 4 (Spring 1981), 93–105.

Jenkins, Reese. *Images and Enterprise: Technology and the American Photographic Industry, 1839–1925.* 1975. Reprint. Baltimore: Johns Hopkins University Press, 1987.

Johnson, Drew Heath, and Marcia Eymann, eds. *Silver & Gold: Cased Images of the California Gold Rush.* Iowa City: University of Iowa Press, 1998.

Johnson, William S., ed. *An Index to Articles on Photography, 1977.* Rochester, N.Y.: Visual Studies Workshop Press, 1978.

————. *International Photography Index.* Boston: G. K. Hall, 1983, 1984– .

————. *Nineteenth-Century Photography: An Annotated Bibliography, 1839–1879.* Boston: G. K. Hall, 1990.

Jones, Bernard E., ed. *Cassell's Cyclopaedia of Photography.* 1911. Reprint. New York: Arno Press, 1973.

Jussim, Estelle. "From the Studio to the Snapshot: An Immigrant Photographer of the 1920s." *History of Photography* 1 (July 1977), 183–99. Reprinted in her *The Eternal Moment: Essays on the Photographic Image.* New York: Aperture, 1989, 161–79.

————. *Visual Communication and the Graphic Arts: Photographic Technologies in the*

Nineteenth Century. 1974. Reprinted with a rev. preface. New York: R. R. Bowker, 1983.

King, Graham. *Say "Cheese"! Looking at Snapshots in a New Way*. New York: Dodd, Mead, 1984.

Koltun, Lilly, ed. *Private Realms of Light: Amateur Photography in Canada, 1839–1940*. Markham, Ontario: Fitzhenry and Whiteside, 1984.

Kotkin, Amy. "The Family Photo Album as a Form of Folklore." *Exposure* 16 (March 1978), 4–8.

Kozloff, Max. *Lone Visions, Crowded Frames: Essays on Photography*. Albuquerque: University of New Mexico Press, 1994.

———. "Nadar and the Republic of Mind." *Artforum* 15 (September 1976), 28–39. Reprinted in his *The Privileged Eye*, 76–89.

———. *Photography and Fascination*. Danbury, N.H.: Addison House, 1979.

———. *The Privileged Eye: Essays on Photography*. Albuquerque: University of New Mexico Press, 1987.

Kreisel, Martha. *American Women Photographers: A Selected and Annotated Bibliography*. Westport, Conn.: Greenwood Press, 1999.

Lalvani, Suren. *Photography, Vision, and the Production of Modern Bodies*. Albany: State University of New York Press, 1996.

Lesy, Michael. "Fame and Fortune: A Snapshot Chronicle." *Afterimage* 5 (October 1977), 8–13.

———. *Real Life: Louisville in the Twenties*. New York: Pantheon Books, 1976.

———. "Snapshots: Psychological Documents, Frozen Dreams." *Afterimage* 4 (October 1976), 12–13.

———. *Time Frames: The Meaning of Family Pictures*. New York: Pantheon Books, 1980.

———. *Wisconsin Death Trip*. 1973. Reprint. New York: Doubleday, 1991.

Library of Congress. *Library of Congress Prints and Photographs: An Illustrated Guide*. Washington, D.C.: Library of Congress, 1995.

Lothrop, Eaton S., Jr. *A Century of Cameras from the Collection of the International Museum of Photography at George Eastman House*. Rev. and expanded ed. Dobbs Ferry, N.Y.: Morgan and Morgan, 1982.

———. "Personality Cameras." *Image* 20 (March 1977), 22–27.

Lury, Celia. *Prosthetic Culture: Photography, Memory and Identity*. New York: Routledge, 1998.

Lyons, Nathan, ed. *Photographers on Photography*. Englewood Cliffs, N.J.: Prentice-Hall, 1966.

Marder, William, and Estelle Marder. *Anthony the Man, the Company, the Cameras: An American Photographic Pioneer*. Ed. Robert G. Duncan. Amesbury, Mass.: Pine Ridge, 1982.

Marien, Mary Warner. *Photography and Its Critics: A Cultural History, 1839–1900*. New York: Cambridge University Press, 1997.

Masteller, Richard N. "Western Views in Eastern Parlors: The Contribution of the Stereograph Photographer to the Conquest of the West." *Prospects: An Annual Journal of American Cultural Studies* 6 (1980), 55–71.

McCauley, Elizabeth Anne. *A.A.E. Disdéri and the Carte de Visite Portrait Photograph*. New Haven, Conn.: Yale University Press, 1985.

McCulloch, Lou W. *Card Photographs: A Guide to Their History and Value*. 1981. Reprint. Exton, Pa.: Schiffer, 1997.

McFarland, Gerald. "The World of the Howes Brothers." In *New England Reflections, 1882–1907: Photographs by the Howes Brothers*, ed. Alan B. Newman. New York: Pantheon, 1981.

McLuhan, H. Marshall. "The Photograph: The Brothel-without-Walls." In *Understanding Media: The Extensions of Man*. 1964. Reprint. Cambridge: MIT Press, 1994, 188–202.

Montana History Society. *F. Jay Haynes Photographer*. Helena: Montana History Society Press, 1981.

Musello, Christopher. "Family Photography." In *Images of Information: Still Photography in the Social Sciences*, ed. Jon Wagner. Beverly Hills, Calif.: Sage, 1979, 101–18.

———. "Studying the Home Mode: An Exploration of Family Photography and Visual Comunication." *Studies in Visual Comunication* 6 (Spring 1980), 23–41.

Newhall, Beaumont. *The Daguerreotype in America*. 3rd rev. ed. New York: Dover, 1976.

———. *The History of Photography from 1839 to the Present*. 5th ed., rev. New York: Museum of Modern Art, 1982.

———. "How George Eastman Invented the Kodak Camera." *Image* 7 (March 1958), 59–64.

———. "Photography." In *Arts in America: A Bibliography*, 4 vols., ed. Bernard Karpel. Washington, D.C.: Smithsonian Institution Press, 1979, vol. 3, n.p.

———. *Photography, Essays and Images: Illustrated Readings in the History of Photography*. New York: New York Graphic Society and Museum of Modern Art, 1980.

Newman, Alan B., ed. *New England Reflections, 1882–1907. Photographs by the Howes Brothers*. New York: Pantheon, 1981.

New York Public Library Research Libraries. *Photographica: A Subject Catalog of Books on Photography*. Boston: G. K. Hall, 1984.

Nolan, Edward W., ed. *Northern Pacific Views: The Railroad Photography of F. Jay Haynes, 1876–1905*. Helena: Montana Historical Society Press, 1983.

Norfleet, Barbara P. *Wedding*. New York: Simon and Schuster, 1979.

Novotny, Ann. *Alice's World: The Life and Photography of an American Original, Alice Austen, 1866–1952*. Old Greenwich, Conn.: Chatham Press, 1976.

Palmquist, Peter E., ed. *A Bibliography of Writings by and about Women in Photography, 1850–1950*. 2nd ed. Arcata, Calif.: Peter E. Palmquist, 1994.

———. *Camera Fiends and Kodak Girls: Fifty Selections by and about Women in Photography, 1840–1930*. New York: Midmarch Art Press, 1989.

———. *Camera Fiends and Kodak Girls II: Sixty Selections by and about Women in Photography, 1855–1965*. New York: Midmarch Art Press, 1995.

———. *Photographers: A Sourcebook for Historical Research*. Brownsville, Calif.: Carl Mautz, 1991.

———. *Shadowcatchers: A Directory of Women in California Photography*. 2 vols. Arcata, Calif.: Peter E. Palmquist, 1990.

Peters, Marsha, and Bernard Mergen. " 'Doing the Rest': The Uses of Photographs in American Studies." *American Quarterly* 29 (1977), 280–303.

Photographers on Disc: An International Index of Photographers, Exhibitions, and Collections. George Eastman House. CD-ROM. New York: G. K. Hall, 1996.

Photography. Modern Art Bibliographical Series, Vol. 2. Santa Barbara, Calif.: American Bibliographical Center and Clio Press, 1982.

Polito, Ronald, comp. *A Directory of Boston Photographers: 1840–1900.* Rev. ed. Boston: Ronald Polito, Department of Art, University of Massachusetts at Boston, 1985.

Pultz, John. *The Body and the Lens: Photography 1839 to the Present.* New York: Harry N. Abrams, 1995.

Rinhart, Floyd, and Marion Rinhart. *The American Daguerreotype.* Athens: University of Georgia Press, 1981.

———. *American Miniature Case Art.* New York: A. S. Barnes, 1969.

Robinson, William F. *A Certain Slant of Light: The First Hundred Years of New England Photography.* Boston: New York Graphic Society, 1980.

Robl, Ernest H. *Picture Sources, No. 4.* Ann Arbor, Mich.: Books on Demand, 1983.

Rodgers, H. J. *Twenty-Three Years under a Skylight, or Life and Experiences of a Photographer.* 1872. Reprint. New York: Arno Press, 1973.

Roosens, Laurent, and Luc Salu. *History of Photography: A Bibliography of Books.* 3 vols. Herndon, Va.: Cassell Academic, 1989, 1994, 1996.

Root, Marcus Aurelius. *The Camera and the Pencil or the Heliographic Art.* 1864. Reprint. Pawlet, Vt.: Helios, 1971.

Rosenblum, Naomi. *A History of Women Photographers.* New York: Abbeville Press, 1994.

———. *A World History of Photography.* 3rd ed. New York: Abbeville Press, 1997.

Ruby, Jay. "The Wheelman and the Snapshooter or, the Industrialization of the Picturesque." In *Shadow and Substance: Essays on the History of Photography in Honor of Heinz K. Henisch,* ed. Kathleen Collins. Bloomfield Hills, Mich.: Amorphous Institute Press, 1990, 261–68.

Rudisill, Richard. "Directories of Photographers: An Annotated World Bibliography." In *Photographers: A Sourcebook for Historical Research,* ed. Peter E. Palmquist. Brownsville, Calif.: Carl Mautz, 1991, 52–98.

———. *Mirror Image: The Influence of the Daguerreotype on American Society.* Albuquerque: University of New Mexico Press, 1971.

———. *Photographers of the New Mexico Territory: 1854–1912.* Santa Fe: Museum of New Mexico, 1973.

Ryder, James F. *Voigtlander and I: In Pursuit of Shadow Catching. A Story of Fifty-Two Years' Companionship with a Camera.* 1902. Reprint. New York: Arno Press, 1973.

Sandweiss, Martha, ed. *Photography in Nineteenth-Century America.* Fort Worth, Tex.: Amon Carter Museum; New York: Harry N. Abrams, 1991.

Schlereth, Thomas J. "Mirrors of the Past: Historical Photography and American History." In his *Artifacts and the American Past.* Nashville: American Association for State and Local History, 1980, 11–48, 240–50.

Seiberling, Grace. *Amateurs, Photography, and the Mid-Victorian Imagination.* Chicago: University of Chicago Press, 1986.

Sekula, Allan. "On the Invention of Photographic Meaning." *Artforum* 13 (January 1975), 36–45. Reprinted in his *Photography against the Grain,* 3–21, and in

Photography in Print: Writings from 1816 to the Present, ed. Vicki Goldberg. Albuquerque: University of New Mexico Press, 1988, 452–73.

———. *Photography against the Grain: Essays and Photo Works, 1973–1983*. Halifax: Press of the Nova Scotia College of Art and Design, 1984.

———. "Photography between Labour and Capital." In *Mining Photographs and Other Pictures 1948–1968*, ed. Benjamin H. D. Buchloh and Robert Wilkie. Photographs by Leslie Shedden. Halifax: Press of the Nova Scotia College of Art and Design, 1983, 193–268.

Sennett, Robert S. *Photographers and Photography to 1900: An Annotated Bibliography*. New York: Garland, 1985.

Snyder, Joel, and Neil Allen. "Photography, Vision and Representation." *Critical Inquiry* 2 (1975), 143–69.

Solomon-Godeau, Abigail. *Photography at the Dock: Essays on Photographic History, Institutions, and Practices*. Minneapolis: University of Minnesota Press, 1991.

Sontag, Susan. *On Photography*. 1977. Reprint. New York: Doubleday, 1990.

Spence, Jo, and Patricia Holland, eds. *Family Snaps: The Meanings of Domestic Photography*. London: Virago, 1991.

Stapp, William F. *Robert Cornelius: Portraits from the Dawn of Photography*. Washington, D.C.: Smithsonian Institution Press, 1983.

Stenger, Erich. *The History of Photography: Its Relation to Civilization and Practice*. Trans. Edward Epstean. Easton, Pa.: Mack Printing, 1939.

Stott, William. *Documentary Expression and Thirties America*. 1973. Reprinted with a new afterword. Chicago: University of Chicago Press, 1986.

Taft, Robert. *Photography and the American Scene: A Social History, 1839–1889*. 1938. Reprint. New York: Dover, 1989.

Tagg, John. *The Burden of Representation: Essays on Photographies and Histories*. Minneapolis: University of Minnesota Press, 1993.

Talbot, George. *At Home: Domestic Life in the Post-Centennial Era, 1876–1920*. Madison: State Historical Society of Wisconsin, 1976.

Thomas, Alan. *Time in a Frame: Photography and the Nineteenth-Century Mind*. New York: Schocken, 1977.

Tissandier, Gaston. *A History and Handbook of Photography*. 2nd ed. 1878. Reprint. New York: Arno Press, 1973.

Towler, John. *The Silver Sunbeam*. 1864. Reprint. New York: Morgan and Morgan, 1969.

Trachtenberg, Alan. "Introduction: Photographs as Symbolic History." In *The American Image: Photographs from the National Archives, 1860–1960*. New York: Pantheon Books, 1979, ix–xxxii.

———. "Mirror in the Marketplace: American Responses to the Daguerreotype, 1839–1851." In *The Daguerreotype: A Sesquicentennial Celebration*, ed. John Wood. Iowa City: University of Iowa Press, 1989, 60–73.

———. "Photography: The Emergence of a Keyword." In *Photography in Nineteenth-Century America*, ed. Martha Sandweiss. Fort Worth, Tex.: Amon Carter Museum, New York: Harry N. Abrams, 1991, 17–47.

———. *Reading American Photographs: Images as History: Mathew Brady to Walker Evans*. New York: Hill and Wang, 1989.

Union Guide to Photograph Collections of the Pacific Northwest. Portland: Oregon Historical Society, 1978.

Vanderbilt, Paul. *Guide to the Special Collections of Prints and Photographs in the Library of Congress.* Washington, D.C.: Government Printing Office, 1955.

Welling, William. *Collector's Guide to Nineteenth-Century Photographs.* New York: Collier-Macmillan, 1976.

———. *Photography in America: The Formative Years 1839–1900.* 1978. Reprint. Albuquerque: University of New Mexico Press, 1987.

Werge, John. *The Evolution of Photography.* 1890. Reprint. New York: Arno Press, 1973.

Willis-Thomas, Deborah. *Black Photographers, 1840–1940: An Illustrated Bio-bibliography.* New York: Garland, 1985.

———. *An Illustrated Bio-Bibliography of Black Photographers, 1940–1988.* New York: Garland, 1989.

Wilson, Edward L., ed. *Wilson's Cyclopaedic Photography: A Complete Handbook of the Terms, Processes, Formulae and Appliances Available in Photography, Arranged in Cyclopaedic Form for Ready Reference.* New York: Edward L. Wilson, 1894.

Wolfman, Augustus, comp. *Wolfman Report on the Photographic and Imaging Industry in the United States.* New York: Diamandis Communications, 1988, 1989.

Wolfman, Augustus, and Lydia Wolfman, comps. *Wolfman Report on the Photographic Industry in the United States.* New York: Modern Photography Magazine and ABC Leisure Magazines, 1952 (and subsequent annual editions).

Wood, John, ed. *America and the Daguerreotype.* Iowa City: University of Iowa Press, 1991.

———. *The Daguerreotype: A Sesquicentennial Celebration.* Iowa City: University of Iowa Press, 1989.

Zeitlin, Steven J., Amy J. Kotkin, and Holly Cutting Baker. *A Celebration of American Family Folklore: Tales and Traditions from the Smithsonian Collection.* 1982. Reprint. Cambridge, Mass.: Yellow Moon Press, 1992.

Zimmerman, Patricia R. "Filming Adventures in Beauty: Pictorialism, Amateur Cinematography, and the Filmic Pleasures of the Nuclear Family from 1897 to 1923." *Afterimage* 14 (December 1986), 8–11.

Periodicals

This checklist of periodicals is divided into three categories. Listed first are nineteenth- and early-twentieth-century photographic periodicals for primary research. The second category of primary materials consists of contemporary, mass-market periodicals aimed at amateur photographers. The third category consists of journals that analyze photography and photographic aesthetics and occasionally contain articles relevant to photography as an artifact of popular culture. A more extensive annotated list of periodicals appears in Beaumont Newhall's "Photography."

Nineteenth- and Early Twentieth-Century Periodicals

American Amateur Photographer. Brunswick, Maine, and New York, 1889–1907.
The American Annual of Photography. Boston and New York, 1887–1953.
American Journal of Photography. Philadelphia, 1879–1900.

American Journal of Photography and the Allied Arts and Sciences. New York, 1852–1867.

American Photography. Boston, 1907–1953.

Anthony's Photographic Bulletin. New York, 1870–1902.

Camera. Philadelphia, 1897–1953.

Camera Craft. San Francisco, 1900–1942.

Camera Notes. New York, 1897–1903.

Camera Work. New York, 1903–1917.

The Daguerreian Journal. New York, 1850–1851.

Humphery's Journal of Photography and the Allied Arts and Sciences. New York, 1852–1870.

The Philadelphia Photographer. Philadelphia, 1864–1888.

Photo-Beacon. Chicago, 1889–1907.

Photo Era Magazine. Boston, 1898–1932.

Photograms of the Year. London, 1895–1925.

The Photographic and Fine Art Journal. New York, 1854–1860.

The Photographic Art Journal. New York, 1851–1853.

Photographic Journal. London, 1853–

Photographic Journal of America. Philadelphia, 1915–1923.

Photographic Mosaics. Philadelphia and New York, 1866–1901.

Photographic Times. New York, 1871–1915.

Photo-Miniature. New York and London, 1899–1936.

Wilson's Photographic Magazine. Philadelphia, 1889–1914.

Contemporary Mass-Market Periodicals

American Photo. New York, 1990– .

American Photographer. New York, 1978–1989.

Camera. Lucerne, Switzerland, 1922–1981.

Camera Thirty-Five. New York, 1957–1982.

Modern Photography. New York, 1937– .

Popular Photography. Chicago, 1937– .

U.S. Camera. New York, 1935–1971.

Contemporary Analytical Periodicals

Afterimage: A Publication of the Visual Studies Workshop. Rochester, N.Y.: 1972– .

Creative Camera. London, 1963– .

Exposure: Journal of the Society for Photographic Education. New York, 1963– .

History of Photography. London, 1977– .

Image: Journal of Photography and Motion Pictures of the International Museum of Photography at George Eastman House. Rochester, N.Y., 1952– .

October. Cambridge, Mass., 1976– .

Studies in the Anthropology of Visual Communication. Philadelphia, 1973–1979.

Studies in Visual Communication. Philadelphia, 1980–1985.

Alexander Gardner's photo setup, 1867. Courtesy of the Library of Congress.

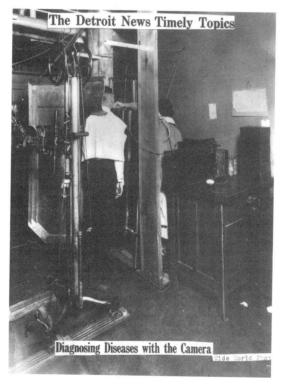

Diagnosing diseases with a camera, ca. 1920. Courtesy of the Library of Congress.

Theodor Horydczak. Courtesy of the Library of Congress.

Photo by Theodor Horydczak. Courtesy of the Library of Congress.

Camera advertisement. Courtesy of George Eastman House

Margaret Bourke-White. Courtesy of the Library of Congress.

Nikon camera. Courtesy of FreeFoto.com

Speed trap camera. Courtesy of FreeFoto.com

Press photographers. Courtesy of FreeFoto.com

POPULAR LITERATURE AND BEST SELLERS

Perry Frank and Suzanne Ellery Greene

Best-selling books have attracted widely varying amounts of attention from scholars depending on their perceived literary values, the predilections of commentators, and changing modes of cultural analysis. Those best sellers determined to have literary merit have been written about many times over and generally are still widely read. A few books, judged to typify the thought of a particular period or considered to have played some major role in influencing the course of history, are read as historical documents. However, until the second half of the twentieth century the vast majority of best-selling novels and nonfiction works had been relegated to the category of popular entertainment and considered unworthy of serious study. Over the last several decades the growing interest in popular culture as a field of scholarly inquiry has sparked the study of best sellers as they reflect and influence audiences. Recent scholarship has also focused on the interrelated elements of the production, distribution, and readership of best sellers as a complex social process.

The definition of the "best seller" is itself problematic. The manner in which sales are counted and best-seller lists are compiled can confuse understanding of a book's impact. Frank Luther Mott's classic study, *Golden Multitudes* (1947), defines a best seller as a book with sales equaling 1 percent of the total population at the beginning of the decade during which it appeared. However, this formula does not take into account sales over time or a book's likely dissemination through libraries or informal networks of readers. Likewise, lists compiled by year can eliminate those that sold well over a multiyear period, as with Benjamin Spock's ubiquitous *Baby and Child Care* (1946), or books that enjoyed a revival of interest, as is happening in 2002 with J.R.R. Tolkein's *Lord of the Rings* trilogy (1954–1955). Also, the proliferation of outlets makes it increasingly difficult to make an accurate count. Finally, the interpenetration of book markets with film, television, various other electronic media, and even museums, theme parks, malls, and consumer products has escalated since the 1960s. As a result, it is increasingly difficult to know if the impact of a best seller comes from reading the book or gleaning its message from the general gestalt.

For these reasons, the term "best seller" is used in this chapter in a colloquial rather than a strict technical sense to include a number of different sales patterns—rapid sales for a short period of time, steady sales over time, revived sales after a dormant period, or sales in conjunction with dissemination through other media, such as film adaptations. The popularity of a "best-selling" author or type of book may also rest on common themes or style in many books, accounting for the influence of genre or cycles. The common denominator is that the message of a book or literary cycle permeates a large segment of the population, and can therefore be said to both impact and reflect the culture in which it is read.

This brief overview describes the types of books that were popular in the United States from the colonial times to the present and will be a guide to reference works and resources most useful to those who wish to study best sellers more thoroughly. Although the Bible, several cookbooks, and a few other reference works have outsold most other books in the United States, these are excluded from this study. All other fiction and nonfiction books are considered. Specific types of genre fiction such as the mystery and the romance are mentioned here as they relate to the best-seller phenomenon; however, since these forms are treated elsewhere in this volume, this chapter will focus on the best seller across genres.

HISTORICAL OUTLINE

The first press in America opened in 1638 in Cambridge, Massachusetts, in conjunction with Harvard College. Its early output consisted of almanacs, sermons, catechisms, and *The Whole Booke of Psalmes*, generally known as *The Bay Psalm Book* (1640). Most books were imported from England, and booksellers reported sales of romances, collections of poetry, school books, and religious books. By the 1660s, American presses had begun to publish books in large enough editions and of sufficient general interest that their products began to gain a wide circulation. Religious books dominated the market, while books about peculiarities of the New World, especially tales of captivity among the Indians, were also popular.

Traditionally, the first American best seller is said to be *The Day of Doom*, an account of the final judgment day written by Michael Wigglesworth in 1662 and printed by Samuel Green in Cambridge. Even a century later, some school children were required to memorize the seemingly endless stanzas about people doomed to an eternity in hell and the lucky few who were chosen by God for heavenly bliss. In 1664 the first of Richard Baxter's four-volume collection of sermons, *A Call to the Unconverted*, appeared. These works were translated by John Eliot for circulation among local Indian tribes. Books such as *The Pilgrim's Progress* by John Bunyan, reprinted in Cambridge in 1681, *Husbandry Spiritualized* (1709) by John Flavel, an anonymous *History of the Holy Jesus* (1745), and James Hervey's *Meditations and Contemplations*, published in Philadelphia in 1750, mark the continued appeal of religious subjects.

The Captivity and Restoration of Mary Rowlandson (1682) and John Williams's *The Redeemed Captive* (1707) exemplify the popular captivity tales. Sensational stories complete with massacres, survival through various sorts of cleverness, and eventual return home, all punctuated by Christian devotion, made lively reading for hard-working colonists who felt threatened by the wilderness outside of their small towns.

As the colonial period progressed, literary concerns grew wider and the philosophical points of view of the authors became more varied. During the 1740s, American editions of Samuel Richardson's sentimental and didactic tale *Pamela* (1744) and Alexander Pope's *Essay on Man* (1747) were best sellers. The decade before the Revolution was marked by the appearance of political best sellers representing diverse points of view: John Dickinson's conservative *Letters from a Farmer in Pennsylvania* (1768), a treatise entitled *Conciliation with America* (1775) written by Edmund Burke, and Thomas Paine's provocative *Common Sense* (1776).

Many of the best sellers that were published from the 1770s came to be considered classics, and despite the Revolution, the majority were by English authors. These include such novels as *The Vicar of Wakefield* (1772) by Oliver Goldsmith, *Clarissa* (1786) by Samuel Richardson, and *Tristram Shandy* (1774) by Laurence Sterne. *Charlotte Temple* (1793, American edition), among the first of a long cycle of novels by and about women, was written by Susanna Rowson, an Englishwoman who spent much of her life in America. Poetry such as William Cowper's *The Task* (1787), and an edition of Robert Burns's *Poems* sold well. Thomas Paine's *Age of Reason* (1794) and Benjamin Franklin's *Autobiography* (1794) were both widely read. *The Federalist* (1788), arguing for the adoption of the new constitution, had a large audience. The popularity of Jonathan Edwards's *Sinners in the Hands of an Angry God* (1741) and John Fox's *Book of Martyrs* (1793) indicate that religion had not been forgotten, although it was less central than it had been a century earlier. It is quite evident that the readers of best sellers in the early Republic had a wide range of interests, were heavily influenced by British literary culture, and also read many American products.

History and heroism dominated the best sellers of the first three decades of the nineteenth century. Books written in America about American subjects predominated for the first time. Parson Mason Weems's *Life of Washington* (1800), in which the cherry tree story first appeared, was received enthusiastically, even in rural areas where it was carried by itinerant book peddlers. Washington Irving's *History of New York* (1809) and his later *Sketch Book* (1819) popularized American life and lore. Jane Porter's novels about patriotic heroes, *Thaddeus of Warsaw* (1804) and *Scottish Chiefs* (1810), helped prepare the way for the enormous success of the tales of adventure and nationalism by Sir Walter Scott, including *Guy Mannering* (1815), *Rob Roy* (1818), *Ivanhoe* (1820), and *Kennilworth* (1821). James Fennimore Cooper created a prototypical American hero in *The Spy* (1821) and the Leatherstocking stories beginning with *The Pioneers* in 1823. *The Last of the Mohicans* (1826) and *The Deerslayer* (1841) were almost as widely read as Scott's novels. The popularity of Scott and Cooper continued through the century.

Book sales exploded in the 1830s and 1840s, in part because the absence of an international copyright law encouraged the practice of issuing cheap reprints. First in newspaper format, then in paperbound books, best sellers became available in twenty-five-cent editions. From this time on, inexpensive editions of popular books were within the reach of even working-class readers. Charles Dickens was an enormously popular author whose novels of sentiment and social reform were snatched up on issue. His sickly children, impoverished innocents, and evil rich men reduced thousands of American readers to tears and helped prepare the way for the American-produced, sentimental novels that followed.

Imitators of Scott, Cooper, and Dickens abounded. The best known were Joseph Hold Ingraham, who wrote thrillers such as *The Pirates of the Gulf* (1836), religious novels such as *The Prince of the House of David* (1855), and novels about life in the city such as *Jemmy Daly, or the Little News Vendor* (1843). Historical novels such as *The Last Days of Pompeii* (1834) by Edward Bulwer-Lytton and *The Three Musketeers* (1844) by Alexandre Dumas were popular, as were histories such as Jared Sparks's *Life of Washington* (1839), William Prescott's *Conquest of Mexico* (1843), and Thomas Macaulay's *History of England* (1849). Maria Monk's *Awful Disclosures* (1836), an anti-Catholic tract purporting to reveal the scandals of life in a nunnery, added a bit of sensationalism to the best-seller list.

Mid-nineteenth-century America supported the rise of the sentimental domestic novel, often written by and about women and their travails, including poverty, prostitution, and drunken and perfidious husbands and lovers. Nathaniel Hawthorne complained that "America is now wholly given over to a d—d mob of scribbling women." Some of the more famous products of this group are *The Wide, Wide World* (1850) by Susan Warner and *The Lamplighter* (1854) by Maria S. Cummins. T. S. Arthur's *Ten Nights in a Bar-Room* (1854), written in a similar vein, was used as a temperance tract by various prohibition societies. Mrs. E.D.E.N. Southwick, the most prolific of the best-selling women authors, wrote over sixty novels. The most popular of these, *Ishmael* (1864) and *Self-Raised* (1864), each sold over two million copies.

While the sentimental novels dealt with many of the problems that concerned the nation's reformers, the most divisive issue of all was largely ignored in the best sellers of the day. *Uncle Tom's Cabin* (1852) by Harriet Beecher Stowe was an exception in directly attacking the slavery system. The book converted many previously disinterested readers into active opponents of slavery, standing as one of the few novels that has had a major, immediate impact on popular thought. Despite her unusual topic, Stowe's heart-rending episodes and moralistic subtext closely resemble those of the other sentimental writers. The book gained power and popularity by emphasizing the physical brutality and destruction of families inherent in slavery while omitting the questions of political rights and racial equality that were of pressing concern primarily to blacks and racial abolitionists.

The period after the Civil War produced some of the most enduring best sellers and also set the stage for popular genres that persist to the present day. One of the best-known and best-selling authors of the period, Mark Twain, owed his popularity to his ability to spoof the type of pieties found in the sentimental literature that abounded. *Innocents Abroad*, his first book (1869), was a best seller, as were *The Adventures of Tom Sawyer* (1876), *Adventures of Huckleberry Finn* (1884), and *Life on the Mississippi* (1883). Twain's books were sold by door-to-door subscription, a distribution method that worked well for a dispersed rural population and was profitable. His reputation grew through reprintings of early sketches in newspapers, and was sustained throughout his life by appearances on the lecture circuit. With Dickens, he was among the first "celebrity" authors who were able to hype their books through other media, anticipating by over one-hundred years

Louisa May Alcott. Courtesy of the Library of Congress

the public performances and endorsements that make a best-selling author's reputation today.

The receptiveness of the post-Civil War population to more realistic fiction was expressed in another very different best seller for youth, *Little Women* (1868), by Louisa May Alcott. Based in part on her own life as daughter of the high-minded if impractical reformer Bronson Alcott, the book offered a picture of a genteel struggle with poverty that resonated with many readers and also dramatized alternatives to stereotypical gender roles. The book is still read with pleasure.

At the same time that Twain and Alcott were experimenting with realism, a new type of popular fiction arose in conjunction with low-cost book production that encouraged wide readership. In 1860 the publishing house of Beadle and Adams brought out the "dime novel," a paperback adventure story drawing on the legacy of Cooper, the captivity narratives, and English detective stories to create tales of heroes and villains engaged in activities far from the experiences of most readers. Through Beadle and several other publishing houses, the cycle flourished and gave us "Deadwood Dick" and "Buffalo Bill." These books, which were created by teams of writers working within strict formula conventions, appealed to a heterogeneous group of readers and foreshadowed the pulp fiction of the twentieth century. Although few, if any, of the books were individual best sellers under Mott's criteria, study of their readership, production, and content sheds light on the best-seller phenomenon and the role of popular fiction in the culture and the economy.

As America moved into the Gilded Age following the Civil War, books purporting to teach the secret of success poured from the presses and were widely read. Several commentators have noted that the homilies avoided concrete advice about business dealings and advised youth to rely on sound moral principles and hard work. The fictional counterpart was expressed in the novels of Horatio Alger, who wrote scores of stories about impoverished street urchins who rose from "rags to riches"—i.e., middle-class respectability—through following these precepts. His best-known tale, *Ragged Dick* (1867), is probably the only one to make Mott's all-time best-seller list, but the books were passed from child to child and undoubtedly had a significant impact until well into the twentieth century.

Reform tracts and utopias were also important as the nation took stock of the dramatic changes wrought by urbanization and industrialization. Two best sellers in these categories that are still appreciated are Henry George's *Progress and Poverty* (1879) and Edward Bellamy's *Looking Backward* (1888). The first, a radical economic tract attacking the capitalist system, paved the way for many economic treatises, although most did not become best sellers. *Looking Backward*, Bellamy's too-optimistic utopia of life in 2000, has been the inspiration for many popular fantasy and science fiction works manipulating time and place.

The period spanning the late nineteenth and early twentieth centuries is marked by the diversity of popular forms, with no one mode predominating. Sentimental and domestic novels, religious books, local-color stories, historical fiction and nonfiction, adventures, some sensationalist exposés, and detective stories were all popular during these decades. Despite the fact that very few of these are read today, even by students of literary history, the period is important in that it established the broad categories of fictional best sellers as they have continued into the twenty-first century.

While Laura Jean Libbey produced sentimental domestic novels of the prewar sort, a new group of "glad-books" began to appear. Many centered on a child character and became children's classics, for example, *Rebecca of Sunnybrook Farm* (1904) by Kate Douglas Wiggin and *Pollyanna* (1913) by Eleanor Porter. These and others by Grace Livingston Hill and Gene Stratton-Porter, called "molasses fiction" by their critics, remained best-selling types through World War I.

Religious novels like *St. Elmo* (1867) by Augusta J. Evans and *Barriers Burned Away* (1872) by Edward Payson Roe prefigured enormously popular writers like Lew Wallace, whose *Ben-Hur* (1880) sold over a million copies through the Sears, Roebuck and Company mail-order catalog alone. Charles Sheldon's *In His Steps* (1897), which purported to show how contemporary people would change their lives if they really followed Christ's teachings, sold even more copies. Harold Bell Wright, in books like *The Shepherd of the Hills* (1907) and *The Eyes of the World* (1914), combined religious morality with the strenuous outdoor life and a love story, thus constructing a successful formula that incorporated the most popular fictional themes. Lloyd C. Douglas, who later produced *The Magnificent Obsession* (1929) and *The Robe* (1942), followed this tradition.

Not all historical novels were religious. Winston Churchill's historical stories such as *Richard Carvel* (1899) and *The Crisis* (1904) made him one of the most popular writers of the turn of the century. Owen Wister's *The Virginian* (1902) created the character that became a prototype for the classic cowboy hero. Zane Grey, whose more than fifty westerns were read by millions, remained on the best-seller lists from the appearance of *The Spirit of the Border* in 1906 through 1924 with *The Call of the Canyon*. Writers like H. Rider Haggard and Rudyard Kipling placed their adventures in the more exotic settings of Africa and India. Jules Verne's fantasies about outer space and the world beneath the sea moved even farther from the familiar. Mystery stories like those of Arthur Conan Doyle, the English creator of Sherlock Holmes, and Mary Roberts Rinehart, who prefigured the thriller, marked the rise of yet another sort of escapist adventure.

Two new kinds of literature caused an enormous sensation in the early twentieth century. The muckrakers' exposés of corrupt business, industry, and political practices were read avidly. Books like Upton Sinclair's *The Jungle* (1906), which chronicled the abuses of the meatpacking industry, shook the public. More sensationally, Elinor Glyn's *Three Weeks* (1907) attracted both enthusiastic readers and an official banning with its vivid account of an affair between an Englishman and a princess.

Popular fiction became more overt in questioning traditional values and behavior during the 1920s. Readers turned away from political writings to popular fiction that commented on the meaning of life in a vastly changed world, overtly or implicitly. Sinclair Lewis's *Main Street* (1920) and *Babbitt* (1922) dramatized the stultifying effect of small-town provincialism. More typical of the best-selling novels of the decade were *The Sheik* (1921) by Edith Hull and *The Private Life of Helen of Troy* (1925) by John Erskine, in which the characters were not bound by the constraints of contemporary life. Fredrick O'Brien's popular books about the South Sea islands also suggest a taste for adventure. Other nonfiction best sellers were histories, biographies, fad books such as *Diet and Health* (1924) by Lulu Hunt Peters, and crossword puzzle books.

The 1930s saw a swing back to historical novels. The leading characters almost invariably stood as successful examples of rugged American individualism. In books like *Drums Along the Mohawk* (1936) by Walter D. Edmonds and *Northwest Passage* (1937) by Kenneth Roberts, the heroes prevailed against overwhelming odds by dint of their hard work and intelligence, perhaps reflecting the hopes of beleaguered Depression-era readers. Two epics headed the best-seller lists for two consecutive years: *Anthony Adverse* by Hervey Allen in 1933 and 1934, and *Gone with the Wind* by Margaret Mitchell in 1936 and 1937. An obvious reach for stability and a moral compass is evident in novels like Pearl Buck's *The Good Earth* (1931) and Lloyd C. Douglas's *Green Light* (1935). Despite the severity of the Depression and the rising tide of Nazism in Germany, neither fiction nor nonfiction best sellers engaged these problems deeply until the very end of the decade.

Best-seller lists from World War II to the present are notable for their variety of topics and treatments—psychology, history, politics, business, and sex are all represented on both fiction and nonfiction lists, and types range from high modernism (*Lolita*, Vladimir Nabokov, 1958) and solid history (*Truman*, David McCullough, 1992), to sensational sex (*Valley of the Dolls*, Jacqueline Susann, 1966), genre fiction (*The Spy Who Came in from the Cold*, John le Carré, 1964), and an amazing array of self-help books (*The Power of Positive Thinking*, Norman Vincent Peale, 1952–1955; *Sylvia Porter's Money Book*, 1975). Several major trends can be identified.

From the appearance of *Mein Kampf* on the list of 1939 through the 1950s, both fiction and nonfiction lists reveal a strong interest in World War II and subjects related to it. Other than that, the best sellers reflected few political concerns until after 1955, when *On the Beach* (1955) by Neville Shute, *Dr. Zhivago* (1958) by Boris Pasternak, *Exodus* (1959) by Leon Uris, and *The Ugly American* (1959) by William Lederer and Eugene Burdick heralded increasing awareness of America in the world. The Watergate affair was the subject of several best sellers, two by the reporters Carl Bernstein and Bob Woodward, *All the President's Men* (1974) and *The Final Days* (1976), as well as several by participants in the scandal such as John Dean and Charles Colson.

Another strong trend since World War II is the increasing incorporation of explicit sex into mainstream, popular books. Perhaps taking inspiration from the experimental novels of elite writers such as James Joyce and D. H. Lawrence, popular novelists such as Hermoun Wouk started including descriptions of the sex act in works such as *Marjorie Morningstar* (1955). Sex also figured heavily in the genre of detective/crime novels, which were helped in their sales by their suggestive covers. In the nonfiction realm, A. C. Kinsey's *Sexual Behavior in the Human Male* (1948) and William E. Masters and Virginia E. Johnson's *Human Sexual Response* (1966) were both best sellers. Continuing in this line are Alex Comfort's hugely successful *The Joy of Sex*, an illustrated manual published in 1973, and a more sociological study, *The Hite Report: A Nationwide Study of Female Sexuality* (1974) by Shere Hite.

The historical romantic adventure story, a leading type of best seller for so long, declined in favor of fiction based on contemporary life. Sometimes presented as novels of manners, these books both modeled and critiqued the increasingly affluent life of the postwar middle class (*A Rage to Live*, John O'Hara, 1949; *The Man in the Gray Flannel Suit*, Sloan Wilson, 1955). The hard-boiled detective novels of Dashiell Hammett, Raymond Chandler, Mickey Spillane, and many others sold millions of copies in the 1940s and 1950s. The morally ambiguous "hard-boiled" hero navigating a recognizable but safely exotic underworld persists as a cultural icon. A new favorite, contemporary suspense stories, arose in the 1970s—for example, *Airport* (Arthur Hailey, 1969) and *The Salzburg Connection* (Helen McInnes, 1974). Many best sellers, like Peter Benchley's sensational *Jaws* (1974), were made into films, further hyping the popularity of the book. Dissemination of best-seller stories and ideologies through film and television adaptations has become commonplace and is a major marketing strategy to boost or sustain sales.

During the 1970s and 1980s a few authors gained extraordinary popularity and a loyal following. Among them are Judith Krantz, Robert Ludlum, Danielle Steel, and Louis L'Amour. John Le Carré, whose caustic spy novels put him on the best-seller lists with his first novel, *The Spy Who Came in from the Cold* (1964), continued to sell well. James Michener's massive historical novels, *Centennial* (1974), *Chesapeake* (1978), *The Covenant* (1980), *Space* (1982), and *Poland* (1983) were all best sellers. The horror stories of Stephen King, *The Dead Zone* (1979), *Firestarter* (1980), *Different Seasons* (1982), *Pet Semetary* (1983), and *It* (1986), were overwhelmingly successful. Novelists more in the elite tradition, including Norman Mailer, E. L. Doctorow, Kurt Vonnegut, Jr., and Saul Bellow also made the best-seller lists in the 1970s and 1980s, but less frequently than the more prolific authors cited above.

The domination of the fiction lists by a few popular novelists was even more striking in the 1990s. During that decade Danielle Steel made the best-seller list an astonishing twenty-one times; Steel, along with Steven King, Robert Ludlum,

Anne Rice, John Grisham, Michael Crichton, and Judith Kranz produced nearly half of the best sellers over the decade, with multiple novels by a handful of relative newcomers accounting for most of the rest. Film versions of some of these books (*The Firm*, John Grisham, 1991), as well as television credits (Crichton is the creator of the popular *E.R.*) undoubtedly helped sell these authors. Other factors include massive advertising campaigns, book-signing tours, and the sheer volume of work produced by each writer.

However, the basic appeal of this group of writers to a large cross-section of the American public is hard to escape. While each of the writers cited has an individual flavor or niche, common factors include topicality, sensational and exotic settings and plot, and models for gender and life-style choices. In Danielle Steel's romantic stories, glamorous surroundings do not shield women from common problems of the heart; Steven King's flawed protagonists find their way through an ambiguous social and moral environment; and Michael Crichton dramatizes national issues related to technology and globalization. Current and future scholarship on these writers, as well as study of the dynamics behind best sellers as a phenomenon, will shed more light on the meaning of these recent trends.

Nonfiction best-seller lists of the postwar period include many works relating to politics (*The Gathering Storm*, Winston Churchill, 1948; *A Thousand Days*, Arthur Schlesinger, Jr., 1965; *Breach of Faith*, Theodore White, 1975) and faith (*Life Is Worth Living*, Fulton J. Sheen, 1953; *Angels: God's Secret Agents*, Billy Graham, 1975). Some serious social commentaries also found their way onto the list, for example, *The Status Seekers* (Vance Packard, 1959).

In the 1960s and 1970s the lists began to include more self-help books, many focusing on sex, relationships and gender roles, health, and success (*Sex and the Single Girl*, Helen Gurley Brown, 1962; *TM: Discovering Energy and Overcoming Stress*, Harold H. Bloomfield, 1975; *Smart Women, Foolish Choices*, Connell Cowan and Melvyn Kinder, 1985). Books such as *In Search of Excellence: Lessons from America's Best-Run Companies* (Thomas J. Peters and Robert H. Waterman, 1982) confirmed the longstanding American interest in formulas for success; the book spawned a television series and seminars for business people. Best-selling nonfiction of the 1970s and 1980s also included biographies of the famous—sometimes infamous—as well as autobiographies and a new genre of fictionalized histories (*Eleanor and Franklin*, Joseph P. Lash, 1971; *Iacocca: An Autobiography*, with William Novak, 1985; and *In Cold Blood*, Truman Capote, 1966).

During the 1990s books of these types proliferated (*Eight Weeks to Optimum Health*, Andrew Weil, 1997; *Couplehood*, Paul Reiser, 1994). Sometimes the categories seemed to conflate with one another and with fictional works, as celebrities offered their life experiences as guidance (*My Story*, The Duchess of York, 1996); biographers used fictional techniques and possibly sources (*Diana: Her True Story*, Andrew Morton, 1997); and a variety of gurus claimed to have the secret of success and happiness (*Homecoming: Reclaiming and Championing Your Inner Child*, John Bradshaw, 1990; *More Wealth Without Risk*, Charles Givens, 1992; *The Seven Spiritual Laws of Success*, Deepak Chopra, 1995; *The Book of Virtues*, William J. Bennett, 1994; and *The Art of Happiness*, the Dalai Lama and Howard C. Cutler, 1999). No doubt it will require much study and analysis to sort out the relationship of recent nonfiction best sellers to the American psyche.

Meanwhile, at the beginning of the twenty-first century, John Grisham's *The Brethren* (2001) reprises recent history by following the activities of three felonious judges imprisoned in Florida during a contested presidential election. Historian David McCullough's *Adams*, helped by aggressive promotion and the engaging speaking style of the author, was a best seller. The children's books by a British author based on a character with supernatural powers but reality-based problems called Harry Potter (*Harry Potter and the Sorcerer's Stone*, J. K. Rowling) created a sensation when published in 1998. The book has topped the paperback and children's best-seller lists in the 2000s and spawned a movie of the same title that led the box office during the 2001 Christmas season. The magical tale is credited with sparking a revival of interest in Tolkein's convoluted *Lord of the Rings* trilogy, which was on some best-seller lists in 2002 and has also been made into a "blockbuster" movie.

REFERENCE WORKS

A wide variety of reference works are available to scholars working on the best seller, although information is scattered among many different kinds of sources and the researcher must dig a bit to find some kinds of data and make connections. However, a few classic and newer sources provide the clear starting point for any study of American best seller.

Frank Luther Mott's 1947 analysis of best-selling books, *Golden Multitudes*, is the best single source for information on earlier books. Mott includes a rationale for his choices of best sellers published before sales figures began to be officially compiled at the end of the nineteenth century. While his "1 percent of readers" method of identifying best sellers does not capture books that fail to sell in great numbers upon publication but nevertheless have tremendous staying power, he makes up for this to some degree by providing a list of "runners up" in an appendix. Although his lists have been reproduced in many places, Mott's book remains valuable for his insightful comments on American reading habits and the publishing industry. James D. Hart's *The Popular Book*, published in 1950, is another survey that combines listings and historically organized analyses of best sellers. His list is selective and is not based on specific sales criteria, but his study includes an exhaustive bibliography for each chapter.

Another basic reference in the field is *80 Years of Best Sellers* by Alice Payne Hackett and James Henry Burke. Hackett and Burke list the top ten best sellers for each year from 1895 to 1975, followed by a brief account of the social context of the period. Separation of fiction and nonfiction lists begins in 1917. The reference includes the total sales figures for the top best sellers and separate lists of novelty books, home reference books, cookbooks, juveniles, mysteries, religious novels, and westerns. The book contains a valuable bibliography of articles on best sellers, although the citations for the later decades are incomplete.

Increased interest has led to some new sources and approaches, although none that attempt the comprehensive lists described above. *American Best Sellers: A Reader's Guide to Popular Fiction* (1989), by Karen Hinckley and Barbara Hinckley, is a comprehensive listing of best-selling hardcover fiction from 1965 to 1985 based on the *World Almanac*'s annual report. Entries are arranged alphabetically by author and include short descriptions, publishing information, biographical information, and movie tie-ins. The book contains analyses of categories, characters, themes, and trends. John Bear's *The #1 New York Times Bestseller* (1992) catalogs the 484 books that have made the *Times* best-seller list since its debut in 1942 and includes interesting facts about the works.

Most recently, Michael Korda, novelist and Simon & Schuster executive, has produced *Making the List: A Cultural History of the American Best Seller, 1900–1999* (2001). Korda's compendium includes the annual fiction and nonfiction lists compiled by *Publisher's Weekly* grouped by decade, along with a breezy overview of social and literary trends. In an introduction and epilogue the author provides anecdotal commentary on the publishing industry, concluding tenuously that "the more things change, the more they stay the same." The book is very handy for analyzing and comparing best-selling trends by decade through the twentieth century. However, his compilation is limited to those books that made the annual best-seller lists, leaving aside the many books that topped weekly charts. The usefulness of the volume to the scholar is marred by an incomplete and virtually microscopic index, and the text no doubt reflects Korda's own publishing role and goals.

A number of sources list books and/or authors and provide very brief information on each. These would provide a useful starting place for facts on a particular writer or best seller. Listing both books and authors are James D. Hart's *The Oxford Companion to American Literature* (1983), which has been updated several times, and *American Authors and Books, 1640–1940* (1943) by William J. Burke and Will D. Howe. Material on recent writers can be found in *Contemporary Authors: A Bio-Bibliographical Guide to Current Authors and Their Works*. Volume 1 was published in 1962, and a cumulative index appears regularly. A new compendium, *Webster's Dictionary of American Authors* (1996), is very useful for research on popular fiction. It contains alphabetically organized biographical sketches, a list of major works, and a section on major groups, movements, and periodicals. The work includes many popular, best-selling authors and books.

American Studies: An Annotated Bibliography, edited by Jack Salzman, is another good resource for the study of popular literature through its extensive, annotated bibliography in the Literature subdivision of its Popular Culture section. Randy F. Nelson's *The Almanac of American Letters* (1981) is an entertaining and informative work, full of interesting anecdotes, odd facts, charts, dates, biographies, statistics, and essays, including one on best sellers, to supplement the more formal histories of American literature.

To aid the scholar working on a specific genre or author, a few specialized checklists and bibliographies have also been published. Albert Johannsen's *The House of Beadle and Adams* (1950–1962) includes an exhaustive list of dime and nickel novels issued by this nineteenth-century publisher. John Y. Cole's *Books in Action: The Armed Services Editions* (1984) is a guide to the special collection of popular military publications at the Library of Congress. *The Dime Novel Companion* (J. Randolph Cox, 2000) contains 1,200 entries on editors, characters, themes and the like, as well as a directory of libraries and museums with significant primary source collections.

Gene DeGruson's *Kansas Authors of Best Sellers: A Bibliography of the Works of Martin and Osa Johnson, Margaret Hill Carpenter, Charles M. Sheldon, and Harold Bell Wright* (1970) is another specialized source. Virginia Gerhardstein's 1981 update of *Dickinson's American Historical Fiction* provides an exhaustive checklist of the genre by period. Maxim Jakubowsky's edited volume, *100 Great Detectives* (1991) includes bibliographies and short essays by different authors. *Edgar Rice Burroughs*, edited by Robert B. Zeuschner (1996), by its own description offers an exhaustive bibliography of that popular early-century icon.

For more detailed information, one can go straight to the source, *Publishers Weekly*, which is published by R. R. Bowker and has reported on best sellers since 1912. The *New York Times* has also published a national list since 1942. Researchers who are interested in a specific genre or subject area will want to familiarize themselves with the many more specialized best-seller lists that are now available. *Publishers Weekly* itself breaks its list down into subject categories, including hardcover, paperback, and audio. Publications targeted to various professions or industries have their own lists. These would include periodicals like *Business Week*, which, naturally, ranks books related to business, and the *New Scientist*, which lists best sellers in the sciences. Amazon.com and other distributors also have lists; although these are obviously skewed by the type of clientele they attract, distributor information can give the researcher a quick feel for the market and can also be used to disaggregate the reading habits of different types of patrons.

A literary magazine, the *Bookman*, contains lists from 1895, when it began publication. In spite of inconsistent and confusing indexing and presentation of information on best sellers, *The Bowker Annual of Library and Book Trade Information* is the best single reference source on recent best sellers. Since the 1974 edition, the book has included a brief essay identifying trends and characteristics of best sellers. A bibliography of sources for making international comparisons can be found in another reference, *The Book Trade of the World* (1972–1984), edited by Sigfred Taubert and Peter Weidhaas. In four volumes, it includes basic information on the international book business and references for more detailed study.

Powerful electronic databases have dramatically extended the researcher's ability to identify and locate books pertaining to best sellers. Researchers seeking studies on specific best-selling authors or books should rely on the *Library of Congress Catalog* and two national bibliographic utilities, *WorldCat* and the *RLIN Catalog*. They provide cataloging information and locations for library materials in academic and public libraries throughout the country and abroad. The on-line version of *Books in Print*, while more limited, contains thumbnail sketches of its listings.

On-line periodical indexes include the *MLA International Bibliography* (1922–   ), and the *Periodicals Contents Index*, which lists articles published in periodicals from 1770 to 1990. The *Arts and Humanities Citations Index* searches for citations by matching names or titles appearing in humanities periodicals, including "little magazines" and book reviews; it is therefore an excellent source for locating reviews or gauging the popularity of works or authors. *Lexis-Nexis* indexes newspapers and trade publications (including *Publishers Weekly*). All of these resources are fee based and most researchers will need to use them through a university, public library, or other institution.

In addition, of course, the now ubiquitous free on-line search tools turn up an amazing variety of information on best sellers, not the least of which are the various best-seller lists. Search engines, which include Alta Vista, HotBot, and Excite, link to Web pages ranked by relevance. Subject directories such as Yahoo! and LookSmart group results into categories, usually alphabetically.

RESEARCH COLLECTIONS

The most useful secondary material can be found in any large library. The best sellers themselves may be more difficult to locate. Recent best sellers are held in the collections of most large public libraries. When that source is exhausted, researchers who have the luxury of time may obtain books through interlibrary loan.

Scholars who wish to work in one place with extensive collections have a number of options. Undoubtedly the richest resource for best sellers is the Library of Congress. The major reason for this is that since 1870 two copies of every copyrighted American book have been deposited in the library. Additionally, the Rare Book and Special Collections Divisions contain materials of special importance to best-seller research. These include the Armed Forces Edition Collection (an archival set of paperbacks published for the American Armed Forces, 1943–1947), the Big Little Book Collection, the Dell Paperback Collection (a virtually complete set from 1943), and the Pulp Fiction Collection. The New York Public Library is also a comprehensive resource. The library owns a collection of over 13,000 volumes of nineteenth-century American literature, as well as vast numbers of twentieth-century fictional works. Special efforts are being made to preserve these collections, especially through microfilming. The holdings are detailed in the New York Public Library's *Dictionary Catalog of the Research Libraries at the New York Public Library, 1911–1971* (1979).

Robert G. Sewell, in his article "Trash or Treasure? Pop Fiction in Academic and Research Libraries," presents a rationale for the acquisition of popular fiction as a primary source resource by academic libraries and describes numerous such collections. In most cases, however, these collections are limited to a specific type of "genre fiction," or publishers' series such as Big Little Books. Many, or most, of the volumes contained in these archives will not be best sellers in the strict sense of the term, although the holdings may be of general value to the scholar of popular literature.

The Center for Research Libraries in Chicago, whose catalogs and handbooks are available at member libraries throughout the nation, has several collections that might be useful in researching the best seller. The American Culture series consists of microfilm copies of 5,200 works published by 1876. The titles are listed in the *Bibliography of American Culture, 1493–1875* (1957), compiled by David R. Weimer. The center houses a 12,000-volume collection of American fiction on microfilm, the titles of which are listed in *American Fiction: A Contribution Towards Bibliography* (1957–1969) compiled by Lyle Wright. The center also owns a collection of nineteenth-century books and 40,000 volumes of children's literature. The Popular Culture Library at Bowling Green State University, the mecca of academic popular culture studies, has a collection of over 50,000 books, comic books, dime novels, Big Little Books, and mass paperbacks.

The Russel B. Nye Popular Culture Collection at Michigan State University, named after the noted scholar of popular culture, has especially noteworthy and relevant materials for best-seller research. These are available in the Special Collection Department of the library and are accessible through many useful finding aids. The University of Minnesota Library owns the Hess Collection, consisting of 70,000 dime and nickel novels published between 1860 and 1890, including an almost complete set of those listed in Albert Johannsen's previously cited *The*

House of Beadle and Adams (1950–1962). The Mugar Memorial Library at Boston University has a valuable research collection in its Twentieth-Century Archives, including manuscripts, journals, diaries, reviews, and correspondence, as well as published works on a number of best-selling twentieth-century authors.

HISTORY AND CRITICISM

This review of the history and criticism of best sellers covers major books, chapters in broader reference sources, and representative articles and dissertations. It is organized into several categories. The first cites the few collections of best-selling or popular works that have been published, since these will ground the beginning student and invariably contain critical commentary as well. The second category, also a logical starting point, includes histories and interpretive works on U.S. best sellers. A third subsection includes studies related to the production and reception of books. Such works focus on the publishing industry and public response.

Important or seminal works on particular types of best sellers such as mysteries or westerns are mentioned as they relate to the broader topic of the best seller; however, much more complete overviews of popular genres are contained in other chapters of this book. Biographies of individual authors and studies of specific best sellers are not included here, since they are readily identified through the indexes cited earlier.

Collections of Popular Literature

The few books that contain excerpts from best sellers do not deal with them exclusively, and most recent anthologies are intended specifically for students who are studying English as a second language. While not in themselves sufficient to provide the basis for new scholarship, all of these books contain interpretive material and can give the researcher an overview of the range of popular publications and an idea of how such texts can extend understanding of American life and thought.

America Through the Looking Glass: A Historical Reader in Popular Culture, edited by David Bruner, Robert D. Marcus, and Jorj Tilson, contains selections from best sellers and other popular writing, both fiction and nonfiction. These are organized chronologically and are selected to reflect the culture of their periods, although the majority of the material does not come from best sellers. *Understanding American History through Fiction*, edited by Warren A. Beck and Myles L. Clowers, also includes portions of best sellers and other fictional works organized around such topics as manifest destiny, slavery, American capitalism, and World War II.

One anthology, Donald McQuade and Robert Atwan's *Popular Writing in America* (1974), contains an extensive section of excerpts from best sellers, both fiction and nonfiction. Selections include not only standard excerpts from *Uncle Tom's Cabin* (1852) and *Poor Richard's Almanac* (1758), but also less common snippets from books such as *Tarzan of the Apes* (1914), Mickey Spillane's *I, the Jury* (1947), Mario Puzo's *The Godfather* (1969), Erich Segal's *Love Story* (1970), Emily Post's *Etiquette* (1923), and Dale Carnegie's *How to Win Friends and Influence People*

(1937). A recent anthology, *Retold American Classic Nonfiction* (1991), contains popular and sometimes best-selling iconic selections such as *Sinners in the Hands of an Angry God* (1741) and *Common Sense* (1776).

Interpretive Works

Except for the lack of anthologies, enough general work on overall patterns of best sellers exists to give the beginning student or researcher a sound start. Russel B. Nye's widely used book on the popular arts in America, *The Unembarrassed Muse* (1970), includes several chapters on popular literature. *Golden Multitudes* by Frank Luther Mott and *The Popular Book* by James D. Hart, cited above, survey and analyze popular literature from the colonial period until the time of their publication (1947 and 1950, respectively). Both include commentary on readership, distribution, and publishing trends, as well as on the best sellers themselves. Their extensive bibliographies are very useful.

Two major interpretive collections containing sections on popular literature have been published within the last fifteen years. *The Columbia Literary History of the United States* (1988), edited by Emory Elliott, Martha Banta, and Houston Baker, while largely canonical, includes some material on popular fiction. *The Columbia History of the American Novel* (1991), edited by Emory Elliott et al., is far more inclusive, and contains numerous essays on popular forms and genres. Another important reference work, the 4-volume *Encyclopedia of American Studies*, edited by George T. Kurian et al., contains several relevant entries, including "Popular Literature," by R. Gordon Kelly; "Popular Culture," by Tom M. Lansford; "Literature and Popular Culture," by Jim Cullen; "Science Fiction," by James Gilbert; and "Romance Novels," by Jaime Harker.

Q. D. Leavis's *Fiction and the Reading Public* (first published in 1932) compares best sellers of different periods and offers commentary on the patterns, styles, and contents of "literary" and "popular" books. Leo Gurko's *Heroes, Highbrows, and the Popular Mind* (1953) describes the most popular heroes of American popular literature and connects evolving trends to changing world conditions. His analysis is quite perceptive. On a less academic note, Geoffrey Bocca's *Best Sellers: A Nostalgic Celebration of the Less-Than-Great Books You Have Always Been Afraid to Admit You Loved* is both wide ranging and fun to read.

Bernard Rosenberg and David Manning White edited *Mass Culture: The Popular Arts in America* (1957), which includes a chapter on mass culture, formula, readers, and the role of paperback books. Another analytical book containing many insightful comments is Carl Bode's *The Half-World of American Culture* (1965), which uses examples of best sellers to make cross-country comparisons.

Literature, Popular Culture, and Society (1961), by Leo Lowenthal, offers a provocative analysis of popular culture from a sociological perspective. Robert Bingham Downs's collection of essays, *Famous American Books* (1971), consists of five-to-ten page studies of fifty books designed to illuminate the impact of books on the course of history. He includes a number of best sellers, from the early *Day of Doom* down through Ralph Nader's *Unsafe at Any Speed* (1965). His selections and analyses are quite good. *Popular Fiction and Social Change* (1984), a collection of theoretical and genre studies edited by Christopher Pawling, examines the ideological underpinnings of popular forms.

Leslie Fiedler's characteristically idiosyncratic *What Was Literature? Class, Culture, and Mass Society* (1982) examines elite and popular literary traditions and changing standards (including his own). In Part One, "Subverting the Standards," Fiedler probes the appeal of best sellers as purveyors of myth. His study is unusual in drawing on classical and Renaissance sources in supporting his analysis. Part Two, "Opening Up the Canon," traces the cultural influence of *Uncle Tom's Cabin* (1852) through *The Clansman* (1905), *Gone with the Wind* (1936), and *Roots* (1976). A more recent book, Resa L. Dudovitz's *The Myth of Superwoman: Women's Bestsellers in France and the United States* (1990), contains two sound chapters on the essence of the best seller and the institutions and cultural contexts that support it, both here and in France. The analysis is especially apt in the light of globalization and its cultural impact. Another book purporting to illuminate the distinctions between elite and popular art forms and readership by Harriett Hawkins, *Classics and Trash: Traditions and Taboos in High Literature and Popular Modern Genres* (1990), proves less useful. The book's argument lacks a clear historical or theoretical basis and forces conclusions into the service of class and gender-role generalizations that have become commonplace.

Political Mythology and Popular Fiction (1988), a collection of essays by political scientists edited by Ernest J. Yanarella and Lee Sigelman (1988), relates popular fiction to political theory and the societal institutions derived from it. The eight essays cover the western, children's literature, sports literature, historical novels, "middle-class" literature, small towns, war, and science fiction. The introduction reviews the myth and symbol approach and its critiques, concluding that only through heuristic analysis of cultural productions along with their audiences and supporting institutions can we use popular fiction to understand our ideals and values. The book contains a suggestive and far-reaching bibliography of works pertaining to the relationship of myth, politics, and popular fiction. John Storey's *Cultural Studies and the Study of Popular Culture: Theories and Methods* (1996), addresses the expressions of hegemony and power in works of popular fiction.

Some studies approach popular literature through a study of genre and its readers. One of the most important of these is John G. Cawelti's *Adventure, Mystery and Romance: Formula Stories as Art and Popular Culture* (1976). *Potboilers: Methods, Concepts and Case Studies in Popular Fiction* (1991), by Jerry Palmer, considers theories of understanding popular texts from a variety of methods. Janice A. Radway, in her influential *Reading the Romance: Women, Patriarchy, and Popular Literature* (1984), interviewed readers to understand the appeal of romances to fans.

One way of looking at the best seller is through its continuing impact in adaptations to stage, screen or television. A provocative interdisciplinary study by Jane Elizabeth Hendler, *Best Sellers and Their Film Adaptations in Postwar America* (2001), explores the reconfiguration of gender identity in the Cold War era through analysis of five widely disparate works, *From Here to Eternity* (James Jones, 1951), *Sayonara* (James Michener, 1954), *Giant* (Edna Ferber, 1952), *Auntie Mame* (Patrick Dennis, 1955), and *Peyton Place* (Grace Metalious, 1956). The reciprocal relationship of Hollywood and popular fiction is the subject of John Parris Springer's *Hollywood Fictions: The Dream Factory in American Popular Literature* (2000).

Period Studies

A number of good period studies exist, some focusing specifically on popular literature, others dealing more generally with the cultural life of a particular era. A work on the colonial period, Thomas Goddard Wright's *Literary Culture in Early New England, 1620–1730* (1920), contains a remarkable list of books held in public and private collections, good material on the Boston booksellers, and interesting information on the reading elite. Although the emphasis is on high culture, the book includes the information necessary to make comparisons between elite and popular literature. Russel B. Nye's *The Cultural Life of the New Nation, 1776–1830* (1960), contains a chapter entitled "The Quest for a National Literature," which concentrates on best sellers. The entire book provides a fine summary of the culture of the period. A more specialized study, Herbert Ross Brown's *The Sentimental Novel in America, 1789–1860* (1940), includes many best sellers in its analysis. Other studies of early American novels are *The Rise of the American Novel* (1948), by Alexander Cowie and *The Early American Novel* (1966), by Lily D. Loshe.

Several books treat best sellers of the mid-nineteenth century. A good starting place is Carl Bode's *The Anatomy of American Popular Culture, 1840–1861* (1959), a thorough study that includes a section on "popular print" that compares trends of that time with those of earlier periods. Bode considers both the works and their reception.

Two recent volumes consider the impact of popular literature related to the sectional conflict on mid-nineteenth century attitudes toward race relations, gender roles, politics, and individual values. Lyde Cullen Sizer's *The Political Work of Northern Women Writers and the Civil War, 1850–1872* (2000) examines the works of nine popular writers, including best-selling authors Lydia Maria Child, Harriett Beecher Stowe, E.D.E.N. Southworth, and Louisa May Alcott. *The Imagined Civil War: The Popular Literature of the North and South, 1861–1865* (2001), by Alice Fahs, looks at a broader range of popular publications but a narrower time period to explore the impact of the war on the publishing industry, reader interests, and literary forms.

Grant C. Knight wrote a study on the final years of the nineteenth century, *The Critical Period in American Literature, 1890–1900* (1951), which integrates the literary and social history of the time. Michael Denning's *Mechanic Accents: Dime Novels and Working-Class Culture in America* (1987) examines popular fiction and blue-collar life, arguing that reading habits became a status marker with the proliferation of cheap literature. *Easterns, Westerns, and Private Eyes: American Matters, 1870–1900* (1994), by Marcus Klein, locates the Ragged Dick cycle, along with versions of the western hero and the cynical private eye, in the massive changes and abuses of the Gilded Age. Forrest G. Robinson's *Having It Both Ways* (1993) explains the enormous popularity of nineteenth- and twentieth-century westerns in terms their ability to evoke, yet diffuse, the enduring tension between individual autonomy and communal authority that is central to a democratic society.

Myths and Mores in American Best Sellers, 1865–1965 (1985), by Ruth Miller Elson, examines the norms and values imparted by typical best sellers to their readers; topics include nature, gender roles, ethnic groups, religion, scholarship and the arts, success, and the law. A final chapter attempts to synthesize the main "selling points" of best sellers, concluding that most combine surface topicality and sensation with a reassuringly conservative world view. This book is insightful and entertaining; however, the author's large project necessitates a broad-brush approach. A more focused but decidedly less readable study of best sellers from the mid-nineteenth through the early twentieth centuries is Karol L. Kelley's *Models for the Multitudes: Social Values in the American Novel, 1850–1920* (1987). The book is based on a computer analysis of paradigms relating to success and gender roles derived from major interpretive works and applied to Mott's list for the selected period. Both the method and the conclusions are unclear, and the results appear not to correlate highly with interpretations accepted by a broad range of scholars. Erik Lofroth's excellent *A World Made Safe: Values in American Best Sellers, 1895–1920* (1983) contends that the temporal nature of the best seller makes it an indicator of values particular to an era.

More has been written about best sellers of the twentieth century than about those of the earlier periods, especially since 1980. A number of classic studies treat twentieth-century literature as a whole, but most are concerned with canonical or at least critically acclaimed works. A few best sellers by modernists such as Ernest Hemingway, William Faulkner, and Thomas Wolfe are included in some of these treatments, but the vast majority are not. For points of comparison it may be useful to look at standard works like Alfred Kazin's *On Native Grounds* (1942) and Malcolm Cowley's *The Literary Situation* (1954); both assume the ascendancy of elite literature, although the latter treats a broader range of authors than the former.

Although much of the material on best sellers since 1945 is in the form of reviews, journal articles, or studies of individual writers, an increasing number of books make a useful introduction to the period. Among these are *The Novel Now* (1967), by Anthony Burgess; *Recent American Fiction: Some Critical Views* (1963), edited by Joseph J. Waldmeir; *Working for the Reader* (1970), by book reviewer Herbert Mitgang; *A Question of Quality* (1976), edited by Louis Filler; and *Bright Book of Life* (1973), by Alfred Kazin.

A number of books analyze the degree to which twentieth-century best sellers reflect the society. Grant C. Knight's integration of literature and social history, *The Strenuous Age in American Literature* (1954), discusses many best sellers that appeared between 1900 and 1910 (1951). In *Novelists' America: Fiction as History, 1910–1940* (1969), Nelson Manfred Blake shows how a group of novels can be used to study social conditions and popular concerns. Although he concentrates on elite writers, best-selling authors like Sinclair Lewis and John Steinbeck are included. Suzanne Ellery Greene's *Books for Pleasure: Popular Fiction, 1914–1945* (1974) uses best sellers to trace changes in popular attitudes and values in such categories as politics and religion, race and ethnicity, class, family, and sex. Her detailed methodology might prove useful to other workers in the field. John Sutherland's *Bestsellers: Popular Fiction of the 1970s* (1981) surveys the most spectacular blockbusters of the decade, and also analyzes the international character of 1970s best sellers. *The American Dream and the Popular Novel* (1985) by Elizabeth Long, examines attitudes toward success as reflected in these books between 1945 and 1975. Another book of possible interest is *The Ethos of Romance at the Turn of the Century* (1994) by William J. Scheick.

Scholarship on best sellers of the twentieth century has also focused on the forms, functions, and political messages of popular literature. One general treatment, Patrick D. Morrow's *The Popular and the Serious in Select Twentieth-Century American Novels* (1992), concludes that popular literature is essentially formulaic. Morrow describes popular genres as "parables" that orient and guide readers in a shifting and complex social environment, a concept that seems to be gaining ground. Ruth Pirsig Wood, in *Lolita in Peyton Place: Highbrow, Middlebrow, and Lowbrow Novels of the 1950s* (1995), contends that lowbrow and highbrow fiction share formal elements and function similarly as models for establishing an individual identity, while "middlebrow" fiction offers a guide for negotiating the social and economic terrain within shared cultural beliefs. Linda Wagner-Martin, in *The Mid-Century American Novel, 1935–1965* (1997) discusses the literary scene, the increasing schisms in reading audiences, and the impact of popular genres such as the detective novel in those decades. A book by Andrew Macdonald, Gina Macdonald, and MaryAnn Sheridan, *Shape Shifting: Images of Native Americans in Recent Popular Fiction* (2000), looks at representations of Native Americans in the western, the romance, detective/crime books, horror stories, and science fiction/fantasy genres.

Topics of Special Interest

The explosion of feminist scholarship has encouraged studies of women authors, the portrayal of women in popular fiction, and types of fiction read mostly by women, such as the romance. Sally Allen McNally's *Who Is in the House? A Psychological Study of Two Centuries of Women's Fiction in America* looks at the development of the domestic novel over time. Helen Waite Papashvily's *All the Happy Endings* (1956) is an early cultural analysis of popular nineteenth-century domestic novels and their authors; Papashvily found social criticism and rebellion beneath conventional moral and gender messages of these books. Nina Baym's *Women's Fiction: A Guide to Novels by and about Women in America, 1820–1870* (1993; 1st ed. 1978) is an excellent overview of the same material; Baym contends that the fiction and lives of domestic novelists were essentially congruent with the social codes of their periods and audiences. The book contains chronological biography of nineteenth-century women's fiction. *Private Woman, Public Stage; Literary Domesticity in Nineteenth-Century America* (1984), by Mary Kelley, extrapolates from women's domestic novels of the period to assumptions about the private experience of female domesticity. Bridging the nineteenth and twentieth centuries, Anne Goodwyn Jones's *Tomorrow Is Another Day: The Woman Writer in the South, 1859–1936* (1981) argues that the best-selling novels of writers such as Augusta Jane Evans and Margaret Mitchell were compelling to their readers because they reflected the conflicts inherent in the ideal of the "southern lady."

Many scholars have treated women in best sellers of the twentieth century. Madonne M. Miner in *Insatiable Appetites* (1984) constructs a twentieth-century "woman's story" based on a content analysis of *Gone with the Wind* (Margaret Mitchell, 1936), *Forever Amber* (Kathleen Windsor, 1944), *Peyton Place* (Grace Metalious, 1956), *Valley of the Dolls* (Jacqueline Susann, 1966), and *Scruples* (Judith Krantz, 1978). Miner's analysis emphasizes the mother-daughter relationship in explaining the content and popularity of twentieth-century romance literature. Carol Thurston, examining paperback fiction of the 1970s and 1980s in her book

The Romance Revolution (1987), shows a healthy skepticism of the oft-repeated assumption that underlying themes of genre literature are fundamentally conservative and tend not to change over time. Using a content analysis of popular romances during her period, she concludes that the expectations, values, and behaviors of women portrayed in these popular novels underwent a marked change in response to the reemergence of feminism in the 1960s. She argues that popular genre literature can perform a transformative function, especially in times of rapid change, by legitimating new worldviews and modes of behavior. Jan Cohn's *Romance and the Erotics of Property: Mass-Market Fiction for Women* (1988) deconstructs the popular romance as exemplified by the Harlequin novels to reveal a heavily coded but subversive social tract empowering the contemporary woman to overturn accepted roles.

Katherine B. Payant, in *Becoming and Bonding: Contemporary Feminism and Popular Fiction by American Women Writers* (1993) traces the impact of feminist theory as expressed by writers including Marge Piercy, Mary Gordon, and Toni Morrison through popular fiction of the 1960s through the 1980s. Her study emphasizes the importance of bonds between women in contemporary feminist theory and popular literature. Patricia Raub, following the approaches of Greene, Lofroth, and Elson cited above, explores the "shared assumptions" of middle-class women as revealed through an analysis of best sellers of the interwar era in *Yesterday's Stories: Popular Women's Novels of the Twenties and Thirties* (1994). The book looks at attitudes toward sexual behavior, marriage, divorce, and work, unsurprisingly concluding that women in the decades immediately following passage of the Nineteenth Amendment for the most part espoused the traditional values of their mothers.

A good deal of recent scholarship related to the best seller has focused on genres expressing the dark side of the American psyche, including mysteries, the hard-boiled detective novels, fantasy, and science fiction. Other chapters in this book, including "Fantasy," "Gothic Novels," "Detective and Mystery Novels," and "Pulps and Dime Novels," treat these forms in depth. However, a few recent works relevant to the study of the best seller are cited here.

Three books focus on the production and influence of hard-boiled detective novels. *Hardboiled America: The Lurid Years of Paperbacks* (1981), by Geoffrey O'Brien, provides an overview of the detective genre as it evolved to feed the fantasies of a mass public in the post-War era. His book includes a checklist of hard-boiled fiction. *Murder in the Millions*, a 1984 study by J. Kenneth Van Dover, documents the enormous popularity of three premier practitioners, Erle Stanley Gardner, Mickey Spillane, and Ian Fleming. Van Dover's introduction borrows from Bruno Bettelheim's analysis of the fairy tale, postulating that the appeal of the works stems from the reader's opportunity to identify with the struggles, not the heroism, of the protagonist. The study includes bibliographies of novels and secondary sources, as well as film and television adaptations. *Whatever Happened to Sherlock Holmes: Detective Fiction, Popular Theology, and Society* (1991), by Robert S. Paul, is an unusual examination of the detective genre from a Christian perspective. Although his approach may put off some and his analysis is not deep, the book shows through its own assemblage of evidence how the genre reflects an increasingly secular society and provides in the various guises of the protagonist a role model and antidote to emptiness. Woody Haut's *Pop Culture: Hardboiled*

Fiction and the Cold War (1995) explores the political implications of the genre, showing how these books supported leftist ideology in the 1930s but had swung to the right by the 1950s. Two appendixes list the fictional works and film adaptations, including writing credits.

In the gothic mode, *American Nightmares: The Haunted House Formula in American Popular Fiction* (1999), by Dale Bailey, traces the trope of the haunted house from its origins through the best sellers of Stephen King and Anne Rice. His book shows how accretions of meaning have subverted the house as a symbol of the "American Dream." David Cochran's *American Noir: Underground Writers and Filmmakers of the Postwar Era* (2000) finds that the morally and culturally ambiguous crime, mystery, science fiction, and fantasy works of the Cold War era indirectly challenged dominant assumptions and prefigured the counterculture of the 1960s. Thomas Newhouse, in *The Beat Generation and the Popular Novel in the United States, 1945–1970* (2000) makes a similar case over a much broader sweep. The book links the quintessential outsiders of *On the Road* (Jack Kerouac, 1957) with the heroes of best-selling novels of Cooper and Twain, as well as dime novels and the more recent hard-boiled detective genres.

Production and Reception

Best sellers cannot be considered without reference to their production and distribution—the circumstances of their composition, the publishing industry, and dissemination of the books. Likewise, it is essential to consider the related issues of readership characteristics and the broad cultural context of a book's reception. Many of the books cited earlier contain commentary on the publishers and readers of the works treated; however, these topics are the primary focus of the books cited in this subsection.

Two excellent histories of the field provide more than enough information for most researchers. John William Tebbel's multivolume *A History of Publishing in the United States* (1972, 1975) contains a short section devoted to best sellers and numerous valuable charts. A briefer study, *Book Publishing in America* (1966), by Charles Allen Madison, includes a chronology of major events and information on book clubs and inexpensive editions. His thorough bibliography lists histories of individual publishing houses, memoirs, literary histories, criticism, and topical studies. *Books: The Culture and Commerce of Publishing* (1982), by Lewis A. Coser, Charles Kadushin, and Walter V. Powell offers a comprehensive, sociological perspective on the publishing scene in the United States as of the early 1980s. Another book from the 1980s is Allen Billy Crider's *Mass Market Publishing in America* (1982). For an overview, *The Columbia History of the American Novel*, cited earlier, surveys the book trade in two sections, "The Book Marketplace I," by Michael T. Gilmore, and "The Book Marketplace II," by John N. Unsworth.

A cynical and disparaging view of modern publishing in America is Thomas Whiteside's *The Blockbuster Complex: Conglomerates, Show Business and Book Publishing* (1981). Whiteside attacks trends in publishing that negate the textual value of the book and treat it as a multimedia commercial property. An intelligent response to Whiteside's critique is found in Elizabeth Long's *The American Dream and the Popular Novel*, cited above.

Some studies focus specifically on publishers of popular books. *Publishers for Mass Entertainment in Nineteenth Century America* (1980), edited by Madeleine B.

Stern, is a collection of histories of such publishers, including Beadle and Adams and Street and Smith, both of which pioneered the dime and nickel novel. Quenton Reynolds's *The Fiction Factory: From Pulp Row to Quality Street; the Story of 100 Years of Publishing at Street and Smith* (1955) is a lively and detailed account of the many publishing ventures of the house that gave the world Ragged Dick, Buffalo Bill, and Frank Merriwell. Albert Johannsen's *The House of Beadle and Adams*, previously cited, is a detailed history of the famous publisher, with an extensive bibliography.

The paperback industry is an especially important aspect of publishing for scholars of twentieth-century best sellers. An early account is Lewis Freeman's *Paper-Bound Books in America* (1952). John William Tebbel's *Paperback Books: A Pocket History* (1964) is a good introduction to the topic. Kenneth C. Davis's *Two-Bit Culture: The Paperbacking of America* (1984), is a readable and insightful account of the origins, development, and economics of modern paperback publishing. His appendix, "Fifty Paperbacks that Changed the World," provides an overview of best-selling paperbacks that had an important impact on American culture and consciousness. William Lyles's *Putting Dell on the Map: A History of the Dell Paperback* (1983) chronicles the history of one important paperback publishing venture.

Taking a somewhat different approach, Clive Bloom's *Pulp Fiction: Popular Reading and Pulp Theory* (1996) broadens his study beyond the cheaply printed paperbacks that proliferated from the 1920s to the 1950s, addressing himself to the "trashy" elements that the term "pulp" connotes. Bloom reprises the long commingled history of publishing and literacy, arguing that technology and business practices created diverse reading publics whose tastes functioned as class markers in England and the United States at mid-twentieth century. Susan Stryker's *Queer Pulp: Perverted Passions from the Golden Age of the Paperback* (2001), explores the forces behind the proliferation of gay- and lesbian-oriented paperbacks in recent decades. While books of this type have not made the national best-seller lists, this account of the reciprocal relationships among the publishing, readers, and cultural attitudes is relevant to the study of the best seller.

Several books on paperbacks include lavish reproductions of the electrifying covers of the 1940s and 1950s that helped to sell the books and reinforced their messages. The earliest of these, Piet Schreuders's *Paperbacks U.S.A.: A Graphic History, 1939–1959* (1981), provides a good overview along with the pictures. Thomas L. Bonn's *Undercover: An Illustrated History of American Mass Market Paperbacks* (1982) is another illustrated history. *Over My Dead Body: The Sensational Age of the American Paperback: 1945–1955* (1994), by Lee Server, focuses on the hard-boiled genre, sex, and the link to the Beat generation; however, its main contribution to scholarship is the chapter on the cover and the book's numerous cover reproductions. Richard A. Lupoff's *The Great American Paperback: An Illustrated Tribute to Legends of the Book* (2001) is a coffee table collection of over 600 reproductions and commentary about publishers, artists, and writers. Unfortunately, the value of this book to the scholar is diminished by its weak index and erratic pagination.

As the preceding comments show, considering the best seller from the perspective of the publishing industry inevitably involves audiences and readers, as well as mediating elements such as book clubs, reviewers, advertising, libraries, and distribution methods. Most studies of readership published since 1930 treat only contemporary statistics, but a few books attempt to describe readers of earlier periods. *The English Common Reader* by Richard D. Altick (1957) surveys the rise of a mass reading public in England of the nineteenth century; his observations on the role of popular magazines, libraries, and reading groups are pertinent to the United States of the same period. Leavis's book (1965), mentioned above, deals with books that were best sellers in Great Britain and in the United States and with the reading public of both countries. Another excellent study of an earlier time is *Literacy in Colonial New England* (1974) by Kenneth A. Lockridge.

Other books treat the effect of publishing practices on literary productions. *Selling the Wild West: Popular Western Fiction, 1860–1960* (1987), by Christine Bold, analyzes the permutations in the western formula from the dime novels to the antiwesterns of the 1970s as responses to the pressures of a commercial publishing system. Bold argues that the factory-like system under which the western genre emerged was responsible for its formulaic content, and that the commercial process and packaging of western formula fiction has sustained interest in the genre. Alf A. Walle's *The Cowboy Hero and Its Audience: Popular Culture as Market Derived Art* (2000) relates changing conventions in the western to economic and social conditions. Isabelle Lehuu's *Carnival on the Page: Popular Print Media in Antebellum America* (2000) examines the democratization of reading before the Civil War. Lehuu contends that the proliferation of readily available reading material in the period transformed readers from "citizens" to "consumers," and encouraged reading as a private, rather than family, activity. Christopher P. Wilson's *The Labor of Words: Literary Professionalism in the Progressive Era* (1985), shows how the increasing standardization of literary and publishing practices during that era helped to shape popular genres.

Three rather technical studies treat readers during the Depression, correlating book sales and library distribution with geographic, cultural, and economic factors. These are Orion Howard Cheney in *Economic Survey of the Book Industry, 1930–1931* (1931); Douglas Waples in *Research Memorandum on Social Aspects of Reading in the Depression* (1937); and Louis R. Wilson in *Geography of Reading* (1938). Roger H. Smith's *The American Reading Public: What It Reads* is a 1964 study.

People and Books by Henry C. Link and Harry Arthur Hopf (1946) is an early, speculative study of reading habits. *Books and the Mass Market* (1953), edited by Harold K. Guinzburg, Robert W. Frase, and Theodore Waller, is a collection of essays on this topic. *Optimum Marketing of Trade Books: Based on Scientific Forecasting Methodology* (1965) by George Blagowidow applies market research to book selling. Another useful volume, not specifically on best sellers, is John Hohenberg's *The Pulitzer Prizes* (1974). Hohenberg lists the prize-winning books, many of which were best sellers, and analyzes changing patterns in the selections. James Calvin Craig's *The Vocabulary Load of the Nation's Best Sellers, 1662–1945* (1954) finds common linguistic patterns in best sellers of various periods. J. Dennis Bounds's *Perry Mason: The Authorship and Reception of a Popular Hero* (1996) looks at the author-reader connection through a study of one popular figure.

Several articles reprinted in Rosenberg and White's *Mass Culture: The Popular Arts in America*, previously cited, deal with reading habits and availability of books; the most useful of these are Bernard Berelson's "Who Reads What Books and Why" and Alan Dutscher's "The Book Business in America." Another collection touching on all aspects of book marketing is *Bookselling, Reviewing, and Reading*

(1978), edited by Peter Davison, Rolf Meyersohn, and Edward Shils. Not entirely, or even primarily, academic, the book brings together selections from a wide variety of sources: Henry Seidel Canby, "Why Popular Novels Are Popular" (*The Century*, 1922); B. F. Page, "Reading for the Workers" (Burns, Oates and Washbourne, 1921); Virginia Smith, "Changes in Bestsellers Since World War One" (*Journal of Popular Culture*, 1968); and Robert Escarpit, "Bookshops and Mass Circulation" (*The Book Revolution*, 1966). Many of these pieces serve as touchstones for researchers looking at attitudes of cultural "gatekeepers" of their periods.

A much more scholarly collection is *Reading in America: Literature and Social History* (1989), edited by Cathy N. Davidson. The twelve essays on audiences explore the ways in which literary texts were used by their readers and the inferences that can be made about a culture based on its readings. Essays such as "Chapbooks in America" (Victor Neuburg); "A Republican Literature: Magazine Reading and Readers in Late Eighteenth-Century New York" (David Paul Nord); and "The Life and Times of *Charlotte Temple*" (Cathy N. Davidson) are applicable to the study of best sellers. Another collection, *Readers in History: Nineteenth-Century American Literature and Contexts of Response* (1993), edited by James L. Machor, contains essays grouped into three sections. Part One focuses on historical and gendered theories of readership. Part Two addresses the role of the real and implied audience on the construction of fiction. Part Three explores the manner in which the treatment of race, gender, and politics in literary texts opens new possibilities of social structure and behavior to readers. While many of the essays deal with reader response to elite figures, the principles and methods expounded by the contributors are eminently applicable to scholars of the best seller.

Many factors mediate between publisher and reader to influence sales of books. According to George Stevens's *Lincoln's Doctor's Dog* (1938), book sales are influenced most by word-of-mouth recommendations. Charles Lee's history of the Book-of-the-Month Club, *The Hidden Public* (1958), is useful for exploring institutions and phenomena that drive book sales, but a richer study of that institution is found in Janice Radway's *A Feeling for Books: The Book-of-the-Month Club, Literary Taste, and Middle Class Desire* (1992). Alice Payne Hackett's "Best Sellers in the Bookstores, 1900–1975," which appeared in Charles E. Anderson's edited collection, *Bookselling in America* (1975), could add to the discussion of book marketing.

More recent works include *The Making of a Middlebrow Culture* (1992) by Joan Rubin, which includes informative chapters on book clubs and radio book programs. A different explanation for the popularity of some books is advanced by *Inside the Bestsellers: Authors Reveal Their Inspiring Stories*, by Jerrold R. Jenkins and Mardi Link (1997). Jenkins and Link chronicle the publishing histories of sixteen best-selling books, concluding that these authors were indefatigable self-promoters who influenced greatly the popularity of their works.

Articles, Dissertations, and Reviews

The best seller is the subject of scholarly articles, dissertations, and reviews, as well as commentary and reviews in general circulation and trade publications. Space prohibits all but a general survey of topics and trends in these materials.

Citations to scholarly articles and dissertations can be searched electronically through numerous on-line data bases as described earlier; two of the best are

America: History and Life and the *MLA International Bibliography.* Three indexes collect citations to reviews of a particular book. The *Book Review Digest* indexes entries by subject and author and publishes a cumulative index every five years. It provides very brief excerpts that indicate the range of reviews. Another good source for locating reviews is the *National Library Service Cumulative Book Review Index, 1905–1974.* In 1965, the Gale Research Company began publishing *Book Review Index,* which lists reviews by author and year. On-line *Dissertation Abstracts* provides brief descriptions of dissertations and selected master's theses accepted at U.S. institutions from 1861.

Overall, the output on the best seller in scholarly articles and dissertations is thin in comparison with the profusion of books over the last ten to fifteen years. However, it is possible that searches under different terms—both broader (i.e., "popular literature") or narrower ("readers")—might turn up some additional materials.

Articles and dissertations added little to bibliographic resources on the best seller in recent years; one exception is a dissertation by Eric Nelson Steinbaugh, "Winston Churchill: An Introduction and Annotated Bibliography of Works by and about the American Author" (1982). A few articles treat aspects of best-seller marketing, including the somewhat neglected importance of bookstores, libraries, and the best-seller lists themselves. More recent articles are "Best-Sellers in Academic Libraries," *College and Research Libraries,* 2001, and Laura J. Miller, "The Best-Seller List as Marketing Tool and Historical Fiction," *Book History,* 2000.

Few scholarly articles or dissertations tackled the theoretical and philosophical issues posed by the dichotomy between popular and elite literature or the dynamic tension between author and reader. Two dissertations that do take this approach are Glenn Stewart Hendler's "Women, Boys, and the American Novel: Figuring the Mass Audience, 1850–1900" (1991) and Deborah Mari Applegate's "The Culture of the Novel and the Consolidation of Middle-Class Consciousness: Henry Ward Beecher and the Uses of Sympathy" (1997). Some articles, however, especially in social science journals, considered the best seller in the context of American values. Examples are Lynn S. Mullins and Richard E. Kopelman, "The Best Seller as an Indicator of Societal Narcissism: Is There a Trend?" *Public Opinion Quarterly,* 1984; Paul Batesel, "Best Sellers and the Public Attitude," *Studies in Popular Culture,* 1989; Gil Troy, "Stumping in the Bookstores: A Literary History of the 1992 Presidential Campaign," *Presidential Studies Quarterly,* 1995.

A handful of articles dealt with early best sellers. Examples are James Southall Wilson's "Best-Sellers in Jefferson's Day," *Virginia Quarterly Review,* 1960, and Kathryn Zabelle Derounian's "The Publication, Promotion, and Distribution of Mary Rowlandson's Indian Captivity Narrative in the Seventeenth Century," *Early American Literature,* 1988. Early dissertations to analyze content in popular books are "Best Sellers: Media of Mass Expression" (1951), by Anna Lee Hopson, which compares the popular novels written from 1907 to 1916 with those written from 1940 to 1949, and "The Good and the Beautiful: A Study of Best-Selling Novels in the United States" (1947), by Dorothy C. Hockey. Suzanne C. Ellery took a historical approach in "The Years of Growth: Best Selling Novels in America, 1918–1927" (*Journal of Popular Culture,* 1969). A recent dissertation touching on values conveyed in best sellers is Thomas E. White's "Popular Religion in America, 1991–1995: A Study of Selected Best Sellers" (1999). Works focusing on genre are exemplified by Patricia Turner, "From Talma Gordon to Theresa Galloway: Images of African American Women in Mysteries" (*The Black Scholar*, 1998); and Steven Penner Rubio's dissertation, "Killer Eyes, Killer Legs, Killer Instincts: An Evolution of the American Hard-Boiled Detective Novel" (1997).

The overwhelming majority of both articles and dissertations, however, clustered around gender studies, focusing especially on representations of women in best-selling fiction. Articles include "Books about Women's Lives: The New Best Sellers" (Linda Hunt, *Radical American*, 1980); "Women's Novels and Women's Minds: An Unsentimental View of Nineteenth-Century American's Women's Fiction," by Nina Baym (*Novel*, 1998); Stephanie Wardrop, "The Last of the Red Hot Mohicans: Miscegenation in the Popular American Romance" (*MELUS*, 1997); J. David Stevens, " 'She Was a Woman': Family Roles, Gender, and Sexuality in Bret Harte's Western Fiction" (*American Literature*, 1997); and David R. Shumway, "Romance in the Romance: Love and Marriage in Turn-of-the-Century Best Sellers" (*Int-Journal of Narrative Theory*, 1999).

The numerous dissertations on gender themes include "Images of Woman in American Best Sellers: 1870–1900" (Diedre Ann Ling Kedesdy, 1976); "What We Must Love: Marriage in the Best-Sellers by Women During the 1930s" (Sue M. Campman, 1987); "Transforming Fictional Genres: Five Nineteenth-Century American Feminist Novelists (Cheri Louise Graves Ross, 1991); "Making Utopia Home: Domestic Discourse and Radical Politics in Nineteenth-Century American Women's Writing" (Susan Lynch Foster, 1997); " 'Strong and Brave': The Culture of Womanhood in the Novels of Maria Susanna Cummins" (Rebecca R. Saulsbury, 1999); "Illegal Fictions: White Women Writers and the Miscegenated Imagination, 1859–1867" (Katharine Nicholson Ings, 2000), and "Sentimental Revolution: American Masculinity and Scenes of Writing, 1790–1860" (Bryce Gordon Traister, 1996).

Trade publications are one of the best sources for contemporaneous information about best-selling books and authors and the book industry. "The One Hundred Leading Authors of Best Sellers in Fiction from 1895 to 1944" (Irving Harlow Hart, *Publishers Weekly*, 1946) noted that in the period from 1919 to 1931 there was an 80 percent correlation between best sellers and the highest circulation library books. "What Makes a Book Sell?" (Robert Banker, *Publishers Weekly*, 1954) provides a nontechnical survey of why readers choose certain books. "Drugs, Big Business and Best Sellers" (Thaddeus Rutkowski, *ADWEEK*, 1986) identified drug abuse and recovery as the "largest thematic concentration" in 1986. General circulation magazines are also a good source for overviews and trends; for example, "Bookshop Journeys . . . and Beyond" (Joanie M. Schrof, *U.S. News and World Report*, 1994) touted the thirst for enlightenment as a key to big sales; and "Audiobooks Get Their Own Niche Stores" (Trudi Miller Rosenblum, *Billboard*, 1994) reported on a new format for books. These citations, often with complete text, can be accessed through on-line data bases described above.

Reviews are another tool for the study of the best seller, providing a window into the popular reception of books at the time of their publication. Long, substantive reviews of some best sellers appear in the *New York Review of Books*, often grouped with others of a similar theme or style and placed in cultural context. The *New York Times Book Review* became a separate section in 1896, and is a source for analyzing popular response. Although it does not review every book, its reviews, like those of the *Bookman*, provide much detail and critical analysis. Other general circulation publications and most newspapers also run reviews of many popular books.

Publishers Weekly, whose best-seller listings began in 1912, has printed reviews of most major books since it first appeared in 1872. The *Library Journal* prints some long reviews and many one-paragraph overviews organized by topic designed primarily for librarians who are considering purchase. Since 1967, R.R. Bowker has published an annual volume collecting many of these under the title *Library Journal Book Review*. Another journal, the *Bookman*, calculated best sellers from its first year in print and reviewed most major books that appeared from 1895 until it ceased publication in 1933. Arno Press published a bound index to reviews from 1896 to 1970. In 1951, the *New York Times* published *A Century of Books*, a selection of one hundred of its reviews.

The *Booklist*, a publication of the American Library Association, provides brief reviews of a large number of books. The *Saturday Review of Literature*, which became the *Saturday Review* in 1951 and ceased publication in the 1970s, ran long reviews of books deemed worthy by its editor. All of these journals contain advertisements that can aid in analyzing publishers' marketing strategies and intended audiences.

Even given some reservations regarding the reach and originality of articles and dissertations dealing with the "best seller" or popular literature more generally, the topic has clearly become one of scholarly, and even popular, interest. The range and quality of books relating to the best seller over the last twenty years are impressive and indicate an increasingly sophisticated understanding of this cultural phenomenon as a subject of serious study. Combined with the contemporaneous commentary widely available in trade and general circulation publications, the researcher approaching this topic will find a rich trove of materials to ground new work.

BIBLIOGRAPHY

Histories and Interpretive Works

Altick, Richard D. *The English Common Reader: A Social History of the Mass Reading Public, 1800–1900.* Chicago: University of Chicago Press, 1957.

Anderson, Charles E., ed. *Bookselling in America and the World: Some Observations and Recollections in Celebration of the 75th Anniversary of the American Booksellers Association.* New York: Quadrangle/New York Times Book Co., 1975.

Appelgate, Deborah Mari. "The Culture of the Novel and the Consolidation of Middle-Class Consciousness: Henry Ward Beecher and the Uses of Sympathy, 1830–1880." Ph.D. dissertation, Yale University, 1997.

Bailey, Dale. *American Nightmares: The Haunted House Formula in American Popular Fiction.* Bowling Green, Ohio: Bowling Green State University Popular Press, 1999.

Banker, Robert. "What Makes a Book Sell?" *Publishers Weekly*, 166 (December 4, 1954), 2179–2182.

Batesel, Paul. "Best Sellers and the Public Attitude."*Studies in Popular Culture*, 12, no. 1 (1989), 15–27.

Baym, Nina. *Women's Fiction: A Guide to Novels by and about Women in America, 1820–1870.* 2d ed. Ithaca, N.Y.: 1993; 1st ed. 1978.

———. "Women's Novels and Women's Minds: An Unsentimental View of Nineteenth-Century American Women's Fiction." *Novel*, 31, no. 3 (Summer 1998), 335–350.

Berelson, Bernard. "Who Reads Books and Why." In Bernard Rosenberg and David Manning White, eds., *Mass Culture: The Popular Arts in America.* Glencoe, Ill.: Free Press, 1957, 119–125. Reprinted from *Contemporary Issues*, 5 (April-May 1954), 38–58.

"Best-Sellers in Academic Libraries." *College and Research Libraries*, 62, no. 3 (May 2001), 216–225.

Blagowidow, George. *Optimum Marketing of Trade Books: Based on Scientific Forecasting Methodology.* New York: R. R. Bowker, 1965.

Blake, Nelson Manfred. *Novelists' America: Fiction as History, 1910–1940.* Syracuse, N.Y.: Syracuse University Press, 1969.

Bloom, Clive. *Cult Fiction: Popular Reading and Pulp Theory.* New York: St. Martin's Press, 1996.

Bocca, Carl. *Best Sellers: A Nostalgic Celebration of the Less-Than-Great Books You Have Always Been Afraid to Admit You Loved.* New York: Wyndham Books, 1981.

Bode, Carl. *The Anatomy of American Popular Culture, 1840–1861.* Berkeley: University of California Press, 1959.

———. *The Half-World of American Culture.* Carbondale: Southern Illinois University Press, 1965.

Bold, Christine. *Selling the Wild West: Popular Western Fiction, 1860 to 1960.* Bloomington: Indiana University Press, 1987.

Bonn, Thomas L. *Undercover: An Illustrated History of American Mass Market Paperbacks.* New York: Penguin, 1982.

Bounds, J. Dennis. *Perry Mason: The Authorship and Reception of a Popular Hero.* Contributions to the Study of Popular Culture, no. 56. Westport, Conn.: Greenwood Press, 1996.

Bowker Lectures on Book Publishing. New York: R. R. Bowker, 1957.

Brown, Herbert Ross. *The Sentimental Novel in America, 1789–1860.* Durham, N.C.: Duke University Press, 1940.

Burgess, Anthony. *The Novel Now.* New York: Norton, 1967.

Campman, Sue M. "What We Must Love: Marriage in the Best-sellers by Women during the 1930s." Ph.D. dissertation, University of Texas, Austin, 1987.

Canby, Henry Seidel. "Why Novels Are So Popular." In *Bookselling, Reviewing, and Reading*, ed. Peter Davidson, Rolf Meyersohn, and Edward Shils. Teaneck, N.J.: Somerset House, 1978, 56–62. Originally published in *The Century*, 104, no. 2, 1922.

Cawelti, John G. *Adventure, Mystery, and Romance: Formula Stories as Art and Popular Culture.* Chicago: University of Chicago Press, 1976.

Cheney, Orion Howard. *Economic Survey of the Book Industry, 1930–1931.* New York: R. R. Bowker, 1931.

Cochran, David. *American Noir: Underground Writers and Filmmakers of the Postwar Era*. Washington, D.C.: Smithsonian Institution Press, 2000.

Cohn, Jan. *Romance and the Erotics of Property: Mass-Market Fiction for Women*. Durham: Duke University Press, 1988.

Coser, Lewis A., Charles Kadushin, and Walter V. Powell. *Books: The Culture and Commerce of Publishing*. New York: Basic Books, 1982.

Cowie, Alexander. *The Rise of the American Novel*. New York: American Book, 1948.

Cowley, Malcolm. *The Literary Situation*. New York: Viking, 1954.

Craig, James Calvin. *The Vocabulary Load of the Nation's Best Sellers, 1662–1945*. Ann Arbor, Mich.: University Microfilms, 1954.

Crider, Allen Billy. *Mass Market Publishing in America*. Boston: G. K. Hall, 1982.

Cullen, Jim. "Literature and Popular Culture." In *Encyclopedia of American Studies*, ed. George T. Kurian, Miles Orvell, Johnella E. Butler, and Jay Mechling. Vol. 3. Danbury, Conn.: Grolier Educational, 2001, 27–29.

Davidson, Cathy N. "The Life and Times of *Charlotte Temple*: The Biography of a Book." In *Reading in America: Literature and Social History*, ed. Cathy N. Davidson. Baltimore: Johns Hopkins University Press, 1989, 157–79.

Davidson, Cathy N., ed. *Reading in America: Literature and Social History*. Baltimore: John Hopkins University Press, 1989.

Davis, Kenneth C. *Two-Bit Culture: The Paperbacking of America*. Boston: Houghton Mifflin, 1984.

Davison, Peter, Rolf Meyersohn, and Edward Shils, eds. *Bookselling, Reviewing, and Reading*. Teaneck, N.J.: Somerset House, 1978.

Denning, Michael. *Mechanic Accents: Dime Novels and Working-Class Culture in America*. London: Verso, 1987.

Derounian, Kathryn Zabelle. "The Publication, Promotion, and Distribution of Mary Rowlandson's Indian Captivity Narrative in the Seventeenth Century." *Early American Literature*, 23, no 3 (1988), 239–261.

Downs, Robert Bingham. *Famous American Books*. New York: McGraw-Hill, 1971.

Dudovitz, Resa L. *The Myth of Superwoman: Women's Bestsellers in France and the United States*. London: Routledge, 1990.

Dutscher, Alan. "The Book Business in America." *Mass Culture: The Popular Arts in America*, ed. Bernard Rosenberg and David Manning White. Glencoe, Ill.: Free Press, 1957, 126–140. Reprinted from *Saturday Review of Literature*, May 12, 1951, 7–8, 30–31.

Ellery, Suzanne C. "The Years of Growth: Best Selling Novels in America, 1918–1927." *Journal of Popular Culture*, 3, no. 3 (1969), 527–552.

Elson, Ruth Miller. *Myths and Mores in American Best Sellers, 1865–1965*. New York: Garland Publishing, 1985.

Escarpit, Robert. "Bookshops and Mass Circulation." In *Bookselling, Reviewing, and Reading*, ed. Peter Davison, Rolf Meyersohn, and Edward Shils. Teaneck, N.J.: Somerset House, 1978, 249–262. Originally published in *The Book Revolution* (Paris: Unesco, 1966).

Fahs, Alice. *The Imagined Civil War: Popular Literature of the North and South, 1861–1865*. Chapel Hill: University of North Carolina Press, 2001.

Fiedler, Leslie. *What Was Literature? Class, Culture, and Mass Society*. New York: Simon and Schuster, 1982.

Filler, Louis, ed. *A Question of Quality: Popularity and Value in Modern Creative Writing*. 2 vols. Bowling Green, Ohio: Bowling Green State University Popular Press, 1976–1980.

Foster, Susan Lynch. "Making Utopia Home: Domestic Discourse and Radical Politics in Nineteenth-Century Women's Writing." Ph.D. dissertation, Cornell University, 1997.

Freeman, Lewis. *Paper-Bound Books in America*. New York: New York Public Library, 1952.

Gilbert, James, "Science Fiction." In *Encyclopedia of American Studies*, ed. George T. Kurian, Miles Orvell, Johnella E. Butler, and Jay Mechling. Vol. 4. Danbury, Conn.: Grolier Educational, 2001, 87–89.

Gilmore, Michael T. "The Book Marketplace I." In *The Columbia History of the American Novel*, ed. Emory Elliott, Cathy N. Davidson, Patrick O'Donnell, Valerie Smith, and Christopher P. Wilson. New York: Columbia University Press, 1991.

Greene, Suzanne Ellery. *Books for Pleasure: Popular Fiction 1914–1945*. Bowling Green, Ohio: Bowling Green State University Popular Press, 1974.

Guinzburg, Harold K., Robert W. Frase, and Theodore Waller, eds. *Books and the Mass Market*. Urbana: University of Illinois Press, 1953.

Gurko, Leo. *Heroes, Highbrows and the Popular Mind*. Indianapolis, Ind.: Bobbs-Merrill, 1953.

Hackett, Alice Payne. "Best Sellers in the Bookstores, 1900–1975." In *Bookselling in America and the World: Some Observations and Recollections*, ed. Charles B. Anderson. In Celebration of the 75th Anniversary of the American Booksellers Association. New York: Quadrangle, New York Times Book Co., 1975.

Hackett, Alice Payne, and James Henry Burke. *80 Years of Best Sellers*. New York: R. R. Bowker, 1977.

Harker, Jaime. "Romance Novels." In *Encyclopedia of American Studies*, ed. George T. Kurian, Miles Orvell, Johnella E. Butler, and Jay Mechling. Vol. 4. Danbury, Conn.: Grolier Educational, 2001, 56–58.

Hart, Irving Harlow. "The One Hundred Leading Authors of Best Sellers in Fiction from 1895 to 1944." *Publishers Weekly*, 149 (January 19, 1946), 285–290.

Hart, James D. *The Popular Book: A History of America's Literary Taste*. New York: Oxford University Press, 1950.

Haut, Woody. *Pulp Culture: Hardboiled Fiction and the Cold War*. London: Serpent's Tail, 1995.

Hawkins, Harriet. *Classics and Trash: Traditions and Taboos in High Literature and Popular Modern Genres*. Theory/Culture 1, ed. Linda Hutcheon and Paul Perron. Toronto: University of Toronto Press, 1990.

Hendler, Glenn Stewart. "Women, Boys, and the American Novel: Figuring the Mass Audience, 1850–1900." Ph.D. dissertation, Northwestern University, 1991.

Hendler, Jane Elizabeth. *Best Sellers and Their Film Adaptations in Postwar America: From Here to Eternity, Sayonara, Giant, Auntie Mame, Peyton Place*. New York: Peter Lang Publishers, 2001.

Hinckley, Karen, and Barbara Hinckley. *American Best Sellers: A Readers' Guide to Popular Fiction*. Bloomington: Indiana University Press, 1989.

Hockey, Dorothy C. "The Good and the Beautiful: A Study of Best Selling Novels in America, 1965–1920." Ph.D. dissertation, Case Western Reserve University, 1947.

Hohenberg, John. *The Pulitzer Prizes*. New York: Columbia University Press, 1974.

Hopson, Anna Lee. "Best Sellers: Media of Mass Expression." Ph.D. dissertation, Radcliff College, 1951.

Hunt, Linda. "Books about Women's Lives: The New Best Sellers." *Radical America*, 14, no. 5 (1980), 45–54.

Ings, Katharine Nicholson. "Illegal Fictions: White Women Writers and the Miscegenated Imagination, 1859–1867." Ph.D. dissertation, Indiana University, 2000.

Jenkins, Jerrold R., and Mardi Link. *Inside the Bestsellers: Authors Reveal Their Inspiring Stories*. Traverse City, Mich.: Rhodes and Easton, 1997.

Jones, Anne Goodwyn. *Tomorrow Is Another Day: The Woman Writer in the South, 1859–1936*. Baton Rouge: Louisiana State University Press, 1981.

Kazin, Alfred. *Bright Book of Life: American Novelists and Storytellers from Hemingway through Mailer*. Boston: Little, Brown, 1973.

———. *On Native Grounds*. New York: Reynal and Hitchcock, 1942.

Kedesdy, Deidre Ann Ling. "Images of Women in the American Best Seller: 1870–1900." Ph.D. dissertation, Tufts University, 1976.

Kelley, Karol L. *Models for the Multitudes: Social Values in the American Popular Novel, 1850–1920*. Contributions to the Study of Childhood and Youth, no. 3. Westport, Conn.: Greenwood Press, 1987.

Kelley, Mary. *Private Woman, Public Stage: Literary Domesticity in Nineteenth-Century America*. New York: Oxford University Press, 1984.

Kelley, R. Gordon. "Popular Literature." In *Encyclopedia of American Studies*, ed. George T. Kurian, Miles Orvell, Johnella E. Butler, and Jay Mechling. Vol. 3. Danbury, N.Y.: Grolier Educational, 2001, 372–375.

Klein, Marcus. *Easterns, Westerns, and Private Eyes: American Matters, 1870–1900*. Madison: University of Wisconsin Press, 1994.

Knight, Grant C. *The Critical Period in American Literature, 1890–1900*. Chapel Hill: University of North Carolina Press, 1951.

———. *The Strenuous Age in American Literature*. Chapel Hill: University of North Carolina Press, 1954.

Korda, Michael. *Making the List: A Cultural History of the American Bestseller, 1900–1999*. New York: Barnes & Noble Publishing, 2001.

Lansford, Tom M. "Popular Culture." In *Encyclopedia of American Studies*, ed. George T. Kurian, Miles Orvell, Johnella E. Butler, and Jay Mechling. Vol 3. Danbury, Conn.: Grolier Educational, 2001, 366–72.

Leavis, Q. D. *Fiction and the Reading Public*. London: Chatto and Windus, 1965. First published 1932.

Lee, Charles. *The Hidden Public: The Story of the Book-of-the-Month Club*. New York: Doubleday, 1958.

Lehuu, Isabella. *Carnival on the Page: Popular Print Media in Antebellum America*. Chapel Hill: University of North Carolina Press, 2000.

Lewis, Freeman. *Paper-Bound Books in America*. New York: New York Public Library, 1952.

Link, Henry C., and Harry Arthur Hopf. *People and Books: A Study of Reading and Book Buying Habits*. New York: Book Industry Committee, Book Manufacturer's Institute, 1946.

Lockridge, Kenneth A. *Literacy in Colonial New England*. New York: Norton, 1974.

Lofroth, Erik. *A World Made Safe: Values in American Best Sellers, 1895–1920*. Studia Anglistica Upsaliensis, no. 45. Uppsala, Sweden: Uppsala Universitet, 1983.

Long, Elizabeth. *The American Dream and the Popular Novel*. Boston: Routledge and Kegan Paul, 1985.

Loshe, Lily D. *The Early American Novel, 1789–1830*. New York: Ungar, 1966.

Lowenthal, Leo. *Literature, Popular Culture, and Society*. Englewood Cliffs, N.J.: Prentice-Hall, 1961.

Lupoff, Richard A. *The Great American Paperback: An Illustrated Tribute to the Legends of the Book*. Berkeley, Calif.: Ten Speed Press, 2001.

Lyles, William H. *Putting Dell on the Map: A History of the Dell Paperback*. Westport, Conn.: Greenwood Press, 1983.

Macdonald, Andrew, Gina Macdonald, and MaryAnn Sheridan. *Shape-Shifting: Images of Native Americans in Recent Popular Fiction*. Contributions to the Study of Popular Culture, no. 71. Westport, Conn.: Greenwood Press, 2000.

Machor, James L., ed. *Readers in History: Nineteenth-Century American Literature and the Contexts of Response*. Baltimore: Johns Hopkins University Press, 1993.

Madison, Charles Allen. *Book Publishing in America*. New York: McGraw-Hill, 1966.

McNall, Sally Allen. *Who Is in the House? A Psychological Study of Two Centuries of Women's Fiction in America, 1795 to the Present*. New York: Elsevier North Holland, 1981.

Miller, Laura J. "The Best-Seller List as Marketing Tool and Historical Fiction." *Book History*, 3 (2000), 266–304.

Miner, Madonne M. *Insatiable Appetites: Twentieth-Century Women's Best Sellers*. Contributions to Women's Studies, No. 48. Westport, Conn.: Greenwood Press, 1984.

Mitgang, Herbert. *Working for the Reader: A Chronicle of Culture, Literature, War and Politics in Books from the 1950s to the Present*. New York: Horizon Press, 1970.

Morrow, Patrick D. *The Popular and the Serious in Select Twentieth-Century American Novels*. Lewiston, N.Y.: Edwin Mellon Press, 1992.

Mullins, Lynn, and Richard E. Kopelman. "The Best Seller as an Indicator of Societal Narcissism: Is There a Trend?" *Public Opinion Quarterly*, 48, no. 4 (1984), 720–30.

Neuburg, Victor. "Chapbooks in America: Reconstructing the Popular Reading of Early America." In *Reading in America: Literature and Social History*, ed. Cathy N. Davidson, 81–113. Baltimore: Johns Hopkins University Press, 1989.

Newhouse, Thomas. *The Beat Generation and the Popular Novel in the United States, 1945–1970*. Jefferson, N.C.: McFarland, 2000.

Nord, David Paul. "A Republican Literature: Magazine Reading and Readers in Late Eighteenth-Century New York." In *Reading in America: Literature and Social History*, ed. Cathy N. Davidson. Baltimore: Johns Hopkins University Press, 1989, 114–139.

Nye, Russel B. *The Cultural Life of the New Nation, 1776–1830*. New York: Harper and Row, 1960.

———. *The Unembarrassed Muse: The Popular Arts in America*. New York: Dial Press, 1970.

O'Brien, Geoffrey. *Hardboiled America: The Lurid Years of Paperbacks*. New York: Van Nostrand Reinhold, 1981.

Page, B. F. "Reading for the Workers: An Undelivered Lecture." In *Bookselling, Reviewing, and Reading*, ed. Peter Davison, Rolf Meyersohn, and Edward Shils. Teaneck, N.J.: Somerset House, 1976, 155–206. Originally published by Burns Oates and Washbourne, London, 1921.

Palmer, Jerry. *Potboilers: Methods, Concepts and Case Studies in Popular Fiction*. Communication and Society, ed. James Curran. London: Routledge, 1991.

Panttaja, Elizabeth Helen. "Seduction and the Heroine in the American Novel, 1850–1920." Ph.D. dissertation, Brandeis University, 1993.

Papashvily, Helen Waite. *All the Happy Endings*. New York: Harper, 1956.

Paul, Robert S. *Whatever Happened to Sherlock Holmes: Detective Fiction, Popular Theology, and Society*. Carbondale: Southern Illinois University Press, 1991.

Pawling, Christopher, ed. *Popular Fiction and Social Change*. London: Macmillan Press, 1984.

Payant, Katherine B. *Becoming and Bonding: Contemporary Feminism and Popular Fiction by American Writers*. Contributions in Women's Studies, no. 134. Westport, Conn.: Greenwood Press, 1993.

Radway, Janice. *A Feeling for Books: The Book-of-the-Month Club, Literary Taste, and Middle-Class Desire*. Chapel Hill: University of North Carolina Press, 1997.

———. *Reading the Romance: Women, Patriarchy, and Popular Literature*. Chapel Hill: University of North Carolina Press, 1984.

Raub, Patricia. *Yesterday's Stories: Popular Women's Novels of the Twenties and Thirties*. Contributions in American Studies, no. 104, ed. Robert H. Walker. Westport, Conn.: Greenwood Press, 1994.

Reynolds, Quenton. *The Fiction Factor: From Pulp Row to Quality Street: The Story of 100 Years of Publishing at Street and Smith*. New York: Random House, 1955.

Robinson, Forrest G. *Having It Both Ways: Self-Subversion in Western Popular Classics*. Albuquerque: University of New Mexico Press, 1993.

Rosenberg, Bernard, and David Manning White, eds. *Mass Culture: The Popular Arts in America*. Glencoe, Ill.: Free Press, 1957.

Rosenblum, Trudi Miller. "Audiobooks Get Their Own Niche Stores; Retailers Struggle, but Remain Committed to Format." *Billboard*, October 22, 1994, 55.

Ross, Cheri Louise Graves. "Transforming Fictional Genres: Five Nineteenth-Century American Feminist Novelists." Ph.D. dissertation, Purdue University, 1991.

Rubin, Joan Shelley. *The Making of Middlebrow Culture*. Chapel Hill: University of North Carolina Press, 1992.

Rubio, Steven Penner. "Killer Eyes, Killer Legs, Killer Instincts: An Evolution of the American Hard-Boiled Detective Novel." Ph.D. dissertation, University of California, Berkeley, 1997.

Rutkowski, Thaddeus. "Drugs, Big Business and Best Sellers." *ADWEEK*, September 8, 1986, n.p. (all editions).

Saulsbury, Rebecca R. " 'Strong and Brave': The Culture of Womanhood in the Novels of Maria Susanna Cummins." Ph.D. dissertation, Purdue University, 1999.

Scheick, William J. *The Ethos of Romance at the Turn of the Century*. Austin: University of Texas Press, 1994.

Schick, Frank L. *The Paperbound Book in America*. New York: R. R. Bowker, 1958.

Schreuders, Piet. *Paperbacks U.S.A.: 1939–1959*. Trans. By Josh Pachter. San Diego, Calif.: Blue Dolphin Enterprises, 1981.

Schrof, Joannie M. "Bookshop Journeys . . . and Beyond." *U.S. News and World Report*, April 25, 1994, 82, 84.

Server, Lee. *Over My Dead Body: The Sensational Age of the American Paperback: 1945–1955*. San Francisco, Calif.: Chronicle Books, 1994.

Shumway, David R. "Romance in the Romance: Love and Marriage in Turn-of-the-Century Best Sellers." *Int-Journal of Narrative Theory*, 29, no. 1 (Winter 1999), 110–134.

Sizer, Lyde Cullen. *The Political Work of Northern Women Writers and the Civil War, 1850–1872*. Chapel Hill: University of North Carolina Press, 2000.

Smith, Roger H. *The American Reading Public: What It Reads*. New York: R. R. Bowker, 1964.

Smith [van Benschoten], Virginia. "Changes in Best Sellers Since World War One." In *Bookselling, Reviewing, and Reading*, ed. Peter Davison, Rolf Meyersohn, and Edward Shils. Teaneck, N.J.: Somerset House, 1978, 89–100. Originally published in *Journal of Popular Culture*, 1, no. 4 (Spring 1968).

Springer, John Parris. *Hollywood Fictions: The Dream Factory in American Popular Literature*. Norman: University of Oklahoma Press, 2000.

Steinbaugh, Eric Nelson. "Winston Churchill: An Introduction and Annotated Bibliography of Works by and about the American Author." Ph.D. dissertation, University of Maryland, 1982.

Stern, Madeleine B., ed. *Publishers for Mass Entertainment in Nineteenth Century America*. Boston: G. K. Hall, 1980.

Stevens, George. *Lincoln's Doctor's Dog*. Philadelphia: J. B. Lippincott, 1938.

Stevens, J. David. " 'She Was a Woman': Family Roles, Gender, and Sexuality in Bret Harte's Western Fiction." *American Literature*, 69, no. 3 (1997), 571–593.

Storey, John. *Cultural Studies and the Study of Popular Culture: Theories and Methods*. Athens: University of Georgia Press, 1996.

Stryker, Susan. *Queer Pulp: Perverted Passions from the Golden Age of the Paperback*. San Francisco: Chronical Books, 2001.

Sutherland, John. *Bestsellers: Popular Fiction of the 1970s*. London: Routledge and Kegan Paul, 1981.

Tebbel, John William. *A History of Book Publishing in the United States.* 2 vols. New York: R. R. Bowker, 1972, 1975.

———. *Paperback Books: A Pocket History.* New York: Pocket Books, 1964.

Thurston, Carol. *The Romance Revolution: Erotic Novels for Women and the Quest for a New Sexual Identity.* Urbana: University of Illinois Press, 1987.

Traister, Bryce Gordon. "Sentimental Revolution: American Masculinity and Scenes of Writing, 1790–1860." Ph.D. dissertation. University of California, Berkeley, 1996.

Troy, Gil. "Stumping in the Bookstores: A Literary History of the 1992 Presidential Campaign." *Presidential Studies Quarterly*, 25 (4) (1995), 697–710.

Turner, Patricia A. "From Talma Gordon to Theresa Galloway: Images of African American Women in Mysteries." *The Black Scholar* (Spring 1998), 23–26.

Unsworth, John N. "The Book Marketplace II." In *The Columbia History of the American Novel*, ed. Emory Elliott, Cathy N. Davidson, Patrick O'Donell, Valerie Smith, and Christopher P. Wilson. New York: Columbia University Press, 1991.

Van Dover, J. Kenneth. *Murder in the Millions: Erle Stanley Gardner, Mickey Spillane, Ian Feming.* New York: Frederick Ungar Publishing, 1984.

Wagner-Martin, Linda. *The Mid-Century American Novel, 1935–1965.* Twayne's Critical History of the Novel. New York: Twayne, 1997.

Waldmeir, Joseph J., ed. *Recent American Fiction: Some Critical Views.* Boston: Houghton Mifflin, 1963.

Walle, Alf H. *The Cowboy Hero and Its Audience: Popular Culture as Market Derived Art.* Bowling Green, Ohio: Bowling Green State University Popular Press, 2000.

Waples, Douglas. *Research Memorandum on Social Aspects of Readers in the Depression.* New York: Social Science Research Council, 1937.

Wardrop, Stephanie. "Last of the Red Hot Mohicans: Miscegenation in the Popular American Romance. *MELUS*, 22, no. 2 (1997), 61–74.

White, Thomas E. "Popular Religion in America: A Study of Selected Best Sellers." Ph.D. dissertation. Catholic University of America, 1999.

Whiteside, Thomas. *The Blockbuster Complex: Conglomerates, Show Business and Book Publishing.* Middletown, Conn.: Wesleyan University Press, 1981.

Wilson, Christopher P. *The Labor of Words: Literary Professionalism in the Progressive Era.* Athens: University of Georgia Press, 1985.

Wilson, James Southall. "Best-Sellers in Jefferson's Day." *Virginia Quarterly Review*, 36, no. 2 (1960), 222–237.

Wilson, Louis R. *The Geography of Reading.* Chicago: American Library Association and University of Chicago Press, 1938.

Wood, Ruth Pirsig. *Lolita in Peyton Place: Highbrow, Middlebrow, and Lowbrow Novels of the 1950s.* Garland Studies in American Popular History and Culture. New York: Garland Publishers, 1995.

Wright, Thomas Goddard. *Literary Culture in Early New England, 1620–1730.* New Haven, Conn.: Yale University Press, 1920.

Yanarella, Ernest J., and Lee Sigelman, eds. *Political Mythology and Popular Fiction.* Contributions in Political Science, no. 197. Westport, Conn.: Greenwood Press, 1988.

Anthologies

Beck, Warren A., and Myles L. Clowers, eds. *Understanding American History through Fiction*. New York: McGraw-Hill, 1975.

Bruner, David, Robert D. Marcus, and Jorj Tilson, eds. *America through the Looking Glass: A Historical Reader in Popular Culture*. Englewood Cliffs, N.J.: Prentice-Hall, 1974.

McQuade, Donald, and Robert Atwan. *Popular Writing in America*. New York: Oxford University Press, 1974.

Myers, Kathleen, and Beth Obermiller, eds. *Retold American Classic Nonfiction*. Logan, Iowa: Perfection Form, 1991.

Print Reference Resources

Bear, John. *The #1 New York Times Bestseller: Intriguing Facts about the 484 Books that Have Been #1 New York Times Bestsellers since the First List in 1942*. Berkeley, Calif.: Ten Speed Press, 1992.

Bowker Annual of Library and Book Trade Information. New York: R. R. Bowker, 1955– .

Burke, William J., and Will D. Howe. *American Authors and Books, 1640–1940*. New York: Gramercy Publishing, 1943.

A Century of Books. New York: New York Times, 1951.

Cole, John Y. *Books in Action: The Armed Services Editions*. Washington, D.C.: Library of Congress, 1984.

Contemporary Authors: A Bio-Bibliographical Guide to Current Authors and Their Works. Detroit: Gale Research, 1962– .

Cox, Randolph J. *The Dime Novel Companion: A Source Book*. Westport, Conn.: Greenwood Press, 2000.

DeGruson, Gene. *Kansas Authors of Best Sellers: A Bibliography of the Works of Martin and Osa Johnson, Margaret Hill Carpenter, Charles M. Sheldon, and Harold Bell Wright*. Pittsburg: Kansas State College of Pittsburg, 1970.

Elliott, Emory, Martha Banta, and Houston A. Baker, eds. *Columbia Literary History of the United States*. New York: Columbia University Press, 1988.

Elliott, Emory, Cathy N. Davidson, Patrick O'Donnell, Valerie Smith, and Christopher P. Wilson, eds. *The Columbia History of the American Novel*. New York: Columbia University Press, 1991.

Gerhardstein, Virginia Brokaw. *Dickinson's American Historical Fiction*. 4th ed. Metuchen, N.J.: Scarecrow Press, 1981.

Hart, James D. *The Oxford Companion to American Literature*. New York: Oxford University Press, 1983.

Jakubowsky, Maxim, ed. *100 Great Detectives, or, The Detective Directory*. New York: Carroll and Graf Publishers, 1991.

Johannsen, Albert. *The House of Beadle and Adams*. 3 vols. Norman: University of Oklahoma Press, 1950–1962.

Kurian, George T., Miles Orvell, Johnnella E. Butler, and Jay Mechling, eds. *Encyclopedia of American Studies*. 4 vols. Danbury, Conn.: Grolier Educational, 2001.

Library Journal Book Review. New York: R. R. Bowker, 1967– .

Mott, Frank Luther. *Golden Multitudes: The Story of Best Sellers in the United States*. New York: Macmillan, 1947.

National Union Catalog Pre-1956 Imprints. 754 vol. London: Mansell, 1968–1981.

National Union Catalogue. Ann Arbor, Mich.: J. W. Edwards, 1958– .

Nelson, Randy F. *The Almanac of American Letters*. Los Altos, Calif.: William Kaufman, 1981.

New York (City) Public Library. *Dictionary Catalog of the Research Libraries at the New York Public Library 1911–1971*. 800 vols. New York: New York Public Library, 1979.

Readers' Guide to Periodical Literature. New York: W. H. Wilson, 1904– .

Salzman, Jack, ed. *American Studies: An Annotated Bibliography*. 3 vols. Cambridge: Cambridge University Press, 1986.

Sewell, Robert G. "Trash or Treasure? Pop Fiction in Academic and Research Libraries." *College and Research Libraries*, 46 (November 1984), 450–461.

Taubert, Sigfred, and Peter Weidhaas, eds. *The Book Trade of the World*. 4 vols. New York: R. R. Bowker and K. G. Saur, 1972–1984.

World Almanac and Book of Facts. New York: Press Publishing, 1923– .

Webster's Dictionary of American Authors. New York: SMITHMARK Publishers, 1996.

Weimer, David R., comp. *Bibliography of American Culture, 1493–1875*. Ann Arbor, Mich.: University Microfilm, 1957.

Wright, Lyle, comp. *American Fiction: A Contribution Towards Bibliography*. 3 vols. San Marino, Calif.: Huntington Library, 1957–1969.

Zeuschner, Robert B. *Edgar Rice Burroughs: The Exhaustive Scholar's and Collector's Descriptive Bibliography of American Periodical, Hardcover, Paperback, and Reprint Editions*. Jefferson, N.C.: McFarland, 1996.

Indexes and Electronic Resources

America: History and Life. New York: Books, 1987– .

Arts and Humanities Citations Index. Philadelphia, Pa.: Institute for Scientific Information, 1976– .

Book History. (Electronic database.) University Park: Pennsylvania State University Press, 1998– .

Book Review Digest. New York, 1905– .

Book Review Index. Detroit, Gale Research, 1965– .

Books in Print. (Electronic database.) Ovid Technologies, 1995– .

Dissertation Abstracts. Ann Arbor, Mich., 1938– .

Humanities Index. New York: H. W. Wilson, 1974.

International Index to Periodicals. New York: H. W. Wilson, 1905–1974.

Library Literature. New York: H. W. Wilson, 1933– .

MLA International Bibliography. (Electronic database.) Boston: SilverPlatter Information, n.d.

National Library Service Cumulative Book Review Index, 1905–1974. Princeton, N.J.: National Library Service Corp., 1975.

New York Times Book Review Index. New York: Arno Press, 1973– .

Periodicals Contents Index. (Electronic database.) Alexandria, Va.: Chadwyck-Healey, 1996– .

RLIN Catalog. (Electronic database.) Research Libraries Information Network, n.d.
Social Sciences and Humanities Index. New York: W. H. Wilson, 1966–1974.
Social Sciences Index. New York: H. W. Wilson, 1974– .
WorldCat (Electronic database.) OCLC, n.d.

Periodicals

ADWEEK. New York, 1985– .
American Literature. Durham, N.C., 1929– .
Billboard. Cincinnati, Ohio, 1963– .
Black Scholar. San Francisco, 1969– .
Book Review Digest. New York, 1905– .
Booklist. Chicago, 1905– .
Bookman. New York, 1895–1933.
Business Week. New York, 1929– .
College and Research Libraries. Chicago, 1939– .
Journal of Popular Culture. Bowling Green, Ohio, 1967– .
Journal of Popular Literature. Bowling Green, Ohio, 1985– .
Library Journal. New York, 1876– .
MELUS. Los Angeles, 1974– .
New York Review of Books. New York, 1863– .
New York Times Book Review. New York, 1896– .
New Scientist. London, 1971– .
Newsweek. Los Angeles, 1933– .
Public Opinion Quarterly. Chicago, 1937– .
Publishers Weekly. New York, 1872– .
Saturday Review. New York, 1952–1973.
Saturday Review of Literature. New York, 1924–1951.
Studies in Popular Culture. New York, 1974– .
U.S. News and World Report. Washington, D.C., 1948– .
Virginia Quarterly Review. Charlottesville, 1925– .

PORNOGRAPHY

Joseph W. Slade

Several factors explain changes in the cultural status of pornography over the last decade. The first is the visible influence of sexually explicit representation on contemporary fiction (from Erica Jong to Nicolson Baker), the Broadway stage (*Puppetry of the Penis*), broadcast (talk shows featuring porn performers) and cable (HBO's *Real Sex*) television,[1] radio (Howard Stern), painting (David Salle et al.), legitimate cinema (Catherine Breillat's *Romance*), music (rap lyrics), high fashion (all genders),[2] journalism (serious analyses in *Talk*, the *New Yorker*, and *The New York Times*), and advertising (Calvin Klein et al.). Thomas Pynchon's niece, Tristan Taormino, exhorts Americans to try anal sex in her syndicated column, "Pucker Up." The nation's bankers and merchandisers copy the transaction technologies, Web page designs, pop-up and flash advertising, and other novelties created by pornographers who helped to build the Internet and who are leading the nation in innovations such as virtual reality. Precisely because courts do not tolerate pornography involving minors, adult discourses now flourish.

A second factor is the muting of an anti-porn feminism once strident in the 1980s. Assertions that pornography directly causes sexual aggression against women have been undercut by successive annual reports of the U.S. Department of Justice, which indicate that rape and sexual assault have fallen dramatically over the last seven years, a period that coincides precisely with booming sales of sex videos and the proliferation of erotic Web sites. Today's feminists promote their own fantasies in the interests of gender equity, a rationale also endorsed by ethnic groups who wish to push their templates of desire into the mainstream. Explicit performance art, often created by former porn stars, both titillates and deconstructs gender, race, age, and ethnicity. For millions of Americans, in fact, *performance* is as central to an appreciation of sex as it is to football; spectators apply similar standards to both.

A third factor is the recapitalization of porn industries by corporate America. Leaving aside "women's porn" such as romances (a billion-dollar-a-year industry) and afternoon soap operas (a lucrative staple of networks), hard-core media are now quasi-respectable, even republican, in their effect on the global economy. General Motors, AT&T, Time Warner, Marriott International, Hilton, and News Corporation market hard-core video directly to hotel rooms and homes.[3] The effect has been to stabilize the finances of production houses, which rely on cable, satellite, and foreign sales to remain profitable. Metro Video trades on the NASDAQ exchange, and Vivid Video will almost certainly go public soon. *The Economist* predicts that western economies will embrace pornography as a legitimate component of national entertainment enterprises, partly as the consequence of demand for content for rapidly expanding media distribution systems.[4]

A fourth factor runs somewhat counter to the third. The adult industry is consolidating as the sheer volume of annual production threatens to lower profits. Five or six companies (Vivid, VCA, Evil Angel, etc.) now dominate the distribution of pornographic videos in this country, much as the big six Hollywood studios dominate the distribution of legitimate movies; the porn majors claim most of the shelves in video rental outlets, just as the Hollywood majors sew up cineplexes. Subsequent shake-outs have led porn companies to seek new marketing niches by pitching videos to women and couples and hiring women and minorities as directors. Given the number of fetishes in play, it is unlikely that any sexual tastes will be overlooked.

Suppressed voices and transgressive images have always driven American culture, but pornography's roles as stimulus and inspiration have never been so obvious. However one thinks about pornography, and there is much to dislike about the vulgarity in its wake, it is clear that many Americans now tolerate it. Or perhaps it is just that transparency has triumphed. Cell phones, surveillance cameras, credit card tracking programs, massive databases, voice- and face-recognition technologies, digital scanners, and reality-based television shows routinely reveal the intimate secrets of our neighbors. Hundreds of thousands of Americans now exchange erotic messages and photos of themselves over the telephone and the Internet.[5] We have become a nation of voyeurs.

But caution seems advisable: If the state could suppress pornography in the past because a majority of citizens tacitly agreed, popular opinion could scapegoat sex again, in the sort of cycle that might be assisted by the bin Ladens and Falwells of our time. Fewer than four decades ago pornographers were despised, artists went to jail, performers suffered mistreatment by producers and police, and consumers (the case of the literary critic Newton Arvin comes to mind[6]) lost reputations and careers to the zeal of censors. Worse to think, repression may be essential if pornography is to retain its power to enrich culture. It is also wise to remember that pornography is profoundly human: If sexual representation enshrines love and longing, it also embodies exploitation and degradation. Human sexuality itself remains mysterious, try as pornographers might to plumb libidos. Pornography also remains largely impervious to research: Despite hundreds of quantitative and qualitative studies of many genres, we know for certain only that some sexual expressions and some images inflame the fantasies of some people, under some circumstances, some of the time—and not much else. An inability to explain pornography's attractions and effects, of course, ensures our continued fascination with it.

HISTORICAL OUTLINE

The history of pornography in America generally resembles that of other cultural artifacts: Most of it was imported until native industries developed. Colonists carved, shaped, or built erotic figurines, weathervanes, and household tools that we today call Primitive or Outsider Art. Among the first domestic printed materials, only Indian Captivity Narratives, which dwelled on the plight of female settlers abducted by savages, might have qualified as pornographic. In the colonies, traffic in pornographic playing cards, music boxes, prints, and books of European origin was large enough to attract attention, but only Massachusetts passed a law (1711) against it, and even then legislators seemed more concerned with sacrilege. The first actual trial for "obscenity," a Pennsylvania case involving crude drawings, was not held until 1815. By 1842, however, Congress curtailed imports of dirty books by tacking federal obscenity legislation onto the new Customs Act. The immediate effect was to stimulate domestic production.

Most pornographers operated in major cities, principally New York's Wall Street area, home to seedy publishers of the "sporting papers" (*The Whip*, *The Flash*, *The Weekly Rake*) that prefigured the underground tabloids (*Screw*, the *Berkeley Barb*) of the 1960s. Overtly political, the sporting press of the Jacksonian era blended calls for reform with smutty stories, guides to masculine amusement, and exposés of corruption and hypocrisy. A surgeon named William Haynes made so much money from reprinting *Fanny Hill* in 1846 that he added 300 titles to his booklist by 1871. Publishers in Philadelphia, Boston, and New Orleans brought out marriage manuals and fictionalized sexual exploits of celebrities, like the anonymously written *The Amorous Intrigues of Aaron Burr* (1848?). (In a democracy, celebrities are the closest thing to royalty that Americans have, and the impulse to debunk them through pornography is irresistible.) The rowdy political scene produced the first genuine domestic pornographic novel, *Venus in Boston* (1849), written by George Thompson, a fiery Jacksonian, and published by James Ramerio, another political hack.

Other "low" novels followed, usually satires of cultural trends, one of the classic functions of pornography: *Flora Montgomery, the Factory Girl* (1856), a parody of the manufacturing system at Lowell, Massachusetts; *Fanny Greely; Or, the Confessions of a Free-Love Sister Written by Herself* (ca. 1850), a sniggering attack on communitarian movements; and *A Plea for Polygamy* (1870), which sent up the Mormons. Exuberance widened the folkways of sexuality, as chronicled by John D'Emilio and Estelle Freedman in *Intimate Matters: A History of Sexuality in America*. Prostitution and vulgar entertainment flourished as people of various sexual persuasions shared fantasies. Docks and harbors gave shelter to homosexuals, and the growth of urban centers encouraged sexual contacts. Freak shows, slave auctions, sleazy "museums" with their "cabinets of curiosity," and carnivals offered nude bodies or sexual performances.

In 1865, the first mail obscenity statute gave postmasters legal authority to seize sexual materials shipped across state lines. By that time, war, urbanization, and rapid industrialization boosted traffic in the salacious. Demand led distributors to offer pamphlets, books, and pictures to Northern and Southern soldiers trying desperately to affirm life in the midst of death. Less readily available were photographs. By 1846, an American shot a daguerrotype of a man gingerly penetrating a woman (it is in the Kinsey Institute), but daguerrotypes could be copied only with difficulty. Veterans of the Civil War wanted the sexually explicit messages made possible by the advent of new negative-positive photographic reproduction and high-speed presses. Lurid magazines such as *Day's Doings*, *Last Sensation*, *Stetson's Dime Illustrated* (all 1868), *Fox's Illustrated Week's Doings* (1883), and *Illustrated Day's Doings and Sporting World* (1885) featured pictures of actresses in tights and corsets.

Nudity in magazines, and even in museums, was still taboo. In fact, American art schools forbade the use of nude models in classes. Nevertheless, nude drawings and photographs began to circulate at bars, fairs, and theaters and through the mails. *Pornography* (the word appears in English in 1857) emerged as a legal and aesthethic category, promoted in part by smut-hunters, who are essential to concepts of the forbidden. The first celebrated crusader had appeared in 1833, when the Reverend John McDowall of New York haunted the canals and brothels of the city, publishing exposés in *McDowell's Journal*. In 1834 he held an exhibit of obscene articles he had collected—books, prints, playing cards, music and snuff boxes, and so on—to the repugnance of other ministers, who detected in McDowall the prurience he sought to uncover.

The transformation of pornography into a species of cultural subversion, however, was largely the work of Anthony Comstock, a grocery clerk who parlayed his YMCA connections into political clout. In 1868, he persuaded the New York State Legislature to pass a law to punish local retailers of material Comstock thought pernicious. He formed the New York Society for the Suppression of Vice and lobbied successfully in 1873 to increase the penalties for obscenity mandated by the 1865 federal postal law. When thirty more states adopted stringent obscenity laws, other watch and ward societies sprang up to ferret out smut. Sexual pathology seems to have motivated Comstock, who would boast in 1913 of having hounded 15 people (including publisher William Haynes) to suicide. Comstock and his successors did not distinguish between erotica, gambling sheets, contraceptive advice, feminist brochures, and sex education pamphlets, to mention only some of their targets. Annual reports of the New York Society listed contraband by number of items or weight, as so much trash, always with a reference to the nationality of those arrested. This practice illustrated the Society's belief in America's vulnerability to infection by sexually active "inferior" races. In actuality, the Society was battling industrialization, immigration, and education.

Genuine pornography, as distinct from borderline material seized by censors, went underground. Ersatz erotica formed a kind of buffer, beyond which, outlawed and therefore largely untouched, hard-core pornography could prosper as an authentic sub-culture. That function cannot be overstated: Gay and lesbian discourse was "pornographic" by definition; it functioned to bond clandestine homosexual communities. As late as the 1930s, artists such as Marsden Hartley and Charles Demuth had to hide their homosexual paintings.

The Progressive Era encouraged urban realists such as John Sloane to draw pictures of prostitutes. During the 1890s, *Munsey's* (1889–1929) ran "nude art," chiefly reproductions of paintings, but occasionally photos of decorously posed models, as did *Nickell Magazine* (1894–1905), *Metropolitan Magazine* (1895–1911), *Broadway* (1898–1911), and *Peterson's* (1842–1898). *Life* magazine promoted the pin-ups drawn by Charles Dana Gibson. Gradually Americans accepted nudity in

Bettie Page, number one pinup girl in 1955. © Bettmann/CORBIS

paintings and sculpture. Marginal publishers grew bolder also, issuing Boccaccio, Aretino, Petronius, Poggio, and Casanova in expensive editions for the wealthy. The *Memoirs of Dolly Morton* (1904), the memoir of a madam, began a less elegant genre that still flourishes today in works like Nell Kimball's *Her Life as an American Madam, by Herself* (written 1922, published 1970) or Pauline Tabor's *Pauline's* (1972).

World war acquainted servicemen with the candor of sexual expression in Europe, and the rhythms of the Jazz Age lent exuberance and good humor to depictions of intercourse, especially in the pornographic cinema of stag films. In 1911, officials investigated the licentious pronoun in Irving Berlin's "Everybody's Doing It Now," and thus set in motion the scrutiny of song lyrics that would peak in the congressional hearings on rap music in the 1980s. Fake scientific works like the reprint of the 1750 *Padlocks and Girdles of Chastity* (1928) emerged, but so did authentic studies of eroticism, like Bronislaw Malinowski's *The Sexual Life of Savages* (1929). Samuel Roth, the most indefatigable of pornographers began his publishing career with such works as *The Strange Confessions of Monsieur Mountcairn* (1928), one of the earliest homosexual novels written in America. Pornography for women, in the form of "confession" magazines like *True Story* (1919), *True Confessions* (1922), and *Modern Romance* (1930), which combined sentiment and sexual transgression, grew explosively. Radclyffe Hall's lesbian novel, *The Well of Loneliness*, created a scandal on its publication in 1928.

Transvestite reviews, secret theatricals, sexual clubs, and obscene performances of the sort satirized in *Huckleberry Finn* (1885) flourished in the eighteenth century, but did not disturb the public until much later. By 1916, Florenz Ziegfeld, followed by the Shuberts, George White, Earl Carroll, and the Minskys, was posing semi-nude showgirls on New York stages. Economic depression and competition from the movies forced theater owners to book strippers into burlesque shows to retrieve audiences, and men's magazines made celebrities of women who could take off their clothes with style. The vogue lasted until 1937, when LaGuardia forced burlesque off the stage in New York City at the behest of merchants concerned about declining property values.

Breasts began to appear in "girlie" magazines such as *Breezy*, *Titter*, and *The Flapper*, often tucked between pages of jokes, cartoons, and arch fiction. The most ribald of these, *Captain Billy's Whiz Bang*, actually began as mimeographed sheets of jokes circulated to American troops during World War I by William Fawcett, who afterward founded the Fawcett publishing house. During the 1920s and 1930s also appeared Tijuana Bibles, known also as "eight-pagers," a particularly demotic form of pornography. These comic books satirized mainstream cartoons like "Dagwood" by depicting Blondie fellating the postman or Dagwood coupling with Mr. Dithers's secretary. They were crudely drawn, and distributed widely by truckdrivers and novelty salesmen, who also sold photographs of actual intercourse. Tijuana Bibles were cheap, plentiful, and aimed at the uneducated, but just as culturally parodistic as more conventional pornography pitched at wealthier pocketbooks.

Writers such as Robert Sewall circulated pornographic novels (*An Oxford Thesis on Love*, 1938) in mimeographed typescript. Marginal publishers released salacious stories in cheap editions: *A Sea-Side Venus at Fifteen* (1933); *Nelly, or The Confessions of a Doctor* (1930); *The Masquerader or the Affairs of Sissie* (c. 1940); *Grushenka* (1933); *The Prodigal Virgin* (1936?); and *Crimson Hairs* (1938), all of them quickly seized by police. Despite attacks on Cabell's *Jurgen* (1919) or Dreiser's *Sister Carrie* (1900) and *An American Tragedy* (1925), books by reputable writers usually escaped prosecution, sometimes because publishers paid off censors. Courts gradually modified the Hicklin principle, which condemned any book that contained a single obscene passage, in a series of highly publicized cases. Even so, the Supreme Court's *Ulysses* decision (1934), which offered protection to serious literature, also spurred censors to excess. By the 1940s and 1950s major publishers chafed at local litigation that cost them money. Massachusetts suppressed Smith's *Strange Fruit* and New York State Wilson's *Memoirs of Hecate County* at the same time that American soldiers returning from World War II brought back Henry Miller's *Tropic of Cancer* (1934), printed in Paris. Respectable publishers did not defend Samuel Roth, who was imprisoned in 1957 for publishing obscenity, but did gamble on individual works of merit and won major cases: *Lady Chatterley's Lover* (Grove Press, 1960), *Tropic of Cancer* (Grove Press, 1961), and *Fanny Hill* (Putnam, 1966).

Caution still governed magazines. Body-building magazines aimed at homosexuals ran pictures of males clad in jock-straps and mineral oil. Fetish journals such as John Willie's *Bizarre* (1946–1959) emphasized sado-masochism and bondage without depicting the genitals that would have invited prosecution. The largest single fetish producer was Irving Klaw, targeted in the 1950s by the Kefauver Committee during a moral panic triggered by sadistic comic books and fear of rampant homosexuality. The decade of the 1950s was significant, however, for declines in the power of censors, especially postal authorities. In Chicago in 1953, Hugh Hefner founded *Playboy*, whose success spawned a host of imitations (*Caper, Escapade, Dude, Scamp, Monsieur*), although none were as adept at blending bare-breasted pin-ups with quality fiction and articles.

Whether it deserves the label or not, the "sexual revolution" of the 1960s liberalized markets for erotica. Driven out of Paris by censorship and encouraged by American court decisions, Maurice Girodias reestablished Olympia Press in New York in 1967, but found that his books were already being openly pirated by California publishers such as Brandon House and Essex House, who were busy hiring writers such as Angelo d'Arcangelo (*The Homosexual Handbook*, 1969), Harriet Daimler (*Darling*, 1973), Alexander Trocchi (*White Thighs*, 1967), Marco Vassi (*Pro Ball Groupie*, 1974), and Charles Bukowski (*Notes of a Dirty Old Man*, 1969). In 1969, Al Goldstein and Jim Buckley, in beginning *Screw*, recreated the "sporting paper" of the 1840s, a sexual tabloid animated by vulgar partisan politics. Its success led to imitators such as the *Berkeley Barb* and the *East Village Other*. Equally political pornographic cartoons began to appear from the pens of illustrators such as R. Crumb, Clay Wilson, Shary Flenniken, and Trina Robbins. Hard-core magazines full of photographs of intercourse streamed from marginal presses.

Pop artists such as Andy Warhol, Larry Rivers, and Tom Wesselman experimented with graphic sexuality. American artists embraced sexual subjects; more to the point, collectors took notice of the investment opportunities. The 1960s created an erotic environment still explored by such painters as Eric Fischl, David Salle, and Jeff Koons. Phyllis and Eberhard Kronhausen, the Scandinavian sexologists, opened a museum of erotic art in San Francisco. The casual nudity of the Hippies found its way onto stages; "topless" and "bottomless" clubs sprang up in major cities, and audiences became accustomed to seeing flesh across the footlights of legitimate theatres. Heady ideals aside, much of this was ugly: Drug addicts performed intercourse in storefronts to feed habits; unscrupulous producers exploited runaways and high school drop-outs; and organized crime took control of the distribution of pornographic magazines and films.

In part because Denmark decriminalized pornography in 1967, with few adverse effects, the President's Commission on Obscenity and Pornography in 1970 concluded that the United States could safely follow suit. The Supreme Court's last major ruling on the subject (*Miller*, 1973), left the door open for local communities to decide for themselves whether works were obscene, provided that such ordinances respected the First Amendment. Radical feminists objected. For them, liberalized sexuality simply victimized women, and pornography shored up male dominance. When Robin Morgan coined the phrase "pornography is the theory, rape the practice" in 1974, sex—and its representations—became ideological. Ten years later, Catharine MacKinnon, a law professor, and Andrea Dworkin, herself the writer of brutal sexual fiction, defined sex *as* violence, argued that pornography was the origin of male aggression against women, and crafted censorship legislation premised on the theory that pornography violated the civil rights of women and was therefore actionable. Anti-porn feminists forced an unparalleled and valuable debate on sexuality and its representations. Pro-sex feminists argued that such legislation would cast women as victims, make them wards of the state, and silence their own voices. They called for using pornography to advance feminist agendas.

Performance artists responded. Significant artists were Hannah Wilke (*Super-T-Art*, 1974), Carolee Schneemann (*Interior Scroll*, 1975), Karen Finley (*I Like the Dwarf on the Table When I Give Him Head*, 1983), and Robbie McCauley, whose protest against female servitude stood her naked on an auction block. Their performances deconstructed issues of sex, race, and gender. But when controversial artists sought federal funds, conservatives such as Senator Jesse Helms in the early '90s attacked the National Endowment for the Arts for its association with "obscene" artists. Some of the performers supported themselves by working in sex industries, principally stripping, sometimes called "pornography set to music." Stripping grew quickly in popularity; by 1995, some 2500 strip clubs had spread across the United States to cater to audiences of all genders.

But in 1986, the conservative Attorney General Meese convened another commission to endorse his belief that pornography had put the nation at risk and enlisted anti-porn feminists to help. Courts struck down feminist anti-porn ordinances as unconstitutional and were scarcely less sympathetic to Meese's tactics, though they did permit zoning as a way of controlling adult businesses and, for a brief period, "forum shopping," the practice of empanelling juries in conservative communities in order to declare obscene materials that were acceptable elsewhere. New technologies soon rendered both strategies futile. Although it grudgingly conceded that print erotica was no longer a menace, the Attorney General's Commission condemned telephone, videotape, and computer pornography as dangerous, thus embracing a classic syndrome—the fear that new communication technologies destabilize morality. Of all such technologies, the moving image has frightened traditionalists the most.

Motion picture censorship boards arose early in many states, encouraged in 1915 by the Supreme Court (*Birth of a Nation*) decision that the cinema was a form of spectacle (like circuses) and therefore not entitled to First Amendment protection. Waves of self-policing by Hollywood—the Hays Office in 1922, the Production Code in 1934, the latter adopted under pressure from the Legion of Decency—staved off federal censorship until the 1950s, when an industry threatened by candid films from Europe and by television at home began to challenge its own code. A series of decisions in the 1950s beginning with *Joseph Burstyn, Inc. v. Wilson* (1952) not only granted First Amendment protection to the cinema but opened the door to treatment of sexual themes and nudity. Well before the 1950s, however, Hollywood had learned to substitute violence for sexuality, a phenomenon documented by Gershon Legman in *Love and Death*. This tendency was pronounced especially in Biblical epics, which allowed directors to shoot scenes of torture sanctioned by religious tradition, but violence overflowed into most melodramas, where embraces would end in aggressively phallic images (say a locomotive penetrating a tunnel), or where death and destruction became satisfying ends in themselves.

Sensationalism also surfaced in "exploitation" films, which promised but rarely delivered nudity and sexual frankness. They began with "exposés" of the white slave traffic in 1913 and reached a kind of apotheosis of trash in the 1930s and

1940s when a group of producer-distributors known as the "Forty Thieves" fed drive-in movies a stream of lurid "educational" films on venereal disease, birth, pre-marital sex, interracial marriage, and contraception. During the 1940s Irving Klaw turned out fetish films featuring women in lingerie, rubber, and leather, sometimes in bondage scenes. The *Garden of Eden* decision (1955) led to several dozen silly "nudies" in which topless women played volleyball. But Russ Meyer (*Faster Pussycat, Kill! Kill!*, 1966) and producers such as David F. Friedman (*Blood Feast*, 1963), as if to borrow a page from Legman, capitalized on the blending of nudity and violence. Unable to depict intercourse, they symbolised it with brutality. When censors accepted this strategem, hundreds of "roughies" poured from sleazy studios. Competition from foreign films such as *The Cousins* (France, 1959), *La Dolce Vita* (Italy, 1959), and *I Am Curious (Yellow)* (Sweden, 1967), forced Hollywood toward greater candor. So did American avant-garde films such as Brakhage's *Lovemaking* (1969), Smith's *Flaming Creatures* (1963), Anger's *Scorpio Rising* (1964), and Warhol's *Blow Job* (1964). More important still was the need to lure audiences away from television; by the 1970s, nudity had become commonplace in Hollywood films, as had serious treatment of sexual themes. Just as significant was the public appearance of hard-core pornographic films.

The early history of genuinely pornographic films is largely anonymous. The earliest surviving American stag, *A Free Ride* (aka *A Grass Sandwich*), involving a man and two women in a Model-T Ford, dates from 1915. Only a few films, like *The Casting Couch* (1920), a lampoon of Mack Sennett, originator of the practice of requiring actresses to sleep with the producer before getting the part, were actually shot in Hollywood. By the late 1920s American amateurs were turning out more stags than those of any other nationality, and continued to do so until the 1950s, when they were outpaced by the English; during the 1960s, the Scandinavians pulled ahead, only to drop behind in the 1970s.

Shot at first on 35mm film stock, then 16mm, the hard-core films were distributed clandestinely, often with the assistance of local authorities and police, who seized them only on complaint. It was a decidedly demotic form, drawing heavily on folklore, deliberately crude and anachronistic; before 1965, only five were shot in sound, only four in color. Because viewers responded uncomfortably to gay behavior, producers rarely depicted homosexual intercourse. Nor did they include violence or underage actors, whose presence distressed the predominantly middle class white male audiences. The 8mm film projector, cheap enough to be available to many, made it possible for individuals to watch films at home rather than in the Legion Hall, and soon producers were turning out copies for specialized audiences who wanted homosexual acts, or anal intercourse, or actresses with red hair. The 8mm reel coexisted briefly with larger format films, which went public in the late 1960s.

The first hard-core film to be shown publicly in the United States was an untitled hour-long 16mm reel exhibited at the Avon Theater in New York City; it was not prosecuted, and subsequent films widened the area of the permissible. "Documentaries" like *Sexual Freedom in Denmark* (1970), under the guise of comment of "socially redeeming importance," made theaters safe for pornography, as did de Renzy's *A History of the Blue Movie* (1970). The market quickly bifurcated into heterosexual and homosexual types, the latter pioneered by Wakefield Poole's *Boys in the Sand* (1972). In 1972, two films, *Deep Throat* and *Behind the Green Door*, attracted enormous audiences. To date, *Deep Throat*, made for around $25,000, has earned through exhibition and videotape copies about $75 million (though exact figures are impossible to ascertain), not much when one considers that a *Harry Potter* (2001) can garner three times that much in a single weekend.

The Adult Film Association holds annual ceremonies modelled on the Academy Awards to recognize directors and performers. Gerard Damiano, who made his reputation with *Deep Throat*, gave way to Svetlana (*Miami Spice*, 1987) and Robert McCallum (*Doll Face*, 1986) and to former performers turned directors such as John Stagliano (the *Buttman* series, 1990–), John Leslie (the *Voyeur* series, 1994–) and Veronica Hart (*Edgewise*, 2001). More than 25,000 women have appeared in hard-core films, the supply continuously replenished by those hoping to become the next Jenna Jameson, who has made millions as a star. Most make nowhere near that, and male performers, of course, are paid a fifth of what the females earn. Vertically integrated American studios now produce more hard-core video-tapes than all other nations combined and export them all over the world.

Pornography drove the development of videotape technology. Sony introduced the Betamax videocassette recorder/player in 1975 but refused to license the for-mat to pornographic filmmakers. The following year JVC released its VHS vid-eocassette, freely licensed its format to hard-core producers, and thus doomed the Betamax design. Well into the 1980s, more than half of all videotapes manufac-tured in the United States were of the pornographic type. In 1999, more than 10,000 new videocassette porn titles brought in $4.2 billion.

Pornography also drove the development of cyberspace. From the outset, Amer-icans used the Internet for erotic messaging, but when Tim Berners-Lee invented the World Wide Web in 1989, porn entrepreneurs established sexual sites. By ruling unconstitutional the Communication Decency Act of 1996, the Supreme Court has forestalled censorship of the Internet. Neither zoning nor selective prosecution can control global distribution technologies; nor can organized crime retain its grip. Americans who object to content must put their faith in technol-ogies such as Internet software filters or V-chips installed on television sets. High demand for sexual materials, coupled with new corporate investment, enhanced distribution systems, and rapidly expanding niche markets, have created oppor-tunities for women and minorities. The future of sexual representation is uncertain but will probably be robust.

REFERENCE WORKS

Archives in several countries contain erotica: The National Museum of Italy in Naples preserves erotic frescoes and statues from excavated Roman cities; the Museu de l'Eròtica in Barcelona, the Sex Museum in Amsterdam, the Museum Erotica in Copenhagen, the Museum für Erotische Kunst in Munich and the Erotik Museum in Berlin display mostly national artifacts; the Museo Nacional in Mexico City shelters erotic Pre-Columbian Art; the Bodleian Library in Oxford, England, keeps a few rare erotic books; the Louvre in Paris has a modest collection of books and paintings, while the Musée de l'Erotisme, also in Paris, contains artifacts; the Russian State Library (formerly the Lenin Library) in Moscow lacks funds to catalog some 11,000 erotic items, mostly from the Soviet Union and Asia[7]; entrepreneurs are assembling items for an erotic museum in New York.

These aside, six western institutions house major collections: the Bibliothèque Nationale (Paris), the British Museum (London), the Victoria and Albert Museum (London), the Library of Congress (Washington), the Institute for the Advanced Study of Sexuality (San Francisco), and the Kinsey Institute for Research in Sex, Gender, and Reproduction (University of Indiana, Bloomington). Although all contain American examples, the Kinsey Institute and the Library of Congress are richest in indigenous articles. Information about collections in the Library of Congress, the Kinsey Institute, SIECUS, Planned Parenthood, and selected research institutions is available in Kara Lichtenberg's *A Research Guide to Human Sexuality*. The essays in Martha Cornog's *Libraries, Erotica, Pornography* discuss many genres and the issues involved in collecting, with lists of repositories. John O. Christensen's *Obscenity, Pornography, and Libraries: A Selective Bibliography* surveys books and articles on library censorship, on collections of erotica/pornography, and on strategies of acquisition and circulation.

The most comprehensive contemporary attempt to cover American pornography is Joseph W. Slade's *Pornography and Sexual Representation: A Reference Guide*. The annotated bibliographies and essays of the three volumes (also available in an on-line, fully searchable, media-linked version) deal with American pornography in twenty sections devoted to history, theory, research, and law, and to genres such as folklore, books, magazines and newspapers, photography, art, motion pictures, comic books, electronic media, and performance. Chronologies, guides to library collections, and materials on child pornography advance discussion further. It is the best starting point for scholars. Also authoritative are bibliographies compiled by the Kinsey Institute, which updates them erratically; these are available as xeroxes. Examples range from "Contemporary Erotic Literature" and "Girlie Magazines" to "Penis in Art" and "Sex Slang Dictionaries." The Institute publishes the monthly *International Directory of Sex Research and Related Fields*, whose pages highlight scholarship on erotica. The *Journal of Sex Research*, the *Journal of the History of Sexuality*, and the *Archives of Sexual Behavior* report on research on forms of sexual representation.

Terence J. Deakin's bibliography of bibliographies, *Catalogi Librorum Eroticorum: A Critical Bibliography of Erotic Bibliographies and Book-Catalogues*, annotates seventy-eight bibliographies and private catalogs of "classic" erotic literature. For later works, scholars should consult *Clandestine Erotic Fiction in English 1800–1930: A Bibliographical Study*, for which Peter Mendes has assembled information on dealers, collectors, and the narratives that occupied them. Modern overviews can be found in *Banned Books*, which covers works censored for various causes. *Banned Books Online*, an electronic exhibit/gallery, is regularly updated. Forthcoming is the *Encyclopedia of Erotic Literature*, which promises international entries edited by Gaëtan Brulotte and John Phillips. Gershon Legman's *The Horn Book: Studies in Erotic Folklore and Bibliography* discusses writers, publishers, and collectors. Lawrence J. Shifreen and Roger Jackson have traced editions, pirated and otherwise, of America's most celebrated "obscene" author in *Henry Miller: A Bibliography of Primary Sources*; questionable works by other famous authors appear in standard literary indexes.

American fiction too candid for publication on this side of the Atlantic was brought out by the Olympia Press in France, as detailed by Patrick Kearney's *The Olympia Press, Paris 1953–1965: A Handlist*, which lists output prior to the press's

William S. Burroughs, 1962. © Bettmann/CORBIS

move to America during the sixties; Kearney's *A Bibliography of the New York Olympia Press* covers subsequent years. The *Erotica-Curiosa-Sexology Catalogs* issued by C. J. Scheiner are authoritative, as are those issued by Ivan Stormgart. Generously annotated entries appear in Stuart Swezey's *Amok: Fifth Dispatch: Sourcebook of the Extremes of Information*. Keyword searches will elicit bibliographic information on specific subjects and fetishes; some Web sites are operated by dealers, others by amateur aficionados of periods or tastes. Typical is Pink Flamingo Publications, which sells books on "Erotic and Spanking Fiction."

In the gendered literature category are *Sex Variant Women in Literature*, a listing of lesbian works in the Kinsey Institute with discussion of writers such as Amy Lowell and Edna St. Vincent Millay, compiled by Jeannette H. Foster; *The Lesbian in Literature: A Bibliography*, compiled by Barbara Grier, Jan Watson, and Robin Jordan; and *Historical, Literary and Erotic Aspects of Lesbianism* by Monica Kehoe. Noel I. Garde annotates 600 entries in *The Homosexual in Literature: A Chronological Bibliography Circa 700 B.C.–1958*. Ian Young's *The Male Homosexual in Literature: A Bibliography*, similarly dated, is still helpful. Two maps to a huge erotic genre are Eileen Fallon's *Words of Love: A Complete Guide to Romance Fiction* and Kristen Ramsdell's *Happily Ever After: A Guide to Reading Interests in Romance Fiction*. Gender shifting is part of the appeal of *Uranian Worlds: A Guide to Alter-*

native Sexuality in Science Fiction, Fantasy and Horror, edited by Eric Garber and Lyn Paleo.

Indispensible for folklorists are Stith Thompson's six-volume *Motif-Index of Folk Literature: A Classification of Narrative Elements in Folktales, Ballads, Myths, Fables, Medieval Romances, Exempla, Fabliaux, Jestbooks, and Local Legends* and *The Types of the Folktale: A Classification and Bibliography* by Antti Aarne and Stith Thompson, a classification scheme derived from Thompson's magnum opus. Their international scope embraces sexual elements in stories, jokes, songs, and legends of all countries. Without peer is Gershon Legman's "Erotic Folksongs and Ballads: An International Bibliography," an erudite annotated bibliography of virtually every notable collection of obscene or bawdy drinking, campfire, music hall, military, cowboy, sailor, college and fraternity, and working songs, as well as sea chanties, folk songs, ballads, and verses, all drawn from classic and fugitive bibliographies, hand- and typewritten manuscripts, xeroxed, mimeographed, and samizdat compilations, private publications, personal contacts, academic papers, and underground resources.

The study of obscene English began with *Slang and Its Analogues*, published by John S. Farmer and William Earnest Henley to compensate for omissions in the *Oxford English Dictionary*; it is an etymological treasure. The only American study to compare with Farmer and Henley's is Allen Walker Read's *Lexical Evidence from Folk Epigraphy in Western North America: A Glossarial Study of the Low Element in the English Vocabulary*, which characterizes graffiti, word play, and other sexual speech as authentic lower class voices. "Sex Similarities and Differences in Language, Speech, and Nonverbal Communication: An Annotated Bibliography," by Barrie Thorne, Cheris Kramarae, and Nancy Henley, is a splendid list of articles, some of which deal with erotic and/or obscene speech. Joseph J. Hayes's "Language Behavior of Lesbian Women and Gay Men: A Selected Bibliography (Part 1)" is comprehensive on academic treatments until the late 1970s; Bruce Rodgers's *The Queen's Vernacular: A Gay Lexicon* is excellent on homosexual expression itself. In *The Language of Sadomasochism: A Glossary and Linguistic Analysis*, Thomas E. Murray and Thomas R. Murrell explore speech patterns of a sexual subculture.

Not surprisingly, few standard indexes include erotic magazines. An exception is David E. E. Sloane's *American Humor Magazines and Comic Periodicals*, which furnishes publication data, brief content analysis, episodes of censorship, and archival locations for magazines such as *Comic Cuties* (1966), *Dash* (1941), and *Dolls and Gags* (1953); other sections include "College Humor Magazines" and "Humor in American Almanacs." Alan Betrock's guides to borderline magazines of the 1950s and 1960s are authoritative, especially his *Complete Guide to Cult Magazines*. Betrock and Hillard Schneider elaborate on celebrities singled out by magazines such as *Confidential* in *The Personality Index to Hollywood Scandal Magazines, 1952–1966*. Information on "girlie" types is available in Betrock's *Pin-Up Mania: The Golden Age of Men's Magazines (1950–1967)*. Entries in *Completely Queer: The Gay and Lesbian Encyclopedia*, edited by Steve Hogan and Lee Hudson, include explicit gay and lesbian magazines. *Words to the Wise: A Writer's Guide to the Feminist and Lesbian Periodicals and Publishers* by Andrea Fleck Clardy, notes magazines hospitable to erotica. The electronic zine *Queer Zine Explosion* describes often short-lived lesbian and gay zines as they appear. The *Report* of the President's Commission on Pornography and Obscenity identifies soft- and hard-core magazines published prior to 1970, while the *Final Report* of the Attorney General's Commission lists 2700 fetish titles. *Access: The Supplementary Index to Periodicals* indexes magazines such as *Playboy, Penthouse*, and local magazines such as the *Village Voice* and *Miami Magazine* that deal with sexualized events. Contemporary soft- and hard-core pornographic magazines can be located in Samia Husni's *Samia Husni's Guide to New Magazines*, an annual compilation.

The fastest source, however, is alt.magazines.pornographic on the Usenet, an up-to-date listing of periodicals devoted to fetishes ranging from rubber, leather, enemas, and lactation to tattoos. Millions of images on the Usenet and Internet have eroded demand for sex magazines; fewer are published every year. Keeping track of erotic categories of electronic zines is the rationale of E-zines Database Menu. Bill Brent's *The Black Book* describes zines devoted to fetishes, but *The World of Zines: A Guide to the Independent Magazine Revolution*, edited by Mike Gunderloy and Cari G. Janice, critiques them more comprehensively, although the monthly *Factsheet Five* updates selections more often. Richard Kadrey's two-volume *Covert Culture Sourcebook* lists outrageous zines, as does Russ Kick's *Outposts: A Catalog of Rare and Disturbing Alternative Information* and its sequel, *Psychotropia*. The best source on scandal tabloids is Gerald S. Greenberg's *Tabloid Journalism: An Annotated Bibliography of English-Language Sources*.

Valuable bibliographies on comic book criticism can be found in Doug Highsmith's "Comic Books: A Guide to Information Sources" and Randall W. Scott's *Comic Books and Strips: An Information Sourcebook*. In *R. Crumb Checklist of Work and Criticism*, Donald M. Fiene lists material by and about the comic artist R. Crumb until 1980; in *Crumb-ology: The Works of R. Crumb, 1981–1994*, Carl Richter advances the bibliography further. Lively and accurate critiques animate *Indy Magazine: The Guide to Alternative Comix and Film*. Indispensable for locating explicit comics are the catalogs of publishers such as Last Gasp, Loompanics Unlimited, Fantagraphics, and Bud Plant (who also publishes the newsletter *Comic Art Update*).

Although focused primarily on painting, Eugene C. Burt's *Erotic Art: An Annotated Bibliography with Essays* cites general histories of pornography, photography, and cinema. Burt lists criticism of individual artists, though nationalities are not always noted. The bibliography appended to Peter Webb's *The Erotic Arts*, though dated, is both precise and global. Cary von Karwath's *Die Erotik in der Kunst* remains the most accurate work on pictorial erotica before 1900; it includes pictures of the erotic murals for Versailles painted by François Boucher; the originals were destroyed by American customs when they were sent to the United States. Jane Clapp discusses 600 images and cross-references critical and biographical with historical data for her *Art Censorship*. Not in the same league, but still informative on controversies in the 1980s is Oliver Trager's collection of newspaper articles for *The Arts and Media in America: Freedom or Censorship?*

The Complete Book of Erotic Art, edited by Eberhard and Phyllis Kronhausen, comments on artists of many nationalities. *The Forbidden Library: An Exhibition of Erotic Illustrations from the 18th Century to the Present Day*, the catalog of an important London show of erotic book illustrations, contains 589 entries on illustrators of books such as *Fanny Hill*. The Erotic Print Society advertises contemporary illustrations. Articles on artists, writers, performers, and themes make up volume 4 of *Studies in Homosexuality*, edited by Dynes and Donaldson.

Materials in the Kinsey Institute have been researched and annotated by Tee Corinne's in *Lesbian Images in the Fine Arts*.

Volume 3 of the *Technical Reports of the Commission on Obscenity and Pornography* outlines traffic in photographs over decades; volume 9 reprints sociological and psychological studies of photos and visual erotica. (Publication of an *Illustrated Presidential Report of the Commission on Obscenity and Pornography*, edited by Earl Kemp, sent the publisher to prison.) Part Two (volume I) of the Attorney General's Commission on Pornography's *Final Report* describes photographs in language as prurient as the images. Steve Sullivan's *Glamour Girls: The Illustrated Encyclopedia* ferrets out nude layouts in magazines and crafts modest biographies of the pin-up models and celebrities.

Dated but still useful is James L. Limbacher's *Sexuality in World Cinema*; annotated filmographies classify 13,000 legitimate and pornographic films into 26 categories. The best quick reference for exploitation films is *Incredibly Strange Films*, edited by Andrea Juno and V. Vale, who add filmographies and bibliographies to analyses of exploitation genres ranging from bikerchick to women-in-prison films. *Russ Meyer—The Life and Films: A Biography and a Comprehensive, Illustrated, and Annotated Filmography and Bibliography* by David K. Frasier is devoted to the director most often identified with soft-core exploitation. For the index of stag films (1915–1960) appended to *Dirty Movies*, Al Di Lauro and Gerald Rabkin merge the shelflist of the Kinsey archive with that of Hugh Hefner's collection. Predominantly heterosexual films and videos are annotated for a audience in the volumes of *The X-Rated Videotape Guide*, authored first by Robert H. Rimmer, then by Rimmer and Patrick Riley, and currently by Riley alone; Riley has compiled *The X-Rated Videotape Star Index* as well. The *Interactive Adult Movie Almanac*, a CD-ROM, reviews 750 porn videos. Reviews can also be found at rame.net, a site incorporating the Adult Movie FAQ and the Internet Adult Film Database. Two other sources are extraordinary: a Web site operated by Luke Ford, whose skepticism about the sex industry lends force to his comments and statistics, and *Adult Video News*, the trade journal, whose statistics on the industry are the most accurate available. *Adult Film World*, another monthly, is occasionally useful if not so reliable as *AVN*. *Adam Black Video Illustrated*, an offshoot of *Adult Film World*, reports on nascent erotica featuring African Americans.

The Ultimate Guide to Lesbian and Gay Film and Video, edited by Jenni Olsen, indexes 2000 entries by subject. The annual *Adam Film World Directory of Gay Adult Video* and *Gay Video: A Guide to Erotica* by John W. Rowberry identify and locate gay films. Angela Cohen and Sarah G. Fox's *The Wise Woman's Guide to Erotic Videos*, Steve and Elizabeth Brent's *The Couple's Guide to the Best Erotic Videos*, and Cathy Winks's *The Good Vibrations Guide to Adult Videos* recommended hardcore for female audiences.

Students of staged eroticism should begin with Arthur Maria Rabenalt's *Mimus Eroticus*. John Gray's *Active Art: A Bibliography of Artists' Performance from Futurism to Fluxus and Beyond* can be helpful on occasionally erotic performance art during the periods indicated in the title. Interviews with sixteen performance artists (e.g., Acker, Finley, Galás, hooks, Hughes, Lunch, Sprinkle) collected by Andrea Juno and V. Vale for *Angry Women* are indispensable. Nick Kaye has gathered scripts and comment from erotic artists such as Carolee Schneeman, Linda Montano, and Richard Foreman in *Art into Theatre: Performance Interviews and Documents*. His-

1291

torians will need the now-defunct journal *High Performance* and the still current *TDR* (*The Drama Review*). The albums on burlesque constructed by Chris Audibert contain ads, programs, reviews, and personal assessments of striptease artists during the 1950s. Professionals consult the annual *Exotic Dancer* for insider dope on agencies, go-go clubs, and nude, topless, and stripper bars; the statistics on more than 2500 venues in *Stripper Magazine*, the trade journal of the exotic dance industry, will surprise the scholar.

The bibliography of bibliographies in "Sexuality and the Mass Media: An Overview" by Jeanne Steele and Jane Brown focuses on broadcasting. The title of Nancy Signorelli's *Role Portrayal and Stereotyping on Television: An Annotated Bibliography of Studies Relating to Women, Minorities, Aging, Sexual Behavior, Health and Handicaps* indicates its scope. *Covert Culture Sourcebook* and *Covert Culture Sourcebook 2.0* by Richard Kadrey and *Bleep! Censoring Rock and Rap Music* by Betty Houchin Winfield and Sandra Davidson review sexually-oriented music. Guides to sexual sites on the Internet include *Alt, Culture: An A-Z Guide to the '90s—Underground, Online, and Over the Counter* by Stephen Daly and Nathaniel Wice; *High Weirdness by Email* by Ivan Stang; *The Woman's Guide to Sex on the Web* by Anne Semans and Cathy Winks; *The Perv's Guide to the Internet* by the Cybersex Consortium; and *The Complete Internet Sex Resource Guide* by Philip Mason.

Censorship: 500 Years of Conflict, edited by William Zeisel, reviews political, economic, and sexual suppression, while *The Encyclopedia of Censorship* by Jonathan Green and *Censorship*, edited by Lawrence Amey, Timothy Hall, Carl Jansen, Charles May, and Richard Wilson, break out cases, personalities, and issues. For *Sourcebook on Pornography*, Franklin Mark Osanka and Sara Lee Johann have assembled studies purporting to demonstrate that sexual representation has effects evil in the extreme, a conclusion that few thoughtful scholars will endorse. Such research suffers from hidden agendas and faulty design, according to Alison King's "Mystery and Imagination: The Case of Pornography Effects Studies."

HISTORY AND CRITICISM

Because they are still developing a discourse appropriate for discussing sexual matters, few critics engage actual pornography. Those who do are more comfortable with print genres than with graphic ones. Tracing literary examples is easier than ascertaining the provenance of songs, jokes, or stag films, about which myths proliferate. Cherished legends include reports of the circulation of "snuff films" in which women are allegedly literally killed at the climax of intercourse (no authentic snuff film has ever been uncovered, although there is a legitimate film with "snuff" as the title, and there do exist filmed records of executions and murders, but *not* coupled with sex); reports that various famous movie actresses started their careers in pornographic movies (various actors and actresses, like Hedy Lamarr in *Ecstacy* or Sylvester Stallone in *Italian Stallion*, have played nude scenes, but no major figure has ever appeared in a hard-core movie; various stag films advertised as starring Marilyn Monroe, Barbara Streisand, and Ronald Reagan are fakes made by look-a-likes); reports that the Nazis flooded Poland with pornography to destroy the moral resistance of the country; and reports that the American OSS dropped pornography on Hitler's headquarters as a way of inducing surrender through masturbation. I. C. Jarvie mentions additional myths: "that there is a hidden agenda in pornography which aims to break down sexual taboos and thus keep women in their place"; and "that there is a connection between viewing/producing pornography and crimes against women."[8] In a larger sense, of course, almost everything humans think they know about pornography (and sexuality) is folklore, and the less evidence available, the stronger the convictions. Disputes about pornography are usually disputes about tastes and ideologies.

Postmodernists view erotic discourses as commodifications of sex, inscriptions of power, subordinations of gender, and programmers of cultural attitudes. Pertinent here are Michel Foucault's *The History of Sexuality*, which finds that sexual and gender taxonomies embody political structures, and Herbert Marcuse's *Eros and Civilization*, which suspects that corporate states eroticize entertainment in order to control fantasies and ensure obedience. Theorists at the other extreme characterize pornography as fundamental to political subversion. In this category are Jean Marie Goulemot's *Forbidden Texts: Erotic Literature and Its Readers in Eighteenth-Century France* and Annie Stora-Lamarre's *L'enfer de la IIIe Republique: Censeurs et pornographes, 1881–1914*, which link pornography to rebellion and the rise of democracy in France. The essays in *The Invention of Pornography: Obscenity and the Origins of Modernity, 1500–1800*, edited by Lynn Hunt, point out that from the sixteenth through the eighteenth centuries, pornography promoted democracy, urbanization, secularism, scientific method, equitable legal systems, technology, and modernity itself.

Beginning with the nineteenth century, middle-class males striving for respectability and fearful of sexual license tried to prevent sexual information from reaching women and the lower classes, says Walter Kendrick's *The Secret Museum: Pornography in Modern Culture*. Forbidding sexual expression shored up a sense of privacy in a society increasingly convinced that democracy and literacy had led to open, public vulgarity. According to Lauren Berlant in *The Queen of America Goes to Washington City: Essays on Sex and Citizenship*, pornography strengthened democracy by reminding Americans that a culture can become authoritarian by trivializing the sexuality of its members. Another argument that pornography is essential to democracy is Joss Marsh's *Word Crimes: Blasphemy, Culture, and Literature in Nineteenth Century England*, which maintains that "lower-class," blasphemous, and obscene speech challenged established institutions. Underclasses often embrace pornography as a political act, say Constance Penley's "Crackers and Whackers: The White Trashing of Porn," Audre Lorde's "Uses of the Erotic: The Erotic as Power," and bell hooks's *Outlaw Culture: Resisting Representations*, all of which discuss racism and class bias behind attacks on erotic expression.

The two greatest cultural critics of pornography, however, are Gershon Legman and Georges Bataille. When depictions of sexuality are suppressed, says Legman in *Love and Death: A Study in Censorship*, they reappear as depictions of violence, the socially acceptable surrogate of sex in modern media. Bataille's *Death and Sensuality* speculates that an increasingly artificial western civilization finds eroticism in artifacts that implicitly deny normal cycles of reproduction; its members actually prefer representations to actual, natural sex. F. M. Christensen, in *Pornography: The Other Side*, claims that opposition to sexual expression derives from false modesty, ignorance, poor education, and differences in taste; pornography can alleviate repression by giving pleasure for those open to erotic experience. Peter Michelson's *Speaking the Unspeakable: Poetics of Obscenity* distinguishes between erotic and pornographic, and applies esthetic criticism to both. At two extremes of feminist criticism are Camille Paglia, whose *Sexual Personae: Art and Decadence from Nefertiti to Emily Dickinson* construes obscenity as essential to moral and esthetic sensibilities, and Susanne Kappeler, whose *The Pornography of Representation* excoriates *all* representations as sexist and ultimately pornographic, and encourages women to destroy western art in its entirety.

Feminist anti-pornography comment seems to be fading. The chief anti-sex text remains Andrea Dworkin's *Pornography: Men's Oppression of Women*, an argument that pornography is the everyday expression of males, all of whom reflexively brutalize women. Dworkin's *Intercourse* blames gender inequity on the act of penetration, and calls for reproductive technologies to replace heterosexual intercourse. According to Catharine A. MacKinnon's *Feminism Unmodified: Discourses on Life and Law* and *Toward a Feminist Theory of the State*, pornography causes discrimination against women, though the thesis falters when she applies it to earlier periods of history. *Pornography: The Production and Consumption of Inequality* by Gail Dines, Robert Jensen, and Ann Russo deconstructs pornography as a discourse of oppression. Of many examples of pro-sex feminist defenses of pornography, some of the best are *"Bad Girls"/"Good Girls": Women, Sex, and Power in the Nineties*, edited by Nan Bauer Maglin and Donna Perry; *XXX: A Woman's Right to Pornography* by Wendy McElroy; *Defending Pornography: Free Speech, Sex, and the Fight for Women's Rights* by Nadine Strossen; and *Talk Dirty to Me: An Intimate Philosophy of Sex* by Sallie Tisdale. Jane Juffer points out that women domesticate pornography in order to eroticize their lives in *At Home with Pornography: Women, Sex, and Everyday Life*. Drucilla Cornell's *Feminism and Pornography* is a balanced sampling of feminist thought from several camps.

Intimate Matters: A History of Sexuality in America by John D'Emilio and Estelle B. Freedman considers pornography of various periods. In *City of Eros: New York City, Prostitution, and the Commercialization of Sex, 1790–1920*, Timothy Gilfoyle roots the origins of domestic pornography in the raucous Jacksonianism of the 1830s and 1840s, especially in tabloids that combined sexual candor with political rivalry. Erotic pictures, books, and novelties sold to troops in the North and South are the subjects of Thomas P. Lowry's *The Story the Soldiers Wouldn't Tell: Sex in the Civil War*, which recovers dealers and products. In *Prurient Interests: Gender, Democracy, and Obscenity in New York City, 1909–1945*, Andrea Friedman examines moral panics caused by the democratization of pleasure; fears that burlesque, motion pictures, and theater degraded women, children, and family life surfaced again in panics more familiar to us. Pornography as a register of experience helps weave together three fine histories: John Heidenry's *What Wild Ecstasy: The Rise and Fall of the Sexual Revolution*, Steve Chapple and David Talbot's *Burning Desires: Sex in America, a Report from the Field*, and James R. Petersen's *The Century of Sex: Playboy's History of the Sexual Revolution, 1900–1999*. Joseph W. Slade's *Pornography in America: A Reference Handbook* details the evolution of various pornographic genres in the United States.

Of several surveys of fiction, the most meticulous and focused (seventeenth to nineteenth centuries) is Patrick J. Kearney's *A History of Erotic Literature*. Peter Wagner's "Erotica in Early America" and "Eros Goes West: European and 'Homespun' Erotica in Eighteenth-Century America" richly evoke the appeal of erotic libraries in the colonial period. David Reynolds identifies the "first" domestically published pornographic novel (George Thompson's *Venus in Boston*, 1843) and ferrets out other clandestine examples in *Beneath the American Renaissance: The Subversive Imagination in the Age of Emerson and Melville*. Joseph Allen Boone ranges along margins in his treatment of mainstream American literature in *Libidinal Currents*, as does G. M. Goshgarian in *To Kiss the Chastening Rod: Domestic Fiction and Sexual Ideology in the American Renaissance*. Any number of texts, of course, deal with sexual representations in canonical literature (see MLA bibliographies).

Jay A. Gertzman's exhaustive study of authors, publishers (e.g., Samuel Roth), and dealers, *Bookleggers and Smuthounds: The Trade in Erotica, 1920–1940*, categorizes genres of erotica (fiction, ballads, jestbooks, romances, and mysteries; anthropological and sociological texts on birth control and prostitution; confessional pamphlets; Tijuana Bibles) against a background of depression and repression; his is easily the best analysis of American traffic in contraband. John de St. Jorre's *Venus Bound: The Erotic Voyages of the Olympia Press* recounts stories of American authors whose erotica was published in Paris. Michael Perkins, in *The Secret Record*, offers perspectives on Richard Amory, Diane di Prima, Mary Sativa, Marco Vassi, Harriet Daimler, and Alexander Trocchi. Maurice Charney's *Sexual Fiction* surveys criticism on Miller, Nin, Roth, Nabokov, Southern, and many others. Miriam Linna's *Smut Peddler* runs essays on erotic paperbacks published between 1959 and 1965. Donald Palumbo's *Erotic Universe: Sexuality and Fantastic Literature* is still the best text on sexual explicitness in science fiction. Advice on formulas, tropes, and dealing with editors is the subject of Mike Bailey's *Writing Erotic Fiction: And Getting Published*, one of several such how-to texts for the novice.

Diverse views of the woman's romance include Jean Radford's *The Progress of Romance: The Politics of Popular Fiction*, Tania Modleski's *Loving with a Vengeance: Mass-Produced Fantasies for Women*, Carol Thurston's *The Romance Revolution: Erotic Novels for Women and the Quest for a New Sexual Identity*, and Janice A. Radway's *Reading the Romance: Women, Patriarchy, and Popular Literature*, all of which outline the genre's pornographic dimensions, but the best overview is *Where the Heart Roams*, a PBS documentary by George Csicsery, which elicits erotic intent from romance authors themselves. Gregory Woods's *A History of Gay Literature: The Male Tradition* surveys gay works; Eve Kosofsky Sedgwick's *Between Men: English Literature and the Male Homosocial Desire* locates "homosocial" connections at the core of all English literature; Earl Jackson's *Strategies of Deviance: Studies in Gay Male Representation* explores the images of gays in several media, especially textual narratives; Lee Edelman's *Homographesis: Essays in Gay Literary and Cultural Theory* analyzes traditional and contemporary texts; and Mark Lilly's *Lesbian and Gay Writing: An Anthology of Critical Essays* tries to establish a gendered esthetic. Excellent critical studies include Bonnie Zimmerman's *The Safe Sea of Women: Lesbian Fiction, 1969–1988*, which identifies themes, motifs, formulas, and structural elements; Susannah Radstone's *Sweet Dreams: Sexuality, Gender and Popular Fiction*, which ranges across high and low gay and lesbian literature; Elizabeth Meese's *(Sem)Erotics: Theorizing Lesbian Writing*, which covers experimental lesbian narratives; and Elaine Hobby and Chris White's *What Lesbians Do in Books*, which examines texts classic and modern.

According to Ken Plummer's *Telling Sexual Stories: Power, Change and Social Worlds*, erotic narrative can construct a sexual self out of erotic tropes to achieve identity and intimacy. By contrast, says Catharine MacKinnon in *Only Words*, sexual language is masculine, aggressive, and literal; pornography, which she defines as systematic discourse for the deliberate oppression of women, is equivalent to rape. Rejecting such theories as mind control, Judith Butler, in *Excitable Speech: A Politics of the Performative*, notes that language is always subordinate to performance and behavior. Three studies of obscene language are valuable: *Blue Streak: Swearing, Free Speech, and Sexual Harassment* by Richard Dooling, who studies biological and linguistic foundations of swearing; *Cursing in America: A Psycholinguistic Study of Dirty Language in the Courts, in the Movies, in the Schoolyards, and on the Streets* by Timothy Jay, who brings wit to bear on obscene phone calls, profanity, and gender stereotypes; and *Wicked Words: A Treasury of Curses, Insults, Put-Downs, and Other Formerly Unprintable Terms from Anglo-Saxon Times to the Present* by Hugh Rawson, who traces etymologies of offensive expressions.

"All folklore is erotic," Gershon Legman has said.[9] Folklorists should begin with Frank Hoffmann's *Analytical Survey of Anglo-American Traditional Erotica*; the special issue of the *Journal of American Folklore* (July 1962) containing the "Symposium on Obscenity in Folklore"; and Rayna Green's "Folk Is a Four-Letter Word: Dealing with Traditional _____ in Fieldwork, Analysis, and Presentation." Alexandra Parson's *Facts and Phalluses: A Collection of Bizarre and Intriguing Truths, Legends, and Measurements* and Rebecca Chalker's *The Clitoral Truth* foreground genital folklore. Gershon Legman's *The Rationale of the Dirty Joke: An Analysis of Sexual Humor* and *No Laughing Matter: Rationale of the Dirty Joke, Second Series* apply impeccable scholarship to hundreds of jokes. In *The Limerick: 1700 Examples, with Notes, Variants, and Index* and *The New Limerick: 2750 Unpublished Examples, American and British*, Legman classifies the form by subject (e.g., "Buggery," "Organs," "Virginity") in order to study themes, origins, meaning, and cultural and class markers. Deft readings of Tijuana Bibles, sex magazines, cartoons, and jokes make Baird Jones's *Sexual Humor* entertaining as well as illuminating. Academic citations also appear on *Urban Legends—Sex*, a Web site of jokes and folklore.

Peter Wagner dissects a quasi-medical magazine of the early 1700s in "The Veil of Medicine and Morality: Some Pornographic Aspects of the *Onania*." Edward Van Every's *Sins of America as Exposed by the Police Gazette* tells the story of the famous early "pornographic" tabloid. Andie Tucher's *Froth and Scum: Truth, Beauty, Goodness, and the Ax-Murder in America's First Mass Medium* traces prurient journalism to nineteenth century newspapers. In *Jazz Journalism: The Story of the Tabloid Newspapers*, Simon Michael Bessie focuses on the *New York Daily News*, the *New York Mirror*, and the *New York Daily Graphic* during the 1920s and 1930s. S. Elizabeth Bird's splendid comment on contemporary journalism is called *For Enquiring Minds: A Cultural Study of Supermarket Tabloids*. Robert J. Glessing's *The Underground Press in America* concentrates on papers such as the *East Village Other* and the *Berkeley Barb*, while in *Politico Frou-Frou: Pornographic Art as Political Protest*, Tuppy Owens insists that such countercultural tabloids were animated by ideological purpose. Stephen Duncombe's *Notes from Underground: Zines and the Politics of Alternative Culture* finds similar imperatives in ephemeral journalism.

Mark Gabor's *The Illustrated History of Girlie Magazines* traces spicy periodicals from the *National Police Gazette* to modern versions, while his *The Pin-Up: A Modest History* outlines stylistic shifts in the pictures in them. Still the best chronicle of "pulps" is Tony Goodstone's *The Pulps: Fifty Years of American Popular*

The novel and film *Candy*, with their open views toward sex, caused quite a stir when they were released. © The Del Valle Archive

Culture, whose chapters fix on the rise of cheap magazines such as *Spicy Detective*, *Spicy Western*, and *Spicy Adventure*. Albert Ellis compares men's magazines (e.g., *Male* and *Argosy*) of the 1950s and 1960s in *The Folklore of Sex*, and Alan Betrock parses genre formulas in *Unseen America: The Greatest Cult Exploitation Magazines, 1950–1966*. Although it attracted a lot of cultural attention in the 1970s, *Playboy* is now an institution critiqued most trenchantly in the financial pages that chart its publicly held stock. By contrast, Laura Kipnis's *Bound and Gagged: Pornography and the Politics of Fantasy in America* focuses on *Hustler* magazine as a lower-class attack on corrupt middle and upper classes. Publisher Larry Flynt agrees in his *An Unseemly Man: My Life as Pornographer, Pundit and Social Outcast*, published at the same time that the movie *The People versus Larry Flynt* (directed by Milos Forman) was released. Louis H. Swartz's "Erotic Witness: The Rise and Flourishing of Genitally Explicit and Sex Act Explicit Heterosexually Oriented Photographic Magazines in the U.S., 1965–1985" tries to establish hierarchies of hard-core periodicals. The best history of homosexual journalism, erotic and otherwise, is Roger Streitmatter's *Unspeakable: The Rise of the Gay and Lesbian Press in America*.

Sex in the Comics by Maurice Horn and *Adult Comics: An Introduction* by Roger

Sabin assess esthetics, sexual themes, gender roles, and cultural weight of erotic comics. Donald H. Gilmore's *Sex in Comics: A History of the Eight Pagers* surveys 500 Tijuana Bibles (of an estimated 700) printed between 1930 and 1965, when social discontent gave bite to raucous humor. In *Tijuana Bibles: Art and Wit in America's Forbidden Funnies, 1930s–1950s*, edited by Bob Adelman, critics investigate languages, images, and formulas of this demotic art. Stefano Piselli and Riccardo Morrocchi introduce the most notorious of fetish cartoonists in *The Art of John Willie: Sophisticated Bondage 1946–1961*. Mark James Estren's *A History of Underground Comics* identifies major artists, their styles, and their fixations, some of them pornographic. Essays gathered by Monte Beauchamp for *The Life and Times of R. Crumb: Commentary from Contemporaries* trace the career of the leading "comix" artist. *From Girls to Grrrlz: A History of ♀ Comics from Teens to Zines* by Trina Robbins and *Women and the Comics* by Robbins and Catherine Yronwode note that women use storylines of emotion and psychology rather than action and technology to create explicit cartoons. Finally, Andrea Juno has edited conversations with underground figures for *Dangerous Drawings: Interviews from Comix & Graphic Artists*.

In *Race, Sex, and Gender in Contemporary Art* Edward Lucie-Smith points out that images called "transgressive," "feminist," and "minority sexuality" signify complex political assumptions. Lucie-Smith's *Sexuality in Western Art* asserts that the need to represent sexuality as lust, affection, spirituality, and power has driven artists from Botticelli to Cindy Sherman. Still worth consulting for its insights is Peter Webb's *The Erotic Arts*. The contributors to Peter Weiermair's *Erotic Art from the 17th to the 20th Century* also bring enormous intelligence to bear. Bradley Smith's *Erotic Art of the Masters: 18th, 19th, 20th Centuries* and *Twentieth Century Masters of Modern Art* are comprehensive in scope and reliable in assessment. Serious students must eventually consult the *Bilderlexicon der Erotik*, whose essays on art and pornography, though dated, are unmatched in scholarship.

The most influential theorist of visual erotica is John Berger, whose *About Looking* and *Ways of Seeing* draw distinctions between nudity and nakedness, between objectification and voyeurism, and between female subordination and male dominance through looking. From Berger's theories spring versions of the "male gaze," a thesis developed primarily by film critic Laura Mulvey, whose "Visual Pleasure and Narrative Cinema," part of her *Visual and Other Pleasures*, asserts that sight has been coopted by males. According to Mulvey, the masculine gaze of a patriarchal society literally constructs a reality from which females are excluded; voyeurism can only be masculine. The most astute feminist critic, however, is Linda Nochlin, who insists that artists can create languages and images in order to assert women's eroticism within a patriarchal culture; her views animate her *Women, Art, and Power, and Other Essays* and *Woman as Sex Object: Studies in Erotic Art, 1730–1970*, edited by Thomas B. Hess and Nochlin. Among many fine books to confront the erotic aspects of art by women are *Erotic Ambiguities: The Female Nude in Art* by Helen McDonald; *Visibly Female: Feminism and Art Today, an Anthology*, edited by Hilary Robinson; *Intimate Distance: Women, Artists and the Body* by Rosemary Betterton; *Women and Art: Contested Territory* by Judy Chicago and Edward Lucie-Smith; all recenter the body in the visions of female artists, and strive for insight rather than political correctness.

Erotic homosexual themes, images, and sensibilities both gay and lesbian have profoundly enriched art, says Emmanuel Cooper in *The Sexual Perspective: Homosexuality and Art in the Last 100 Years in the West*. "Lesbian Art and Artists," a special issue of *Heresies*, is the best single source on pornography as an architect of lesbian identities. Philip Rawson's *Primitive Erotic Art* delves into native Central and North American artifacts. Some of those, and demotic erotic art of the subsequent three centuries, assume enormous importance for Milton Simpson in *Folk Erotica: Celebrating Centuries of Erotic Americana*, which understands erotic folk art as an upwelling of passion and vitality. *The Great American Nude: A History in Art* by William H. Gerdts is a solid, accurate, and instructive chronicle of American representations of nakedness.

Authoritative on the early erotic photograph is *Das Aktfoto: Ansichten vom Körper im fotografischen Zeitalter: Ästhetik—Geschichte—Ideologie*, edited by Michael Köhler and Gisela Barche, who contextualize splendid reproductions. Just as astute on contemporary images is *Eros and Photography: An Exploration of Sexual Imagery and Photographic Practice*, edited by Donna-Lee Phillips and Lew Thomas. Valerie Steele's *Fetish: Fashion, Sex and Power* addresses images that speak to gender identification, erotic attraction, and "perverse" behaviors. Margaret Walters's *The Male Nude* is the most persuasive of theoretical works on photos of males that emphasize phallic power through scrupulously rendered genitals. Hal Fischer in *Gay Semiotics: A Photographic Study of Visual Coding Among Homosexual Men* and Richard Dyer in *The Matter of Images: Essays on Representations* grapple with what Dyer calls the "enormously complex sign systems" that code for gender in erotic photos. Thomas Waugh's *Hard to Imagine: Gay Male Eroticism in Photography and Film from Their Beginnings to Stonewall* is a gritty, intelligent cultural history with no equal. The Kiss and Tell lesbian collective challenges stereotypes promoted by anti-porn feminists for *Her Tongue on My Theory: Images, Essays and Fantasies*. Also recommended is *Nothing but the Girl: The Blatant Lesbian Image, a Portfolio and Exploration of Lesbian Erotic Photography*, edited by Susie Bright and Jill Posener.

Most theories of cinematic eroticism derive from "Style and Medium in Moving Pictures," in which Erwin Panofsky traces the origins of cinema to pornographic folklore. Variations on this argument drive Amos Vogel's *Film as a Subversive Art*, which characterizes the rise of film from "taboo to freedom." Eric Schaefer's *Bold! Daring! Shocking! True!: A History of Exploitation Films, 1919–1959* demystifies softcore genres (sexual hygiene, miscegenation, drug, nudist, burlesque, white slavery) as produced by Louis Sonney, Kroger Babb, Herschel Gordon Lewis, David Friedman, and other pioneers. Anecdotes can be found in *Grindhouse: The Forbidden World of "Adults Only" Cinema* by Eddie Muller and Daniel Faris.

The principal scholar of early hard-core films is Kurt Moreck, whose *Sittengeschichte des Kinos* (A Moral History of the Cinema) tracks stag films until the mid-1920s. Joseph W. Slade is preparing *Shades of Blue: A History of the Clandestine Film*, on stags of several countries. Slade's "Violence in the Hard-Core Pornographic Film: A Historical Survey" explains the lack of aggression in hard-core genres. Linda Williams's *Hard-Core: The Frenzy of the Visible*, more focused on recent features, compares their formulas to those of musicals. "Capitalism in the raw" is the term applied to adult industries by Laurence O'Toole's *Pornocopia: Porn, Sex, Technology and Desire*, which considers videos as responses to demand. In David Flint's *Babylon Blue: An Illustrated History of Adult Cinema*, insiders speak well or badly, but always revealingly of their profession.

Ian Gittler's *Pornstar*, by a photographer who shoots stills for the porn video industry, is a non-judgmental look at performers and producers. Autobiographies by performers, some insightful, most not, include Tina Russell's *Porno Star*, Harry Reems's *Here Comes Harry Reems!*, Marc Stevens's *Ten and a Half*, Marilyn Chambers's *My Story*, Jerry Butler's *Raw Talent: The Adult Film Industry as Seen by Its Most Popular Male Star*, and Peter (Beercan) North's *Penetrating Insights*. Linda Lovelace's indictment of the industry in *Ordeal* and *Out of Bondage* should be contrasted with her recent mellow remarks to Eric Danville in *The Complete Linda Lovelace*. Anthony Petkovich interviews actresses, directors, and cinematographers for *The X Factory: Inside the American Hardcore Industry*. Robert J. Stoller's psychological exploration of the industry, *Porn: Myths for the Twentieth Century*, asserts that sexual hostility pervades the industry, as does his *Coming Attractions: The Making of an X-Rated Video*, coauthored with I. S. Levine, which discovers similar aggression in a capitalist cultural that dotes on exploitation of sex. David McCumber's *Rated-X: The Mitchell Brothers, a True Story of Sex, Money, and Death* and John Hubner's *Bottom Feeders: From Free Love to hard Hard Core—The Rise and Fall of Counterculture Heroes Jim and Artie Mitchell* attempt to comprehend the bizarre story of the producers of *Behind the Green Door* (1973). Interviews and carefully derived facts support analysis in the often overlooked *Porn Gold: Inside the Pornography Business* by David Hebditch and Nick Anning, a period study of the industry. John R. Burger's *One-Handed Histories: The Eroto-Politics of Gay Male Video Pornography* views videos as an agent of "popular memory" that builds culture and gives visibility to gays. Material on gay stars can be found in *The Jack Wrangler Story: What's a Nice Boy Like You Doing in a Business Like This?* by Jack Wrangler; *Autopornography: A Memoir of Life in the Lust Lane* by "Spunk" O'Hara; *Wonder Bread and Ecstacy: The Life and Death of Joey Stefano* by Charles Isherwood; *Making It Big: Sex Stars, Porn Films, and Me* by Chi Chi LaRue; and *Sorry I Asked: Intimate Interviews with Gay Porn's Rank and File* by Dave Kinnick.

Well to the margins of the legitimate urban stage are three strains of explicit theater. The first, avant-garde performance has been chronicled by Roselee Goldberg in *Performance Art: From Futurism to the Present*. Rebecca Schneider's *The Explicit Body in Performance* contextualizes feminist performance art (e.g., Carolee Schneemann, Kathy Acker, Karen Finley) and can be read with Annie Sprinkle's *Post Porn Modernist*, a manifesto on explicitness staged to enlighten. The second strain is the "low" performance associated with carnivals, burlesque, and striptease. In *Girl Show: Into the Canvas World of Bump and Grind*, A. W. Stencell draws on first-hand experience in carnivals. The origins of burlesque intrigue Robert Allen in *Horrible Prettiness: Burlesque and American Culture*, which subjects popular amusement to stringent academic theory. Field research in sixty clubs in seven major cities persuaded Katherine H. Liepe-Levinson that male and female striptease shores up and simultaneously subverts gender roles, a thesis that drives her *Strip Show*. For *Red Light: Inside the Sex Industry*, Sylvia Plachy and James Ridgeway report on working conditions against a background of class and economic discrimination. The third strain is the clandestine performance of staged sex. The chief theoretical work is Karl Toepfer's *Theatre, Aristocracy, and Pornocracy: The Orgy Calculus*, a fascinating history of gender and class values. Along with dozens of texts on sado-masochism as theater, Lynda Hart's *Between the Body and the Flesh:*

Performing Sadomasochism characterizes sado-masochism, especially in its "queer" guises, as a means for "bearing witness" to the power of sexuality.

"Sex on Prime-Time in the 90s," a cultivation study by Nancy Signorielli, determined that numbers of sexual images declined in the 1990s but were still used for comic and dramatic purposes (sex was treated humorously in four out of ten programs); broadcast (as opposed to cable) audiences do not seem to prize sexual content, a conclusion borne out by Nielsen ratings. Americans do not demand challenging programming out of fear that their children will be corrupted by the screen, says Marjorie Heins in *Not in Front of the Children: "Indecency," Censorship, and the Innocence of Youth*. Standards of appropriateness, though more liberal than before, are still enforced by broadcast censors, says Tad Friend in "Department of Broadcasting: You Can't Say That." Suzanne Garment's *Scandal: The Culture of Mistrust in American Politics* examines bidding wars between newspapers, magazines, and television tabloid shows for rights to stories of sexual scandal, while David J. Krajicek's *Scooped! Mass Media Miss Real Story on Crime while Chasing Sex, Sleaze, and Celebrities* recounts similar diversions. Tabloid talk shows help to change social attitudes toward deviant, marginal, or alternative sexual lifestyles, says Joshua Gamson in *Freaks Talk Back: Tabloid Talk Shows and Sexual Nonconformity*. Sheila Nevins, originator of HBO's "Shock Video" and "Real Sex," tells James Sterngold that cable audiences demand candid treatment of sex in "HBO Programmer Likes to Kindle Both Heat and Light." *Dreamworlds II: Desire/Sex/Power in Rock Video*, a video by Sut Jhally, attacks Music Television as sexist and misogynistic. Two often amusing accounts of the (now waning) telephone sex industry are *Dirty Talk: Diary of a Phone Sex "Mistress"* by Gary Anthony, a female impersonator who enjoyed great success conversing with male clients, and *The Fantasy Factory: An Insider's View of the Phone Sex Industry* by Amy Flowers, an ethnographic study of operators and clients by a scholar-worker.

Worth looking at as folkore in the making is "Marketing Pornography on the Information Superhighway," a notoriously hyperbolic hoax by Martin Rimm, who claimed that pornography dominates the Internet (it actually constitutes 3% of content). In "A Content Analysis of Sex in Usenet Newsgroups," William E. Brigman, having methodically surveyed hundreds of newsgroups, breaks out images of specific sexual behavior in terms of gender and racial characteristics of those groups. Electronic transformations of the body into representations and the radical reconfigurations of erotic fantasies that follow are major themes of *The War of Desire and Technology at the Close of the Machine Age* by Allucquère Roseanne Stone and *Electronic Eros: Bodies and Desire in the Postindustrial Age* by Claudia Springer, but the boldest views are enunciated in *Virtual Reality* by Howard Rheingold, who coins the term "teledildonics" for electronic simulations of sex.

Despite dozens of experiments often flawed by runaway variables or the sexual pathologies of researchers, no respectable study has established a convincing causal connection between sexual materials and anti-social behavior. In "Does Pornography Cause Violence? The Search for Evidence," Lynne Segal believes that myth and confusion arise when laypeople misinterpret reports by social scientists. Students impressed by hyperbolic claims should look at "Uneasy Bedfellows: Social Science and Pornography," a suite of articles whose authors discuss the politics, assumptions, and limitations of research methodologies. Also on the wane are the debates over the constitutionality of sexual expression that roiled the 1980s (pornography is quite legal in the United States, partly because it is so difficult to prove obscenity); Marjorie Heins's *Sex, Sin, and Blasphemy: A Guide to America's Censorship Wars* recaps the period neatly. Of a host of fairly recent texts on the subject, Kent Greenawalt's *Fighting Words: Individuals, Communities, and Liberties of Speech* sheds the most light on the conflict, while in *The Pleasure Police: How Bluenose Busybodies and Lily-Livered Alarmists Are Taking All the Fun Out of Life*, a much wittier than usual analysis, David Shaw attacks activist opponents of smoking, porn, fast food, and risky behavior. Alan Hyde's novel riffs on the legal status of penises and vaginas and their representations render his *Bodies of Law* more trenchant than most legal texts. Andrea Tone's *Devices and Desires: A History of Contraceptives in America* begins with the Comstock Act of 1873, which criminalized birth control as a species of pornography, and follows the movement of reproductive information out of legal shadows. Frederick S. Lane provides statistics in *Obscene Profits: The Entrepreneurs of Pornography in the Cyber Age*, although articles such as Timothy Egan's "Technology Sent Wall Street into Market for Pornography" are more up to date.

ANTHOLOGIES AND REPRINTS

Anthologies of various genres of pornography—or, as they are more likely to be called, *erotica*—vary enormously in sweep and explicitness. Any number of coffee-table volumes sanitize texts and images. Making such images "safe" is part of the dynamic by which a culture assimilates the marginal.

Anthologies of erotic fiction fill shelves in major bookstores. Widely available are *The Mammoth Book of International Erotica* and *The Mammoth Book of New Erotica*, both edited by Maxim Jakubowski; *Erotic Literature: A Connoisseur's Guide*, edited by Donald McCormick; *The Literary Companion to Sex: An Anthology of Prose and Poetry*, edited by Fiona Pitt-Kethley; and *The Bloomsbury Guide to Erotic Literature*, edited by Jane Mills; all are miscellanies of familiar pieces. An interesting compilation of recent fiction is *Too Darn Hot: Writing About Sex Since Kinsey*, for which Judy Bloomfield, Mary McGrail, and Lauren Sanders have anthologized writers from William Burroughs to Scarlet Harlot. Susie Bright puts together annuals titled *The Best American Erotica* to include stories by authors major and minor.

Salacious feminine fantasies fill the *Herotica: A Collection of Women's Erotic Fiction* series, the first volume edited by Susie Bright, the second by Bright and Joanni Blank, the third by Bright, and the fourth, fifth, and sixth by Marcy Sheiner; all indulge heterosexual, homosexual, and bisexual caprice. Readers can sample erotica by 39 female writers and artists in *The Girl Wants To: Women's Representation of Sex and the Body*, edited by Lynn Crosbie. *Lip Service: Alluring New Lesbian Erotica*, edited by Jess Wells, and *The Very Thought of You: Erotic Love Stories by Naiad Press Authors*, edited by Barbara Grier and Christine Cassidy, give free rein to lesbian lust. As John Preston observes in *Flesh and the Word: An Anthology of Erotic Writing*, in the past there was no gay *erotica*; "anything written about [gay men] had to be declared pornography" (II, 2). Preston and Michael Lowenthal have edited a third volume of *Flesh and the Word*, and Lowenthal himself yet a fourth. Gender bending fantasies stock *Best Bisexual Erotica*, edited by Bill Brent and Carol Queen. Writers commissioned by Queen and Lawrence Schimel experiment in

Switch Hitters: Lesbians Write Gay Male Erotica and Gay Men Write Lesbian Erotica. *Erotique Noire: Black Erotica*, edited by Miriam Decosta-Willis, Reginald Martin, and RoseAnn P. Bell, and *Dark Eros: Black Erotic Writings*, edited by Martin alone, include erotica by Alice Walker, Chester Hines, Trey Ellis, Calvin Hernton, and others. Blanche Richardson targets *Best Black Women's Erotica* even more precisely. Geraldine Kudaka's *On a Bed of Rice: An Asian-American Erotic Feast*, which anthologizes Korean, Filipino, Japanese, East Indian, Vietnamese, Chinese, and Thai examples, Marcy Sheiner's *The Oy of Sex: Jewish Women Write Erotica*, and Ray Gonzalez's *Under the Pomegranate Tree: The Best New Latino Erotica*, address the erotic imaginations of other ethnic groups.

William Cole's *Erotic Poetry: The Lyrics, Ballads, Idyls and Epics of Love—Classical to Contemporary* is basically an updating of T. R. Smith's *Poetica Erotica: A Collection of Rare and Curious Amatory Verse* to include Anne Sexton and other contemporary American poets. Less bowdlerized are Alan Bold's *Making Love: The Picador Book of Erotic Verse*, Derek Parker's *An Anthology of Erotic Verse*, and John Whitworth's *The Faber Book of Blue Verse*. The poems in *Wanting Women: An Anthology of Erotic Lesbian Poetry*, edited by Jan Hardy, have uncommon edge. *The Male Muse: Gay Poetry Anthology*, edited by Robert Duncan and others, and *Eros: An Anthology of Friendship*, edited by Alistair Sutherland and Patrick Anderson, reproduce gay erotic poems, including some by Americans such as Hart Crane.

The classic compilation of American stories and jokes is the 1927 *Anecdota Americana, Being Explicitly an Anthology of the Tales in the Vernacular* by Joseph Fliesler. Also in 1927, T. R. Smith, an editor at Boni and Liveright, surreptitiously published *Immortalia: An Anthology of American Ballads, Sailors' Songs, Cowboy Songs, College Songs, Parodies, Limericks, and Other Humorous Verses and Doggerel Now for the First Time Brought Together in Book Form by a Gentleman About Town*. Although sanitized anthologies of bawdy songs and poems were common, censors suppressed authentic collections. A. Reynolds Morse's *Folk Poems and Ballads: An Anthology: A Collection of Rare Verses and Amusing Folk Songs Compiled from Scarce and Suppressed Books as Well as from Verbal Sources, which Modern Prudery, False Social Customs and Intolerance Have Separated from the Public and Historical Record* (1948) was banned for four decades. A pornographic house issued E. R. Linton's *The Dirty Song Book* in the 1960s, but Guy Logsdon's bawdy *"The Whorehouse Bells Were Ringing," and Other Songs Cowboys Sing* did not appear until 1989. Other landmarks include *Pissing in the Snow & Other Ozark Folktales* (1976), *Roll Me in Your Arms: "Unprintable" Ozark Folksongs and Folklore* (1992), and *Blow the Candle Out: "Unprintable" Ozark Folklore* (1997); all are materials gathered by Vance Randolph, who could not publish them during his lifetime. Sexually explicit jokes fill any number of volumes, whose popularity can be assessed by the steady sales of the eleven volumes of *Gross Jokes*, collected by Julius Alvin, and the eleven volumes of *Truly Tasteless Jokes*, edited by Blanche Knott. The "dirtiest" collection of limericks is *The Limerick: A Facet of Our Culture* by A. Reynolds Morse; this book, like the Morse collection mentioned above, was instantly censored.

Historically very important is *Free Press Anthology*, a group of articles mostly on pornography and censorship compiled from alternative papers by the noted Constitutional lawyer Theodore A. Schroeder in 1909. Gene and Jayne Barry Smith have reprinted articles, graphics, cartoons, illustrations, and advertisements from 1878 to 1897 for the nostalgic *The Police Gazette*. *The Tijuana Bible Reader*, edited by Douglas H. Gamelin, excerpts stories from crude pamphlets called "Bibles" before the term came to designate eight-page "dirty" comic books. The entire run of the leading bondage and discipline magazine of the 1940s and 1950s appears in *Bizarre: The Complete Reprint of John Willie's Bizarre, vols. 1–13*; reprints of 36 issues of a similar fetish periodical make up *Exotique: A New Magazine of the Bizarre and Unusual*. C. G. Martignette and L. K. Meisel have compiled mostly covers in *The Best of American Girlie Magazines*; their value is the spectrum of types. The contents of Gretchen Edgren's *The Playboy Book: Forty Years. The Complete Pictorial History* seem tame by modern standards.

Microfilm editions such as *Underground Newspaper Microfilm Collection*, and *Alternative Press Collection*, and *Underground Press Collection* (the latter two by University Microfilms) reproduce the "dildo journalism" of the 1960s and 1970s. Selected articles appear in *Underground Press Anthology*, compiled by Thomas King Forcade, and *Underground Reader*, compiled by Mel Howard and Forcade. *The Screw Reader*, put together by the tabloid's editors Al Goldstein and Jim Buckley, recalls rowdy and/or erotic features. *Apocalypse Culture*, edited by Adam Parfrey, collects essays from fringe publications, as does *Beneath the Underground* by Bob Black. Zines, frequently sexual, furnish material for *Sensoria from Censorium*. *The Complete Reprint of Physique Pictorial, 1951–1990* reproduces the gay photo magazine of the Athletic Model Guild. Jim Kepner has gathered articles for *Rough News—Daring Views: 1950s Pioneer Gay Press Journalism*, a period when writing as a homosexual required bravery. *Flaunting It: A Decade of Gay Journalism from the Body Politic*, edited by Ed Jackson and Stan Persky, and *Gay Roots: Twenty Years of Gay Sunshine* and *Gay Roots: An Anthology of Gay History, Sex, Politics, and Culture, Volume 2*, edited by Winston Leyland, reproduce fiction, essays, humor, and cartoons from gay presses.

Of numerous collections of American Tijuana Bibles, the best are *Little Dirty Comics* and *More Dirty Little Comics*, edited by R. G. Holt. Bélier Press publishes the arcane *Bizarre Comix*; 24 volumes reproduce bondage and domination fetish comics from the 1950s and 1960s by Stanton, Mario, Ruiz, Eneg, "Jim," and others commissioned by Irving Klaw. Bélier Press's edition of John Willie's *The Adventures of Sweet Gwendolyn* is now a classic, and it, together with other materials from the Bélier archives, are the basis for a seven-cassette video series of the same title. *The Complete Crumb* retrieves fugitive pieces by the greatest underground comix artist, who has now achieved cultural stardom. Artists selected by Winston Leyland for *Meatmen: An Anthology of Gay Male Comics* and *More Meatmen: An Anthology of Gay Comics* include Tom of Finland and American cartoonists. Examples of the work of Julie Doucet, Phoebe Gloeckner, Penny Moran Van Horn, M. K. Brown, Aline Kominsky Crumb, Carel Moiseiwitsch, Mary Fleener, Leslie Sternbergh, and others can be found in Diane Noomin's *Twisted Sisters: A Collection of Bad Girl Art* and *Twisted Sisters: Volume II: Drawing the Line*. Trina Robbins has published an excellent, occasionally explicit anthology called *A Century of Women Cartoonists*.

Edward Lucie-Smith's selection of paintings for *Ars Erotica: An Arousing History of Erotic Art* includes a few very explicit novelties mixed with classic choices. Charlotte Hill and William Wallace scatter drawings and paintings throughout *Erotica: An Illustrated Anthology of Sexual Art and Literature*, although most are European and the attributions erratic. *Fisher's Erotic Encyclopedia*, a CD-ROM, is loaded with hundreds of examples of erotic art. Gilles Néret's *Erotica Universalis*, perhaps the most comprehensive collection of reproductions from all periods, contains no comment. By contrast, Néret's *Erotic Art* discusses nineteenth and twentieth century paintings by Europeans from Matisse to Bellmer, while his *Twentieth Century Erotic Art* foregrounds such Americans as O'Keeffe, Oldenburg, Pollock, Fischl, Warhol, Koons, Lichtenstein, Pearlstein, Rivers, Salle, and Sherman. Constance Franklin quotes the artists themselves on their illustrations in *Erotic Art by Living Artists*. John S. Barrington depends on drawings, paintings, and photographs from homosexual magazines to chronicle gay visual expression during the late 1960s and early 1970s in *Contemporary Homo-Erotic Art*. The most comprehensive anthology of painted pin-up illustrations is *The Great American Pin-Up* by Charles G. Martignette and L. K. Meisel; included are over 900 reproductions of calendars, magazine covers, centerfolds, playing cards, and other formats by artists (e.g., Rolf Armstrong, Zöe Mozert, and Alberto Vargas) working from World War II until the mid-1970s.

The five volumes of *Bizarre Classix* feature fetish photographs (bondage and discipline, sado-masochism, flagellation, rubber and leather garments, and so on) from 1920 to 1960; the four volumes of *Bizarre Fotos: From the Archives of Irving Klaw* offer similar subjects from 1930 to 1950; the four volumes of *Betty Page: Private Peeks* display photos of Klaw's famous fetish model (others can be found on 2000+ Web sites devoted to Page). Mark Rotenberg marshalls soft-core nudes for the extensive *Cheesecake: The Rotenberg Collection*, while his *Forbidden Erotica: The Rotenberg Collection* is more explicit. The *Vasta Collection*, a CD-ROM, contains images assembled by Joseph Vasta, the principal American dealer in erotic photographs. Five hundred *Playboy* Playmates (1953 to 1996) make up *The Playmate Book: Five Decades of Centerfolds*, their biographies written by Gretchen Edgren. The Internet, of course, is rife with photos in endless categories; one accurate historical site is John Cox's archive@badpuppy.com/; it documents 800,000 gay images from 1950 to 1980.

Forays into pornographic realms highlight careers of major American photographers, most notably Nan Goldin, beginning with her *The Ballad of Sexual Dependency*; this volume, compiled with friends, illustrates "real" sexuality among ordinary people. The most notorious artist is the late Robert Mapplethorpe; *Mapplethorpe* gathers more than 300 photos, including those of sexual undergrounds. For others whose work is tinged by the pornographic, see *Teenage Lust* and *Larry Clark, 1992*, volumes of images of oral sex, intercourse, drugs, and violence by Larry Clark, who translated his obsession with decadence into his first film, *Kids*; the three volumes titled *Roy Stuart* by Roy Stuart, whose eye transforms gritty transgression into ravishing moments of desire; *Orgasm* by Tony Ward, whose pictures, he says, "further define the genre" of hard core; and *Pôr' ne-graf'.n* by Ken Probst, who documents the shooting of a gay porn video.

Two videotape compilations of short bondage reels of the 1940s and 1950s by Irving Klaw, featuring Bettie Page and other popular models, are marketed as the *Classic Films of Irving Klaw: Volumes I and II*. Kit Parker Films spliced footage from exploitation stalwarts into a history called *Sex and Buttered Popcorn*, complete with interviews with David P. Friedman and other exploitation pioneers. Mike Varney has compiled two video series, the first called *Nudie Cuties* (just nude scenes), the second *Twisted Sex* (classic exploitation scenes). Playboy Video's *The Story of X:*

100 Years of Adult Film and Its Stars includes clips from historically important porn films, with commentary by Andrea Dworkin, Donald Wildmon, and Russ Meyer, among others. Cass Paley's *Wadd: The Life and Times of John C. Holmes* is a non-exploitive look at the industry's most notorious male star and should be viewed along with *Boogie Nights*, Marc Ahlberg's Hollywood *cinéma à clef* based on Holmes's career.

Ralph G. Allen, who reproduced famous routines for the road-show *Sugar Babies*, published them as *The Best Burlesque Sketches as Adapted for Sugar Babies and Other Entertainments*. *Live Girls Nude Unitel*, a documentary directed by Julia Query and Vicky Funari, deals with the struggle of strippers to unionize the Lusty Lady Theater in Seattle. *Strippers: The Naked Stages*, produced by Anthony Radziwill, visits a few of the more than 2500 strip clubs and interviews a few of the more than 250,000 women who dance in them. Lenora Champagne, Ellie Covan, Diane Torr, Robbie McCauley, Arlene Raven, Rachel Rosenthal, Martha Wilson, Carolee Schneemann, Laurie Anderson, Holly Hughes, and Diamanda Galás perform sequences in Maria Beatty's videotape, *Sphinxes without Secrets: Women Performance Artists Speak Out*.

Torn Shapes of Desire: Internet Erotica by Mary Anne Mohanraj is one of the very few print collections of messages drawn from digital narratives and from e-mail, chat rooms, and other pathways. Another is *Susie Bright's Sexual Reality: A Virtual Sex World Reader*, whose chapters range from television broadcasts to erotic exchanges in cyberspace. Also of interest is *Hot off the Net: Erotica and Other Sex Writings from the Internet*, edited by Russ Kick. Web sites, of course, cluster their own selections. For *The Mammoth Book of Sex, Drugs, and Rock 'n' Roll*, Jim Driver includes essays on erotic aspects of the music scene.

Margaret C. Jasper excerpts leading cases and important decisions in *The Law of Obscenity and Pornography*. Arthur S. Leonard's *Sexuality and the Law: An Encyclopedia of Major Legal Cases* is comprehensive, if slightly dated. Current decisions of U.S. Courts of Appeals for all districts can be found in the periodical *Federal Reporter*, and rulings by the Supreme Court appear in the monthly *United States Reports*. Some information on prosecutions of pornography can be found in *Crime in the United States*, the Uniform Crime Reports published annually by the FBI.

NOTES

1. Jim Rutenberg, "Seamy or Serious, It's Now Center Stage," *New York Times*, 21 March 2001, p. B5.

2. Guy Trebay, "Men's Fashion Does without the Clothes," *New York Times*, 20 March 2001, p. A22.

3. Timothy Egan, "Technology Sent Wall Street into Market for Pornography," *New York Times*, October 23, 2000, pp. A1, A20.

4. "The Sex Industry," *The Economist*, 346 (14–20 February 1998): 21–23.

5. See for example www.voyeurweb.com.

6. See Barry Werth, *The Scarlet Professor: Newton Arvin: A Literary Life Shattered by Scandal* (New York: Nan Talese/Doubleday, 2001).

7. Josephine Schmidt, "Psst, Comrade: Check Out the Erotica in the Library," *New York Times* (September 5, 2001), p. B2.

8. Jarvie, *Thinking About Society*, p. 412.

9. Legman quoted by Helen Dudar, "Love and Death (and Schmutz): G. Legman's Second Thoughts," *Village Voice*, 1 May 1984, p. 42.

BIBLIOGRAPHY

Aarne, Antti, and Stith Thompson. *The Types of the Folktale: A Classification and Bibliography*. Folklore Fellows Communication, 184. Helsinki: Suomalainen Tiedekatemia, 1961.

Access: The Supplementary Index to Periodicals, 1975– . Syracuse, NY: Gaylord Professional Publishers, 1975–1977; Evanston, IL: J. G. Burke Publishers, 1978– .

Adelman, Bob, ed. *Tijuana Bibles: Art and Wit in America's Forbidden Funnies, 1930s–1950s*. New York: Simon and Schuster, 1997.

Allen, Ralph G. *The Best Burlesque Sketches as Adapted for Sugar Babies and Other Entertainments*. New York: Applause Theatre Books, 1995.

Allen, Robert C. *Horrible Prettiness: Burlesque and American Culture*. Chapel Hill: University of North Carolina Press, 1991.

alt.magazines.pornographic

Alvin, Julius. *Gross Jokes*. 11 vols. New York: Zebra Books, 1983–1991.

Amey, Lawrence, Timothy Hall, Carl Jansen, Charles May, and Richard Wilson, eds. *Censorship*. 3 vols. Pasadena, CA: Salem Press, 1997.

Anthony, Gary, with Rockey Bennett. *Dirty Talk: Diary of a Phone Sex "Mistress."* Buffalo, NY: Prometheus Books, 1997.

Attorney General's Commission on Pornography. *Final Report*. 2 vols. Washington DC: U.S. Government Printing Office, 1986.

Audibert, Chris. Burlesque Albums, 1950–1959. 4 vols. Billy Rose Theatre Collection, New York Public Library, Lincoln Center for the Performing Arts, New York, New York.

Ayres, Michael. *English Homosexual Poetry of the 19th and 20th Centuries*. London: Michael de Hartington, 1972.

Bailey, Mike. *Writing Erotic Fiction: And Getting Published*. Lincolnwood, IL: NTC Contemporary Publishing, 1998.

Banned Books. 4 vols. New York: Facts on File, 1998.

Banned Books Online. www.cs.cmu.edu/Web/People/spok/

Barrington, John S. *Contemporary Homo-Erotic Art*. London: S & H, 1974.

Bataille, Georges. *Death and Sensuality: A Study of Eroticism and the Taboo*. New York: Ballantine Books, 1962; rpt. *Eroticism: Death and Sensuality*, trans. Mary Dalwood. San Francisco: City Light Books, 1986; both are translations of *Eroticism*. Paris: Editions de Minuit, 1957.

Beauchamp, Monte, ed. *The Life and Times of R. Crumb; Commentary from Contemporaries*. New York: St. Martin's/Griffin, 1998.

Berger, John. *About Looking*. New York: Random House, 1991.

———. *Ways of Seeing*. London: BBC/Penguin, 1986.

Berlant, Lauren. *The Queen of America Goes to Washington City: Essays on Sex and Citizenship*. Durham, NC: Duke University Press, 1997.

Bessie, Simon Michael. *Jazz Journalism: The Story of the Tabloid Newspapers*. New York: Dutton, 1938.

Betrock, Alan. *Complete Guide to Cult Magazines*. Brooklyn, NY: Shake Books, 1998.

———. *Pin-Up Mania: The Golden Age of Men's Magazines (1950–1967)*. Brooklyn, NY: Shake Books, 1996.

———. *Unseen America: The Greatest Cult Exploitation Magazines, 1950–1966*; rev. of *One Hundred Greatest Cult Exploitation Magazines, 1950–1965*. Brooklyn, NY: Shake Books, 1990.

Betrock, Alan, and Hillard Schneider. *The Personality Index to Hollywood Scandal Magazines, 1952–1966*. Brooklyn, NY: Shake Books, 1990.

Betterton, Rosemary. *Intimate Distance: Women, Artists and the Body*. New York: Routledge, 1996.

Betty Page: Private Peeks. 4 vols. New York: Belier Press, 1980.

Bilderlexicon der Erotik, Ein bibliographisches und biographisches Nachschlagewerk, eine Kunst- und Literaturgeschichte für die Gebiete der erotischen Belletristik . . . von der Antike zur Gegenwart. 6 vols. Vienna and Hamburg: Verlag für Kulturforschung, 1928–1931, 1963. Edited by Leo Schidrowitz: I: *Kulturgeschichte*; II: *Literatur und Kunst*; III: *Sexualwissenschaft*; IV: *Ergänzungsband*. Edited by Armand Mergen: V and VI: *Sexualforschung: Stichwort und Bild*.

Bird, S. Elizabeth. *For Enquiring Minds: A Cultural Study of Supermarket Tabloids*. Knoxville: University of Tennessee Press, 1992.

Bizarre Classix. 5 vols. New York: Bélier Press, 1977–1982.

Bizarre Comix. 24 vols. New York: Bélier Press, 1975–87.

Bizarre Fotos: From the Archives of Irving Klaw. 4 vols. New York: Bélier Press, 1978.

Black, Bob. *Beneath the Underground*. Portland, OR: Feral House, 1994.

Bloomfield, Judy, Mary McGrail, and Lauren Sanders, eds. *Too Darn Hot: Writing About Sex Since Kinsey*. New York: Persea, 1998.

Bold, Alan, ed. *Making Love: The Picador Book of Erotic Verse*. London: Picador, 1978.

Boone, Joseph Allen. *Libidinal Currents*. Chicago: University of Chicago Press, 1998.

Brent, Bill, ed. *The Black Book*. Editions 1–5. Brent/Amador, P.O. Box 31155, San Francisco, CA 94131–0155, 1993–1998.

Brent, Bill, and Carol Queen, eds. *Best Bisexual Erotica*. New York: Seven Story Press, 2000.

Brent, Steve, and Elizabeth Brent. *The Couple's Guide to the Best Erotic Videos*. New York: St. Martin's, 1997.

Bright, Susie. *Susie Bright's Sexual Reality: A Virtual Sex World Reader*. Pittsburgh, PA: Cleis Press, 1992.

———, ed. *The Best American Erotica*. New York: Collier, 1993, 1994, 1995, 1996, 1997; New York: Touchstone, 1998, 1999, 2000, 2001.

———. *Herotica: A Collection of Women's Erotic Fiction*. Burlingame, CA: Down There Press, 1988.

———. *Herotica III: A Collection of Women's Erotic Fiction*. New York: Plume, 1994.

Bright, Susie, and Joannie Blank, eds. *Herotica II: A Collection of Women's Erotic Fiction*. New York: Plume, 1991.

Bright, Susie, and Jill Posener, eds. *Nothing but the Girl: The Blatant Lesbian Image*, *a Portfolio and Exploration of Lesbian Erotic Photography*. London: Wellington House, 1995.

Brigman, William E. "A Content Analysis of Sex in Usenet Newsgroups." Paper presented to Popular Culture Association, Philadelphia, 13 April 2001; available from author at University of Houston–Downtown.

Brulotte, Gaëtan, and John Phillips, eds. *Encyclopedia of Erotic Literature*. London: Fitzroy Dearborn, forthcoming.

Bud Plant Company. *Bud Plant's Incredible Catalog* and *Comic Art Update*. P.O. Box 1689, Grass Valley, CA 95945, current.

Burger, John R. *One-Handed Histories: The Eroto-Politics of Gay Male Video Pornography*. New York: Harrington Park Press/Haworth Press, 1995.

Burt, Eugene C. *Erotic Art: An Annotated Bibliography with Essays*. Boston: G. K. Hall, 1989.

Butler, Jerry, with Robert Rimmer and Catherine Tavel. *Raw Talent: The Adult Film Industry as Seen by Its Most Popular Male Star*. Buffalo, NY: Prometheus Books, 1989.

Butler, Judith. *Excitable Speech: A Politics of the Performative*. New York: Routledge, 1997.

Chalker, Rebecca. *The Clitoral Truth: The Secret World at Your Fingertips*. New York: Seven Stories Press, 2000.

Chambers, Marilyn. *Marilyn Chambers: My Story*. New York: Warner Books, 1975.

Chapple, Steve, and David Talbot. *Burning Desires: Sex in America, a Report from the Field*. New York: Signet, 1990.

Charney, Maurice. *Sexual Fiction*. New York: Methuen, 1981.

Chicago, Judy, and Edward Lucie-Smith. *Women and Art: Contested Territory*. New York: Watson-Guptill, 1999.

Christensen, F. M. *Pornography: The Other Side*. New York: Praeger, 1990.

Christensen, John O. *Obscenity, Pornography, and Libraries: A Selective Bibliography*. Monticello, IL: Vance Bibliographies, 1991.

Clapp, Jane. *Art Censorship*. Metuchen, NJ: Scarecrow Press, 1972.

Clardy, Andrea Fleck. *Words to the Wise: A Writer's Guide to the Feminist and Lesbian Periodicals and Publishers*. Ithaca, NY: Firebrand Pubs., 1986.

Clark, Larry. *Larry Clark, 1992*. New York: Thea Westreich, and Köln: Gisela Captain, 1992.

———. *Teenage Lust*. New York: Clark, 1983.

Cohen, Angela, and Sarah G. Fox. *The Wise Woman's Guide to Erotic Videos*. New York: Broadway Books, 1997.

Cole, William, ed. *Erotic Poetry: The Lyrics, Ballads, Idyls and Epics of Love—Classical to Contemporary*. New York: Random House, 1963.

The Complete Reprint of Physique Pictorial, 1951–1990. 3 vols. Berlin: Benedikt Taschen, 1997.

Cooper, Emmanuel. *The Sexual Perspective: Homosexuality and Art in the Last 100 Years in the West*. London: Routledge and Kegan Paul, 1986; 2nd ed. 1994.

Corinne, Tee. *Lesbian Images in the Fine Arts*. San Francisco: Privately issued, 1978.

Cornell, Drucilla. *Feminism and Pornography*. New York: Oxford University Press, 2000.

Cornog, Martha. *Libraries, Erotica, Pornography*. Phoenix, AZ: Oryx Press, 1991.

Cox, John. www.archive@badpuppy.com

Crosbie, Lynn, ed. *The Girl Wants To: Women's Representation of Sex and the Body*. Toronto: Coach House, 1993.

Crumb, Robert. *The Complete Crumb*. 10 vols. Seattle: Fantagraphics, 1986–1994.

Cybersex Consortium. *The Perv's Guide to the Internet*. New York: Masquerade, 1996.

Daly, Stephen, and Nathaniel Wice. *Alt. Culture: An A-Z Guide to the '90s—Underground, Online, and Over the Counter*. New York: HarperPerennial, 1995.

Danville, Eric. *The Complete Linda Lovelace*. New York: Power Process Publishing, 2001.

Deakin, Terence. *Catalogi Liborum Eroticum*. London: Cecil & Amelia Woolf, 1964.

Decosta-Willis, Miriam, Reginald Martin, and RoseAnn P. Bell, eds. *Erotique Noire: Black Erotica*. New York: Doubleday, 1992.

D'Emilio, John, and Estelle B. Freedman. *Intimate Matters: A History of Sexuality in America*. New York: Harper and Row, 1988.

Di Lauro, Al, and Gerald Rabkin. *Dirty Movies: An Illustrated History of the Stag Film, 1915–1970*. New York: Chelsea House, 1976.

Dines, Gail, Robert Jensen, and Ann Russo. *Pornography: The Production and Consumption of Inequality*. New York: Routledge, 1998.

Dooling, Richard. *Blue Streak: Swearing, Free Speech, and Sexual Harassment*. New York: Random House, 1996.

Driver, Jim, ed. *The Mammoth Book of Sex, Drugs, and Rock 'n' Roll*. New York: Carroll & Graf, 2001.

Duncan, Robert, et al. *The Male Muse: Gay Poetry Anthology*. Freedom, CA: Crossing Press, 1973.

Duncombe, Stephen. *Notes From Underground: Zines and the Politics of Alternative Culture*. New York: Verso, 1997.

Dworkin, Andrea. *Intercourse*. New York: Free Press, 1987.

———. *Pornography: Men Possessing Women*. New York: Putnam's, 1980.

Dyer, Richard, ed. *The Matter of Images: Essays on Representations*. New York: Routledge, 1993.

Dynes, Wayne R., and Stephen Donaldson, eds. *Studies in Homosexuality*. 13 vols. Hamden, CT: Garland, 1990.

E-zines Database Menu. www.dominis.com/Zines/

Edelman, Lee. *Homographesis: Essays in Gay Literary and Cultural Theory*. New York: Routledge, 1994.

Edgren, Gretchen, ed. *The Playmate Book: Five Decades of Centerfolds*. Los Angeles: General Publishing Group, 1996.

———. *The Playboy Book: Forty Years, The Complete Pictorial History*. Santa Monica CA: General Publishing Corp., 1994.

Egan, Timothy. "Technology Sent Wall Street into Market for Pornography." *New York Times*, October 23, 2000, pp. A1, A20.

Ellis, Albert. *The Folklore of Sex*, aka *Sex Beliefs and Customs*. New York: Charles Boni, 1951; and *The Folklore of Sex*. New York: Grove Press, 1961.

Erotic Print Society. *Catalogs*. P.O. Box 10645, London SW10 9ZT, UK, or www.eps.org.uk

Estren, Mark James. *A History of Underground Comics*. San Francisco: Straight Arrow, 1974.

Exotique. New York: Burmel Publications, 1957–1963; 36 issues reprinted as *Exotique: A New Magazine of the Bizarre and Unusual*. 3 vols. Cologne: Benedikt Taschen, 1998.

Fallon, Eileen. *Words of Love: A Complete Guide to Romance Fiction*. New York: Garland, 1984.

Fantagraphics. *The Ultimate Comics Catalog*. Seattle, WA: Fantagraphics, current.

Farmer, John S., and William Earnest Henley. *Slang and Its Analogues*. 7 vols. London: Privately printed, 1890–1904; rpt. *Slang and Its Analogues, Past and Present*. 3 vols. Millwood, NY: Kraus Reprint, 1989.

Federal Bureau of Investigation. Uniform Crime Reports. *Crime in the United States*. Washington, DC: Government Printing Office, annual.

Fiene, Donald M. *R. Crumb Checklist of Work and Criticism*. Cambridge, MA: Boatner Norton Press, 1981.

Fischer, Hal. *Gay Semiotics: A Photographic Study of Visual Coding Among Homosexual Men*. Berkeley: NFS Press, 1978.

Fisher's Erotic Encyclopedia. Dream Catcher Interactive, 265 Rim Rock Road, Toronto M3J3C6 Canada, or www.eroticencyclopedia.com

[Fliesler, Joseph]. *Anecdota Americana, Being Explicitly an Anthology of the Tales of the Vernacular. Elucidatory Preface by J. Mortimer Hall*. Boston [New York]: Humphrey Adams, 1927; reset and expanded, same publisher, 1932. Second edition, also reset but not expanded, published as *Anecdota Americana. Being Explicitly an Anthology of the Tales in the Vernacular*. [New York: Gotham Book Mart, 1927–1928]; reprinted as *The Classic Book of Dirty Jokes*. New York: Bell, 1981. Sanitized editions by Samuel Roth: *Anecdota Americana: Five Hundred Stories for the Amusement of the Five Hundred Nations that Comprise America*. New York: William Faro, 1933; also New York: Golden Hind Press, 1933; rpt. New York: Nesor Publishing Company, 1933; rev. ed. *The New Anecdota Americana*. New York: Grayson, 1944. Probably not by Fliesler: *Anecdota Americana. An Anthology of Tales in the Vernacular Edited without Expurgation*. By J. Mortimer Hall. Second Series. Boston [New York]: Humphrey Adams [Vincent Smith], 1934; rpt. as *The Unexpurgated Anecdota Americana*. 2 vols. North Hollywood, CA: Brandon House, 1968.

Flint, David. *Babylon Blue: An Illustrated History of Adult Cinema*. London: Creation Books, 1999.

Flowers, Amy. *The Fantasy Factory: An Insider's View of the Phone Sex Industry*. Philadelphia: University of Pennsylvania Press, 1998.

Flynt, Larry. *An Unseemly Man: My Life as Pornographer, Pundit and Social Outcast*. New York: Penguin/Dove, 1996.

The Forbidden Library: An Exhibition of Erotic Illustrations From the 18th Century to the Present Day, with intro. by Peter Webb. London: Hobart and Maclean, 1986.

Forcade, Thomas King, comp. *Underground Press Anthology*. New York: Ace Books, 1972.

Ford, Luke. www.LukeFord.com

Foster, Jeannette H. *Sex Variant Women in Literature*. New York: Vantage Press, 1956; 3rd ed. Tallahassee, FL: Naiad Press, 1985.

Foucault, Michel. *The History of Sexuality*, trans. Robert Hurley. 3 vols. New York: Pantheon, 1978–1987.

Franklin, Constance, ed. *Erotic Art By Living Artists*. Vol. 1. Renaissance, CA: Directors Guild Pub., 1988; Vol. 2. Los Angeles: ArtNetwork, 1994.

Frasier, David K. *Russ Meyer—the Life and Films: A Biography and a Comprehensive, Illustrated, and Annotated Filmography and Bibliography*. Jefferson, NC: McFarland, 1990.

Friedman, Andrea. *Prurient Interests: Gender, Democracy, and Obscenity in New York City, 1909–1945*. New York: Columbia University Press, 2000.

Friend, Tad. "Department of Broadcasting: You Can't Say That." *New Yorker*, 19 November 2001, pp. 44–46, 48–49.

Gabor, Mark. *The Illustrated History of Girlie Magazines*. New York: Harmony, 1984.

———. *The Pin-Up: A Modest History*. New York: Universe Books, 1972.

Gamelin, Douglas H., ed. *The Tijuana Bible Reader*. San Diego: Greenleaf, 1969.

Gamson, Joshua. *Freaks Talk Back: Tabloid Talk Shows and Sexual Nonconformity*. Chicago: University of Chicago Press, 1998.

Garber, Eric, and Lyn Paleo, eds. *Uranian Worlds: A Guide to Alternative Sexuality in Science Fiction, Fantasy and Horror*. 2nd ed. New York: Macmillan, 1990.

Garde, Noel I. *The Homosexual in Literature: A Chronological Bibliography Circa 700 B.C.–1958*. New York: Village Press, 1959.

Garment, Suzanne. *Scandal: The Culture of Mistrust in American Politics*. New York: Doubleday/Anchor, 1992.

Gerdts, William H. *The Great American Nude: A History in Art*. New York: Praeger, 1974.

Gertzman, Jay A. *Bookleggers and Smuthounds: The Trade in Erotica, 1920–1940*. Philadelphia: University of Pennsylvania Press, 1999.

Gilfoyle, Timothy J. *City of Eros: New York City, Prostitution, and the Commercialization of Sex, 1790–1920*. New York: Norton, 1992.

Gilmore, Donald H. *Sex in Comics: A History of the Eight Pagers*. 4 vols. San Diego, CA: Greenleaf Classics, 1971.

Gittler, Ian. *Pornstar*. New York: Simon and Schuster, 1999.

Glessing, Robert J. *The Underground Press in America*. Bloomington: Indiana University Press, 1970.

Goldberg, RoseLee. *Performance Art: From Futurism to the Present*. New York: Harry Abrams, 1988; rev. of *Performance: Live Art 1909 to the Present*. New York: Abrams, 1979.

Goldin, Nan, Marvin Heifernan, Mark Holborn, and Suzanne Fletcher. *The Ballad of Sexual Dependency*. New York: Aperture, 1986.

Goldstein, Al, and Jim Buckley, eds. *The Screw Reader*. New York: Lyle Stuart, 1971.

Gonzalez, Ray, ed. *Under the Pomegranate Tree: The Best New Latino Erotica*. New York: Washington Square Press, 1996.

Goodstone, Tony. *The Pulps: Fifty Years of American Popular Culture*. New York: Chelsea House, 1970.

Goshgarian, G. M. *To Kiss the Chastening Rod: Domestic Fiction and Sexual Ideology in the American Renaissance*. Ithaca, NY: Cornell University Press, 1992.

Goulemot, Jean Marie. *Ces livres qu'on ne lit que d'une main: Lecture et lecteurs de livres pornographiques au XVIIIe siècle*. Aix-en-Province: Alines, 1991; rpt. *Forbidden Texts: Erotic Literature and Its Readers in Eighteenth-Century France*. Philadelphia: University of Pennsylvania Press, 1995.

Gray, John. *Active Art: A Bibliography of Artists' Performance from Futurism to Fluxus and Beyond*. Westport, CT: Greenwood, 1993.

Green, Jonathan. *The Encyclopedia of Censorship*. New York: Facts on File, 1990.

Green, Rayna. "Folk Is a Four-Letter Word: Dealing with Traditional _____ in Fieldwork, Analysis, and Presentation." *Handbook of American Folklore*, ed. Richard M. Dorson. Bloomington: Indiana University Press, 1983, pp. 525–532.

Greenawalt, Kent. *Fighting Words: Individuals, Communities, and Liberties of Speech*. Princeton, NJ: Princeton University Press, 1995.

Greenberg, Gerald S. *Tabloid Journalism: An Annotated Bibliography of English-Language Sources*. Westport, CT: Greenwood Press, 1996.

Grier, Barbara, and Christine Cassidy, eds. *The Very Thought of You: Erotic Love Stories by Naiad Press Authors*. Tallahassee, FL: Naiad Press, 1999.

Grier, Barbara, Jan Watson, and Robin Jordan. *The Lesbian in Literature: A Bibliography*. 3rd ed. Tallahassee, FL: Naiad Press, 1981.

Gunderloy, Mike, and Cari G. Janice, eds. *The World of Zines: A Guide to the Independent Magazine Revolution*. New York: Penguin, 1992.

Hardy, Jan, ed. *Wanting Women: An Anthology of Erotic Lesbian Poetry*. Pittsburgh: Sidewalk Revolution Press, 1990.

Hart, Lynda. *Between the Body and the Flesh: Performing Sadomasochism*. New York: Columbia University Press, 1998.

Hayes, Joseph J. "Language Behavior of Lesbian Women and Gay Men: A Selected Bibliography (Part 1)." *Journal of Homosexuality*, 4 (1978): 201–212.

Hebditch, David, and Nick Anning. *Porn Gold: Inside the Pornography Business*. London: Faber and Faber, 1988.

Heidenry, John. *What Wild Ecstacy: The Rise and Fall of the Sexual Revolution*. New York: Simon and Schuster, 1997.

Heins, Marjorie. *Not in Front of the Children: "Indecency," Censorship, and the Innocence of Youth*. New York: Hill and Wang, 2001.

———. *Sex, Sin, and Blasphemy: A Guide to America's Censorship Wars*. New York: New Press, 1993.

Hess, Thomas B., and Linda Nochlin, eds. *Woman as Sex Object: Studies in Erotic Art, 1730–1970*. New York: Newsweek, 1972 (rep. vol. 38 of *Art News Annual*); London: Allen Lowe, 1973.

Highsmith, Doug. "Comic Books: A Guide to Information Sources." *Riverside Quarterly*, 27 (Winter 1987): 202–209.

Hill, Charlotte, and William Wallace. *Erotica: An Illustrated Anthology of Sexual Art and Literature*. 3 vols. New York: Carroll and Graf, 1992, 1993, 1995.

Hobby, Elaine, and Chris White, eds. *What Lesbians Do in Books*. London: Women's Press, 1991.

Hoffmann, Frank. *Analytical Survey of Anglo-American Traditional Erotica*. Bowling Green, Ohio: Popular Press, 1973.

Hogan, Steve, and Lee Hudson, eds. *Completely Queer: The Gay and Lesbian Encyclopedia*. New York: Henry Holt, 1998.

Holt, R. G., ed. *Little Dirty Comics* and *More Dirty Little Comics*. San Diego, CA:

Socio Library, 1971; Terence Atkinson is listed as editor on the second volume.

hooks, bell. *Outlaw Culture: Resisting Representations*. New York: Routledge, 1994.

Horn, Maurice. *Sex in the Comics*. New York: Chelsea House, 1985.

Howard, Mel, and Thomas King Forcade, comps. *Underground Reader*. New York: Plume, 1972.

Hubner, John. *Bottom Feeders: From Free Love to Hard Core—The Rise and Fall of Counterculture Heroes Jim and Artie Mitchell*. New York: Doubleday, 1993.

Hunt, Lynn, ed. *The Invention of Pornography: Obscenity and the Origins of Modernity, 1500–1800*. Cambridge, MA: MIT Zone, 1993.

Husni, Samia. *Husni Samia's Guide to New Magazines*. University: Department of Journalism, University of Mississippi, 1986– , annual.

Hyde, Alan. *Bodies of Law*. Princeton, NJ: Princeton University Press, 1997.

Interactive Adult Movie Almanac. Los Angeles: New Machine Publishing, 1994.

Isherwood, Charles. *Wonder Bread and Ecstacy: The Life and Death of Joey Stefano*. Boston: Alyson, 1996.

Jackson, Earl, Jr. *Strategies of Deviance: Studies in Gay Male Representation*. Bloomington: Indiana University Press, 1995.

Jackson, Ed, and Stan Persky, eds. *Flaunting It: A Decade of Gay Journalism from the Body Politic*. Vancouver: New Star Books, 1982.

Jakubowski, Maxim, ed. *The Mammoth Book of International Erotica*. New York: Carroll and Graf, 1996.

———. *The Mammoth Book of New Erotica*. New York: Carroll and Graf, 1997.

Jarvie, I. C. "Methodological and Conceptual Problems in the Study of Pornography and Violence." *Thinking About Society: Theory and Practice*. Dordrecht, Holland: Reidel, 1985, pp. 390–475.

Jasper, Margaret C. *The Law of Obscenity and Pornography*. Dobbs Ferry, NY: Oceana Publications, 1996.

Jay, Timothy. *Cursing in America: A Psycholinguistic Study of Dirty Language in the Courts, in the Movies, in the Schoolyards, and on the Streets*. Philadelphia: John Benjamins, 1992.

Jones, Baird. *Sexual Humor*. New York: Philosophical Library, 1987.

Juffer, Jane. *At Home with Pornography: Women, Sex, and Everyday Life*. New York: New York University Press, 1998.

Juno, Andrea, ed. *Dangerous Drawings: Interviews with Comix & Graphic Artists*. New York: Juno Books, 1997.

Juno, Andrea, and V. Vale, eds. *Angry Women*. San Francisco: RE/Search, 1991.

———. *Incredibly Strange Films*. San Francisco: RE/Search, 1986.

Kadrey, Richard. *Covert Culture Sourcebook*, and *Covert Culture Sourcebook 2.0*. New York: St. Martin's, 1993, 1994; updates available from kadrey@well.sf.ca.us

Kappeler, Susanne. *The Pornography of Representation*. Minneapolis: University of Minnesota Press, 1986.

Karwath, Cary von. *Die Erotik im der Kunst*. Vienna: C. W. Stern, 1908.

Kaye, Nick. *Art into Theatre: Performance Interviews and Documents*. Amsterdam: Harwood Academic Publishers, 1996.

Kearney, Patrick J. *A Bibliography of the New York Olympia Press*. Santa Rosa, CA: Scissors and Paste Bibliographies, 1988.

———. *A History of Erotic Literature*. London: Macmillan, 1982.

———. *The Olympia Press, Paris 1953–1965: A Handlist*. London: Privately printed, 1975; rpt. *The Paris Olympia Press*. London: Black Spring, 1987.

Kehoe, Monika, ed. *Historical, Literary and Erotic Aspects of Lesbianism*. New York: Haworth Press, 1986; rpt. special issue *Journal of Homosexuality*, 12 (May 1986).

Kemp, Earl, ed. *The Illustrated Presidential Report of the Commission on Obscenity and Pornography*. San Diego, CA: Greenleaf Classics, 1970.

Kendrick, Walter. *The Secret Museum: Pornography in Modern Culture*. New York: Viking, 1987.

Kepner, Jim. *Rough News—Daring Views: 1950s Pioneer Gay Press Journalism*. Binghamton, NY: Haworth Press, 1997.

Kick, Russ, ed. *Hot off the Net: Erotica and Other Sex Writings from the Internet*. New York: Black Books, 2000.

———. *Outposts: A Catalog of Rare and Disturbing Alternative Information*. New York: Carrol and Graf/Richard Kasak, 1995.

———. *Psychotropia*. Manchester, UK: Headpress, 1998.

King, Alison. "Mystery and Imagination: The Case of Pornography Effects Studies." *Bad Girls and Dirty Pictures: The Challenge to Reclaim Feminism*, ed. Alison Assiter and Avedon Carol. Boulder, CO: Pluto Press, 1993, pp. 57–87.

Kinnick, Dave. *Sorry I Asked: Intimate Interviews with Gay Porn's Rank and File*. New York: Badboy, 1993.

Kinsey Institute for Research in Sex, Gender, and Reproduction. *Bibliographies*. Information Service, Kinsey Institute for Research in Sex, Gender, and Reproduction, Indiana University, Bloomington.

Kipnis, Laura. *Bound and Gagged: Pornography and the Politics of Fantasy in America*. New York: Grove Press, 1996.

Kiss and Tell [Blackbridge, Persimmon, Lizard Jones, and Susan Stewart]. *Her Tongue on My Theory: Images, Essays and Fantasies*. Vancouver: Press Gang Publishers, 1994; East Haven, CT: InBook Publishing, 1994.

Knott, Blanche. *Truly Tasteless Jokes*. 11 vols. New York: Ballantine, 1982–1991.

Köhler, Michael, and Gisela Barche, eds. *Das Aktfoto: Ansichten vom Körper im fotografischen Zeitalter: Ästhetik—Geschichte—Ideologie*. Munich: C. J. Bucher/Stadtmuseum, 1985.

Krajicek, David J. *Scooped! Mass Media Miss Real Story on Crime while Chasing Sex, Sleaze, and Celebrities*. New York: Columbia University Press, 1998.

Kronhausen, Eberhard and Phyllis. *The Complete Book of Erotic Art*. New York: Bell, 1978.

Kudaka, Geraldine, ed. *On a Bed of Rice: An Asian-American Erotic Feast*. New York: Anchor/Doubleday, 1995.

Lane, Frederick S., III. *Obscene Profits: The Entrepreneurs of Pornography in the Cyber Age*. New York: Routledge, 2000.

LaRue, Chi Chi [Paciotti, Larry], with John Erich. *Making It Big: Sex Stars, Porn Films, and Me*. Los Angeles: Alyson Books, 1997.

Last Gasp Catalog. 777 Florida Street, San Francisco 94110.

Legman, Gershon. "Erotic Folksongs and Ballads: An International Bibliography." *Journal of American Folklore*, 103 (October/December 1990): 417–501.

———. *The Horn Book: Studies in Erotic Folklore and Bibliography*. New York: University Books, 1964.

———. *The Limerick*. Paris: Les Hautes Etudes, 1953.

———. *The New Limerick: 2750 Unpublished Examples, American and British*. New York: Crown Publishers, 1977.

———. *Love and Death: A Study in Censorship*. New York: Breaking Point, 1949.

———. *No Laughing Matter: Rationale of the Dirty Joke, Second Series*. New York: Grove Press, 1975.

———. *The Rationale of the Dirty Joke: An Analysis of Sexual Humor*. New York: Grove Press, 1968.

Leonard, Arthur S. *Sexuality and the Law: An Encyclopedia of Major Legal Cases*. New York: Garland, 1993.

"Lesbian Art and Artists." Special Issue of *Heresies*, 3 (1977).

Leyland, Winston, ed. *Gay Roots: Twenty Years of Gay Sunshine* and *Gay Roots: An Anthology of Gay History, Sex, Politics, and Culture, Volume 2*. San Francisco: Gay Sunshine Press, 1991, 1993.

———. *Meatmen: An Anthology of Gay Male Comics* and *More Meatmen: An Anthology of Gay Male Comics*. San Francisco: G. S. Press, 1986.

Lichtenberg, Kara. *A Research Guide to Human Sexuality*. Hamden, CT: Garland, 1993.

Liepe-Levinson, Katherine H. *Strip Show*. New York: Routledge, 2001.

Lilly, Mark, ed. *Lesbian and Gay Writing: An Anthology of Critical Essays*. New York: Macmillan, 1990.

Limbacher, James L. *Sexuality in World Cinema*. 2 vols. Metuchen, NJ: Scarecrow Press, 1983.

Linna, Miriam. *Smut Peddler*. P.O. Box 646, Cooper Station, NYC 10003, 1993– .

Linton, E. R. [Edward B. Cray], comp. *The Dirty Song Book: American Bawdy Songs*. Los Angeles: Medco Books, 1965; updated as *The Erotic Muse*. New York: Oak Publications, 1969.

Logsdon, Guy. *"The Whorehouse Bells Were Ringing," and Other Songs Cowboys Sing*. Urbana: University of Illinois Press, 1989.

Loompanics Unlimited. *Catalog*. P.O. Box 1197, Port Townsend, WA 98368.

Lorde, Audre. "Uses of the Erotic: The Erotic as Power." *Sister Outsider: Essays and Speeches by Audre Lorde*. Trumansbury, NY: Crossing Press, 1984, pp. 53–59.

Lovelace, Linda, with Mike Brady. *Ordeal*. New York: Citadel, 1980.

———. *Out of Bondage*. Secaucus: Lyle Stuart, 1986.

Lowenthal, Michael, ed. *Flesh and the Word 4: Gay Erotic Confessionals*. New York: Plume, 1997.

Lowry, Thomas P. *The Story the Soldiers Wouldn't Tell: Sex in the Civil War*. Mechanicsburg, PA: Stackpole Books, 1994.

Lucie-Smith, Edward. *Ars Erotica: An Arousing History of Erotic Art*. New York: Rizzoli, 1997.

———. *Race, Sex and Gender: Issues in Contemporary Art*. New York: Abrams, 1994.

———. *Sexuality in Western Art*. London: Thames and Hudson, 1991; rev. of *Eroticism in Western Art*. New York: Praeger, 1972.

MacKinnon, Catharine A. *Feminism Unmodified: Discourses on Life and Law*. Cambridge, MA: Harvard University Press, 1987.

———. *Only Words*. Cambridge, MA: Harvard University Press, 1993.

———. *Toward a Feminist Theory of the State*. Cambridge, MA: Harvard University Press, 1989.

Maglin, Nan Bauer, and Donna Perry, eds. *"Bad Girls"/"Good Girls": Women, Sex, and Power in the Nineties*. New Brunswick, NJ: Rutgers University Press, 1996.

Mapplethorpe, Robert, with an Introduction by Arthur Danto. *Mapplethorpe*. New York: Random House, 1992.

Marcuse, Herbert. *Eros and Civilization: A Philosophical Inquiry into Freud*. Boston: Beacon, 1955.

Marsh, Joss. *Word Crimes: Blasphemy, Culture, and Literature in Nineteenth Century England*. Chicago: University of Chicago Press, 1998.

Martignette, C. G., and L. K. Meisel. *The Best of American Girlie Magazines*. Cologne: Benedikt Taschen, 1998.

———. *The Great American Pin-Up*. Berlin: Benedikt Taschen, 1995.

Martin, Reginald, ed. *Dark Eros: Black Erotic Writings*. New York: St. Martin's, 1997.

Mason, Philip. *The Complete Internet Sex Resource Guide*. alt.magazines. pornographicPhilip@iglou.com. Request by e-mail (message area: Send Sex Surfer Catalog).

McCumber, David. *Rated-X: The Mitchell Brothers, a True Story of Sex, Money, and Death*. New York: Simon and Schuster, 1992.

McDonald, Helen. *Erotic Ambiguities: The Female Nude in Art*. New York: Routledge, 2001.

McElroy, Wendy. *XXX: A Woman's Right to Pornography*. New York: St. Martin's Press, 1995.

Meese, Elizabeth. *(Sem)Erotics: Theorizing Lesbian: Writing*. New York: New York University Press, 1992.

Mendes, Peter. *Clandestine Erotic Fiction in English 1800–1930: A Bibliographical Study*. Aldershot, England: Scolar Press, 1993.

Michelson, Peter. *Speaking the Unspeakable: A Poetics of Obscenity*. Albany: State University of New York Press, 1993; rev. and enl. of *The Aesthetics of Pornography*. New York: Herder & Herder, 1971.

Mills, Jane, ed. *The Bloomsbury Guide to Erotic Literature*. London: Bloomsbury, 1993.

Modleski, Tania. *Loving With a Vengeance: Mass-Produced Fantasies for Women*. New York: Metheun, 1984.

Mohanraj, Mary Anne, with photos by Tracy Lee. *Torn Shapes of Desire: Internet Erotica*. Philadelphia, PA: Intangible Assets Manufacturing, 1996.

Moreck, Curt [Konrad Hammerling]. *Sittengeschichte des Kinos*. Dresden: Paul Aretz, 1926.

[Morse, A. Reynolds]. *The Limerick: A Facet of Our Culture*. Mexico City: Cruciform Press, 1944 [1948].

———, comp. *Folk Poems and Ballads: An Anthology: A Collection of Rare Verses and Amusing Folk Songs Compiled from Scarce and Suppressed Books as Well as from Verbal Sources, which Modern Prudery, False Social Customs and Intolerance*

Have Separated from the Public and Historical Record [1948]. Waukesha, WI: Maledicta Press, 1984.

Muller, Eddie, and Daniel Faris. *Grindhouse: The Forbidden World of "Adults Only" Cinema*. New York: St. Martin's, 1996.

Mulvey, Laura. "Visual Pleasure and Narrative Cinema." *Screen*, 16:3 (1975): 6–18; rpt. in *Visual and Other Pleasures*. Bloomington: Indiana University Press, 1989.

Murray, Thomas E., and Thomas R. Murrell. *The Language of Sadomasochism: A Glossary and Linguistic Analysis*. Westport, CT: Greenwood Press, 1989.

Néret, Gilles. *Erotic Art*. Berlin: Benedikt Taschen, 1994.

———. *Erotica Universalis*. Berlin: Benedikt Taschen, 1994.

———. *Twentieth Century Erotic Art*, ed. Angelika Muthesias and Burkhard Riemschneider. Berlin: Benedikt Taschen, 1994.

Nochlin, Linda. *Women, Art, and Power, and Other Essays*. New York: Harper and Row, 1989.

Noomin, Diane, ed. *Twisted Sisters: A Collection of Bad Girl Art*. New York: Penguin, 1991.

———. *Twisted Sisters: Volume II: Drawing the Line*. Northampton, MA: Kitchen Sink, 1995.

North, Peter. *Penetrating Insights*. Los Angeles: Privately printed, 1992.

O'Hara, Scott "Spunk." *Autopornography: A Memoir of Life in the Lust Lane*. Binghamton, NY: Haworth Press, 1998.

Olsen, Jenni, ed. *The Ultimate Guide to Lesbian and Gay Film and Video*. New York: Serpent's Tail/High Risk Books, 1996.

Osanka, Franklin Mark, and Sara Lee Johann. *Sourcebook on Pornography*. Lexington, MA: Lexington Books, 1989.

O'Toole, Laurence. *Pornocopia: Porn, Sex, Technology and Desire*. Rev. ed. New York: Serpent's Tail, 2000.

Owens, Tuppy. *Politico Frou-Frou: Pornographic Art as Political Protest*. New York: Cassell, 1996.

Paglia, Camille. *Sexual Personae: Art and Decadence From Nefertiti to Emily Dickinson*. New York: Vintage, 1991.

Palumbo, Donald, ed. *Erotic Universe: Sexuality and Fantastic Literature*. Westport, CT: Greenwood, 1986.

Panofsky, Erwin. "Style and Medium in the Motion Pictures" [1934]. *Film Theory and Criticism*, ed. Gerald Mast and Marshall Cohen. 2nd ed. New York: Oxford University Press, 1979, pp. 243–263.

Parfrey, Adam, ed. *Apocalypse Culture*. Portland, OR: Feral House, 1987.

Parker, Derek. *An Anthology of Erotic Verse*. London: Constable, 1980.

Parsons, Alexandra. *Facts and Phalluses: A Collection of Bizarre and Intriguing Truths, Legends, and Measurements*. New York: St. Martin's, 1990.

Penley, Constance. "Crackers and Whackers: The White Trashing of Porn." *White Trash: Race and Class in America*, ed. Matt Wray and Annalee Newitz. New York: Routledge, 1997, pp. 89–112.

Perkins, Michael. *The Secret Record: Modern Erotic Literature*. New York: William Morrow, 1977.

Petersen, James R. *The Century of Sex: Playboy's History of the Sexual Revolution, 1900–1999*. New York: Grove Press, 1999.

Petkovich, Anthony. *The X Factory: Inside the American Hardcore Industry*. Manchester, UK: Headpress, 1997.

Phillips, Donna-Lee and Lew Thomas, eds. *Eros and Photography: An Exploration of Sexual Imagery and Photographic Practice*. San Francisco: Camerawork/ NFS Press, 1977.

Pink Flamingo Publications. "Erotic and Spanking Fiction." www.pinkflamingo. com

Piselli, Stefano and Riccardo Morrocchi, eds. *The Art of John Willie: Sophisticated Bondage 1946–1961*. 2 vols. Milan: Glittering Images, 1990.

Pitt-Kethley, Fiona, ed. *The Literary Companion to Sex: An Anthology of Prose and Poetry*. New York: Random House, 1993.

Plachy, Sylvia, and James Ridgeway. *Red Light: Inside the Sex Industry*. New York: Powerhouse Books, 1996.

Plummer, Ken. *Telling Sexual Stories: Power, Change and Social Worlds*. New York: Routledge, 1995.

President's Commission on Obscenity and Pornography. *Report of the Commission on Obscenity and Pornography*. Washington, DC: Government Printing Office, 1970; New York: Bantam, 1970.

———. *Technical Report of the Commission on Obscenity and Pornography*. 9 vols. Washington, DC: Government Printing Office, 1971–1972. I: *Preliminary Studies*; II: *Legal Analysis*; III: *The Marketplace: The Industry*; IV: *The Marketplace: Empirical Studies*; V: *Societal Control Mechanisms*; VI: *National Survey*; VII: *Erotica and Antisocial Behavior*; VIII: *Erotica and Social Behavior*; IX: *The Consumer and the Community* (and index of authors).

Preston, John, ed. *Flesh and the Word: An Anthology of Erotic Writing*. Vols. 1 and 2. New York: Plume, 1992, 1993.

Preston, John, and Michael Lowenthal, eds. *Flesh and the Word 3: An Anthology of Gay Erotic Writing*. New York: Plume, 1995.

Probst, Ken. *Pôr' ne-graf'.n*. Sante Fe, NM: Twin Palms, 1998.

Queen, Carol, and Lawrence Schimel, eds. *Switch Hitters: Lesbians Write Gay Male Erotica and Gay Men Write Lesbian Erotica*. Pittsburgh, PA: Cleis Press, 1996.

Rabenalt, Arthur Maria. *Mimus Eroticus*. 5 vols. Hamburg: Verlag für Kulturforschung, 1965–1967.

Radford, Jean, ed. *The Progress of Romance: The Politics of Popular Fiction*. London: Routledge, 1986.

Radstone, Susannah, ed. *Sweet Dreams: Sexuality, Gender and Popular Fiction*. London: Lawrence and Wishart, 1988.

Radway, Janice A. *Reading the Romance: Women, Patriarchy, and Popular Literature*. Chapel Hill: University of North Carolina Press, 1984.

rame.net ("The Official Website of Recarts, Movies, Erotica"). www.rame.net; incorporates Adult Movie FAQ (www.rame.net.faq) and the Internet Adult Film Database (www.iafd.com).

Ramsdell, Kristen. *Happily Ever After: A Guide to Reading Interests in Romance Fiction*. Englewood, CO: Libraries Unlimited, 1987.

Randolph, Vance. *Blow the Candle Out: "Unprintable" Ozark Folklore*, ed. Gershon Legman. Vol. II. Fayetteville, AR: University of Arkansas Press, 1997.

———. *Pissing in the Snow & Other Ozark Folktales*, ed. Frank Hoffmann. Urbana: University of Illinois Press, 1976.

———. *Roll Me in Your Arms: "Unprintable" Ozark Folksongs and Folklore*, ed. Gershon Legman. Vol. I. Fayetteville, AR: University of Arkansas Press, 1992.

Rawson, Hugh. *Wicked Words: A Treasury of Curses, Insults, Put-Downs, and Other Formerly Unprintable Terms from Anglo-Saxon Times to the Present*. New York: Crown, 1989.

Rawson, Philip. *Primitive Erotic Art*. New York: Putnam, 1973.

Read, Allen Walker. *Lexical Evidence from Folk Epigraphy in Western North America: A Glossarial Study of the Low Element in the English Vocabulary*. Paris: Privately printed, 1935; rpt. *Classic American Graffiti*. Waukesha, WI: Maledicta Press, 1977.

Reems, Harry. *Here Comes Harry Reems!* New York: Pinnacle Books, 1975.

Reynolds, David. *Beneath the American Renaissance: The Subversive Imagination in the Age of Emerson and Melville*. New York: Knopf, 1988.

Rheingold, Howard. *Virtual Reality*. New York: Summit Books, 1991.

Richardson, Blanche, ed. *Best Black Women's Erotica*. San Francisco: Cleis Press, 2001.

Richter, Carl. *Crumb-ology: The Works of R. Crumb, 1981–1994*. Sudbury, MA: Water Row Press, 1995.

Riley, Patrick. *The X-Rated Videotape Guide*. Vols. 5–8. Amherst, NY: Prometheus Books, 1995, 1996, 1998, 2000.

———. *The X-Rated Videotape Star Index*. 3 vols. Amherst, NY: Prometheus Books, 1997, 1998, 1999.

Rimm, Martin. "Marketing Pornography on the Information Superhighway: A Survey of 917,410 Images, Descriptions, Short Stories, and Animations Downloaded 8.5 Million Times by Consumers in Over 2000 Cities in Forty Countries, Provinces, and Territories." *Georgetown Law Review*, 83 (June 1995): 1849–1958.

Rimmer, Robert H. *The X-Rated Videotape Guide*. New York: Arlington House, 1984; rev. ed. New York: Crown, 1986; rpt. Buffalo, NY: Prometheus Books, 1988.

———. *The X-Rated Videotape Guide II*. Buffalo, NY: Prometheus Books, 1991.

Rimmer, Robert H., and Patrick Riley. *The X-Rated Videotape Guide*. Vols. 3 and 4. Buffalo, NY: Prometheus Books, 1993, 1994.

Robbins, Trina, ed. *A Century of Women Cartoonists*. Princeton, WI: Kitchen Sink Press, 1992.

———. *From Girls to Grrrlz: A History of ♀ Comics From Teens to Zines*. San Francisco: Chronicle Books, 1999.

Robbins, Trina, and Catherine Yronwode. *Women and the Comics*. Forestville, CA: Eclipse Press, 1990.

Robinson, Hilary, ed. *Visibly Female: Feminism and Art Today, An Anthology*. New York: Universe Books, 1987.

Rodgers, Bruce. *The Queen's Vernacular: A Gay Lexicon*. San Francisco: Straight Arrow Books, 1972; rpt. as *Gaytalk*. New York: Paragon, 1979.

Rotenberg, Mark Lee. *Cheesecake: The Rotenberg Collection*. Cologne: Taschen, 1999.

———. *Forbidden Erotica: The Rotenberg Collection*. Cologne: Taschen, 2001.

Rowberry, John W. *Gay Video: A Guide to Erotica*. San Francisco: G. S. Press, 1986.

Russell, Tina. *Porno Star*. New York: Lancer Books, 1973.

Sabin, Roger. *Adult Comics: An Introduction*. New York: Routledge, 1993.

Sagarin, Edward. *The Anatomy of Dirty Words*. New York: Lyle Stuart, 1962.

Schaefer, Eric. *Bold! Daring! Shocking! True!: A History of Exploitation Films, 1919–1959*. Durham, NC: Duke University Press, 1999.

Scheiner, C. J. *Erotica-Curiosa-Sexology Catalog*. 275 Linden Blvd, Brooklyn, New York: 1978– .

Schneider, Rebecca. *The Explicit Body in Performance*. New York: Routledge, 1997.

Schroeder, Theodore A., comp. *Free Press Anthology*. New York: Free Speech League and Truth Seeker Publishing, 1909.

Scott, Randall W. *Comic Books and Strips: An Information Sourcebook*. Phoenix, AZ: Oryx Press, 1988.

Sedgwick, Eve Kosofsky. *Between Men: English Literature and the Male Homosocial Desire*. New York: Columbia University Press, 1985.

Segal, Lynne. "Does Pornography Cause Violence: The Search for Evidence." *Dirty Looks: Women, Pornography, Power*, ed. Pamela Church Gibson and Roma Gibson. London: British Film Institute, 1993, pp. 5–21.

Semans, Anne, and Cathy Winks. *The Woman's Guide to Sex on the Web*. San Francisco: HarperSanFrancisco, 1999.

Sensoria from Censorium. 2 vols. Toronto, Ontario: Mangajin Books, 1991, 1993.

Shaw, David. *The Pleasure Police: How Bluenose Busybodies and Lily-Livered Alarmists Are Taking All the Fun Out of Life*. New York: Doubleday, 1996.

Sheiner, Marcy, ed. *Herotica 4*. New York: Plume, 1996.

———. *Herotica 5*. New York: Plume, 1997.

———. *Herotica 6*. San Francisco: Down There Press, 1999.

———. *The Oy of Sex: Jewish Women Write Erotica*. Pittsburgh, PA: Cleis Press, 1999.

Shifreen, Lawrence J., and Roger Jackson. *Henry Miller: A Bibliography of Primary Sources*. Author, 1993.

Signorelli, Nancy. *Role Portrayal and Stereotyping on Television: An Annotated Bibliography of Studies Relating to Women, Minorities, Aging, Sexual Behavior, Health and Handicaps*. Westport, CT: Greenwood Press, 1985.

———. "Sex on Prime-Time in the 90s." *Communication Research Reports*, 17: 1 (Winter 2000): 70–78.

Simpson, Milton: *Folk Erotica: Celebrating Centuries of Erotic Americana*. New York: HarperCollins, 1994.

Slade, Joseph W. *Pornography and Sexual Representation: A Reference Guide*. 3 vols. Westport, CT: Greenwood Press, 2001.

———. *Pornography in America: A Reference Handbook*. Los Angeles: ABC-Clio, 2000.

———. *Shades of Blue: A History of the Clandestine Film*. Forthcoming.

———. "Violence in the Hard-Core Pornographic Film: A Historical Survey." *Journal of Communication*, 34 (Summer, 1984): 148–63.

Sloane, David E. E. *American Humor Magazines and Comic Periodicals*. Westport, CT: Greenwood Press, 1987.

Smith, Bradley. *Erotic Art of the Masters: 18th, 19th, 20th Centuries*. Rev. ed. La Jolla, CA: Gemini Smith, 1981.

————. *Twentieth Century Masters of Modern Art*. La Jolla, CA: Gemini Smith, 1985.

Smith, Gene, and Jayne Barry Smith, eds. *The Police Gazette*. New York: Simon and Schuster, 1972.

[Smith, T. R.], ed. *Immortalia: An Anthology of American Ballads, Sailors' Songs, Cowboy Songs, College Songs, Parodies, Limericks, and Other Humorous Verses and Doggerel Now for the First Time Brought Together in Book Form by a Gentleman About Town*. [New York]: Privately printed, 1927; rpt. Venice, CA: Parthena Press, 1969.

————. *Poetica Erotica: A Collection of Rare and Curious Amatory Verse*. 3 vols. New York: Boni and Liveright, 1921–1922.

Springer, Claudia. *Electronic Eros: Bodies and Desire in the Postindustrial Age*. Austin: University of Texas Press, 1996.

Sprinkle, Annie [Ellen F. Steinberg]. *Post Porn Modernist*. Amsterdam: Art Unlimited, 1991.

St. Jorre, John de. *Venus Bound: The Erotic Voyages of the Olympia Press*. New York: Random House, 1996.

Stang, Ivan. *High Weirdness by Email*. email address: mporter@nyx.cs.du.edu

Steele, Jeanne, and Jane Brown. "Sexuality and the Mass Media: An Overview." *Siecus Report* (April/May 1996): 3–9.

Steele, Valerie. *Fetish: Fashion, Sex and Power*. New York: Oxford University Press, 1995.

Stencell, A. W. *Girl Show: Into the Canvas World of Bump and Grind*. Toronto: ECW Press, 1999.

Sterngold, James. "HBO Programmer Likes to Kindle Both Heat and Light." *New York Times*, 15 April 1998, p. B2.

Stevens, Marc. *Ten and a Half*. New York: Kensington, 1975.

Stinson, Bryon. "Pin-Ups of the Civil War." *Civil War Times Illustrated*, 8 (August 1969), 38–41.

Stoller, Robert. *Porn: Myths for the Twentieth Century*. New Haven, CT: Yale University Press, 1991.

Stoller, Robert, and I. S. Levine. *Coming Attractions: The Making of an X-Rated Video*. New Haven, CT: Yale University Press, 1993.

Stone, Allucqère Roseanne. *The War of Desire and Technology at the Close of the Machine Age*. Cambridge, MA: MIT Press, 1995.

Stora-Lamarre, Annie. *L'enfer de la IIIe Republique: censeurs et pornographes, 1881–1914*. Paris: Imago, 1990.

Stormgart, Ivan. *Catalogs*. P.O. Box 470883, San Francisco, CA 94147–0883.

Streitmatter, Roger. *Unspeakable: The Rise of the Gay and Lesbian Press in America*. Boston: Faber and Faber, 1995.

Strossen, Nadine. *Defending Pornography: Free Speech, Sex, and the Fight for Women's Rights*. New York: Doubleday, 1996.

Stuart, Roy. *Roy Stuart*. 3 vols. (Volume 3 edited by Nina Schmidt). Cologne: Benedikt Taschen, 1997, 1998, 2000.

Sullivan, Steve. *Glamour Girls: The Illustrated Encyclopedia*. New York: St. Martin's, 1999.

Sutherland, Alistair, and Patrick Anderson. *Eros: An Anthology of Friendship*. New York: Arno, 1975.

Swartz, Louis H. "Erotic Witness: The Rise and Flourishing of Genitally Explicit and Sex Act Explicit Heterosexually Oriented Photographic Magazines in the U.S., 1965–1985." *Porn 101: Eroticism, Pornography, and the First Amendment*, ed. James Elias, Veronica Diehl Elias, Vern L. Bullough, Gwen Brewer, Jeffrey J. Douglas, and Will Jarvis. Amherst, NY: Prometheus Books, 1999, pp. 414–426.

"Symposium on Obscenity in Folklore," ed. Frank Hoffmann and Tristram Coffin. *Journal of American Folklore*, 75 (1962): 187–265.

Swezey, Stuart, ed. *Amok: Fifth Dispatch: Sourcebook of the Extremes of Information*. Los Angeles: Amok Books, 1999.

Thompson, Stith. *Motif-Index of Folk Literature: A Classification of Narrative Elements in Folktales, Ballads, Myths, Fables, Medieval Romances, Exempla, Fabliaux, Jest-books, and Local Legends*. 6 vols. Bloomington: Indiana University Press, 1955–1958.

Thorne, Barrie, Cheris Kramaae, and Nancy Henley, eds. "Sex Similarities and Differences in Language, Speech, and Nonverbal Communication: An Annotated Bibliography." *Language, Gender and Society*. Rowley, MA: Newbury House, 1983, pp. 151–331.

Thurston, Carol. *The Romance Revolution: Erotic Novels for Women and the Quest for a New Sexual Identity*. Champaign, IL: University of Illinois Press, 1987.

Tisdale, Sallie. *Talk Dirty to Me: An Intimate Philosophy of Sex*. New York: Doubleday, 1994.

Toepfer, Karl. *Theatre, Aristocracy, and Pornocracy: The Orgy Calculus*. New York: PAJ Publications, 1991.

Tone, Andrea. *Devices and Desires: A History of Contraceptives in America*. New York: Hill and Wang, 2001.

Trager, Oliver, ed. *The Arts and Media in America: Freedom or Censorship?* New York: Facts on File, 1991.

Tucher, Andie. *Froth and Scum: Truth, Beauty, Goodness, and the Ax-Murder in America's First Mass Medium*. Chapel Hill: University of North Carolina Press, 1994.

Underground Newspaper Microfilm Collection. 147 reels. Wooster, OH: Bell and Howell and the Underground Press Syndicate, 1965–1973.

"Uneasy Bedfellows: Social Science and Pornography": "British, Canadian, and U.S. Commissions" by Edna F. Einsiedel; "Pornography, Politics, and the Press: The U.S. Attorney General's Commission on Pornography" by David L. Paletz; and "Methods and Merits of Research" by Daniel Linz, Edward Donnerstein, Dolf Zillmann, and Jennings Bryant. *Journal of Communication*, 38: 2 (Spring 1998): 107–136.

University Microfilm International. *Alternative Press Collection: A Guide to the Microfilm Collection*. Ann Arbor, MI: UMI, 1990.

———. *Underground Press Collection: A Guide to the Microfilm Collection*. Ann Arbor, MI: UMI, 1988.

Urban Legends—Sex. www.snopes.com/sex

Van Every, Edward. *Sins of America as Exposed by the Police Gazette*. New York: Stokes, 1931.

Vasta Collection. Body Cello, P.O. Box 910531, Sorrento Valley, CA 92191.

Vogel, Amos. *Film as a Subversive Art*. New York: Random House, 1974.

Wagner, Peter. "Erotica in Early America." *Eros Revived: Erotica of the Enlightenment in England and America*. London: Secker and Warburg, 1988, pp. 292–302.

———. "Eros Goes West: European and 'Homespun' Erotica in Eighteenth-Century America." *The Transit of Civilization from Europe to America: Essays in Honor of Hans Galinsky*, ed. Winfried Herget and Karl Ortseifen. Tübingen: G. Narr, 1986, pp. 145–165.

———. "The Veil of Medicine and Morality: Some Pornographic Aspects of the *Onania*." *British Journal for Eighteenth-Century Studies*, 6 (1983): 179–184.

Walters, Margaret. *The Male Nude*. London: Paddington Press, 1978.

Ward, Tony. *Orgasm*. Paris: Editions Alixe, 2000.

Waugh, Tom. *Hard to Imagine: Gay Male Eroticism in Photography and Film from Their Beginnings to Stonewall*. New York: Columbia University Press, 1997.

Webb, Peter. *The Erotic Arts*. Boston: New York Graphic Society, 1975.

Weiermair, Peter, ed. *Erotic Art from the 17th to the 20th Century*. Zurich: Edition Stemmle, 1995.

Wells, Jess. *Lip Service: Alluring New Lesbian Erotica*. Boston: Alyson Press, 1999.

Whitworth, John. *The Faber Book of Blue Verse*. Boston: Faber and Faber, 1990.

Williams, Linda. *Hard Core: Power, Pleasure, and the Frenzy of the Visible*. Berkeley: University of California Press, 1989.

Willie, John [J.A.S. Coutts]. *The Adventures of Sweet Gwendolyn*. New York: Bélier Press, 1974; also available in seven video cassettes from Alain Siritzky, ASP 29, rue de Marignan, Paris 75008.

———. *Bizarre: The Complete Reprint of John Willie's Bizarre, vols. 1–13*, ed. Eric Kroll. Berlin: Benedikt Taschen Verlag, 1995.

Winfield, Betty Houchin, and Sandra Davidson. *Bleep! Censoring Rock and Rap Music*. Westport, CT: Greenwood, 1999.

Winks, Cathy. *The Good Vibrations Guide to Adult Videos*. Burlingame, CA: Down There Press, 1998.

Woods, Gregory. *A History of Gay Literature: The Male Tradition*. New Haven, CT: Yale University Press, 1998.

Wrangler, Jack, and Carl Johnes. *The Jack Wrangler Story; What's a Nice Boy Like You Doing in a Business Like This?* New York: St. Martin, 1984.

Young, Ian. *The Male Homosexual in Literature: A Bibliography*. Metuchen, NJ: Scarecrow Press, 1975.

Zeisel, William, ed. *Censorship: 500 Years of Conflict*. New York: New York Public Library, 1984.

Zimmerman, Bonnie. *The Safe Sea of Women: Lesbian Fiction, 1969–1988*. Boston: Beacon, 1990.

PERIODICALS

Adam Black Video Illustrated. Los Angeles, 1995– .

Adam Film World and Adult Video Guide. Los Angeles: Knight Publishing, 1968– .

Adam Film World Directory of Gay Adult Video. Los Angeles, CA, annual, 1994– .

Adult Video News. Upper Darby, PA, 1983–1996; Van Nuys, CA, 1996– ; www.adultvideonews.com/

Archives of Sexual Behavior. New York, 1971– .

Exotic Dancer: Directory of Gentlemen's Clubs. ERI Productions, 3437 W. 7th St., Fort Worth, TX 76107, annual.

Factsheet Five. 1982–1991, 6 Arizona Avenue, Rensselaer, NY 12144; 1992–present, Box 170099, San Francisco, CA 94117; email: jerod23@well.sf.ca.us

Federal Reporter. Washington, DC: Government Printing Office, current.

High Performance: A Quarterly Magazine for the New Arts Audience. Los Angeles, 1969–1999.

Indy Magazine: The Guide to Alternative Comix and Film. Gainesville, FL, 1994– .

International Directory of Sex Research and Related Fields. Bloomington, IN, 1976– .

Journal of Sex Research. Philadelphia, 1965.

Journal of the History of Sexuality. Chicago, 1990– .

Queer Zine Explosion. Box 591276, San Francisco, CA 94159, 1997– .

Screw. New York, 1969.

Stripper Magazine. New York, 1993– .

TDR (formerly *Tulane Drama Review*, now *The Drama Review*). New York, 1966– .

United States Reports. Washington, DC: Government Printing Office, current.

FILMOGRAPHY/VIDEOGRAPHY

Ahlberg, Marc, dir. *Boogie Nights.* Los Angeles: New Line Cinema/Home Video, 1997.

Beatty, Maria, dir. *Sphinxes without Secrets: Women Performance Artists Speak Out.* New York: Beatty, 1991 (distributed by San Francisco Art Commission).

Clark, Larry, dir. *Kids.* Los Angeles: Shining Excaliber Films/Miramax, 1995.

Csicsery, George, dir. *Where the Heart Roams.* Point of View documentary series, Public Broadcasting System, first aired 4 August 1991.

Forman, Milos, dir. *The People vs. Larry Flynt.* Los Angeles: Sony Pictures, 1996.

Jhally, Sut, prod. *Dreamworlds II: Desire/Sex/Power in Rock Video.* Amherst, MA: Foundation for Media Education, 1995.

Kit Parker Films. *Sex and Buttered Popcorn*, hosted by Ned Beatty. Monterey, CA: Kit Parker Films/Main Street Movies, 1989.

Klaw, Irving, dir. *Classic Films of Irving Klaw: Volumes I and II.* London: London Enterprises, 1984.

Paley, Cass, prod. and dir. *Wadd: The Life and Times of John C. Holmes.* Chatsworth, CA: VCA Pictures, 2000.

Playboy Videos. *The Story of X: 100 Years of Adult Film and Its Stars.* Los Angeles: Playboy Entertainment/Calliope Film, 1998.

Query, Julia, and Vicky Funari, dirs. *Live Girls Nude Unite!* Brooklyn, NY: First Run/Icarus Films, 2000.

Radziwill, Anthony, prod. *Strippers: The Naked Stages.* HBO America Undercover Series. New York: HBO, 1998.

Varney, Mike, comp. *Nudie Cuties.* 13 reels. P.O. Box 33664, Seattle, WA: Something Weird Video, 1991–1993.

———. *Twisted Sex.* 3 reels. P.O. Box 33664, Seattle, WA: Something Weird Video, 1991.

PROPAGANDA

Richard Alan Nelson

However unclearly we perceive it, propaganda—especially when cloaked as education or information—influences our understanding of the world around us. Each one of us has been indoctrinated since childhood, and daily we continue to be bombarded with intrusive messages attempting to inform, manipulate, motivate, redirect, and even placate us.

Propaganda is worth studying for numerous reasons, if only because it so permeates American culture and institutions. Widespread technological diffusion and urbanization, prerequisites at the core of contemporary mass society, are essential components explaining the emergence of propaganda as an everyday factor in the American experience. The growth of propaganda in modern life has resulted largely from applied usage of certain inventive media developments over the last two centuries (including high-speed print, telegraphy, films, radio, television, and, more recently, satellites) which provided governments and private interests with an unprecedented mind manipulation arsenal useful in times of both war and peace.

The impact of propaganda seems self-evident today, although this has not always been the case. While public opinion was recognized as an important component of the American political experiment, most nineteenth-century political theorists felt that governing institutions reflected rather than directed popular attitudes. Struggles by Populist, muckraker, and other reform forces used media to bring about middle-class awareness and helped spur change. But the blatant manipulation of news and public opinion during World War I through persuasive campaigns by government and various special interests was a revelation to scholars, forcing an abandonment of prior theories about a benign public-private compact. Disillusioned by the distortion practiced by the warring powers for often inconsistent and changing war aims, they began applying critical perspectives to understand better those patterns shaping social influence.

Most propaganda research in the 1920s and 1930s was largely impressionistic, pacifistic, and aimed at educating a broad public about the continuing dangers presented by the persuasion industries. This revisionist line of inquiry, drawing upon rhetorical scholarship and progressive ideology, came to be known as "propaganda analysis." However, such research emphases presented a problem for those who sought to investigate propaganda more dispassionately. Gradually, influenced by the increasing precision of the social sciences, those in this competing school turned to statistical and experimental methodologies. Abandoning the term *propaganda analysis* entirely, they preferred to define themselves as empirical communication researchers. Over time this emphasis on quantifiable documentation has become the dominant paradigm or approach to research. As a result, contemporary studies of power groups and propaganda using qualitative historical-critical research tools tend to be written by Marxist, libertarian, and other ideologically motivated scholars still actively committed to social change.

Many people give little thought to their culture, assuming that most of life is just "there." We now know that propaganda plays a great role in shaping mass society's "psychic economy" as part of a broader "culture industry"—terms popularized by Marxist philosopher and art theoretician Theodor Wiesengrund-Adorno (1903–1969). In fact there is a social, economic, and political context to the institutions and power relationships in a nation as diverse as the United States. Culture, particularly popular culture, is of importance in the study of propaganda since it reflects the indigenous nature of a people and incorporates the cumulative short-term and long-term residual influence of mass-mediated messages in the collective national consciousness.

In discussing ideology, thinkers such as Marx have also been correct in their observation that we are dominated by ideas that bear no accurate relationship to the reality we live. One reason is that in a "propaganda environment," opinion and belief are manipulated by social managers more interested in control than freedom. Where propaganda is widespread, cultural conditioning occurs so that the illusion of choice is maintained while truly independent thought is discouraged. The result is a channeling away from broadly participatory processes, what some have termed a cynical short-circuiting of critical thinking through subversion of political and economic discourse, into more predictable "rituals" where prepackaged commodities ranging from candidates to products are not so much chosen as rubber-stamped. Certainly, an objective observer is forced to conclude that we live at a time when propaganda—far from abating—is becoming an increasingly pervasive force in democratic as well as totalitarian states. For example, almost all governments maintain that they legitimately represent the will of the people. But this means that whether they be a capitalist democracy or a people's republic, their leaderships must devote vast resources to "engineering" and maintaining that consent.

Despite the continuing role played by commercial advertising and political propaganda in defining our national culture and institutions, Americans by and large bear a traditional antipathy toward the idea (if not the practice) of propaganda. The sobering thought that arises in preparing a topical reference guide such as this is that, notwithstanding an overwhelmingly negative literature condemning propaganda as inimical to freedom (an argument that itself is open to question but that nevertheless represents a consensus of published opinion), very little has been done to control its spread. That the term continues to hold a strongly pejorative—even sinister—connotation is somewhat surprising since it was Americans who pioneered the implementation of attitudinal methodologies, mass-marketing strategies, and media technologies now considered essential to widespread persuasive communication.

What, then, constitutes propaganda? Unfortunately, there is no easy answer. Although we have progressed beyond the insular "us versus them" belief that propaganda is something only our enemies engage in (facetiously described as the other side's case put so convincingly as to be annoying!), a definition remains largely a matter of perspective. Writers on the topic regularly devote entire chapters to this one problem due to the imprecision of propaganda and related terms such as *ideology*, *persuasion*, and *rhetoric*. Propaganda has been interpreted variously to include such functions as advertising, public relations, publicity, political communication, special interest lobbying, radical agitation, psychological warfare, and even education. There is, however, general agreement that propaganda is a form of manipulative communication designed to elicit some predetermined response.

We can divide such persuasive communication into activities that require impersonal use of media as a way of linking sender to audience and those conducted interpersonally. Messages can also be conveniently separated into those that encourage us to buy a commercial product and those that seek to direct our belief structure and personality in a more fundamental way. While not all persuasive communication is equally embracive, pervasive, or effective in what the persuader asks us to think or do, nevertheless we can agree that propaganda is purposive. In many cases, the job of today's propagandist involves not so much changing minds as finding the right audience in order to reinforce and extend existing attitudes.

Some have seen propaganda as the organized spreading of special doctrines, beliefs, ideas, or information to promote or injure a nation, cause, or group. This is perhaps too generic, however. For purposes of this chapter, *propaganda is defined as the systematic attempt to influence the emotions, attitudes, opinions, and actions of specified target audiences for ideological, political, or commercial purposes through the controlled transmission of one-sided messages via mass and direct media channels.*

As we have seen, part of the confusion in terminology stems from the interdisciplinary nature and differing emphases of propaganda studies. Some authors argue that all propaganda is corrosive and a menace, whereas a minority state that propaganda is a neutral tool that can be put to either good or bad uses depending on the purpose of the source. A number of books have focused on the use of propaganda by governments in wartime; others choose a broad historical rather than case study approach. Another way of looking at propaganda favored by social scientists and linguists codifies and analyzes in "cookbook" form various motivational devices and techniques used by propagandists (such as the "glittering generality"). A fourth methodology often used by psychologically oriented communications researchers tests various hypotheses about attitude formation and behavioral change. These are loosely grouped under the banner of "persuasion" studies. Because we still lack clear theoretical bases for understanding the persuasive process, these conclusions (particularly those evaluating the effectiveness of propaganda) remain tentative and are not necessarily generalizable to mass groups. Despite scientific trappings, for example, we still cannot predict with absolute certainty that a particular campaign design will lead to the desired results in a target population.

HISTORICAL OUTLINE

One can trace the origins of propaganda to remote antiquity. More than 2,500 years ago Chinese strategist Sun Tzu was writing in *The Art of War* about the military importance of manipulating information. Plato points out that the foundations of ancient democracy were connected with the emergence of professional communicators skilled in using language to move other people to action. The Greeks were among the first to see the need for selecting spokesmen to represent various interest groups in the community; they called a person who could effect one-to-many argumentation a *rhetor*. In the *Phaedrus* the famed philosopher defines the practice of rhetoric as "a universal art of winning the mind by arguments, which means not merely arguments in the courts of justice and all other sorts of public councils, but in private conference as well." Aristotle was Plato's pupil and, although they disagreed on some fundamental principles, Aristotle's *Rhetoric* even today remains a valuable guide to propaganda techniques despite the passage of more than two millennia.

By the Middle Ages, the introduction of the printing press in Europe and the spread of literacy were encouraging greater use of books and tracts designed to sway opinion. Much of this literature was religious, particularly by independent Protestants boldly attempting to get biblical scriptures and doctrinal commentaries into the hands of the common people. This was perceived as a radical threat to royal governments and state religious unity, with many of the reformers sentenced to torture and death for their publishing activities. The term *propaganda* was first used widely by the Roman Catholic Church in 1622, with the founding of the Congregatio de propaganda fide (Congregation for the Propagation of Faith) during the Counter-Reformation.

Drawing on this European heritage, religionists coming to America during the pre-revolutionary period became active publishers not only of biblical texts but also of literature extolling the virtues of the new land. In this endeavor they were joined by wealthy colonial trading companies, which issued a number of misleading promotional advertisements designed to encourage settlement of their commercial plantations. The political foundations for modern propaganda emerged late in the eighteenth century, when the idea of inalienable rights advanced during the Enlightenment found flower in the colonial republics. The use of printing technologies in America allowed for expression both supportive and critical of the Crown. The now famous "JOIN, or DIE" political cartoon by Benjamin Franklin appeared in a 1754 issue of the *Pennsylvania Gazette* urging the people of the colonies to unite in fighting the French and Indian War. Little more than twenty years later, the Declaration of Independence, penned by Thomas Jefferson, was widely distributed. This proved itself a masterful propaganda document not only by clearly expressing the philosophy of the Revolution in language that all colonists could understand but also by justifying the American cause overseas and presaging the rise in importance of public opinion.

One should remember, however, that the American Revolution was not a spontaneous popular uprising. Contrary to myth, it was in reality the work of a small group of dedicated persuaders who created our first national propaganda and agitation campaign in order to overthrow a monarchical government. Even today the work of James Otis, Samuel Adams, Patrick Henry, Benjamin Franklin, and

Thomas Paine (whose *Common Sense* in 1776 and *The American Crisis* in 1776–1783 helped cement opposition to the Crown) continues to be studied by propaganda researchers. Among the techniques these radical pamphleteers inaugurated that are still utilized in contemporary ideological communication are (1) the realization that propaganda, to be effective, requires organization (the Sons of Liberty and Committees of Correspondence acted as conduits for revolutionary propaganda throughout the colonies); (2) the creation of the identifiable emotive symbols (the Liberty Tree) and slogans ("Don't tread on me" and "Taxation without representation is tyranny"), which simplify issues and arouse emotions; (3) the utilization of publicity and staged events (such as the Boston Tea Party) to attract media attention and enlist support of key cooperators (religious leaders whose sermons were widely published and distributed); (4) the exploitation of differences rather than emphasizing similarities of specified groups as well as mass audiences with monolithic reportage on a sustained and unrelenting basis through control of key organs of opinion (press, pamphlets, broadsides, even songs). The "Patriots" proved expert at publicizing their grievances first so as to establish the agenda for debate, while simultaneously discrediting their Loyalist opponents.

During the period of controversy surrounding adoption of the federal Constitution to replace the Articles of Confederation after the war, a series of newspaper articles now known collectively as *The Federalist Papers* (1787–1788) were anonymously prepared by Alexander Hamilton, James Madison, and John Jay to sell Americans on the new government. These proved an effective instrument of propaganda among opinion leaders as well as a thoughtful political treatise of more lasting interest. The freedoms secured by the Constitution led to the development early in the nineteenth century of clearly defined political parties and special interest organizations that readily adopted propaganda techniques and technologies for their own purposes. Leading American propagandists of the early 1800s include Theodore Dwight, an effective spokesman for the Federalist cause, and Amos Kendall, who served as Andrew Jackson's chief adviser and later earned the title of "first presidential public relations man."

Fears of undue foreign influence in the new republic led to a series of "anti" campaigns (anti-Illuminati, anti-Mason, anti-Catholic, anti-Irish, anti-Jewish, anti-Mormon, and so on), which even today flourish sporadically. Early propaganda books, typified by Rebecca Reed's *Six Months in a Convent*, which first appeared in 1835, helped to focus hatred and were often underwritten by interests anxious to control immigrant blocs politically and keep their wages artificially low. The outstanding propaganda novel of the century was Harriet Beecher Stowe's powerful indictment of slavery, *Uncle Tom's Cabin* (1851), which sold an unprecedented 300,000 copies during its first year of publication and contributed significantly to the abolitionist movement. Proslavery forces were also active in the period up through the Civil War, issuing tracts and lobbying for support in Congress. In this they were secretly aided by "Manifest Destiny" expansionists in the North, who flooded the country with literature designed to raise patriotic fervor for war with Mexico. In a real sense, words as much as bullets helped to win the West.

As sectional differences became more pronounced and a war between the states inevitable, leaders in both the North and South recognized the importance of propaganda to the struggle. Particularly in the North, where the war remained unpopular (there were draft riots in New York in 1863, and the so-called Copperhead movement fielded peace candidates as late as 1864), propaganda was utilized to mobilize public opinion both at home and abroad. Many of the trappings of contemporary journalism such as the press conference, press pass, and author byline were instituted by military leaders in order to censor battle reportage unfavorable to the Union. Lincoln also personally dispatched up to 100 special agents to Britain along with a boatload of foodstuffs for unemployed English cotton textile workers so as to counter propaganda gains made by the Confederacy. In the North, too, the art of pamphleteering was advanced by the unceasing efforts of private organizations such as the Loyal Publication Society and the Union League Board of Publications.

The full impact of industrialism and the importance of public opinion began to be felt by 1865. Public opinion, which was at first narrowly defined to include only educated white male landowners, gradually came to be extended to the middle and lower working classes (and later, in the twentieth century, to women and minorities, changes themselves brought about in part by propaganda). Groups such as the Fenian Brotherhood, a body of Irish patriots and exiles organized in 1857 to bring about Ireland's revolutionary independence from England, sought to mobilize sympathy in the United States by becoming more active in issuing propaganda following the Civil War. In the Fenians' case, they sought to energize anti-British sentiment by staging an invasion of Canada with 800–900 men in 1866, actually capturing Fort Erie in an uprising leaders hoped would inflame annexationist sentiment in the United States. Even though military success proved fleeting, the Brotherhood organization was not suppressed, and its propagandistic activities for some time contributed to Canadian-U.S. border tensions.

Growing urbanism was accompanied by sweeping improvements in communication, which extended the power of the press as a corridor into the minds of millions. In the era of yellow journalism (roughly 1890–1914) much of the news was, as it is today, artificial, that is, created and promoted by the news media, which reported the stories as bona fide events. Although the impact of the press as a propaganda organ dates back before the Revolution, by this period the chains of publications controlled by press barons such as William Randolph Hearst had unrivaled influence on American thought. His *New York Journal* is largely credited with exciting the United States to challenge Spain over Cuba in 1898. Besides quadrupling Hearst's circulation, the events leading up to the war also marked the first time motion pictures were utilized meaningfully for propagandistic purposes. Highly patriotic short films such as *Tearing Down the Spanish Flag!* (1898) electrified U.S. audiences when the hated European emblem was replaced by "Old Glory." The tremendous popular success of this picture (although it was actually shot on a rooftop in New York) spawned a host of imitators once actual hostilities broke out. Since cameramen were often prohibited from gaining access to authentic battleground footage because of military censorship, much of the visual "reportage," such as the series released under the title *The Campaign in Cuba* (1898), was surreptitiously filmed in the wilds of New Jersey. Screen propaganda already had shown flagrant disregard for truth, but this proved secondary to audiences who clamored for the lifelike images on the screen. This power of "actuality" and "documentary" freed propagandists for the first time from nearly complete reliance on publications and the printed word.

As the United States emerged to become a more important twentieth-century international political factor, European nations competing for continental leadership soon realized that the United States could play a pivotal role in the next war. As early as 1910, Germany began an active propaganda campaign to counteract pro-British biases in the leading organs of U.S. opinion. With the outbreak of hostilities in Europe, both Irish American and German American propagandists such as George Sylvester Viereck sought to combat the much more pervasive pro-intervention views spread by English agents working through a well-organized network of native sympathizers, press contacts, cultural exchanges, and business and banking ties. Overcoming isolationist impulses thanks to clumsy German diplomacy, American gullibility, and the huge investments made in United Kingdom war bonds by U.S. financial interests, the British view prevailed. The country was successfully maneuvered into collective hatred of all things German through widespread dissemination of maliciously false (but effective) "anti-Hun" atrocity stories and other propaganda.

Even though the United States was the last major power to enter the war, it ironically was the first belligerent to establish an open, fully coordinated propaganda unit, known as the Committee on Public Information (CPI). Headed by advertising executive George Creel, the CPI was given the commission to "sell the War to America." To do this, the CPI organized a national speakers' bureau of "four-minute men" who galvanized audiences with carefully timed short propaganda messages supporting Liberty Bond sales drives. Recognizing the power of the screen, the Creel Committee also arranged for cooperation between the private film industry (including newsreel companies) and the military. The poster also emerged at this time as an effective mass war medium, and individual governments flooded their nations with millions of propaganda posters designed to muster public support for total victory. Among the American artists who lent themselves to the war effort were Norman Rockwell, James Montgomery Flagg (whose "I Want You for U.S. Army" Uncle Sam recruiting poster is the best-known example from the period), and Charles Dana Gibson (creator of the "Gibson Girl"). Under CPI auspices alone, more than 100 million enthusiastically patriotic posters and other publications were distributed.

Although in the end much of the propaganda effort by Creel and his Allied counterparts proved (like Wilson's famous "Fourteen Points" as the basis for a just peace) more hyperbole than fact, World War I is important historically because it commemorates the inaugural deployment of contemporary mass propaganda. While the history of propaganda is indelibly linked to war, the seemingly interminable stalemate that marked most of the years of fighting propelled propaganda to the forefront as an important tool of government for sustaining homeland morale and maintaining ties of alliance. With the end of the war, however, Americans' desire to return to "normalcy" led to the quick disbanding of the CPI and a limiting of U.S. government propaganda efforts. On the other hand, during the 1920s and 1930s privately originated propaganda increased as numerous pressure groups formed in attempts to influence individual thought and actions as well as to affect government policies by harnessing mass opinion swelled by newly enfranchised women voters.

Later, when the social upheavals wrought by the Great Depression led to installation of an activist Democratic administration promising a "New Deal," official U.S. propaganda took off once more. The expansion of government powers and the introduction of new Social Security, public works, labor, housing, agricultural, military, and other policies required unparalleled peacetime publicity, with federal authorities committed to mobilizing a shared public consensus. Motion picture advertising (which had already been used for partisan political purposes) was extended, and the Roosevelt leadership further commissioned the filming of a number of documentary films with strong social messages. *The Plow That Broke the Plains* (1936) and *The River* (1937), for example, both pointed to the need for government intervention in conserving natural resources, and their success helped establish a federally controlled U.S. Film Service. Perhaps the most controversial of the early New Deal propaganda campaigns involved the National Recovery Administration (NRA). The totalitarian methods favored by NRA administrators, including enforced display of the blue NRA eagle emblem by "cooperating" businesses, were seen by many as a threat to American democratic principles. Partially on the basis of the propagandistic excesses of its supporters, the NRA was declared unconstitutional and nullified by the Supreme Court.

World propaganda had already entered a new phase with the successes of the communists in Russia and the national socialists in Germany. Attention to propaganda issues was further exacerbated by the uncertain economic climate of the period and increases in the West of ideological movements willing to utilize propaganda unhesitatingly for both internal and external distribution. As early as 1919–1920, the United States had been engulfed in a "Red Scare," but despite this temporary setback Marxist propaganda continued to circulate with growing effectiveness among disenchanted American intellectuals and workers. The sheer amount of propaganda issued by the totalitarian states forced the leading democracies (notably Britain and the United States) to respond with a series of investigations and by upgrading their own intelligence and propaganda apparatuses. Much of the latter was again interventionist in nature, particularly after 1939 and the outbreak of World War II in Europe. Until Pearl Harbor, U.S. antiwar sentiment (epitomized by the America First Committee and the radio sermons of Catholic firebrand preacher Father Charles Edward Coughlin) openly competed against the line promoted by Anglophile organizations such as the Fight for Freedom Committee. Even as early as 1938, the United States was moving to shore up its position in Latin America by forming a Division of Cultural Relations in the Department of State, which rigorously issued propaganda designed to portray the United States as an altruistic benefactor in a common struggle against possible foreign aggression. That same year Congress also passed the Foreign Agents Registration Act, specifying that individuals and organizations engaged in disseminating propaganda or related activities on behalf of another country must file public reports with the Justice Department's Criminal Division. While the act includes some exemptions for commercial, religious, academic, scientific, and artistic pursuits, it has tended to be used arbitrarily as a way of controlling domestic dissent and limiting access to print and visual political materials produced outside the United States.

With the coming of World War II, official American propaganda efforts were mostly directed by the Office of War Information (OWI), which was responsible for internal and external information. The Office of Strategic Services (OSS) conducted clandestine anti-Axis psychological warfare or so-called black propaganda programs as well as more conventional spy missions. Coordinating the European operations of the OWI and OSS for military needs was the Psychological Warfare Division at Allied Supreme Headquarters. There were marked differences between U.S. propaganda and that of the Axis powers, which generally proved more adept at utilizing the latest advances in technology until battlefield reverses curtailed their effectiveness. National socialist magazines such as *Signal* were published in lavish color versions in all the major languages of Europe (including English). Similarly, well-produced German newsreels and documentaries were masterful propaganda devices screened widely not only in the Greater Reich and occupied Europe, but also in many neutral countries (among them the United States prior to 1942). Much of the enemy effort, however, relied heavily on radio. The sarcastic broadcasts of "Lord Haw Haw" (William Joyce) and "Axis Sally" from Germany, "Tokyo Rose" and "The Zero Hour" from Japan, and American expatriate poet Ezra Pound from Italy were listened to widely by U.S. servicemen. Apart from Allied counter-broadcasts, the Allies utilized a number of other propaganda methods—notably air-dropped leaflets. How effective these were in undermining enemy morale is still debated, but there is no doubt that internally the overall U.S. propaganda effort was successful.

On the home front, the major media willingly cooperated in the war effort. The Hollywood studios actively collaborated with federal authorities in grinding out hundreds of racist anti-Japanese and anti-German war epics. In the changed political climate after the war, some pro-Soviet films also made at this time were to prove more controversial. Numerous government agencies, including the Treasury Department, took to the airwaves with highly propagandistic patriotic radio programs such as "Treasury Star Parade" (1943–1944) to sell war bonds and maintain enthusiasm for continuing the fight. Newspapers and newsreels, too, carried regular government-inspired reports and voluntarily censored potentially demoralizing news. Gigantic posters dominated factories and military shipyards to spur production, and even comic books and pulp literature were enlisted to put the country on a war footing unenvisioned even in the darkest and most regimented days of World War I.

With the defeat of fascist Italy, Germany, and Japan, U.S. propaganda took on a new direction. Largely because of the struggle with the Soviet Union for postwar dominance, much of the official propaganda issued by the United States since the mid-1940s has been directed at Eastern Europe and the emerging Third World states. The Voice of America, which transmits news, entertainment, and propaganda worldwide in dozens of languages, is a division of the United States Information Agency (USIA, briefly renamed the United States International Communication Agency during the Carter administration). The USIA also supervises the anti-Castro Radio Marti, maintains information offices and libraries in approximately sixty countries, and operates an extensive press and broadcast assistance service. Secret operations are usually the function of the Central Intelligence Agency (CIA), which for years helped to support the ostensibly private anticommunist Radio Free Europe and Radio Liberty broadcasts.

Many other government departments and divisions are responsible for information gathering and/or communication. Today the federal government, rather than any Madison Avenue firm or corporate entity, constitutes the single greatest "propaganda machine" in the United States. Despite cutback attempts in the Reagan presidency, specialists in an estimated forty-seven different federal agencies currently spend over $2.5 billion each year attempting to influence the way Americans think. The government, for example, is the nation's leading publisher and film producer, distributing thousands of magazines and books, hundreds of motion pictures and videocassettes, and countless press releases annually. The Treasury Department continues to underwrite production of special video episodes for internal government use, using some of Hollywood's top television series stars to promote purchases of savings bonds by federal employees. Taxpayers are also underwriting the military as one of the country's largest advertisers, whose messages urge young people to join up—not to preserve peace or ensure foreign policy objectives, but rather so recruits can "find a great place to start" to "be all you can be."

Earlier government intervention in the broadcast advertising marketplace helped to spur development of so-called public service announcements (PSAs) that continue to ask the public to support a variety of "approved" causes ranging from the innocuous to the controversial. Despite deregulatory elimination of many controversial communication restrictions, agencies such as the Federal Trade Commission and the Federal Communications Commission retain great powers over media and ancillary industries. Uncertainty exists about how far broadcast deregulation should go and whether electronic communicators should have the same First Amendment rights as their print counterparts. The convergence of communications and computer technologies as well as widespread group ownership of media properties in several fields are blurring the once clear distinction between print and broadcast, important legally as well as in popular culture terms. National newspapers such as the *Wall Street Journal* and *USA Today*, for example, now daily use satellites to get copies of their lithographed pages to printing plants across the country for localized editing and distribution. Should related technologies such as teletext and videotex (which use print on video screens) be regulated according to broadcast or print standards? Taking advantage of these uncertainties and the cutback in governmental controls, so-called hate groups have allegedly been more actively using electronic media in recent years. At the same time, one questionable impact of the FCC-authored "Fairness Doctrine" (which remained in effect until 1987 and may yet be reimposed) was to restrict discussions of major issues and limit the content of serious broadcast advertising (such as "advertorials" and "informationals"). The experience in deciding such questions leaves open the possibility of greater (rather than less) government intervention in American media over the long term.

What of the future of propaganda in America? It is somewhat interesting to note that the elitist critics who most decry propaganda tend to view it as a direct form of indoctrination mindlessly swallowed by the mass audience. Implied is a personal superiority by virtue of their intellectual isolation from the naive propaganda consumer. This is a false and dangerously parochial dichotomy because wealthy intellectuals are just as susceptible to well-targeted propaganda as are the poor or ignorant. The naive assumptions voiced by some that federal controls and "rational education" would somehow neutralize "irrational propaganda" have not been borne out by experience, nor are they likely to be in coming years.

For numerous private groups operating nationally, the battle of propaganda is as much as anything a fight for access to political decision makers and the channels of mass dissemination. Political action committees, trade and education groups, foundations, and other organizations that must compete and lobby for support are often forced to rely on the techniques of propaganda if they are successfully to reach their own institutional goals. Increased use of direct mail and new technological breakthroughs may well open additional doors and opportunities for ideational propagandists, as well as those more interested in purely commercial advertising and public relations marketing efforts.

Today we can expect additional refinements in propaganda technique. Indeed, the previous work chronicled in this bibliographic essay soon may unfortunately seem like child's play. The relatively new concept of "narrowcasting" to highly specialized, homogeneous audiences will allow for cost-effective message placement to specific population subgroups on an unprecedented scale. Widespread private ownership of audio- and videocassette players, for example, encouraged "Pat" Robertson to distribute free tapes (or "electronic campaign buttons") to targeted voting groups with his message unedited by network newscasters. The result: political professionals were surprised by the unexpected early caucus voter turnouts for Robertson in the 1988 Republican presidential nomination race.

Other new telecommunications technologies (including international direct satellite-to-home transmission and extension of optic two-way capacity) promise to redefine our informational environment dramatically in ways only dimly perceived. The revolution in information technology is making classical closed-door diplomacy less viable, as nations begin responding to internal challenges by counteracting propaganda from outsider groups and expanding their own initiatives directed at various "publics" in other countries. As U.S. Information Agency Director Charles Wick pointed out at a "Public Diplomacy in the Information Age" meeting in 1987, "Today the success or failure of foreign policy undertakings is frequently affected more profoundly by what people think and say than by the workings of judical diplomacy." Some recent examples include the the training of Afghan rebels to use minicams to document for Western newscasts the armed struggle during the 1980s against the Soviet occupation; improvements in broadcast technology that make it possible for American USIA satellite television as well as radio to reach around the world and cut through the Iron Curtain; the aggressive image campaign by Mikhail Gorbachev to undercut NATO and restructure the European and American political landscape by presenting a more open view of Soviet life and decision making; and the largely private distribution of cassette tapes, which can result in a revolution such as the one that brought Ayatollah Khomeini to power in Iran.

Like all powerful forces, propaganda must be understood and wisely used if an unintended disastrous backlash is to be avoided. For example, the possibilities for genetic alteration and cloning are expanding. Combined with the specter of controlled mind-altering drugs and gases, this, frighteningly, may lead some to seek a permanent redirection of society through media-supported biochemical means. As a neutral weaponry system, propaganda can be used either to support or to combat this horrific possibility. If uncertain economic and social conditions in the United States worsen, some no doubt will be tempted to embrace these developments to impose order through more totalitarian controls. So beware when the rights of various organizations to communicate—even organizations you dislike—are restricted "in the public interest," for this will mean that access to information is being interfered with, possibly prefiguring a drift toward an authoritarian dictatorship.

At the same time, propaganda is now such an indelible part of life that it may take on a less heinous stature as more individuals come to see that one-sided communication can be an essential component not only of free speech but of civilization itself. Indeed, given the pluralistic nature of contemporary society, some forms of propagandistic social engineering may be necessary if we hope to reach consensus on the many vital (but perhaps controversial) issues facing us. Raucous views are not so much the problem as not having the opportunity to publicly dispute them. The best antidote to abuse continues to be the absolutely free libertarian marketplace of ideas endorsed by America's Founding Fathers, who more than two centuries ago recognized that the common good is advanced most effectively when private individuals and organizations are allowed to compete openly in pursuing their own self-interests.

Just as in Shakespeare's day, we are still players living on a world stage. Unlike his plays, though, our scenario remains unfinished. Only one certainty exists—we have entered an exciting new era for the propagandists, but a challenging and potentially haunting one for the rest of us.

REFERENCE WORKS

Given the divergent sources of propaganda, its literature is enormous. Relevant references run into the tens of thousands. Obviously, an introductory guide cannot hope to provide more than a representative overview of the more important works and collections. The appended bibliography, however, lists a number of specialized studies cited in the text that are definitive for their topic or offer interesting insights on propaganda in America. Included are selected books, doctoral dissertations, master's theses, and government documents, along with pertinent journals and magazine articles.

Despite propaganda's long history and the large number of publications devoted to its analysis, serious study of the phenomenon has largely been limited to the last seventy years. Most pre-World War I reference works (including the venerable *Encyclopedia Britannica*) do not even mention the topic. However, the widespread utilization of propaganda in World War I and the extension of radical ideology in the 1920s led a number of thoughtful writers to reflect on the problems as well as the promises of propaganda.

The late political scientist Harold D. Lasswell may well be referred to as the father of propaganda study in the United States. His doctoral dissertation, published as *Propaganda Technique in the World War* in 1927 (more recently reissued as *Propaganda Technique in World War I*), even led one critic to suggest that such "a Machiavellian textbook . . . should be destroyed." Lasswell's importance stems from the fact that he made a number of contributions toward the development of a comprehensive theoretical basis for analyzing propaganda. This book holds continuing interest because it provides an objective overview of the structure and strategies utilized by the propaganda services in the belligerent governments. Lasswell was one of the first to observe that the propagandist usually works within a specific culture in which strategies are circumscribed by the availability of media; the value norms of targeted audiences, which limit the variance of messages from current norms; and other preexisting constraints that are not necessarily universal in character. He further notes that war, by extending beyond established frontiers, forces the military propagandist to adapt or fail. The new edition includes a valuable introduction by Lasswell and Jackson A. Giddens summarizing the field after fifty years of subsequent research. Unfortunately, the appended bibliography remains unannotated, and the index is inadequate.

Despite these shortcomings, a number of later studies issued during the revisionist period of the 1930s built upon Lasswell without substantially altering his conclusions. Today much of the work appears rather primitive. One glaring weakness of the pioneering propaganda scholars was their cursory treatment of the origin and historical development of propaganda in the United States. Even today, there are relatively few in-depth documentary analyses detailing the historicity of the propaganda phenomenon. Nevertheless, it was only after Lasswell's groundbreaking work that the first serious questions were raised and tentative answers proposed about the nature of attitude change and the effects of persuasive communications. Lasswell himself later turned to the problems of methodology in *World Revolutionary Propaganda* (1939, coauthored by Dorothy Blumenstock) and received support from the Rockefeller Foundation to develop a statistical method of content analysis. An outstanding overview essay describing the underlying reasons for his and others' significant shift away from propaganda to communication analysis is found in J. Michael Sproule's essay "Propaganda Studies in American Social Science."

Another useful jumping-off point is the three-volume *Propaganda and Communication in World History* series (1979–1980), edited by Lasswell, Daniel Lerner, and Hans Speier. Volume 1, subtitled *The Symbolic Instrument in Early Times*, covers the period before the emergence of America as a nation. However, volume 2, subtitled *The Emergence of Public Opinion in the West*, includes nineteen essays (many original to the work) that begin with the invention of the printing press and trace the development of mass communication and symbol management to the present day. Volume 3 features fourteen chapters on *A Pluralizing World in Formation* which analyze contemporary marketing, advertising, public relations, and media planning from a social science perspective. Lasswell concludes this last volume with a prophetic look at the future of world communication and propaganda, written shortly before his death in 1978. Each volume has its own introduction, a comprehensive index, and brief biographies of contributors. But while virtually a who's who forum for leading political and communication scholars, these compendiums suffer from the weaknesses common to all anthologies by not being a true encyclopedia of propaganda—a work sorely needed despite the welcome new addition to the literature of *The International Encyclopedia of Communications*, edited by Erik Barnouw.

The Fine Art of Propaganda: A Study of Father Coughlin's Speeches, edited by Alfred McClung Lee and Elizabeth Briant Lee, remains one of the most significant books on propaganda ever published. First issued in 1939 and now available in several reprint editions, the work cuts across several fields. Although only 140 pages, the book's influence stems from its clear organizational analysis and labeling of the seven chief devices utilized by professional propagandists (such as "name calling" and "band wagon"). Updating this seminal study, Alfred McClung Lee in 1952 published the probing *How to Understand Propaganda*. Rather than taking a communication-oriented approach, Lee describes how we are all consumers of propaganda. Using numerous illustrations taken from the popular press, he writes that the only way to combat propaganda is to recognize it. Although Lee typically sees propaganda as an often debilitating force assaulting individual free will, he nevertheless points out that propaganda is also used to achieve a variety of desirable socioeconomic and political ends. A similar emphasis is found in *The Analysis of Propaganda* by William Hummel and Keith Huntress. After offering a general introduction and describing how propaganda can be detected in everyday life, the authors provide a justification for its further study. A rather eclectic reader, ranging from writings by Benjamin Franklin to those of John Steinbeck, is appended. Unfortunately, there is no bibliography, and the book is disappointing when contrasted to the publications by Alfred and Elizabeth Lee.

The leading theoretical analyses of propaganda today are Terence H. Qualter's *Opinion Control in the Democracies* (1985) and Jacques Ellul's *Propaganda: The Formation of Men's Attitudes*, published twenty years earlier. Both challenge many traditional notions (that education is the antidote to propaganda, that there are significant differences between so-called democratic and totalitarian propagandas, that the principal purpose of propaganda is to change belief rather than reinforce existing attitudes or motivate people to action) and provide a theoretical base from which to examine it as an important social force. In particular, the brilliant French theorist presents a convincing case for the corrosive effect of propaganda despite its necessity. After an introductory review of major trends in propaganda analysis, Ellul describes the primary characteristics and categories of propaganda as he sees them, discusses the underlying conditions that contribute to the widespread existence of propaganda, analyzes the necessity of propaganda for individuals and states, and reviews the results of propaganda. Two appendixes probe the effectiveness and limits of propaganda and dissect the brainwashing techniques used in Mao's China. Included are a bibliography and index. No illustrations and a lack of statistical data are the major weaknesses of the work (he argues that small-group experiments are unnecessary if we are to understand the psychology of propaganda), but clearly Ellul—like Qualter—is obligatory reading. In an interesting attempt at making this more relevant for Americans, Robert W. Raspberry's *The "Technique" of Political Lying* applies Ellul's propaganda theories, using the Watergate incident as its primary case study.

For those looking for a solid one-stop guide to the entire field, a major book has appeared: Garth S. Jowett and Victoria O'Donnell's *Propaganda and Persuasion*. Their work fills an important void in the literature. The authors' attempt to distinguish between persuasion and propaganda is useful but bound to be somewhat controversial, since others use the terms almost interchangeably. Although arguing that Ellul's views about propaganda's pervasiveness are too inclusive, Jowett and O'Donnell are also forced to be somewhat expansive in labeling the subtleties of social influence that propaganda incorporates. Aside from these criticisms and a few minor factual errors (for e.g., Charles I rather than James II was beheaded after being deposed, p. 51), this is a major contribution that will certainly help stimulate a revival of propaganda studies. Indeed, *Propaganda and Persuasion* is ideally suited as a primer to the subject and should be the starting text of choice for most classes on the subject. The authors present an overview of the history of propaganda, a review of the social scientific research on its effects, and an examination of its applications. Early chapters offer an original, systematic analysis and evaluation of propaganda from a communication perspective. This is followed by five detailed case studies of propaganda in modern times: the banning of cigarette advertising on radio and television, religious evangelism on television (which needs updating in a second edition because of recent developments), the *Pueblo* incident, the controversy over legalized abortion, and South African activities in the United States. The model, accompanying narrative describing the process and social-historical context for propaganda is very well done. A useful bibliography, index, and illustrations are appended.

Oliver Thomson's *Mass Persuasion in History: A Historical Analysis of the Development of Propaganda Techniques* is another compact primer valuable for beginning students because of its brevity. After a thoughtful introduction to the problems of historical analysis, Thomson divides propaganda into seven main categories ranked according to the objectives of the propagandist (political, economic, war/military, diplomatic, didactic, ideological, and escapist aimed at achieving social acquiescence). He treats message construction in terms of style, structure, and theme, then follows it with a pragmatic review of propagandistic philosophy and methodologies used for determining effectiveness. Also useful, given the transient nature and unavailability of much propaganda product, is a photographic section illustrating appended historical case studies ranging from the Roman Empire through the mobilization propaganda of the Western democracies. The work is faulted, though, by the limited bibliography and index.

Unfortunately, the more detailed *3000 Jahre Politische Propaganda* (3000 Years of Political Propaganda) by Alfred Sturminger remains untranslated. Although this profusely illustrated work concentrates on the history of propaganda in Europe, it is useful for its inclusion of such media as postage stamps and cancellations as propaganda tools. Besides art, another interesting section traces pro- and antireligious propaganda. Standard bibliographic data and indexing facilitate the book's use.

The title of Frederick E. Lumley's *The Propaganda Menace* adequately describes his attitude to the practice. Unlike others who typically lament the barrage of distortion while neglecting historical precedent, Lumley devotes considerable space to the prior development of propaganda. Considering that he wrote over fifty years ago, the book holds up well and reflects credibly on his scholarship. One of its valuable attributes is the division into specific topic areas. In addition to the obligatory "Propaganda and War" section, later chapters discuss politics, race, education, and religion as forums for persuasive communication. His fear that then-current trends would make propaganda an increasingly powerful factor in society has been borne out. Lumley's somewhat depressing conclusion that the only antidote for propaganda is the ability to think straight seems as true as ever. One oversight is that no illustrations or photographs are used.

Following closely in Lumley's tradition is Michael Choukas' *Propaganda Comes of Age*. Choukas, who holds a doctoral degree from Columbia University, writes with some authority since he served in the propaganda arm of the OSS during World War II. In tracing the evolution of the vast domestic propaganda network in this country, he argues that, because of its deliberately manipulative nature, propaganda is not an informational tool. Rather, says Choukas, propaganda and democracy are at odds, and without strong controls on advertising, lobbying, and so forth the country faces a totalitarian future. Nevertheless, he approves of propaganda directed at foreign audiences in pursuit of governmental policies. The book is enhanced by numerous cartoons, advertisements, leaflets, and so on, but these are not always keyed directly to the text. A serious deficiency is the lack of an index or bibliography.

Despite a rather sensational title, Robert Sobel's *The Manipulators: America in the Media Age* is a serious—if flawed—look at the development of U.S. communications. Writing from a passionate fear that the media are contributing to national instability by the blurring of fact and fiction, Sobel has compiled a big book (458 pages) that documents the emergence of America's newspapers, the role of the university as a training ground for the journalistic elite, the wartime propaganda blitz of the Committee on Public Information, the anti-Axis co-optation of the motion picture industry, and the rise of television and other new technologies as a force in contemporary society. More than simply a history, Sobel raises important questions about the future of our propagandistic culture. The value of this work as a scholarly reference, however, is undermined by the inclusion of numerous careless factual errors, which work to negate the credibility of Sobel's argumentation.

Also of interest is Barry Marks' doctoral dissertation, "The Idea of Propaganda in America" (1957), which traces the origin of the concept of propaganda as a malevolent new social force after World War I, analyzes the "marriage" of propaganda and anti-intellectualism as a challenge to democracy, and treats the influence of propagandistic impact in American progressive education. Marks' study certainly deserves a wider audience.

Two books sharing the same title, *Public Opinion and Propaganda*, by Frederick C. Irion and Leonard W. Doob, respectively, were both geared to the college market but given the dramatic changes in media statistics and sociological perspectives have become rather dated. Irion also lacks a bibliography. Each, however, has some historic interest because of the wealth of detail included; thus they are recommended for overviews of the field up to the date of their publication. Doob, particularly, has been an important figure in U.S. propaganda studies since the publication of his *Propaganda: Its Psychology and Technique*. Less useful for the specialist is *Propaganda Handbook* by D. Lincoln Harter and John Sullivan. The book reflects the Cold War period in which it appeared and, despite the embracive title, is rather simplistic. Largely based on secondary sources, its major strength is in synthesis of more original work.

Among the first to catalog the growing literature systematically were Kimball Young and Raymond D. Lawrence, whose annotated *Bibliography on Censorship and Propaganda*, issued serially in 1928, is still useful for early newspaper and magazine citations dating from the nineteenth century not usually found in later compendiums.

Expanding upon this pioneering work were Harold D. Lasswell, Ralph D. Casey, and Bruce L. Smith, whose *Propaganda and Promotional Activities: An Annotated Bibliography* quickly became a standard reference upon publication in 1935 and remains an indispensable guide to the seminal literature. A 1969 reissue includes a new introduction by Lasswell summarizing his thoughts after nearly forty years of propaganda study. Lasswell (whose communication formula "who says what, in which channel, to whom, with what effect?" remains the basic starting point for most empirical studies) notes that despite scientific advances we are still without a comprehensive theory that can accurately explain as well as analyze human behavior—including the interplay of propaganda. Originally prepared for the Social Science Research Council, the bibliography has seven divisions. Theories of propaganda management are discussed in a thirty-five-page section, which is followed by references to the propagandas of governments, international agencies, political parties, and other organizations classified by type (business, labor, professional, and so on). Later sections classify propaganda according to the response sought, the symbols manipulated, and the channels used. Also listed are early measurement studies and references that describe the impact of propaganda and censorship on modern society. An author-subject index is appended, helping to compensate for the somewhat loose topical categorization.

The same authors (but with Bruce L. Smith listed first) updated this in 1946 with *Propaganda, Communication, and Public Opinion: A Comprehensive Reference Guide*, which includes four essays on the science of mass communication and within a similar organizational framework provides an excellent, selectively annotated bibliography of 2,558 books and articles published for the most part between 1934 and 1943. Bruce L. Smith has additionally coauthored with Chitra M. Smith the supplemental *International Communication and Political Opinion: A Guide to the Literature*. This features another 2,500 entries (among them government documents and unpublished studies) released between 1943 and 1955. Stress is placed on the international and political aspects of propaganda. Both of the preceding works include author and subject indexes.

Reference should also be made to Harwood L. Childs, *A Reference Guide to the Study of Public Opinion* (1934), which is organized topically and continues to hold interest despite the lack of annotations, and to the brief *List of Bibliographies on Propaganda*, prepared for publication by the U.S. Library of Congress in 1940. Warren C. Price's *The Literature of Journalism: An Annotated Bibliography* includes a short section devoted specifically to selected books and articles on "public opinion, propaganda, and public relations" (177 citations). Again, a subject-author index provides cross-references. Price supplements this volume with *An Annotated Journalism Bibliography: 1958–1968*, coauthored with Calder M. Pickett. This work has 2,172 listings (most not related specifically to propaganda) organized alphabetically by author rather than subject. To compensate for this stylistic change, the index has been expanded to fifty pages.

Of more direct relevance are Scott M. Cutlip's *A Public Relations Bibliography to 1965*, with 6,000 entries organized topically; Robert L. Bishop's *Public Relations: A Comprehensive Bibliography—Articles and Books on Public Relations, Communication Theory, Public Opinion, and Propaganda, 1964–1972*, which follows Cutlip with another 4,500 subject-divided citations; and the subsequent annual updates by Bishop and Albert Walker that appear in special issues of *Public Relations Review*. Even though more than 300 periodical and other sources were searched in compiling the Cutlip-Bishop-Walker bibliographies, there are, unfortunately, still numerous omissions. The more recent Walker-prepared guides, for example, appear far less comprehensive, particularly in the area of government and think-tank reports. Each follows a similar format, indexing author names and government agencies as well as listing occasional names of companies and countries.

Researchers interested in government publications on the topic of propaganda should not overlook George D. Brightbill's *Communications and the United States Congress: A Selectively Annotated Bibliography of Committee Hearings, 1870–1976*, which provides chronologically arranged guidance to some 1,100 titles issued by the House and Senate. Material on censorship is included, although publishing references are not. This work is further limited because documents, reports, and committee prints are also excluded. William W. Buchanan and Edna A. Kanely, *Cumulative Subject Index to the Monthly Catalog of United States Government Publications 1900–1971*, published by Carrollton Press, is invaluable for wading through the wealth of available material. Neglected by many researchers has been another Carrollton service called the "Declassified Documents Reference System." The basic collection includes 16,000 official documents made available through the Freedom of Information Act. These are summarized, indexed, photo-duplicated on microfilm, and supplied to subscribing research libraries with annual updates (1976 to the present). The importance of the system is that it includes sensitive material previously unavailable to the public, taken directly from the files of the CIA, the FBI, and other government agencies.

A very different orientation is found in *Marxism and the Mass Media: Towards a Basic Bibliography*, issued intermittently by the International Mass Media Research Center (1972 to present) as part of an ongoing periodical series whose purpose is to compile a global, multilingual, annotated bibliography of left studies on all aspects of communication (including propaganda). As a result this reference journal covers ground often overlooked by others. Affiliated researchers to the center have additionally prepared *Marxist Readings: A Bibliography of over 4,000 Books, Pamphlets, and Reprints in English, German and Italian—Volume 1*, a source worth reviewing. Also of considerable reference value is Thomas F. Gordon and Mary Ellen Verna's *Mass Communication Effects and Processes: A Comprehensive Bibliography, 1950–1975*. The bibliography, although not annotated, has a useful narrative introduction to the literature and features over 2,700 citations arranged alphabetically by author. The subject index is detailed, and there is an unusual index of secondary authors which allows the user to find specific citations.

On political propaganda, see *Political Campaign Communications: A Bibliography and Guide to the Literature* (1974) by Lynda Lee Kaid, Keith R. Sanders, and Robert O. Hirsch, the first comprehensive summary of the literature in this specialized area. Included is an annotated introduction to the fifty most important reference books plus an unannotated supplemental listing of hundreds of relevant periodical citations, updated in 1985 and 1986 by two follow-up books. Dan Nimmo (whose earlier *The Political Persuaders: The Techniques of Modern Election Campaigns* is still required reading for understanding the importance of image over issue in determining most electoral outcomes) has also recently published a helpful analysis entitled *Political Communication and Public Opinion in America*. This latter work presents a useful summary of available knowledge with comments on the general area of political communication as well as the roles played by expert communicators, the language and symbols manipulated, persuasion (including propaganda, advertising, and rhetoric), media channels, and other contemporary pragmatic approaches to influencing voter behavior.

In *Information Sources in Advertising History* (1979), edited by Richard W. Pollay, four essays assess the literature and discuss sources, but the book's centerpiece is an annotated bibliography of 1,600 titles arranged by subject, with strength in literature prior to 1940. Although "propaganda" as such is not one of the topics, related areas such as the psychology and sociology of advertising, marketing, public relations, and broadcasting are covered. Two directories list professional associations and describe special collections and archival holdings.

General overviews of the history and literature of propaganda (often prepared by leading authorities) can be found in most encyclopedias. Among the more complete and analytical are those of Harwood L. Childs in *Collier's Encyclopedia*, W. E. Barber in *Dictionary of American History*, Jackson Giddens in *Encyclopedia Americana*, Harold D. Lasswell in *Encyclopaedia Britannica* and the classic first edition of the *Encyclopaedia of the Social Sciences* found in most good reference libraries, Bruce L. Smith in *The New Encyclopaedia Britannica* and the *International Encyclopedia of the Social Sciences*, and Horst Reimann in *Marxism, Communism and Western Society: A Comparative Encyclopedia*.

Researchers interested in the more recent serious periodical literature should also consult the basic volume and yearly updates entitled *Public Opinion, Mass Behavior and Political Psychology*, issued as part of the Political Science, Government, and Public Policy series published since 1967. Through use of a computerized keyword system, literally thousands of citations appearing in social and behavioral science literature are cataloged under the heading "Edu/Prop . . . Education, Propaganda, Persuasion." This is well worth reviewing.

Standard business indexes list media/business topics. Recent publications can also be searched using keywords and the unique cross-referenced citation listings of *Social Sciences Citation Index* and the *Arts and Humanities Citation Index*, supplemented by up-to-date title page reprints in *Current Contents/Social and Behavioral Sciences* and *Current Contents/Arts and Humanities*. Other reference guides regularly summarizing current propaganda writing include *America: History and Life*, *Communication Abstracts*, *Historical Abstracts*, *International Political Science Abstracts*, *Sociological Abstracts*, and *Topicator* (for advertising).

The *Insider Newsletter*, published by the Heritage Foundation, is a particularly useful free monthly summary of recent conservative and libertarian publications, conferences, and legal cases. In contrast, the slicker magazine-format *Propaganda Review*, produced by the Media Alliance (a San Francisco–based collective of left-oriented media professionals), serves as an interesting forum for critiques of the pervasive "propaganda environment." Writers cover topics ranging from public relations/advertising campaigns to disinformation activities by intelligence agencies. This replaces an earlier tabloid predecessor, *Propaganda Analysis Review* (1985–1987).

Communication Booknotes, published monthly by policy academic Christopher Sterling at George Washington University, is another effective and timely source; in addition to thoughtful commentary on new publications, it devotes one issue per year to federally issued literature (including reports by propaganda agencies such as the USIA). See also selected articles and the review sections of journals such as *Critical Studies in Mass Communication*, *Historical Journal of Film, Radio and Television*, *Journal of Broadcasting and Electronic Media*, *Journal of Communication*, *Journalism Quarterly*, *Political Communication and Persuasion: An International Journal*, *Public Affairs Review*, and *Quarterly Review of Doublespeak*.

Countless articles, monographs, and books have also appeared under the catchall heading "persuasion research." This, like public opinion, often involves surveys and experimental control studies reported in psychology, sociology, political science, and communications journals. One distinction made is that, although all propaganda attempts to persuade, not all persuasion is propaganda. As a result, much of this material is directed to an empirical audience and is thus far removed from the popular culture literature. (Major exceptions include Vance Packard's popularized *The Hidden Persuaders*, first published in 1957, and Wilson Bryant Key's pseudoscientific *The Subliminal Seduction: Ad Media's Manipulation of a Not So Innocent America*.) The student of propaganda in America, however, should at least be aware that this body of research writing exists and may want to cross-reference it with a review of the broader rhetorical and ideological literature, which can be given here no more than cursory discussion.

Useful in distinguishing between persuasion, propaganda, debate, brainwashing, and coercion is the introductory chapter in Austin J. Freeley, *Argumentation and Debate: Critical Thinking for Reasoned Decision Making*. Although not as structurally integrated as one would hope, *Introduction to Rhetorical Theory* by Gerard A. Hauser does provide a rather useful compilation summarizing the literature of rhetorical theory. On the other hand, Richard M. Weaver's *The Ethics of Rhetoric* is a classical study that insists that analyzing rhetoric can reveal the degree to which a person's or organization's use of language expresses or betrays his or her underlying values. "The use of language is, in short, an ethical undertaking, bearing with it high obligations to the true and the good." *Iconology: Image, Text, Ideology* by W.J.T. Mitchell argues that distinctions between images and words reflect ideological values and interests of a culture rather than any naturally based differences. The book then critiques the question of ideology itself. This is heavy reading, not for the beginner without solid grounding in philosophy. Similarly, *The Concept of Ideology and Political Analysis: A Critical Examination of Its Usage by Marx, Lenin, and Mannheim*, authored by Walter Carlsnaes, tries to come to grips with the widely used but imprecise term *ideology*. This unenviable task is complicated by the almost endless variety of meanings applied by those writing about the topic, particularly in the literature of the left.

Fortunately, there are several guides to help the neophyte interested in bridging these gaps for a fuller discussion of the literature dealing specifically with persuasion. Two useful critical introductions are "Persuasion" by Gerald R. Miller and "Persuasion Research: Review and Commentary" by Miller and Michael Burgoon, which complement "Persuasion, Resistance, and Attitude Change" by William J. McGuire.

Among the more widely circulated general works, all of which provide an overview of this specialized field, are Erwin P. Bettinghaus and Michael J. Cody, *Persuasive Communication*; Winston Brembeck and William Howell, *Persuasion: A Means of Social Influence*; Gary Cronkhite, *Persuasion: Speech and Behavioral Change*, which has a particularly thoughtful analysis; George N. Gordon, *Persuasion: The Theory and Practice of Manipulative Communication*; Carl Hovland and others, *Communication and Persuasion*; Marvin Karlins and Herbert Abelson, *Persuasion: How Opinions and Attitudes Are Changed*; Andrew King, *Power and Communication*; Charles U. Larson, *Persuasion: Reception and Responsibility*; Wayne Minnick, *The Art of Persuasion*; Michael Roloff and Gerald R. Miller, editors, *Persuasion: New Directions in Theory and Research*; Herbert W. Simons, *Persuasion: Understanding, Practice and Analysis*; Mary John Smith, *Persuasion and Human Action: A Review and*

Critique of Social Influence Theories; Wayne N. Thompson, *The Process of Persuasion: Principles and Readings*; and Philip Zimbardo, Ebbe B. Ebbeson, and Christina Maslach, *Influencing Attitudes and Changing Behavior*. Gary C. Woodward and Robert E. Denton Jr.'s *Persuasion and Influence in American Life* is a recent comprehensive text describing the processes that apply for both constructing and analyzing persuasive messages used by businesses, politicians, and others.

Among the newer persuasion periodicals that should be referenced are *Human Communication Research* and *Social Science Monitor*. The latter, which is aimed at public relations and advertising executives, summarizes findings from behavioral science journals that have implications for the pragmatist interested in "getting the right information into the right minds." Hugh Rank's *The Pitch* evaluates the typical five-part strategy used by most advertisers to get attention, build confidence, stimulate desire, press urgency, and seek an action response. Later, in *The Pep Talk*, he similarly reviews the common patterns of political persuasion. Both are worthwhile attempts to create a contemporary pedagogy of propaganda analysis, using numerous illustrations to reinforce understanding of the often nonrational structures utilized in such persuasive messages. Also of relevance is Steuart Henderson Britt's *Psychological Principles of Marketing and Consumer Behavior*, which collates a wealth of data. Now must reading for the contemporary propagandist, his book is organized to describe both what happens in the psyche of a person exposed to directed communication and how the mass of available empirical data can be more effectively applied in persuasive campaigns.

Anthologies and Reprints

Thirty-one of the most important books issued originally between 1920 and 1962 have now been made available in an International Propaganda and Communications collection by Arno Press. Included are a number of seminal studies cited elsewhere in this book. Greenwood Press also has reprinted a variety of titles on mass persuasion covering the fields of public opinion, advertising, and psychology. A particular service is making Gallup poll data from 1935 on conveniently available. In addition, publication has begun on a one-volume annual, *Index to International Public Opinion*, edited by Elizabeth and Philip Hastings, with comprehensive worldwide coverage of polling data issued by more than fifty leading research organizations.

Despite earlier citations of several excellent reference anthologies, no definitive collation of propaganda essays exists. Given the breadth of the literature, such a work is probably impossible. Among the first to study the relationship of pressure groups and propaganda was Harwood Childs, who assembled a series of topical papers by twenty-eight leading authorities and students for a special issue of the *Annals* of the American Academy of Political and Social Sciences in May 1935. Much of this was previously unpublished and, although somewhat dated, continues to have historical and theoretical interest. By the 1950s, as a result of the propaganda onslaught in World War II and the beginnings of the Cold War, a number of readers began to appear. These include *Propaganda in War and Crisis: Materials for American Foreign Policy*, edited by Daniel Lerner, *America's Weapons of Psychological Warfare*, edited by R. E. Summers, and *Political Opinion and Propaganda: A*

Book of Readings, edited by Daniel Katz and other noted researchers for the Society for the Psychological Study of Social Issues.

Most such books are geared to the needs of undergraduates, offering a rather eclectic review of public opinion and propaganda as a social science discipline. Updating these with more recent material are massive works such as *Reader in Public Opinion and Communication*, edited by Bernard Berelson and Morris Janowitz, and *Voice of the People: Readings in Public Opinion and Propaganda* by Reo M. Christenson and Robert O. McWilliams. For the less academic, *Language in Uniform: A Reader on Propaganda*, edited by Nick Aaron Ford, and *Propaganda, Polls, and Public Opinion: Are the People Manipulated?*, compiled by Malcolm Mitchell, provide a more directed and simplified introduction.

Teaching about Doublespeak is a useful primer prepared for classroom use by Daniel Dietrich. Published by the National Council of Teachers of English, it includes a number of readings designed to make students more informed about their daily intake of propaganda (including advertising). A useful, sixteen-page bibliography is appended. Note should also be made of the collection of articles "On Propaganda" in the Summer 1979 issue of *ETC.: A Review of General Semantics*. Authors include Jacques Ellul on "The Role of Persuasion in a Technical Society," Thomas Steinfatt on "Evaluating Approaches to Propaganda Analysis," Elizabeth Briant Lee and Alfred McClung Lee on "The Fine Art of Propaganda Analysis—Then and Now," and others. Journals such as *Public Opinion Quarterly* also occasionally devote entire issues to the subject of propaganda (some earlier *POQ* compilations are included in the Arno Press collection cited earlier). For more on available advertising reprints, see the chapter on "Advertising" elsewhere in this *Handbook*.

HISTORY AND CRITICISM

Since numerous studies exist covering specialized topical areas and historical periods, subdivisions have been included in this section to enable readers to identify more easily what is most useful for their particular research interests.

Revolutionary War Period

The American Revolution was a conflict of political ideals in which both warring sides were convinced of the rightness of their cause. Conveniently available in reprint is *A Short Narrative of the Horrid Massacre in Boston*, first prepared in 1770 by a partisan committee chaired by James Bowdoin. Featured are eyewitness interviews of ninety-six military men, citizens, and others who testified about their experiences on that fateful day when a group of frightened British soldiers opened fire on a threatening crowd of demonstrators, killing or wounding eleven. Perhaps overemphasized is the impact of actions taken in cities such as Boston on the rest of the colonies, a fault remedied by Robert W. Smith in his unpublished thesis "What Came After?: News Diffusion and the Significance of the Boston Massacre in Six American Colonies, 1770–1775." Smith traces the media coverage of the "massacre" and concludes that the Patriotic view of the British army as a major threat to liberty had meaning only for Massachusetts and was relatively unimportant in terms of its propaganda value outside the Bay Colony.

Philip Davidson's *Propaganda and the American Revolution, 1763–1783* remains the standard history of American propaganda before and during the Revolution. Included are sections on Whig and Patriotic propaganda, as well as the efforts of the Tory-Loyalist counterattack. Although the topical arrangement at times results in some repetition, Davidson's careful scholarship not only forms a solid contribution to the study of the early American experience but also points to the many similarities to be found within all modern revolutionary movements. Challenging many supposed facts about U.S. history (since much of what we "know" about the Revolution has derived from the propaganda of that era), the author stresses the importance of ideas in deciding the conflict of arms.

Supplementing Davidson, by concentrating more directly on the actual war years, is the revised edition of *Broadsides & Bayonets: The Propaganda War of the American Revolution* by Carl Berger. Unlike most studies, which focus primarily on pamphlets and newspapers, Berger explores other efforts involving "secret arts and machinations" to influence the course of the war. Particularly interesting are the chapters entitled "American Propaganda and the Struggle for Canada," "The Campaign to Win the Indians' Allegiance," "The Incitement of Negro Insurrection," and "Overseas Propaganda." The notes and bibliography are useful as well. Readers interested in a related aspect of the Revolutionary struggle should also refer to "Lafayette as a Tool of American Propaganda," a neglected doctoral study completed by Marguerite Bloxom in 1970.

Useful guides to available original propaganda publications of the pre-Constitutional period include Charles F. Heartman, compiler, *The Cradle of the United States, 1765–1789: Five Hundred Contemporary Broadsides, Pamphlets, and a Few Books Pertaining to the History of the Stamp Act, the Boston Massacre and Other Pre-Revolutionary Troubles, the War for Independence and the Adoption of the Federal Constitution*; Ruth Lampham, compiler, *Check List of American Revolutionary War Pamphlets in the Newberry Library*; and the unattributed *Manuscripts of the American Revolution in the Boston Public Library: A Descriptive Catalog*. Heartman had one of the finest collections of its type, alphabetically listing each item "bibliographically, historically and sometimes sentimentally" with an index to materials issued anonymously. Lampham similarly describes 754 tracts issued by American and British sources between 1750 and 1786, including a specific section devoted to Revolutionary propaganda held by the Chicago research facility. The Boston collection has the advantage of being larger because of the more recent date of collation but otherwise differs little from its predecessors. Useful insights and references to contemporary materials are also found in Bernard Bailyn's *Ideological Origins of the American Revolution*, which complements his earlier *Pamphlets of the American Revolution, 1750–1776*. The latter reprints original texts selected on the basis of representativeness, contemporary fame, originality of thought, literary distinction, and/or importance of the author.

Of the American propagandists, Samuel Adams and Thomas Paine have been written about the most. John C. Miller's *Sam Adams: Pioneer in Propaganda* supersedes Ralph Volney Harlow's *Samuel Adams, Promoter of the American Revolution: A Study in Psychology and Politics* as the standard biographical reference for Adams' propagandistic career. Miller draws a picture of the "father of the American Revolution" that is not entirely flattering. The omission of an introduction (which would have been useful in appraising Adams' significance) and a bibliography weaken an otherwise fine book. The later edition does add a brief one-page bibliography of works appearing after 1941, but for details one must struggle through the footnotes. While Harlow takes an intriguing Freudian approach in interpreting Adams' motivations and psyche, he tends at times to be inaccurate in detail and biased in his use of supporting evidence. Among early works, *The Life and Public Services of Samuel Adams* by great-grandson William Vincent Wells is of interest. Published in three volumes in 1865, the biography is naturally laudatory but nonetheless demonstrates careful and thorough attention to research as well as a wealth of fascinating minutiae. Of the newer studies, see John R. Galvin, *Three Men of Boston*, which focuses on the interrelationship among Adams, James Otis, and Governor Thomas Hutchinson; Stewart Beach, *Samuel Adams: The Fateful Years, 1764–1776*; and Cass Canfield, *Sam Adams' Revolution (1765–1776)*, published in the Bicentennial. While Galvin offers an excellent interpretive account, Canfield unfortunately tells us little we do not already know about Adams. Beach, drawing extensively from Adams' state papers, correspondence, and political essays, believes he was neither the extremist nor as violent as he is depicted in more conventional biographies. By approaching the Revolution through the eyes of Adams, Beach presents a reappraisal of the whole period which cannot simply be shunted aside. Although lacking footnotes, the book has a particularly useful bibliographic essay, which is must reading for anyone interested in Adams and the Revolution. Note also that *The Writings of Samuel Adams 1764–1802* was collected and edited by Harry Alonzo Cushing in four volumes appearing between 1904 and 1908. Only Adams' own surviving writings appear. Letters from others to him, although numerous in the manuscript collections, are not included.

The materials on Paine are, if anything, more voluminous. The basic biography is the 500-page *Paine*, by David Freeman Hawke, who has written knowledgeably about the colonial era in numerous other books. Paine, despite an active public career in America and Europe, proves to be a surprisingly introspective and exceedingly private man. Because few of Paine's personal papers survive, the task of the historian is at once complicated and simplified—complicated, because questions must remain unanswered and details undiscovered; simplified, because most of the remaining Paine materials have been collected under one roof. In readable, even exciting style, Hawke traces Paine's life from his humble origins working as a ladies corset maker in Britain to his spectacular rise as a major Revolutionary pamphleteer in America and France, through his later imprisonment and bittersweet return to the United States he helped create. The bibliography, albeit extensive, lacks references to publishers and cities of publication for all citations, an unfortunate omission. Other studies of interest include the overly journalistic but still fascinating *Tom Paine: America's Godfather, 1737–1809* by W. E. Woodward (featuring a chapter entitled "Paine as Propagandist"); Arnold Kinsey King, "Thomas Paine in America, 1774–1787," an unpublished 1952 dissertation, which exhaustively covers Paine's Revolutionary influence; and Alfred Owen Aldridge, *Man of Reason: The Life of Thomas Paine*, which points out that Paine's writings were important not because of his style but because of the substantive appeal and compelling logic they employed. Aldridge includes full chapter notes and fleshes out his narrative with information overlooked by previous researchers.

Recent biographies such as Samuel Edwards' *Rebel! A Biography of Tom Paine* and *Tom Paine* by Jerome D. Wilson and William F. Ricketson are designed more for the popular market. Wilson and Ricketson do, however, include a useful select annotated bibliography; Edwards' book, on the other hand, despite pretensions as an authoritative text, lacks documentation and is rather free in handling sources. Better are Audrey Williamson's *Thomas Paine: His Life, Work and Times* and Eric Foner's *Tom Paine and Revolutionary America*. Williamson includes newly researched details about Paine's life and benefits not only from a rather comprehensive treatment but also the author's British perspective. Foner, rather than pursuing a traditional biography, explores key moments in Paine's career. He suggests that Paine's influence was not merely propagandistic but transcended narrow economic interests when he became an innovative political communicator who really believed in the utopian vision of an egalitarian American society.

No complete collection of Paine's public and private writings is as yet available. *The Writings of Thomas Paine*, collected and edited by Moncure Daniel Conway in four volumes from 1894 to 1896, filled a gap at the time of publication but is now superseded by later works such as the ten-volume large-print *The Life and Works of Thomas Paine*, edited by William van der Weyde and published in 1925; and Philip S. Foner's *The Complete Writings of Thomas Paine*, issued in two volumes in 1945. Unfortunately, all are seriously flawed. Although Foner's is perhaps the most comprehensive, occasional misdating of letters, editorial deletions, a topical organization that makes it difficult to work chronologically, the inclusion of an inadequate index, and the failure to collate all available Paine material point to the need for a new and truly definitive collection. Numerous student editions of Paine's political writings also exist. Among the best, because of its useful introduction to Paine's career with full explanatory notes, is *Common Sense and Other Political Writings* (1953), edited by Nelson F. Adkins.

Propaganda in a New Nation, 1785–1825

The years between the Revolutionary and Civil Wars saw great change, yet they remain among the most neglected in the history of U.S. propaganda. The outstanding document influencing the constitutional debate is, of course, *The Federalist Papers* by Alexander Hamilton, James Madison, and John Jay. A number of editions of the collected papers exist, but the most used reference text is that edited by Clinton Rossiter based on what is known as the McLean edition of 1788. Included are an informative introduction describing the political and social background, an expanded table of contents with a brief precis for each of the eighty-five essays, an appendix containing the Constitution with cross-references to pertinent sections within the papers, and an index of ideas, which helps search out the major political concepts. See also John Heller's unpublished "The Selling of the Constitution: The Federalist Papers Viewed as an Advertising Campaign." After tracing the historical development of constitutionalism in the United States, Heller describes the reasons advanced for adopting the Constitution contained within the papers and provides factual data on the authors. Using a content analysis, Heller concludes that the advocacy methodology of the proponents strongly resembles issue-oriented advertising campaigns common today.

Most of the other important scholarly materials commenting on U.S. propaganda in this period appear in journals or remain unpublished. Of value in terms of background, however, is Gustavus Myers' monumental *History of Bigotry in the*

United States, which gives a very serviceable guide to not only the immediate post-Revolutionary period but more modern eras as well. The footnotes are extensive, although one wishes that they had been organized into a bibliography.

Emergence of Political Parties and Factions, 1826–1860

The Antimasonic Party was the first influential minor or third party in the United States and introduced the technique of the national presidential nominating convention to the nation in 1831. The avowed goal of its members was the destruction of Freemasonry and all secret societies because of Masonry's alleged subversive, unchristian, undemocratic character and activities. Later the Antimasonry Crusade was incorporated into the reform wing of the Whig Party and declined as more pressing issues, such as slavery, came to dominate national attention. Its story is well told by William Preston Vaughn in *The Antimasonic Party in the United States, 1826–1843*. This remains the best reference source, although specialists interested in political rhetoric should review Leland M. Griffin's doctoral dissertation, "The Antimasonic Persuasion: A Study of Public Address in the American Antimasonic Movement, 1826–1838." For comparison, see also Powrie Vaux Doctor's "Amos Kendall, Propagandist of Jacksonian Democracy."

An in-depth scholarly study exploring every aspect of the struggle to rid the country of slavery is contained in Dwight Lowell Dumond's *Antislavery: The Crusade for Freedom in America*. For the student of propaganda, the book details the organization and development of antislavery societies, the continuing communication efforts to win over public opinion by activists such as William Lloyd Garrison, and the emergence of partisan activity in the Liberty Party that eventually led "free soilers" to fuse their interests by forming the Republican Party. In contrast, Joel H. Silbey argues in a series of provocative revisionist essays that slavery was not the most important issue in American politics in the period just prior to the outbreak of war in 1861. In *The Partisan Imperative: The Dynamics of American Politics before the Civil War* he discusses the importance of local issues, ethnic and religious attitudes, and the role of the national parties in influencing the drift toward secession. For background, see James Constantine's 1953 doctoral dissertation, "The African Slave Trade: A Study of Eighteenth Century Propaganda and Public Controversy," which thoroughly covers the topic.

The Civil War

Every American war has brought a heated debate over the extent to which national security will permit protesters to exercise constitutional guarantees of free speech. Frank L. Klement's *The Limits of Dissent: Clement L. Vallandigham and the Civil War* is an intellectual biography of the passionate critic who led the pro-peace faction in the North opposed to Lincoln's policies by insisting that no circumstance—not even a divisive war—could deprive a citizen of the right to oppose governmental decisions freely and openly. In the resulting fiercely fought propaganda battle for mass opinion, Vallandigham risked everything—including arrest, imprisonment, and exile—to defend free speech for all. "Valiant Val" became a symbol of the dissenter; his case raises civil rights questions of continuing relevance today as documented in this important book.

The North-South conflict has the "advantage" of being the first major war fought in the United States when there was general literacy. Given the strong philosophical and ideological differences between the northern and southern leaderships, the increasing presence of large numbers of foreign-born immigrants who needed to be "Americanized," and the lack of enthusiasm for the war among large segments of the nonsecessionist population, it is not surprising that the staple of pre-twentieth-century propagandists—pamphlets and broadsides—proliferated in the effort to rally support for what it soon was realized would be a protracted fight.

For northern publications see *Union Pamphlets of the Civil War, 1861–1865*, compiled in two volumes by Frank B. Freidel. This is the standard introduction to this material, reprinting fifty-two selected texts. Organization here is similar to that employed for the Revolutionary War Collection edited by Bailyn. Each pamphlet appears in its entirety, along with appendixes and associated matter (including a fact-filled introduction supplemented by representative illustrations). Numerous works on the life of Harriet Beecher Stowe are not included here, but reference should be made to "Generative Forces in Union Propaganda: A Study in Civil War Pressure Groups" by George Winston Smith, written in 1940 during another era of crisis; and to "The Pictorial Reporting and Propaganda of the Civil War" by William F. Thompson Jr., a fascinating exploration of the role played by wartime illustrators, photographers, cartoonists, and commercial artists in shaping northern public opinion.

The Confederacy also issued literally thousands of imprints. Fortunately, guides and catalogs do exist to assist the researcher in locating pertinent references. Basic works include Marjorie Lyle Crandall, *Confederate Imprints: A Check List Based Principally on the Collection of the Boston Athenaeum*, in two volumes, with 5,121 citations; Richard Harwell, *More Confederate Imprints*, two volumes, with 1,773 citations; and Ray O. Hummel Jr., *Southeastern Broadsides before 1877: A Bibliography*, with over 5,000 entries. Although not every publication can be classified as propaganda, each guide contains references to official publications by state as well as by topic area for unofficial publications ("Slavery and the Negro," "Religious Tracts," and so on), an author index, and authoritative introductions. Of specialized interest is Charles P. Cullop's *Confederate Propaganda in Europe, 1861–1865*. The work is currently unique, features a six-page bibliography, but is only 160 pages long.

Following the defeat of the Confederacy, post–Civil War reactionaries formed the Ku Klux Klan as a political and social movement to reestablish white supremacy in the South, but soon its influence began to be felt nationwide and has not yet died out. There are many books on the Klan, but a serviceable introduction and overview are found in *Hooded Americanism: The History of the Ku Klux Klan* by David M. Chalmers, now out in a third edition.

Spanish-American War

Not surprisingly, the flashpoint of propaganda studies in the years between the Civil War and World War I is yet another armed conflict—the Spanish-American War. Two basic references are Marcus M. Wilkerson, *Public Opinion and the Spanish-American War: A Study in War Propaganda*, and Joseph E. Wisan, *The*

Cuban Crisis as Reflected in the New York Press, 1895–1898. Of the two, Wisan's book is by far the more complete, but each has contrasting insights on the role played by such New York papers as the *Journal* and *World* in whipping up interventionist enthusiasm. Wilkerson is particularly damning in his indictment of the publishers, whose primary concern was circulation rather than human rights. Often overlooked, however, is the role played by Cuban nationalists in encouraging U.S. involvement. See, for example, the article by George Auxier, "The Propaganda Activities of the Cuban Junta in Precipitating the Spanish-American War, 1895–1898," which appeared in the *Hispanic American Historical Review.*

Rise of Populism, Progressivism, and the Muckrakers

Set against the power of rawboned industrialization were two movements that sought to constrain the increasingly unbridled power of business and finance. The muckrakers were journalistic supporters of the Progressives, the middle-class counterpart to the more agrarian Populists. The efforts of these reformers were fostered by the growing numbers of magazines seeking to enlarge their circulations, particularly during the first two decades of this century. For example, *McClure's Magazine* became the leading outlet for reformist material. Muckraking investigative reporters such as David Graham Phillips, Frank Norris, Lincoln Steffens, Upton Sinclair, Ida Tarbell, and others rallied to expose irresponsibility rampant in industry, as in Tarbell's damning *History of the Standard Oil Company* and Steffens' *The Shame of the Cities.* Books such as Norris' *The Pit* (1903) and Sinclair's *The Jungle* (1906) fostered a national discussion, which led to passage of the Pure Food and Drug Act and the Federal Meat Inspection Act of 1906, two major victories for Progressive reform.

Indeed, the Progressive movement influenced American life so decisively from the 1890s through World War I that historians have labeled the period the Progressive Era. Benjamin Parke DeWitt's *The Progressive Movement: A Non-partisan, Comprehensive Discussion of Current Tendencies in American Politics,* first published in 1915 and now reprinted with a new introduction by Arthur Mann, despite often being overlooked by later scholars, remains a particularly useful contemporary analysis of Progressivism's manifestations in various political parties. Although a true believer in the reform effort, DeWitt wrote soberly and without sentimentalism about its impact on the U.S. political scene. Compare this to the cogent outline found in *The Progressive Movement: Its Principles and Its Programme* by Samuel Duncan-Clark, published in 1913, and the more recent reassessment in Robert M. Cruden's *Ministers of Reform: The Progressives' Achievement in American Civilization, 1889–1920.*

About the same time, Populism culminated in the formation of yet another party organization that despite a relatively brief existence in the 1890s had a lasting effect on American politics and society. An outstanding biography-history of the life of the movement's foremost spokesman is *Populism and Politics: William Alfred Peffer and the People's Party* by Peter H. Argersinger. The book documents how Populism succumbed to the very factors in American politics that it sought to destroy: prejudice, corruption, indifference, expediency, and elite manipulation.

Increasingly sophisticated lobby efforts by middle-class reformers and labor interests over time encouraged a rethinking of the public interest. For example, the rising importance of public relations, as Walter Lippmann notes in *Drift and Mastery*, by 1914 reflected dramatic changes not only in the public perception of business but also in management attitudes toward corporate social responsibility. Readers further interested in the propaganda of the Populist and Progressive movements should consult *Progressivism and Muckraking* by Louis Filler, part of a bibliographic series issued by the R. R. Bowker Company. While the emphasis is on in-print materials, there is much valuable commentary and annotation for the person interested in these traditional undercurrents in U.S. history extending from early roots to the contemporary political and news scenes. Appended are useful author, subject, and title indexes.

World War I

The "war to end all wars" failed to accomplish that goal but does mark a major break with the past. The public lies about national aims, the wasteful policy of attrition, and the wearing down of social barriers as the carnage continued help explain the onset of postwar disillusionment. Each side emphasized propaganda but differed in its approach toward the United States. An excellent resource is "German Propaganda in the United States, 1914–1917," a doctoral dissertation completed by David Hirst at Northwestern University in 1962. It identifies the major propaganda agencies and their leaders and also analyzes pro-German reportage as it appeared in books, films, pamphlets, periodicals, and newspapers (including the *New York Evening Mail* secretly purchased by representatives of the Kaiser in 1915). A graduate thesis by Elizabeth Gaines, "*The Fatherland*: An American Vehicle for German Propaganda, 1914–1917," presents an independent analysis of another publication. Gaines' review indicates that the four major propaganda themes stressed by George S. Viereck's publication were maintaining U.S. neutrality, promoting closer U.S.-German political and commercial ties, warning of the dangers of an entangling alliance with Great Britain, and exposing the pro-Ally bias of U.S. news media.

In studying various movements, one often overlooks the people behind the propaganda. This is unfortunate, for very often these men and women prove more interesting than the dogmas they attempt to spread. A case in point is Phyllis Keller's unusual *States of Belonging: German-American Intellectuals and the First World War*. Keller tracks the impact of World War I as a decisive turning point for individuals representative of Western civilization in her illuminating combination of cultural, governmental, and psychological history. She explores the conflicting group loyalties and allegiances of three similar men who chose different political paths: Viereck, the poet-publicist embracing the German side; Hugo Munsterberg, opting for the middle of the road; and Hermann Hagedorn, also a writer, turning to American superpatriotism. Viereck himself later published several works in which he describes his career. See, for example, his *Spreading Germs of Hate* and *My Flesh and Blood: A Lyric Autobiography with Indiscreet Annotations*.

Unlike the Germans, who attempted to keep the United States out of the war, leaders in the United Kingdom sought U.S. intervention. Their ultimate success is chronicled in Horace C. Peterson's *Propaganda for War: The Campaign against American Neutrality, 1914–1917*, James D. Squires' *British Propaganda at Home and in the United States from 1914 to 1917*, and Cate Haste's *Keep the Home Fires*

Burning: Propaganda in the First World War. Of the three, Peterson's remains the most definitive and despite the passage of years holds up well in its basic approach. Extensive notes and ten pages of bibliographic references are also useful, although the index is inadequate. Squires' slim book is largely a summary of other works but presents a serviceable and occasionally brilliant outline of the topic. While Haste emphasizes internal propaganda in Britain rather than that designed for overseas consumption, the book benefits from inclusion of thirty-seven illustrations and particularly incisive chapters describing the nature of propaganda in World War I, the impact of prewar images on later propaganda efforts, the organizational machinery used by the British government to mobilize the press and other propaganda cooperators, and the long-term implications that the propaganda onslaught unleashed by England had for postwar stability. This latter theme is treated in greater depth by George C. Bruntz in *Allied Propaganda and the Collapse of the German Empire in 1918*, which despite occasional lapses in the quality of the translation from the original German is objective and well documented. See also the representative studies by Victor S. Mamatey, *The United States and East Central Europe, 1914–1918: A Study in Wilsonian Diplomacy and Propaganda*, which utilizes printed sources, State Department files, plus diaries of key governmental officials and foreign materials to describe the contradictory U.S. policies and propaganda messages that contributed to the breakup of the Hapsburg Empire; Arthur Posonby, *Falsehood in War-time*, which, although brief, exposes the fabrications, distortions, and official-unofficial lies circulated by the belligerent powers; James M. Read, *Atrocity Propaganda, 1914–1919*, an excellent, comprehensive summary of the motives, methods, and notorious untruths widely disseminated during the war and after; Albert R. Buchanan, "European Propaganda and American Public Opinion, 1914–1917," a dissertation; and George T. Blakey, *Historians on the Homefront: American Propagandists for the Great War*.

The American propaganda effort spearheaded by George Creel is well recounted in a number of works. The standard history, *Words That Won the War: The Story of the Committee on Public Information, 1917–1919* by James R. Mock and Cedric Larson, is based on the papers of the CPI now in the National Archives. The authors trace the background on American public opinion and the coming of wartime censorship, the committee's use of various media in cooperating with educators, labor organizations, and corporate leaders to create an effective internal propaganda campaign, as well as "the fight for the mind of mankind" overseas. Although there is no bibliography as such, the notes are well organized and are supplemented with numerous illustrations. A more recent scholarly reinterpretation of the CPI is contained in Stephen L. Vaughn's *Holding Fast the Inner Lines: Democracy, Nationalism, and the Committee on Public Information*. This 397-page tome, issued as a supplementary volume to the Papers of Woodrow Wilson series, concentrates on the domestic operations of the CPI. While covering much of the same ground as Mock and Larson, the book is an important addition to the literature of propaganda administration. An extensive bibliography is appended, along with an intriguing, twenty-page comparative essay on primary and secondary sources.

While the overall communicative structure of advertising changed over time, as Robert L. Craig documents in his doctoral dissertation, many individuals such as Creel willingly defended the need for government involvement in the emerging field. The CPI leader proudly recounts his experiences in *How We Advertised America: The First Telling of the Amazing Story of the Committee on Public Information That Carried the Gospel of Americanism to Every Corner of the Globe*. Despite Creel's jingoism, evident from the title he chose, this is an important work since Creel reveals the congressional attempt to suppress his public report describing the true nature of the CPI's propaganda activities. Creel himself was unapologetic for his wartime activities and details the history of the CPI's domestic and foreign sections along with an account of the unhappy period of demobilization. A documentary listing of CPI publications along with photographs and an index make this a valuable reference. Creel also later wrote an autobiography, *Rebel at Large: Recollections of Fifty Crowded Years*, in which he reviews his World War I experiences.

For further reference readers may wish to peruse "American Foreign Propaganda in World War I," a relevant doctoral study by Jackson Giddens; and Kent and Gretchen Kreuter's *An American Dissenter: The Life of Algie Martin Simons, 1870–1950*, a fascinating biography tracing the intellectual odyssey of one of the journalists who founded the American socialist movement. Simons' subsequent disillusionment led him to work in World War I for the ultrapatriotic CPI and later as a researcher and pamphleteer attacking health insurance on behalf of the American Medical Association.

The Interwar Period, 1919–1941

The Bolshevik victory in Russia and other radical uprisings in Europe following World War I caused the United States to be swept by a wave of fear that revolution could similarly happen here. This paranoia was fueled by release of sensational propaganda emanating from supposedly responsible governmental agencies as much as by left- and right-wing extremist groups. The standard account of this phenomenon is Robert Murray's meticulously researched *Red Scare: A Study in National Hysteria, 1919–1920*. Although the federal government conducted several hearings and issued a report on foreign propaganda activities in the United States (see the bibliography for a selective listing of important U.S. documents on communist and Nazi propaganda), the most complete and detailed published repository of radical propaganda literature is found in a four-volume report released in 1920 by a New York State Senate committee chaired by Clayton R. Lusk. The resulting *Revolutionary Radicalism: Its History, Purpose, and Tactics* ("Lusk Report") totals 10,983 pages and is a unique collation of original documents, manifestos, and the like. Care, however, must be maintained in utilizing this collection since the conclusions reached by the committee members on the basis of their investigation are open to question.

While much has been written about the growth of the Ku Klux Klan during these years, relatively little has been said about the propaganda methods utilized by its leaders in building their organization. John Shotwell's thesis, "Crystalizing Public Hatred: Ku Klux Klan Public Relations in the Early 1920s," is the first detailed study of the effective, though sometimes nefarious, campaign waged by the Klan to influence key opinion leaders and elites.

Also of interest is Ralph Droz Casey's pioneering doctoral study of propaganda in the 1928 election. Most of the key studies chronicling the very effective use of mass communication by the Franklin D. Roosevelt administration for political purposes are referenced later and in a later section on media. Worth noting here is "The Propaganda Program of the National Recovery Administration," Carol Jean Holgren's unpublished 1962 thesis investigating the NRA as an example of government abuse of its public trust during the 1930s. This is must reading for the topic, particularly for its treatment of the New Deal program as a harbinger of a type of American fascism.

Isolationism vs. Interventionism

A book by Justus Doenecke, *Anti-interventionism: A Bibliographical Introduction to Isolationism and Pacifism from World War I to the Early Cold War*, provides a long-needed critical overview to the literature. This is the place to start in sorting out what has been written about those opposed to "foreign military adventures." Readers interested in the interventionist versus isolationist controversy leading up to the U.S. alliance with Britain and the Soviet Union also might wish to consult Selig Adler, *The Isolationist Impulse: Its Twentieth Century Reaction*. It is an accessible, classic text that attempts to place the history of American isolationism in context with other developments and forces active in the world. The book serves as a good narrative to the philosophy that connected La Follette's Progressive Party with later developments such as the Nye Committee antiwar investigation of 1934 and the subsequent Neutrality Law that (unsuccessfully) sought to keep America out of overseas conflicts. Special attention is given to Charles Lindbergh's involvement with the America First Committee and the post-World War II reemergence of isolationism, culminating in the dramatic anticommunist hearings chaired by Senator Joseph McCarthy in the 1950s. While Adler is not particularly sympathetic with the conservative and Populist views that underscored isolationist thought, he does summarize well the key underlying issues that troubled American society while the nation rose to prominence as a world power. The notes and bibliography are still pertinent.

Adler's reading of history should be compared to Harold Lavine and James Wechsler, *War Propaganda and the United States*, originally prepared for the Institute for Propaganda Analysis in 1940 and subsequently reprinted in several editions; Walter Johnson, *The Battle against Isolation*; Letty Bergstrom, "The Battle for America: German-English Language Propaganda in the U.S. from 1933 to 1941"; Jane Schwar, "Interventionist Propaganda and Pressure Groups in the United States, 1937–1941," a detailed 1973 doctoral study of prewar organizations actively encouraging U.S. involvement in Europe; and Michele Flynn Stenejhem, *An American First: John T. Flynn and the America First Committee*. The latter details the career and philosophy of one of the nation's leading revisionist journalists, concentrating on the 1940–1941 period, when Flynn sought to strengthen the U.S. commitment to neutrality. Six appendixes, more than 100 cited references, and an extensive bibliography help provide access to other relevant works. Also of some interest is Larry Ceplair's *Under the Shadow of War: Fascism, Anti-Fascism, and Marxists, 1918–1939*, which analyzes the failure of the antifascist movement during the interwar years; and Alan Brinkley's *Voices of Protest: Huey Long, Father Coughlin and the Great Depression*, a highly praised study of "two fascinating, disturbing political figures whose brief but vast popularity explains much about Depression-age America."

World War II

Of course, everything changed following the attack on Pearl Harbor by the Japanese. The resulting avalanche of books can overwhelm the reader interested in pursuing propaganda issues from the war years. Two of the more interesting, in that they concentrate on propaganda as a creative cultural phenomenon, are John Morton Blum's *V Was for Victory: Politics and American Culture during World War II* and Richard R. Lingeman's *Don't You Know There's a War On? The American Home Front, 1941–1945*. The former is an intriguing (if somewhat fawning) look at the legacy of FDR's presidency in shaping American popular culture. The first fifty pages detail the efforts by the Office of War Information to sell the war domestically. Also discussed in this serious account written by a Yale history professor are other official (and unofficial) propaganda activities, including a particularly trenchant review of wartime popular novels. Despite the catchy title of Lingeman's book, his is more than simply a nostalgic overview. Written in an evocative style, *There's a War On* is a solidly researched and richly detailed history of the war years. Included is a discussion of the propagandistic and escapist purposes to which books, motion pictures, comics, and music were put in cooperation with the government.

Several excellent studies covering visual aspects of the propaganda war have appeared in recent years, among them J. Darracott and B. Loftus, *Second World War Posters*; Denis Judd, *Posters of World War Two*; Anthony Rhodes, *Propaganda—The Art of Persuasion: World War II*; and Zbynek Zeman, *Selling the War: Art and Propaganda in World War II*. Darracott and Loftus concentrate on materials from the Imperial War Museum. Although there are some inaccuracies, as well as mediocre integration of the lengthy text and pictorial matter, Judd does provide a basic introduction to the use of posters. Rhodes tends to follow a similar organization to that of Judd (with long sections by country, including the United States), but coverage is broader, with more than 270 color and a like number of black-and-white illustrations superbly reproduced in a lavish, oversize 9" × 12" volume. Rhodes also gives attention to recordings, radio, and the cinema as propaganda channels, noting how different nations dealt with common themes. Additionally, there are an afterword by Daniel Lerner on the American psychological warfare campaign against Germany and a fifteen-page filmographic essay, as well as a short bibliography and complete index. Zeman, an authority on Nazi propaganda, reprints 100 of the most effective wartime posters issued by Allied and Axis propagandists (with an emphasis on European rather than American contributions). The strength of the work is in his analysis of what such visual propaganda reveals about the political, military, and moral conditions that lay behind it. The text itself is brief, supplemented with a limited bibliography and index.

Highly critical of U.S. policy is Benjamin Colby's *'Twas a Famous Victory: Deception and Propaganda in the War with Germany*. The author argues in common with several other revisionist historians that Roosevelt deliberately deceived the American people by telling them that American survival—like Britain's—depended on U.S. entry into the war. After reviewing administration cover-ups of

World War II propaganda poster. Courtesy of the Library
of Congress

Soviet atrocities and distortions of Hitler's true war aims, Colby asserts that Roosevelt bears the blame for the needless deaths of thousands of GIs through his propaganda policy designed to cause war. Mobilization of American media (through such institutions as the OWI, the Writers War Board, and the Hollywood studios), again to create hatred of the Germans and build enthusiasm for the alliance with the Soviets, is also covered. Colby, a former *New York Times* and Associated Press staff journalist, organizes his case well but relies largely on secondary sources for his evidence. That there was a secret conspiracy between Roosevelt and Churchill, however, is now known. The links between the highly clandestine British Security Coordination organization and the American OSS were revealed following the declassification of a number of sensitive wartime documents in recent years. The standard recitals include R. Harris Smith, *OSS: The Secret History of America's First Central Intelligence Agency*, and Bradley F. Smith, *The Shadow Warriors: O.S.S. and the Origins of the C.I.A.* For an authoritative account of British intelligence and propaganda activities both before and during World War II, see William Stevenson's *A Man Called Intrepid: The Secret War*.

Four major studies document the history of the OWI. See Allan M. Winkler, *The Politics of Propaganda: The Office of War Information, 1942–1945*; Lamar MacKay, "Domestic Operations of the Office of War Information in World War

II"; Robert L. Bishop, "The Overseas Branch of the Office of War Information"; and Sydney Weinberg's massive "Wartime Propaganda in a Democracy: America's Twentieth Century Information Agencies." Winkler's text, drawn heavily from original documents in the National Archives, is organized into four chapters describing the OWI's origins, its use of propaganda at home (where the OWI was prohibited from distributing materials directly to the public), political propaganda abroad, and overseas military propaganda. As all four authors make clear, the OWI was limited by its temporary wartime mandate and the fact that it had powerful congressional enemies. Also hampering the agency (which at its height had 11,000 employees) were the lack of clear-cut U.S. goals other than unconditional victory, the failure to develop long-range policies for the postwar period, personality conflicts within the OWI itself, and continued public distrust of government-issued propaganda. Bishop's study is particularly useful for its discussion of the operations of the Voice of America, directed originally by OWI's Overseas Branch.

In a heavily annotated (and at times repetitious) history with the virtues and weaknesses common to doctoral studies converted to books, Leila J. Rupp's *Mobilizing Women for War: German and American Propaganda, 1939–1945* nevertheless adds dimension to our understanding of the effectiveness of mobilization propaganda. Rupp contrasts the image of women carried within popular periodicals and other media with the reality of wartime conditions in both countries. Working from a feminist perspective, she demonstrates that such propaganda was more extensive in the United States and proved critically important in converting women to industrial work so that men could be freed to fight overseas. Scrupulous documentation and a wide-ranging use of sources are confirmed by an extensive, fifty-page bibliography.

The U.S. military's postwar de-Nazification efforts at reeducating the German people to support democracy are reported in Albert Norman's *Our German Policy: Propaganda and Culture*. The focus of the book, which relies heavily on primary sources acquired by the author while a member of the occupation government, is a history of the policies and practices applied by U.S. forces in reshaping the media and cultural institutions of a defeated Germany. The Western allies slowly abandoned all systematic reeducation attempts and eventually resorted to a series of piecemeal measures. More recent scholarship investigating this period is found in "Propaganda and the Control of Information in Occupied Germany: The U.S. Information Control Division at Radio Frankfort 1945–1949," a Ph.D. dissertation completed by Lawrence Raymond Hartenian at Rutgers University in 1984; and in *The Political Re-education of Germany and Her Allies after World War II*, edited by Nicholas Pronay and Keith Wilson.

Psychological Warfare

Propaganda as a manipulative art naturally has an interest in psychology and human attitudes. An offshoot of World War II, the Korea and Vietnam conflicts, and the establishment of a permanent U.S. governmental news and propaganda ministry in the United States Information Agency has increased emphasis on what is known as psychological warfare or psy-war. A basic introduction is Terence H. Qualter's *Propaganda and Psychological Warfare*, which offers both a philosophical and historical treatment of the subject. Daniel Lerner's *Sykewar: Psychological War-*

fare against Germany, D-Day to VE-Day is the definitive history of Allied wartime efforts in the European theater by an actively involved scholar. Chapters discuss policy, personnel, media, operations, and effectiveness. See also Charles G. Cruickshank's *The Fourth Arm: Psychological Warfare 1938–1945*, emphasizing the British perspective. Writers such as Murray Dyer in *The Weapon on the Wall: Rethinking Psychological Warfare* and Robert T. Holt and Robert W. van de Velde in *Strategic Psychological Operations and American Foreign Policy* have questioned the assumptions underlying American propaganda and psy-war overseas by arguing that U.S. naïveté and overreliance on military aspects of political communication undercut the effectiveness of messages to other peoples. Other basic references include Paul Linebarger's *Psychological Warfare*, a very useful summary of thinking on the topic through time of publication, and William E. Dougherty and Morris Janowitz's *Psychological Warfare Casebook*, which during the Vietnam years served as the chief psy-warrior text. Updating these are Joseph J. McDonough's "Analysis of Official U.S. Military Psychological Warfare Efforts in the Vietnam Conflict," Phillip Paul Katz's *A Systematic Approach to Psyop Information*, and the 1982 book edited by Ron D. McLaurin called *Military Propaganda: Psychological Warfare and Operations*. Less valuable is Charles Roetter's historical *The Art of Psychological Warfare, 1914–1945*, which lacks notes or bibliography and is rather shallow in its coverage.

A review of case studies makes it clear that the "hypodermic theory" model (a blatant campaign organized from the top down in order to inject the populace with information) does not work particularly well and in no way guarantees message reception, understanding, acceptance, or desired action. This points to the central problem facing psychological warfare and propaganda researchers: how does one adequately measure effectiveness? In contrast to advertising—where syndicated research is widely available because of the competitive needs of media, agencies, and clients—when one wades through the mass of military propaganda literature generated since World War I, this area is usually glibly, simplistically, and inadequately addressed. Even in the Korean conflict, very little evaluation was carried out. Since Vietnam, however, the beginnings of a true social science effort to evaluate the output of psychological warfare message systems and activities have been evident.

Recommended reading includes Edward Hunter's *Brainwashing: The Story of the Men Who Defied It*, a lucidly reported popular account of the horror techniques used against American POWs in Korea; more recently supplemented by Edgar Schein and others, *Coercive Persuasion: A Socio-Psychological Analysis of the "Brainwashing" of American Civilian Prisoners by the Chinese Communists*; Alan W. Scheflin and Edward M. Opton Jr., *The Mind Manipulators*; and John Marks' shocking *The Search for the "Manchurian Candidate": The CIA and Mind Control—The Story of the Agency's Secret Efforts to Control Human Behavior*. Schein notes that the essential prerequisite is to close off the outside environment. Once this condition is met, as in a POW camp or closed psychiatric ward, all kinds of successful manipulations are possible. This is one reason that the United States placed so much reliance on broadcasting in Vietnam in order to break down the local communication structure and replace it with a tightly controlled new one. However, as Thomas William Hoffer points out in his massive two-volume dissertation, "Broadcasting in an Insurgency Environment: USIA in Vietnam, 1965–1970," U.S. advisers underestimated competing propaganda strategies used by the insurgents, who acted effectively to limit U.S.–South Vietnam efforts. Adding to the value of Hoffer's analysis are extensive appendixes that reprint a number of rare government reports, memoranda, and other documents. Also worthwhile is Peter Braestrup's massive, two-volume analysis of media performance, *Big Story! How the American Press and Television Reported and Interpreted the Crises of Tet 1968 in Vietnam and Washington.*

U.S. Information Agency

For a quick introduction and independent overview see the special report "USIA: A Battered but Powerful Propaganda Tool" in *U.S. News & World Report.* Note that the USIA operates an Office of Public Liaison (Washington, D.C. 20547). This publishes a free newsletter called *USIA Update* and provides fact sheets and other materials describing current agency activities. Since 1953 the USIA has also issued a series of reports to Congress that contain a wealth of statistical and policy information on operations of the agency, including Voice of America broadcasting (see later). Also of interest are the independent oversight studies prepared by the General Accounting Office for congressional hearings on budget requests before the House Committee on Foreign Affairs, often providing extensive coverage of current issues.

Many of the relevant data, along with an expert introduction to working with government documents, have been collected in *The Mass Media: Aspen Institute Guide to Communication Industry Trends* by Christopher H. Sterling and Timothy R. Haight. Dr. Sterling, as noted earlier, also edits an indispensable monthly review of new literature called *Communication Booknotes*, which features a special annual issue summarizing the major government studies from the previous year of interest to researchers.

Of the available histories, the most valuable books on the USIA include Robert Elder's *The Information Machine: The United States Information Agency and American Foreign Policy*, John W. Henderson's *The United States Information Agency*, and Leo Bogart's *Premises for Propaganda: The United States Information Agency's Operating Assumptions in the Cold War.* The latter, for example, is based on 142 interviews with key USIA personnel conducted during the 1950s. The book is actually an abridgment of a five-volume report that remained restricted for more than twenty years. These sources are further supplemented by personalized subjective accounts such as Edward W. Barrett's *Truth Is Our Weapon* and Thomas C. Sorenson's *The World War: The Story of American Propaganda.* Critical studies of the USIA also include George N. Gordon and Irving A. Falk, *The War of Ideas: America's International Identity Crisis*, Eugene W. Castle's polemical *Billions, Blunders and Baloney: The Fantastic Story of How Uncle Sam Is Squandering Your Money Overseas*, and L. Skvortsov, *The Ideology and Tactics of Anti-Communism*, which contains an interesting section entitled "The Aims and Tactics of Propaganda," written from a pro-Soviet perspective.

The Voice of America, Radio Free Europe, Radio Liberty, Radio Marti, Worldnet, and Other Broadcasting Efforts

The success of Voice of America encouraged other post-1945 efforts once the Cold War got under way. Former OSS officers used secret CIA funding to establish Radio Free Europe (1950) and Radio Liberty several years later. Much of this history is summarized in an important 1983 work by Sig Mickelson, *America's Other Voice: The Story of Radio Free Europe and Radio Liberty*. The former president of CBS News, who headed RFE/RL from 1975 to 1978, argues the widely presented case that such broadcasts provide not propaganda but "free information" to censored societies behind the Iron Curtain.

In recent years there has been a greater effort—particularly by the USIA—to upgrade communications equipment and take advantage of new technological advances. Worldnet, for example, is an interactive audiovisual satellite service competing against foreign efforts to influence media coverage affecting public opinion in Europe and Asia. USIA's Express File was inaugurated in 1987 to transmit news and information about the United States directly into the newsrooms of foreign news organizations (wire services, newspapers, magazines, and broadcasters) over the communications circuits of United Press International (UPI). To limit potential criticism, the Express File is clearly labeled as USIA material. An estimated 130 million adults listen to direct broadcasts by the Voice of America at least once a week, according to a 1986 survey released by the USIA, an increase of 11 million people over 1985. Not included in the figures are audiences for the VOA-operated Radio Marti (broadcasting to Cuba), VOA Europe, or rebroadcasts of VOA programs on foreign radio stations.

In the absence of definitive legal controls over international radio broadcasting, nations may engage in diplomacy, jamming, counterpropaganda, and other responses. For standard overviews of U.S. government radio and television propaganda, consult David Abshire, *International Broadcasting: A New Dimension in Western Diplomacy*; Julian Hale, *Radio Power: Propaganda and International Broadcasting*; Maury Lisann, *Broadcasting to the Soviet Union: International Politics and Radio*; K.R.M. Short, *Western Broadcasting over the Iron Curtain*; plus a number of other government reports and unpublished scholarly works listed in the bibliography. The Board for International Broadcasting, for example, now coordinates the various nonmilitary overseas radio and television services operated by the government. It has issued a series of useful *Annual Reports* (1974 to the present), which, when combined with the published record of the House of Representatives Committee on Foreign Affairs *Oversight Hearings*, document activities of Radio Liberty and Radio Free Europe.

Broadcasting to Latin America by U.S. interests dates back to the 1920s, as pointed out by Fred Fejes in *Imperialism, Media and the Good Neighbor: New Deal Foreign Policy and United States Shortwave Broadcasting to Latin America*, published in 1986. Unfortunately, Fejes' work is not definitive, for he overlooks several major collections of source material and inadequately documents his claims of U.S. dominance. Worse, he fails to explore the actual content of American broadcasts and nowhere defines imprecise terminology such as "cultural diplomacy" or "propaganda." Two independent views on the more current Radio Marti experience are

Hazel G. Warlaumont's 1986 thesis, "Radio Marti and the U.S.-Cuban Radio War: Strategies Used in the Absence of Definitive Legal Controls over International Broadcasting as Compared with Strategies Used in the U.S.-USSR Radio War," and Howard H. Frederick's *Cuban-American Radio Wars: Ideology in International Telecommunications.* Both present the story of pro- and anti-Castro radiocasts, although the latter book reflects a leftist "progressive" approach to content analysis in propounding a "theory of inter-ideological state propaganda apparatuses."

Other Recent Latin American Developments

Beginning in 1985, the State Department engaged in a secret effort to generate congressional and public support for President Reagan's Central American policies. As part of this campaign, the State Department's Office of Public Diplomacy for Latin America and the Caribbean began awarding numerous contracts to outside public relations consultants to help "favorably influence" the image of the Nicaraguan Contra rebels. A National Security Council memo outlining some of these activities by Oliver North to National Security Adviser Robert McFarlane, "Timing and the Nicaraguan Resistance Vote," dated March 20, 1985, was released two years later as a result of the Iran-Contra hearings. A reprint of the complete memo and twelve-page confidential chronology is available from *Propaganda Review* in San Francisco. In 1987 these and related covert "white propaganda" activities were held by the General Accounting Office, the investigative arm of Congress, to violate congressional restrictions curbing the use of federal funds for publicity or propaganda purposes.

Much of this government effort (which also included authorizing the FBI to conduct surveillance on individuals prominently associated with support for immigration amnesty for Salvadorans and other Latin American refugees) stemmed from frustrations by federal policymakers over the successful propaganda efforts of pro-Sandinista supporters in the United States. See, for example, two monographs by the leftist Institute for Media Analysis published in 1987: *The Reagan Administration and Nicaragua: How Washington Constructs Its Case for Counterrevolution in Central America* by Professors Noam Chomsky, Morris Morley, James Petras, and Michael Parenti; and *Packaging the Contras: A Case of CIA Disinformation* by Edgar Chamorro, former dean at the University of Central America and a direct descendant of four Nicaraguan presidents. Both argue that the U.S. government manipulated journalists and media institutions to create a false image of the "freedom fighter" rebels as "the democratic alternative" to Daniel Ortega's government. Three critical, yet well-documented, recent briefs upholding the administration's position include James L. Tyson, *Prophets or Useful Idiots? Church Organizations Attacking U.S. Central America Policy*; J. Michael Waller, "CISPES: A Terrorist Propaganda Network"; and Allan C. Brownfeld and J. Michael Waller, *The Revolution Lobby.* Are religious groups lobbying for radical political causes? Yes, says Tyson, who reports on the extensive propaganda and support network American churches have provided the Sandinista regime in Nicaragua as well as to Cuban-supported insurgencies in El Salvador and throughout Central America. The other studies by Waller listed earlier present overviews of the various organizations supporting dovish policy toward Latin America and the Caribbean, particularly their communication efforts to affect political decision making.

Intelligence

Decoding the garbled terminology of government-orchestrated propaganda campaigns and intelligence operations often requires a guidebook. Three paperbacks that help are Henry S.A. Becket, *The Dictionary of Espionage: Spookspeak into English*, incorporating little-known facts and interesting anecdotes in clear definitions to over 2,000 words of tradecraft used by covert organizations worldwide; Bob Burton, *Top Secret: A Clandestine Operator's Glossary of Terms*, identifying more than 800 common espionage terms; and Roy Colby, *A Communese-English Dictionary*, containing over 1,000 Marxist expressions and idioms de-semanticized for anticommunist audiences. Compare the latter book to the more sympathetic *A Dictionary of Marxist Thought*, edited by Tom Bottomore. While propaganda is inexplicably neglected here, a useful review of ideology is included. So while these works are not necessarily individually definitive, they have collectively proven helpful.

For an in-depth, "up close and personal" introduction to the major superpowers, readers should consult Jeffrey T. Richelson's *The U.S. Intelligence Community* and *Sword and Shield: Soviet Intelligence and Security Apparatus*. These superb companion volumes dispense with rhetorical excess to document the organizational structure and activities that each country would prefer to remain hidden. While differing in philosophy and approach, both powers agree that they have a right to manipulate mass opinion and intervene in the affairs of other countries. Although the CIA gets most of the publicity, actually the American intelligence community is much broader and includes numerous lesser-known agencies described here. Depending on point of view, you will either be reassured or concerned over the extent of activities ranging from information gathering, to policy/issue management, to covert activities (including propaganda) that government employees undertake to enforce U.S. interests. Soviet propaganda measures are directed by the Politburo and Central Party Secretariat through an International Information Department linking various news organizations and embassy information departments; an International Department operating clandestine radio stations in addition to coordinating foreign communist parties, front organizations and friendship societies; and the KGB, specializing in more direct active measures. These are must reading for the serious student. Richelson's *American Espionage and the Soviet Target*, published in 1987, is also recommended.

Other provocative studies include James Bamford's very revealing *The Puzzle Palace: A Report on NSA, America's Most Secret Agency*, republished by Penguin Books in 1983 with a new afterword outlining government attempts to quash the book. Philip Agee's *Inside the Company: A CIA Diary* created an uproar when first published in 1975 by chronicling the author's growing estrangement as it described classified operations in which he participated. Very downbeat is Agee's latest book, coedited with Louis Wolf. *Dirty Work: The CIA in Western Europe* exposes the seamy side of American espionage, including the secret portfolio of dirty work done under the guise of national security—from the routine planting of phony news stories to assassinations and the overthrow of governments. Jonathan Kwitny's *The Crimes of Patriots: A True Tale of Dope, Dirty Money, and the CIA* also persuasively argues that a secret government does exist, actively engaging in widespread corruption and media manipulation. One of the more balanced books by disgruntled former agents incorporating newly declassified materials is the updated 1983 version of *The CIA and the Cult of Intelligence* by Victor Marchetti and John D. Marks.

For a controversial overview of the William Casey era, see Bob Woodward's *Veil: The Secret Wars of the CIA, 1981–1987*. He gives the impression that "ideological overdrive" by Casey on the subject of Soviet active measures led the United States wrongfully to upgrade its own propaganda efforts. This supplements—yet contrasts with—the views of Ernest W. Lefever and Roy Godson, who concentrate on the troubled 1974–1979 period in *The CIA and the American Ethic: An Unfinished Debate*. The authors say that the arguments over CIA activities have proven inadequate. They believe that national media (led by the commercial television networks, which regularly criticized the CIA while giving scant attention to Soviet KGB activities) and individual congressmen were strongly influenced by an aggressive and well-financed "anti-intelligence lobby" determined to diminish American clandestine operations and covert action. Subsequently this distorted flow of information resulted in congressional restrictions that temporarily crippled CIA intelligence capabilities.

That lobby has not disappeared. The Institute for Media Analysis (IMA), for example, is a New York-based nonprofit organization formed in 1986. The IMA is devoted to monitoring, analyzing, and reporting on propaganda and disinformation, making available a newsletter entitled *Right to Know* and specialized monographs as noted earlier. Codirectors Ellen Ray and Bill Schaap are also the publishers of *Covert Action Information Bulletin*, which for more than a decade has critically covered the role of the intelligence community in the "worldwide power struggle."

Knowing what to believe can prove a serious problem. One example involves the attack on a Korean Airlines passenger plane by Soviet fighter defense forces, killing all on board, including a U.S. congressman. This proved a propaganda bonanza for the Reagan administration. But what actually occurred? Detailed studies include R. W. Johnson's *Shootdown: Flight 007 and the American Connection*, which indicates, in a chapter titled "The Media War," that U.S. officials misled the public and engaged in a cover-up; it is well complemented by Seymour M. Hersh's *"The Target Is Destroyed"—What Really Happened to Flight 007 and What America Knew about it*. The updated 1987 edition outlines a controversial, carefully researched account of the plane's secret spy mission describing "how intelligence is collected and abused as well as used."

Disinformation and Deception

Disinformation, according to Ladislav Bittman, is a false message leaked to the opponents in order to deceive the decision makers or the public. It works because it is deliberately designed to confirm the darkest suspicions of the recipients. It serves to convince people to believe what they already want to believe. Bittman should know, as he was intimately involved with creating such campaigns as deputy commander of the disinformation department of the Czechoslovak intelligence service. After the Soviet invasion of his country in 1968, Bittman left and received political asylum in the United States, where he now is on the faculty of Boston University. His two books, *The KGB and Soviet Disinformation: An Insider's View* and *The Deception Game*, are authoritative introductions to the theory and Marxist application of intelligence, black propaganda, and disinformation. Also valuable reading from specialists expert in the field is *Dezinformatsia: Active Measures in Soviet Strategy* by Richard H. Shultz and Roy Godson. Recent developments can be followed in *Disinformation and Subversion Update*, a new weekly newsletter addressing various themes relating to Soviet active measures campaigns and perceived incorrect reporting in the U.S. media.

Several KGB-initiated disinformation coups in 1980 proved the susceptivity of U.S. and world media to cleverly planted false stories. One involved a forged "Presidential Review Memorandum NSC 46," supposedly urging a tilt of U.S. policy toward total support for South Africa, complete with a program to monitor and divide American blacks to neutralize their political influence on this issue. Copies of the supposed document were widely circulated to black UN delegates and U.S. media outlets. Subsequent denials by confused Carter White House staffers proved so lame that they enhanced the credibility of the forgery. Another forged document, a State Department "dissent" paper that year recommended what was called the "Zimbabwe option" in El Salvador. This suggested that the United States could limit Soviet and Cuban influence by aiding the Marxist opposition to win them to the American side. A number of leftist columnists encouraged the administration to the heed the recommendations before the window of opportunity to influence the guerrillas was lost. Only later was it shown to be a Soviet-manipulated, disinformation campaign.

More specifically focusing on KGB activities inside the United States are several in-depth studies: John Barron's KGB: *The Secret Work of Soviet Secret Agents* and the more recent *KGB Today: The Hidden Hand* are well-documented essential reading for those interested in digging below the surface to study systematic Soviet attempts to influence U.S. mass opinion. James L. Tyson, *Target America: The Influence of Communist Propaganda on U.S. Media,* by the former research director of Time-Life International, is also a highly regarded conservative critique outlining the extent of communist influence in American mass communication. *Soviet Hypocrisy and Western Gullibility* by Sydney Hook, Vladimir Bukovsky, and Paul Hollander discusses the susceptibility of intellectuals, religious leaders, and politicians to Soviet propaganda, and even lies about totalitarianism in the twentieth century. Each essayist, writing from personal experience, decries what is called the hypocrisy of Soviet life and information, and the silly—but by no means harmless—gullibility of many Westerners to the ideology of Marx and the glasnost of Gorbachev.

Soviet Influence Activities, issued in 1987 by the U.S. Department of State's Bureau of Intelligence and Research, describes active measures by the USSR in America and names Soviet front groups spreading disinformation aimed at discrediting the United States. The Soviet AIDS disinformation campaign as well as propaganda about the USSR's role in Afghanistan are examined in great detail. This complements *Contemporary Soviet Propaganda and Information,* a 337-page report summarizing the research findings of experts brought together by the U.S. Department of State and the Central Intelligence Agency in 1985; and *Soviet*

Covert Action (The Forgery Offensive) and *Soviet Active Measures*, published records of oversight hearings conducted in 1980 and 1982 by the U.S. House of Representatives Permanent Select Committee on Intelligence.

Terrorism/Counterterrorism

Terrorism, accentuated by the events of September 11, 2001, has often been described as "propaganda of the deed"—a strategy used by activists when their socially acceptable information efforts are inadequate to effect change. However, it was not until 1970 that the term *terrorism* first entered the *New York Times Index*. Selecting the term *terrorist* rather than other options such as "freedom fighter," "member of a liberation front," "resistance leader," or even "guerrilla" implies that the specific action is illegitimate or criminal. On the other hand, use of one of the alternative labels encourages the reader, viewer, or listener to accept a particular incident—even if it involves kidnapping, bombing, or killing—as a legitimate attention-getting tactic in an unequal struggle for social justice.

Clearly, terrorism is not simply going to wither away. A solid introductory grounding to the phenomenon is found in *The Terrorism Reader*, edited in a new edition by Walter Laqueur and Yonah Alexander. The history of terrorism, including contemporary developments, is well covered. This should be compared to *Alchemists of Revolution: Terrorism in the Modern World* by Richard E. Rubenstein, offering "a clear-eyed look at the terrorist mentality, its origins, and consequences"; *The Never-Ending War: Terrorism in the 80's* by Christopher Dobson and Ronald Payne, with a who's who guide to terrorism today; and *Beating International Terrorism: An Action Strategy for Preemption and Punishment* by Stephen Sloan, which, despite being a short monograph, clearly defines issues and terminology before opting for military control of American antiterrorist activities.

Television has often been accused of promoting the cause of terrorist violence. Although written from a British perspective, or perhaps because of it, *Televising "Terrorism": Political Violence in Popular Culture* by Philip Schlesinger, Graham Murdock, and Philip Elliot might be profitably read by students and analysts in the United States. After discussing the work of critics on both the left and right, the book argues for a more sophisticated understanding of the way in which television coverage of terrorism is conducted. The authors also outline an approach to analysis that incorporates not only factual news coverage but also fictional representations that could be usefully applied in an American context.

Claire Sterling, *The Terror Network: The Secret War of International Terrorism*, and Edward S. Herman, *The Real Terror Network: Terrorism in Fact and Propaganda* come to opposite conclusions. Sterling's book supports the conservative position that most terrorism movements are globally interlocked and manipulated by KGB agent provocateurs to support Soviet aims indirectly. Herman disputes this U.S. government-supported "official" account, arguing that Sterling and those like her are right-wing Cold Warriors dispensing pseudoscientific disinformation to direct attention away from American-backed state terrorism in Latin America, Israel, South Africa, Indonesia, and other countries.

Also of interest is *Low Intensity Warfare: Counterinsurgency, Proinsurgency, and Antiterrorism in the 80s*, edited by Michael Klare and Peter Kornbluh. This brings together eight experts who investigate the nature and future of American war-fighting capabilities as they are reoriented toward unconventional conflict situations in the Third World—what the Pentagon calls "low-intensity warfare." The contributors are associated with three important Washington-based policy analysis centers: the Institute for Policy Studies, the Center for Defense Information, and the Carnegie Endowment for International Peace.

Ongoing scholarship is reported in *Terrorism*, a major new journal published by Taylor and Francis. This presents the results of original research by social scientists, humanists, public officials, and diplomats on the types, causes, consequences, control, and management of all forms of terrorism. The approach is interdisciplinary, with articles examining the historical, legal, sociological, psychological, philosophical, political, biological, and economic aspects of the subject.

Political Definitions

Dictionary of Modern Political Ideologies, edited by Michael A. Riff, is a sourcebook tracing the origins of most modern ideologies to ideas born of the European Enlightenment, particularly in the tumult of the French Revolution and its aftermath. Rather than simply offering a chronological history of various Western political movements, the contributors discuss the subsequent development of these ideas and their manifestation in approximately 200 distinct "isms" today. See also *Beyond Liberal and Conservative* by William S. Maddox and Stuart A. Lilie, which shows the need to incorporate populist and libertarian categories in demographic research if ideological diversity in the political terrain is to be effectively analyzed in the future. Another reference to consult is *Right Minds: A Sourcebook of American Conservative Thought* by Gregory Wolfe. This features a detailed bibliography of important conservative writings and serves as a convenient desktop reference to leaders, organizations, foundations, publishers, and so on (including addresses and phone numbers). More conventional is Louis Filler, *Dictionary of American Conservatism*, which should be consulted but does not really live up to its jacket billing as "the first complete guide to issues, people, events, organizations." For example, it includes Jimmy Carter but leaves out Willis Carto and Liberty Lobby.

Pressure/Power Special Interest Groups and Lobbying

If you have been in a major American air terminus, you have likely encountered dedicated individuals distributing attractive books, magazines, and *The New Federalist* newspaper—all literature representing the political philosophies of Lyndon LaRouche and his supporters. Given the growth of the government sector in our society, it is not surprising that such special interests attempt to influence the opinions of selected audiences. Lobbying actually is protected in the First Amendment, a right jealously guarded by those seeking redress of grievances. For example, opponents of Judge Robert Bork's nomination to the Supreme Court conducted an unprecedented public campaign to prevent his confirmation in 1987. Heavy news coverage resulted from updated releases of polling data and a steady stream of other media events. Grassroots contact with senators was encouraged in broadcast and print ads as well as through sophisticated computerized phone lists used to direct calls to targeted homes. Organizational supporters of Bork such as We the People were outraged and responded by charging that the anti-Bork forces spent millions of dollars to create a hate campaign. Bork opponents such as the American Civil Liberties Union and the National Organization of Women shrugged off the criticism as sour grapes and said that they were clarifying the record to encourage democratic citizen participation in a decision with far-reaching social implications.

Literally hundreds of other policy think tanks such as the conservative Heritage Foundation or the liberal Brookings Institution compete for influence in government, media, and public opinion. Heritage, for example, sponsors seminars, liaisons with other like-minded organizations and academics, produces an *Annual Guide to Public Policy Experts*, coordinates testimony, lobbies, conducts studies, sponsors a booth at media trade conventions such as the annual meeting of the Radio-Television News Directors Association, and produces a wide variety of "audience positioned" informational materials. These range from a newsletter such as *Heritage Today*, summarizing activities and collating reprints of news articles mentioning the foundation and its members, to a prestigious, academic-style intellectual journal, *Policy Review*, to position papers and backgrounders on topical subjects and critical issues such as trade, national security, Taiwan, and the United Nations, to books on the merits of enterprise zones. Similarly, *Policy Analysis* is an interesting libertarian think-tank publication by the feisty Cato Institute, typically poking holes in conventional public policy arguments through well-thought-out summaries and alternative proposals.

Among the first to study this relationship of pressure groups and propaganda in depth was Harwood Childs, who assembled a series of topical papers by twenty-eight leading authorities and students for a special issue of the *Annals* of the American Academy of Political and Social Sciences in May 1935. Much of this was previously unpublished; although somewhat dated, it continues to have historical and theoretical interest. Also of historical relevance are *Interest Groups in American Politics* by L. Harmon Ziegler and Wayne C. Peak and *Pressure Groups in American Politics* by H. R. Mahood.

For current detailed overviews of 250 leading advocacy groups supplemented with commentaries by noted policy experts, see the latest edition of *Public Interest Profiles*, edited by Douglas J. Bergner of the Foundation for Public Affairs. *The Washington Lobby*, updated regularly and published by the staff of *Congressional Quarterly*, also provides an unbiased, comprehensive overview of contemporary lobbying tactics in the United States. Introductory material includes a compact history of lobbying and federal attempts to regulate it. Additional sections describe how the executive branch lobbies in behalf of the White House; trace the development and impact of political action committees (PACs); profile major business, labor, and public interest lobbies; and analyze the work of foreign lobbyist organizations working in the United States. There are an index and a detailed bibliography of pertinent books, articles, and documents. All in all, *The Washington Lobby* is mandatory reading for its subject.

If you ever wondered why Congress couldn't balance the budget and why money keeps getting spent on projects and programs you don't like, William Ashworth's *Under the Influence: Congress, Lobbies, and the American Pork-Barrel System* has the answer. The answer, of course, is that the pork barrel isn't just dams and other public works. It involves almost every decision made by Congress, particularly when questions of the public interest are raised. This is a no-nonsense guide to the reality of Washington lobbying and how self-interests couch their rhetoric to influence public policy. Additional information is in the report prepared by the Congressional Research Service for the U.S. Senate's Committee on Government Affairs, *Congress and Pressure Groups: Lobbying in a Modern Democracy*, published in 1986.

Detailed case studies can be especially instructive, as is the case with the fascinating *Showdown at Gucci Gulch: Lawmakers, Lobbyists, and the Unlikely Triumph of Tax Reform* by Jeffrey H. Birnbaum and Alan S. Murray. Probably the best and most critical survey of how the process can be manipulated by sophisticated insiders, however, is found in *Destroying Democracy: How Government Funds Partisan Politics* by James T. Bennett and Thomas J. DiLorenzo. They document how every year governments give hundreds of millions of taxpayer dollars to organizations that use the money for political advocacy—lobbying, campaigning, grassroots organizing, and more. Although Congress has prohibited the use of federal funds for political activities and lobbying, abuses of the law are widespread and flagrant. A 1987 study by the Postal Rate Commission, for example, found that 21 percent of nonprofit subsidized mail contains political advocacy.

Equally controversial is the impact of foreign lobbyists, who have often proved very adept at representing their national interests in American corridors of power. For example, in 1974 Arab nations began a coordinated program outlined in a highly confidential document, "Public Affairs Program for the Arab World," to spend as much as $15 million annually employing a network of Washington lobbyists, influential lawyers, public relations experts, political consultants, and other highly paid specialists to shift American public opinion away from the Israelis. How successful they have been is argued in *Pro-Arab Propaganda in America: Vehicles and Voices*, a research brief published by the Anti-Defamation League of B'nai B'rith. Contrast this with the challenging anti-Zionist thesis in *They Dare to Speak Out: People and Institutions Confront Israel's Lobby* by former Congressman Paul Findley.

Joining the traditional corridor lobbyists (an estimated 15,000 currently work Capitol Hill pleading causes for their clients) are increasing numbers of PACs, which utilize all available channels from personal contact to direct mail and advocacy advertising in order to create support for their business, labor, or ideological agenda. Corporations are barred by law from making direct political contributions but following a 1974 ruling of the Federal Election Commission that said that there was nothing illegal about businesses soliciting voluntary donations from employees for electoral purposes, the number of business PACs alone jumped from less than 100 to nearly 4,000. *National Trade and Professional Associations of the United States* has annual listings of more than 6,000 groups. While PACs are excluded from this work, they do appear in a companion directory issued yearly called *Washington Representatives*. Another useful research reference is the *Encyclopedia of Associations*, updated continuously and published in multiple volumes. This is the most complete guide to nonprofit membership organizations with national scope. Listed are the name, location, size, objectives, and other useful data for over 14,000 organizations. All of the preceding are thoroughly cross-referenced. Current editors are Karin E. Keak and Susan Boyles Martin.

Several recent studies analyze the rise and status of important contemporary movements. *Persuasion and Social Movements* by Charles J. Stewart, Craig Smith, and Robert E. Denton Jr. synthesizes previous research in the study of persuasion and applies the findings to investigations of current social movements (the radical right and pro-life movements) and non-traditional discourse (songs, slogans, and obscenities). Also worth looking at is Irwin Unger's *The Movement: A History of the American New Left, 1959–1972*, a concise, objective survey of the emergence and decline of the romanticized student political rebellion against middle-class values characterized by rock and roll, posters of Che Guevara, and marches against the war in Vietnam. Some of this same moral enthusiasm has been applied to tackling the problems of racism and poverty. See, for example, Robert Tomshoi's survey of the Hispanic immigration struggle in the sympathetic *The American Sanctuary Movement*.

Taking a very different topic, Joni Lovenduski and Joyce Outshoorn have edited *The New Politics of Abortion*. This is a useful guide to understanding the complexities of abortion arguments, networks, and pressure group activities as they influence political agendas here in the United States and Europe. Similarly, *The New Women's Movement: Feminism and Political Power in Europe and the U.S.A.*, edited by Drude Dahlerup, concentrates on how decentralized, grassroots organizing has been able to effect political change. Mary Frances Berry's *Why ERA Failed: Politics, Women's Rights, and the Amending Process of the Constitution* is a balanced analysis of the ERA campaign, placing its rise and fall in constitutional, political, and ideological contexts.

While the scandals facing some prominent televangelists have dominated the headlines, much religious activity of interest to propaganda researchers is happening behind the scenes. For specialized—if biased—looks at some of the more controversial organizations and activists, see Dave Hunt, *The Cult Explosion*; Marilyn Ferguson, *The Aquarian Conspiracy: Personal and Social Transformation in the 1980s*; and Constance Cumby, *The Hidden Dangers of the Rainbow: The New Age Movement and Our Coming Age of Barbarism*.

Public Relations, Advertising, and Issues Management

The art of opinion molding is practiced in even the most primitive tribes, with evidence reaching back to the earliest written records. But advertising and public relations, as specialized research-based vocations concerned with image building, did not develop as recognized professions until relatively recently. The rise of the Western democracies, including the United States, meant that greater attention needed to be paid to public opinion both in expanding markets for consumer goods and informing political policies reflecting a national consensus. Thus the growth in public relations parallels the rise of advertising as key components of twenty-first-century society.

Business leaders realize that public opinion and government regulation are likely to be a major part of corporate decision making for the future despite the often capricious nature of public opinion. We seem to be in a period of accelerating change and uncertainty. But because no single clear-cut public interest standard exists, any attempt to influence issue development and policy implementation is open to controversy. For example, business critics such as Michael Schudson in *Advertising, the Uneasy Persuasion* warn that "deep pocket" corporate advocacy can distort the public policy process and result in dangerous "information inequality."

Other commentators argue that such communication is narrowing the gap between corporate performance and public expectations by harmonizing corporate practices to public interests.

Art Stevens' *The Persuasion Explosion: Your Guide to the Power and Influence of Contemporary Public Relations* sounds like an exposé. While essentially anecdotal, the author's breezy style and use of numerous examples to illustrate his thesis that public relations is a necessary part of society make for a useful quick-read introduction to modern PR practices. In terms of basic public relations textbooks, the market is flooded with them. Among the best and most widely taught from are the latest editions of Otis Baskin and Craig Aronoff, *Public Relations: The Profession and the Practice*; Scott M. Cutlip, Allen H. Center, and Glen M. Broom, *Effective Public Relations*; S. Watson Dunn, *Public Relations: Contemporary Approach*, with a more marketing-oriented focus; James E. Grunig and Todd Hunt, *Managing Public Relations*, structured to emphasize systems theory; and Doug Newsom, Alan Scott, and Judy Vanslyke Turk, *This Is PR*.

The historical development of public relations is generally covered in these texts, but numerous lacunae need to be filled in by specialists. The earliest public relations practitioners—individuals such as James Ellsworth, George Michaelis, and Ivy Lee—were former journalists whose newspaper background made them valuable press agents for big business. Over time, however, they saw the need to shape as well as explain corporate policy. Edward L. Bernays, the nephew of Freud who rejected individual psychotherapy to concentrate on linking psychological principles to practical mass applications, helped focus attention on how meaningful public relationships might be collectively engineered with his seminal books *Crystallizing Public Opinion* and *Propaganda*.

Among the more intriguing published studies tracing the development of public relations as a managerial function, led by defenders of railroads and utilities against labor unrest and political hostility, is Alan R. Raucher's *Public Relations and Business, 1900–1929*. While Raucher outlines some of the ethical problems facing these corporate defenders, his approach is essentially sympathetic. Much more critical is Marvin N. Olasky, who argues for the elimination of public relations entirely. Olasky takes on Bernays and argues that the ongoing purpose of most corporate public relations has been to erect a mask of social responsibility behind which management can ruthlessly collude with government to stifle competition. Writing in *Corporate Public Relations: A New Historical Perspective*, Olasky uses a number of case studies to paint a sad portrait of continuing manipulation and to raise ongoing questions about the ethical role of business in American society today.

Olasky's pessimistic conclusions are open to question, however, even though today the new bottom line is public acceptance: this has necessitated a radical shift from the traditional adherence to profit making at any cost, to a more socially responsible balance of interests. Though corporate attempts at issues management occurred as early as the nineteenth century, evidence is mounting that it is evolving into a specialized strategic planning process requiring broader organizational involvement than traditional public relations/affairs campaigns. These important developments stem from the desire by executive leaderships to integrate with long-term social changes through proactive—as compared to reactive—intervention in the public interest process. Issues management functions include (1) integrating public policy issues analysis and audits into corporate strategic planning; (2) monitoring standards of corporate performance to discover the opinions and values key publics hold that may affect corporate operations; (3) developing and implementing codes of corporate social accountability; (4) assisting senior management decision making, particularly in readjusting corporate goals and operating policies vis-à-vis public opinion; (5) identifying, prioritizing, and analyzing empirically those issues of greatest operational, financial, and political significance to the organization; (6) creating multidimensional proactive and reactive response plans from among the range of available issue change strategy options; (7) communicating on issues important to various key publics to direct opinion and stall or mitigate the development and effects of undesirable regulation; and (8) evaluating the impact of these efforts to make ongoing improvements in recommendations to the management core.

A still timely and comprehensive introduction to what business advocates are doing is found in *The Public Affairs Handbook*, edited by Joseph S. Nagelschmidt. The forty-one successful practitioners featured draw upon their experience to describe the evolution of the public affairs function, explain how such departments are commonly structured, reveal the ways public policy issues are identified by government/business political relations specialists, and discuss resulting grassroots mobilization programs. This should be updated and contrasted with S. Prakash Sethi's more critical *Advocacy Advertising and Large Corporations: Social Conflict, Big Business Image, the News Media, and Public Policy*; his *Handbook of Advocacy Advertising: Concepts, Strategies, and Applications*, offering numerous case histories and hundreds of illustrated examples from the print and broadcast media; and *Business and Public Policy: Dimensions of Conflict and Cooperation*, coedited by Sethi and Cecilia McHugh Falbe.

W. Howard Chase (a founding father of both the Public Relations Society of America and the Issues Management Association) and Raymond P. Ewing (at Allstate Insurance Companies) pioneered in applying futures research and developing contemporary advocacy advertising. Chase's *Issue Management: Origins of the Future* and Ewing's *Managing the New Bottom Line: Issues Management for Senior Executives* are excellent insider-written primers directed at a management audience. Drawing upon years of practical experience, they explain and illustrate step by step the basics of identifying potential public policy issues, analyzing them, selecting from appropriate change strategy options, creating action programs, and conducting continuing evaluation. More in-depth in terms of outlining the actual methods and techniques used by successful practitioners is the highly recommended *Issues Management: How You Can Plan, Organize, and Manage for the Future* by Joseph F. Coates, Vary T. Coates, Jennifer Jarratt, and Lisa Heinz. The book also contains numerous charts and graphs. *Issues Management: Corporate Public Policymaking in an Information Society* by Robert L. Heath and Richard Alan Nelson is more scholarly. After reviewing the history and practice of issues management, Heath and Nelson demonstrate that efforts by business to communicate to targeted audiences—even when propagandistic—are an important antidote to information imbalance created by artificial government regulatory restrictions on business speech. Coverage of broadcast Fairness Doctrine and IRS deductibility issues is particularly detailed, and an impressive reference and case law bibliography is appended. In conjunction with leading practitioners and scholars, Heath in 1988 extended research in the area by editing *Strategic Issues Management: How*

Organizations Influence and Respond to Public Interests and Policies. This offers specific advice on creating a comprehensive corporate survival strategy for the 1990s.

Oscar H. Gandy, Jr.'s *Beyond Agenda Setting: Information Subsidies and Public Policy* takes a different approach in examining advocacy attempts. *Beyond Agenda Setting* is a thought-provoking, but at times strident, analysis of the often successful manipulations applied to mass media and other communication channels by corporations, bureaucrats, politicians, and consumer advocates. Gandy warns that organizations are successfully using indirect as well as more open means to influence the outcome of policy debates to their—not necessarily the public's—advantage. The book begins with a discussion of agenda setting as it is traditionally explored. Building on insights from political economy and decision theory, the author then provides numerous illustrations and examples that describe the flow of information and influence in the areas of science, technology, education, and social service delivery. Interestingly integrated are discussions of corporate issue advertising, government information as subsidized news, the growth of television docudrama as a replacement for the documentary, and information inequity. The final chapter identifies problems and possible goals for structured research into the ideological role of information subsidies in the public policy process. The extensive bibliography includes congressional hearings, corporate publications, and research reports.

Propaganda and Education, authored by William Wishart Biddle in 1932, was an early exploration of the business linkage between propaganda and education. It has been updated with the insurance of *Hucksters in the Classroom: A Review of Industry Propaganda in Schools* by Sheila Harty. Published by the Ralph Nader-organized Center for the Study of Responsible Law, the book examines four major areas of current controversy (nutrition education, nuclear power advocacy, environmental education, and economics education). A major conclusion is that American schoolteachers have been largely dependent on business-produced educational materials. Harty is particularly critical of sponsored films and videos distributed by organizations such as Modern Talking Picture Service. For more on the role of sponsored film from a less strident perspective, see Jay E. Gordon, *Motion Picture Production for Industry*, and Walter Klein, *The Sponsored Film*.

Labor Union Propaganda

In contrast, *Labor's New Voice: Unions and the Mass Media* by Sara U. Douglas is an important study of public relations activities by unions. The book explores relevant history, legal and regulatory factors, economic constraints, and short- and long-term goals—incorporating several case studies to show how the labor movement in recent years has again been more active in advocacy communication. An important theme throughout is access. The publisher of the book is Ablex, based in Norwood, New Jersey, which has fast become an important source of information for critical studies in the field of communication and information science. While the slant is usually politically leftist, the research is well documented and often at the cutting edge of developments of interest to students of propaganda.

It is important to note that federal, state, and local governments have historically worked to support corporate interests by suppressing more radical labor organizations. Various means, including deportation of foreign-born leaders, have been utilized at different times. Eldridge Foster Dowell's *History of Criminal Syndicalism Legislation in the United States*, first published in 1939, is a valuable pioneering study of legal attempts to suppress radical worker movements such as the Industrial Workers of the World (IWW or "Wobblies"). *The Price of Vigilance* by Joan Jensen traces in scholarly style the history of the American Protective League, a World War I–period business organization that promoted vigilante action to combat militant labor groups. Similarly, Louis F. Post's *The Deportations Delirium*, originally appearing in 1923, features disclosures by the assistant secretary of labor on antiradical raids of 1919–1920. However, William Preston Jr.'s *Aliens and Dissenters* is the benchmark study, standing as the basic work on this subject. Preston utilized correspondence in the National Archives to document federal acquiescence to pressure by business groups for repression of activist labor organizations during World War I and after. Following publication of the book in 1963, FBI director J. Edgar Hoover ordered a review of archival holdings which restricted access to some of the cited materials and removed other "sensitive" materials from public files.

Contemporary revelations that the FBI investigated organizations outspokenly opposed to the Reagan administration's Central American policies are newsworthy but not particularly unique, as we have seen. Frank J. Donner's *The Age of Surveillance: The Aims and Methods of America's Political Intelligence System* is a devastating critique of the limits of democracy written by a noted attorney while director of the American Civil Liberties Project on Political Surveillance. This monumental book rather chillingly documents how, from the Red Scare of World War I to the Watergate scandals of the 1970s, continuing (often illegal) attempts were made to suppress political dissenters and other movements seeking social change. These clandestine campaigns against Americans were conducted by officials of their own government. Although left-leaning progressives were often targeted, legal activities by rightist organizations also were regularly victimized by disinformation. The exercise of civil liberties by potentially subversive individuals and organizations highlights the ongoing constitutional tension between investigative information gathering and more aggressive uses of surveillance to disrupt political free speech. Also worth reading in this same vein is Athan Theoharis' *Spying on Americans: Political Surveillance from Hoover to the Huston Plan*. This is a solid history of the abuses of the American domestic intelligence system from 1936, when President Franklin Roosevelt verbally authorized investigation of fascist and communist activities, until 1978, when proposals were made to lift existing restrictions under White House direction. An eye-opening chapter is devoted to exposing a variety of government political counterintelligence programs (COINTELPROs) secretly conducted to neutralize opposition to federal policies.

In studying labor history and propaganda, a number of useful reference guides to workers' movements exist. Since the amount of overlap material is relatively small, serious researchers should consult them all. Among the most important are Gulik, Ockert, and Wallace's *History and Theories of Working Class Movements—A Select Bibliography*; two bibliographies by the Institute of Labor and Industrial Relations at the University of Illinois entitled *American Labor in Journals of History* and *Labor History in the United States*; James McBrearty's *American Labor History and Comparative Labor Movements—A Selected Bibliography* (which includes a brief but intriguing section on labor novels); Maurice Neufeld's *A Representative Bibli-*

ography of American Labor History; and Gerald Friedberg's annotated "Sources for the Study of Socialism in America, 1901–1919." Also helpful are two pamphlets: John Evansohn et al.'s *Literature of the American Working Class* and a descriptive introduction to the "Wobblies" prepared by IWW members entitled "A Reading List on IWW History," with pro-union citations on a variety of topic areas.

The standard labor history, sympathetic to the aspirations of workers, is Philip S. Foner's multivolume *History of the Labor Movement in the United States*. Also important in analyzing labor theory and ideology, especially its more radically politicized elements, are several master's theses and doctoral studies, including Thomas Howard McEnroe, "The International Workers of the World: Theories, Organizational Problems and Appeals as Revealed Principally in *Industrial Worker*"; Donald Barnes, "Ideology of the IWW"; and John Crow, "Ideology and Organization."

Most IWW magazines were not archived by libraries when first published, but Greenwood Press has conveniently republished a number of key journals in bound form with introductions by recognized academic labor historians. These include *International Socialist Review* (Chicago, 1900–1918), *Industrial Union Bulletin* (Chicago, 1907–1990), *Industrial Worker* (Spokane, 1909–1913), *One Big Union Monthly* (Chicago, 1919–1928), *Industrial Pioneer* (Chicago, 1921–1926), and *Industrial Unionist* (Portland, Oregon, 1925–1926), *Rebel Voices, an IWW Anthology*, edited by Joyce Kornbluh, draws from the files of these IWW publications and other hard-to-come-by materials to reproduce a representative sample of articles, poems, photographs, and cartoons.

Contemporary journals with valuable labor material include *Labor History* (1960–present), the resurrected *Industrial Worker*, *Radical America*, and other publications. For example, an interesting reminiscence on IWW use of colorful stickers for organizing is well discussed in an illustrated article in *American West* by Tony Bubka.

Free Speech, the Mass Media, and Propaganda

Surveys reveal that most people in the United States endorse freedom of speech for the views they believe in but welcome censorship of positions they oppose. This general misunderstanding of the rationale for constitutional speech guarantees and the ongoing history of attempted controls point to a continuing need for defenders of the First Amendment to articulate its worth even when media are used as a conduit for propaganda.

For a history lesson see Thomas L. Tedford's *Freedom of Speech in the United States*, an important new book summarizing the history of control on free speech, stressing the ethical responsibilities of sender and receiver. Valuable appendixes explain the federal court system, chart underlying First Amendment theory, and index 310 key cases. For an overview of some major historical turning points, see Craig R. Smith's *The Flight for Freedom of Expression: Three Case Studies*, written by a leading contemporary media civil libertarian. The case studies involve events surrounding passage of the Alien and Sedition Acts of 1798, the Reconstruction Acts following the Civil War, and the Subversive Activities Control Act of 1950, which set the stage for Senator Joseph McCarthy's anticommunist investigations. Appendixes include reprints of pertinent documents and speeches.

More detailed is Leonard W. Levy's *Emergence of a Free Press*, a greatly revised and enlarged edition of his landmark 1960 book, *Legacy of Suppression*. That work created a storm of controversy when it was first published by challenging the absolutist position on the freedom of the press. He maintained that it was not the intention of the framers of the First Amendment to overturn the common law of seditious libel, the principal means of suppressing political dissent. On the basis of further research, however, Levy has revised some of his earlier views and deepened others. He now contends that the early press was far more robust in its criticisms of public officials and policies than existing laws and theoretical tradition would seem to have allowed. That makes the new book a major source work, now much more supportive of the libertarian absolutist view. Thomas C. Leonard's *The Power of the Press: The Birth of American Political Reporting* is a pioneering look at the birth of political journalism. It traces the rise of political reporting, beginning with the exposés that helped trigger the revolution in 1776 through the emergence of muckraking at the beginning of the twentieth century. Supplementing these is Jeffery A. Smith, *Printers and Press Freedom: The Ideology of Early American Journalism*, which tracks the origins of the freedom-of-the-press clause in the First Amendment and includes discussion of how "libertarian press theory" was translated into practice by Benjamin Franklin and others.

The Press as a Propaganda Conduit

The continuing interaction of politics, media, and propaganda is well documented in such historical works as the popularized *Political Power and the Press* by CBS Washington bureau manager William Small; *The Press, Politics, and Patronage: The American Government's Use of Newspapers, 1789–1875* by Culver Smith; the early muckraking *Our Press Gang; or, A Complete Exposition of the Corruptions and Crimes of the American Newspapers*, first published in 1859 by Lambert A. Wilmer; the similarly outspoken report on the early twentieth-century press, *The Brass Check: A Study in American Journalism* by Upton Sinclair; and the engrossing analysis of the death of truth in wartime by Phillip Knightley entitled *The First Casualty—From the Crimea to Vietnam: The War Correspondent as Hero, Propagandist, and Myth Maker*, which supplements Oscar W. Riegel's gloomily prophetic *Mobilizing for Chaos: The Story of the New Propaganda*. See also George Seldes' angry exposé of corrupt media, *The Facts Are . . . A Guide to Falsehood and Propaganda in the Press and Radio*, and Kent Cooper's *The Right to Know: An Exposition of the Evils of News Suppression and Propaganda*. Less satisfying is David Wise's *The Politics of Lying: Government Deception, Secrecy and Power*. Overly dramatic in tone (befitting Wise's experience as a journalist) and somewhat simplistic in analysis, the book provides a rather vitriolic view of the Nixon administration's attempts to manipulate public opinion by ahistorically condemning it as the first to condone habitual lying. Wise's basic problem is that he fails to recognize the failings of the news media themselves and he is guilty of many of the same faults he criticizes, such as concealing sources. Also refer to C. Richard Hofstetter's *Bias in the News: Network Television Coverage of the 1972 Election Campaign*, which argues that McGovern—not Nixon—was the real media victim. For a contrasting view see Victor Lasky, *It Didn't Start with Watergate*.

The up-to-date *The Interplay of Influence: Mass Media and Their Publics in News,*

Advertising, Politics, by Kathleen Hall Jamieson and Karlyn Kohrs Campbell, explains how key mass media systems interact with society and respond to a variety of commercial, political, group, self-imposed, and other pressures. A number of case studies document the commercial limitations and persuasive nature of news, audience analysis, advertising, and political versus product campaigns. The book encourages readers to go beyond claims of media manipulation to become activists themselves. W. Lance Bennett's textbook *News: The Politics of Illusion* presents a well-documented critique of the news to demonstrate how government leaders, journalists, and the general public all contribute to the illusory nature of mass media reporting in the United States—particularly how mass prejudices and stereotypes are reinforced.

Much of the recent criticism has emanated from conservative authors who perceive a deliberate leftist bias in media (particularly broadcasting). Representative publications include *Distortion by Design: The Story of America's Liberal Press* by the Reverend Billy James Hargis; *The News Twisters* and *How CBS Tried to Kill a Book,* both by *TV Guide* columnist Edith Efron, which detail controversies in the early 1970s over her findings that there were indeed anti-Nixon media tendencies at the three major networks; Joseph Keeley's somewhat rambling *The Left Leaning Antenna: Political Bias in Television;* Tim La Haye's pro-Christian exploration of humanism's "stranglehold" on the media in *The Hidden Censors;* and the work of Accuracy in Media (AIM), a Washington-based conservative watchdog organization. See particularly AIM chairman Reed Irvine's collection of columns entitled *Media Mischief and Misdeeds. The Media Elite: America's New Powerbrokers* by S. Robert Lichter, Stanley Rothman, and Linda S. Lichter is the most scientific and serious of the books demonstrating that journalists working for the major national media share common political perspectives and exercise growing influence over public opinion. To keep tabs on their current research, the Lichters edit *Media Monitor,* a research publication of the Center for Media and Public Affairs.

In contrast, Martin Linsky's *Impact: How the Press Affects Federal Policy-making* and the companion volume he coauthored with Jonathan Moore, Wendy O'Donnell, and David Whitman, *How the Press Affects Federal Policymaking: Six Case Studies,* attempt to demonstrate that the press are neither passive, detached observers of government nor liberal interventionists who heavy-handedly impose their views through selective reporting. Linsky and his collaborators do agree, however, that the media act to frame issues and influence government policy. Cases cover three administrations and include the 1969 reorganization of the Postal Department, the resignation of Vice President Agnew, the decision of President Carter not to deploy the neutron bomb, the Love Canal chemical tragedy, the struggle over Bob Jones University's attempt to retain tax exemption, and the 1984 case on the suspension of Social Security disability reviews. Although rich in anecdotes, the books lack any theoretical underpinning, which weakens their presentation.

A timely and important series, Presidents and the Press, copublished by the White Burkett Miller Center of Public Affairs and the University of Virginia, includes several studies of interest. Blaire Atherton French, *The Presidential Press Conference: Its History and Role in the American Political System,* is a monograph answering questions about the origins of the press conference and how and why it came to be as we find it today. *The White House Press on the Presidency: News*

Management and Co-option, by Frank Cormier, James Deakin, and Helen Thomas, offers "insider" opinions by three senior White House correspondents about how the news media are co-opted by the officials they cover. Also included as an appendix is a reprint of *The Report of the Commission on Presidential Press Conferences*. Finally, John E. Mueller's *War, Presidents and Public Opinion* is a minor classic presenting rigorous reanalysis of public opinion on the wars in Korea and Vietnam. In showing how polling results were often misused, the author develops many unconventional conclusions including, for example, the argument that the press and the antiwar movement probably had little special impact on attitudes toward the Vietnam conflict.

Dale Minor's *The Information War* is a practical primer on how the government has intervened in the news process. Drawing on his experience as a Pacifica Radio correspondent, Minor traces the cynical cooperation (and occasional confrontation) between government and media gatekeepers in manipulating, censoring, and directing the news for their own corrupt practices. Events in Vietnam form the backdrop for much of Minor's report. Specialized analyses of contemporary U.S. military propaganda activities include former U.S. Senator J. William Fulbright's *The Pentagon Propaganda Machine* and a post-Vietnam update by Juergen Arthur Heise titled *Minimum Disclosure: How the Pentagon Manipulates the News*. This latter work is based on the author's personal encounters with military information officers.

For a variety of views, see a current reader. One that raises fundamental questions about how the mass media shape public opinion and serve as propaganda conduits is *When Information Counts: Grading the Media*, edited by Bernard Rubin. Herbert I. Schiller's *The Mind Managers*, written in the early 1970s, is still useful to counteract the more chauvinistic "us versus them" views, angrily surveying the role the communications industry plays as a purveyor of propaganda. Updating the work of thoughtful leftist critics such as Schiller and George Seldes is Ben H. Bagdikian's *The Media Monopoly*, which presents an insightful and readable introduction to how news is being used by propagandists. Contrast these views with those of the equally critical Michael Parenti in *Inventing Reality: The Politics of the Mass Media*. Parenti is angry, too, in outlining a provocative thesis. However, he says that a continuing pattern of press misrepresentation works to uphold capitalistic ideological values while distorting Marxist criticism that might lead to a more genuine discourse on what needs to be done to change the world for the better. The book is worth reading. Another Marxist perspective is provided in James Aronson's now dated *Packaging the News: A Critical Survey of Press, Radio, TV*.

Also of interest is Robert Cirino's mildly left critique, *Don't Blame the People: How the News Media Use Bias, Distortion and Censorship to Manipulate Public Opinion*. See particularly the chapter titled "The Importance of Propaganda." Cirino argues that the news media manipulated attitudes toward the Vietnam War, minorities, car safety, crime, abortion, pollution, safety, population increase, dissenters, the hazards of smoking, and hunger in America—not to serve liberal causes but to serve the mass media's and the corporate establishment's own profit-making and political interest. For these reasons the author, a history teacher, blames the news media and not the people (hence the book's title) for what he sees as the mistaken priorities and policies that have made America unnecessarily pay so high a price in lives, resources, environmental quality, and worldwide respect. In another work by Cirino called *We're Being More than Entertained*, rather than simply decrying the propagandistic nature of mass media, he creatively allows the reader to construct his or her own "propaganda detector." The book encourages rewriting of scripts using four basic political viewpoints (liberal, conservative, socialist, and libertarian) to study the impact of various social and political objectives on what we see. Overall this is an unusual, fun, and perceptive short analysis of the so-called entertainment industry.

International News Issues

As an antidote to unwavering acceptance of U.S. government or media claims, one might want to read the booklet *The Big Lie: Analysis of U.S. Press Coverage of the Grenada Invasion*, published by the International Organization of Journalists in cooperation with the National Alliance of Third World Journalists. Author Glen Ford, a former host and producer for the syndicated television news program *America's Black Forum*, argues that despite minor differences with the government, American reporters served U.S. ruling class interests by deceitfully setting up the Cubans as villains and romantically justifying the resulting military aggression against the Grenadan government as a "rescue mission."

Ze'ev Chafets' *Double Vision: How the Press Distorts America's View of the Middle East*, by the former director of the Israeli Government Press Office during the Menachem Begin administration, argues that a closed and impenetrable Arab world, by restricting correspondent access (a fact reporters generally do not mention), and a relatively open Israel (with the largest number of foreign correspondents per capita of any country in the world) create the impression of an Israel constantly in turmoil and a relatively dull Arab world where basically nothing is going on. For a more official U.S. view, see the House Committee on Foreign Affairs hearing summary *The Media, Diplomacy, and Terrorism in the Middle East*, which analyzes the role of television network coverage in unwittingly aiding terrorists.

William A. Hachten and C. Anthony Giffard comprehensively document the history of legal and political constraints on the press in South Africa in *The Press and Apartheid: Repression and Propaganda in South Africa*, with a description of media conditions current to the date of publication. Of particular interest is the chapter on "Muldergate," which details the South African Information Department's failed efforts to influence U.S. political opinion by secretly acquiring control of the *Washington Star* through bank-rolling sympathetic conservative American media owner John McGoff.

Taking a less narrow topical approach, *The World News Prism: Changing Media, Clashing Ideologies* by William A. Hachten traces the growth of the global news network, especially the impact of developing technology in placing new pressures on both news organizations and governments. A new chapter in the second edition on public diplomacy and propaganda provides a good introduction to international radio and the ongoing efforts of governments to influence world opinion by manipulating foreign news media. The ever prolific Herbert I. Schiller weighs in with another important related book, *Information and the Crisis Economy*, which portrays the future information society as a nightmare rather than a blessing.

Beyond the scope of this chapter are studies attacking American television and film exports as a form of "media imperialism." Along with similar critiques decrying Western domination of the major world news and information agencies, they provide a fascinating perspective on the cultural and propaganda implications of media. Most of the fundamental issues and supporting documents are collected in *The New International Information and Communication Order*, edited by Kaarle Nordenstreng et al. Readers interested in exploring the topic further can do so by referring to Jeremy Tunstall's *The Media Are American: Anglo-American Media in the World* and other current international communications literature (particularly recent UNESCO reports and the English-language issues of *The Democratic Journalist* published in Czechoslovakia).

Films That Lie

During the period of U.S. neutrality before World War II, motion pictures were already established as propaganda vehicles attempting to sway public opinion, a trend accelerated by the CPI's wartime involvement and subsequent governmental utilization of Hollywood in World War II and Korea. Current estimates of federal propaganda film work range as high as $500 million a year. (This figure omits commercial, educational, state-financed, and privately produced "sponsored" motion pictures.) Again the literature is large, and a bibliographic review must be selective. A basic starting point is *Politics and Film*, a collation of available secondary sources with refreshingly objective perspective by Leif Furhammer and Folke Isaksson, which traces the troubled origins of movie propaganda, details the fervently patriotic efforts of 1914–1918 through more current releases, and includes a well-organized analysis of the aesthetics and principles of the genre. Kevin Brownlow's *The War, the West and the Wilderness* is a massive study of silent films. The largest section of the book, more than 200 pages, examines the motion picture in the Spanish-American War and World War I. In addition to published material, the author conducted interviews with many newsreel and propaganda filmmakers active in the period and had access to previously unpublished letters, diaries, and logbooks. The work is lavishly illustrated, with excellent notes and a detailed index. A thoughtful study of the overuse of war themes by motion picture propaganda, with recommendations on how the screen might have been used for more uplifting purposes, is found in William Marston Seabury's *Motion Picture Problems: The Cinema and the League of Nations*. Also of interest is Winifred Johnston's *Memo on the Movies: War Propaganda, 1914–1939*, a short but nonetheless intriguing polemical study of how "peace-loving people" "turned to ways of hate" by filmic distortion. One might compare it to more recent critiques of television as a propaganda medium.

The upheavals wrought by the two world wars and the continuing struggle between the Soviet Union and United States for international influence have spurred ongoing interest by scholars in the impact of communications on public opinion. Much of what we know about information control and the psychology of propaganda stems from earlier efforts by Harold Lasswell and others to describe propaganda techniques and analyze both private and government attempts to mobilize targeted publics and populations. One value of propaganda analysis is to be predictive of emerging trends, particularly for those of us who see the future in terms of the past. While the propaganda literature is large, a need exists for more in-depth historical studies of official propaganda by democratic and other powers in war and peace, drawing upon new research advances and the wealth of recently declassified state documents.

That is the value of Nicholas Pronay and D. W. Spring, *Propaganda, Politics and Film, 1918–1945*, and K.R.M. Short, *Film & Radio Propaganda in World War II*. These two books, each edited by a leading world scholar, bring together specialists of the first rank in the field of propaganda and communication to make an important contribution to our current knowledge of the workings and effects of propaganda. Both are organized logically. Pronay and Spring divide their volume into four parts: the official projection of Britain, film propaganda in Britain and France between the world wars, film propaganda in Britain in World War II, and the projection of the Soviet Union. Short similarly utilizes four sectional groupings but is far more expansive in the range of topical coverage. An introduction to propaganda in international politics by Philip Taylor is followed by aspects of the Allied experience ranging from racial ambiguities and attempts in American films at fighting anti-Semitism to broadcasts by Radio Luxembourg in 1944–1945; then the book's coverage moves to propaganda in fascist Europe and concludes with Japanese persuasive communication. The twenty-eight chapters (thirteen and fifteen, respectively) stem from papers presented at international conferences in which co-participation by academicians and individuals personally involved in government propaganda efforts took place.

One wishes the two books had been jointly released, for not only do they share similar perspectives but a number of authors have integrative essays appearing in each volume. Among them are studies by Pronay (on news as propaganda and other topics), David Ellwood (who examines cultural propaganda by Britain and then turns southward to report on fascist propaganda from Italy), Elizabeth Strebel (on prewar and Vichy cinema), Sergei Drobashenko (describing Soviet film), and Taylor (on interwar propaganda efforts).

While such collaborative publications are often uneven, through expert editing both volumes demonstrate unusual coherence and focus as references. Pronay, Spring, and Short (at the time all senior lecturers in history at major British universities) were well qualified for the task. Short, particularly, is well known for his *Films as History* and as editor of the influential *Historical Journal of Film, Radio and Television*. Pronay, like Spring, has held leadership positions in the Inter-University History Film Consortium and is widely published, including coauthorship with Frances Thorpe of *British Official Films in the Second World War: A Descriptive Catalogue*.

Although all countries to some extent engage in progaganda, the British early proved particularly adept at using media for political mobilization—a point later noted by Hitler in *Mein Kampf* when outlining the communication strategy he would ultimately impose on Germany. British politics is confusing to many Europeans as well as Americans, and Pronay provides a useful introduction to the turbulent social context of interwar Britain in *Propaganda, Politics and Film*. He describes how a variety of class factors influenced continued reliance on propaganda—despite claims to the contrary—by politicians worried that democratic institutions might well collapse from powerful internal as well as external evolutionary and revolutionary challenges. This is supplemented by Pronay's informative evaluation in Short of the role played by leftist documentarists in pushing socialist causes while working in the British Ministry of Information under Conservative party administrations.

Pronay's views are also well complemented by Philip Taylor's lead essay appearing in *Film & Radio Propaganda in World War II*. As Taylor observes, the "communications revolution" we are now experiencing parallels the technological innovations of the 1920s and 1930s beyond mass print, which spurred greater usage of broadcasting, newsreels, and feature motion pictures as propaganda tools during a crisis period of world history. Taylor outlines development in various industrial countries including the United Kingdom, arguing that Britain's decline as a power forced it to exploit the new media but with questionable effectiveness (particularly in the United States and the Soviet Union). Ultimately, he says, "Truth was a casualty long before the actual fighting began."

Recognizing that some contributing authors might resent the term, the books are nevertheless revisionist in that many of the articles reflect changing views on the nature of propaganda. They agree that once war began, propaganda was practiced widely by both Allied and Axis governments. Several authors point to the lack of unified policy in France, the United States, and other belligerents, which led to contradictory propaganda campaign efforts and resulting uncertainty as to the long-term effects on intended audiences.

Generally speaking, however, Pronay, Taylor, and most of their fellow contributors fail to agree on a clear definition of propaganda—usually equating the term uncertainly with political communication. This umbrella usage is not atypical, given the imprecision and vagaries associated with its use. Commonly, "propaganda" is used as a pejorative appellation for the communication efforts of others, while the euphemism "information" is retained for one's own activities, thus the value of Kenneth Short's insightful commentary on the problems "propaganda" has caused both for scholars and lexicologists attempting to grapple with its ambiguity. While recognizing that there are differences in propaganda styles, particularly between totalitarian one-party states and those nations with multiple political/economic/religious social organizations, Short realistically points out that "propaganda," "information," and "education" are often used interchangeably to mean "persuasion" in democracies as well as dictatorships. Indeed, he argues, because of the need to build social consensus through ideological conditioning, "a world in which *propagandas* compete for dominance and allegiance would appear to be our earthly lot."

Even though some chapters are not particularly illuminating because of the wealth of previously available material (e.g., David Welch's review of wartime newsreels by national socialist Germany offers little new), overall *Film and Radio Propaganda in World War II* is greatly strengthened by analyses of Italian, Japanese, and French topics not well covered in English. Gordon Daniel's interesting overview of Japanese domestic radio and cinema propaganda from 1937 to 1945 reports on the sustained emphasis placed on social continuity despite wartime stress. This is coupled with the unusually frank insider assessment by Namikawa Ryo of the imperial government's Central Information Bureau and Japanese short-wave transmissions such as the "Zero Hour" broadcast to Allied troops in the Pacific. Even topics well covered elsewhere, such as David Culbert's review of the social engineering aspects of the American *Why We Fight* series, receive fresh analysis.

There are some things to criticize in the two books, among them occasional typographical errors, the failure except in one instance to publish organizational charts clearly defining the chain of command and linkages in various propaganda agencies, the lack of photographs, no comprehensive frontispiece listing of figures and tables, inconsistent inclusion of filmographies, which would have been useful for most chapters instead of only a few, the decision not to append glossaries of terms and biographical details on key personalities mentioned in the text, and the elimination of comprehensive reference bibliographies (instead each chapter has endnotes). For the most part these excisions are likely victims of the publishers' need to keep production costs within reasonable limits, and such complaints are minor in comparison to the value of each volume. In addition to suggesting the diversity of methodological approaches useful in the study of film and broadcast, both books reinforce the importance of understanding the process of dissemination and control of information. They certainly are must reading for propaganda historians and contemporary researchers seeking to learn from the past rather than repeat it.

The documentary film is an ideal vehicle for propaganda, for it combines the advantages of believability through "reality" and image manipulation (subject/shot selection plus control over the audience response to the screen dialectic via edit juxtapositioning). A number of outlets such as Third World Cinema Group, October Films, Tricontinental Film Center, and Films for Social Change arose out of the student protests in the 1960s to distribute noncommercial documentaries in actively creating a "new consciousness." Tricontinental, for example, found itself the target of a U.S. Justice Department order in 1976 to register as a "foreign agent" under the provisions of the Foreign Agents Registration Act of 1938. The law requires that registered organizations must attach a "foreign propaganda" label to their printed materials and similarly identify films with a preceding leader. In addition, all officers and employees are required to register, organizational records must be kept open to FBI investigation, and sales and rental data, including the names and addresses of customers, must be filed with the government. These and similar rules are now undergoing various legal challenges.

The interrelationship of the "factual" motion picture and propaganda is further explored in a number of other published studies. These include Thomas Bohn, *An Historical and Descriptive Analysis of the "Why We Fight" Series*; Raymond Fielding, *The American Newsreel: 1911–1967*; Richard Dyer MacCann, *The People's Films: A Political History of U.S. Government Motion Pictures*; Richard A. Maynard, *Propaganda on Film: A Nation at War*, a basic reader comparing Soviet, German, and U.S. responses to film propaganda; Tom Perlmutter, *War Movies*; Clyde Jeavons, *A Pictorial History of War Films*; Joe Morella, Edward Z. Epstein, and John Griggs, *The Films of World War II*; Ken Jones and Arthur McClure, *Hollywood at War: The American Motion Picture Industry and World War II*, with a useful introductory essay and filmography of over 400 releases; and Roger Manvell, *Films and the Second World War*, in which Manvell provides parallels between what actually was happening in the world and how that was presented in film. All told, from 1939 to 1945 some 2,500 pictures were released in the United States. Valuable additions to the literature are the more recent *Mission to Moscow: The Feature Film as Official Propaganda*, edited by David Culbert, and *Hollywood Goes to War: How Politics, Profits, and Propaganda Shaped World War II Movies* by Clayton R. Koppes and Gregory D. Black. *Film and Propaganda in America: A Documentary History*, also edited by Culbert, consists of four volumes of new textual analysis and photographs, which provide a veritable archive of original documents and other materials reproduced in affordable format.

Continuing interest in the topic is also reflected by the growing number of critical histories and anthologies. Lewis Jacobs' *The Documentary Tradition* collates a wide variety of works by theoreticians, critics, and filmmakers to survey mostly American and European developments. Arranged chronologically in five decade-long sections starting in 1922, it serves as a useful—though incomplete—summary. Richard M. Barsam's two major works in this area—*Nonfiction Film: A Critical History* and *Nonfiction Film: Theory and Criticism*—have been criticized for promoting a dichotomy between art and politics in arguing that documentaries can be analyzed in terms of their artistic qualities irrespective of the ideology of the filmmaker. Nevertheless, for the beginning student they are serviceable introductions to the field and incorporate adequate—if predictable—discussion of major topics related to war propaganda and government films by the USIA and other agencies. More extensive and detailed (reflecting his background as a media—as compared to simply film—historian) is Erik Barnouw's *Documentary: A History of the Non-fiction Film*, which focuses on the different roles that documentary films and filmmakers have played in society. The illustrations are thoughtful and help the text chronicle major developments in the history of documentary and its use as a forum for the socially committed. Coverage outside America is also more extensive than the preceding books. The short (115 pages) *About Documentary: Anthropology on Film* by Robert Edmunds is worth noting for its discussion of the fallacy of the notion of objectivity in film. Its primary value is for someone interested in teaching documentary. The book features an introduction by Lewis Jacobs and incorporates a course outline, filmography, and bibliography.

F. D. Klingender and Stuart Legg's *Money behind the Screen*, first published in 1937, documents the economic consolidation of the major studios that saw them all come under the financial control of either Morgan or Rockefeller interests by the mid-1930s. This helps amplify explanations of the continuing cooperation between the motion picture industry and the federal government, evident in features and numerous patriotic shorts made by the studios over the years to demonstrate their patriotism. Propaganda documentaries such as *Why Korea?* (1951, Twentieth Century Fox-Movietone News) were distributed without charge, in this case to bolster Truman administration foreign policy intervention. The same basic theme was again used in *Why Viet Nam?*, a 1965 Defense Department production that revived Cold War rhetoric and analyses. Among the more ambitious anticommunist films was *Red Nightmare* (Warner Brothers, 1962; reissued 1965), produced under the personal supervision of Jack L. Warner. Narrated by television star-producer Jack Webb and featuring popular actors such as Jack Kelley and Robert Conrad, such educational pictures helped cement a long-lasting formal alliance with Pentagon project cosponsors such as the Department of Defense Directorate for the Armed Forces and Educational Information.

In part these releases were designed to combat the image of Hollywood as a virtual Soviet enclave. Among those leading the charge against communism was Myron C. Fagan, who edited the Cinema Educational Guild's *News-Bulletin* (first published in 1949) and later authored *Red Treason on Broadway: Stage, Television,*

Radio, Red Treason in Hollywood, and *Documentation of the Red Stars in Hollywood* to focus attention on the use of front tactics by leftist media groups. Fagan, a prolific playwright with successes, found himself out of favor as his work became more political. Concerned that the entertainment industry and Jewish organizations seemed to be moving further to the left, Fagan authored two controversial plays: *Thieves Paradise* (about travails in Iron Curtain Bulgaria) and *Red Rainbow* (an exposé of communist infiltration in America). His subsequent blacklisting (as an anti-communist) led him into pamphleteering for a cleanup of Hollywood and Broadway. He heartily endorsed calls for investigation of un-American practices in numerous publications issued by his Cinema Educational Guild (originally known briefly as Citizens United for American Principles), which operated from the late 1940s until the 1960s. His oversize paperback books contain a fascinating combination of personal observation, historical philosophizing, and reprints from news items, books, and government reports. Differing perspectives can be found in alternative journals such as *Cinéaste*, *Jump Cut*, and *Cultural Correspondence: A Journal of Popular and Left Culture*, important sources of Marxist media ideology and history. They often feature interviews with leading activists that supplement more standard, book-length studies.

American Radio and Television Broadcasting

The essential starting point for study of American broadcasting, tracing the history of radio and television from 1900 to 1970, is the 1,200-page trilogy (*A Tower in Babel*, *The Golden Web*, and *The Image Empire*) by Erik Barnouw. Each volume contains a wealth of material including texts of significant documents, chronology, and full bibliography. Although not particularly sympathetic to the media moguls, Barnouw avoids open editorializing until end-of-book summaries. The widespread popularity of broadcasting only underscores the importance of the long and largely successful struggle by corporate, military, and civilian government agencies to control the medium. The growth of the industry, move to commercial sponsorship, formation of the networks, emergence of "public interest" regulatory bodies co-opted by industry, limitations on private broadcasters in wartime, and official government propaganda "information" programming efforts ranging from the Armed Forces Radio and Television Service to Radio Free Europe, Radio Free Asia, Radio Liberation, and the Voice of America are all well discussed here. The result is a monument to scholarship. Interestingly, the wartime cooperation with the government proved profitable: in 1939 the industry as a whole earned 67.1 percent before-tax profits; by 1944 the figure was 222.6 percent, which helped underwrite the move of the radio networks into television.

Richard W. Steele's *Propaganda in an Open Society: The Roosevelt Administration and the Media, 1933–41* is more useful for the footnotes than the narrative. Ultimately the book fails to hang together and in actuality is more a series of articles than a coherent analysis. This is unfortunate, since there is a wealth of material here on news management and attempts to create a national propaganda agency. Readers should compare this to David Culbert's more satisfying *News for Everyman: Radio and Foreign Affairs in Thirties America* and Qualter's *Opinion Control in the Democracies*, cited earlier. On communism and television, the literature is well summarized in J. Fred McDonald's *Television and the Red Menace*. Additional studies related to broadcasting are described in *Television: A Guide to the Literature* by Mary B. Cassata and Thomas Skill, as well as in other chapters of this *Handbook*.

Political Advertising

A good place to begin is *Political Communication in America* by Robert E. Denton Jr. and Gary C. Woodward. This encyclopedic overview of history, theory, and practices ranges from presidential marketing to mass media effects on contemporary politics. All in all, it is an excellent primer on how the "engineering of consensus" occurs. See also Robert G. Meadow's *Politics as Communication*, a useful, left-oriented introduction to the theories of political communication. It discusses how manipulation of political image and myth via news, advertising, and entertainment are expanding through new technologies.

Kathleen Hall Jamieson's *Packaging the Presidency: A History and Criticism of Presidential Campaign Advertising* is somewhat misleadingly titled. Actually the book concentrates on the 1952–1980 campaigns, although an introductory chapter provides an overview of early practices through the 1940s. The themes, issues, candidates, agencies, finances, media, images, and slogans of each campaign are identified. *The Spot: The Rise of Political Advertising on Television* is now a standard reference work. But while widely praised, this is not an exhaustive scholarly treatment even in its revised edition. Authors Edwin Diamond and Stephen Bates still largely gloss over motion picture and radio broadcasting origins to such advertising; they also leave room for more thorough investigation, particularly of nonpresidential television campaigns.

Of related interest is David Paletz, Robert Pearson, and Donald Willis, *Politics in Public Service Advertising on Television*, which notes the growing role of and the highly politicized atmosphere surrounding production and airing of corporate "advertorials" and nonprofit PSAs. Access to major media is dominated by the private Advertising Council, established in 1942 to support the war effort. Since then it has publicized information and positions for hundreds of organizations on such wide-ranging issues as drunken driving prevention, savings bonds, Social Security, safety belt education, the U.S. Bicentennial, the United Nations, and world hunger problems. In 1987 alone, more than $1.1 billion in free broadcast airtime and print advertising space was contributed to the Ad Council's "public service" campaigns. See also *Public Communication Campaigns*, edited by Ronald E. Rice and William J. Paisley. Following three chapters that provide historical and theoretical linkages to the long tradition of nonpartisan mobilization via mass communication in America, the book presents seven case studies of various public service campaigns and concludes with ways to analyze how these social marketing efforts can be measured in terms of effectiveness. The bibliography and index are valuable.

Music as Propaganda

Popular music has always reflected political and cultural attitudes. Advertisers, of course, use music to sell products because of its unique ability to establish mood. In recent years, rock-and-roll artists in particular have used their songs as a forum to communicate ideas, expressing their protests in styles ranging from folk to heavy metal to Christian rock. However, overtly partisan music tends to be confined to a more narrow spectrum of specialized recordings. A number of companies such as Brass Tacks Music of New Haven, Connecticut, market records and cassettes with radical political messages—in this case albums such as *Paint the Town Red* with songs such as the "Young Communist League Song" and "You Ain't Done Nothing if You Ain't Been Called a Red." See Philip S. Foner's *American Labor Songs of the Nineteenth Century*. However, the best overall information source for further study is Arnold Perris' *Music as Propaganda*, published by Greenwood Press.

RESEARCH COLLECTIONS

Much of the material of the propagandist is ephemeral. Leaflets, broadsides, banners, posters, pamphlets, broadcasts, commercials, and even motion pictures are not designed to be long-lasting. The propagandist usually is time-bound and concerned with effecting specific, measurable goals rather than creating permanent monuments to "truth." Therefore, specialized reference and research collections are critical for serious historical research involving the propaganda activities of particular organizations, agencies, and individuals. Unfortunately, important materials are widely scattered. The difficulty is compounded because reference aids and guides to special collections are inadequately cross-referenced.

With this caveat, the logical place to begin the study of American propaganda is in Washington, D.C. Indispensable in working one's way through the maze of government records is the U.S. National Archives and Records Services' *Guide to the National Archives of the United States*, issued in 1974. All photographic and paper holdings in the National Archives are organized by government agency "Record Groups" (RG), now numbering over 400. A list of record groups is available on request from the archives; many RGs have printed "preliminary inventories" of real value in tracking down specific documents, manuscripts, and other materials. Demonstrating the extent of media involvement, an estimated seventy-five federal agencies have made motion pictures at one time or another. The National Archives now houses over 35,000 sound recordings, 50,000 reels of film, and more than 4.5 million photographic items. Among the more important RGs relating to federal propaganda and informational activities are the following:

RG 44—Office of Government Reports (OGR). This office acted as a clearinghouse for government information and helped coordinate home-front aspects of the defense and war effort in World War II until being consolidated with other agencies to form the Office of War Information in 1942. Later, the OGR was briefly reestablished to provide motion picture advertising and liaison services. Within this large collection, for example, are the records of the Office of the Coordinator of Government Films, 1941–1942; still photos and posters issued by the OWI's Division of Public Inquiries, 1942–1945 (14,150 items); and other pertinent propaganda materials from the Division of Press Intelligence, which issued summaries and digests of radio and press comments.

RG 63—Committee on Public Information (CPI). More than 110 linear feet of reports, correspondence, posters, bulletins, speeches, films, clippings, and other documentation detailing both the domestic and foreign work of the CPI from 1917 to 1919 are housed in this collection. Included are materials describing the

Vietnamese government propaganda. © Painet

anti-Bolshevik propaganda campaign conducted by the United States in Russia following the collapse of the Czarist regime.

RG 111—Office of the Chief Signal Officer. Preserved here are propaganda and informational films and newsreels made by the Signal Corps since World War I, the immense bulk of production files for World War II releases, plus other related post–1945 material.

RG 131—Office of Alien Property. Minutes, reports, pamphlets, press releases, periodicals, films, and other documents seized from German and Italian organizations operating in the United States (such as the German-American Bund) at the time of American entry into World War II are collected in this record group. For a comprehensive introduction to the more general topic of "Germany and German Film, 1930–1945" and attempts to sway American audiences, see the comprehensive three-part research bibliography by Richard Alan Nelson published by the *Journal of the University Film Association* in 1977–1978.

RG 200—National Archives Gift Collection. This is a motion picture and newsreel treasure house covering the years from 1919 to 1967. Included in the collection are issues of the *Official War Review, March of Time, Paramount News, Ford Animated Weekly* (1914–1921), and eight commercial films investigated by a Senate subcommittee just prior to Pearl Harbor for their alleged war propaganda. The useful *Guide to the Ford Film Collection in the National Archives* by Mayfield Bray, documenting the auto manufacturer's motion picture interests, appeared in 1970.

RG 208—Office of War Information. This is the main source of OWI documentation. Among the extensive holdings are a complete run of *Victory* magazine, 1943–1946.

RG 216—Office of Censorship. The records of this office, established by executive order to coordinate U.S. press censorship in World War II, still have restricted entry, suggesting that such activities must have been more extensive and coordinated than commonly recognized.

RG 226—Office of Strategic Services. The major archival depository for the OSS. The long-classified U.S. War Department's *War Report of the O.S.S.*, however, was published in 1976 and provides a revealing look at the organization's clandestine psychological operations.

RG 229—Office of Inter-American Coordinator. Records here describe Nelson Rockefeller's work in promoting a favorable U.S. image in Latin America during World War II, particularly through the efforts of the Walt Disney studios.

RG 262—Foreign Broadcast Intelligence Service. Contained are 512 cubic feet of documents from the period 1940–1947. Included are English translations of monitored foreign broadcasts and actual recordings by U.S. citizens such as Edward Delaney, Douglas Chandler, and Fred Keltenback aired over German radio. Tokyo Rose broadcasts from Japan and speeches by Allied leaders are also preserved. Note that the Center for Research Libraries in Chicago has microfilm copies of the *Daily Report of Foreign Radio Broadcasts* (1941–) transcribed into English, Voice of America broadcast scripts in English (1953–present), foreign broadcasts monitored by CBS (1939–1945), and other related wide-ranging deposits of potential interest.

RG 306—United States Information Agency. These consist primarily of audiovisual materials, including sound recordings (387 items) issued by the Voice of America from 1950 to 1965. However, unclassified materials relating to USIA's later role in Vietnam are also now available for study.

The National Audio-Visual Center operated by the National Archives and Record Service also rents and/or sells prints of more than 9,000 motion pictures produced by the federal government since the 1930s. Included are many classic propaganda films from World War II, as well as more recent USIA productions. The USIA maintains its own library in Washington, D.C., with a large clipping and document collection (much of it devoted to the persuasive efforts of the USIA and its predecessor organizations). Note should also be made of the State Department library, which has tightly restricted entry into its large holdings, including extensive propaganda documentation. The library of Congress, however, tends to be much more cooperative with independent researchers and offers a wealth of material for the propaganda historian. The *Catalog of Holdings, the American Film Institute Collection and the United Artists Collection at the Library of Congress* lists the 14,124 motion pictures acquisitioned through September 1977. Most of these are commercial features, but a number are of interest for their political messages. The Rare Book Division, by way of further illustration, has a very large collection of early political broadsides (including over 250 relating to the Continental Congress and the Constitutional Convention of 1787). The Prints and Photographs Division is also rich with posters and political cartoons of all periods, as well as World War II photos issued by the OWI and others. On deposit at the Library of Congress are many important collections of private papers, such as those of CPI director George Creel. The library also houses the records of the National Board for

Historical Service (which in World War I conducted an enemy press intelligence service), the Elmer Gertz Papers (with important materials relating to the career of George Viereck), and a series of bound volumes containing pamphlets issued by U.S. radical groups since the early 1900s.

The National Association of Broadcasters' Library and Information Center is an important reference service administered by the NAB's Public Affairs and Communications Department in Washington, D.C. In nearby Lexington, Virginia, the George C. Marshall Research Foundation and Library boasts much more than the general's private papers (themselves of great interest). There is also a small but excellent twentieth-century war poster collection (nearly 700 issued in the United States, Germany, and France), over 6,000 uncatalogued U.S. Signal Corps and OWI photos, and other military propaganda materials. A useful illustrated guide to the poster holdings written by Anthony Crawford, with an informed sixteen-page introduction by former OWI propaganda analyst O. W. Riegel, was published in 1979. For more on other available resources, see *Scholars' Guide to Washington D.C. Film and Video Collections* by Rowan, Culbert, Cripps, and Lichty and *Scholars' Guide to Washington, D.C. for Audio Resources* by James Heintze.

As to the country as a whole, also refer to *The Directory of Archives and Manuscript Repositories*, published by the National Historical Publications and Records Commission. This is a guide to 3,200 archives and manuscript repositories in the United States, arranged by state and town. Additional access is provided by a name-subject index, as well as special lists of different types of repositories. Bibliographic references accompany some of the entries.

Outside the greater Washington area, New York offers perhaps the single greatest concentration of library research materials for the study of American propaganda. The Radio Free Europe/Radio Liberty (RFE/RL) Reference Library in New York City is open to the public by appointment. Although its abundant holdings largely document current developments in the Soviet Union, there are also runs of RFE/RL publications and other pertinent materials detailing international broadcast propaganda. All in all, this is an exceptional research library that attracts scholars from across the globe interested in Soviet studies. Note that the papers of Frank Altschul, former chairman of Radio Free Europe, are in the Lehman Collection at Columbia University.

Anti- and pro-Semitic propaganda from here and abroad is collected at the four major Jewish libraries in New York City: the Jacob Alson Memorial Library of the Anti-Defamation League of B'nai B'rith, the Blaustein Library of the American Jewish Committee, the YIVO Institute for Jewish Research Library and Archives, and the Zionist Archives and Library. The Jewish Division of the New York Public Library also has a large collection of extremist literature. The American Jewish Archives (AJA) in Cincinnati is another source worth consulting as it includes the papers of important figures such as Jacob Schiff, Samuel Untermeyer, Felix Warburg, and Isaac Wise. The records of the House Special Committee on Un-American Activities, 1934–1939, focusing on Nazi propaganda in the United States, have been donated to the AJA by the family of Representative Samuel Dickstein. Similarly, an extensive collection of anti-Jewish propaganda materials issued between 1922 and 1967 is on deposit at the Minnesota Historical Society.

The New York Public Library's American History Division additionally houses a plethora of political propaganda materials, including party pamphlets, presidential campaign buttons, posters, ribbons, coins, and similar material (cataloged on over 100 cards). Its research libraries also have a strong advertising collection and regular deposit of newer publications and materials from groups such as the Advertising Council (which has had great agenda-setting influence on national "public service" issues). There are also twenty-nine Civil War enlistment posters and bound photographic volumes of over 2,000 World War I posters. The Bancroft Collection of original manuscripts from the American Revolution at the library includes the papers of the Boston Committee of Correspondence. The New York Public Library also has the papers of Samuel Adams and his grandson, Samuel Adams Wells. While considerable, these personal effects of Adams represent only a small portion of his total correspondence since much of what he wrote suffered from neglect or was destroyed in an effort to protect his reputation. Wells' papers consist of his manuscript notes and partial drafts for an unfinished biography of his grandfather, later utilized by subsequent writers. (Specialized materials on Samuel Adams and other revolutionary leaders can also be reviewed at the Massachusetts Historical Society Research Library in Boston.)

Other materials at the New York Public Library of interest to propaganda researchers include wide-ranging antislavery materials (including runs of early abolitionist propaganda periodicals such as the *Anti-Slavery Reporter*), over 11,000 pamphlets from World War I (many of them propagandistic; see also the Socialism Collection), a number of psychological warfare leaflets distributed in Europe and Asia during World War II, and substantial holdings of press releases and other publications issued by various government information services (such as those of the U.S. Central Intelligence Group from the years 1942–1947). Note that the papers of the Institute for Propaganda Analysis, long held privately by Alfred McClung Lee, have also been donated to the New York Public Library. Other materials on the institute can be consulted in the Kirtley F. Mather Collection, Harvard University Archives, Cambridge, Massachusetts. Mather was secretary for the institute.

For students of radical literature, the Tamiment Labor History Collection of New York University's Bobst Library is a mecca. There are extensive holdings of AFL-CIO materials, and the Oral History of the American Left Project serves as a repository for veterans of radicalism in unions, politics, and culture. A free guide can be obtained on request. Also in New York, the American Institute for Marxist Studies, headed for many years by Herbert Aptheker, has an interesting collection of "progressive" literature and publishes the bimonthly *AIMS Newsletter* (1964–) describing current activities in the field of Marxist thought, including bibliographical listings of interest to students of left propaganda.

The New York Historical Society tends to take a longer view and so is another source for early Revolutionary and Civil War propaganda broadsides. The society also houses the Landauer Collection of American Advertising—more than 1 million pictorial items demonstrating the power and art of U.S. business propaganda. Nearby, the library at Fairleigh Dickinson University in Madison, New Jersey, has been the official depository of the Outdoor Advertising Industry since 1972. Manuscripts, pamphlets, slides, photographs, and even full-sized billboards make up this most unusual collection.

Brooklyn College of the City University of New York is the home of the papers of Norman Cousins. These cover the years 1942–1958 and include his work with the OWI. The school's Department of Television and Radio also houses an unusual collection of black-and-white television commercials produced between 1948 and 1958. Across town, the Museum of Broadcasting (founded in 1976 with seed money from CBS) has already acquired a number of historical materials, including copies of World War II Axis English-language propaganda programs. It is also establishing a collection of landmark radio and television commercials that will be the only one of its kind to be thoroughly accessible to the public. Supplementing these is the University of Arizona's Bureau of Audio-Visual Services Archive Collection of Television Commercials, which includes more than 2,000 spots, mostly from the 1960s to the present. See also the holdings of the American Advertising Museum in Portland, Oregon. The collection contains more than 1,700 original advertising prints dating from 1673, impressive runs of pertinent trade journals, and a representative selection of broadcast commercials tracing back to the early 1920s. Of related interest is the Broadcast Promotion Association Archive in the Telecommunications Department Library at San Diego State University. This is the world's largest collection of tape, film, and print materials created by radio and television professionals to promote and advertise stations and programs.

The Public Relations Society of America operates a Research Information Center from its New York offices. This lending and reference library is primarily for members, but the library and vertical file holdings are open to the public. Although "propaganda" is not a specific subject area, related topics (particularly those of interest to contemporary public relations practitioners) are well covered. The New York State Library in Albany contains extensive propaganda poster holdings from World War I (including the Benjamin Walworth Arnold Collection), World War II (with civilian and war industries issues featured), the United Nations, and a number of other miscellaneous items. Also archived there are records of the now defunct New York State Board of Censors (1910–1966), which reviewed all films screened in the state. Scripts were required for purposes of rating and approval, and copies of these (which number over 70,000) have been indexed by title and transferred to the jurisdiction of the library's Manuscripts and Special Collections Division. Unfortunately, photocopying is restricted, but the collection forms a unique reference for the polemical as well as the purely entertainment film. The Sarah Lawrence Library in Bronxville also reportedly has propaganda-related materials.

The Rockefeller Archive Center in Pocantico Hills, New York, contains family and business papers of interest to students of Rockefeller-endowed organizations and people. Among the presidential libraries, the Franklin D. Roosevelt Library in Hyde Park is well organized and has collections and other manuscripts indispensable for research into the 1933–1945 New Deal period. A useful pamphlet describing historical materials in the library is available on request. Except for the Rutherford B. Hayes Library in Fremont, Ohio, the other presidential collections are administered by the National Archives and continue to receive relevant documents and publications. These include the Herbert Hoover Library in West Branch, Iowa; the Harry S Truman Library in Independence, Missouri; the Dwight D. Eisenhower Library in Abilene, Kansas; the Lyndon B. Johnson Library in Austin, Texas; the John F. Kennedy Library in Dorchester, Massachusetts; the Gerald R. Ford Library in Ann Arbor, Michigan; the Jimmy Carter Library in Atlanta; and the Ronald Reagan Library in California. Unfortunately, in the Johnson and Kennedy complexes a number of propaganda and psychological warfare documents from the Vietnam period remain classified. The difficulty former President Nixon had in locating a home for his library, including disputes over who owns what materials, further restricted serious political communication research for several years. For helpful suggestions, see the step-by-step advice of Kathleen Turner on getting started.

The presidential libraries also house political advertisements. For example, copies of selected Democratic ads for 1956–1964 are found in the Lyndon B. Johnson Library and for 1952–1968 in the John F. Kennedy Library. Fortunately, there are numerous other locations for campaign propaganda. The Kanter Political Archives at the University of Oklahoma is a particularly important collection, especially for broadcast materials—the place to head to if you can go to only one source. Materials in the archives, collected over more than thirty years by Julian Kanter, come from all across the country and represent candidates for every office from president to city council member. The collection today consists of more than 10,000 television spots and uncounted radio announcements. Rarities include a cartoon for Eisenhower, with a "We Like Ike" sound-track song—the only animated commercial ever made by the Disney Studio for a political campaign. Some of the other major archives include the University of Rhode Island, which has complete sets of the Eisenhower-Stevenson 1952 spots in the Wood and Devlin Collections, supplemented by a large number of later polispots, mostly from presidential campaigns. The Television Archives of the News Study Group in the Department of Political Science at the Massachusetts Institute of Technology has collected hundreds of commercials plus other political television materials. All of this is available on videotape for public inspection. In addition, a number of VHS compilations are beginning to appear for home and teaching use. Among the best is a sixty-minute documentary hosted by former Senator Eugene McCarthy entitled *The Classics of Political Television Advertising* (Washington, D.C.: Campaigns and Elections, 1986). David Beiler has written a very informative accompanying viewer's guide to this outstanding collection.

Befitting its historic Revolutionary heritage, Pennsylvania boasts several important propaganda collections. The American Philosophical Library in Philadelphia houses the vast Richard Gimbel Collection, formerly at Yale University, of published and unpublished materials by and about Thomas Paine. Other documents have been added to make this the single greatest reference center for the study of Paine's life and work. The Historical Society of Pennsylvania has cataloged the papers of U.S. Senator Jonathan Roberts (1771–1854), which are rich for study of national political history in the post-Revolutionary/pre–Civil War period (particularly the agitation for war with England in 1812 and controversies relating to the charter of the Bank of the United States).

The World War II Collection in the library of the Historical Society of Pennsylvania is also strong in broadsides, posters, and other forms of federal publicity and propaganda issued by U.S. government agencies. One of the country's largest collections of war posters and radical-racist literature is found nearby at the Balch Institute in Philadelphia. Temple University's Rare Books and Manuscripts Room also stores over 3,000 U.S. and foreign war posters dating from 1914 through the end of the Vietnam conflict. A card guide exists for World War I issues. The university's Contemporary Culture Center has equally impressive holdings of alternative and radical left- and right-wing press ephemera and polemical writings. These are supplemented by microfilm documents and taped interviews with neo-Nazi leaders and others.

See also the Quaker Collection at Haverford College in Pennsylvania, which includes the records (1821–1857) of the Indian Society of Anti-Slavery Friends and the diary of William Charles Allen, which discusses at some length the effect of propaganda on American public attitudes in World War I. Swarthmore College, besides material from World War I, also holds propaganda materials issued by the Women's Information League for Peace and Freedom, the League of Nations Association, and the Emergency Peace Campaign of 1937. The Harry S. Baird Papers in the U.S. Army Military History Research Collection at Carlisle Barracks, Pennsylvania, include a scrapbook of propaganda leaflets dropped over Japan in World War II. For other related materials consult the librarian directly.

Another useful source is the Thomas Newcommen Memorial Library and Museum in Exton, Pennsylvania, one of the finest specialized business and industrial history libraries in the world. Since propaganda has depended so closely upon technological advances, this library, with its extensive corporate documentation, should be canvassed by those interested in business elites' relationship to mass persuasion.

Cambridge and Boston are rightly regarded as among our greatest library centers. In addition to the John F. Kennedy Library, one can consult the Widener Library at Harvard, which has a simply overwhelming collection of Americana primary and secondary materials dating back to the seventeenth century. Researchers working in Cambridge should also visit the Edward L. Bernays Public Relations Library, which features one of the nation's largest propaganda collections. Because of its leadership role in recognizing public relations as an academic discipline, Boston University also has strong propaganda holdings including a number of war posters.

The papers of veteran newscaster Edward R. Murrow and his personal library (with much describing his years as USIA director) are now at the Murrow Center of Public Diplomacy, Fletcher School of Law and Diplomacy, Tufts University in Medford, Massachusetts. These contain scripts, research notes, and correspondence and are now available on fifty reels from Microfilming Corporation of America, a *New York Times* company. See the printed *Edward R. Murrow Papers, 1927–1965: A Guide to the Microfilm Edition* for more information.

In other New England institutions, the Yale University holdings in New Haven, Connecticut, make it one of the premier library collections in the United States. Besides general references, of interest are the extensive holdings of twentieth-century war posters plus the papers of Ezra Pound (whose propaganda broadcasts from Italy favorably comparing Mussolini to Thomas Jefferson were held by the victorious Allies to be clear proof of his insanity).

Rhode Island's history as an antislavery capital is reflected in the Harris Collection on the American Civil War and Slavery, archived at the Providence Public Library. It includes propaganda pamphlets, books, periodicals, broadsheet music, and other eighteenth- and nineteenth-century materials reflecting both sides of the controversy. Archiving more than eighty-five editions of *Uncle Tom's Cabin* in fourteen languages is typical of the thoroughness of the collection. Use is restricted, however, as is photocopying. Benefiting from the trend to microfilm scarce documents has been the Anti-Slavery Collection at Oberlin College in Ohio, now widely available.

The Newberry Library in Chicago, Northwestern University Library in Evanston, and the Illinois Historical Society Library at the University of Illinois in Urbana all have important holdings dealing with U.S. radicalism and related social, political, and labor struggles. Newberry's is perhaps the strongest for the nineteenth century. The files of the Church League of America in Wheaton, Illinois, offer an unusually detailed clipping collection of materials documenting communist and leftist propaganda in the United States. Included in this conservative research and lobby organization are complete sets of the hearings and reports issued by the U.S. House and California State Un-American Activities committees. Large holdings of right-wing political literature, documentation on controversial public relations pioneer Ivy Lee, and propaganda from World War I (including twelve file drawers of correspondence and business records from the Council on Books in Wartime) are now housed at the Princeton University Library in New Jersey. For researchers interested in acquiring reasonably priced works by radical rightist authors, many of which are out of print or unavailable elsewhere because of what the distributors call a "historical blackout," an indispensable source is the Sons of Liberty, P.O. Box 214, Metairie, La. 70004. A free booklist of hundreds of titles is available.

The University of Kansas also encompasses strong holdings in radical ephemera from the United States, much of which is cataloged. The Leon Josephson Collection there of pamphlets on modern socialism is particularly definitive with regard to the Communist Party of America. The University of Michigan has an excellent radical literature collection (except for Populism) dating from the nineteenth century. These include recordings of rightist figures in addition to limited collections of World War I posters (320 items) and election advertisements dating from the 1950s (500-plus items from the United States, Canada, and Europe). Note should additionally be made of the Archives of Labor and Urban Affairs in the Walter P. Reuther Library, Wayne State University, Detroit, where materials relevant to labor struggles as well as interesting collections such as the papers of Heber Blankenhorn (a journalist and economist who played an important role in World War II army psychological warfare efforts) are on deposit.

The State Historical Society of Wisconsin is yet another surprising source of documents and audiovisual material, particularly in relation to communist propaganda in the motion picture industry. Papers of Dalton Trumbo, Albert Maltz, Melvyn Douglas, Samuel Ornitz, the Progressive Citizens of America/Hollywood Democratic Committee, plus Robert Morris and Robert Kenny (lawyers who defended the Hollywood 10) are all available at the Wisconsin Center for Theatre Research, sponsored jointly by the society and the University of Wisconsin at Madison Department of Communication Arts. Other extensive film and television material is located there, including episodes of the controversial FBI-supported *I Led Three Lives* program aired during the McCarthy era of the 1950s. The papers of Frank Early Mason, also in the society's collections, contain private records of his radio propaganda activities as special assistant to the secretary of the navy in World War II. The university's School of Journalism and Mass Communication additionally operates a reading room with vertical file holdings on propaganda and public opinion. The University of Wisconsin campus at Milwaukee houses in its library an interesting collection of propaganda-related materials documenting third-party movements in U.S. politics.

Other state libraries such as the one at the University of Iowa maintain important reference archives. For example, at Iowa one can consult runs of more than 900 propaganda periodicals issued by right-wing groups since the 1920s. The basic collection is now available on microfilm for purchase by other research centers. The University of Iowa also holds the letters, papers (including a confidential psychiatric report), and legal documents of German-American propagandist George Sylvester Viereck. Nearly 1,300 items are included, covering the years 1896–1959, which reflect his long activist career (including representation of the National Socialist government prior to World War II). The American Archives of the Factual Film at Iowa State University now has close to 2,000 "sponsored" films in its collection and is the only major repository of its kind for business, educational, and informational motion pictures prepared for private distribution.

The University of Nebraska at Lincoln is another source for limited-circulation materials. The Rare Books and Special Collections Room there has posters, pamphlets, clippings, and other fugitive propaganda issues from World War II numbering over 1,000 items. The papers of Horace C. Peterson archived in the University of Oklahoma Library include original references used in writing his book *Propaganda for War: The Campaign against American Neutrality, 1914–1917*, supplemented by reviews and other documentation of reaction to publication. Of a different nature are the sixty-nine microfilm reels of administrative records for the *Congregatio de propaganda fide* covering Catholic activities in the Americas and Great Britain from 1622 to 1865, housed, appropriately, at the University of Notre Dame Archives. A guide to these documents by Finbar Kenneally has been published.

In the South, the U.S. Infantry Museum at Fort Benning (Columbus, Georgia) includes a collection of posters and other militaria from both world wars. The U.S. Army Institute for Military Assistance Library (formerly the Special Warfare School Library) at Fort Bragg, North Carolina, has more than 45,000 pamphlets and documents related to military strategy and counterintelligence (including propaganda leaflets from World War II and Korea). The University of Louisville's Belknap Campus Library and Allen Hite Art Institute have strong U.S. government-issue poster holdings from both world wars, Red Cross posters from the 1915–1921 period, and numerous posters issued by the anti-Vietnam War movement. The University of Georgia Library has a noted Confederate Imprint Collection with eighty broadsides and other persuasive documents (official and unofficial) issued between 1861 and 1865.

The Vanderbilt Television News Archive in Nashville is a unique collection of nearly 10,000 hours of videotaped news and public affairs programs issued since August 1968 (indexed and abstracted since 1972). Disputes over news bias and propaganda in electronic journalism can at last be objectively researched, with individual programs and complications available at nominal cost for noncommercial purposes. A regional News Archive center also exists at George Washington University in Washington, D.C. The Purdue University Public Affairs Video Archive in West Lafayette, Indiana, began recording Cable-Satellite Public Affairs Network (C-SPAN) programming in October 1987. The archive is developing a catalog that will list C-SPAN material by type of event, content, and time reference. Educators can purchase unedited C-SPAN airings or single-subject packaged tapes.

In Texas, several centers other than the Lyndon B. Johnson Presidential Library are of interest. The University of Texas Library at Austin, for example, owns the Frances Harvey Papers, which discuss use of newspaper propaganda in the Southwest following the Civil War. The Edward A. Peden papers at the University of Texas-Austin trace his work distributing U.S. propaganda materials in Germany after World War I.

One of the finer specialized collections of atheist, free-thought, and anti-church propaganda in the country is the Society of Separationists Library in Austin, Texas. Unfortunately, the books and other materials are not properly cataloged because of financial constraints and are displayed in rather haphazard condition. The Library of the American Association for the Advancement of Atheism in San Diego, California, reflects similar interests and encompasses another useful reference center for this topic. Researchers, however, are requested to make prior arrangements before traveling to the library. More narrow is the Richard Alan Nelson Mormon Film and Television Collection, which supplements other archived communications holdings at Brigham Young University in Provo, Utah, to document pro- and anti-Mormon media portrayals over the years.

In contrast, the Hoover Institution of War, Revolution, and Peace at Stanford University is the largest private repository in the United States. Its library, begun in 1919, alone houses over 1.25 million book volumes dealing with all aspects of modern social, economic, and political change. However, it is for the library's collection of propaganda posters (more than 50,000), letters, leaflets, newspapers, rare photos, diaries, personal records, and limited-circulation street propaganda that the Hoover Institution is justly famed. Several surveys of holdings and library catalogs have been published, indicating the importance of this research treasure house.

Another Nothern California resource is the Pacific Studies Center (founded in 1969) in Mountain View, which maintains a library with information files covering a wide variety of propaganda-related titles. The center also publishes the bimonthly *Pacific Research*, a critical journal focusing on U.S. foreign policy and power structure studies concerning the activities of multinational corporations. The DataCenter is an unusual user-supported library and information center in Oakland, California, which collects, organizes, and provides access to a treasure trove of information on economic, social, and political issues. It also offers specialized search, clipping, and other services. PeaceNet, a San Francisco-based computer network for "progressives," links users throughout the United States and in over seventy countries. It offers electronic mail, on-line bulletin boards, data bases, and Telex services to share information.

For the historian, access to scarce left radical propaganda is possible at the Southern California Library for Social Studies and Research in Los Angeles. More than 15,000 volumes on Marxism, a like number of rare pamphlets dating back more than eighty-five years, over 2,000 tape recordings of contemporary antiestablishment leaders ranging from Angela Davis to Martin Luther King Jr., plus 150,000 news clips broken down into 800 categories (including propaganda) and selected news films made in the 1930s are arranged for easy use. Also maintained are files documenting hundreds of labor, social, and political campaigns and groups active before World War I.

California State University, Fullerton, has a small but interesting Freedom Center of Political Ephemera which has runs of over 800 labor publications dating from the late 1800s, election propaganda and campaign buttons from the twentieth century, and the nearly complete papers of the League of Nations. Yet another archive is found at the University of California at Davis, whose library has a substantial collection of over 6,000 pamphlets issued by U.S. radical and social change organizations (1890 to the present) and a more limited number of U.S. and Japanese war posters from the 1940s. The University of Wyoming similarly has literally thousands of collections of papers, many relating to propaganda (such as those of Lyman Munson, Frank Capra's boss for the *Why We Fight* motion picture series). Also of interest is the collection of U.S. and French World War I propaganda posters (over 1,000) and pamplets on file at the Tacoma, Washington, Public Library. An unusually comprehensive resource is the KIRO-CBS Collection of Broadcasts of the World War II Years and After, in the Phonoarchive of the University of Washington, which preserves inclusive sound recordings of one radio network's fare during the 1940s. A guide to this collection exists, prepared by Milo Ryan.

This brief overview of available materials gives some idea of the immensity of the topic. Not all sources for the study of American propaganda, however, are to be found within the United States. The Imperial War Museum in London is a major propaganda research center. The museum's library is very strong in twentieth-century pamphlets, film (with over 37 million feet from the two world wars and an increasing collection of post-1945 footage, including Vietnam), artwork (the poster collection exceeds 50,000 items, among them significant U.S. issues), and photographs, as well as standard book and clipping file materials. Another British contact is the Psywar Society of England, headed by Reginald Auckland, which publishes a fact-filled journal called *The Falling Leaf* and acts as a clearinghouse for psychological warfare memorabilia collectors. Auckland, for example, has a personal collection of over 9,000 items (including many rare U.S. Army leaflets). On the continent, the Radical Communication Research Library at the Institute of Social Studies, The Hague, Netherlands (formerly the International Mass Media Research Center Library in Bagnolet, France) library, serves as a documentary archive for those interested in worldwide Marxist studies involving all aspects of communications (including propaganda). The center also publishes useful bibliographical catalogs.

BIBLIOGRAPHY

Books, Articles, and Unpublished Scholarly Works

Abshire, David. *International Broadcasting: A New Dimension in Western Diplomacy.* Beverly Hills, Calif.: Sage, 1976.

Adams, Samuel. *The Writings of Samuel Adams 1764–1802.* 4 vols. Collected and ed. Harry Alonzo Cushing. New York: Putnam's, 1904–1908.

Adler, Selig. *The Isolationist Impulse: Its Twentieth Century Reaction.* New York: Free Press, 1966.

Agee, Philip. *Inside the Company: A CIA Diary*. New York: Stonehill, 1975.

Agee, Philip, and Louis Wolf, eds. *Dirty Work: The CIA in Western Europe*. Secaucus, N.J.: L. Stuart, 1978.

Aldridge, Alfred Owen. *Man of Reason: The Life of Thomas Paine*. Philadelphia: J. B. Lippincott, 1959.

Altschull, J. Herbert. *Agents of Power: The Role of the News Media in Human Affairs*. White Plains, N.Y.: Longman, 1984.

Altheide, David L., and John M. Johnson. *Bureaucratic Propaganda*. Boston: Allyn and Bacon, 1980.

Archival and Manuscript Materials at the Hoover Institution on War, Revolution and Peace: A Checklist of Major Collections. Stanford, Calif.: Hoover Institution Press, 1978.

Argersinger, Peter H. *Populism and Politics: William Alfred Peffer and the People's Party*. Lexington: University Press of Kentucky, 1974.

Aristotle. *Rhetoric*. Trans. Lane Cooper. New York: Appleton-Century, 1932.

Armor, John C. *Substance and Shadows: The Original Meaning of Freedom of the Press*. Washington, D.C.: Freedom of Expression Foundation, 1984.

Aronson, James. *Packaging the News: A Critical Survey of Press, Radio, TV*. New York: International, 1971.

Ashworth, William. *Under the Influence: Congress, Lobbies, and the American Pork-Barrel System*. New York: Hawthorn/Dutton, 1981.

Auxier, George. "The Propaganda Activities of the Cuban Junta in Precipating the Spanish American War, 1895–1898." *Hispanic American Historical Review* 19 (August 1939), 286–305.

Bagdikian, Ben H. *The Media Monopoly*. Boston: Beacon Press, 1983.

Bailey, R. N. "Issues Management: A Survey of Contemporary Practice." Master's thesis, University of Florida, 1983.

Bailyn, Bernard. *Ideological Origins of the American Revolution*. Cambridge: Belknap Press of Harvard University Press, 1967.

———, ed. *Pamphlets of the American Revolution, 1750–1776*. Cambridge: Belknap Press of Harvard University Press, 1965.

Bamford, James. *The Puzzle Palace: A Report on NSA, America's Most Secret Agency*. New York: Penguin Books, 1983.

Barber, W. E. "Propaganda." In *Dictionary of American History*. Rev. ed. New York: Scribner's, 1976, V: 41–43.

Barghoorn, Frederick C. *Soviet Foreign Propaganda*. Princeton, N.J.: Princeton University Press, 1964.

Barnes, Donald. "Ideology of the IWW." Ph.D. diss., Washington State University, 1962.

Barnouw, Erik. *Documentary: A History of the Non-fiction Film*. New York: Oxford University Press, 1974.

———. *The Golden Web: A History of Broadcasting in the United States, 1933–1953*. New York: Oxford University Press, 1968.

———. *The Image Empire: A History of Broadcasting in the United States from 1953*. New York: Oxford University Press, 1970.

———. *A Tower in Babel: A History of Broadcasting in the United States to 1933*. New York: Oxford University Press, 1966.

————, ed. in chief. *The International Encyclopedia of Communications*. 4 vols. New York: Oxford University Press, 1989.

Barrett, Edward W. *Truth Is Our Weapon*. New York: Funk and Wagnalls, 1953.

Barron, John. *KGB: The Secret Work of Soviet Secret Agents*. New York: Reader's Digest Press, 1974.

————, *KGB Today: The Hidden Hand*. New York: Reader's Digest Press, 1983.

Barsam, Richard M. *Nonfiction Film: A Critical History*. New York: E. P. Dutton, 1973.

————, ed. *Nonfiction Film: Theory and Criticism*. New York: E. P. Dutton, 1976.

Bartlett, F. C. *Political Propaganda*. Cambridge, England: Cambridge University Press, 1940. Reprint. New York: Octagon, 1973.

Baskin, Otis, and Craig Aronoff. *Public Relations: The Profession and the Practice*. 2nd ed. Dubuque, Iowa: William C. Brown, 1988.

Beach, Stewart. *Samuel Adams: The Fateful Years, 1764–1776*. New York: Dodd, Mead, 1965.

Becket, Henry S.A. *The Dictionary of Espionage: Spookspeak into English*. New York: Dell, 1987.

Beiler, David. *The Classics of Political Television Advertising: A Viewers Guide*. Washington, D.C.: Campaigns and Elections, 1986. This accompanies a sixty-minute VHS videotape documentary hosted by former Senator Eugene McCarthy.

Bennett, James T., and Thomas J. DiLorenzo. *Destroying Democracy: How Government Funds Partisan Politics*. Washington, D.C.: Cato Institute, 1985.

Bennett, W. Lance. *News: The Politics of Illusion*. 2nd ed. White Plains, N.Y.: Longman, 1988.

Berelson, Bernard, and Morris Janowitz. *Reader in Public Opinion and Communication*. 2nd ed. New York: Free Press, 1966.

Berger, Carl. *Broadsides & Bayonets: The Propaganda War of the American Revolution*. Rev. ed. San Rafael, Calif.: Presidio Press, 1976.

Bergner, Douglas J., ed. *Public Interest Profiles, 1986–1987*. 5th ed. Washington, D.C.: Foundation for Public Affairs, 1986.

Bergstrom, Letty. "The Battle for America: German-English Language Propaganda in the U.S. from 1933 to 1941." Master's thesis, Northwestern University, 1948.

Bernays, Edward L. *Crystalizing Public Opinion*. New York: Boni and Liveright, 1923. 2nd ed. New York: Liveright, 1961.

————. *Propaganda*. New York: Horace Liveright, 1928.

Berry, Mary Frances. *Why ERA Failed: Politics, Women's Rights, and the Amending Process of the Constitution*. Bloomington: Indiana University Press, 1986.

Bettinghaus, Erwin P., and Michael J. Cody. *Persuasive Communication*. 4th ed. New York: Holt, Rinehart, and Winston, 1987.

Biddle, William Wishart. *Propaganda and Education*. New York: Teachers College Press, Columbia University, 1932.

Birnbaum, Jeffrey H., and Alan S. Murray. *Showdown at Gucci Gulch: Lawmakers, Lobbyists, and the Unlikely Triumph of Tax Reform*. New York: Random House, 1987.

Bishop, Robert L. "The Overseas Branch of the Office of War Information." Ph.D. diss., University of Wisconsin at Madison, 1966.

————. *Public Relations: A Comprehensive Bibliography—Articles and Books on Public Relations, Communication Theory, Public Opinion, and Propaganda, 1964–1972.* Ann Arbor: University of Michigan Press, 1974.

————. "Public Relations: A Comprehensive Bibliography of Articles and Books on Public Relations, Communication Theory, Public Opinion, and Propaganda, 1973–1974." *Public Relations Review* 1 (Winter Supplement 1975–76), 1–200.

————. "Public Relations: A Comprehensive Bibliography of Articles and Books on Public Relations, Communication Theory, Public Opinion, and Propaganda, 1975." *Public Relations Review* 3 (Summer 1977), 1–145.

Bittman, Ladislav. *The Deception Game.* Syracuse, N.Y.: Syracuse University Research Corp. 1972.

————. *The KGB and Soviet Disinformation: An Insider's View.* Washington, D.C.: Pergamon-Brassey's 1985.

Blakey, George T. *Historians on the Homefront: American Propagandists for the Great War.* Lexington: University of Kentucky Press, 1970.

Bloxom, Marguerite. "Lafayette as a Tool of American Propaganda." Ph.D. diss., University of Maryland, 1970.

Blum, John Morton. *V Was for Victory: Politics and American Culture during World War II.* New York: Harcourt Brace Jovanovich, 1976.

Bogart, Leo. *Premises for Propaganda: The United States Information Agency's Operating Assumptions in the Cold War.* New York: Free Press, 1976.

Bohn, Thomas. *An Historical and Descriptive Analysis of the "Why We Fight" Series.* New York: Arno Press, 1977.

Bottomore, Tom, ed. *A Dictionary of Marxist Thought.* Cambridge: Harvard University Press, 1983.

Bowdoin, James, Joseph Warren, and Samuel Pemberton. *A Short Narrative of the Horrid Massacre in Boston, Perpetrated in the Evening of the Fifth Day of March, 1770, by Soldiers of the 29th Regiment, which with the 14th Regiment Were Then Quartered There; with Some Observations on the State of Things Prior to that Catastrophe.* Boston: Town of Boston, 1770. Republished with notes and illustrations. New York: John Doggett Jr., 1849. Photo-republication of 1849 ed. Williamstown, Mass.: Corner House, 1973.

Braestrup, Peter. *Big Story! How the American Press and Television Reported and Interpreted the Crisis of Tet 1968 in Vietnam and Washington.* 2 vols. Boulder, Colo.: Westview Press, 1977.

Brembeck, Winston, and William Howell. *Persuasion: A Means of Social Influence.* 2nd ed. Englewood Cliffs, N.J.: Prentice-Hall, 1976.

Brightbill, George D. *Communications and the United States Congress: A Selectively Annotated Bibliography of Committee Hearings, 1870–1976.* Washington, D.C.: Broadcast Education Association, 1978.

Brinkley, Alan. *Voices of Protest: Huey Long, Father Coughlin and the Great Depression.* New York: Alfred A. Knopf, 1982.

Britt, Steuart Henderson. *Psychological Principles of Marketing and Consumer Behavior.* Lexington, Mass.: Lexington Books/Heath, 1978.

Brownfeld, Allan C., and J. Michael Waller. *The Revolution Lobby.* Washington, D.C.: Council for Inter-American Security and the Inter-American Security Educational Institute, 1985.

Brownlow, Kevin. *The War, the West and the Wilderness*. New York: Alfred A. Knopf, 1979.

Bruntz, George C. *Allied Propaganda and the Collapse of the German Empire in 1918*. Stanford, Calif.: Stanford University Press, 1938.

Bubka, Tony. "Time to Organize!: The IWW Stickerettes." *American West* 5 (January 1968), 21–27, 73.

Buchanan, Albert R. "European Propaganda and American Public Opinion, 1914–1917." Ph.D. diss., Stanford University, 1935.

Buchanan, William W., and Edna A. Kanely, comps. *Cumulative Subject Index to the Monthly Catalog of United States Government Publications 1900–1971*. 15 vols. Washington, D.C.: Carrollton Press, 1973–75.

Buchholz, Rogene. *Essentials of Public Policy for Management*. Englewood Cliffs, N.J.: Prentice-Hall, 1985.

Burton, Bob. *Top Secret: A Clandestine Operator's Glossary of Terms*. New York: Berkley Books, 1987.

Canfield, Cass. *Sam Adams' Revolution (1765–1776)*. New York: Harper and Row, 1976.

Carlsnaes, Walter. *The Concept of Ideology and Political Analysis: A Critical Examination of Its Usage by Marx, Lenin, and Mannheim*. Westport, Conn.: Greenwood Press, 1981.

Carroll, Wallace. *Persuade or Perish*. Boston: Houghton Mifflin, 1948.

Casey, Ralph Droz. "Propaganda Technique in the 1928 Presidential Campaign." Ph.D. diss., University of Wisconsin, 1929.

Cassata, Mary B., and Thomas Skill. *Television: A Guide to the Literature*. Phoenix: Oryx Press, 1985.

Castle, Eugene W. *Billions, Blunders and Baloney: The Fantastic Story of How Uncle Sam Is Squandering Your Money Overseas*. New York: Devin-Adair, 1955.

Ceplair, Larry. *Under the Shadow of War: Fascism, Anti-Fascism, and Marxists, 1918–1939*. New York: Columbia University Press, 1987.

Chafets, Ze'ev. *Double Vision: How the Press Distorts America's View of the Middle East*. New York: William Morrow, 1985.

Chaitkin, Anton. *Treason in America from Aaron Burr to Averell Harriman*. 2nd ed. New York: New Benjamin Franklin House, 1985.

Chalmers, David M. *Hooded Americanism: The History of the Ku Klux Klan*. 3rd ed. Durham, N.C.: Duke University Press, 1987.

Chamorro, Edgar. *Packaging the Contras: A Case of CIA Disinformation*. New York: Institute for Media Analysis, 1987.

Chase, W. Howard. *Issue Management: Origins of the Future*. Stamford, Conn.: Issue Action Publications, 1984.

Childs, Harwood L. *An Introduction to Public Opinion*. New York: Wiley, 1940.

———. "Propaganda." In *Collier's Encyclopedia*. New York: Macmillan, 1979, XIX: 410–17.

———. *A Reference Guide to the Study of Public Opinion*. Princeton, N.J.: Princeton University Press, 1934. Reprint. Ann Arbor, Mich.: Gryphon Books; 1971.

———, ed. "Pressure Groups and Propaganda." *Annals* of the American Academy of Political and Social Sciences, 179 (May 1935). Special issue.

Childs, Harwood L., and John B. Whitton, eds. *Propaganda by Short Wave* (1942). Bound with C. A. Rigby's *The War on Short Waves* (1943) in a new joint edition as part of the International Propaganda and Communication series. New York: Arno Press, 1972.

Chomsky, Noam, Morris Morley, James Petras, and Michael Parenti. *The Reagan Administration and Nicaragua: How Washington Constructs Its Case for Counter-revolution in Central America.* New York: Institute for Media Analysis, 1987.

Choukas, Michael. *Propaganda Comes of Age.* Washington, D.C.: Public Affairs Press, 1965.

Christenson, Reo M., and Robert O. McWilliams, comps. *Voice of the People: Readings in Public Opinion and Propaganda.* 2nd ed. New York: McGraw-Hill, 1967.

Cigler, Allan J., and Burdett A. Loomis, eds. *Interest Group Politics.* 2nd ed. Washington, D.C.: Congressional Quarterly Books, 1986.

Cirino, Robert. *Don't Blame the People: How the News Media Use Bias, Distortion and Censorship to Manipulate Public Opinion.* New York: Vintage/Random House, 1972.

———. *We're Being More than Entertained.* Honolulu: Lighthouse Press, 1977.

Coates, Joseph F., Vary T. Coates, Jennifer Jarratt, and Lisa Heinz. *Issues Management: How You Can Plan, Organize, and Manage for the Future.* Mt. Airy, Md.: Lomond, 1986.

Colby, Benjamin. *'Twas a Famous Victory: Deception and Propaganda in the War with Germany.* New Rochelle, N.Y.: Arlington House, 1974.

Colby, Roy. *A Communese-English Dictionary.* Boston: Western Islands, 1972.

Congressional Quarterly. *The Washington Lobby.* 5th ed. Washington, D.C.: Congressional Quarterly Books, 1987.

Constantine, James. "The African Slave Trade: A Study of Eighteenth Century Propaganda and Public Controversy." Ph.D. diss., Indiana University, 1953.

Conway, Moncure D. *The Life of Thomas Paine.* 2 vols. New York: Putnam's, 1892. Reprint. New York: Benjamin Blom, 1969.

Cooper, Kent. *The Right to Know: An Exposition of the Evils of News Suppression and Propaganda.* New York: Farrar, Straus, and Cudahy, 1956.

Cormier, Frank, James Deakin, and Helen Thomas. *The White House Press on the Presidency: News Management and Co-option.* Lanham, Md.: University Press of America, 1983.

Craig, Robert L. "The Changing Communicative Structure of Advertisements, 1850–1930." Ph.D. diss., University of Iowa, 1985.

Crandall, Marjorie Lyle. *Confederate Imprints: A Check List Based Principally on the Collection of the Boston Athenaeum.* 2 vols. Boston: Boston Athenaeum, 1955.

Crawford, Anthony R., ed. *Posters of World War I and World War II in the George C. Marshall Research Foundation.* Charlottesville: University Press of Virginia, 1979.

Creel, George. *How We Advertised America: The First Telling of the Amazing Story of the Committee on Public Information That Carried the Gospel of Americanism to Every Corner of the Globe.* New York: Harper and Brothers, 1920. Reprint. New York: Arno Press, 1972.

———. *Rebel at Large: Recollections of Fifty Crowded Years.* New York: Putnam's, 1947.

Cronkhite, Gary. *Persuasion: Speech and Behavioral Change*. Indianapolis: Bobbs-Merrill, 1969.

Crow, John. "Ideology and Organization." Master's thesis, University of Chicago, 1958.

Cruickshank, Charles G. *The Fourth Arm: Psychological Warfare 1938–1945*. London: Davis-Poynter, 1977.

Crunden, Robert M. *Ministers of Reform: The Progressives' Achievement in American Civilization, 1889–1920*. New York: Basic Books, 1982.

Culbert, David. *News for Everyman: Radio and Foreign Affairs in Thirties America*. Westport, Conn.: Greenwood Press, 1976.

———, ed. in chief. *Film and Propaganda in America: A Documentary History*. 4 vols. Westport, Conn.: Greenwood Press, 1990–1991.

———, ed. *Mission to Moscow: The Feature Film as Propaganda*. Madison: University of Wisconsin Press, 1980.

Cullop, Charles P. *Confederate Propaganda in Europe, 1861–1865*. Coral Gables, Fla.: University of Miami Press, 1969.

Cumby, Constance. *The Hidden Dangers of the Rainbow: The New Age Movement and Our Coming Age of Barbarism*. Rev. ed. Shreveport, La.: Huntington House, 1983.

Cutlip, Scott M. *A Public Relations Bibliography to 1965*. 2nd ed. Madison: University of Wisconsin Press, 1965.

Cutlip, Scott M., Allen H. Center, and Glen M. Broom. *Effective Public Relations*. 6th ed. Englewood Cliffs, N.J.: Prentice-Hall, 1985.

Dahlerup, Drude, ed. *The New Women's Movement: Feminism and Political Power in Europe and the U.S.A.* Newbury Park, Calif.: Sage, 1987.

Darracott, J., and B. Loftus. *Second World War Posters*. London: Imperial War Museum, 1972.

Davidson, Philip. *Propaganda and the American Revolution, 1763–1783*. Chapel Hill: University of North Carolina Press, 1941. Reprinted as *Propaganda in the American Revolution*. New York: W. W. Norton, 1973.

de Borchgrave, Arnaud, and Robert Moss. *The Spike*. New York: Avon Books, 1981.

Denton, Robert E. Jr., and Gary C. Woodward. *Political Communication in America*. New York: Praeger, 1985.

DeWitt, Benjamin Parke. *The Progressive Movement: A Non-partisan, Comprehensive Discussion of Current Tendencies in American Politics*. New York: Macmillan, 1915. Republished with a new introduction by Arthur Mann. Seattle: University of Washington Press, 1968.

Diamond, Edwin, and Stephen Bates. *The Spot: The Rise of Political Advertising on Television*. Cambridge: MIT Press, 1984. Rev. ed. 1988.

Dietrich, Daniel, ed. *Teaching about Doublespeak*. Urbana, Ill.: National Council of Teachers of English, 1976.

Dizard, Wilson P., Jr. *The Coming Information Age: An Overview of Technology, Economics and Politics*. 2nd ed. White Plains, N.Y.: Longman, 1985.

Dobson, Christopher, and Ronald Payne. *The Never-Ending War: Terrorism in the Eighties*. New York: Facts on File, 1987.

Doctor, Powrie Vaux. "Amos Kendall, Propagandist of Jacksonian Democracy." Ph.D. diss., Georgetown University, 1940.

Doenecke, Justus. *Anti-interventionism: A Bibliographical Introduction to Isolationism and Pacifism from World War I to the Early Cold War*. New York: Garland, 1987.

Donner, Frank J. *The Age of Surveillance: The Aims and Methods of America's Political Intelligence System*. New York: Vintage Books, 1981.

Doob, Leonard W. *Propaganda: Its Psychology and Technique*. New York: Holt, 1935.

———. *Public Opinion and Propaganda*. 2nd ed. Hamden, Conn.: Archon Books, 1966.

Dougherty, William E., and Morris Janowitz. *Psychological Warfare Casebook*. Baltimore: John Hopkins University Press, 1958.

Douglas, Sara U. *Labor's New Voice: Unions and the Mass Media*. Norwood, N.J.: Ablex, 1986.

Dowell, Eldridge Foster. *History of Criminal Syndicalism Legislation in the United States*. Studies in Historical and Political Science, Series LVII, No. 1. Baltimore: Johns Hopkins University, 1939. Reprint ed. New York: Da Capo Press, 1970.

Dumond, Dwight Lowell. *Antislavery: The Crusade for Freedom in America*. New York: W. W. Norton, 1966.

Duncan-Clark, Samuel. *The Progressive Movement: Its Principles and Its Programme*. Boston: Small, Maynard, 1913.

Dunham, Donald C. *Kremlin Target: U.S.A.; Conquest by Propaganda*. New York: I. Washburn, 1961.

Dunn, S. Watson. *Public Relations: A Contemporary Approach*. Homewood, Ill.: Irwin, 1986.

Dyer, Murray. *The Weapon on the Wall: Rethinking Psychological Warfare*. Baltimore: Johns Hopkins University Press, 1959.

Edmunds, Robert. *About Documentary: Anthropology on Film*. Dayton, Ohio: Pflaum, 1974.

Edward R. Murrow Papers, 1927–1965: A Guide to the Microfilm Edition. Sanford, N.C.: Microfilming Corporation of America, 1981.

Edwards, Samuel. *Rebel! A Biography of Tom Paine*. New York: Praeger, 1974.

Efron, Edith. *The News Twisters*. Los Angeles: Nash, 1971.

Efron, Edith, and Clytia Chambers. *How CBS Tried to Kill a Book*. Los Angeles: Nash, 1972.

Elder, Robert. *The Information Machine: The United States Information Agency and American Foreign Policy*. Syracuse, N.Y.: Syracuse University Press, 1968.

Ellul, Jacques. *Propaganda: The Formation of Men's Attitudes*. New York: Alfred A. Knopf, 1965. Reprint. New York: Vintage Books, 1973.

Evans, Frank Bowen, ed. *Worldwide Communist Propaganda Activities*. New York: Macmillan, 1955.

Evansohn, John, et al. *Literature of the American Working Class*. San Francisco: Bay Area Radical Education Project, [1969].

Ewing, Raymond P. *Managing the New Bottom Line: Issues Management for Senior Executives*. Homewood, Ill.: Dow Jones-Irwin, 1988.

Fagan, Myron C. *Documentation of the Red Stars in Hollywood*. Hollywood, Calif.: Cinema Educational Guild, [ca. 1950].

————. *Red Treason in Hollywood*. Hollywood, Calif.: Cinema Educational Guild, 1949.

————. *Red Treason on Broadway: Stage, Television, Radio*. Hollywood, Calif.: Cinema Educational Guild, 1954.

Fejes, Fred. *Imperialism, Media and the Good Neighbor: New Deal Foreign Policy and United States Shortwave Broadcasting to Latin America*. Norwood, N.J.: Ablex, 1986.

————. *The U.S. in Third World Communications: Latin America, 1900–1945*. Journalism Monographs, No. 86. Columbia, S.C.: Association for Education in Journalism and Mass Communication, November 1983.

Ferguson, Marilyn. *The Aquarian Conspiracy: Personal and Social Transformation in the 1980s*. Updated ed. Los Angeles: J. P. Tarcher, 1987.

Fielding, Raymond. *The American Newsreel: 1911–1967*. Norman: University of Oklahoma Press, 1972.

Filler, Louis. *Dictionary of American Conservatism*. New York: Philosophical Library, 1987.

————. *Progressivism and Muckraking*. New York: R. R. Bowker, 1976.

Findley, Paul. *They Dare to Speak Out: People and Institutions Confront Israel's Lobby*. Westport, Conn.: Lawrence Hill, 1985.

Fitzgerald, Richard. "The Images of Power in American Political Cartoons." *Praxis: A Journal of Radical Perspectives on the Arts* 1 (Winter 1976), 1–8.

Foner, Eric. *Tom Paine and Revolutionary America*. New York: Oxford University Press, 1976.

Foner, Philip S. *History of the Labor Movement in the United States*. 6 vols. New York: International Publishers, 1947–82.

————, ed. *American Labor Songs of the Nineteenth Century*. Urbana: University of Illinois Press, 1975.

Ford, Glen. *The Big Lie: Analysis of U.S. Press Coverage of the Grenada Invasion*. Prague: International Organization of Journalists in cooperation with the National Alliance of Third World Journalists, 1985.

Ford, Nick Aaron. *Language in Uniform: A Reader on Propaganda*. New York: Odyssey Press, 1967.

Fraser, Lindley. *Propaganda*. New York: Oxford University Press, 1957.

Frederick, Howard H. *Cuban-American Radio Wars: Ideology in International Telecommunications*. Norwood, N.J.: Ablex, 1986.

Freeley, Austin J. *Argumentation and Debate: Critical Thinking for Reasoned Decision Making*. 6th ed. Belmont, Calif.: Wadsworth, 1986.

Freidel, Frank. B., comp. *Union Pamphlets of the Civil War, 1861–1865*. Cambridge: Belknap Press of the Harvard University Press, 1967.

French, Blaire Atherton. *The Presidential Press Conference: Its History and Role in the American Political System*. Lanham, Md.: University Press of America, 1982.

Friedberg, Gerald. "Sources for the Study of Socialism in America, 1901–1919." *Labor History* 6 (Spring 1965), 159–65.

Fulbright, J. William. *The Pentagon Propaganda Machine*. New York: Liveright, 1970.

Furhammer, Leif, and Folke Isaksson. *Politics and Film*. New York: Praeger, 1971.

Gaines, Elizabeth. "*The Fatherland*: An American Vehicle for German Propaganda, 1914–1917." Master's thesis, Indiana University, 1971.

Galvin, John R. *Three Men of Boston*. New York: Crowell, 1976.

Gandy, Oscar H., Jr. *Beyond Agenda Setting: Information Subsidies and Public Policy*. Norwood, N.J.: Ablex, 1982.

Giddens, Jackson. "American Foreign Propaganda in World War I." Ph.D. diss., Fletcher School of Law and Diplomacy, Tufts University, 1967.

———. "Propaganda." In *The Encyclopedia Americana*. International ed. Danbury, Conn.: Americana, 1979, xxii: 656–60.

Giffard, C. Anthony. *UNESCO and the Media*. White Plains, N.Y.: Longman, 1988.

Gimbel, Richard. *Thomas Paine: A Bibliographical Check List of "Common Sense," with an Account of Its Publication*. New Haven, Conn.: Yale University Press, 1956.

Gipson, Henry Clay. *Films in Business and Industry*. New York: McGraw-Hill, 1947.

Glazier, Kenneth M., and James R. Hobson. *International and English-Language Collections: A Survey of the Holdings at the Hoover Institution on War, Revolution and Peace*. Stanford, Calif.: Hoover Institution Press, 1971.

Goehlert, Robert U., and Fenton S. Martin. *The American Presidency: A Bibliography*. Washington, D.C.: Congressional Quarterly Books, 1987.

———. *American Presidents: A Bibliography*. Washington, D.C.: Congressional Quarterly Books, 1987.

Gordon, George N. *Persuasion: The Theory and Practice of Manipulative Communication*. New York: Hastings House, 1971.

Gordon, George N., and Irving A. Falk. *The War of Ideas: America's International Identity Crisis*. New York: Hastings House, 1973.

Gordon, George N., and William Hodapp. *The Idea Invaders*. New York: Hastings House, 1963.

Gordon, Jay E. *Motion Picture Production for Industry*. New York: Macmillan, 1961.

Gordon, Thomas F., and Mary Ellen Verna. *Mass Communication Effects and Processes: A Comprehensive Bibliography, 1950–1975*. Beverly Hills, Calif.: Sage, 1978.

Gould, Frederick James. *Thomas Paine (1737–1809)*. Boston: Small, Maynard, 1925.

Graber, Doris A. *Mass Media and American Politics*. 3rd ed. Washington D.C.: Congressional Quarterly Books, 1988.

———, ed. *Media Power in Politics*. Washington, D.C.: Congressional Quarterly Books, 1984.

Greenstadt, Melvin. "A Critical Survey of United States Government Films in World War I." Master's thesis, University of Southern California, 1949.

Griffin, Leland M. "The Antimasonic Persuasion: A Study of Public Address in the American Antimasonic Movement, 1826–1838." Ph.D. diss., Cornell University, 1950.

Grunig, James E., and Todd Hunt. *Managing Public Relations*. New York: Holt, Rinehart, and Winston, 1984.

Gulik, Charles, Roy Ockert, and Raymond Wallace. *History and Theories of Working Class Movements—A Select Bibliography*. Berkeley: Institute of Industrial Relations, University of California, 1955.

Hachten, William A. *The World News Prism: Changing Media, Clashing Ideologies*. 2nd ed. Ames: Iowa State University Press, 1987.

Hachten, William A., and C. Anthony Giffard. *The Press and Apartheid: Repression and Propaganda in South Africa*. Madison: University of Wisconsin Press, 1984.

Hale, Julian. *Radio Power: Propaganda and International Broadcasting*. Philadelphia: Temple University Press, 1975.

Hamilton, Alexander, James Madison, and John Jay. *The Federalist Papers*. Intro. Clinton Rossiter. New York: New American Library/Mentor Books, 1961.

Hapgood, Norman, ed. *Professional Patriots: An Exposure of the Personalities, Methods and Objectives Involved in the Organized Effort to Exploit Patriotic Impulses in These United States during and after the Late War*. New York: Boni, 1927.

Hargis, Billy James. *Distortion by Design: The Story of America's Liberal Press*. Tulsa, Okla.: Christian Crusade, 1965.

Harlow, Ralph Volney. *Samuel Adams, Promoter of the American Revolution: A Study in Psychology and Politics*. New York: Holt, 1923.

Hartenian, Lawrence Raymond. "Propaganda and the Control of Information in Occupied Germany: The U.S. Information Control Division at Radio Frankfort 1945–1949." Ph.D. diss., Rutgers University, 1984.

Harter, D. Lincoln, and John Sullivan. *Propaganda Handbook*. Philadelphia: Twentieth Century, 1953.

Harty, Sheila. *Hucksters in the Classroom: A Review of Industry Propaganda in Schools*. Washington, D.C.: Center for the Study of Responsible Law, 1980.

Harwell, Richard. *More Confederate Imprints*. 2 vols. Richmond: Virginia State Library, 1957.

Haste, Cate. *Keep the Home Fires Burning: Propaganda in the First World War*. London: Alien Lane/Penguin Books, 1977.

Hauser, Gerard A. *Introduction to Rhetorical Theory*. New York: Harper and Row, 1986.

Hawke, David Freeman. *Paine*. New York: Harper and Row, 1974.

Heartman, Charles F., comp. *The Cradle of the United States, 1765–1789: Five Hundred Contemporary Broadsides, Pamphlets, and a Few Books Pertaining to the History of the Stamp Act, the Boston Massacre and Other Pre-Revolutionary Troubles, the War for Independence and the Adoption of the Federal Constitution*. Perth Amboy, N.J.: Privately printed, 1922.

Heath, Robert L., et al. *Strategic Issues Management: How Organizations Influence and Respond to Public Interests and Policies*. San Francisco: Jossey-Bass, 1988.

Heath, Robert L., and Richard Alan Nelson. *Issues Management: Corporate Public Policymaking in an Information Society*. Beverly Hills, Calif.: Sage, 1986.

Heintze, James R. *Scholars' Guide to Washington, D.C. for Audio Resources: Sound Recordings in the Arts, Humanities and Social, Physical and Life Sciences*. Washington, D.C.: Smithsonian Institution Press, 1985.

Heise, Juergen Arthur. *Minimum Disclosure: How the Pentagon Manipulates the News*. New York: W. W. Norton, 1979.

Heller, John. "The Selling of the Constitution: The Federalist Papers Viewed as an Advertising Campaign." Master's thesis, University of Florida, 1974.

Henderson, John W. *The United States Information Agency*. New York: Praeger, 1969.

Herman, Edward S. *The Real Terror Network: Terrorism in Fact and Propaganda*. Boston: South End Press, 1982.

Hersh, Seymour M. *"The Target Is Destroyed"—What Really Happened to Flight 007 and What America Knew about It*. Updated ed., with new preface. New York: Vintage Books, 1987.

Hirst, David. "German Propaganda in the United States, 1914–1917." Ph.D. diss., Northwestern University, 1962.

Hitler, Adolf. *Mein Kampf*. Unexpurgated annotated translation. New York: Reynal and Hitchcock, 1940. Sentry Edition, Ralph Manheim translation. Boston: Houghton Mifflin, 1943.

Hoffer, Thomas William. "Broadcasting in an Insurgency Environment: USIA in Vietnam, 1965–1970." Ph.D. diss., University of Wisconsin, 1972.

Hofstetter, C. Richard. *Bias in the News: Network Television Coverage of the 1972 Election Campaign*. Columbus: Ohio State University Press, 1976.

Holgren, Carol Jean. "The Propaganda Program of the National Recovery Administration." Master's thesis, University of Washington, 1962.

Holt, Robert T., and Robert W. van de Velde. *Strategic Psychological Operations and American Foreign Policy*. Chicago: University of Chicago Press, 1960.

Hook, Sydney, Vladimir Bukovsky, and Paul Hollander. *Soviet Hypocrisy and Western Gullibility*. Lanham Md.: University Press of America, 1987.

Hosmer, James K. *Samuel Adams*. Boston: Houghton Mifflin, 1917.

Hovland, Carl, et al. *Communication and Persuasion*. New Haven, Conn.: Yale University Press, 1953.

Howe, Quincy. *England Expects Every American to Do His Duty*. New York: Simon and Schuster, 1937.

Howe, Russell Warren, and Sarah Hays Trott. *The Power Peddlers: How Lobbyists Mold America's Foreign Policy*. Garden City, N.Y.: Doubleday, 1977.

Hummel, Ray O., Jr. *Southeastern Broadsides before 1877: A Bibliography*. Richmond: Virginia State Library, 1971.

Hummel, William, and Keith Huntress. *The Analysis of Propaganda*. New York: William Sloane, 1949.

Hunt, Dave. *The Cult Explosion*. Eugene, Oreg.: Harvest House, 1980.

Hunter, Edward. *Brainwashing: The Story of the Men Who Defied It*. New York: Farrar, Straus, and Cudahy, 1956.

Industrial Workers of the World. *IWW Little Red Songbook*. Chicago: Industrial Workers of the World, n.d.

———. "A Reading List on IWW History." Rev. pamphlet. Chicago: Industrial Workers of the World, August 1973.

Institute of Labor and Industrial Relations. *American Labor in Journals of History*. Urbana: Institute of Labor and Industrial Relations, University of Illinois, 1962.

———. *Labor History in the United States*. Urbana: Institute of Labor and Industrial Relations, University of Illinois, 1961.

International Propaganda/Communications: Selections from the Public Opinion Quarterly. New York: Arno Press, 1972.

Irion, Frederick C. *Public Opinion and Propaganda*. New York: Crowell, 1950.

Irvine, Reed. *Media Mischief and Misdeeds*. Chicago: Regnery Gateway, 1984.

Irwin, Will. *Propaganda and the News; or, What Makes You Think So?* New York: McGraw-Hill, 1936. Reprint. Westport, Conn.: Greenwood Press, 1970.

Jacobs, Lewis, ed. *The Documentary Tradition.* New York: Hopkinson and Blake, 1971.

Jamieson, Kathleen Hall. *Packaging the Presidency: A History and Criticism of Presidential Campaign Advertising.* New York: Oxford University Press, 1984.

Jamieson, Kathleen Hall, and Karlyn Kohrs Campbell. *The Interplay of Influence: Mass Media and Their Publics in News, Advertising, Politics.* 2nd ed. Belmont, Calif.: Wadsworth, 1988.

Jeavons, Clyde. *A Pictorial History of War Films.* Secaucus, N.J.: Citadel Press, 1974.

Jensen, Joan. *The Price of Vigilance.* New York: Rand McNally, 1968.

Johnson, R. W. *Shootdown: Flight 007 and the American Connection.* New York: Penguin Books, 1986.

Johnson, Walter. *The Battle against Isolation.* Chicago: University of Chicago Press, 1944.

Johnston, Winifred. *Memo on the Movies: War Propaganda, 1914–1939.* Norman, Okla.: Cooperative Books, 1939.

Jones, Ken and Arthur McClure. *Hollywood at War: The American Motion Picture Industry and World War II.* New York: Castle Books, 1973.

Jowett, Garth S., and Victoria O'Donnell. *Propaganda and Persuasion.* Newbury Park, Calif.: Sage, 1986.

Judd, Denis. *Posters of World War Two.* New York: St. Martin's Press, 1973.

Kaid, Lynda Lee, Keith R. Sanders, and Robert O. Hirsch. *Political Campaign Communications: A Bibliography and Guide to the Literature.* Metuchen, N.J.: Scarecrow Press, 1974.

Kaid, Lynda Lee, and Anne J. Wadsworth. *Political Campaign Communications: A Bibliography and Guide to the Literature, 1973–1982.* Metuchen, N.J.: Scarecrow Press, 1985.

Kaid, Lynda Lee, et al., eds. *New Perspectives on Political Advertising.* Carbondale: Southern Illinois University Press, 1986.

Karlins, Marvin, and Herbert Abelson. *Persuasion: How Opinions and Attitudes Are Changed.* 2nd ed. New York: Springer, 1970.

Katz, Daniel, et al. *Public Opinion and Propaganda: A Book of Readings.* New York: Dryden, 1954.

Katz, Phillip Paul. *A Systematic Approach to Psyop Information.* Washington, D.C.: Center for Research in Social Systems, 1970.

Keeley, Joseph. *The Left-Leaning Antenna: Political Bias in Television.* New Rochelle, N.Y.: Arlington House, 1971.

Keller, Phyllis. *States of Belonging: German-American Intellectuals and the First World War.* Cambridge: Harvard University Press, 1979.

Kenneally, Finbar. *United States Documents in the Propaganda Fide Archives: A Calendar.* 7 vols. Washington, D.C.: Academy of American Franciscan History, 1966–1971.

Key, Wilson Bryant. *The Subliminal Seduction: Ad Media's Manipulation of a Not So Innocent America.* Englewood Cliffs, N.J.: Prentice-Hall, 1973.

King, Andrew. *Power and Communication.* Prospect Heights, Ill.: Waveland Press, 1987.

King, Arnold Kinsey. "Thomas Paine in America, 1774–1787." Ph.D. diss. University of Chicago, 1952.

Klare, Michael, and Peter Kornbluh, eds. *Low Intensity Warfare: Counterinsurgency, Proinsurgency, and Antiterrorism in the 80s*. New York: Random House/Pantheon, 1988.

Klein, Walter. *The Sponsored Film*. New York: Hastings House, 1976.

Klement, Frank L. *The Limits of Dissent: Clement L. Vallandigham and the Civil War*. Lexington: University Press of Kentucky, 1970.

Klingender, F. D., and Stuart Legg. *Money behind the Screen*. London: Lawrence and Wishart, 1937.

Knightley, Phillip. *The First Casualty—From the Crimea to Vietnam: The War Correspondent as Hero, Propagandist, and Myth Maker*. New York: Harcourt Brace Jovanovich, 1976.

Koek, Karin E., and Susan Boyles Martin, eds. *Encyclopedia of Associations, 1988*. 22nd ed. 4 vols. Detroit: Gale Research, 1987.

Koppes, Clayton R., and Gregory D. Black. *Hollywood Goes to War: How Politics, Profits, and Propaganda Shaped World War II Movies*. New York: Free Press, 1987.

Kornbluh, Joyce L., ed. *Rebel Voices, an IWW Anthology*. Ann Arbor: University of Michigan Press, 1964. Rev. ed. Chicago: Charles H. Kerr, 1985.

Kreuter, Kent, and Gretchen Kreuter. *An American Dissenter: The Life of Algie Martin Simons, 1870–1950*. Lexington: University Press of Kentucky, 1969.

Kwitny, Jonathan. *The Crimes of Patriots: A True Tale of Dope, Dirty Money, and the CIA*. New York: W. W. Norton, 1987.

La Haye, Tim. *The Hidden Censors*. Old Tappan, N.J.: Fleming H. Ravell Co., 1984.

Lampham, Ruth, comp. *Check List of American Revolutionary War Pamphlets in the Newberry Library*. Chicago: Newberry Library, 1922.

Laqueur, Walter, and Yonah Alexander, eds. *The Terrorism Reader*. Rev. ed. New York: NAL Penguin, 1987.

Larson, Charles U. *Persuasion: Reception and Responsibility*. 4th ed. Belmont, Calif.: Wadsworth, 1986.

Lasky, Victor. *It Didn't Start with Watergate*. New York: Dell, 1978.

Lasswell, Harold D. "Propaganda." In *Encyclopaedia Britannica*. Chicago: Encyclopaedia Britannica, 1973, XVIII: 624–39.

———. "Propaganda." In *Encyclopaedia of the Social Sciences*. New York: Macmillan, 1933, XII: 521–28.

———. *Propaganda Technique in the World War*. London: Kegan Paul, Trench, Trubner, 1927. Reprinted as *Propaganda Technique in World War I*. Cambridge: MIT Press, 1971.

Lasswell, Harold D., and Dorothy Blumenstock. *World Revolutionary Propaganda*. New York: Alfred A. Knopf, 1939.

Lasswell, Harold D., Ralph D. Casey, and Bruce L. Smith. *Propaganda and Promotional Activities: An Annotated Bibliography*. Minneapolis: University of Minnesota Press, 1935. Reprint. Chicago: University of Chicago Press, 1969.

Lasswell, Harold D., Daniel Lerner, and Hans Speier, eds. *Propaganda and Com-*

munication in World History, Volume 1: The Symbolic Instrument in Early Times. Honolulu: University Press of Hawaii, 1979.

———. *Propaganda and Communication in World History, Volume 2: The Emergence of Public Opinion in the West*. Honolulu: University Press of Hawaii, 1979.

———. *Propaganda and Communication in World History, Volume 3: A Pluralizing World in Formation*. Honolulu: University Press of Hawaii, 1980.

Lavine, Harold, and James Wechsler. *War Propaganda and the United States*. New Haven, Conn.: Yale University Press for the Institute for Propaganda Analysis, 1940. Reprint. New York: Arno Press, 1972.

Lee, Alfred McClung. *How to Understand Propaganda*. New York: Holt, Rinehart, 1952.

Lee, Alfred McClung, and Elizabeth Briant Lee. *The Fine Art of Propaganda: A Study of Father Coughlin's Speeches*. New York: Harcourt, Brace, 1939. Reprint. New York: Octagon, 1972; San Francisco: International Society for General Semantics, 1979.

Lefever, Ernest W., and Roy Godson. *The CIA and the American Ethic: An Unfinished Debate*. Washington, D.C.: Ethics and Public Policy Center of Georgetown University, 1979.

Leonard, Thomas C. *The Power of the Press: The Birth of American Political Reporting*. New York: Oxford University Press, 1986.

Lerner, Daniel. "Propaganda." In *Funk and Wagnalls Standard Reference Encyclopedia*. New York: Standard Reference Works, 1959, xx: 7266–68.

———. *Sykewar: Psychological Warfare against Germany, D-Day to VE-Day*. New York: George W. Stewart, 1949.

———, ed. *Propaganda in War and Crisis: Materials for American Foreign Policy*. New York: George W. Stewart, 1951. Reprint. New York: Arno Press, 1972.

Levy, Leonard W. *Emergence of a Free Press*. New York: Oxford University Press, 1985.

———. *Legacy of Suppression: Freedom of Speech and Press in Early American History*. Cambridge: Belknap Press of Harvard University Press, 1960.

Lichter, S. Robert, Stanley Rothman, and Linda S. Lichter. *The Media Elite: America's New Powerbrokers*. Bethesda, Md.: Adler and Adler, 1986.

Linebarger, Paul. *Psychological Warfare*. 2nd ed. Washington, D.C.: Combat Forces Press, 1954. Reprint. New York: Arno Press, 1972.

Lingeman, Richard R. *Don't You Know There's a War On? The American Home Front, 1941–1945*. New York: Putnam's, 1970.

Linsky, Martin. *Impact: How the Press Affects Federal Policymaking*. New York: W. W. Norton, 1986.

Linsky, Martin, Jonathan Moore, Wendy O'Donnell, and David Whitman. *How the Press Affects Federal Policymaking: Six Case Studies*. New York: W. W. Norton, 1986.

Lippmann, Walter. *Drift and Mastery: An Attempt to Diagnose the Current Unrest*. Englewood Cliffs, N.J.: Prentice-Hall, 1961.

———. *Public Opinion*. New York: Harcourt, Brace, 1922. Rev. ed. New York: Free Press, 1965.

Lisann, Maury. *Broadcasting to the Soviet Union: International Politics and Radio*. New York: Praeger, 1975.

Lovenduski, Joni, and Joyce Outshoorn, eds. *The New Politics of Abortion*. Newbury Park, Calif.: Sage, 1986.

Lowenthal, Leo, and Norbert Guterman. *Prophets of Deceit: A Study of the Techniques of the American Agitator*. 2nd ed. Palo Alto, Calif.: Pacific Books, 1970.

Lumley, Frederick E. *The Propaganda Menace*. New York: Century, 1933.

MacKay, Lamar. "Domestic Operations of the Office of War Information in World War II." Ph.D. diss., University of Wisconsin, 1966.

Maddox, William S., and Stuart A. Lilie. *Beyond Liberal and Conservative*. Washington, D.C.: Cato Institute, 1984.

Mahood, H. R. *Pressure Groups in American Politics*. New York: Scribner's, 1967.

Mamatey, Victor S. *The United States and East Central Europe, 1914–1918: A Study in Wilsonian Diplomacy and Propaganda*. Princeton, N.J.: Princeton University Press, 1957.

Manuscripts of the American Revolution in the Boston Public Library: A Descriptive Catalog. Boston: G. K. Hall, 1968.

Manvell, Roger. *Films and the Second World War*. New York: Dell, 1974.

Marchetti, Victor, and John D. Marks. *The CIA and the Cult of Intelligence*. Updated paperback ed. New York: Laurel/Dell, 1983.

Marks, Barry. "The Idea of Propaganda in America." Ph.D. diss., University of Minnesota, 1957.

Marks, John. *The Search for the "Manchurian Candidate": The CIA and Mind Control—The Story of the Agency's Secret Efforts to Control Human Behavior*. New York: Times Books, 1979.

Marxist Readings: A Bibliography of over 4,000 Books, Pamphlets, and Reprints in English, German and Italian—Volume 1. Bagnolet, France: Critiques Livres, 1970.

Maynard, Richard A. *Propaganda on Film: A Nation at War*. Rochelle Park, N.J.: Hayden Books, 1975.

MacCann, Richard Dyer. *The People's Films: A Political History of U.S. Government Motion Pictures*. New York: Hastings House, 1973.

McBrearty, James. *American Labor History and Comparative Labor Movements—A Selected Bibliography*. Tucson: University of Arizona Press, 1973.

McDonald, J. Fred. *Television and the Red Menace: The Video Road to Vietnam*. New York: Praeger, 1985.

McDonough, Joseph J. "Analysis of Official U.S. Military Psychological Warfare Efforts in the Vietnam Conflict." Master's thesis, Boston University, 1968.

McEnroe, Thomas Howard. "The International Workers of the World: Theories, Organizational Problems and Appeals as Revealed Principally in the *Industrial Worker*." Ph.D. diss., University of Minnesota, 1960.

McGuire, William J. "Persuasion, Resistance, and Attitude Change." In *Handbook of Communication*, ed. Ithiel de Sola Pool, Wilbur Schramm, et al. Chicago: Rand McNally, 1973, 216–52.

McLaurin, Ron D., ed. *Military Propaganda: Psychological Warfare and Operations*. New York: Praeger, 1982.

Meadow, Robert G. *Politics as Communication*. Norwood, N.J.: Ablex, 1980.

Mickelson, Sig. *America's Other Voice: The Story of Radio Free Europe and Radio Liberty*. New York: Praeger, 1983.

Miller, Gerald R. "Persuasion." In Charles R. Berger and Steven H. Chaffee, eds., *Handbook of Communication Science*. Newbury Park, Calif.: Sage, 1987.

Miller, Gerald R., and Michael Burgoon. "Persuasion Research: Review and Commentary." In *Communication Yearbook 2*, ed. Brent Ruben. New Brunswick, N.J.: Transaction Books, 1978, 29–47.

Miller, John C. *Sam Adams: Pioneer in Propaganda*. Stanford, Calif.: Stanford University Press, 1936.

Minnick, Wayne. *The Art of Persuasion*. 2nd ed. Boston: Houghton Mifflin, 1968.

Minor, Dale. *The Information War*. New York: Hawthorn Books, 1970.

Mitchell, Malcolm. *Propaganda, Polls, and Public Opinion: Are the People Manipulated?* Englewood Cliffs, N.J.: Prentice-Hall, 1970.

Mitchell, W.J.T. *Iconology: Image, Text, Ideology*. Chicago: University of Chicago Press, 1986.

Mock, James R., and Cedric Larson. *Words That Won the War: The Story of the Committee on Public Information, 1917–1919*. Princeton, N.J.: Princeton University Press, 1939. Reprint. New York: Russell and Russell, 1968.

Morella, Joe, Edward Z. Epstein, and John Griggs. *The Films of World War II*. New York: Citadel Press, 1973.

Mueller, John E. *War, Presidents and Public Opinion*. New York: Wiley, 1973. Reprint. Lanham, Md.: University Press of America, 1985.

Murray, Robert. *Red Scare: A Study in National Hysteria, 1919–1920*. Minneapolis: University of Minnesota Press, 1955. Reprint. New York: McGraw-Hill, 1964.

Murty, B. S. *Propaganda and World Public Order: The Legal Regulation of the Ideological Instrument of Coercion*. New Haven, Conn.: Yale University Press, 1968.

Myers, Gustavus. *History of Bigotry in the United States*. Rev. ed. New York: Capricorn Books, 1960.

Nagelschmidt, Joseph S., ed. *The Public Affairs Handbook*. New York: Amacom, 1982.

Neilson, Francis. *Escort of Lies: War Propaganda*. Brooklyn, N.Y.: Revisionist Press, 1979.

Nelson, Richard Alan. *A Chronology and Glossary of Propaganda in the United States*. Westport, Conn.: Greenwood Press, 1996.

———. "Commercial Propaganda in the Silent Film: A Case Study of *A Mormon Maid* (1917)." *Film History: An International Journal* (1987), 149–62.

———. "Germany and the German Film, 1930–1945: An Annotated Research Bibliography. Part I: Books, Dissertations, and Pamphlets." *Journal of the University Film Association* 29 (Winter 1977), 45–66.

———. "Germany and the German Film, 1930–1945: An Annotated Research Bibliography. Part II: Articles and Periodicals." *Journal of the University Film Association* 29 (Spring 1977), 67–80.

———. "Germany and the German Film, 1930–1945: An Annotated Research Bibliography. Part III: Research Libraries, Archives, and Other Sources." *Journal of the University Film Association* 30 (Winter 1978), 53–72.

———. "Mormons as Silent Cinema Villains: Propaganda and Entertainment." *Historical Journal of Film, Radio and Television* 4 (March 1984), 3–14.

Neufeld, Maurice. *A Representative Bibliography of American Labor History*. Ithaca, N.Y.: Cornell University Press, 1964.

Newsom, Doug, Alan Scott, and Judy Vanslyke Turk. *This Is PR: The Realities of Public Relations*. 4th ed. Belmont, Calif.: Wadsworth, 1985.

Nimmo, Dan. *Political Communication and Public Opinion in America*. Santa Monica, Calif.: Goodyear, 1978.

———. *The Political Persuaders: The Techniques of Modern Election Campaigns*. Englewood Cliffs, N.J.: Prentice-Hall, 1970.

Nordenstreng, Kaarle, E. G. Manet, and W. Kleinwächter. *The New International Information and Communication Order*. Prague: International Organization of Journalists, 1987.

Norman, Albert. *Our German Policy: Propaganda and Culture*. New York: Vintage Books, 1951.

Norris, Frank. *The Pit: A Story of Chicago*. New York: Doubleday, 1903.

Olasky, Marvin N. *Corporate Public Relations: A New Historical Perspective*. Hillsdale N.J.: Lawrence Erlbaum Associates, 1988.

"On Propaganda." *ETC.: A Review of General Semantics* 36 (Summer 1979). Special issue.

Packard, Vance. *The Hidden Persuaders*. New York: McKay, 1957. Rev. ed. New York: Pocket Books, 1980.

Paine, Thomas. *Common Sense and Other Political Writings*. Ed. Nelson F. Adkins. Indianapolis: Bobbs-Merrill, 1953.

———. *The Complete Writings of Thomas Paine*. Ed. Philip S. Foner. 2 vols. New York: Citadel Press, 1945.

———. *The Life and Works of Thomas Paine*. Ed. William van der Weyde. 10 vols. New Rochelle, N.Y.: Thomas Paine National Historical Association, 1925.

———. *The Writings of Thomas Paine*. Ed. Moncure Daniel Conway. 4 vols. New York: Putnam's, 1894–1896. Reprint. New York: AMS Press, 1967.

Paletz, David, Roberta Pearson, and Donald Willis. *Politics in Public Service Advertising on Television*. New York: Praeger, 1977.

Parenti, Michael. *Inventing Reality: The Politics of the Mass Media*. New York: St. Martin's Press, 1986.

Perlmutter, Tom. *War Movies*. New York: Castle Books, 1974.

Perris, Arnold. *Music as Propaganda*. Westport, Conn.: Greenwood Press, 1985.

Peterson, Horace C. *Propaganda for War: The Campaign against American Neutrality, 1914–1917*. Norman: University of Oklahoma Press, 1939. Reprint. Port Washington, N.Y.: Kennikat Press, 1968.

Philippe, Robert. *Political Graphics: Art as a Weapon*. New York: Abbeville Press, 1982.

Pirsein, Robert W. *The Voice of America*. New York: Arno Press, 1979.

Plato. *Phaedrus*. Ed. R. Hackworth. Cambridge, England: Cambridge University Press, 1972.

Pollay, Richard W., ed. *Information Sources in Advertising History*. Westport, Conn.: Greenwood Press, 1979.

Pool, Ithiel de Sola, Wilbur Schramm, et al., eds. *Handbook of Communication*. Chicago: Rand McNally, 1973.

Posonby, Arthur. *Falsehood in War-time*. New York: E. P. Dutton, 1928.

Post, Louis F. *The Deportations Delirium of Nineteen-Twenty: A Personal Narrative of an Historic Official Experience*. Chicago: Charles H. Kerr, 1923. Reprint. New York: Da Capo Press, 1970.

Preston, William, Jr. *Aliens and Dissenters: Federal Suppression of Radicals, 1903–1933*. Cambridge: Harvard University Press, 1963. Reprint. New York: Harper and Row, 1963.

Price, Warren C. *The Literature of Journalism: An Annotated Bibliography*. Minneapolis: University of Minnesota Press, 1959.

Price, Warren C., and Calder M. Pickett. *An Annotated Journalism Bibliography: 1958–1968*. Minneapolis: University of Minnesota Press, 1970.

Pro-Arab Propaganda in America: Vehicles and Voices. New York: Anti-Defamation League of B'nai B'rith, 1983.

Pronay, Nicholas and D. W. Spring, eds. *Propaganda, Politics and Film, 1918–1945*. Atlantic Highlands, N.J.: Humanities Press, 1982.

Pronay, Nicholas, and Keith Wilson, eds. *The Political Re-education of Germany and Her Allies after World War II*. London: Croom Helm, 1985.

Public Opinion, Mass Behavior and Political Psychology. Vol. 6 of the Political Science, Government, and Public Policy Series. Princeton, N.J.: Princeton Research/IFI/Plenum Data, 1967. With annual supplements, 1967– .

Qualter, Terence H. *Opinion Control in the Democracies*. New York: St. Martin's Press, 1985.

———. *Propaganda and Psychological Warfare*. New York: Random House, 1962.

Rank, Hugh. *The Pep Talk: How to Analyze Political Language*. Park Forest, Ill.: Counter-Propaganda Press, 1984.

———. *The Pitch: How to Analyze Advertising*. Park Forest, Ill.: Counter-Propaganda Press, 1982.

Raspberry, Robert W. *The "Technique" of Political Lying*. Washington, D.C.: University Press of America, 1981.

Raucher, Alan R. *Public Relations and Business, 1900–1929*. Baltimore: Johns Hopkins University Press, 1968.

Read, James M. *Atrocity Propaganda, 1914–1919*. New Haven, Conn.: Yale University Press, 1941. Reprint. New York: Arno Press, 1972.

Reed, Rebecca Theresa. *Six Months in a Convent*. Boston: Rusell, Odiorne and Metcalf, 1835.

Reimann, Horst. "Propaganda" and "Public Opinion." In *Marxism, Communism and Western Society: A Comparative Encyclopedia*. London: Herder and Herder, 1973, vii: 67–68, 113–23.

Rhodes, Anthony. *Propaganda—The Art of Persuasion: World War II*. New York: Chelsea House, 1976. Reprint. Secaucus, N.J.: Wellfleet Press, 1987.

Rice, Ronald E., and William J. Paisley, eds. *Public Communication Campaigns*. Beverly Hills, Calif.: Sage, 1981.

Richelson, Jeffrey T. *American Espionage and the Soviet Target*. New York: William Morrow, 1987.

———. *Sword and Shield: Soviet Intelligence and Security Apparatus*. Cambridge, Mass.: Ballinger, 1986.

———. *The U.S. Intelligence Community*. Cambridge, Mass.: Ballinger, 1985.

Riegel, Oscar W. *Mobilizing for Chaos: The Story of the New Propaganda*. New Haven, Conn.: Yale University Press, 1934. Reprint. New York: Arno Press, 1972.

Riff, Michael A., ed. *Dictionary of Modern Political Ideologies*. New York: St. Martin's Press, 1987.

Robison, John. *Proofs of a Conspiracy against All the Religions and Governments of Europe, Carried on in Secret Meetings of Free Masons, Illuminati, and Reading Societies, Collected from Good Authorities*. 4th ed. New York: George Forman, 1798. Reprint, with new introduction. Boston and Los Angeles: Western Islands, 1967.

Roetter, Charles. *The Art of Psychological Warfare, 1914–1945*. New York: Stein and Day, 1974.

Roloff, Michael, and Gerald R. Miller, eds. *Persuasion: New Directions in Theory and Research*. Beverly Hills, Calif.: Sage, 1980.

Rowan, B. G., with D. Culbert and consultants T. Cripps and L. Lichty. *Scholars' Guide to Washington D.C. Film and Video Collections*. Washington, D.C.: Smithsonian Institution Press and Woodrow Wilson International Center for Scholars, 1980.

Rubenstein, Richard E. *Alchemists of Revolution: Terrorism in the Modern World*. New York: Basic Books, 1987.

Rubin, Bernard, ed. *When Information Counts: Grading the Media*. Lexington, Mass.: Lexington Books, 1985.

Rupp, Leila J. *Mobilizing Women for War: German and American Propaganda, 1939–1945*. Princeton, N.J.: Princeton University Press, 1978.

Ryan, Milo. *History in Sound: A Descriptive Listing of the KIRO-CBS Collection of Broadcasts of the World War II Years and After, in the Phonoarchive of the University of Washington*. Seattle: University of Washington Press, 1963.

Salisbury, Allen. *The Civil War and the American System*. New York: Campaigner Publications, 1978.

Scheflin, Alan W., and Edward M. Opton Jr. *The Mind Manipulators: A Non-Fiction Account*. New York: Paddington Press, 1978.

Schein, Edgar, et al. *Coercive Persuasion: A Socio-Psychological Analysis of the "Brainwashing" of American Civilian Prisoners by the Chinese Communists*. New York: W. W. Norton, 1971.

Schiller, Herbert I. *Information and the Crisis Economy*. New York: Oxford University Press, 1986.

———. *The Mind Managers*. Boston: Beacon Press, 1973.

Schlesinger, Philip, Graham Murdock, and Philip Elliott. *Televising "Terrorism": Political Violence in Popular Culture*. London: Comedia Publishing Group, 1983.

Schudson, Michael. *Advertising, the Uneasy Persuasion*. New York: Basic Books, 1985.

Schwar, Jane. "Interventionist Propaganda and Pressure Groups in the United States, 1937–1941." Ph.D. diss., Ohio State University, 1973.

Seabury, William Marston. *Motion Picture Problems: The Cinema and the League of Nations*. New York: Avondale Press, 1929. Reprint. New York: Arno Press, 1978.

Seldes, George. *The Facts Are . . . A Guide to Falsehood and Propaganda in the Press and Radio*. New York: In Fact, 1942.

Sethi, S. Prakash. *Advocacy Advertising and Large Corporations: Social Conflict, Big*

Business Image, the News Media, and Public Policy. Lexington, Mass.: Lexington Books/Heath, 1977.

———. *Handbook of Advocacy Advertising: Concepts, Strategies, and Applications.* Cambridge, Mass.: Ballinger/Harper and Row, 1987.

Sethi, S. Prakash, and Cecilia McHugh Falbe, eds. *Business and Public Policy: Dimensions of Conflict and Cooperation.* Lexington, Mass.: Lexington Books/ D. C. Heath, 1987.

Severin, Werner J., and James W. Tankard Jr. *Communication Theories: Origins— Methods—Uses.* New York: Hastings House, 1979.

Shaheen, Jack G. *The TV Arab.* Bowling Green, Ohio: Bowling Green State University Popular Press, 1984.

Short, K.R.M., ed. *Film and Radio Propaganda in World War II.* Knoxville: University of Tennessee Press, 1983.

———. *Films as History.* Knoxville: University of Tennessee Press, 1981.

———. *Western Broadcasting over the Iron Curtain.* London: Croom Helm, 1986.

Shotwell, John. "Crystalizing Public Hatred: Ku Klux Klan Public Relations in the Early 1920s." Master's thesis, University of Wisconsin at Madison, 1974.

Shultz, Richard H., and Roy Godson. *Dezinformatsia: Active Measures in Soviet Strategy.* Washington, D.C.: Pergamon-Brassey's, 1984.

Silbey, Joel H. *The Partisan Imperative: The Dynamics of American Politics before the Civil War.* New York: Oxford University Press, 1985.

Simons, Herbert W. *Persuasion: Understanding, Practice and Analysis.* 2nd ed. New York: Random House, 1986.

Sinclair, Upton. *The Brass Check: A Study in American Journalism.* Pasadena, Calif.: Privately printed, 1919. Reprint. New York: Arno Press, 1974.

———. *The Jungle.* New York: Doubleday, 1906.

Skvortsov, L. *The Ideology and Tactics of Anti-Communism.* Moscow: Progress, 1969.

Sloan, Stephen. *Beating International Terrorism: An Action Strategy for Preemption and Punishment.* Maxwell Air Force Base, Ala.: Air University Press, December 1986.

Small, William. *Political Power and the Press.* New York: W. W. Norton, 1972.

Smith, Bradley F. *The Shadow Warriors: O.S.S. and the Origins of the C.I.A.* New York: Basic Books, 1983.

Smith, Bruce L. "Propaganda." In *International Encyclopedia of the Social Sciences.* New York: Macmillan, 1968, XII: 579–89.

———. "Propaganda." In *The New Encyclopaedia Britannica.* Macropaedia. Chicago: Encyclopedia Britannica, 1974, XV: 36–45.

Smith, Bruce L., Harold D. Lasswell, and Ralph D. Casey. *Propaganda, Communication, and Public Opinion: A Comprehensive Reference Guide.* Princeton, N.J.: Princeton University Press, 1946.

Smith, Bruce L., and Chitra M. Smith. *International Communication and Political Opinion: A Guide to the Literature.* Princeton, N.J.: Princeton University Press, 1956. Reprint. Westport, Conn.: Greenwood Press, 1972.

Smith, Craig R. *The Fight for Freedom of Expression: Three Case Studies.* Washington, D.C.: Institute for Freedom of Communication, 1985.

Smith, Culver. *The Press, Politics, and Patronage: The American Government's Use of Newspapers, 1789–1875.* Athens: University of Georgia Press, 1977.

Smith, George Winston. "Generative Forces in Union Propaganda: A Study in Civil War Pressure Groups." Ph.D. diss., University of Wisconsin, 1940.

Smith, Jeffrey A. *Printers and Press Freedom: The Ideology of Early American Journalism*. New York: Oxford University Press, 1987.

Smith, Mary John. *Persuasion and Human Action: A Review and Critique of Social Influence Theories*. Belmont, Calif.: Wadsworth, 1982.

Smith, R. Harris. *OSS: The Secret History of America's First Central Intelligence Agency*. Berkeley: University of California Press, 1972.

Smith, Robert W. "What Came After?: News Diffusion and the Significance of the Boston Massacre in Six American Colonies, 1770–1775." Ph.D. diss., University of Wisconsin at Madison, 1972.

Sobel, Robert. *The Manipulators: America in the Media Age*. Garden City, N.Y.: Doubleday, 1976.

Sorensen, Thomas C. *The Word War: The Story of American Propaganda*. New York: Harper and Row, 1968.

Spannaus, Nancy, and Christopher White. *The Political Economy of the American Revolution*. New York: Campaigner Publications, 1977.

Sproule, J. Michael. "Propaganda Studies in American Social Science: The Rise and Fall of the Critical Paradigm." *Quarterly Journal of Speech* 73 (February 1987), 60–78.

Squires, James D. *British Propaganda at Home and in the United States from 1914 to 1917*. Cambridge: Harvard University Press, 1935.

Steele, Richard W. *Propaganda in an Open Society: The Roosevelt Administration and the Media, 1933–41*. Westport, Conn.: Greenwood Press, 1985.

Steffens, Lincoln. *The Shame of the Cities*. New York: McClure, Phillips, 1904.

Stenejhem, Michele Flynn. *An American First: John T. Flynn and the American First Committee*. New Rochelle, N.Y.: Arlington House, 1976.

Sterling, Christopher H., and Timothy R. Haight. *The Mass Media: Aspen Institute Guide to Communication Industry Trends*. New York: Praeger, 1978.

Sterling, Claire. *The Terror Network: The Secret War of International Terrorism*. London: Weidenfeld and Nicolson, 1981.

Stevens, Art. *The Persuasion Explosion: Your Guide to the Power and Influence of Contemporary Public Relations*. Washington, D.C.: Acropolis Books, 1985.

Stevenson, William. *A Man Called Intrepid: The Secret War*. New York: Harcourt Brace Jovanovich, 1976.

Stewart, Charles J., Craig Smith, and Robert E. Denton Jr. *Persuasion and Social Movements*. Prospect Heights, Ill.:Waveland Press, 1984.

Stoetzer, Carlos. *Postage Stamps as Propaganda*. Washington, D.C.: Public Affairs Press, 1953.

Stowe, Harriet Beecher. *The Annotated Uncle Tom's Cabin*. Ed., with an intro. Phillip Van Doren Stern. New York: Eriksson, 1964.

Stridsberg, A. B., in conjunction with International Advertising Association. *Controversy Advertising: How Advertisers Present Points of View in Public Affairs*. New York: Hastings House, 1977.

Sturminger, Alfred. *3000 Jahre Politische Propaganda*. Vienna: Herold, 1960.

Summers, R. E., ed. *America's Weapons of Psychological Warfare*. New York: H. W. Wilson, 1951.

Tarbell, Ida. *The History of the Standard Oil Company*. New York: McClure, Phillips, 1904.

Tedford, Thomas L. *Freedom of Speech in the United States*. New York: Random House, 1985. Carbondale: Southern Illinois University Press, 1985.

Theoharis, Athan. *Spying on Americans: Political Surveillance from Hoover to the Huston Plan*. Philadelphia: Temple University Press, 1978.

Thompson, Wayne N. *The Process of Persuasion: Principles and Readings*. New York: Harper and Row, 1975.

Thompson, William F. "The Pictorial Reporting and Propaganda of the Civil War." Ph.D. diss., University of Wisconsin, 1959.

Thomson, Charles. *Overseas Information Service of the United States Government*. Washington, D.C.: Brookings Institution, 1948.

Thomson, Oliver. *Mass Persuasion in History: A Historical Analysis of the Development of Propaganda Techniques*. Edinburgh: Paul Harris Publishing, 1977.

Thorpe, Frances, and Nicholas Pronay, with Clive Coultass. *British Official Films in the Second World War: A Descriptive Catalogue*. Santa Barbara, Calif.: Clio Press, 1980.

Tomshoi, Robert. *The American Sanctuary Movement*. Austin: Texas Monthly Press, 1987.

Tunstall, Jeremy. *The Media Are American: Anglo-American Media in the World*. New York: Columbia University Press, 1977.

Turner, Kathleen J. "The Presidential Libraries as Research Facilities: An Analysis of Resources for Rhetorical Scholarship." *Communication Education* 35 (July 1986), 243–53.

Tyson, James L. *Prophets or Useful Idiots? Church Organizations Attacking U.S. Central America Policy*. Washington, D.C.: Council for the Defense of Freedom, 1987.

———. *Target America: The Influence of Communist Propaganda on U.S. Media*. Chicago: Regnery Gateway, 1981.

Tzu, Sun. *Sun Tzu, the Art of War*. Trans. Samuel Griffith. London: Oxford University Press, 1963.

Unger, Irwin. *The Movement: A History of the American New Left, 1959–1972*. New York: Dodd, Mead, 1974.

"USIA: A Battered but Powerful Propaganda Tool." Special Report. *U.S. News and World Report* (March 5, 1984), 58–61.

Vaughn, Stephen L. *Holding Fast the Inner Lines: Democracy, Nationalism, and the Committee on Public Information*. Chapel Hill: University of North Carolina Press, 1980.

Vaughn, William Preston. *The Antimasonic Party in the United States, 1826–1843*. Lexington: University Press of Kentucky, 1983.

Viereck, George S. *My Flesh and Blood: A Lyric Autobiography with Indiscreet Annotations*. New York: Horace Liveright, 1931.

———. *Spreading Germs of Hate*. New York: Horace Liveright, 1930.

Walker, Albert. "Public Relations Bibliography: Sixth Edition, 1976–77." *Public Relations Review* 4 (Winter 1978), 1–94. Subsequent annual updates appear in the Winter issues of *Public Relations Review*, 1979–   .

Waller, J. Michael. "CISPES: A Terrorist Propaganda Network." Special Report. Washington, D.C.: Council for Inter-American Security, 1984.

Warlaumont, Hazel G. "Radio Marti and the U.S.-Cuban Radio War: Strategies Used in the Absence of Definitive Legal Controls over International Broadcasting as Compared with Strategies Used in the U.S.-USSR Radio War." Master's thesis, California State University-Fullerton, 1986.

Weaver, Richard M. *The Ethics of Rhetoric*. Chicago: Henry Regnery, 1953. Reprint. Davis, Calif.: Hermagoras Press, 1985.

Weinberg, Sydney. "Wartime Propaganda in a Democracy: America's Twentieth Century Information Agencies." Ph.D. diss., Columbia University, 1969.

Wells, William Vincent. *The Life and Public Services of Samuel Adams*. 3 vols. Boston: Little, Brown, 1865.

White, Carol. *The New Dark Ages Conspiracy: Britain's Plot to Destroy Civilization*. New York: New Benjamin Franklin House, 1980.

Wilkerson, Marcus M. *Public Opinion and the Spanish-American War: A Study in War Propaganda*. Baton Rouge: Louisiana State University Press, 1932.

Williamson, Audrey. *Thomas Paine: His Life, Work and Times*. London: Allen and Unwin, 1973.

Wilmer, Lambert A. *Our Press Gang; or, a Complete Exposition of the Corruptions and Crimes of the American Newspapers*. Philadelphia: J. T. Lloyd, 1859. Reprint. New York: Arno Press, 1970.

Wilson, Jerome D., and William F. Ricketson. *Tom Paine*. Boston: Twayne/Hall, 1978.

Winkler, Allan M. *The Politics of Propaganda: The Office of War Information, 1942–1945*. New Haven, Conn.: Yale University Press, 1978.

Wisan, Joseph. *The Cuban Crisis as Reflected in the New York Press, 1895–1898*. New York: Columbia University Press, 1934. Reprint. New York: Octagon Books, 1965.

Wise, David. *The Politics of Lying: Government Deception, Secrecy and Power*. New York: Vintage Books, 1973.

Wolfe, Gregory. *Right Minds: A Sourcebook of American Conservative Thought*. Chicago: Regnery Gateway, 1987.

Woodward, Bob. *Veil: The Secret Wars of the CIA, 1981–1987*. New York: Simon and Schuster, 1987.

Woodward, Gary C., and Robert E. Denton, Jr. *Persuasion and Influence in American Life*. Prospect Heights, Ill.: Waveland Press, 1988.

Woodward, W. E. *Tom Paine: America's Godfather, 1737–1809*. New York: E. P. Dutton, 1945.

Wright, Quincy, ed. *Public Opinion and World-Politics*. Chicago: University of Chicago Press, 1933. Reprint. New York: Arno Press, 1972.

Young, Kimball, and Raymond D. Lawrence. *Bibliography on Censorship and Propaganda*. University of Oregon Journalism Series, No. 1 Eugene: University of Oregon Press, 1928.

Zeman, Zbynck. *Selling the War: Art and Propaganda in World War II*. London: Orbis, 1978.

Ziegler, L. Harmon, and Wayne C. Peak. *Interest Groups in American Politics*. 2nd ed. Englewood Cliffs, N.J.: Prentice-Hall, 1972.

Zimbardo, Philip, Ebbe B. Ebbesen, and Christina Maslach. *Influencing Attitudes and Changing Behavior*. 2nd ed. New York: Random House, 1977.

State and Federal Government Documents

American Film Institute. *Catalog of Holdings, the American Film Institute Collection and the United Artists Collection at the Library of Congress*. Washington, D.C.: American Film Institute, 1978.

"Declassified Documents Reference System." Official U.S. documents photoduplicated, summarized, and indexed from Freedom of Information requests. Washington, D.C.: Carrollton Press, 1976– .

National Historical Publications and Records Commission. *The Directory of Archives and Manuscript Repositories*. Washington, D.C.: National Historical Publications and Records Commission, 1978.

New York State Senate. Lusk Committee. *Revolutionary Radicalism: Its History, Purpose, and Tactics*. 4 vols. Albany, N.Y.: J. B. Lyon, 1920.

The Psychological Warfare Division, Supreme Headquarters, Allied Expeditionary Force. An Account of Its Operations in the Western European Campaign, 1944–45. Bad Homburg, Germany: S.H.A.E.F., 1945.

U.S. Advisory Commission on Public Diplomacy. *Public Diplomacy: Lessons from the Washington Summit*. Washington, D.C.: U.S. Advisory Commission on Public Diplomacy, March 1988.

U.S. Arms Control and Disarmament Agency. *Soviet Propaganda Campaign against NATO*, by Charles A. Sorrels. Washington, D.C.: U.S. Arms Control and Disarmament Agency, October 1983.

U.S. Board for International Broadcasting. *Annual Report*. Washington, D.C.: Government Printing Office, 1974– .

U.S. Committee on Public Information. *Complete Report of the Chairman of the Committee on Public Information: 1917, 1918, 1919*, by George Creel ("Creel Report"). Washington, D.C.: Government Printing Office, 1920. Reprint. New York: Da Capo Press, 1972.

U.S. Congress. General Accounting Office. *Suggestions to Improve Management of Radio Free Europe/Radio Liberty*. Report No. ID-76–55. Washington, D.C.: General Accounting Office, June 25, 1976.

———. *Telling America's Story to the World—Problems and Issues*. Report No. B-118654. Washington, D.C.: General Accounting Office, March 25, 1974.

U.S. Congress. House. Committee on Foreign Affairs. *Authorizing Appropriations for Fiscal Years 1980–81 for the Department of State, the International Communication Agency, and the Board for International Broadcasting, Hearings. February 1979*. Washington, D.C.: Government Printing Office, 1979.

———. *The Media, Diplomacy and Terrorism in the Middle East, Hearing July 30, 1985*. Washington, D.C.: Government Printing Office, 1985.

———. *Oversight of the Board for International Broadcasting, Hearing, June 17, 1986*. Washington, D.C.: Government Printing Office, 1986.

———. *Oversight of the Bureau of International Communications and Information Policy. Hearing, June 16, 1986*. Washington, D.C.: Government Printing Office, 1986. (Note: First extensive coverage of what until recently had been a smaller office in the Department of State.)

———. *Radio Free Europe and Radio Liberty, September 14, 21, 1971*. Washington, D.C.: Government Printing Office, 1972.

———. *Soviet Active Measures. Hearings before the Subcommittee on Europe Affairs,*

September 12–13, 1985. Washington, D.C.: Government Printing Office, 1985.

———. *USIA: Authorization for Fiscal Year 1973. March, May, 1972.* Washington, D.C.: Government Printing Office, 1972.

———. *U.S. Information Agency Operations.* 2 parts. *Part I: Survey of the U.S. Information Service, December 1972; Part II: Hearings on the United States Information Agency, July 1970, September–October 1971.* Washington, D.C.: Government Printing Office, 1973.

———. *Winning the Cold War: The U.S. Ideological Offensive.* Hearings before the Subcommittee on International Organizations and Movements of the Committee on Foreign Affairs. 9 parts. Washington, D.C.: Government Printing Office, 1963–1966.

U.S. Congress. House. Committee on Un-American Activities. *Annual Reports.* Washington, D.C.: Government Printing Office, 1946–1969.

———. *Cumulative Index to Publications of the Committee on Un-American Activities, 1938–1954.* Washington, D.C.: Government Printing Office, January 29, 1955.

———. *Supplement to Cumulative Index to Publications of the Committee on Un-American Activities, 1950 through 1960.* Washington, D.C.: Government Printing Office, June 1961. (Note: Between 1945 and 1969, when the House Un-American Activities Committee [HUAC] became the Internal Security Committee, approximately 600 publications were issued covering a variety of "un-American" activities. These include transcripts of public hearings, reports, and other documents. Many deal specifically with the effects of subversive propaganda. Rather than list each here, readers are recommended to consult the HUAC indexes, previously cited guides to U.S. government publications, and general studies critically analyzing the work of the committee.)

U.S. Congress. House. Permanent Select Committee on Intelligence. *Soviet Active Measures. Hearings, July 13–14, 1982.* Washington, D.C.: Government Printing Office, 1982.

———. Subcommittee on Oversight. *Soviet Covert Action (The Forgery Offensive). Hearings, February 6 and 19, 1980.* Washington, D.C.: Government Printing Office, 1980. (Note: Includes the "Central Intelligence Agency Study: Soviet Covert Action and Propaganda.")

U.S. Congress. House. Special Committee on Un-American Activities. *Appendixes.* 9 parts. Washington, D.C.: Government Printing Office, 1940–1944. See particularly Part 3, *Preliminary Report on Totalitarian Propaganda in the United States* (1941); and Part 9, *Communist Front Organizations* (Committee Print, 1944).

———. *Hearings.* 16 vols. Washington, D.C.: Government Printing Office, 1938–43.

———. *Investigation of Nazi and Other Propaganda.* Report No. 153. Washington, D.C.: Government Printing Office, 1935.

———. *Investigation of Nazi Propaganda Activities and Investigation of Certain Other Propaganda Activities. Public Hearings.* 6 vols. Washington, D.C.: Government Printing Office, 1934.

————. *Investigation of Un-American Activities and Propaganda*. House Report No. 2. Washington, D.C.: Government Printing Office, January 3, 1939.

————. *Investigation of Un-American Activities and Propaganda*. House Report No. 1476. Washington, D.C.: Government Printing Office, January 3, 1940.

————. *Investigation of Un-American Activities and Propaganda*. House Report No. 1. Washington, D.C.: Government Printing Office, January 3, 1941.

U.S. Congress. House. Special Committee to Investigate Communism in the United States. *Hearings*. 6 parts. Washington, D.C.: Government Printing Office, 1930.

————. *Investigation of Communist Propaganda*. Report No. 2290. Washington, D.C.: Government Printing Office, 1931.

U.S. Congress. Senate. Committee on Foreign Relations. *Foreign Relations Authorization Act, Fiscal Years 1980 and 1981*. Washington, D.C.: Government Printing Office, March 1979.

————. *Foreign Relations Authorization Act. Hearings*. Washington, D.C.: Government Printing Office, April 1977. (Note: Includes Board for International Broadcasting and USIA. See earlier and subsequent years, as well as publications listed later for other related source information.)

————. *Russian Propaganda. Hearings before a Subcommittee of the Senate Committee on Foreign Relations Pursuant to S. Res. 263*. Washington, D.C.: Government Printing Office, 1920.

U.S. Congress. Senate. Committee on Government Affairs. *Congress and Pressure Groups: Lobbying in a Modern Democracy*, by Congressional Research Service. Washington, D.C.: Government Printing Office (Committee Print, Senate Print 99–161), June 1986.

U.S. Congress. Senate. Committee on Interstate Commerce. *Propaganda in Motion Pictures. Hearings before a Subcommittee of the Senate Committee on Interstate Commerce Pursuant to S. Res. 152*. Washington, D.C.: Government Printing Office (Committee Print), 1942.

U.S. Congress. Senate. Committee on the Judiciary. *Bolshevik Propaganda. Hearings before a Subcommittee of the Committee on the Judiciary, Feb. 11, 1919 to March 10, 1919*. Washington, D.C.: Government Printing Office, 1919.

————. *Brewing and Liquor Interests and German and Bolshevik Propaganda. Report, Doc. No. 61*. Washington, D.C.: Government Printing Office, 1919.

————. *The Technique of Soviet Propaganda. A Study Presented by the Subcommittee to Investigate the Administration of the Internal Security Act and Other Internal Security Laws of the Committee on the Judiciary*, by Suzanne Labin. Washington, D.C.: Government Printing Office, 1960.

U.S. Department of State. *Memorandum on the Postwar International Information Program of the United States*, by Arthur W. MacMahon. Publication 2348. Washington, D.C.: Government Printing Office, 1945. Reprint. New York: Arno Press, 1972.

U.S. Department of State. Bureau of Intelligence and Research, Active Measures Analysis and Response. *Soviet Influence Activities*. Washington, D.C.: Department of State, 1987.

U.S. Department of State. Bureau of Public Affairs. *Soviet Active Measures: An Update*. Special Reports No. 101 and 110. Washington, D.C.: Department of State, July 1982 and September 1983.

U.S. Department of State. International Information Program. *Telling America's Story Abroad: The State Department's Information and Educational Exchange Program*. Washington, D.C.: Government Printing Office, 1951.

———. *The Voice of America: 1950–1951*. Washington, D.C.: Department of State, 1951.

U.S. Department of State. Library Division. *Psychological Warfare in Support of Military Operations: A Bibliography of Selected Materials with Annotations*. Washington, D.C.: Department of State, Library Division, 1951.

U.S. Department of State and Central Intelligence Agency. *Contemporary Soviet Propaganda and Information: A Conference Report, Airlie, Virginia, June 25–27, 1985*. Publication 9536. Washington, D.C.: Department of State, Bureau of Intelligence and Research, Office of the Executive Director, March 1987.

U.S. Foreign Broadcast Intelligence Service. *The Daily Report of Foreign Radio Broadcasts*. Washington, D.C.: Foreign Broadcast Intelligence Service, 1940–1947.

U.S. Information Agency. *Propaganda and Information: An Annotated Bibliography*. Washington, D.C.: USIA Library, July 1973.

———. *Report to the Congress*, nos. 5, 10–11, 38. Washington, D.C.: Government Printing Office, 1955, 1958, 1972.

———. *Report to the Congress*, nos. 43–46. Washington, D.C.: Government Printing Office, 1974–1978.

———. *Review of Operations*, nos. 1–4, 6–9, 12–32, 35. Washington, D.C.: Government Printing Office, 1953–1955, 1956–1957, 1959–1960, 1970.

———. *Semiannual Report to the Congress*, nos. 34, 36–37, 39–42. Washington, D.C.: Government Printing Office, 1970, 1971, 1972–1974.

———. *Semiannual Review of Operations*, no. 33. Washington, D.C.: Government Printing Office, 1969.

———. *Soviet Foreign Propaganda: An Annotated Bibliography*, by Anne Boyer. Washington, D.C.: USIA Library, 1971.

———. *The United States Information Agency: A Bibliography*. 2nd ed. Washington, D.C.: USIA Library, 1976.

U.S. International Communication Agency. Office of Congressional and Public Liaison. *International Communication Agency Fact Sheet*. Washington, D.C.: USICA, October 1979.

———. *Report to Congress 1978–1979*. Washington, D.C.: Government Printing Office, 1980.

U.S. Library of Congress. *A List of Bibliographies on Propaganda*, by Grace Hadley Fuller. Compiled under the direction of Florence S. Hellman. Washington, D.C.: Library of Congress, Division of Bibliography, 1940.

U.S. National Archives and Records Service. *Guide to the Ford Film Collection in the National Archives*, by Mayfield Bray. Washington, D.C.: National Archives and Records Service, General Services Administration, 1970.

———. *Guide to the National Archives of the United States*. Washington, D.C.: National Archives and Records Service, 1974.

U.S. National Security Council. "Timing and the Nicaraguan Resistance Vote." Secret NSC memo and 12-page confidential chronology from Oliver L.

North to Robert C. McFarlane, March 20, 1985. Reprint. San Francisco: *Propaganda Review*, 1987.

U.S. War Department. *Guide to the Use of Information Materials*. War Department Pamphlet, no. 20–3. Washington, D.C.: Government Printing Office, September 1944.

———. Strategic Services Unit. History Project. Office of the Assistant Secretary of War. *War Report of the O.S.S. (Office of Strategic Services)*, vol. 1; *The Overseas Targets: War Report of the O.S.S. (Office of Strategic Services)*, vol. 2. Previously classified and unavailable. Reprinted with a new introduction by Kermit Roosevelt. New York: Walker, 1976.

Periodicals and Annuals

AIMS Newsletter. New York, 1964– .
America: History and Life. Santa Barbara, Calif., 1964– .
Annals of the American Academy of Political and Social Sciences. Newbury Park, Calif., 1891– .
Annual Guide to Public Policy Experts. Washington, D.C.: Heritage Foundation, 1982– .
Anti-Slavery Reporter. New York, 1825–1832; 1840–1844.
Arts and Humanities Citation Index. Philadelphia, 1976– .
Business and Home TV Screen (formerly *Business Screen*). New York, 1939–1977.
Cinéaste. New York, 1967– .
Communication Abstracts. Newbury Park, Calif., 1978– .
Communication Booknotes (formerly *Mass Media Booknotes*). Washington, D.C., 1969– .
Communication Monographs (formerly *Speech Monographs*). Annandale, Va., 1934– .
Communication Research: An International Quarterly. Newbury Park, Calif., 1974– .
Covert Action Information Bulletin. Washington, D.C., 1978– .
Critical Studies in Mass Communication. Annandale, Va., 1984– .
Cultural Correspondence: A Journal of Popular and Left Culture. New York, 1976– .
Current Contents/Arts and Humanities. Philadelphia, 1979– .
Current Contents/Social and Behavioral Sciences. Philadelphia, 1969– .
The Democratic Journalist (English-language ed.). Prague, Czechoslovakia, 1953– .
Disinformation and Subversion Update. Washington, D.C., 1988– .
The Falling Leaf. Birmingham, England, 1958– .
The Gallup Poll, 1935– . Wilmington, Del.: Scholarly Resources, 1972– . Annual.
The Gallup Report (formerly *Gallup Opinion Index* and *Gallup Political Index*). Princeton, N.J., 1965– .
Heritage Today. Washington, D.C., 1984– .
Historical Abstracts. Santa Barbara, Calif., 1955– .
Historical Journal of Film, Radio and Television. Oxford, England, 1981– .
Human Communication Research. Newbury Park, Calif., 1974– .
Index to International Public Opinion, 1978– . Westport, Conn.: Greenwood Press, 1980– . Annual.
Industrial Pioneer. Chicago, 1921–1926.
Industrial Union Bulletin. Chicago, 1907–1909.

Industrial Unionist. Portland, Ore. 1925–1926.
Industrial Worker. Spokane, 1909–1913.
Industrial Worker. Chicago, 1909– .
In Fact. New York, 1940–1950.
The Insider Newsletter. Washington, D.C., 1980– .
Insurgent Sociologist. Eugene, Ore., 1969– .
International Historic Films Videocassette Catalog. Chicago, 1982– .
International Political Science Abstracts. Oxford/Paris, 1951– .
International Socialist Review. Chicago, 1900–1918.
International Socialist Review. New York, 1939– .
Journal of Broadcasting and Electronic Media (formerly *Journal of Broadcasting*).
    Washington, D.C., 1956– .
Journal of Communication. Philadelphia, 1951– .
Journal of Historical Review. Torrance, Calif., 1980– .
JQ: Journalism Quarterly. Columbus, S.C., 1924– .
Jump Cut. Berkeley, 1974– .
Labor History. New York, 1960– .
McClure's Magazine. New York, 1890–1918.
Marxism and the Mass Media: Towards a Basic Bibliography. Bagnolet, France, and
    New York, 1972–1988.
Media Monitor. Washington, D.C., 1987– .
National Trade and Professional Associations of the United States. Washington, D.C.:
    Columbia Books, 1966– . Annual.
The New Federalist. Leesburg, Va., 1987– .
News-Bulletin. Hollywood, Calif., 1949–1965.
New Solidarity. New York, 1973–1987.
One Big Union Monthly. Chicago, 1919–1928.
Pacific Research. Mountain View, Calif., 1969– .
Policy Analysis. Washington, D.C.: Cato Institute, 1981– .
Policy Review. Washington, D.C.: Heritage Foundation, 1976– .
Political Communication and Persuasion: An International Journal. New York, 1981– .
Praxis: A Journal of Cultural Criticism. Los Angeles, 1975– .
Propaganda Analysis. New York, 1937–1941.
Propaganda Analysis Review. San Francisco, 1985–1987.
Propaganda Review. San Francisco, 1987– .
Psychological Abstracts. Washington, D.C., 1927– .
Public Affairs Review. Washington, D.C., 1980– .
Public Opinion Quarterly. Chicago, 1937– .
Public Relations Review. College Park, Md., 1975– .
Quarterly Journal of Speech. Annandale, Va., 1915– .
Quarterly Review of Doublespeak. Urbana Ill., 1973– .
Radical America. Somerville, Mass., 1967– .
Radical History Review. New York, 1973– .
Radio Free Europe Research Reports on Eastern Europe. Munich and New York,
    1956– .
Right to Know. New York: Institute for Media Analysis, 1988– .
Signal. Paris, 1940–1944. Berlin, 1944–1945. (Published in some twenty languages,
    including English.)

Socialist Review (formerly *Socialist Revolution* and *Studies on the Left*, 1959–67). Berkeley, 1970– .

Social Science Monitor. College Park, Md., 1979– .

Social Sciences Citation Index, 1956– . Philadelphia, 1972– .

Sociological Abstracts. San Diego, 1953– .

The Spotlight. Washington, D.C., 1975– .

Terrorism. New York, 1988– .

Topicator: Classified Article Guide to the Advertising/Communications/Marketing Periodical Press. Clackamas, Ore., 1967– .

USIA Update: News from the United States Information Agency. Washington, D.C.

Victory. Washington, D.C.: Office of War Information, 1943–1946.

Washington Representatives. Washington, D.C.: Columbia Books, 1977– . Annual.